**The Thebaid in Times of Crisis**

# CHRONOI
Zeit, Zeitempfinden, Zeitordnungen
Time, Time Awareness, Time Management

―

Edited by

Eva Cancik-Kirschbaum, Christoph Markschies and Hermann Parzinger

on behalf of the Einstein Center Chronoi

## Volume 13

# The Thebaid in Times of Crisis

Revolt and Response in Ptolemaic Egypt

Edited by
Ralph Birk and Laurent Coulon

DE GRUYTER

ISBN 978-3-11-160784-9
e-ISBN (PDF) 978-3-11-160805-1
e-ISBN (EPUB) 978-3-11-160855-6
ISSN 2701-1453
DOI https://doi.org/10.1515/9783111608051

This work is licensed under the Creative Commons Attribution-NonCommercial-NoDerivatives 4.0 International License. For details go to https://creativecommons.org/licenses/by-nc-nd/4.0.

Creative Commons license terms for re-use do not apply to any content (such as graphs, figures, photos, excerpts, etc.) that is not part of the Open Access publication. These may require obtaining further permission from the rights holder. The obligation to research and clear permission lies solely with the party re-using the material.

**Library of Congress Control Number: 2024947504**

**Bibliographic information published by the Deutsche Nationalbibliothek**
The Deutsche Nationalbibliothek lists this publication in the Deutsche Nationalbibliografie; detailed bibliographic data are available on the internet at http://dnb.dnb.de.

© 2025 the author(s), editing © 2025 Ralph Birk and Laurent Coulon, published by Walter de Gruyter GmbH, Berlin/Boston
The book is published open access at www.degruyter.com.

Typesetting: Integra Software Services Pvt. Ltd.

www.degruyter.com
Questions about General Product Safety Regulation:
productsafety@degruyterbrill.com

# Acknowledgements

This volume results from the international conference "The Thebaid in Times of Crisis" held at the Berlin-Brandenburg Academy of Sciences and Humanities and the Freie Universität Berlin, organised by Ralph Birk, Laurent Coulon and Tonio Sebastian Richter. From 9 to 11 May 2019, scholars from Egyptology, Papyrology, and Ancient History spent three days presenting and discussing crisis phenomena in Ptolemaic Egypt at the BBAW as well as the FU Berlin, made possible by generous financial support of different institutions, namely the Center for International Cooperation at the Freie Universität Berlin, the Einstein-Center Chronoi (FU Berlin) and the École Pratique des Hautes Études (PSL-AOROC) in Paris. Before, during and after the conference, the organisers were grateful for the relentless help of Antje Müller and Leonie Meier (both FU Berlin), Angela Böhme and Ralf Wolz (both BBAW), as well as Aurore Bezi, Jérôme Billaud and Olivier Piprot (EPHE PSL-AOROC).

The editors, Ralph Birk and Laurent Coulon, would like to express their heartfelt gratitude towards the Einstein Center Chronoi and its board, Eva Cancik-Kirschbaum (FU Berlin), Christoph Markschies (BBAW) and Hermann Parzinger (SMB-PK), for accepting their volume to the Chronoi series and for providing generous financial support; but first and foremost for creating with the Einstein Center Chronoi a very stimulating intellectual setting for this conference.

For us (post)modern contemporaries, dealing with crisis phenomena is part of our daily routines. However, when a global crisis strikes, even academic routines halt – and the COVID-19 pandemic was such a crisis that delayed the timely publication of these acts. Given the unbowed importance of the topic in our fields, we hope that the diversity and erudition of the presented case studies will compensate for the loss in time.

Berlin and Paris, August 2024
Ralph Birk and Laurent Coulon

# Contents

**Acknowledgements —— V**

Ralph Birk
**Introduction —— 1**

Ralph Birk
**Rebellious Priests of Thebes? —— 27**

Stefano G. Caneva and Stefan Pfeiffer
*Stratēgos* **Kallimachos II of the Thebaid: the Honours for a Royal Local Official in the Context of the Epigraphical Records from the Hellenistic World —— 55**

Marie-Pierre Chaufray
*Lésôneis* **en Thébaïde : avant et après les crises —— 91**

Laurent Coulon
**Les cimetières osiriens, témoins de la politique des Lagides et de ses aléas —— 105**

Thomas Faucher
**How Did Coins Survive the Theban Crises in the Ptolemaic Period? —— 123**

Joseph G. Manning
**Volcanoes, Floods, and Social Unrest: The Theban Unrest in Its Social and Environmental Context —— 143**

Martina Minas-Nerpel
**Arsinoe, Berenice, and Cleopatra: The 'ABC' of the Ptolemaic Ruler Cult in the Times of Crisis —— 155**

Jan Moje
**The Great Revolt 206–186 BCE in the Demotic Sources from Elephantine —— 189**

Alexandra Nespoulous-Phalippou
**Native Revolts from South Thebes to North Thebes: Historical Facts and Royal Ideology According to the Priestly Decrees from Ptolemy V Epiphanes' reign (204–180 BCE)** —— 203

René Preys
**Révoltes, meurtres et intrigues : L'histoire des Ptolémées d'après les parois des temples égyptiens** —— 229

Felix Relats Montserrat
**La destruction des temples pendant les révoltes : un état de la question à partir de l'exemple de Médamoud** —— 255

Anne-Emmanuelle Veïsse
**De la « Grande Révolte de la Thébaïde » aux événements de 88 : un siècle d'insurrection thébaine ?** —— 297

Daniel von Recklinghausen
**Der große Aufstand in der Thebais nach den Aussagen in dem Synodaldekret Philensis II** —— 331

**List of Contributors** —— 353

**Names and Places Index** —— 355

**Sources Index** —— 363

**Res Notabiles Index** —— 369

Ralph Birk
# Introduction

In 30/29 BCE,[1] after military victories in several cities of the Thebaid, the *praefectus aegypti* C. Cornelius Gallus famously declared the region to be no less than a "common horror of all kings" (*communi omnium regum formidine*).[2] Although the multilingual stela is a rhetoric self-adulation of the praefect, the evocation of a disloyal and unstable region harkens back to the revolts and crises of earlier Ptolemaic times that shook the Thebaid from the onset of the late 3rd century BCE and lasted for more than 200 years. All phenomena discussed in this volume, from small-scale insurgencies, famine, and civil wars, to full-fledged secession during the Great Theban Revolt (206–186 BCE), are covered by the term "crisis" – i.e. "a situation or period characterised by intense difficulty, insecurity, or danger" (OED). The term itself has been described, not only from a contemporary perspective, as "omnipresent,"[3] thus "there is virtually no area of life that has not been examined and interpreted through this concept."[4] This introduction gives an overview of crisis conceptualisations offering a theoretical foundation for the following case studies that take a closer look at the Thebaid in times of crisis during the Ptolemaic period.

## 1 Times of Crisis – Crisis of Time

Broadly, crises are moments that tip the scales.[5] As states of imbalance, they are resolved through decisions, as suggested by the etymology from the Greek *krínô* – "to choose, give judgment and accuse." The concept of crisis, within its Greco-Roman context, had acquired a central role in both medical and legal practices. Following Galen, a crisis represents a decisive moment that determines life or

---

[1] This volume uses an adapted version of the referencing style for Egyptology of the IFAO (Cairo) for English and French. For the German contribution, guidelines were developed based on the English referencing style.
[2] The Greek version even states that the Thebaid had not been subdued by (Ptolemaic) kings before, cf. for comment on this passage: Hoffmann, Minas-Nerpel, Pfeiffer 2009, pp. 144–145. The Egyptian version does conspicuously not take note of the rebellious character of the Thebaid.
[3] Roitman 2013, p. 3.
[4] Koselleck 2006b, p. 358; Nassehi 2023, p. 189 and also the compendium in Stern 2022.
[5] Liddell-Scott, s.v. "krínô". For the following the still basic conceptual history of the term, see Koselleck 2006b and also Goldstone 2016, p. 9.

death for the ill;⁶ in Aristotle, the term encompasses a political dimension where judicial decisions serve the maintenance of civic order. In late Hellenism, the concept underwent a religious and teleological shift through its use in the Septuagint and the New Testament, particularly in the expectation of the Last Judgment, when ultimate justice would be served.⁷ All these notions – medical, political, and theological – share the requirement of resolute action, whether by a civic agent, a physician, or Christ as the judge of the world. At the same time, these acts are characterised by a *telos*, a goal or state towards which the crisis should be resolved, be it the maintenance and restoration of civic order, physical recovery, or the ultimate salvation or damnation of humankind. In modernity, especially from the late 18th century onwards, crisis was integrated as a central concept in Western philosophical discourses on history: From designating a specific, decisive point in time, it was expanded to a transitional phase, as in J. G. Herder's "epochal crisis" (1793) denoting the choice between evolution and revolution,⁸ or, more drastically in Diderot's words "l'esclavage ou la liberté" – "slavery or freedom."⁹ For thinkers like Diderot, the nature of a crisis is defined by its goal, by anticipating the outcome in a moment of instability through two prognostic poles. A crisis is therefore defined through "its ending,"¹⁰ for agents who are thrown into a situation of crisis, forced to develop prognostic scenarios, or for historians who structure the flow of events *post hoc* into meaningful segments. In modernity, history has – as F. Hartog pointed out – assumed the role of the apocalyptic judge of the world at the end of time.¹¹ From this perspective, crisis becomes the signature of modernity¹² and subsequently the very notion of how history is "located, recognized, comprehended, and even posited."¹³ The concept of crisis therefore shows very different sorts of temporalities: From a decisive turning point in time, or a period of transition, to a permanent condition, in which agents cannot live *through* it, but only *in* it.¹⁴

Sociologists emphasize that these different temporalities – or semantics of time – serve as coping mechanisms for dealing with the structural conditions

---

6 Singer 2022, pp. 102–106.
7 Koselleck 2006b, pp. 358–361.
8 Cited after: Koselleck 2006b, p. 378.
9 Cited after: Koselleck 1973, p. 144.
10 Koselleck 1973, p. 145.
11 Hartog 2020, pp. 230–243. Or in Schiller's poetic words: "World History is the Last Judgment" – "Die Weltgeschichte ist das Weltgericht" (Resignation, eine Phantasie, 1786), cited after: Koselleck 2006b, p. 371.
12 Koselleck 2006a.
13 Roitman 2013, p. 7.
14 Vigh 2008; Nassehi 2023, pp. 189–190; 204–207.

within a given society,[15] particularly in times of internal and external challenges. Given these different temporal modes of crises, one might inquire how these dynamics are to be analytically framed, compared, and differentiated on one given scale, without cultural, temporal or spatial limitations. Reinhart Koselleck famously declared the onset of modernity as a *Sattelzeit*, marked by a distinct temporal shift that drove a wedge between the space of experience (*Erfahrungsraum*) and the horizon of expectation (*Erwartungshorizont*).[16] In this framework, he posited that the societal and political experiences of pre-revolutionary Europe, across various scales and social domains – from agriculture to political practices – failed to adequately prepare agents in and for a post-revolutionary world, when they were compelled to adapt to fast-paced political and social changes in the new modernist time regime. According to Koselleck, individual biographical, societal, and political temporalities, each with their own rhythm and structure, become superposed, so that time becomes the multi-layered phenomenon coined as the *contemporaneous of the non-contemporaneous*. Recently, this approach has gained traction, as the coexistence of different time regimes in a given society has been recognized not only as multi-layered, but also as intertwined, interacting and, potentially, in conflict with each other. For example, did a "new ecology of temporal regimes" reconfigure the short and long-term rhythms of post-1789 France, the new revolutionary calendar being only a case in point, representing the most evident example of an attempt to counter the religious premises of the 7-day week during the *ancien régime*.[17]

Contemporaries in 3$^{rd}$ century BCE Egypt experienced significant shifts of their temporal regimes, a period culminating in the secession of the Thebaid. Firstly, disruptions in natural cycles profoundly impacted the agricultural backbone of Ptolemaic Egypt: Low Nile floods, triggered by large-scale environmental pressures, resulted in poor harvests and ultimately led to a famine outbreak in the mid-3$^{rd}$ century BCE, as documented in the Decree of Canopus in 238 BCE.[18] The consequences of inadequate inundations were so severe and out of the ordinary that wheat had to be imported *to* Egypt from the Levant and Cyprus to alleviate the crisis. Secondly, the Ptolemies initiated administrative reforms that affected the traditional rhythms of the temple, regarding cultic services through-

---

**15** Nassehi 1993, p. 379.
**16** Koselleck 1979, pp. 349–375.
**17** Edelstein, Geroulanos, Wheatley 2020, pp. 27–29. For the implementation of the calendar reform in the administration see for example Meinzer 1988.
**18** Cf. Pfeiffer 2004. I thank Andreas Winkler for pointing out to me the study by Zelinskyi 2020, dealing with the exact dating of the famine between 243 and 238 BCE. See also the contribution by J. G. Manning in this volume.

out the year (reform of the phylae-system through the introduction of the fifth phyle in relation to the lunar calendar),[19] as well as the genealogical traditions of titleholders by turning hereditary positions non-hereditary. This last measure, affecting for example notaries,[20] disrupted the inheritance cycles that were a central theme in private inscriptions, framed, in the words of Ph. Collombert, as the "eternal succession of generations."[21] Even the domain of calendars underwent challenges and reorganizations during this period. The synod convened in Canopus in 238 BCE sought to introduce a leap day to the civil calendar as a sixth epagomenal day every four years, aiming to realign the cultic feasts and processions with the seasonal cycle. However, this reform was never properly implemented, at least not during the Ptolemaic period,[22] indicating a reluctance on the ground to adopt the new Ptolemaic time regime.

These multi-layered political and societal responses to a profound ecological, economic, and humanitarian crisis also reshaped the period's horizon of expectation. In its most pronounced form, the new Ptolemaic time regime triggered, i.a., literary responses, such as the resurgence of an "apocalyptic sensitivity" in the Demotic literature of the 3$^{rd}$ and 2$^{nd}$ centuries BCE.[23] The *Demotic Chronicle* – predicting a ruler who shall come after the Greeks (2,25) – is likely to have been redacted at that time, though its core text is supposedly of earlier date.[24] Given their onomastics, even the rebel pharaoh(s) Haronnophris and Chaonnophris, who headed the Great Theban Revolt, can be attributed with a messianic quality, embodying an *Osiris redivivus* and his successor, and thus emulating a mythical model as a promise for the future.[25] Although this introduction can only outline these developments in very broad strokes, it becomes evident that the 3$^{rd}$ and 2$^{nd}$ centuries BCE were not just times of crisis, but also marked a crisis of (the perception of) time itself.

---

19 Bennett 2008, pp. 542–543.
20 See R. Birk in this volume.
21 Collombert 1998.
22 Lippert 2009, p. 186 and Bennett 2011, pp. 179–186.
23 Baslez 2020. See in this volume J. G. Manning on the *Oracle of the Potter* and L. Coulon on the Osirian character of the rebel king(s) Haronnophris and Chaonnophris.
24 Quack 2009, pp. 37–38. See there for the different interpretations of the texts, partly highly divergent, by scholars such as J. Johnson and H. Felber. It would be interesting to contrast these Egyptian apocalyptic texts with Egyptian historiography of the 3$^{rd}$ century BCE, especially the case of Manetho, cf. Moyer 2011a.
25 See Veïsse 2004, p. 99 and the discussion by L. Coulon in this volume.

## 2 Revelatory Crises

Anthropologists have posited the role of natural disasters as "revelatory crises," when the "fundamental features of society and culture are laid bare in stark relief by the reduction of priorities to basic social, cultural, and material necessities."[26] Given the contingent character of historical sources, these emerging fundamental features need to be differentiated, according to the agent's or observer's particular "gaze, interests, and positionality."[27] But in crises, contingency figures into the concept as a fundamental experience of difference and reflexivity, when the seemingly self-evident is suddenly subjected to scrutiny as routines begin to break down.[28] In the same vein, J. Goldstone defines the crisis of the state as a "shift in elite or popular attitudes toward the state," which, in turn, would be "incapable of performing necessary tasks of governance."[29] Therefore, the study of crises in a given society is both fundamental and specific: When studying societal collapse, taking individual and multiple perspectives into account generates insights on "fundamental features of society and culture."[30]

With this volume, we embark on a broad analysis of crises in Ptolemaic Egypt as such multi-perspective phenomena, while being critically aware of the teleological overtones, intrinsic dichotomies and temporalities that the crisis concept entails.[31] For Ptolemaic Egypt, crises have become one of the field's major topics, engaging scholars from Greek and Demotic Papyrology, Ancient History, Egyptology and Classical Archaeology.[32] Since P. W. Pestman's groundbreaking article "Haronnophris and Chaonnophris. Two Indigenous Pharaohs in Ptolemaic Egypt (205-186 B.C.)" in 1995 and A.-E. Veïsse's seminal monograph "Les 'révoltes égyptiennes'" in 2004,[33] the framework of sources for rebellions in Ptolemaic Egypt, and especially of the so-called "Great Theban Revolt" of 206–186 BCE, had been set. By using this framework for the past twenty years, researchers have been differentiating causes of revolts, identifying agents and their specific moti-

---

[26] Oliver-Smith 1996, p. 304; see also List 2012, p. 73.
[27] Barrios 2017, p. 155; as Habermas remarks: "Crisis cannot be separated from the viewpoint of the one who is undergoing it": Habermas 1992 [1976], p. 1.
[28] Nassehi 2023, p. 205; List 2012 and Vigh 2008, pp. 16–19. For the contingency of truth claims cf. also Roitman 2016, pp. 29–30.
[29] Goldstone 2016, p. 8.
[30] Oliver-Smith 1996, p. 304.
[31] The period of 204–180 BCE has been explicitly coined as "Die Krise des Reichs zur Zeit Ptolemaios' V." by Werner Huß in his monumental history of Ptolemaic Egypt: Huß 2001.
[32] Jördens, Quack (eds.) 2011; Collins, Manning (eds.) 2016; Wackenier, Gorre (eds.) 2020; Fischer-Bovet, Reden (eds.) 2021; Pfeiffer, Weber (eds.) 2021; Kosmin, Moyer (eds.) 2022.
[33] Pestman 1995; Veïsse 2004. See most recently Veïsse 2022.

vations, developing models of interaction, conflict and reconciliation, and, eventually, drawing conclusions on the "fundamental features" of Ptolemaic society, its cohesive characteristics, but also its lines of conflict.

The Great Theban Revolt is not only central to these narratives because of its sheer length of roughly 20 years, its large territorial extension, from Abydos in the north to Philae in the south, but also because it separates the Early Ptolemaic Period up until Ptolemy IV Philopator, with the battle of Raphia in 217 BCE marking the largest territorial expansion of the Ptolemaic empire, from the Middle and Late Ptolemaic Periods, which traditionally are treated as a period of decline of foreign and domestic power – under the increasing influence of Rome.[34] The Great Revolt therefore served as an interpretative key for two central notions on Ptolemaic Egypt through a negative lens: Synchronically, the ethnic *divide* between 'Greeks' and 'Egyptians' and diachronically, the grand narrative of *decline* that the Ptolemaic kingdom suffered after the crisis of the early 2$^{nd}$ century BCE, until its integration into the Roman Empire.[35] This grand narrative of decline with its "tendency to teleology,"[36] can be retraced to the historiography of the *fin de siècle*, for example in Maspero's influential *Histoire ancienne des peuples de l'Orient*.[37] Therefore, we find both characteristics of crisis centre stage in the disciplinary discourses on societal conflicts in Ptolemaic Egypt: The dichotomous choice between being Greek and Egyptian – as a choice between foreign rule and autochthonous rebellion – on one side, and teleologies at work, where crisis leads to the ultimate demise of the Ptolemaic state, implying a permanent state of crisis.[38] But how to critically reassess revolts as multi-perspectival phenomena in Ptolemaic Egypt, when divide and decline have been dominating the academic discourse for so long?

## 3 Reassessing Narratives of Ethnic Divide and Historical Decline

In the last years, both notions – historical decline and ethnic division – have been variously challenged in inspiring ways. Though their influence is still perceptible

---

[34] See also the comments in: Wackenier, Gorre 2020, pp. 1–2. Manning (2009, p. 30) brands this strand of scholarship as the "brief Summer and endless Autumn" school (after James Davidson).
[35] Fischer-Bovet 2015.
[36] Jambon 2015, p. 202.
[37] Jambon 2015.
[38] See A.-E. Veïsse's contribution in this volume.

in modern scholarship,³⁹ recent synthesises conspicuously refrain from this teleological narrative⁴⁰ so that crises of the 3rd to 2nd century BCE become trigger events for "reorganisation"⁴¹ instead of "decline"⁴² as "catalysts for transformation,"⁴³ stressing the innovative force of societal crises⁴⁴. Case studies from the 2nd century BCE contributed to this re-evaluation through different perspectives, from political history to daily routines in the countryside.⁴⁵ It is only in such a recalibrated historiographical framework that the agency of local, regional, and central actors, however active or passive, and their interactions, be they collaborative or hostile, can be reassessed in illustrating "elite or popular attitudes to the state."⁴⁶

Ever since the concept of crisis has been in use, one of its core characteristics has been the radical choice between dichotomous alternatives: life or death, salvation or damnation. What qualifies a crisis has been though subject to change. Therefore, these alternative pairs have multiplied over time, reflecting the specific perspectives of actors and their diagnosis of and prognosis for the crisis at hand.⁴⁷ A strong current in scholarship has been the diagnosis of an ethnic dichotomy in Ptolemaic sources, antagonizing Greek(s) and Egyptian(s), based on – though not exclusively – linguistic (and therefore also disciplinary) grounds. This has heavily influenced premises, analytical categories and research questions in the field. The Great Theban Revolt plays a key role in this segment of the literature. Taken to the extreme, this dichotomous view of Ptolemaic Egypt led to the assessment that "nationalistic" Egyptians revolted against "foreign" Greek rule – at a time when Macedonian rulership was already more than 100 years old and "foreign" rulership was by no means foreign to Egyptians of the first millennium.⁴⁸

---

39 Cf. the grand narratives in Huß 2001; Hölbl 1994.
40 See Veïsse 2019; Agut-Labordère, Moreno-García 2016, pp. 679–726 or, thematically structured: Manning 2009 and Fischer-Bovet 2015, pp. 224–231.
41 Veïsse 2019, pp. 44–47.
42 Huß 2001, pp. 537–670.
43 Vandorpe 2011, p. 295.
44 See also, from a paleoclimatic perspective, Ludlow, Manning 2021, p. 314: "Our results also suggest that the 'decline' of the Ptolemaic state after 200 BCE has probably been exaggerated. The social dynamics were more complex." For crises as moments of innovation, cf. List 2012, p. 72.
45 Jördens, Quack (eds.) 2011; Wackenier, Gorre (eds.) 2020.
46 See also now the recent synthesis by D. Agut-Labordère and J.-C. Moreno-García (2016, pp. 679–725) treating Hellenistic Egypt from a social and institutional viewpoint.
47 Koselleck 2006b, p. 370.
48 Famously McGing 1997 and McGing 2016; but see also Huß 2001, p. 441. On the apparent dichotomy see also now Pfeiffer 2021.

For Egypt, the focus on ethnic distinction has been counterbalanced by a shift towards modes of interaction, exchange and hybridity,[49] which does not take the alleged dichotomy between 'Greeks' and 'Egyptians' as a given but works towards a nuanced analysis, building the argument on eloquent case studies that transgress linguistic, cultural, and societal boundaries.[50] This does not entail disposing of ethnic identity as a category entirely, though it sees in groups and individuals multiple facets of identity at work, such as language and onomastics, social status, gender, and religious affiliations – with ethnic (self-)ascription being only one of many qualities.[51] In turn, studies have also stressed the dynamism and fluidity of ethnic designations in the sources, be it group or individual ethnics, for example in the case of *Macedonians* which became a pseudo-ethnic in the Ptolemaic army at the beginning of the 2$^{nd}$ century BCE,[52] or as markers of social status.[53] Instead of being indicative of a rigid ethnic affiliation, they convey "social mobility on a large scale"[54] – such as Egyptian *misthophoroi*-soldiers who gain fiscal privileges when joining the ranks of "Persians" in 2$^{nd}$-century BCE Pathyris and Latopolis.[55] Complementing these efforts, new readings of ancient historians as well as officially sanctioned texts, such as the Philensis II decree or Pausanias' testimony of Thebes' total destruction in 88 BCE, offer a historiographical top-down critique.[56] One thinks for example of Polybius' short, though very influential depiction of the Great Revolt (*History* V.107) where the levied 20,000 Egyptian troops (*machimoi*) in the battle of Raphia during the Fourth Syrian War are portrayed as the main catalysts of the Great Revolt, armed by and eventually turned against the Ptolemies. This narrative not only contracts time – ten years lie between both events – but also overemphasises the conscription of Egyptian soldiers as the *one*

---

**49** See also the fruitful concept of the middle ground and its application for Ptolemaic Egypt: Moyer 2011b and Gorre 2017, based on the historical model of interaction developed by Richard White (2011); see also its analogous application to the Seleucid Middle East: Hoffmann-Salz (ed.) 2021. For Greco-Egyptian interaction see most recently: Moyer 2011a; Rutherford 2016; Escolano-Poveda 2020.
**50** Collombert 2000; Coulon 2001; Veïsse 2007; Klotz 2009; Thompson, Vandorpe, Christensen 2017, pp. 44–46; Moyer 2022; Birk 2023; Fischer-Bovet 2023. See also the contribution by S. Caneva and S. Pfeiffer in this volume.
**51** See most recently: Clarysse 2019; Veïsse 2014. For polyonymy and identification methods in general: Coussement 2016 and Depauw, Coussement (eds.) 2014.
**52** Fischer-Bovet 2014, pp. 177–191; Johstono 2018.
**53** Veïsse 2014, p. 208.
**54** Vandorpe 2011, pp. 305–307.
**55** Vandorpe 2008.
**56** Honigman, Veïsse 2021, p. 302; for Philensis II: Recklinghausen 2018. See also the author's and A. Nespoulous-Phalippou's treatment of Philensis II and A.-E. Veïsse's critique of Pausanias in this volume.

decisive factor – without a before or an after, pathing the way to Egyptian nationalism *avant la lettre*.[57] When societal division based on ethnicity is relegated to one phenomenon among many, other causes for insurgency come to the fore as well. The causes and contexts of conflict are typically described along the lines of socioeconomic, political, military, and religious factors, besides ethnicity.[58] Economic and social explanations have been part of the debate since Claire Préaux's article in 1936,[59] in which she stated that "'chasser le grec' est peut-être un de ces cris de guerre; ce n'est ni le but premier, ni la cause profonde de l'inlassable révolte égyptienne."[60] Among these "causes profondes" are certainly environmental pressures during the 3$^{rd}$ and 2$^{nd}$ centuries BCE that prompted societal responses on different levels: one important – and long-time neglected – factor. The analysis of paleoclimatic datasets points to heavy volcanic activity in that timeframe, leading ultimately to massive failures of the annual Nile flood, right before the onset of the Great Theban Revolt in 207/206 BCE,[61] but also for the troubled period of the 160s BCE.[62] Fine-grained paleoclimatic datasets and their use as proxies to detect Nile flood variability and – in the worst case – Nile failure, form independent correlates of the written and material record from Ptolemaic Egypt.[63] However, as has been stressed by F. Ludlow and J. G. Manning, these analyses become only meaningful when properly contextualized within the cultural record.[64] Whereas malignant Nile failures are treated in Demotic literary and para-literary texts of the Ptolemaic and Roman period, coined also as 'apocalyptic', the Famine Stela – probably to be dated to the 2$^{nd}$ century BCE, in a particularly heated period – historicizes a crisis of provision in the distant past, in the time of Djoser of the 3$^{rd}$ Dynasty. In the text, famine gains a supra-temporal quality, even though the text

---

**57** See the analysis of Fischer-Bovet 2023 and the comments on Polybios' framing of Ptolemy IV and V in Veïsse 2016; but cf. also the illuminating points made already in Préaux 1936 and Peremans 1975, taken up by McGing 1997, pp. 280–282. For a critique on nationalism *avant la lettre* see: Gehrke 2021, p. 199. For the role of Egyptian soldiers in the revolts, see Fischer-Bovet 2015, Pfeiffer 2021, p. 112; a nationalist reading is offered by McGing 2012, pp. 514–515.
**58** Veïsse 2004 analyses these factors in relation to specific agents.
**59** Préaux 1936.
**60** Préaux 1936, p. 552.
**61** Ludlow, Manning 2016; Ludlow, Manning 2021.
**62** Singh et al. 2023.
**63** Erdkamp, Manning, Verboven (eds.) 2021, p. IX.
**64** Ludlow, Manning 2021, p. 309. For natural catastrophes in pre-Ptolemaic Egypt, see Dirksen 2021.

deals with the concrete status of the Dodekaschoinos-region.[65] Nile failure, drought, and famine trigger responses on very different social scales. There is active crisis management within Ptolemaic administration and leadership, as can be inferred e.g. from the measures detailed in the Canopus decree (238 BCE), such as the reduction of taxes and importation of grain – itself possibly triggered by a *domestica seditio* as reported by Justin.[66] Royal ordinances command that wheat shall be prioritized for Alexandria (240s BCE) or be brought mandatorily to the capital – on the threat of death – in 50 BCE.[67] But there are also local elites raising to the task, as in the famous case of the *strategos* Kallimachos II, whose family administered the Thebaid in the 1st century BCE, and who was honoured as the "saviour of the city" by the Theban priesthood in 40/39 BCE in a situation of Nile failure.[68]

For Ptolemaic Thebes, the 1992 milestone colloquium "Hundred-Gated Thebes" in Leiden transgressed the disciplinary separations between philology and archaeology, fostering a productive intersection of these fields.[69] With the 2019 Berlin conference and this ensuing volume, we took this contextualizing impulse to have a closer look at how Ptolemaic Egypt dealt with and coped with times of crisis, specifically on a regional scale, with a focus on Thebes and the larger Thebaid. The following summaries are thematically structured, yet the papers appear in alphabetic order of authors in the volume.

In his contribution, **Joseph G. Manning** underscores the potential for significantly advancing our comprehension of historical crises by employing new theoretical models and fostering a meaningful dialogue among diverse and distinct categories of sources. In *Volcanoes, Floods, and Social Unrest. The Theban Unrest in Its Social and Environmental Context* Manning aligns with Karl Butzer's vision, in which societal crises are embedded in coupled systems of constant human-environment interaction, in a complex interplay involving a "great tapestry of variables."[70] Manning contends that the structural tensions of Ptolemaic society extended well beyond new fiscal regimes and ethnic conflicts. He emphasizes the often-overlooked role of the non-elite population, acknowledging its significance

---

[65] See most recently: Quack 2012; the same supratemporal quality can be deduced from the *Book of the Temple*, where Nile failure is reported from the distant past, from the reign of King Neferkasokar: Quack 2012, pp. 348–350.
[66] Justin, XXVII, I, see Veïsse 2004, pp. 3–5; Ludlow, Manning 2021, p. 307.
[67] *P. Tebt.* 703: Ludlow, Manning 2016, p. 157; prostagma of 50/49 BCE: *BGU* VIII 1843, see also the contribution by S. Caneva and S. Pfeiffer in this volume.
[68] See S. Caneva and S. Pfeiffer in this volume with further references.
[69] Vleeming (ed.) 1995.
[70] See Butzer 2012, p. 3633.

even if it remains mostly a blind spot in the sources. To address this gap, Manning suggests using proxies, such as paleoclimatic datasets, to understand environmental pressures in Ptolemaic Egypt – and their correlation with the phenomena of social unrest. Recognizing that societal responses to trigger events can manifest in various ways, Manning proposes a promising avenue for understanding these dynamics through re-evaluations of literary sources. One compelling example he cites is the Oracle of the Potter, a text that delves into a broad spectrum of interconnected phenomena – from Nile failures and fiscal pressures to the emergence of social unrest, showcasing the multifaceted nature of societal reactions during critical moments.

By re-evaluating and reshaping the framework of sources in this manner, we might not only gain new insights into societal pressures on the whole but also, more specifically, into the diverging roles of often largely anonymous social groups and individuals who remain opaque in scholarly discourses. The proactive roles of Upper Egyptian priests can be illuminated through a comprehensive and thorough analysis of private and temple texts, as well as imagery. This approach veers away from simply assigning roles to them within a presumed drama of conflict and decline. It brings about a renewed interest in the historical context's impact on the evolution, variation and adaptation of highly formalized 'Ptolemaic' temple texts by the priesthood.[71] **René Preys** analyses in his contribution how priests actively sought to reflect dynastical changes in scenes of the royal cult, especially in the ritual scenes showing the "transmission of the *imi.t-pr*" to the reigning couple and those depicting the ancestor cult of the deceased king(s) and queen(s) in Karnak and Edfu. This theme, appearing already during the reign of Ptolemy III in the Decree of Canopus, is traced through the troublesome 2$^{nd}$ and 1$^{st}$ centuries BCE, in response to the Great Theban Revolt during Epiphanes' reign, but also in reaction to the dynastic strife from Ptolemy VI Philometor until Ptolemy IX Soter II, under whose second reign the scenes are attested for a last time. At first glance, rigid elements of these ritual scenes were conceptually moulded to the specific dynastic constellation, such as the royal triad of Ptolemy VI with his mother Cleopatra II and his wife Cleopatra III being split into two *imi.t-pr*-scenes. In one extraordinary case, these scenes also become subject to material alterations *ex-post*, such as the image of Ptolemy IX's mother, most likely Cleopatra III, became the focus of a targeted attack that may become meaningful in the aftermath of her falling out with her son after 107 and her assassination in 101 BCE. For Preys, priests in Edfu were thus not practising a refined yet self-

---

[71] See the contributions in: Coppens (ed.) 2021; and also, besides the research of Preys, Caßor-Pfeiffer 2008a; Caßor-Pfeiffer 2008b.

referential theology in a secluded, sacred space, but actively involved in shaping royal ideologies and reacting to historical events as political actors, not in the sphere of the royal court but in sacred space.

How these royal ideologies shifted during Ptolemaic rule is taken up by **Martina Minas-Nerpel** in her contribution on *Arsinoe, Berenice, and Cleopatra: The 'ABC' of the Ptolemaic Ruler Cult in the Times of Crisis* – from the perspective of Ptolemaic queens, before, during, and after the Great Theban Revolt. After a thorough diachronic investigation of Ptolemaic ruler cults, implementing Greek and Egyptian traditions in Alexandria and the *chora*, she develops how the Great Theban Revolt marks a turning point for the roles of queens in textual and pictorial representations. Those were not only affected materially during the revolt – as in the case of the decoration of Taharqa's Kiosk in Karnak, halted in the time of Ptolemy V – but also conceptually, as Ptolemaic queens are attributed with more agency after the revolt than before: With the Seleucid-born Cleopatra I, Ptolemaic queens redefine their position in the framework of the royal cult. They begin appearing as active agents in temple imagery, be it in the form of statues (Cleopatra I – as mentioned in the Philensis I Decree) or as ritual agents in innumerable temple scenes, as in the case of Cleopatra II and III, seizing the opportunity to mirror their decisive roles in the political struggle during the reigns of Ptolemy VI and VIII. But they are also building on continuities that stretch over the hiatus of the revolt: Arsinoe II, whose eponymous cult was implemented in 270 BCE, and Berenice II, the first queen bearing the epithet of "female Horus," became influential role models for all following queens of the dynasty.

The introduction of the ruler cults during the 3$^{rd}$ century BCE is accompanied by substantial royal investments in the divine liturgies and cemeteries of Osiris all over Egypt. However, given the Osirian programme formulated in the rebels' titularies – Haronnophris and Chaonnophris, incorporating both the Osirian epithet *wn-nfr* – of the Great Theban Revolt, **Laurent Coulon** takes a closer look at the evolution of the Osirian cemeteries as contested sites between the Ptolemies and their adversaries. He first carefully reviews the archaeological and epigraphic evidence of Osirian cemeteries in different regions, north and south: From the catacombs in Giza, related to the necropolis of ancient Ro-Setau, to the cemetery of Sokar in Abusir, the Osirian catacombs in Oxyrhynchos and finally Karnak, some patterns emerge: First, the attestations are contemporaneous with the implantation of the royal cult in the *chora*. Second, the wealth of sources particularly in the time of Ptolemy IV indicates that Osirian cultic practices were systematized and intensified during his reign. Third, these Osirian necropoleis lack any sign of hellenization. Instead, they build on long-standing cultic traditions from the Pharaonic era, each with their distinct local specificities. Particularly noteworthy is the annual rhythm of burials dictated by the ritual of Khoiak, which creates an excellent framework for discussing cultic continuities and the impact of crises in the Thebaid and beyond. Coulon stresses that it is difficult to outline how – and if – the related rituals were performed during rebel rule, as the evidence remains fragmentary. There is though probable cause for the discontinuation of Osirian burials both in Karnak during the Great Revolt as well as in Oxyrhynchos during the autonomy of Cleopatra II in the $2^{nd}$ century BCE. Even if Osirian cemeteries were apparently not targeted during the Great Revolt, individuals involved in the dynastic cult may have suffered another fate, as suggested by the dossier of the priestess Takhybiat. The association of both the Lagids and the rebels with the divine and resurrected king Osiris, be it in cultic practice or onomastics, points towards a shared ideological repertoire at the verge of the $3^{rd}$ to the $2^{nd}$ century BCE – transgressing enemy lines.

One central corpus for the analyses of these shifting royal ideologies, shaped by historical dynamics, is the Ptolemaic Synodal Decrees, issued by representatives of the Egyptian priesthood in favour of the king (and queen), a genre that attests to the crisis management of the Ptolemies and their elites in the $3^{rd}$ and $2^{nd}$ century BCE.[72] The contributions by **Daniel von Recklinghausen** and **Alexandra Nespoulous-Phalippou** offer two complementary perspectives on the decrees of Ptolemy V Epiphanes and Philensis II in particular. Although the Memphis (196 BCE), Philensis II (186 BCE), and Philensis I (185 BCE) decrees constitute one of the most important historical sources for the reconstruction of the Great Theban Revolt during the reign of Ptolemy V, Daniel von Recklinghausen reminds us in his contribution *Der große Aufstand in der Thebais nach den Aussagen in dem Synodaldekret Philensis II* that they were primarily destined for the realm of the temple, using theological phraseology, mythological comparanda – with the revolt being only the trigger event. The rendition of military conflicts through a mythological lens not only draws on older Egyptian sources going back at least to the Ramesside period but also renders the unthinkable – the disturbance of Pharaonic kingship from the inside – manageable. While von Recklinghausen sets the framework of how these texts work in sacred contexts, which rules they obey and what discourses they partake in, Alexandra Nespoulous-Phalippou focuses on the shifting image of Ptolemy V in the decrees and the growing importance of two of his generals, Aristonikos and Komanos. In *Native Revolts from South Thebes to North Thebes. Historical Facts and Royal Ideology According to the Priestly Decrees from Ptolemy V Epiphanes' Reign (204–180 BCE)* she demonstrates, how a subtle analysis of the formalized phraseology of the decrees can reveal historical dynamics behind the ideological curtain. From the fiction that

---

72 See also the contribution by J. G. Manning in this volume.

makes out of the 5-year-old Ptolemy V the central actor in the Memphis Decree (196 BCE), the priestly authors shift towards the introduction of Aristonikos and Komanos as the main agents in the Revolt. Conspicuously, they use the given framework: In Philensis II, both generals are commemorated during feasts of royal dynastic worship. This evolution culminates in the statement that Aristonikos won the "victory like a sovereign" in the Memphis Decree of 182 BCE, reducing royal euergetism to nothing more than a cliché. Aristonikos became, as the author stresses, the main interlocutor of the crown with Egyptians and Greeks, priests, soldiers and other groups.

Whereas the priestly interlocutors of Aristonikos remain anonymous, they come into clearer focus, complete with names and identities, when examined in the realm of private documentation. In *Rebellious Priests of Thebes?*, **Ralph Birk** delves into one of the central yet largely anonymous actors of the Great Theban Revolt, the Theban priesthood. He begins by delineating the Lagid reforms of Egyptian temples during the $3^{rd}$ century BCE, highlighting the weakening of the temple's autonomy economically and the establishment of new leading figures before the revolt, the so-called "Great Governors of Thebes." To discern the direct repercussions of the rebellion, he zooms in on two specific case studies: the family of the royal scribe Pakhnoum and the Theban high clergy, especially the First Prophet of Amun. Pakhnoum, a royal scribe who witnessed the outbreak of the revolt was directly impacted. The author renders likely that his family might have relocated north to the nome of Memphis during the rebellion, only to return after the Ptolemies reconquered Thebes in 191/190 BCE to resume their position. Pakhnoum's dossier underlines the mobility of priests during crises – and that they had to adapt to novel situations, not only personally, but even rhetorically in biographical texts on private statuary. Through his survey of the evidence, Birk analyses the genealogical continuities and breaks of the Theban high clergy surrounding the Great Theban Revolt. Conspicuously, no First Prophet is attested during the revolt, though this vacancy leaves room for interpretation. The author pleads cautiously for the possible scenario of a targeted action against the First Prophet during the revolt. After the secession of the Thebaid, the structural weakening of the Theban high clergy was accentuated, as the Great Governors were recruited from a larger group of priestly families, distributing power and inhibiting priestly dynasties. In view of these case studies, Birk contends that the Theban clergy comprised a diverse community. They navigated a landscape of collaboration or resistance vis-à-vis rebel rulers and Ptolemaic kings, actively negotiating their roles in a volatile environment, before, during, and after the revolt.

Zooming out to the broader Thebaid, **Marie-Pierre Chaufray**, in her contribution titled *Lésôneis en Thébaïde : avant et après les crises*, introduces another pivotal official of the late Egyptian temple, the *lesonis*. This figure served as head of the temple administration and held responsibility for the temple's revenues and taxes directed towards the state. While evidence for *lesoneis* in Thebes and Edfu is abundant during the Early Ptolemaic Period, it becomes scarce in the aftermath of the revolt. Particularly revealing is the data from Pathyris, where two *lesoneis* emerge in contemporaneous documents from the revolt. The continued existence of this office during the revolt not only indicates the acknowledgement of Chaonnophris' rule by the local temple administration, as evidenced in Pathyris from his first regnal year, but also suggests that Chaonnophris took advantage of the existing financial liaison between the temple and the state for his counter-administration and the financing of the revolt. In Pathyris, the families of these administrators retained their positions in the temple of Hathor even after the Ptolemies had reclaimed the Thebaid. Remarkably, this occurred despite their families being implicated during the rule of Chaonnophris and Haronnophris, showcasing the pragmatic attitudes adopted by both the local priesthood and state alike.

In his contribution, *The Great Revolt 206–186 BCE in the Demotic Sources from Elephantine*, **Jan Moje** takes us to the southern border of the Thebaid. Elephantine presents a unique case, as the city seemingly never capitulated to the Great Theban Revolt, despite being surrounded by rebel territory. Moje sets the scene by introducing the quantitative evidence of Demotic sources. Even though Elephantine continued to function as a Ptolemaic garrison during the rebellion, there was a marked decrease in the production of tax receipts written in Demotic from the reign of Ptolemy IV. However, private and religious documents in this idiom persist throughout the Ptolemaic Period. The author draws a correlation between this shift with the increased prevalence of Greek in both mono- and multilingual documents following the Great Revolt. This observation suggests that the revolt played a pivotal role in influencing the linguistic landscape of Elephantine, prompting a shift towards Greek in administrative and official documentation, while Demotic retained its relevance in domains of private and religious life. Moje progresses with a thorough examination of the rich textual evidence from Elephantine, shedding light on coping strategies and movements of priests at border zones in and out of enemy lines.

While these last contributions primarily focus on textual evidence, we expand our viewpoint with the following two by **Thomas Faucher** and **Felix Relats Montserrat** concentrating on the numismatic material from Thebes and the larger Thebaid, and, respectively, on the archaeological record in Medamud. Both contributions not only enlarge the analytical framework by their change of focus, but fundamentally problematize, how military, political, and social crises become perceptible in material culture. In his contribution, Faucher starts from the observation that there is – compared to other regions – only a limited numismatic corpus in the Thebaid. Gold, silver, and bronze coins were nevertheless circulating and used in the region for all purposes, appearing in the record as stray and hoard finds in Karnak and Luxor. From the now generally accepted ten subsequent series of Ptolemaic bronze coinage, only a limited number come from Thebes in the Early Ptolemaic Period. After 261 BCE, bronze coins are well represented until the end of the Ptolemaic period. Through his survey of the evidence, he concludes that shortly before or at the beginning of the Great Revolt, most coins were withdrawn from circulation. Some of these last coins in the reign of Ptolemy IV were deposited in a hoard under the Bubastide portal in Karnak, though linking it to the outbreak of the rebellion in 205 BCE remains circumstantial. Nevertheless, coins probably also circulated after the beginning of the Revolt, at least early in the $2^{nd}$ century BCE with a new coin series. It is noteworthy, how local actors adopted non-official coinage practices, before the revolt (non-official countermarking of coins) and during the $2^{nd}$ century BCE (minting at the chapel of Osiris neb djefau in Karnak). Faucher finally asserts that after the Great Revolt the monetization process was in full swing and that coins were fully used by the local population – independent from the tumultuous political circumstances.

Relats Montserrat engages in his contribution *La destruction des temples pendant les révoltes : Un état de la question à partir de l'exemple de Médamoud* critically with the still influential notion that Medamud's temple precinct was destroyed during the Great Theban Revolt, brought to the fore by the site's early $20^{th}$-century excavator F. Bisson de la Roque. According to the latter, Philopator's reign marked a critical turning point in the temple's history, demarcating a distinct before (*le temple "latéral"*) and after (*le temple de Montou*), serving as material evidence of how rebels targeted the temples in the Thebaid – a perspective influenced by the Synodal Decrees. Through a meticulous deconstruction of this dichotomous opposition, Relats Montserrat exposes various presuppositions and blind spots that lead to Bisson de la Roque's assessment and proposes a new evolutionary model of Medamud's sacred landscape during the Ptolemaic Period, based on a comprehensive examination of the archaeological and architectural evidence on-site. He is able to dismiss the evidence for Bisson de la Roque's "*temple latéral*" and Epiphanes' rebuilding of the temple of Month, as the temple's extant masonry reaches back as far as the New Kingdom. Instead, he proposes a constant pattern of dismantling and rebuilding during the Early Ptolemaic Period, modifying the temple of the New Kingdom, restructuring the backside of the temple, constructing a pylon next to the so-called "tribune," as well as a peribolos-court and several porticoes. Though the Great Theban Revolt – as the conflict between Philometor and Euergetes II in the $2^{nd}$ century BCE – meant the interruption of the royal building programme at Medamud, it resumed ostentatiously with Philometor, as an affirmation of Lagid presence in the Theban region.

In her contribution *De la « Grande Révolte de la Thébaïde » aux événements de 88 : Un siècle d'insurrection thébaine ?* **Anne-Emmanuelle Veïsse** shifts the perspective from a specific, critical point in time to an alleged continuous era of crisis spanning from 206 to 88 BCE. Veïsse notes that still, a widely accepted notion holds that the Theban revolt of 88 BCE stands in continuity with the Great Revolt, an assertion that she carefully reviews. Veïsse proceeds by first discussing the papyrological evidence of the armed conflict in 88 BCE, revolving mainly around the so-called 'Pathyrite dossier', containing five Greek letters of the *strategos* Platon to local stakeholders in Pathyris. These letters address imminent threats and the impending arrival of general Hierax to suppress the rebellion. In the aftermath, Pathyris not only lost its legal status but all of its inhabitants. Secondly, Veïsse critically examines Pausanias' testimony, of Thebes' destruction in the aftermath of the rebellion and his chronology of events, by confronting them with papyrological and archaeological evidence of the 1$^{st}$ century BCE. In order to better understand the nature and extent of the revolt, Veïsse then turns to the causes of the events in 88 BCE in the second part of her contribution. She meticulously dissects the onset of the brotherly wars in the toxic triangle of Ptolemy IX Soter II, Cleopatra III and Ptolemy X Alexander I at the turn of the 1$^{st}$ century BCE. Ptolemy IX's efforts to regain the throne after 103 BCE are next, followed by Ptolemy X's defeat in 88 BCE. Veïsse concludes that the revolt of 88 BCE, and consequently also the role of Pathyris and Thebes, must be interpreted against the backdrop of the civil war between Soter II and Alexander I. In this reading, Hierax aimed to specifically punish Alexander's loyal partisans in Upper Egypt – not to crush a full-fledged rebellion against the Ptolemaic state, setting the rebellion of 88 BCE apart from the Great Theban Revolt. By breaking down continuous crisis narratives into distinct, multifaceted conflicts in the Thebaid, Veïsse exemplifies here the structuring power of crises.

This differentiating approach can benefit significantly from a broader comparatist perspective, with respect to scale and duration, causes and occasions of conflict, means and media of uprising and the specific modes of resolution.[73] This comparative viewpoint examines local crises and their structural features in a wider geographical, transcultural scope – be it in the context of ancient empires,[74] Hellenistic kingdoms in the East,[75] and also in differentiating between

---

73 See Gehrke 2021, p. 198.
74 Collins, Manning (eds.) 2016.
75 Fischer-Bovet, Reden (eds.) 2021; Kosmin, Moyer (eds.) 2022.

Hellenistic poleis and kingdoms.[76] In their contribution, **Stefano Caneva** and **Stefan Pfeiffer** offer new comparative perspectives of this kind into the rich dossier of the strategos Kallimachos (II), known by the bilingual decree in his honour. The authors start from the observation that Kallimachos enters the stage in a particularly troublesome period, characterized by insufficient Nile floods in the 50s and 40s. The subsequent food shortages brought the Thebaid, as the decree states, close to starvation. In this situation of distress emerges Kallimachos as the saviour of Thebes and its inhabitants. The authors closely analyse both his deeds and his epithets in diachronic depth within Egyptian private texts of the Late and Ptolemaic Period and show, at the same time, that his benefactions and honours resonate as well in the broader context of Hellenistic euergetism of the 1$^{st}$ century BCE. Given these local and transregional ties of Kallimachos' traits, deeds, and honours, such as the celebration of his birthday as an eponymous day, the authors conclude that the decree is not a testimony of political opposition to the rule of Cleopatra VII and Ptolemy XV, neither by the issuing party, namely the Theban priests and elders, nor by Kallimachos himself. By shifting their viewpoint from the local to the global, from the specific to the general, Caneva and Pfeiffer propose therefore a renewed, de-isolated vision of the socio-political landscape of the Thebaid in the 1$^{st}$ century BCE, as a place of ethnic and cultural heterogeneity, where Theban priests and elders appear as agents of a *polis*, who, in turn, portray Kallimachos as an Egyptian royal official in the tradition of grand predecessors such as the Chief Steward of the God's wife Harwa of the 25$^{th}$ Dynasty – without integrating him into the Theban priesthood. This fruitful cooperation was, as the authors conclude, a key to saving the Thebaid from political and military anarchy that had ravaged other regions of the late Hellenistic kingdoms.

The presented case studies in this volume investigate crises and their subsequent societal responses in Ptolemaic Egypt by critically reflecting on the concept's underlying notions of teleology and dichotomy through three overlapping strategies: diversifying the source material and analytical perspectives, challenging dominant narratives in scholarly literature, and re-evaluating the evidence from Ptolemaic Egypt through a comparative lens.

In regard to the sources, documentary papyri have been at the heart of the field's discourse on Ptolemaic crises,[77] a rich corpus that still plays a major role. However, our contributions seek to bring a wider variety of sources to the discussion, such as palaeoclimatic datasets (Manning), archaeological (Coulon, Relats Montserrat) and numismatic material (Faucher), monumental temple inscriptions, religious and his-

---

76 Pfeiffer, Weber (eds.) 2021.
77 See the state of the art in: Veïsse 2004, pp. XI–XVI.

torical (Minas-Nerpel, Preys, Nespoulous-Phalippou, von Recklinghausen), private monuments and documentation (Birk, Chaufray, Coulon, Minas-Nerpel, Moje, Pfeiffer/Caneva, Veïsse), as well as literary (Manning) and historical sources (especially Veïsse). It is important to note that only a few of the presented and studied sources refer to crises and their specific societal responses directly. The Elephantine letters discussed by Moje, the Pathyrite Dossier in Veïsse's contribution, or the Ptolemaic Synodal Decrees (see von Recklinghausen and Nespoulous-Phalippou respectively) are exceptional cases. The authors analyse many of these sources as proxies, requesting a refined methodological line-up that lets them resonate. Approaches can involve studying continuities and breaks before, during and after crises, in order to measure their immediate impact, e.g., in the case of genealogies of priests, officials and their respective duties (Birk, Chaufray) and the Osirian catacombs in Karnak and beyond (Coulon). These shifts can be traced also in the evolution of concepts and ideologies, such as with the increasing importance of Ptolemaic queens in texts and iconography in Ptolemaic temples after the Great Revolt (Minas-Nerpel) or changes in decorum, as in the case of the victorious generals Komanos and Aristonikos in the Synodal Decrees of Ptolemy V (Nespoulous-Phalippou) or with the strategos Kallimachos, whose decree is crowned by a royal lunette depicting the reigning Queen and King, Cleopatra VII and Ptolemy XV (Caneva/Pfeiffer). Whether these individuals enter into a relationship of rivalry with the king is a delicate question that has to be carefully addressed, as Caneva and Pfeiffer point out. That rivalry is one of the central internal features of the Ptolemaic dynasty and a central reason for the crises of the $2^{nd}$ century BCE was beyond doubt, but that it shows itself in ritual scenes of Ptolemaic temples in Upper Egypt is a promising avenue of research (Preys).

Crisis-induced breaks can also have a concrete material impact, reaching from the (temporary) suspension of cults (Coulon) or building activities, for example in Medamud (Relats Montserrat) or Karnak (Minas-Nerpel) during the Great Revolt, to the destruction of whole cities, as in the case of Pathyris and Krokodilopolis in and after 88 BCE (Veïsse). Especially Relats Montserrat's contribution on Medamud explores how methodologically difficult it is to attribute the dismantling of an architectural structure to a targeted, hostile act of destruction, a topic touched upon also in relation to private monuments in the case of the Theban priesthood (Birk, Coulon). An analogous problem arises with the interpretation of hoard and stray finds of coins in the Thebaid (Faucher). The correlation between coin series and datable archaeological contexts narrows down possible dates of deposition, as in the case of the hoard underneath the Bubastide Portal in Karnak – the result of priests who wanted to save their savings at the onset of the revolt? Though Thomas Faucher remains cautious in his interpretation of these specific cases, he underlines adamantly, how coins can become highly indicative of how fiscal procedures were implemented on the ground and, thus, how the Thebaid was "ptolemaicized," before and after the Great Revolt.

Some contributions highlight the structuring power of crises by critically addressing tipping points and radical choices between dichotomous alternatives that have dominated scholarly discourses, and which have, in turn, relegated alternative readings to the periphery. The notion that the Great Revolt inaugurated a century of crises in the 2$^{nd}$ century BCE, culminating in Thebes' destruction 88 BCE ("l'inlassable révolte égyptienne" in Préaux's words) is re-evaluated by Veïsse, while Relats Montserrat puts into practice the analytical shift from identifying one critical, decisive point in time – the Great Revolt – to a non-teleological model of constant change that does justice to the complexity of the archaeological evidence of Medamud's temples, not the other way around. Likewise, other contributions highlight the active, creative and diverse role of the Egyptian priesthood as "politicians in the temple" (Preys). Priests in Ptolemaic Egypt were thus far from being a monolithic block, either supporting or combatting the Ptolemies. Judging from the Elephantine letters (Moje) or the analysis of Theban private monuments (Birk), supporters or adversaries of the rebellion could change sides, sometimes in the same family. This is true also for the Ptolemaic high administration, as can be induced from the famous case of the strategos Platon, who put his faith in the hand of Ptolemy X as his "very great god Soter," overcompensating his stained allegiance after switching sides (Veïsse). Viewing the ancients as acting in a field of possibilities, instead of caging them into a role ex-post, enables also contributors like Caneva and Pfeiffer to deconstruct Kallimachos' alleged role of a usurper in Thebes at the end of Ptolemaic rule, by embedding him into a network of ties with the Egyptian past and the Hellenistic, international present. It is this comparative approach that renders the allegedly exceptional comprehensible.

The authors' de-isolating and thus contextualising impulse can be deemed imperative for all contributions in this volume, analysing crises as revelatory, not for the alleged roles of their actors in a historiographic drama of decline and division, but for the diverse, highly adaptive and sometimes conflicting choices that made actors in Ptolemaic Thebes and beyond live in and through a crisis.

# Bibliography

Agut-Labordère, Moreno-García 2016
    Agut-Labordère, D., Moreno-García, J.C., *L'Égypte des pharaons. De Narmer à Dioclétien, 3150 av. J.-C.-284 apr. J.-C*, Mondes anciens, Paris, 2016.
Barrios 2017
    Barrios, R.E., "What Does Catastrophe Reveal for Whom? The Anthropology of Crises and Disasters at the Onset of the Anthropocene", *Annual Review of Anthropology* 46/1, 2017, pp. 151–166.

Baslez 2020
 Baslez, M.-F., "L'émergence d'une sensibilité apocalyptique dans l'histoire", *Recherches de Science Religieuse* 108/1, 2020, pp. 13–26.

Bennett 2008
 Bennett, C., "Egyptian Lunar Dates and Temple Service Months", *BiOr* 65, 2008, pp. 525–554.

Bennett 2011
 Bennett, C., *Alexandria and the Moon: An Investigation into the Lunar Macedonian Calendar of Ptolemaic Egypt*, StudHell 52, Leuven, Paris, Bristol, CT, 2011.

Birk 2023
 Birk, R., "D'un monde à l'autre. Prophètes thébains et fonctionnaires lagides dans la statuaire privée à la fin de l'époque ptolémaïque", in R. Roure (ed.), *Le multilinguisme dans la Méditerranée antique*, Diglossi@ 1, Pessac, 2023, pp. 115–140.

Butzer 2012
 Butzer, K.W., "Collapse, Environment, and Society", *PNAS* 109/10, 2012, pp. 3632–3639.

Caßor-Pfeiffer 2008a
 Caßor-Pfeiffer, S., "Zur Reflexion ptolemäischer Geschichte in den ägyptischen Tempeln unter Ptolemaios IX. Philometor II./Soter II. und Ptolemaios X. Alexander I. (116–80 v. Chr.) – Teil 1: Die Bau- und Dekorationstätigkeit", *JEH* 1/1, 2008, pp. 21–77.

Caßor-Pfeiffer 2008b
 Caßor-Pfeiffer, S., "Zur Reflexion ptolemäischer Geschichte in den ägyptischen Tempeln unter Ptolemaios IX. Philometor II./Soter II. und Ptolemaios X. Alexander I. (116–80 v. Chr.) – Teil 2: Kleopatra III. und Kleopatra Berenike III. im Spiegel der Tempelreliefs", *JEH* 1/2, 2008, pp. 235–265.

Clarysse 2019
 Clarysse, W., "Ethnic Identity: Egyptians, Greeks, and Romans", in K. Vandorpe (ed.), *A Companion to Greco-Roman and Late Antique Egypt*, Blackwell Companions to the Ancient World, Hoboken, NJ, 2019, pp. 299–313.

Collins, Manning (eds.) 2016
 Collins, J.J., Manning, J.G. (eds.), *Revolt and Resistance in the Classical World and the Near East: In the Crucible of Empire*, CHANE 85, Leiden, Boston, 2016.

Collombert 1998
 Collombert, P., "La succession éternelle des générations. À propos d'une formule des autobiographies tardives", *RdE* 49, 1998, pp. 47–58.

Collombert 2000
 Collombert, P., "Religion égyptienne et culture grecque. L'exemple de Διοσκουρίδης", *CdE* 75, 2000, pp. 47–63.

Coppens (ed.) 2021
 Coppens, F. (ed.), *Continuity, Discontinuity and Change: Case studies from the New Kingdom to the Ptolemaic and Roman Era*, Prague, 2021.

Coulon 2001
 Coulon, L., "Quand Amon parle à Platon (La statue Caire JE 38033)", *RdE* 52, 2001, pp. 85–125.

Coussement 2016
 Coussement, S., *'Because I am Greek': Polyonymy as an Expression of Ethnicity in Ptolemaic Egypt*, StudHell 55, Leuven, Paris, Bristol, CT, 2016.

Depauw, Coussement (eds.) 2014
 Depauw, M., Coussement, S. (eds.), *Identifiers and Identification Methods in the Ancient World: Legal Documents in Ancient Societies III*, OLA 229, Leuven, Paris, Walpole, MA, 2014.

Dirksen 2021
: Dirksen, S., "'Nicht wurde dergleichen gesehen seit der Zeit der Vorfahren': Naturkatastrophen im Alten Ägypten", in K. Gabler, A. Verbovsek, S. Bickel, E. Hemauer (eds.), *Formen kultureller Dynamik, Impuls – Progression – Transformation: Beiträge des zehnten Basler und Berliner Arbeitskreises Junge Aegyptologie (BAJA 10), 29.11.–1.12.2019*, GOF IV/68, Wiesbaden, 2021, pp. 91–104.

Edelstein, Geroulanos, Wheatley 2020
: Edelstein, D., Geroulanos, S., Wheatley, N., "Chronocenosis: An Introduction to Power and Time", in D. Edelstein, S. Geroulanos, N. Wheatley (eds.), *Power and Time: Temporalities in Conflict and the Making of History*, Chicago, London, 2020, pp. 1–49.

Erdkamp, Manning, Verboven (eds.) 2021
: Erdkamp, P., Manning, J.G., Verboven, K. (eds.), *Climate Change and Ancient Societies in Europe and the Near East: Diversity in Collapse and Resilience*, Palgrave Studies in Ancient Economies, Cham, 2021.

Escolano-Poveda 2020
: Escolano-Poveda, M., *The Egyptian Priests of the Graeco-Roman Period: an Analysis on the Basis of the Egyptian and Graeco-Roman Literary and Paraliterary Sources*, SSR 29, Wiesbaden, 2020.

Fischer-Bovet 2014
: Fischer-Bovet, C., *Army and Society in Ptolemaic Egypt*, Armies of the Ancient World, Cambridge, 2014.

Fischer-Bovet 2015
: Fischer-Bovet, C., "A Challenge to the Concept of Decline for Understanding Hellenistic Egypt: From Polybius to the Twenty-first Century", in D. Agut-Labordère, M.-P. Chaufray, A.-E. Veïsse (eds.), *Le thème du "déclin" dans l'historiographie de l'Égypte et de l'Orient ancien. Actes de la 5ème table ronde de l'Atelier Aigyptos à Paris, 25 juin 2011*, Topoi 20, Paris, 2015, pp. 209–237.

Fischer-Bovet 2023
: Fischer-Bovet, C., "Hellenistic Warfare and Egyptian Society", in D. Candelora, N. Ben-Marzouk, K. Cooney (eds.), *Ancient Egyptian Society: Challenging Assumptions, Exploring Approaches*, Abingdon, Oxon, New York, 2023, pp. 182–194.

Fischer-Bovet, Reden (eds.) 2021
: Fischer-Bovet, C., Reden, S. von (eds.), *Comparing the Ptolemaic and Seleucid Empire: Integration, Communication, and Resistance*, Cambridge, 2021.

Gehrke 2021
: Gehrke, H.-J., "Zusammenfassung und Perspektivierung", in S. Pfeiffer, G. Weber (eds.), *Gesellschaftliche Spaltungen im Zeitalter des Hellenismus (4. bis 1. Jahrhundert v. Chr.)*, Oriens et Occidens 35, Stuttgart, 2021, pp. 197–205.

Goldstone 2016
: Goldstone, J.A., *Revolution and Rebellion in the Early Modern World: Population Change and State Breakdown in England, France, Turkey, and China, 1600–1850, 25th Anniversary Edition*, New York, 2016.

Gorre 2017
: Gorre, G., "The Satrap Stela: A Middle Ground Approach", *JEH* 10/1, 2017, pp. 51–68.

Habermas 1992 [1976]
: Habermas, J., *Legitimation Crisis*, Cambridge, 1992 [1976].

Hartog 2020
: Hartog, F., *Chronos. L'occident aux prises avec le temps*, Bibliothèque des Histoires, Paris, 2020.

Hoffmann, Minas-Nerpel, Pfeiffer 2009
: Hoffmann, F., Minas-Nerpel, M., Pfeiffer, S., *Die dreisprachige Stele des C. Cornelius Gallus: Übersetzung und Kommentar*, AfP Beihefte 9, Berlin, New York, 2009.

Hoffmann-Salz (ed.) 2021
    Hoffmann-Salz, J. (ed.), *The Middle East as Middle Ground? Cultural Interaction in the Ancient Middle East Revisited*, Vienna, 2021.

Hölbl 1994
    Hölbl, G., *Geschichte des Ptolemäerreiches: Politik, Ideologie und religiöse Kultur von Alexander dem Großen bis zur römischen Eroberung*, Darmstadt, 1994.

Honigman, Veïsse 2021
    Honigman, S., Veïsse, A.-E., "Regional Revolts in the Seleucid and Ptolemaic Empires", in C. Fischer-Bovet, S. von Reden (eds.), *Comparing the Ptolemaic and Seleucid Empire: Integration, Communication, and Resistance*, Cambridge, 2021, pp. 301–328.

Huß 2001
    Huß, W., *Ägypten in hellenistischer Zeit. 332–30 v. Chr.*, Munich, 2001.

Jambon 2015
    Jambon, E., "'Fin de siècle' ou 'belle époque'? Réflexions sur la représentation de l'Égypte tardive chez Gaston Maspero et Ernest A. Wallis Budge", in D. Agut-Labordère, M.-P. Chaufray, A.-E. Veïsse (eds.), *Le thème du "déclin" dans l'historiographie de l'Égypte et de l'Orient ancien. Actes de la 5$^{ème}$ table ronde de l'Atelier Aigyptos à Paris, 25 juin 2011*, Topoi 20, Paris, 2015, pp. 187–208.

Johstono 2018
    Johstono, P., "'No Strength To Stand': Defeat at Panium, the Macedonian Class, and Ptolemaic Decline", in J.H. Clark, B. Turner (eds.), *Brill's Companion to Military Defeat in Ancient Mediterranean Society*, Warfare in the Ancient Mediterranean World 2, Leiden, Boston, 2018, pp. 162–187.

Jördens, Quack (eds.) 2011
    Jördens, A., Quack, J.F. (eds.), *Ägypten zwischen innerem Zwist und äußerem Druck: die Zeit Ptolemaios' VI. bis VIII. – Internationales Symposion Heidelberg 16.–19.9.2007*, Philippika 45, Wiesbaden, 2011.

Klotz 2009
    Klotz, D., "The Statue of the *dioikêtês* Harchebi/Archibios: Nelson-Atkins Museum of Art 47-12", *BIFAO* 109, 2009, pp. 281–310.

Koselleck 1973
    Koselleck, R., *Kritik und Krise: Eine Studie zur Pathogenese der bürgerlichen Welt*, Frankfurt am Main, 1973.

Koselleck 1979
    Koselleck, R., *Vergangene Zukunft: Zur Semantik geschichtlicher Zeiten*, Frankfurt am Main, 1979.

Koselleck 2006a
    Koselleck, R., *Begriffsgeschichten: Studien zur Semantik und Pragmatik der politischen und sozialen Sprache*, Frankfurt am Main, 2006.

Koselleck 2006b
    Koselleck, R., "Crisis", *Journal of the History of Ideas* 67/2, 2006, pp. 357–400.

Kosmin, Moyer (eds.) 2022
    Kosmin, P.J., Moyer, I.S. (eds.), *Cultures of Resistance in the Hellenistic East*, Oxford, 2022.

Liddell-Scott, s.v. "krínô"
    Liddell-Scott, *A Greek-English Lexicon*, Oxford, 1996, p. 996, s.v. "krínô".

Lippert 2009
    Lippert, S.L., "*Au clair de la lune*: The Organisation of Cultic Service by Moon Calendar in Soknopaiou Nesos", in G. Widmer, D. Devauchelle (eds.), *Actes du IXe congrès international des études démotiques Paris, 31 août–3 septembre 2005*, BdE 147, Kairo, 2009, pp. 183–194.

List 2012
: List, E., "Einbruch ins Selbstverständliche: Katastrophen als Kontingenzerfahrung", in A. Berlejung (ed.), *Disaster and Relief Management: Katastrophen und ihre Bewältigung*, Forschungen zum Alten Testament 81, Tübingen, 2012, pp. 67–83.

Ludlow, Manning 2016
: Ludlow, F., Manning, J.G., "Revolts under the Ptolemies: A Paleoclimatical Perspective", in J.J. Collins, J.G. Manning (eds.), *Revolt and Resistance in the Classical World and the Near East: In the Crucible of Empire*, CHANE 85, Leiden, Boston, 2016, pp. 154–171.

Ludlow, Manning 2021
: Ludlow, F., Manning, J.G., "Volcanic Eruptions, Veiled Suns, and Nile Failure in Egyptian History: Integrating Hydroclimate into Understandings of Historical Change", in P. Erdkamp, J.G. Manning, K. Verboven (eds.), *Climate Change and Ancient Societies in Europe and the Near East: Diversity in Collapse and Resilience*, Palgrave Studies in Ancient Economies, Cham, 2021, pp. 301–320.

Manning 2009
: Manning, J.G., *The Last Pharaohs: Egypt under the Ptolemies, 305–30 BC*, Princeton, 2009.

McGing 1997
: McGing, B., "Revolt Egyptian Style: Internal Opposition to Ptolemaic Rule", *AfP* 43/2, 1997, pp. 273–314.

McGing 2012
: McGing, B., "Revolt in Ptolemaic Egypt: Nationalism Revisited", in P. Schubert (ed.), *Actes du 26$^e$ Congrès international de papyrologie*s, Recherches et Rencontres 30, Geneva, 2012, pp. 509–516.

McGing 2016
: McGing, B., "Revolting Subjects – Empires and Insurrection: Ancient and Modern", in J.J. Collins, J.G. Manning (eds.), *Revolt and Resistance in the Classical World and the Near East: In the Crucible of Empire*, CHANE 85, Leiden, Boston, 2016, pp. 141–153.

Meinzer 1988
: Meinzer, M., "Der französische Revolutionskalender und die 'Neue Zeit'", in R. Koselleck, R. Reichardt (eds.), *Die Französische Revolution als Bruch des gesellschaftlichen Bewußtseins: Vorlagen und Diskussionen der internationalen Arbeitstagung am Zentrum für Interdisziplinäre Forschung der Univ. Bielefeld, 28. Mai – 1. Juni 1985*, Ancien Régime, Aufklärung und Revolution 15, Munich, 1988, pp. 23–60.

Moyer 2011a
: Moyer, I.S., *Egypt and the Limits of Hellenism*, Cambridge, 2011.

Moyer 2011b
: Moyer, I.S., "Finding a Middle Ground: Culture and Politics in the Ptolemaic Period", in P.F. Dorman, B.M. Bryan (eds.), *Perspectives on Ptolemaic Thebes*, SAOC 65, Chicago, 2011, pp. 115–145.

Moyer 2022
: Moyer, I.S., "Revolts, Resistance, and the Materiality of the Moral Order in Ptolemaic Egypt", in P.J. Kosmin, I.S. Moyer (eds.), *Cultures of Resistance in the Hellenistic East*, Oxford, 2022, pp. 148–174.

Nassehi 1993
: Nassehi, A., *Die Zeit der Gesellschaft: Auf dem Weg zu einer soziologischen Theorie der Zeit*, Opladen, 1993.

Nassehi 2023
: Nassehi, A., *Gesellschaftliche Grundbegriffe: Ein Glossar der öffentlichen Rede*, Munich, 2023.

Oliver-Smith 1996
: Oliver-Smith, A., "Anthropological Research on Hazards and Disasters", *Annual Review of Anthropology* 25/1, 1996, pp. 303–328.

Peremans 1975
> Peremans, W., "Ptolémée IV et les Égyptiens", in J. Bingen, G. Cambier, G. Nachtergael (eds.), *Le monde grec. pensée, littérature, histoire, documents. Hommages à Claire Préaux*, Brussels, 1975, pp. 393–402.

Pestman 1995
> Pestman, P.W., "Haronnophris and Chaonnophris. Two Indigenous Pharaohs in Ptolemaic Egypt (205–186 B.C.)", in S.G. Vleeming (ed.), *Hundred-Gated Thebes. Acts of a Colloquium on Thebes and the Theban Area in the Graeco-Roman Period.* P.L.Bat. 27, Leiden, New York, Cologne, 1995, pp. 101–137.

Pfeiffer 2004
> Pfeiffer, S., *Das Dekret von Kanopos (238 v. Chr.)*, AfP Beihefte 18, Munich, Leipzig, 2004.

Pfeiffer 2021
> Pfeiffer, S., "Innere Konflikte und herrschaftliche Versöhnungsstrategien im ptolemäischen Ägypten (3.–2. Jh. v. Chr.)", in S. Pfeiffer, G. Weber (eds.), *Gesellschaftliche Spaltungen im Zeitalter des Hellenismus (4. bis 1. Jahrhundert v. Chr.)*, Oriens et Occidens 35, Stuttgart, 2021, pp. 107–128.

Pfeiffer, Weber (eds.) 2021
> Pfeiffer, S., Weber, G. (eds.), *Gesellschaftliche Spaltungen im Zeitalter des Hellenismus (4. bis 1. Jahrhundert v. Chr.)*, Oriens et Occidens 35, Stuttgart, 2021.

Préaux 2009
> Préaux, C., "Esquisse d'une histoire des révolutions égyptiennes sous les Lagides", *CdE* 11, 1936, pp. 522–552.

Quack 2009
> Quack, J.F., "Menetekel an der Wand? Zur Deutung der 'Demotischen Chronik'", in M. Witte, J. F. Diehl (eds.), *Orakel und Gebete: interdisziplinäre Studien zur Sprache der Religion in Ägypten, Vorderasien und Griechenland in hellenistischer Zeit*, Forschungen zum Alten Testament, 2. Reihe 38, Tübingen, 2009, pp. 23–51.

Quack 2012
> Quack, J.F., "Danaergeschenk des Nil? Zu viel oder zu wenig Wasser im Alten Ägypten", in A. Berlejung (ed.), *Disaster and Relief Management: Katastrophen und ihre Bewältigung*, Forschungen zum Alten Testament 81, Tübingen, 2012, pp. 333–381.

Recklinghausen 2018
> Recklinghausen, D. von, *Die Philensis-Dekrete: Untersuchungen über zwei Synodaldekrete aus der Zeit Ptolemaios' V. und ihre geschichtliche und religiöse Bedeutung*, ÄA 73, Wiesbaden, 2018.

Roitman 2013
> Roitman, J., *Anti-Crisis*, Durham, 2013.

Roitman 2016
> Roitman, J., "Africa Otherwise", in B. Goldstone, J. Obarrio (eds.), *African Futures: Essays on Crisis, Emergence, and Possibility*, Chicago, 2016, pp. 23–38.

Rutherford (ed.) 2016
> Rutherford, I. (ed.), *Greco-Egyptian Interactions : Literature, Translation, and Culture, 500 BCE–300 CE*, Oxford, 2016.

Singer 2022
> Singer, P.N., *Time for the Ancients: Measurement, Theory, Experience*, Chronoi 3, Berlin, Boston, 2022.

Singh et al. 2023
> Singh, R., Tsigaridis, K., LeGrande, A.N., Ludlow, F., Manning, J.G., "Investigating Hydroclimatic Impacts of the 168–158 BCE Volcanic Quartet and their Relevance to the Nile River Basin and Egyptian History", *Climate of the Past* 19/1, 2023, pp. 249–275.

Stern 2022
> Stern, E.K., *The Oxford Encyclopedia of Crisis Analysis*, Oxford, 2022.

Thompson, Vandorpe, Christensen 2017
> Thompson, D.J., Vandorpe, K., Christensen, T., *Land and Taxes in Ptolemaic Egypt: An Edition, Translation and Commentary for the Edfu Land Survey (P. Haun. IV 70)*, Cambridge classical studies, Cambridge, 2017.

Vandorpe 2008
> Vandorpe, K., *Persian Soldiers and Persians of the Epigone: Social Mobility of Soldiers-herdsmen in Upper Egypt*, AfP 54, 2008, pp. 87–108.

Vandorpe 2011
> Vandorpe, K., "A Successful, but Fragile Biculturalism: The Hellenization Process in the Upper-Egyptian Town of Pathyris under Ptolemy VI and VIII", in A. Jördens, J.F. Quack (eds.), *Ägypten zwischen innerem Zwist und äußerem Druck: die Zeit Ptolemaios' VI. bis VIII. – Internationales Symposion Heidelberg 16.–19.9.2007*, Philippika 45, Wiesbaden, 2011, pp. 292–308.

Veïsse 2004
> Veïsse, A.-E., *Les "révoltes égyptiennes": Recherches sur les troubles du règne de Ptolémée III à la conquête romaine*, StudHell 41, Leuven, Paris, Dudley, MA, 2004.

Veïsse 2007
> Veïsse, A.-E., "Les identités multiples de Ptolémaios, fils de Glaukias", *AncSoc* 37, 2007, pp. 69–87.

Veïsse 2014
> Veïsse, A.-E., "Pour situer le débat. L'identité ethnique en Égypte aux époques perse, ptolémaïque et romain", *DHA-Suppl.* 10, 2014, pp. 207–218.

Veïsse 2016
> Veïsse, A.-E., "Polybe, les Lagides et les rebelles", *Cahiers du centre Gustave Glotz* 27, 2016, pp. 199–213.

Veïsse 2019
> Veïsse, A.-E., "The Last Pharaohs: The Ptolemaic Dynasty and the Hellenistic World", in K. Vandorpe (ed.), *A Companion to Greco-Roman and Late Antique Egypt*, Blackwell Companions to the Ancient World, Hoboken, NJ, 2019, pp. 35–49.

Veïsse 2022
> Veïsse, A.-E., "The 'Great Theban Revolt', 206–186 BCE", in I.S. Moyer, P.J. Kosmin (eds.), *Cultures of Resistance in the Hellenistic East*, Oxford, 2022, pp. 57–73.

Vigh 2008
> Vigh, H., "Crisis and Chronicity: Anthropological Perspectives on Continuous Conflict and Decline", *Ethnos* 73/1, 2008, pp. 5–24.

Vleeming (ed.) 1995
> Vleeming, S.P. (ed.), *Hundred-Gated Thebes: Acts of a Colloquium on Thebes and the Theban Area in the Graeco-Roman Period*, P.L.Bat. 27, Leiden, New York, Cologne, 1995.

Wackenier, Gorre (eds.) 2020
> Wackenier, S., Gorre, G. (eds.), *Quand la fortune du royaume ne dépend pas de la vertu du prince. Un renforcement de la monarchie lagide de Ptolémée VI à Ptolémée X (169–88 av. J.-C.)?*, StudHell 59, Leuven, Paris, Bristol, CT, 2020.

White 2011
> White, R., *The Middle Ground – Indians, Empires, and Republics in the Great Lakes Region, 1650-1815: Twentieth-anniversary Edition*, Studies in North American Indian History, Cambridge, New York, 2011.

Zelinskyi 2020
> Zelinskyi, A., "ГОЛОД В ЕГИПТЕ ПРИ ПТОЛЕМЕЕ III ЭВЕРГЕТЕ: ПЕРЕСМОТР ДАТИРОВКИ И ИСТОЧНИКОВОЙ БАЗЫ [The Famine in Egypt under Ptolemy III Euergetes: the Revision of the Date and the List of Sources]", *Восток (Oriens)* 3, 2020, pp. 65–73.

Ralph Birk
# Rebellious Priests of Thebes?

## 1 Introduction

The Great Theban Revolt, which held the Thebaid in its grip for 20 years (206–186 BCE), involved several key players: On the one side were the two rebel kings Haronnophris and Chaonnophris,[1] while on the other side were their dynastic antagonists Ptolemy IV Philopator and especially Ptolemy V Epiphanes, along with their victorious generals, Komanos and Aristonikos.[2] Another group that is omnipresent in modern historiography as a rebellious faction in the Thebaid is the Theban priesthood. But despite the prominence assigned to them, they remain generally anonymous in these accounts.[3] This is owed to the fact that based on the known sources, especially documentary papyri, it is difficult to draw conclusions as to their mindset, intentions, and allegiances during the revolt.[4] Yet, the assumption that the priesthood was affected by and potentially, in turn, had an effect on events during the revolt is worth considering. The length of the revolt suggests a deep influence on more than one generation in the Theban high clergy: a person born in 206 BCE came off age at the end of the revolt – having lived most of their life under rebel rule, with Ptolemaic interregna in 199 and 198 BCE. On the other hand, priestly successions in hereditary offices probably had to continue during that time if the offices still existed.

Therefore, this chapter suggests a different approach: an analysis of the evolution of families of the high clergy before, during, and after the revolt in combination with individual case studies to shed light on the varied and complicated role(s) of priests in a time of upheaval.

---

[1] For the possible identification of the two kings as one individual who changed his name after 199 BCE: Veïsse 2013, pp. 513–514.
[2] See A. Nespoulous-Phalippou in this volume and Nespoulous-Phalippou 2015a; Nespoulous-Phalippou 2015b.
[3] E.g. Huß 2001, p. 448; "die thebanischen Amunspriester": Pfeiffer 2021, p. 113; "priests of Thebes": Moyer 2022, p. 163; but see the differentiated view in Veïsse 2013, pp. 228–243.
[4] See the methodological considerations in Moyer 2022; Pfeiffer 2021, pp. 113–116 and Veïsse 2004, pp. 228–232.

Open Access. © 2025 the author(s), published by De Gruyter. This work is licensed under the Creative Commons Attribution-NonCommercial-NoDerivatives 4.0 International License.
https://doi.org/10.1515/9783111608051-002

## 2 The Prelude to the Revolt: Evolutions in the 3rd Century BCE

Before the revolt, during the 3rd century BCE, the Ptolemies took measures that reshaped the relationship between the central government and the Egyptian temples in the *chora* and in Thebes, administratively, economically, and institutionally.[5]

A first piece of evidence for royal reforms might be the famous Karnak Ostracon (oKarnak L.S. 462,4). Its dating has been debated in recent scholarship, as Chauveau proposed a Saite original of this Ptolemaic copy by reading "Psammetich" instead of a royal epithet referring to Ptolemy II.[6] The newest proposition by Thomas/Ray is to read the questioned group as *p3 nsw bἰk* – "the falcon king" as an epithet of Ptolemy II,[7] corroborating a date that had been advanced already by Bresciani in the first edition.[8] If we accept this dating to the reign of Ptolemy II, in the year 258 BCE ("year 28", l. 2), we might draw the following conclusions: On royal command, probably based on a royal *prostagma* and without being necessarily a literal translation of a Greek ordonnance,[9] "scribes" (*sḥ.w*, l. 4) and "agents" (*rd.w*, l. 4) are sent to report on the state and the dimensions of the cultivated land of temples and the crown, also in respect to the irrigation system and other entities, such as crops and vineyards. This cadastre is not only an account of agricultural farmland, but also involves inspecting the "income of the priesthoods" (*p3 b3k n3 w'b.w*, l. 15) and of the "king's servants" (*šms.w pr-ꜥ3*),[10] thus accounting for the income by temple priests, also in Karnak, where the ostracon has been found in the priestly quarter east of the sacred lake.[11] If dated correctly, the find spot of the ostracon indicates the important role of the Theban priesthood in implementing royal ordonnances on the ground in the early Ptolemaic period. But we are also aware of smaller-scale land surveys in the Fayum from the 3rd century BCE.[12] An inventory of the priesthoods, as described in the ostracon, be it from Thebes or elsewhere, enables the palace to gain a fuller picture not only of the income of temple priests but also of the organisation of the priesthood.

---

5 See Veïsse 2022, pp. 70–72 with further literature.
6 Chauveau 2011 and Thomas, Ray 2014, pp. 332–336. See also G. Vittmann's German translation (with Chauveau's readings): *Thesaurus Linguae Aegyptiae*, KX4HSHA5BJAP7PCO2UVLM6DORA.
7 Thomas, Ray 2014.
8 Bresciani 1978; Bresciani 1983.
9 Thomas, Ray 2014, pp. 343–344.
10 Bresciani 1983, pp. 16–17; 28.
11 For the findspot: Bresciani 1983, Vandorpe 1995, p. 214 and Masson-Berghoff 2021, p. 633.
12 Muhs 2005, pp. 17–19; cf. also Armoni 2012.

During the 3ʳᵈ century BCE, reforms affect the hierarchical structure of the priesthood and the economic and fiscal competencies of the temple and its staff. During the reign of Ptolemy III, first administrative reforms of the temples become tangible. In the Canopus Decree (238 BCE), one of the decisions taken by the priestly synod is to reform the phyle structure of the temples: a new, fifth phyle is added to the rotating system of four phyle.[13] Secure attestations for the 5ᵗʰ phyle in priestly titles in Theban sources date to the 2ⁿᵈ century BCE, after the revolt.[14] It is therefore difficult to establish the impact of the phyle-reform on the ground in Thebes directly after the issue of the Canopus Decree in 238 BCE, even though this process is attested for the high priest of Ptah in Memphis Harmachis. He changed to the 5ᵗʰ phyle from his father Anemher II's 3ʳᵈ phyle most likely as early as the 3ʳᵈ century BCE.[15] The reform also encompassed the introduction of a 5ᵗʰ Prophet of Amun, who enlarged the college of traditionally four Prophets of Amun.[16] Furthermore, there is a clear link between the hierarchical position of these priests and their service in the corresponding phyle (*imi-3bd=f ḥr s3 dpi / 2.nw / 3.nw / 4.nw / 5.nw*), as exemplified by the dossiers of the First Prophet of Amun Osoroeris III (1ˢᵗ half 3ʳᵈ century BCE), the Second Prophet of Amun Spotus (2ⁿᵈ half 4ᵗʰ century BCE), and the Third Prophet of Amun Nechtmonthes I (3ʳᵈ–2ⁿᵈ centuries BCE).[17] Consequently, the new phyle also affected the hierarchical positions in Thebes: Two 5ᵗʰ Prophets of Amun are known from Thebes, but dating most likely after the Great Revolt: Monthemhet III, son of the 4ᵗʰ Prophet of Amun Horos III, probably from the second half of the 2ⁿᵈ century BCE, and Osoroeris, whose family background remains obscure.[18] The introduction of the fifth phyle and implicitly also of the fifth prophet was bound to the king himself, as the "fifth phyle of the beneficient gods". The presence of the Ptolemaic ruler in the realm of the temples was reinforced by the introduction of the dynastic cult.[19] Individual title holders appear in Thebes during the time of Ptolemy III, as shown by the ample dossier of Harendotes.[20]

Moreover, two new positions come to the fore in Karnak during the 3ʳᵈ century BCE, the so-called "Great Governor in Thebes" (*ḥ3ti-ʿ wr m W3s.t*) and "Second Governor in Thebes" (*ḥ3ti-ʿ m-ḥt m W3s.t*).[21] These titles are frequently associated with

---

13 Pfeiffer 2004, pp. 110–121.
14 Birk 2020, pp. 252–253.
15 Pfeiffer 2004, p. 117; Reymond 1981, pp. 92–94; Quaegebeur 1971, p. 250.
16 Birk 2020, pp. 249–260.
17 Birk 2020, p. 210.
18 Birk 2020, pp. 249–260.
19 For the royal cult as one of the main reasons for the Synodal Decrees, cf. Gorre, Veïsse 2020.
20 Quaegebeur 1995, pp. 142–144.
21 Birk 2020, pp. 281–428.

the function of "Chief of the Prophets in Thebes" (*ỉmỉ-r' ḥm.w-nṯr m W3s.t*). The association between the two titles is so close that they form a unity, with the toponym juxtaposed at the end: *ḥ3tỉ-' wr ỉmỉ-r' ḥm.w-nṯr m W3s.t*.[22] The fact that in the 4th century BCE the function of "Chief of the Prophets" still belonged to the 1st Prophet of Amun Spotus I[23] indicates that the "Governors" replaced the 1st Prophet of Amun in this role during the early Ptolemaic period making them the leading priests in the temple.

However, the dating of the earliest "Governors in Thebes" is problematic, as they are only attested indirectly in the genealogies of their descendants, on monuments of much later date (Tab. 1).[24] Their approximate lifetime can be projected via a stable generation period, here fixed at 25 years.[25]

**Tab. 1:** Earliest Great Governors in Thebes.

| | *ḥ3tỉ-' wr m W3s.t* | *ỉmỉ-r' ḥm.w-nṯr m W3s.t* | Other titles | Generations to descendant | Dating | Dating of monument | Family |
|---|---|---|---|---|---|---|---|
| Spotus[26] | X | X | – | 7 | ~ 1st half/mid-3rd c. BCE | Begin 1st c. BCE | 1st PA? |
| Chapochonsis[27] | X | – | 3rd PA | 2 | ~ mid-3rd c. BCE | First half 2nd c. BCE | 3rd PA |
| Monthemhet[28] | X | – | – | 3 | ~ end 3rd c./ begin 2nd c. BCE | Second half 2nd c. BCE | 4th PA |

All three probably come from families occupying the highest echelons of the Theban hierarchy: Chapochonsis was a 3rd Prophet of Amun and Monthemhet is related to the 4th Prophets of Amun. The case for Spotus is not as clear-cut, as he and his descendants share common, typical features with the early Ptolemaic 1st Proph-

---

22 Birk 2020, p. 389.
23 Birk 2020, pp. 15–22.
24 For the dating of the Great and Second Governors in Thebes see Birk 2020, pp. 377–386.
25 Birk 2020, pp. 377–381. For other systems, in favor of a 30-year-generation see Jansen-Winkeln 2006; Payraudeau 2014, pp. 112–115. A 30-year-generation would extend the families even more back into the 3rd century BCE.
26 Statue Cairo, TR 20/2/25/4, Birk 2020, pp. 298–305.
27 Statue Cairo, SR 218, Birk 2020, pp. 189–193; Rashed, Abdelrahman 2016; a new edition is prepared by L. Coulon and R. Birk.
28 Statue New York, Private Collection, see Birk 2020, pp. 249–254; Klotz 2016a, pp. 446–453.

ets, in onomastics (Spotus, Osoroeris) and titles (ḥm-nṯr wḥm n Ỉmn), but no monument of this family exhibits the title of "Great Governor".[29] It is therefore also possible that he is to be identified with one of the early Ptolemaic 1st Prophets of Amun, e.g. Spotus II or Spotus III (see *infra*). In any case, the genealogies point to the existence of "Great Governors" in Thebes already in the 3rd century BCE.[30]

What becomes clear is that these new offices brought a new dynamic. After the Macedonian conquest, the hierarchy consisting of 1st – 4th Prophets of Amun was, in Thebes, accepted by the Argeads and Ptolemies. The family of the 1st Prophets of Amun is continuously attested from the early Sebennytic era in the 4th century BCE to the 2nd half of the 3rd century BCE, and even after the Great Revolt scattered evidence indicates the maintenance of the office.[31] It seems that introducing the new offices of "Great" and "Second Governors" was one of the royal measures to break the hereditary system they inherited from the 30th dynasty and that survived the 2nd Persian period. The charge of leading the prophets in Karnak then switched families, even the three earliest "Great Governors" come from different families, but from the same milieu. Presiding over the prophets of Karnak was then no longer a hereditary task that was monopolised by one family, to the detriment of the 1st Prophets of Amun. In the beginning, this need not have been an administrative reform that deprived the high clergy of their powerful positions in the hierarchy, as six of ten families, which counted a "Governor" among their ranks, were associated through relatives with the 1st to 5th Prophets of Amun. But the automatism of a hereditary system was in any case broken up. However, we do not know how a "Great Governor" acquired his position – be it by royal ordonnance, by acquisition in a bidding process, or by election through peers.[32]

Attestations of the Great and Second Governors in other temples and regions, from the private statuary in Tanis to the processions of the New Year in Dendera and Edfu,[33] speak to the fact that this has been a concerted, national reform.[34] One of these non-Theban Great Governors is Psentesoys from Xois, whose group

---

[29] A fragmentary, feminine statue now in the Abu-Gud-Magazine in Luxor (Register of Mut & Khonsu Chapel in Luxor temple, Nr. 121) probably mentions a "Second (?) Governor" and 1st Prophet of Amun Osoroeris, *non vidi*.

[30] The next attested Great Governor would be the forefather of the extended family of the pJoseph Smith, Osoroeris, whose fragmentary statue (Baltimore, Walters Art Museum 22.213) might belong to the verge from the 3rd to the 2nd century BCE: Birk 2020, pp. 306; 312–313.

[31] See *infra* and Birk 2020, pl. 1.

[32] For the involvement of the palace: Birk 2020, p. 443.

[33] See inscription on the statue CG 689 of Teos, son of Apries: Zivie-Coche 2004, pp. 148–155; Birk 2020, p. 425 and the role of the governors in the processions of the new year: Rickert 2019, p. 532; Birk 2020, pp. 426–428; Birk 2016.

[34] Birk 2020, pp. 390–391; 424–428.

statue has been found in the cachette of Karnak (Cairo, JE 36576).³⁵ Like his Theban counterparts, he inhabits leading positions in the Xoite priesthood (sḥḏ ḥm.w-nṯr m Ḥw.t-nswy.t – "Overseer of Prophets in Ḥw.t-nswy.t", ḥm-nṯr dpỉ ḥm-nṯr 3.nw n Bȝ-nb -Ḏd – "First and Third Prophet of Banebdjed").³⁶ The statue is, judging by iconography and style, difficult to date. While it most likely forms part of the archaising tendency of the 30ᵗʰ dynasty and early Ptolemaic period,³⁷ there are other categories which point to the early Ptolemaic period, such as Ptolemaic orthographies, the use of a Saite formula (not securely attested after the 2ⁿᵈ half of the 3ʳᵈ century BCE)³⁸ and the title rḫ-nsw, which most probably also disappears after the early Ptolemaic period.³⁹ Hence, it is unlikely that Psentesoys' dossier dates after the 3ʳᵈ century BCE. By consequence, this early Ptolemaic non-Theban "Great Governor" renders the first appearance of "Great Governors of Thebes" for the 3ʳᵈ century BCE quite probable.⁴⁰

However, it is important to mention that neither the positions nor their introduction in the temple hierarchy appear in any of the Ptolemaic synodal decrees. In the preamble, the first priests listed as in attendance at the synod are the ỉmỉ.w-rʾ gs.w-pr.w – "Chiefs of the Temple Domains" (*Égyptien de Tradition*), corresponding to the "Lesoneis" (mr-šn.w) in Demotic and the archiereis in Greek (ἀρχιερεῖς).⁴¹ Thus, the hieroglyphic title does not correspond to the Governor's typical prerogative of being "Chief of the Prophets". While the "Prophets" (*Égyptien de Tradition*/Demotic: ḥm.w-nṯr, Greek: προφῆται) are mentioned as the following group of priests, their designation does not entail any inner hierarchical quality. Likewise, the First Prophets (ḥm-nṯr dpỉ) of a god were not mentioned in the decrees either. It seems nevertheless reasonable to contextualise the introduction of the "Great" and "Second Governors" during the reign of Ptolemy III, when the hierarchical structures of the temple are adapted in the decree of Canopus (238 BCE) through the

---

35 Guermeur 2004; Jansen-Winkeln 2001.
36 Jansen-Winkeln 2001, pp. 137; 146 (text e); Guermeur 2004, pp. 261–262.
37 Jansen-Winkeln 2001, p. 139; Guermeur 2004.
38 Jansen-Winkeln 2000. See now also Jansen-Winkeln 2020 as a reaction to Klotz 2016b. For the dating: De Meulenaere 1993, p. 64.
39 De Meulenaere 1995, p. 84. For Ptolemaic attestations of this title in a Panopolitan and religious context: Gorre 2009a.
40 Another piece of evidence might be the mentioning of the ḥȝtỉ.w-ʿ (without differentiation) as one of the status groups that shall come together on ordonnance of Ptolemy II in Alexandria, as mentioned by the Stela of Sais in 266/265 BCE, Thiers 1999, pp. 426, 429. However, the following group of the ḥkȝ.w-ḥw.t rather indicates that these "Governors" are not considered to be priests, but royal representatives, as suggested by Collombert 2008, p. 92. See now also the comments in: Gorre, Veïsse 2020, p. 120. In the 2ⁿᵈ century BCE, the "Governors" appear in the decree from 161 BCE, in a heavily destroyed passage (l. 15): Panov, Lanciers 2023, pp. 45–46.
41 El-Masry, Altenmüller, Thissen 2012, pp. 79–80; Nespoulous-Phalippou 2015b, pp. 166–174.

introduction of the title "priest of the theoi euergetai", the 5$^{th}$ phyle and the reform of the *boulê* – "the council" of priests to 25 priests instead of 20.[42] It is important to note that the reforms of Canopus are directly related to the king and the royal cult of the *theoi euergetai*: a new position of "prophet of the theoi euergetai", a 5$^{th}$ phyle in honour of the *theoi euergetai* and consequently a replenished *boulê* by the new phyle. In addition, we see that in a Theban marriage contract from 220 BCE the scribe Psenchonsis writes – for the first time – in the name of the priests of Amun and the deified Ptolemies "of the five phylae".[43] This first attestation of the notary's office with the mention of the five phylae shows how the Theban priesthood was conceived as being devoted – even as an administrative entity – to Amun and the deified Ptolemies.

The introduction of the new positions of Governors need not have been disguised as a synodal decision of the priests, as was the fifth phyle in the Canopus decree.[44] Most likely, it was a top-down decision by the Ptolemies which was enforced on the ground, *before* the Great Revolt.

These new offices coincide with a firmer grip of the Ptolemies on Upper Egypt in the economic sphere and with administrative reforms during the second half of the 3$^{rd}$ century BCE.[45] From the early Ptolemaic period to the second half of the 3$^{rd}$ century BCE, the notaries and royal scribes in Thebes came mostly from one large and influential Theban family.[46] Title holders are attested through four generations in their ranks and it seems that the office was hereditary. These royal scribes were also involved in the legal proceedings of private transactions as notaries. The ample and varied religious titles of the "royal scribe of Upper Egypt" Harnouphis, attested on his striding statue (Lausanne, EG 7) from the first half of the 3$^{rd}$ century BCE, demonstrates how deeply embedded these scribes were in the local cults.[47] The last member of this family, Psenchonsis, signs a contract in Oct. 220 BCE – the last document witnessing their activity in Thebes,[48] but also the first mention of the newly established notary's office of the priests of Amun in Karnak.

---

42 Pfeiffer 2004, pp. 234–241.
43 *pEheverträge 22* (Oct. 220 BCE), Lüddeckens 1960, pp. 48–51; Arlt 2009, p. 30. For attestations of the fifth phyle in titles, found in hieroglyphic texts see Birk 2020, pp. 252–253.
44 Pfeiffer 2004, pp. 115–117.
45 Honigman, Veïsse 2021, pp. 302; 307–309; Pfeiffer 2021, p. 113; Manning 2003, pp. 160–164.
46 Quaegebeur 1995, pp. 152–154; Arlt 2011.
47 Wild 1954. The missing head of the statue Lausanne, Musée de Beaux-arts EG 7 is now in the Metropolitan Museum of Art (1980.422), for the attribution: De Meulenaere 1995, pp. 87–88. See also for the discussion of his titulary: Gorre 2009b.
48 Arlt 2011, p. 29: *pEheverträge 22*: Lüddeckens 1960, pp. 48–51.

The establishment of the notary's office of the priests of Amun in Karnak in the late 3rd century BCE and the disappearance of one single family of notaries appear to be, therefore, related events, indicating the shift from a monopolised family business to an institutionalisation of the Theban notary. After the revolt, notaries are attested foremost in Greek documents and form an integral part of the Ptolemaic hierarchic administration of the nome, bearing also – in some cases – Greek names.[49] Afterwards, except for the family of Pakhnoum, who, himself, was a witness of the Great Revolt and which will be discussed in detail below,[50] "royal scribes" from the 2nd century BCE do not appear to be related to each other.[51] This seems to be an analogous development to the introduction of the "Great" and "Second Governors", namely turning a hereditary function that is prone to monopolisation by certain families ("First Prophets" / "royal scribes") non-hereditary, be it by the introduction of new functions, e.g. the Governors in the temple, or by adjustment of old ones, e.g. the royal scribes.

At the same time, further administrative and fiscal reforms are implemented. We are informed that from 220 BCE onward, the harvest tax (in kind) is still collected by the temple, but brought to the royal granary in Thebes – as the oldest Greek tax receipts from Thebes show.[52] And texts from Edfu demonstrate that taxes were no longer transferred to the granary of the temple of Amun in Karnak, but to the royal granaries.[53] The lack of income of the temple was then at some time before 196 BCE compensated by the introduction of the *syntaxis*-payments, as is mentioned in the Memphis Decree as an already established practice.

All in all, before the outbreak of the Great Revolt, the autonomy of the Theban temples and their clergy was affected severely by Lagid reforms, be it institutionally or financially.

---

[49] Armoni 2012, pp. 11–15; 262. For the appointment procedure of notaries in the 2nd century BCE (probably from Arsinoites), involving the epistates, the archiereis and the laokritai, see *pRylands Gr. IV 572* and Manning 2003, p. 54.
[50] For their dossier, see *infra*.
[51] Arlt 2011, p. 21; Veïsse 2022, pp. 61–68.
[52] Vandorpe 2000, pp. 177; 195; 199; Pfeiffer 2021, pp. 113–114.
[53] Vandorpe 2000.

## 3 The Theban Priesthood During the Revolt – the Case of Pakhnoum

From the onset of the revolt, Thebes was a cornerstone of Haronnophris' "new state"[54], ideologically drawing heavily from Theban theology, given the rebel king's titulary ("beloved by Isis, beloved by Amunrasonther, the Great God") found mostly in the dating formulas of Demotic contracts, while also developing an administrative structure of his own. The earliest account is the limestone tablet Cairo, JE 38258 from the first year of his reign, found in Karnak.[55] Even if this literary letter may have been re-dated to Haronnophris' first year,[56] recently published documentary papyri from Pathyris attest to the first year of his reign,[57] indicating the implementation of administrative structures early on in his reign in the Thebaid. This extended to the establishment of a royal court in Thebes, as "those of the palace of pharaoh" (na pr Pr-'3) and the "scribe of the directive" (sḥ n p(3) wḫ3) are mentioned in the limestone tablet from year one of his reign.[58] It remains open, where such a rebel royal court would have sojourned in Thebes.

In this context, Thebes and the temples of Karnak have been stipulated to be the place where Haronnophris was crowned as Pharaoh by the Theban high priest, analogous to the coronation of the Ptolemies.[59] But if and how the Ptolemies underwent a "coronation" or – more accurately – a royal initiation ritual, and by whom this ritual might have been performed has been recently critically reassessed by Stadler, von Recklinghausen, and Lanciers/Panov,[60] discussing the Ptolemaic evidence from synodal decrees and temple texts. Sources pointing to a ritualized form begin with Ptolemy III. In the Alexandria Decree (243 BCE), the priests mention the day "on which his majesty received the kingship from his father",[61] a simple statement that is repeated in Canopus (238 BCE).[62] Then, under Ptolemy V, the information is amplified in the Memphis Decree (196 BCE): The king receives his office from his father in the

---

54 See last Veïsse 2022, pp. 61–64 and Moyer 2022, pp. 149–150.
55 Pestman 1965, p. 158; Pestman 1995, p. 101; Veïsse 2004, pp. 86–87; 96–99; Depauw 2006; Chaufray, Wegner 2016, p. 35. The tablet was found in Karnak by Legrain: Spiegelberg 1912, p. 34.
56 Depauw 2006, p. 102.
57 Chaufray, Wegner 2016, pp. 35–36.
58 Depauw 2006, p. 97.
59 Huß 2001, p. 446; Pestman 1995, pp. 105; 112–113.
60 Stadler 2012; Recklinghausen 2018, pp. 341–353 and now Panov, Lanciers 2023, pp. 67–70.
61 El-Masry, Altenmüller, Thissen 2012, pp. 131–134.
62 Pfeiffer 2004, pp. 73, 80–81.

context of a feast (ḥꜣb), during which members of the revolt from Lykopolis were executed.[63] In the time of Ptolemy V and VI, the role of the sḫmtï-crown is furthermore elaborated upon in the decrees, as the king appeared with the crown after having undergone the "initiation (bsi̯.t) of the king into the temple when he received his great office".[64] Only in late Ptolemaic times (41 BCE), a specific role for the Memphite high priest is attested on the stela of the high priest of Ptah Pasherenptah (BM, EA 886),[65] where a recurrent ritual involving the uraeus(-diadem) of the king, and not an initial coronation ceremony, was most probably meant. This raises the question, of when the initiation ritual was carried out. In comparing the given – yet scanty – data of the 2nd and 1st centuries BCE, Lanciers and Panov conclude that there is no clear temporal correlation between the king's ascension to the throne and the attested "coronation" rites, these could be performed even years later.[66] Considering this temporal gap between ascension and initiation in the temple, it is questionable, if the coronation would have been a necessary prerequisite for Haronnophris' rule in Thebes. Besides, even the existence of a royal titulary is not conditioned on a coronation, as exemplified by Macedonian pharaohs with a full titulary who were practically not present in Egypt.[67] A Theban ritual, administered by a priestly authority from Karnak, is therefore only a conclusion by analogy – but whose analogon already stands on shaky grounds.[68] And even if such a ritual is assumed, it would be difficult to ascribe it to the First Prophet of Amun, as this position might have been vacant during the revolt (see *infra*). This illustrates how methodologically difficult it is to attribute specific attitudes to the Theban priesthood as a corporation or individual priests, ranging from collaboration to full-fledged resistance.

One Theban priest who did witness the beginning of the revolt in 206 BCE is the "royal accounting scribe of the king of the gods" (sḫꜣw nsw ḥsb n nsw nṯr.w) Pakhnoum, son of Patous. H. De Meulenaere treated his dossier, revolving around his striding statue Cairo, JE 37456 (see Fig. 1).[69] He recognized that his burial is mentioned in two transactions of choachytes, in 195 BCE (pBM Andrews 11) and 175 BCE (pBM Andrews 5).[70] Possibly, another Demotic document may be added

---

63 Urk. II, 183, 5, Stadler 2012, 68–69 and Veïsse 2004, pp. 187–194.
64 Urk. II, 192, 7 (Memphis Decree, 196 BCE); Recklinghausen 2018, pp. 145–155 (Philensis I, 185 BCE); Panov, Lanciers 2023, pp. 59–60 (Memphis Decree of 161 BCE). For older parallels from the New Kingdom see the references in Panov, Lanciers 2023, p. 59 n. 71.
65 Panov 2012.
66 Panov, Lanciers 2023, p. 68.
67 Stadler 2012, pp. 61–62; 65.
68 Veïsse 2004, p. 232.
69 Coulon, Jambon 2017, B-CK 141.
70 See De Meulenaere 1997, pp. 23–24. For the papyri see: Andrews 1990, pp. 29–30, pl. 15–18; 45, pl. 33.

**Fig. 1:** Statue Cairo, JE 37456 (after De Meulenaere 1997, pp. 18; 20, figs. 1–2).

to this dossier, a money receipt that records a transaction of a Pakhnoum (without titles), son of Patous, to a certain Pabel (V DO Uppsala 1027). It is dated to a regnal year 22, on day 8 of Mecheir, which may correspond – as being early Ptolemaic by palaeography – to Ptolemy II (263 BCE), as suggested by Wångsted, or possibly to Ptolemy III (225 BCE). If the latter is correct, then we might see in this ostracon Pakhnoum being active roughly 20 years already before the beginning of the revolt, here in a private transaction.

That "royal scribes" were part of the rebel administration under Haronnophris is suggested by the letter Cairo, JE 38258 from his first regnal year, where a "royal scribe" and "scribe of the directive" (sḫ n pꜣ wḫꜣ) whose name is lost in the lacuna, is addressed as a "superior" (ḥry) of the "scribe of the trench of the water of Thebes" (sḫ n tꜣ ꜥ.t pꜣ mw Nw.t).[71] In the letter, the "scribe of the trench" informs the royal scribe that he would see to it that the water would not be let out of the trenches under his watch. As Depauw suggests, this might have had military reasons, as the flooding of canals prevented adversaries from landing on the shores of the city. This text clearly shows how the measurement and administra-

---

71 Depauw 2006, p. 97; Veïsse 2022, pp. 61–62.

tion of fields was not only a central element of the Ptolemaic fiscal system[72] but could serve also a military rationale that implicated "royal scribes" much more than other actors in Thebes during the Great Revolt. It is thus safe to assume that Pakhnoum was – as a royal scribe – directly affected by the rebellion.

From the choachyte papyri, we know that Pakhnoum died before 195 BCE, but not exactly when. Three possibilities arise: Either Pakhnoum passed away before the rebellion started, or he was coopted into the administrative structure of rebellious Karnak under Haronnophris, or he might as well have been discharged for being a "Ptolemaic" royal scribe. On his statue, the particular phrasing of the title "royal accounting scribe" is an important cue, as he is subordinated to the "king of the gods" and thus integrated into the temple administration.[73] This peculiar rendering of the title points, at least, to the changed circumstances under which Pakhnoum most probably died. Similarly, notaries signed their contracts only in the name of the priests of "Amunrasonther" – while omitting the Ptolemies, who were, under Ptolemy IV, still part of the formula.[74] It is hence very likely that Pakhnoum died after the revolt erupted.

Even if Pakhnoum was let go at the beginning of Haronnophris' rule, his family was able to pay the choachytes and the involved priests the necessary fees for embalming and burial in or rather sometime before 195 BCE.[75] It is thus not plausible that the rebels confiscated all of Pakhnoum's and his family's possessions.[76]

The son and grandson of Pakhnoum are also present in the documentation, namely his son Patous and his grandson Phibis, through two statues, Cairo, JE 38004, and Cairo, JE 37436.[77] All three statues from three subsequent generations, share – in pairs – different elements: The statues of Pakhnoum and his son Patous (JE 37456 and JE 38004) are of the same type, depicting a striding priest with a shaven head, holding a statue of Osiris by its base.[78] Both priests are clothed in an enveloping robe up to their chest, with a prominent bulge on the upper margin and a marked vertical edge on the left. Underneath this robe, they wear a garment that is knotted on their left shoulder, leaving the right shoulder bare. The statues of Osiris show slight differences in iconography: While the hands of Pakhnoum's

---

72 For this role of the royal scribes: Armoni 2012, pp. 172–178.
73 See already Birk 2020, p. 270.
74 See Pestman 1995, pp. 131–132.
75 See for this topic most recently: Cannata 2020, pp. 217–223 and *passim*.
76 Johstono 2015, pp. 194–195.
77 Coulon, Jambon 2017, B-CK 560 and B-CK 269.
78 For this type of statue see De Meulenaere 1997 and Klotz 2016a, p. 435 n. 14.

Osiris are not rendered, Patous' Osiris holds a *heqat*-sceptre and *nekhakha*-flagellum in his hands. The son's statue is also a bit larger (~ 30,4 cm)[79] than his father's (22,5 cm), although both are currently lacking their feet and base.

The two later statues of Patous and his son Phibis (Cairo, JE 38004 and JE 37436) share the same formula (*ḥsb(=i) n=k 3ḥ.t* . . . – "I counted for you (= Amonrasonther) fields . . .") on their back-pillar. And in all three generations, the topos of filial succession is mentioned:

| | | |
|---|---|---|
| Pakhnoum (before 195 BCE) | *s3=k ḥr ns.t=k* [. . .] "may your son be on your throne [. . .]" | Cairo, JE 37456, back pillar[80] |
| Patous | *s3(=i) ḥr s.t(=i) nḥḥ* "may (my) son be in (my) place, eternally" | Cairo, JE 38004, back pillar |
| Phibis | *s3(=i) ḥr s.t(=i) nn 3bw rʿ nb* "may (my) son be on (my) throne, incessantly, every day" | Cairo JE 37436, back pillar, l. 2 |

Although all three also attest to the same title of royal scribe, it is rendered differently between the first and the latter generations:[81]

| Name | Title | |
|---|---|---|
| Pakhnoum (before 195 BCE) | *sh3w nsw ḥsb n nsw nṯr.w* | Royal accounting scribe of the king of the gods |
| Patous | *sh3w nsw n t3š Nîw.t Înb.w-ḥḏ* | Royal scribe of the nome of Thebes (and) of Memphis |
| Phibis | *sh3w nsw n t3š Nîw.t t3š Înb.w-ḥḏ* | Royal scribe of the nome of Thebes and the nome of Memphis |

As De Meulenaere pointed out, Patous and Phibis exercised their duties of counting the fields for Amonrasonther on "order of the king of Upper and Lower Egypt" (*m wḏ (n) nsw-bîtî*).[82] Furthermore, he raised the possibility that this anon-

---

79 Patous' statue Cairo, JE 38004 is headless (measuring 24,4 cm). Laurent Coulon attributed the head Cairo, TR 25/12/26/2 (Coulon, Jambon 2017, CK 1051, height 6 cm), to the statue which matches perfectly, see his remarks in Coulon, Jambon 2017, CK 560.
80 On the pictures of this statue from the *Corpus of Late Egyptian Sculpture*, only "your son" (𓅭𓊃) is still visible at the bottom of the inscription. Legrain noted though in his manuscript for the Catalogue Général (Ms LK III/4) the whole phrase (𓅭𓊃𓏏𓊪𓏤), an addition that is phraseologically beyond doubt. The last group (𓏏𓊪) may be now hidden in the modern base of the feetless statue.
81 See De Meulenaere 1997.
82 Cairo, JE 38004, back pillar; Cairo, JE 37436, back pillar, l. 2.

ymous king might have been one of the rebel rulers, Haronnophris or Chaonnophris.[83] It is striking though, that both royal scribes execute their role not only in the "nome of Thebes", but also in the "nome of Memphis"[84] – and that their ancestor Pakhnoum did not exert any duty in the Memphite nome.

The Upper Egyptian revolt never reached Memphis,[85] to the contrary, the corridor to Memphis was open only during the Ptolemaic interregnum of rebel rule in the Thebaid between 199 and 197 BCE. At this time, it was possible to transport the deceased mother cow of the Apis-bull downstream to Memphis from the Thebaid.[86] And, concurrently, information on the current eponymous priests of the Ptolemaic ruler cults reached Thebes upstream in 199/198 BCE together with the Greek troops, as shown in the Demotic contracts. But in 197 BCE, the corridor to the north closed and the notaries kept on using the names of the eponymous priests from 199/198 BCE.[87] Given the correlation between the title of "royal scribe in the nome of Memphis" and a "royal order", it is more probable to attribute this order to Ptolemy V or even, after the death of the king in 180 BCE, to Ptolemy VI. The question remains: How could Patous acquire a Memphite title during this period?

After Pakhnoum's burial, his son Patous might have taken his chances and moved north at the beginning of the revolt or in the open corridor of 199/198 BCE to Memphis, where he could settle and perform similar duties as royal scribe, thus acquiring his Memphite title. The papyrological record points to the mobility of Egyptians – and of priests – during the revolt, be it as rebels or as refugees.[88] In pBaraize (= SB V 8033, found in Deir el-Bahari), a Greek petition from 182 BCE to the strategos Daimachos of the Peritheban nome,[89] the case of the farmer Pemsais and his wife Tsenonpmus sheds light on these movements during the revolt. Tsenonpmus, owning 80 *arura* of land, went to "northern areas" after the revolt began. When she came back, her land had been partly confiscated and sold during rebel rule, which is contested in 182 BCE by her husband, the now-widowed farmer Pemsais. For the royal scribe Patous, one might reconstruct an analogous

---

83 De Meulenaere 1997, pp. 22–24.
84 See the comment by De Meulenaere: "Loin de relever de la pure vantardise, ces mentions doivent être liées à des circonstances particulières qui ont marqué la carrière des personnages concernés", De Meulenaere 1997, p. 23 n. 24. He admits at the same time that he is unable to explain the concomitance of Memphite and Theban titles in the titularies of Patous and Phibis.
85 For the extension of the revolt cf. Veïsse 2004, pp. 18–19. For possibly local insurgent activities in the Fayum and Middle Egypt cf. Johstono 2017.
86 Smith 1972, pp. 185–186; Veïsse 2004, p. 19.
87 Pestman 1995, pp. 132–134.
88 Pfeiffer 2021, pp. 114–116.
89 Armoni, Jördens 2018; Veïsse 2004, p. 136.

scenario: A couple of years later, after Ptolemaic troops retook the city of Amun in 191/190 BCE,[90] Patous possibly moved back to Thebes and took possession – again – of his family's position as "royal scribe", executing his office now on order from the "King of Upper and Lower Egypt", not only in the district of Memphis but also in the district of Thebes.

Emphasising the royal order on their statues might have become necessary, as direct filial succession as "royal scribe" was no longer the norm in the 2nd century BCE.[91] In this vein, stressing the succession from father to son in all three generations ("may your/my son be on your/my throne (. . .)") loses its topical quality and becomes a strategic argument. Even after the *prostagmata* of Ptolemy V in 186 BCE, it would be comprehensible that the Ptolemaic administration relied on trustworthy royal scribes, as most of them bear Greek names in the 2nd century BCE. In the documentation of "royal scribes of the Thebaid" from this time, there are significant gaps in the documentation, which would leave space for the activity of Patous and his son Phibis.[92]

Given the similarity in type, iconography, and style of Pakhnoum's and Patous' statues, one might even speculate that it was after Patous' return to Thebes that he erected a statue in his father's name, then again under Ptolemaic rule. In that case, Pakhnoum's family would have been in a quandary. On the one side, the family's claim to the title needed to be made clear, but even an indirect reference to the rebel ruler – hiding for the contemporaries potentially behind the anonymous "king" in the title of *sḥ3w nsw ḥsb* – had to be avoided. Subsuming the "royal accounting scribe" under the authority of Amunrasonther, the "king of the gods", acknowledged the autonomy of the temple at the time of the revolt by referencing Amun's divine kingship – which elegantly solves the dilemma. Furthermore, the long genealogy on Pakhnoum's statue covers not only Pakhnoum's father, Patous, but also his grandfather Pakebis and his grand-grandfather Patous, emphasising diachronic family ties, those that connect him with Thebes before the Great Revolt.

The testimony of the three statues is much less explicit than documentary evidence in the papyrological record would be, but points nonetheless to the impact of the revolt on their biographies. This reconstruction integrates the given pieces of information into a coherent plot that interprets Patous as a refugee from rebel rule in the Thebaid. In this reconstruction, Patous' alleged return to Thebes made his family regain the important position of royal scribe in the Thebaid – and his

---

90 Pestman 1995, pp. 108–109.
91 See *supra* n. 51. It is possible though that the royal order refers strictly to the counting of fields, without any legitimising overtones.
92 Armoni 2012, p. 262: attestations from 191–187 BCE (Harendotes), 182 BCE (Theon), 144 BCE (Themnestos), 133–130 BCE (Heliodoros) and 117 BCE (NN).

family was – again – well established in Thebes, as we can infer from a sale of liturgies (pTor Choach. 7)[93] from 98 BCE. The sale not only mentions the mummies of Patous, son of Pakhnoum, but also of his wife, their children, and their "servants" (b3k.w), including also their "nurse" (mn'.t) and their "praised ones" (ḥsy.w). This indicates that after Patous' alleged return to Thebes, his family thrived during the 2nd century BCE and was well established after the revolt – as witnessed by the two statues of Patous and Phibis.

## 4 The Theban High Clergy During and After the Revolt

It is furthermore worthwhile asking whether the revolt had a lasting impact on the Theban families of the high clergy. We could suspect that fervent supporters of rebel rule amidst the high clergy would have suffered repercussions after the Ptolemies re-established their rule in Thebes in 191/190 BCE, even though general amnesties were ordained in the synodal decrees, be it in the Rosettana in 196 BCE or in Philensis II in 186 BCE.[94] To tackle this question, we would have to look for breaks in genealogies of the high clergy, namely the First to Fourth Prophet of Amun that might correlate with the turn from the 3$^{rd}$ to the 2$^{nd}$ century BCE, as an indicator of measures taken during or after the revolt.

While the family of the First Prophets of Amun is well attested from the 30$^{th}$ dynasty to the middle of the 3$^{rd}$ century BCE, no linear genealogy is traceable from the end of the 3$^{rd}$ century BCE into the 2$^{nd}$ century BCE.[95] The last securely attested First Prophet of Amun is Spotus III (~ mid/late 3$^{rd}$ century BCE).[96] In this family of high priests, papponymy is strong, alternating between the names of Spotus and Osoroeris, from Osoroeris I and Spotus I (1$^{st}$ half 4$^{th}$ century BCE) to Spotus III and Osoroeris IV (mid/late 3$^{rd}$ century BCE). But it is noteworthy that Osoroeris IV, the youngest representative of this family line and closest chronologically to the Great Theban Revolt, is not a high priest anymore.[97] He probably died childless, as it was his brother who performed the rites of the "beloved son"

---

[93] pTor. Choach. 7 (=pSurvey 73, pTurin Cat. 2132, TM 44019), see Pestman 1992, pp. 77–85; pl. 66–67; Pestman 1993, p. XL.
[94] Veïsse 2004, pp. 171–177.
[95] Birk 2020, pp. 436–439; pl. 20.
[96] He is attested in the dossiers of his sons: Birk 2020, pp. 50–63. Possibly Spotus III could be identified with Spotus IV, son of Senchonsis: Birk 2020, pp. 67–68.
[97] For his dossier see Birk 2020, pp. 50–53.

during his burial.⁹⁸ But who was the First Prophet of Amun at that time? On the basis of papponymy, it would have been consistent to see in Osoroeris IV the designated pretender to the title of First Prophet. It is theoretically conceivable that the impact of the Great Revolt in 205 BCE might have prevented an initiation of Spotus III's son Osoroeris IV as high priest of Amun – if he lived that long, which is doubtful. In any case, the genealogical gap does correlate with the time of the revolt.⁹⁹ Yet establishing why the seat was vacant is rather complicated. Haronnophris might have deposed the successor of Spotus III or the succession was disturbed because of other factors, such as family disputes that Osoroeris IV's early demise might have caused. Given the lack of sources for the generation after Osoroeris IV, it is difficult to weigh these scenarios against one another. Something certain though, is that according to the known sources, there is no link between the pre-revolt family of First Prophets to the scattered First Prophets of Amun dating to the 2$^{nd}$ century BCE, Spotus V (~ 2$^{nd}$ century BCE) and Espmetis II (end of 2$^{nd}$ century BCE). It remains obscure, whether the two – unrelated – high priests of Amun from the 2$^{nd}$ century BCE belong to the early Ptolemaic family.

Given these prosopographical considerations, we might ask whether or how the residential areas in Karnak were affected by the revolt. One of these priestly quarters lies southeast of the sacred lake in the temple precinct, a residential and artisanal area that was inhabited in various constellations from the Third Intermediate through the Ptolemaic period.¹⁰⁰ In Hellenistic times, two phases of occupation, phases 14a and 14b, can be differentiated denoting the transition from the end of the 3$^{rd}$ century BCE (end of phase 14a) to the 2$^{nd}$ century BCE (beginning of phase 14b). This transition, concurrent with the time of the Great Revolt, becomes perceptible in the southern corner of the excavated area. There, the house "J" and the adjacent street to the west are subject to a rearrangement during the 2$^{nd}$ century BCE.¹⁰¹ Before the reconstruction of building "J" in the 2$^{nd}$ century BCE, a couple of waste pits were dug in the street west of the building. Then, the former building "J" was demolished and the street was filled with its debris. One of these pits was F 44, covering the whole area of the street next to building "J".¹⁰² Amid large quantities of pottery, a sandstone fragment was found, bearing a two-column hieroglyphic inscription that mentions the "First Prophet of Amunrasonther". The name is lost in the lacuna.¹⁰³ The material from pit F 44 corrobo-

---

98 The identification of Nechtmonthes in the back-pillar's l. 2 is due to Klotz 2022, p. 16.
99 For gaps in priestly successions during times of trouble see Thompson 2011, pp. 18–19.
100 Masson-Berghoff 2021, pp. 653–660.
101 Masson-Berghoff 2021, pp. 157–171.
102 Masson-Berghoff 2021, pp. 163–167; 657.
103 Block 7373.22, Masson-Berghoff 2021, pp. 165; 609 and 611, fig. 405.1.

rates a dating at the turn from the 3rd to the 2nd century BCE. But whether this sandstone fragment was part of the decoration of a contemporaneous Ptolemaic building from the 3rd century BCE is not certain – it might belong to an earlier structure. However, the dismantlement of a building that belonged to the First Prophet of Amun at the end of the 3rd century BCE or the beginning of the 2nd century BCE, during or after the revolt, could be correlated with the vacant seat of the Theban high priest shortly before or during the revolt. It is impossible to discern whether this dismantlement might have been induced by rebel activity – in any form – against the First Prophet of Amun – or after the breakdown of the revolt by local agents.

Unfortunately, there is no attestation of the First Prophet of Amun amid the numerous seal impressions from the priestly quarters in that timeframe that could have provided a name or filiation, leaving the sandstone fragment as an isolated attestation.[104] In any case, the two phases 14a and 14b do point to a restructuration of the area after the revolt, but without any signs of destruction or abandonment.[105] The fragment might then show a targeted effort against the First Prophet of Amun. Violence against temples and priests during the revolt in the Thebaid is highlighted in the Philensis-II-decree, where it serves as a counter-discourse to Ptolemaic euergetism.[106] Besides, private houses that were burnt and destroyed during the revolt north of the precinct of Karnak in the quarter of the "House of the Cow" show, how the outskirts of Thebes, beyond the enclosure walls of the temples of Karnak, were a battleground during the revolt;[107] similar patterns may be inferred from remains of burnt houses in front of the first pylon.[108] Targeted political violence, taking place in public or semi-public spaces inside the temple's enclosure walls, has been recently studied by Moyer in the case of the Karnak stela of the Canopus Decree, which has been defaced at some point after its erection in 238 BCE.[109] He ingeniously makes the case for a violent "public gesture", performatively nullifying the promulgations of the decree and delegitimising Ptolemy III and Lagid authority within Karnak, a gesture that would be meaningful during the Great Revolt, especially as the decrees were deemed to be set up in the "most conspicuous place" of the temple.[110] Destroying the First Prophet's house would be – again in a semi-public space within the te-

---

104 For those see Masson-Berghoff 2021, pp. 435–458.
105 Masson-Berghoff 2021, p. 658.
106 Recklinghausen 2018, pp. 61–69.
107 See Ryholt 2022.
108 Lauffray 1995.
109 Moyer 2022, pp. 158–166.
110 Moyer 2022, p. 165.

menos of the temple – an equivalent violent act, aimed not at royal authority, but at a representative of those who implemented Ptolemy III's reforms in Thebes, with all due caution.

Apart from the First Prophets of Amun, the high clergy consists of four more (Second, Third, Fourth, and Fifth Prophets of Amun) priests that form an interesting case. While prosopographical research could not yield enough data to answer the question of continuity concerning the Second and Fourth Prophets of Amun, the large family of Third Prophets might add to the emerging picture. During the transition from the $3^{rd}$ to the $2^{nd}$ century BCE, two family lines follow one after the other – without any link.[111] It is also striking that the statue of the last Third Prophet of Amun from the line ending in the $3^{rd}$ century BCE, Nechtmonthes I, was mutilated after being set up in the temple. The nose was cut off and his and his daughter's depictions on the statue were destroyed, although their names were left intact.[112] Not only might this mutilation be judged as an act of *damnatio memoriae*, but the statue's physical integrity was also rehabilitated afterwards, as the nose was later reconstructed. This happened possibly two generations after Nechtmonthes I: Peculiarly, it was at this time that a statue of his brother Hersenef was erected by Hersenef's grandson Kapefhakhonsou. This constellation of a priest erecting a statue for his grandfather might point to the fact that this had not been possible before. So, possibly, the violent conflict surrounding Nechtmonthes I was resolved two generations later. It is nevertheless difficult to determine whether the underlying social conflict and the revolt were interlinked.

In sum, it has to be highlighted that all four hierarchical positions of the high clergy are attested after the revolt, together with the Fifth Prophet of Amun – who is added to the echelon through the reform of the phylae-system by the Canopus decree.[113]

The structural changes in the Theban high clergy that persisted in the $2^{nd}$ century BCE, namely non-hereditary "Great and Second Governors" as the leading roles in the temple and the diminished presence of the First Prophets in the sources does not necessarily speak towards a concrete action against the Theban clergy by the Ptolemies after the revolt, but is rather the effect of a national reform of the administrative and cultic structure of the temple that already began in the $3^{rd}$ century BCE. Great and Second Governors are not only present in the larger Thebaid but also in the Delta, in Tanis, likely already before the Great Re-

---

111 Birk 2020, pp. 227–230; 437–439.
112 For this dossier and the following see Birk 2020, pp. 137–147; Birk, Delvaux, Labrique 2022, pp. 46–48.
113 See for the Fifth Prophets of Amun: Birk 2020, pp. 249–260.

volt.¹¹⁴ It is striking though that after the revolt, Great and Second Governors also stem from families of lower status, meaning not those of the First to Fourth/Fifth Prophets of Amun. These families sometimes show characteristic cultic titles which are inherited from one generation to another, like the family of "Prophets of Min, who massacres his enemies", of "Khonsu, who governs in Thebes"¹¹⁵, or the family of the "scribes of the god's book" (*sẖ3w.w mḏ3.t-nṯr*)¹¹⁶. Nevertheless, in the 2nd century BCE, there are also members of the larger families of Third and Fourth Prophets of Amun who reach the highest ranks of the clerical hierarchy.¹¹⁷ Hence, the affiliation of the Governors' status groups diversified in the 2nd century BCE, as is power and influence among the Theban high clergy. In whatever way the Governors were appointed, be it by royal ordonnance or through a different procedure, the distribution of power among a larger group of families is an important feature of Ptolemaic structural reform in the 2nd century BCE, as is also suggested by the non-hereditary tasks of royal scribes after the revolt.¹¹⁸ Concomitantly, at the beginning of the 2nd century BCE, the introduction of a system of honorific titles at the Ptolemaic court corresponding to specific functions formalized access to the court and extended it beyond Alexandria into the *chora*.¹¹⁹ The introduction of the Governors in the temple (3rd century BCE) and the diversification of the involved families (2nd century BCE), as well as the extension of the court into the chora, can be seen as reforms that aimed at controlling social status, be it at the royal court (against grown social networks of interpersonal *philía* between king and courtiers) or in the temple (against a system of hereditary offices, e.g. the First Prophet of a god).¹²⁰ Moreover, there are structural parallels: Both the system of honorific titles of functionaries and the epithets of the Great and Second Governors in Thebes relate to the intimacy of the titular to the king or the god, as "relative" (*syngenés*) or "one of the first friends" (*ton próton phílon*) vs. "one who is alone with the king of the gods" (*wʿ wʿ.w ḥnʿ nsw nṯr.w*).¹²¹ These reforms of temple and court can be – with

---

**114** Birk 2020, pp. 425–428. Another example from Elkab can be added to those cited there, the statue CLES 1483, a striding draped male figure of a "*Ḥr-m-*[. . .]" (?) with the titles *ḥ3tî-ʿ* [*wr?*] *imi-r' ḥm.w-nṯr*), see Lanciers 1991, p. 142. For this type of statue see now Cafici 2021.
**115** This is the Great Governor Osoroeris, the forefather of the family, Birk 2020, pp. 305–336.
**116** Birk 2020, pp. 281–297.
**117** Birk 2020, pp. 384–386.
**118** See *supra* n. 51.
**119** Mooren 1975; Mooren 1977; Weber 1997, pp. 55–56; Huß 2001, pp. 524–525; Moyer 2011, pp. 20–21; Manning 2019, p. 116; on the date of the introduction see Lanciers 2018 and on the (non-)rigidity of the honorific title system: Lanciers 2020.
**120** On the role of land auction by the state as an analogous phenomenon see: Hogan 2019, pp. 117–119.
**121** For this epithet of the Governors: Birk 2020, pp. 391–419, esp. 418–419.

all due caution – situated in the timeframe from Ptolemy III to Ptolemy V, when domestic and foreign conflicts forced the Ptolemies and the priesthood to take measures – the heyday of the synodal decrees.[122]

# 5 Conclusion

The private documentation of Ptolemaic Thebes cannot yield direct traces of the high clergy's attitude towards the rebels during the Great Revolt. It is thus difficult to subscribe to an Egyptian-Greek antagonism that was felt and lived by the priests of Amun in Thebes.[123] Nevertheless, prosopography can highlight continuities and breaks within genealogies of high-status families and their title holders which might be correlated with the impact of the revolt and its aftermath – whether induced by rebel kings or the Ptolemies. Besides this question, the analysis of specific dossiers of priests who witnessed the revolt, such as the royal scribe Pakhnoum and his son Patous, offers a punctual, exemplary insight into the effects of the revolt.

Concerning continuities and breaks, there is no clear attestation of a First Prophet of Amun during the Great Revolt, as the seat might have been vacant at the end of the $3^{rd}$ century BCE. Why the seat was vacant is difficult to establish, as it is impossible to discern whether Haronnophris disposed of the successor of Spotus III or if the succession was disturbed because of other factors, such as family disputes. The contemporaneous dismantlement of a building that belonged to a First Prophet might be a material trace of a targeted effort against the First Prophet of Amun.

After the revolt, First Prophets are attested again, even if the evidence remains scattered and cannot be attached to the earlier, continuous line of First Prophets before the Great Revolt. This scarcity of monuments of the First Prophets of Amun after the revolt stands in contrast to the prevalence of Great and Second Governors in the record. All other hierarchical positions of the high clergy, the Second to Fifth Prophets of Amun, are known from the $2^{nd}$ century BCE as well. These structural changes in the hierarchy of priests were most likely already introduced before the revolt by the Ptolemies – but they gained momentum in the $2^{nd}$ century when new families came to the fore. This might well be a result of the insurrection in the Thebaid, in whose aftermath the Ptolemies tried to extend their control of the chora, also by distributing power.

---

122 See now Gorre, Veïsse 2020.
123 See f. ex. the strong opinion in Huß 2001, p. 448 and now the differentiated view in Moyer 2022.

Besides the question of genealogical continuity and breaks, the individual dossier of the royal scribe Pakhnoum and his son Patous can be contextualized within the time of the Great Revolt. Given their supposed loyalty to the Ptolemaic administration as royal scribes, the revolt might have forced Patous to move northwards to Memphis, only returning to Thebes once the Ptolemies regained control of the city in 190 BCE. This scenario enables us to reconcile the given evidence of titles and epithets into a coherent plot. It also demonstrates an example of individual mobility during times of crisis, over long distances, from Thebes to Memphis and back again. If reconstructed correctly, this interpretation sheds light on the various positions taken by Theban priests vis-à-vis the rebellion. Finally, it shows that the Theban high clergy was no monolithic block, but a complex society tied together by family, governmental and personal relations that were constantly negotiated between these groups – in times of peace and crisis.

# Bibliography

Andrews 1990
    Andrews, C.A., *Ptolemaic Legal Texts from the Theban Area*, Catalogue of Demotic Papyri in the British Museum 4, London, 1990.

Arlt 2009
    Arlt, C., "Die thebanischen Notare", in G. Widmer, D. Devauchelle (eds.), *Actes du IXe congrès international des études démotiques Paris, 31 août–3 septembre 2005*, BdE 147, Cairo, 2009, pp. 29–49.

Arlt 2011
    Arlt, C., "Scribal Offices and Scribal Families in Ptolemaic Thebes", in P.F. Dorman, B.M. Bryan (eds.), *Perspectives on Ptolemaic Thebes*, SAOC 65, Chicago, 2011, pp. 17–34.

Armoni 2012
    Armoni, C., *Studien zur Verwaltung des Ptolemäischen Ägypten: Das Amt des Basilikos Grammateus*, PapCol 36, Paderborn, 2012.

Armoni 2018
    Armoni, C., Jördens, A., "Der König und die Rebellen: Vom Umgang der Ptolemäer mit strittigen Eigentumsfragen im Gefolge von Bürgerkriegen", *Chiron* 48, 2018, pp. 77–106.

Birk 2016
    Birk, R., "Genormt? Zur überregionalen Normierung von priesterlichen Epitheta in der Ptolemäerzeit", in M. Ullmann (ed.), *10. Ägyptologische Tempeltagung – Ägyptische Tempel zwischen Normierung und Individualität: München, 29.–31. August 2014*, KSG 3.5, Wiesbaden, 2016, pp. 17–35.

Birk 2020
    Birk, R., *Türöffner des Himmels: Prosopographische Studien zur thebanischen Hohepriesterschaft der Ptolemäerzeit*, ÄA 76, Wiesbaden, 2020.

Birk, Delvaux, Labrique 2022
    Birk, R., Delvaux, L., Labrique, F., "Mémoire de l'élite thébaine tardive et culte des ancêtres", in G. Lenzo, C. Nihan, M. Pellet (eds.), *Les cultes aux rois et aux héros dans l'Antiquité. Continuités et changements à l'époque hellénistique*, ORA 44, Tübingen, 2022, pp. 27-58.

Bresciani 1978
    Bresciani, E., "La spedizione di Tolomeo II in Siria in un ostrakon demotico inedito da Karnak", in H. Maehler, V.M. Strocka (eds.), *Das ptolemäische Ägypten*, Mainz, 1978, pp. 31-37.

Bresciani 1983
    Bresciani, E., "Registrazione catastale de ideologia politica nell'Egitto tolemaico. A completamento di 'la spedizione di Tolomeo II in Siria in un ostrakon demotico inedito da Karnak'", *EVO* 6, 1983, pp. 15-31.

Cafici 2021
    Cafici, G., *The Egyptian Elite as Roman Citizens: Looking at Ptolemaic Private Portraiture*, HES 14, Leiden, Boston, 2021.

Cannata 2020
    Cannata, M., *Three Hundred Years of Death: The Egyptian Funerary Industry in the Ptolemaic Period*, CHANE 110, Boston, 2020.

Chaufray, Wegner 2016
    Chaufray, M.-P., Wegner, W., "Two Early Ptolemaic Documents from Pathyris", in S. Lippert, M. Schentuleit, M.A. Stadler (eds.), *Sapientia Felicitas: Festschrift für Günter Vittmann zum 29. Februar 2017*, CENiM 14, Montpellier, 2016, pp. 23-49.

Chauveau 2011
    Chauveau, M., "Le saut dans le temps d'un document historique. Des Ptolémées aux Saïtes", in D. Devauchelle (ed.), *La XXVI$^e$ dynastie : continuités et ruptures. Promenade saïte avec Jean Yoyotte*, Paris, 2011, pp. 39-46.

Collombert 2008
    Collombert, P., "La 'stèle de Saïs' et l'instauration du culte d'Arsinoé II dans la 'chôra'", *AncSoc* 38, 2008, pp. 83-101.

Coulon 2016
    Coulon, L. (ed.), *La Cachette de Karnak. Nouvelles perspectives sur les découvertes de Georges Legrain*, BdE 161, Cairo, 2016.

Coulon, Jambon 2017
    Coulon, L., Jambon, E., *Cachette de Karnak*, online database, https://www.ifao.egnet.net/bases/cachette, version 28 Aug. 2017, accessed 30 August 2024.

De Meulenaere 1993
    De Meulenaere, H., "Trois membres d'une famille sacerdotale thébaine", *CdE* 68, 1993, pp. 45-64.

De Meulenaere 1995
    De Meulenaere, H., "La prosopographie thébaine de l'époque ptolémaïque à la lumière des sources hiéroglyphiques", in S.P. Vleeming (ed.), *Hundred-Gated Thebes : Acts of a Colloquium on Thebes and the Theban Area in the Graeco-Roman Period*, P.L.Bat. 27, Leiden, New York, Cologne, 1995, pp. 83-90.

De Meulenaere 1997
    De Meulenaere, H., "La statuette du scribe du roi Pakhnoum", *CdE* 72, 1997, pp. 17-24.

Depauw 2006
    Depauw, M., "Egyptianizing the Chancellery during the Great Theban Revolt (205-186 BC): A New Study of Limestone Tablet Cairo 38258", *SAK* 34, 2006, pp. 97-105.

El-Masry, Altenmüller, Thissen 2012
El-Masry, Y.; Altenmüller, H.; Thissen, H.-J., *Das Synodaldekret von Alexandria aus dem Jahr 243 v. Chr.*, SAK/B 11, Hamburg, 2012.

Gorre 2009a
Gorre, G., "*Rḫ-nswt*. Titre aulique ou titre sacerdotal 'spécifique'?", *ZÄS* 136, 2009, pp. 8–18.

Gorre 2009b
Gorre, G., "La place des scribes des temples dans l'administration lagide du troisième siècle. Confrontation des archives papyrologiques et de la documentation épigraphique", in P. Piacentini, C. Orsenigo (eds.), *Egyptian Archives – Proceedings of the First Session of the International Congress Egyptian Archives / Egyptological Archives*: Milano, September 9–10, 2008, Quaderni di Acme 111, Milan, 2009, pp. 127–142.

Gorre, Veïsse 2020
Gorre, G., Veïsse, A.-E., "Birth and Disappearance of the Priestly Synods in the Time of the Ptolemies", in S. Wackenier, G. Gorre (eds.), *Quand la fortune du royaume ne dépend pas de la vertu du prince. Un renforcement de la monarchie lagide de Ptolémée VI à Ptolémée X (169–88 av. J.-C.) ?*, StudHell 59, Leuven, 2020, pp. 113–139.

Guermeur 2019
Guermeur, I., "Le groupe familial de Pachéryentaisouy. Caire JE 36576", *BIFAO* 104, 2004, pp. 245–289.

Hogan 2019
Hogan, A., "The Auction of Pharaoh Revisited", in F. Naether (ed.), *New Approaches in Demotic Studies: Acts of the 13th International Conference of Demotic Studies*, Berlin, Boston, 2019, pp. 107–121.

Honigman, Veïsse 2021
Honigman, S., Veïsse, A.-E., "Regional Revolts in the Seleucid and Ptolemaic Empires", in C. Fischer-Bovet, S. von Reden (eds.), *Comparing the Ptolemaic and Seleucid Empire: Integration, Communication, and Resistance*, Cambridge, 2021, pp. 301–328.

Howe, Brice 2015
Howe, T., Brice, L.L. (eds.), *Brill's Companion to Insurgency and Terrorism in the Ancient Mediterranean*, Brill's Companions to Classical Studies: Warfare in the Ancient Mediterranean World 1, Leiden, Boston, 2015.

Huß 2001
Huß, W., *Ägypten in hellenistischer Zeit. 332–30 v. Chr.*, München, 2001.

Jansen-Winkeln 2000
Jansen-Winkeln, K., "Zum Verständnis der 'Saitischen Formel'", *SAK* 28, 2000, pp. 83–124.

Jansen-Winkeln 2001
Jansen-Winkeln, K., *Biographische und religiöse Inschriften der Spätzeit aus dem Ägyptischen Museum Kairo – Teil 1: Übersetzungen und Kommentare; Teil 2: Texte und Tafeln*, ÄAT 45, Wiesbaden, 2001.

Jansen-Winkeln 2006
Jansen-Winkeln, K., "The Relevance of Genealogical Information for Egyptian Chronology", *Ä&L* 16, 2006, pp. 257–273.

Jansen-Winkeln 2020
Jansen-Winkeln, K., "Imperativ oder Passiv: Noch einmal zur 'Saitischen Formel'", *SAK* 49, 2020, pp. 73–92.

Johstono 2015

Johstono, P., "Insurgency in Ptolemaic Egypt", in T. Howe, L.L. Brice (eds.), *Brill's Companion to Insurgency and Terrorism in the Ancient Mediterranean*, Brill's Companions to Classical Studies: Warfare in the Ancient Mediterranean World 1, Leiden, Boston, 2015, pp. 183–220.

Johstono 2017

Johstono, P., "Rebels in the Arsinoites: Reconsidering the Extent of the Great Revolt", *AfP* 63/1, 2017, pp. 48–58.

Klotz 2016a

Klotz, D., "A Good Burial in the West: Four Late Period Theban Statues in American Collections", in L. Coulon (ed.), *La Cachette de Karnak. Nouvelles perspectives sur les découvertes de Georges Legrain*, BdE 161, Cairo, 2016, pp. 433–464.

Klotz 2016b

Klotz, D., "Get Thee behind Me, City God! New Kingdom Versions of the So-called 'Saite Formula'", *ZÄS* 143/2, 2016, pp. 204–213.

Klotz 2022

Klotz, D., "Review of R. Birk, Türöffner des Himmels: Prosopographische Studien zur thebanischen Hohepriesterschaft der Ptolemäerzeit, ÄA 76, Wiesbaden, 2020", *OLZ* 117/1, 2022, pp. 14–18.

Lanciers 1991

Lanciers, E., "Die ägyptischen Priester des ptolemäischen Königskultes", *RdE* 42, 1991, pp. 117–145.

Lanciers 2018

Lanciers, E., "The Emergence of the Ptolemaic Honorific Court Titles", *AncSoc* 48, 2018, pp. 49–82.

Lanciers 2020

Lanciers, E., "The Evolution of the Court Titles of the Ptolemaic *Dioiketes* in the Second Century", *AncSoc* 50, 2020, pp. 99–128.

Lauffray 1995

Lauffray, J., *La chapelle d'Achôris à Karnak* I, Paris, 1995.

Lippert, Schentuleit, Stadler 2016

Lippert, S., Schentuleit, M., Stadler, M.A. (eds.), *Sapientia Felicitas. Festschrift für Günter Vittmann zum 29. Februar 2017*, CENiM 14, Montpellier, 2016.

Lüddeckens 1960

Lüddeckens, E., *Ägyptische Eheverträge*, ÄA 1, Wiesbaden, 1960.

Manning 2003

Manning, J.G., *Land and Power in Ptolemaic Egypt: The Structure of Land Tenure*, Cambridge, 2003.

Manning 2019

Manning, J.G., "The Ptolemaic Governmental Branches and the Role of Temples and Elite Groups", in K. Vandorpe (ed.), *A Companion to Greco-Roman and Late Antique Egypt*, Blackwell Companions to the Ancient World, Hoboken, NJ, 2019, pp. 103–117.

Masson-Berghoff 2021

Masson-Berghoff, A., *Le quartier des prêtres dans le temple d'Amon à Karnak*, OLA 300, Leuven, Paris, Bristol, CT, 2021.

Mooren 1975

Mooren, L., *The Aulic Titulature in Ptolemaic Egypt: Introduction and Prosopography*, Brussels, 1975.

Mooren 1977
: Mooren, L., *La hiérarchie de cour ptolémaïque. Contribution à l'étude des institutions et des classes dirigeantes à l'époque hellénistique*, StudHell 23, Leuven, 1977.

Moyer 2011
: Moyer, I.S., "Court, Chora and Culture in Late Ptolemaic Egypt", *AJP* 132/1, 2011, pp. 15–44.

Moyer 2022
: Moyer, I.S., "Revolts, Resistance, and the Materiality of the Moral Order in Ptolemaic Egypt", in P.J. Kosmin, I.S. Moyer (eds.), *Cultures of Resistance in the Hellenistic East*, Oxford, 2022, pp. 148–174.

Muhs 2005
: Muhs, B. P., *Tax Receipts, Taxpayers, and Taxes in Early Ptolemaic Thebes*, OIP 126, Chicago, 2005.

Nespoulous-Phalippou 2015a
: Nespoulous-Phalippou, A., "Aristonikos, fils d'Aristonikos. Floruit d'un eunuque et commandant en chef de la cavalerie sous le règne de Ptolémée Épiphane", *RdE* 66, 2015, pp. 151–183.

Nespoulous-Phalippou 2015b
: Nespoulous-Phalippou, A., *Ptolémée Épiphane, Aristonikos et les prêtres d'Égypte : Le Décret de Memphis (182 a.C.). Édition commentée des stèles Caire RT 2/3/25/7 et JE 44901*, CENiM 12, Montpellier, 2015.

Panov 2012
: Panov, M., "Die Stele des Pascherenptah", *LingAeg* 20, 2012, pp. 185–208.

Panov, Lanciers 2023
: Panov, M., Lanciers, E., "The Memphite Sacerdotal Decree of 161 BCE (Plates I–V)", *JEH* 16, 2023, pp. 30–82.

Payraudeau 2014
: Payraudeau, F., *Administration, société et pouvoir à Thèbes sous la XXII$^e$ dynastie bubastite*, BdE 160, Cairo, 2014.

Pestman 1965
: Pestman, P.W., "Harmachis et Anchmachis, deux rois indigènes du temps des Ptolémées", *CdE* 40, 1965, pp. 157–170.

Pestman 1992
: Pestman, P.W., *Il processo di Hermias e altri documenti dell'archivio dei Choachiti (P. Tor. Choachiti)*, CMT 6, Turin, 1992.

Pestman 1993
: Pestman, P.W., *The Archive of the Theban Choachytes (Second Century B.C.): A Survey of the Demotic and Greek Papyri Contained in the Archive*, StudDem 2, Leuven, 1993.

Pestman 1995
: Pestman, P.W., "Haronnophris and Chaonnophris: Two Indigenous Pharaohs in Ptolemaic Egypt (205–186 v. Chr.)", in S.P. Vleeming (ed.), *Hundred-Gated Thebes: Acts of a Colloquium on Thebes and the Theban Area in the Graeco-Roman Period*, P.L.Bat. 27, Leiden, New York, Cologne, 1995, pp. 101–137.

Pfeiffer 2004
: Pfeiffer, S., *Das Dekret von Kanopos (238 v. Chr.)*, AfP Beihefte 18, Munich, Leipzig, 2004.

Pfeiffer 2021
: Pfeiffer, S., "Innere Konflikte und herrschaftliche Versöhnungsstrategien im ptolemäischen Ägypten (3.-2. Jh. v. Chr.)", in S. Pfeiffer, G. Weber (eds.), *Gesellschaftliche Spaltungen im Zeitalter des Hellenismus (4. bis 1. Jahrhundert v. Chr.)*, Oriens et Occidens 35, 2021, pp. 107–128.

Quaegebeur 1971
   Quaegebeur, J., "A cult of Arsinoe Philadelphos at Memphis", *JNES* 30/4, 1971, pp. 239–270.
Quaegebeur 1995
   Quaegebeur, J., "À la recherche du haut clergé thébain", in S.P. Vleeming (ed.), *Hundred-Gated Thebes: Acts of a Colloquium on Thebes and the Theban Area in the Graeco-Roman Period*, P.L.Bat. 27, Leiden, New York, Cologne, 1995, pp. 139–162.
Rashed, Abdelrahman 2016
   Rashed, M.G., Abdelrahman, A.A., "The Statue of Ankhef-Khonsou from Karnak Cachette (CK 1164)", *SAK* 45, 2016, pp. 295–306.
Recklinghausen 2018
   Recklinghausen, D. von, *Die Philensis-Dekrete: Untersuchungen über zwei Synodaldekrete aus der Zeit Ptolemaios' V. und ihre geschichtliche und religiöse Bedeutung*, ÄA 73, Wiesbaden, 2018.
Reymond 1981
   Reymond, E.A., *From the Records of a Priestly Family from Memphis I*, ÄA 28, Wiesbaden, 1981.
Rickert 2019
   Rickert, A., *Das Horn des Steinbocks: die Treppen und der Dachkiosk in Dendara als Quellen zum Neujahrsfest*, SSR 23, Wiesbaden, 2019.
Ryholt 2022
   Ryholt, K., "On the Theban Archive of Amenothes Son of Harsiesis and Chibois, and the Acquisition of Ruined Houses after the Great Theban Rebellion", in A. Almásy-Martin, M. Chauveau, K. Donker van Heel, K. Ryholt (eds.), *Ripple in Still Water When There is no Pebble Tossed: Festschrift in Honour of Cary J. Martin*, GHP Egyptology 34, London, 2022, pp. 3–25.
Smith 1972
   Smith, H.S., "Dates of the Obsequies of the Mothers of Apis", *RdE* 24, 1972, pp. 176–187.
Spiegelberg 1912
   Spiegelberg, W., "Zwei Kalksteinplatten mit demotischen Texten", *ZÄS* 50, 1912, pp. 32–36.
Stadler 2012
   Stadler, M.A., "Die Krönung der Ptolemäer zu Pharaonen", *WJA* 36, 2012, pp. 59–94.
*Thesaurus Linguae Aegyptiae Thesaurus Linguae Aegyptiae*, online database, <https://thesaurus-linguae-aegyptiae.de> accessed 30 August 2024.
Thiers 1999
   Thiers, C., "Ptolémée Philadelphe et les prêtres de Saïs. La stèle Codex Ursinianus, fol. 6 r° + Naples 1034 + Louvre C.123", *BIFAO* 99, 1999, pp. 423–445.
Thomas, Ray 2014
   Thomas, S., Ray, J.D., "The Falcon King: Ptolemy Philadelphus and the Karnak Ostracon", in M. Depauw, Y. Broux (eds.), *Acts of the Tenth International Congress of Demotic Studies: Leuven, 26–30 August 2008*, OLA 231, Leuven, Paris, Walpole, MA, 2014, pp. 331–345.
Thompson 2011
   Thompson, D., "The Sons of Ptolemy V in a Post-secession World", in A. Jördens, J.F. Quack (eds.), *Ägypten zwischen innerem Zwist und äußerem Druck: die Zeit Ptolemaios' VI. bis VIII. - Internationales Symposion Heidelberg 16.–19.9.2007*, Philippika 45, Wiesbaden, 2011, pp. 10–23.
Vandorpe 1995
   Vandorpe, K., "City of many a Gate, Harbour for many a Rebel", in S.P. Vleeming (ed.), *Hundred-Gated Thebes: Acts of a Colloquium on Thebes and the Theban Area in the Graeco-Roman Period*, P.L. Bat. 27, Leiden, New York, Cologne, 1995, pp. 203–239.
Vandorpe 2000
   Vandorpe, K., "The Ptolemaic Epigraphe or Harvest Tax (*shemu*)", *AfP* 46/2, 2000.

Veïsse 2004
Veïsse, A.-E., *Les "révoltes égyptiennes". Recherches sur les troubles du règne de Ptolémée III à la conquête romaine*, StudHell 41, Leuven, Paris, Dudley, MA, 2004.

Veïsse 2013
Veïsse, A.-E., "Retour sur les 'révoltes égyptiennes'", *Topoi (L) Suppl.* 12, 2013, pp. 507–516.

Veïsse 2022
Veïsse, A.-E., "The 'Great Theban Revolt', 206–186 BCE", in P.J. Kosmin, I.S. Moyer (eds.), *Cultures of Resistance in the Hellenistic East*, Oxford, 2022, pp. 57–73.

Weber 1997
Weber, G., "Interaktion, Repräsentation und Herrschaft: Der Königshof im Hellenismus", in A. Winterling (ed.), *Zwischen "Haus" und "Staat". Antike Höfe im Vergleich*, HistZeit Beiheft 23, München, 1997, pp. 27–71.

Wild 1954
Wild, H., "Statue de Hor-néfer au Musée des Beaux-Arts de Lausanne", *BIFAO* 54, 1954, pp. 173–222.

Zivie-Coche 2004
Zivie-Coche, C., *Statues et autobiographies de dignitaires. Tanis à l'époque ptolémaïque*, TTR 3, Paris, 2004.

Stefano G. Caneva and Stefan Pfeiffer

# *Stratēgos* Kallimachos II of the Thebaid: the Honours for a Royal Local Official in the Context of the Epigraphical Records from the Hellenistic World

In memory of Prof. Heinz Heinen (1941–2013)

## 1 In Search for the Big Picture: De-isolating 1st-Cent. BCE Thebaid

The way we intend to contribute to this interdisciplinary reappraisal of the history of 1st–cent. BCE Thebaid is to look at the socio-political trends characterising this region in comparison with the contemporaneous affirmation of local elites in other areas of the late-Hellenistic world.

Our focus will switch from the specific to the general. Our specific case study is provided by a Greek and Demotic honorific decree issued at Thebes for Kallimachos son of Kallimachos, the member of an elite family of Ptolemais Hermiou and the *strategos* of the Perithebas nome, around 40 BCE (Fig. 1). The decree was issued by the priests of Amun-Re at Karnak and the local community of Thebes and praises Kallimachos for his euergetic activity towards Thebes, the people of the Thebaid, and the local temples. As a consequence, Kallimachos receives honours comparable to a certain extent to those for Greek or Egyptian holders of monarchic power: the Macedonian *basileis* or the indigenous pharaohs.

On the basis of the outstanding deeds of Kallimachos in Thebes, scholars have generally interpreted this Ptolemaic official either as a usurper overtly preparing a secession from Alexandria, or at any rate as a "warlord" opportunisti-

---

**Note:** All English translations of Egyptian and Greek texts, if not otherwise stated, are of the authors. We wish to thank Cathy Lorber for discussing our paper with us and for the improvements she has brought to our English text. We also owe great thanks to Ralph Birk for his further references to the Egyptian biographic texts. Of course, we remain solely responsible for any mistake or lack of precision in this paper.

∂ Open Access. © 2025 the author(s), published by De Gruyter. (cc) BY-NC-ND This work is licensed under the Creative Commons Attribution-NonCommercial-NoDerivatives 4.0 International License.
https://doi.org/10.1515/9783111608051-003

cally taking advantage of the severe crisis in the Thebaid to acquire more power to the detriment of the legitimate but far sovereigns.[1]

The only voice outside the chorus was that of Heinz Heinen.[2] In his view, in order to fully understand the socio-political implications of the decree, we should go beyond searching for a direct equation between the honorific rhetoric employed by the community of Thebes and the actual exercise of a semi-monarchic power by Kallimachos. Rather, as argued by Heinen, the honorific strategy of the Theban community would more fruitfully be compared with the contemporaneous trends of honorific decrees in the Hellenistic world, which shed light on the growing power of local elites and on the proliferation of honours similar to those granted to monarchs in the early Hellenistic period.

In our paper we will embrace and further explore the research path suggested by Heinen, arguing not only that Kallimachos' actions and honours are explainable in relation to the social and cultural life of the elites in 1$^{st}$-cent. Upper Egypt, but also that these local trends show some significant similarities with the contemporaneous developments which are known in other regions in the Eastern Mediterranean world. This comparative effort will also help us better focus on what ultimately made the situation in 1$^{st}$-cent. Thebaid special in relation to both the rest of Egypt and the Eastern Mediterranean.

## 2 The Thebaid under the Kallimachoi

Let us first deal with the human and environmental causes of the crisis of the Thebaid in the 1$^{st}$ cent. BCE.[3] A turning point for the history of this region was

---

[1] According to the first editor of the text, Hutmacher 1965, p. 6, the decree would reflect a historical situation in which Kallimachos acted as a *de facto* local lord. Blasius 2001, pp. 92–93, concludes that Kallimachos "mit königlichen Tugenden für Stadt und Tempel königliche Taten vollbracht hat" and the Thebans in exchange honoured him like a king, or at least established him as a factual ruler of Upper Egypt or the Thebaid. For McGing 2004, p. 136, "the priests of Thebes honour Kallimachos like a king [. . .] and it seems as if the Thebaid was virtually his personal chiefdom." The definition of Kallimachos as a warlord is proposed by Manning 2003, pp. 37, 230. By and large, scholars see Kallimachos as the new champion of an untamed Thebaid wanting to secede once again from Ptolemaic rule.

[2] Heinen 2006.

[3] For a broader overview of the political and economic history of Ptolemaic Thebaid, see Manning 2011, focusing on the factors that led to the progressive decline of Thebes: the political role of Ptolemais Hermiou, the economic competition of Edfu in relation to the control over the caravan routes from the Red Sea, and the numerous unsuccessful rebellions leading to the augmentation of the Ptolemaic military presence, interfering with the agenda of the local elites.

**Fig. 1:** The reused Egyptian stela from Karnak, with the decree in honour of Kallimachos; Turin, Museo Egizio, Cat. 1764. © Nicola Dell'Aquila and Federico Taverni/Museo Egizio.

marked by the repression of the last revolt of the Ptolemaic period in 88 BCE, when the army of Ptolemy IX Soter II crushed the resistance of the rebellious Thebaid and destroyed Thebes as an ultimate act of punishment. According to the Greek author Pausanias, who wrote two centuries later, royal repression had been so severe that the ancient capital of the pharaohs lost any trace of its past prosperity forever.[4] And yet new challenges were to strike the Thebaid during the last decades of the Ptolemaic kingdom. The years 50s and 40s seem to have been times of insufficient Nile floods, which repeatedly resulted in food shortage and famine amongst the population. There is the likely possibility that the situation was made even more problematic by the export of Ptolemaic crops to provision the armies of Roman generals fighting the Civil Wars in the East. The dire situation of food shortage in Egypt after an insufficient Nile flood is evoked by a *prostagma* of Kleopatra VII and her brother Ptolemy XIII from 50 BCE.[5] The two sovereigns ordered:

"No one purchasing wheat or pulse from the nomes above Memphis shall carry it down to the low country or yet carry it up to the Thebaid on any pretext, though all may transport it to Alexandria free of question, on pain of being liable to death if detected."[6]

The security of food supply could not be guaranteed anymore without harsh measures. One can imagine the distress such emergency resolutions could cause to the local population of Egypt. Problems may have been even bigger in Upper Egypt and in particular in a region like the Thebaid, which had a record of conflictual relationships with the central power. Eight years after this *prostagma*, two insufficient Nile floods took place one after the other in 43/2 and 42/1 BCE. As the decree for Kallimachos reports, this brought the Thebaid close to starvation.[7]

This particular historical background must be borne in mind when we deal with the role played by Kallimachos and the intentions of the Theban community who honoured him. But who exactly was Kallimachos? His family belonged to the elite of Ptolemais Hermiou,[8] the administrative centre of Upper Egypt and the

---

[4] Paus. 1.9.3. On this episode, see Ritner 2011, pp. 102–104; McGing 1997, pp. 296–299; Veïsse 2004, pp. 64–74; Van 't Dack et al. 1989, pp. 136–150. See also the article by A.-E. Veïsse in this volume.

[5] *BGU* VIII 1843 (50/49 BCE): διὰ τὴν γεγονυεῖαν ἐν τῇ κώμῃ ἀβροχίαν ἐν τῶι ἐνεστῶτι γ (ἔτει); see also *BGU* VIII 1842 (50/49 BCE); cf. Ioseph., *Ap.* 2.58.

[6] *BGU* VIII 1730. Engl. trans. from *Sel.Pap.* II 209 see now however the objections of Käppel 2021, 441–444.

[7] On the dates: Hutmacher 1965, pp. 28–29; Sen., *Q.Nat.* 4.2.16. See Appendix for the Greek text and translation.

[8] The dossier of Kallimachos I (*TM* People 9563) makes it clear that this family belonged to the citizens of Ptolemais. For his son Kallimachos II (*TM* People 9560), however, it may be surprising that line 12 of our decree compares the honorand's euergetic efforts towards Thebes with those

only urban settlement with a Greek *polis* government south of the Delta. Both Kallimachos (II) and his homonymous father were gymnasiarchs in Ptolemais;[9] his father Kallimachos (I) was also *archiprytanis*, that is, he held the most prominent institutional charge of the city.[10] At the regional level, Kallimachos I had been *stratēgos* and *epistratēgos* of the Thebaid with responsibility over the Red Sea and the Indian Ocean.[11] The first document surely mentioning him is dated 62 BCE,[12] but it is likely that he was already acting as *epistratēgos* as early as 74/3 BCE.[13] A new published Demotic graffito presents him making a *proskynēma* to Amun-Nakht at the temple of Ain Birbiyeh in 58 BCE.[14] Kallimachos I had also been the donor of a sanctuary of Isis for the well-being of Kleopatra VII at the southern outskirts of his fatherland Ptolemais.[15]

His son Kallimachos II, the recipient of our decree, was hipparch, *strategos* and financial manager (*epi tōn prosodōn*) of the Perithebas nome. His brother Kronios is also attested as *epistratēgos* in documents from Philae.[16] In relation to the Alexandrian court hierarchy, the family of Kallimachos held the highest-ranking aulic title of *syngenēs* of the king, a title held by all the *stratēgoi* of the Thebaid since 135 BCE onwards.[17] Besides, the text (lines 24–26) compares the pious initiative of Kallimachos II with that of his grandfather, who had renovated the traditional processions and festivals held in the temple of Amun at Karnak,

---

of a father taking care of his own home and children. However, since Thebes was no Greek *polis* – and therefore Kallimachos could not have citizenship there – we must understand this expression in a figurative sense: the Thebans would be ready to recognise Kallimachos as one of them, and even symbolically as their father, because of all that he had done in their favour. On the family of Kallimachos see also Blasius 2015.
9 For the *gymnasiarchy* of Kallimachos I, see *SB* I 2264; cf. Heinen 2006, pp. 32–33 for the debate about whether the place where Kallimachos II served as gymnasiarch was Ptolemais or Thebes itself.
10 *SB* I 2264.
11 *I.Philae* I 52, 53, 56; *SB* I 2264; *C.Ord.Ptol.* 67; *I.Prose* 46. In *SB* V 8036, the name of Kallimachos I is restored in lacuna. If the integration is correct, then this text would let us know yet another member of this family: his brother Apollodoros, *stratēgos* of the Diospolites and possibly hipparch.
12 *I.Philae* I 52.
13 Blasius 2001, pp. 93–94, pointing to *SB* V 8036.
14 Vleeming 2015, no. 2265.
15 *SB* I 3926. Manning 2003, p. 230 surmises that in Thebes, Kallimachos' family might even have taken over the prominent position of the local high-priest, "by which political and economic power was asserted." However, this inference is not supported by the ancient evidence. If Manning was correct, then the lack of any reference to Kallimachos' priestly duties would be a striking silence in a stela by which the priests of Karnak intended to honour their benefactor.
16 *I.Philae* I 57, 58, 61; Ricketts 1982, p. 164; Ricketts 1990, pp. 82–83, n. 77; 103, n. 109 (n.v.); Blasius 2001, p. 97; *TM People* 16146.
17 Moyer 2011a, p. 21.

probably after an interruption following the defeat of the rebels in 88 BCE. This glimpse at the public role of Kallimachos' grandfather suggests that his family had been active in the Thebaid at least from the period directly following the end of the rebellion, and that its euergetic attitude towards the main Theban sanctuary may have fostered a new collaboration between the Ptolemaic administration and the Egyptian priestly elite while also allowing this family to achieve great prestige at the regional level.

## 3 The Decree of Thebes in Honour of Kallimachos

### 3.1 The Stela

Shortly after the drought of 43/2 and 42/1, and most probably in 40 or 39 BCE,[18] the community of Thebes granted honours to Kallimachos II and commemorated his benefactions in a honorific decree whose Greek and Demotic text was inscribed on an Egyptian stela erected on the front terrace of the Karnak temple of Amun. The decree follows the typical structure of Greek honorific decrees – opening, motivations, resolution, and the final practical clauses – just as was the habit for 3rd and 2nd-cent. priestly decrees for the Ptolemies.[19] Regrettably, the Demotic text, which is severely worn, has never received a publication, which hampers a linguistic comparison between the two versions. The first position in the list of the honours' issuers is occupied by the priests of Amun-Re, followed by "the elders and all the others". The identification of these categories has been debated, but a convincing explanation is that they refer to the council of elders of Thebes and to the inhabitants of the city. As aptly pointed out by Heinen, these defini-

---

**18** Blasius 2001, p. 85, n. 36, proposes 18th of March 39 BCE.
**19** Turin, Museo Egizio, Cat. 1764; cf. Spier, Potts, Cole 2018, pp. 170–171, no. 102. For the Greek text, see *OGIS* I 194; *SEG* XXIV 1217; *I.Prose* 46 (with French trans.); Engl. trans. in Burstein 1985, pp. 144–146, no. 111; *TM* 6325; a new edition of the text will appear in *CPI* II 387. See now also Rossini 2022, whose analysis already takes into account our arguments as expressed in the text of our Berlin communication in 2019. In the Appendix we provide a version of the Greek text based on *I.Prose* 46, together with a new translation. Here we only draw attention to a problematic passage at line 26, where the editor Bernand reads ἤ ἐστιν ἀρχεῖον, ὃ σταθ[μίο]ν and consequently interprets Thebes as the city "qui est le siège du gouvernement et de la garnison." Bernand's interpretation points to the possibility that after 88 BCE, Thebes hosted – at least at times – a Ptolemaic garrison, yet this detail is unparalleled in the contemporaneous evidence. Therefore, we publish this emendation in the Appendix for sake of completeness, but we accompany it with a question mark.

tions are the closest the Theban community could get to the formula "council and *dēmos*" which identifies the issuing legal authority of Greek civic decrees.[20]

The text honouring Kallimachos was inscribed on a reused Egyptian stela of the New Kingdom, or perhaps of the 25th dynasty. The stela presents a lunette whose original decoration depicted the double scene of a pharaoh performing an offering to the god Monthu (right) and Amun-Re (left), standing back to back in the middle. When the new decree was inscribed, the representation of the original pharaoh was replaced on the left side by a pharaoh offering a *sechet*-field and on the right side by a queen offering wine and flowers – a traditional symbol of a pharaonic donation of land to a temple. Although the dating formula of the decree surely identifies the sovereigns as Kleopatra VII and her son Ptolemy XV, the cartouches of the king and queen were left blank (Fig. 2).[21]

**Fig. 2:** Pediment of the stela. © Nicola Dell'Aquila and Federico Taverni/Museo Egizio.

---

[20] Heinen 2006, pp. 31–32, with the previous refs. Together with the repeated use of the term *polis* in relation to Thebes (lines 5, 10, 16, 26, 28), this vocabulary shows that the Theban community aimed to describe itself as a cohesive and autonomous corporation legally capable of issuing a honorific decree, even though Thebes was not formally an autonomous *polis* as Ptolemais Hermiou. In this respect, see also the reference at line 26 to the city as the seat of Ptolemaic power.
[21] Lines 1–2. On the problem of the empty cartouches: Blasius 2001, pp. 94–95.

Scholars interpreting the decree as a sign of the renewed separatist intentions of the Thebaid elite have established a comparison with the Satrap stela for Ptolemy I.[22] However, the actual reasons for the missing cartouches on the Satrap stela are highly debated by scholars and their interpretation as a mark of overt opposition against the absent ruler, Alexander IV, cannot be taken as certain.[23] Moreover, in the case of Kallimachos' stela, another detail calls for caution: the decree shows no trace of the explicit contrast the Satrap stela makes between the legitimate but only virtual monarch, who lived far away from Egypt (*Urk.* II, 13, line 2), and the decisive intervention of the satrap Ptolemy. As a consequence, the inference that the empty cartouches are a sign of political opposition against the central rule ultimately relies on the assumption that the Thebans wanted to explicitly present Kallimachos as a usurper, which is a circular argument.

Other interpretations are possible. For instance, one may notice that the palimpsest is carved in a dilettantish way, which makes it possible that the cartouches were not left empty, but painted. In this case, we simply cannot know whether or not the cartouches contained the names of the ruling sovereigns.

## 3.2 The Decree

The prescript of the decree is followed by an extensive motivation (introduced by ἐπειδή), which legitimates the resolution of honours for Kallimachos (after the formula ἀγαθῆι τύχηι). The motivations consist of four points. The first section (lines 4–9) deals with the past merits of Kallimachos towards Thebes and its surroundings. He is said to have taken over and restored the ruined *polis* and to have guaranteed the peace in the area, proving particularly benevolent towards the sanctuaries and the priests. The following two sections more specifically focus on the conduct of Kallimachos at the time of the recent food crisis and should be considered as the main cause for the decree. In order to face the devastating famine affecting Thebes and the region, Kallimachos behaved like a father with his children. With the favour (εὐμένεια) of the gods, he saved nearly everyone by providing food supplies (lines 9–13). A second, even more serious famine occurred the following year, by which the city fell into a severe crisis and the population

---

[22] Written in 311/0 BCE, only a few years before Ptolemy took up the royal title (305/4 BCE), this text issued by the priests of Buto in the Delta mentioned the legitimate pharaoh Alexander IV in the dating formula but left the cartouche blank. Moreover, the priests praised Ptolemy for his benefactions and referred to the satrap with honorific terms equating him with a *de facto* ruler. For comparison with the decree for Kallimachos, see in particular Blasius 2001, pp. 95–96.

[23] See the commentary in Schäfer 2011, pp. 62–66.

was in total despair for its survival. With the help of the god Amonrasonther, Kallimachos managed to save the city by relying only on his own financial resources, "shining for all as an Agathos Daimon and a bright star" (lines 14–20). The decree then provides a general evaluation of the euergetic behaviour of Kallimachos. The first and most important thing he did was to take care of the sanctuaries of Thebes as already his grandfather had done before (lines 20–26).

The resolution declares that Kallimachos was proclaimed "Saviour of the city". He received three portraits – one in bronze and two in a hard stone, probably granite – which were to be erected on his birthday at the most conspicuous places in the sanctuary. This indication plausibly points to the temple forecourt, the only area accessible to persons other than the priests.[24] Furthermore, the birthday of Kallimachos was to be declared an eponymous day: called "the day of Kallimachos", it would host offerings and feasts celebrated in his honour for the gods (lines 26–30). The decree then ends up with instructions concerning the inscription of the bilingual text, which was to be posted on a stela on the external terrace of the sanctuary of Amonrasonther in Karnak (lines 30–32).

# 4 Kallimachos in the Light of Egyptian Ideals about Good Rulers and Officials

Although, to date, the Greek text is the only way we can approach the decree for Kallimachos, and even though the structure of the decree is typically Greek, Thebes always remained a prominently Egyptian settlement. Moreover, as we have seen, the Egyptian priests of Amun-Re were the first issuers of the decree. Accordingly, in our analysis we will first deal with Kallimachos' acts and honours in relation to Egyptian ideals of a good official.[25]

Taking care for the cults, financing the building and renovation of temples, feeding the people in times of distress: at first view, all these actions are clear obligations of the pharaoh. This is not only shown by the synodal decrees of the

---

[24] As argued by Stanwick 2002, p. 50, the chosen materials provide information about the style of the statues: the bronze portrait would present Kallimachos in Greek fashion, the two stone statues in an Egyptian way. The priests had to finance one statue, whereas the city would pay for two, including the more expensive portrait made of bronze.

[25] This approach is also justified by the importance of Egyptian high-ranking agents in the government of late-Ptolemaic Thebaid. Thus, even though Kallimachos was certainly a Greek, the initiatives of the Theban community were embedded in an established tradition of honorific responses to the euergetism of Greco-Egyptian officials. On this point, see in particular Moyer 2011a and 2011b.

Egyptian priests of Ptolemaic times, but also by nearly every temple inscription in Egypt. However, as we will see, such obligations could, or even had to, be taken over on a local level by royal officials in their capacities as agents of the pharaoh.

## 4.1 The Deeds of Kallimachos

The euergetic initiatives of Kallimachos find clear parallels in the so-called autobiographies of Egyptian priests.[26] These texts are arranged according to the set of norms exposed in the negative confessions of Chapter 125 of the *Book of the Dead*. Negative confessions inform us *e contrario* about the ideals by which a good Egyptian official should abide,[27] norms that are also explained in the so-called instructions and wisdom literature. In their turn, these norms were modelled after inscriptions of the good deeds of a pharaoh.[28] Thus, the fact that a royal official could be praised for the same virtues as the monarch should be considered as a natural consequence of the ideology of a good official, rather than an exception to it.

To provide only a few examples, the dossier of the priest Hor, son of Tutu/Thotoes, from Sais, closely recalls the description of Kallimachos' euergetic deeds. Hor calls himself the one "who answers to the prayers of the beggar" and "grants protection".[29] The text of another priest with the same name Hor, found near Alexandria but coming from Hermoupolis and most probably dating to the late reign of Kleopatra VII, presents himself as the one "who protects (*nḏ*) the wretched man against the mighty man."[30] A priest called Panemerit from Tanis calls himself the one "who makes his city splendid"[31] in the time of Ptolemy XII.

---

**26** On the problems related to this terminology, see Stadler 2009, p. 124, n. 14; on earlier autobiographies: Frood 2007.
**27** Assmann 2001, pp. 106–115; Kloth 2002, pp. 1–2; Gnirs 1996, pp. 194–206.
**28** Otto 1954, p. 78.
**29** Statue Berlin, ÄM 2271. Lembke, Vittmann 1999, pp. 299–313, Blasius 2001, p. 87, n. 40, and Gorre 2009, no. 71, with further references.
**30** CG 697: Jansen-Winkeln 1998, p. 229; for the 26th dynasty cf. Heise 2007, pp. 152, 220; see also the Theban dossiers from the (early) Ptolemaic period: Espmetis (Block statue Cairo, JE 37169) (= B-CK no. 356), left side, l. 6–7: "one who is free of defaming someone else, who sits in the council of victorious Thebes, in order to divide the needy and the strong one, who wards off the powerful one" (Jansen-Winkeln 2001, p. 248); Khnumibre (Block statue Cairo, JE 36918) (= B-CK no. 136): "I separated two enemies in the *qnb.t*-court, without being partial <towards> the weak one, because of the one who was greater than him" (Jansen-Winkeln 2007, pp. 49–79); statue group Cairo, JE 36576, back, line 24 (early Ptolemaic): "who gives bread to the hungry, beer to the thirsty, clothes <to him>, who is naked, who puts his arms around the prophets of Thebes (already) for a long time, a protector, who knows no fatigue" (cf. also back pillar, lines 15–16): Jansen-Winkeln 2001, p. 150; see also Birk 2023.
**31** Statue Cairo, JE 67094: Zivie-Coche 2004, pp. 256–259; Gorre 2009, no. 83.

Besides these general deeds, more specific benefactions of Egyptian priests also find their parallel in the praise of Kallimachos. Some priests state that they have financed temple buildings and decorations as well as the erection of statues of gods out of their own means.[32] Even the saving of a city from a famine can be counted among one's good deeds.[33] In his autobiography, the priest Teos from Tanis (3$^{rd}$/2$^{nd}$ cent. BCE) calls himself "Hapy (= Nile) for his city when the two lands were in drought."[34] We read exactly the same in the autobiography of the priest Hor of Herakleopolis.[35]

The intention of commemorating such euergetic actions was not only to pass the judgement of the dead before Osiris, but also to earn everlasting fame in the local community. Self-promotion emerges from the inscriptions of Harwa, a notable of the 25$^{th}$ dynasty, "a very rich man who nourishes the hungry of his province".[36] Comparable claims appear everywhere in texts from his dossier:

> I have raised up what is submerged; a high Nile am I; the barley of my land is good; my seed-corn is profitable to my city. I have protected the old man; I have given gifts to (?) the widow; I give my hand to him who is in sore sorrow (?).[37]
>
> I have done what men like and what the gods praise, a really honoured one without fault, who gives bread to the hungry and clothes to the naked, who destroys pain and removes calamity; who buries the honoured ones and succours(?) the old; who takes away the distress of the destitute . . . . I have done these things, knowing the reward of them; may their recompense from others be an abiding in the mouth (of men) without perishing for ever, and a good remembrance in after years.[38]

---

[32] See, for instance, Ankh-pa-khered/Chapokrates in Thebes (time of Philip Arrhidaios): Jansen-Winkeln 2013, pp. 1–12 (the inscription does not explicitly mention a financing activity, yet Chapochrates bears the title ḥrp k3.t, which means "director of works"; Amun appointed him; for the dossier see Birk 2020, pp. 18–22); Kapef-ha-Monthu (late Ptolemaic period?): Jansen-Winkeln 2005, pp. 35–39; Iah-mes (30$^{th}$ dynasty): Mekis 2016, pp. 383–395; see also the Theban dossiers of Pamonthes (middle 1$^{st}$ century BCE; commentary *supra*) and of the general Petimuthes (end 2$^{nd}$/ beginning 1$^{st}$ century BCE), who restored a deposit in Karnak: Gorre 2009, no. 73 and Quaegebeur 1989, pp. 88–108; on the famous case of Petosiris, the priest in Hermopolis-Magna, see Gorre 2009, no. 39; for his building activities at the Nehemetaway-temple and in other locations, Birk et al. forthcoming. On the theme of financing temple building projects in general, see Thiers 2006.

[33] That the good governor knows how to overcome a famine is a recurrent topic in Egyptian historical and pseudo-historical narratives: see Heinen 2006, pp. 41–42.

[34] Zivie-Coche 2004, p. 103; Gorre 2009, no. 80.

[35] Vercoutter 1950, p. 103; Gorre 2009, no. 41.

[36] Cairo, CG 48606; hieroglyphic text: Jansen-Winkeln 2009, p. 282; translation: Gunn, Engelbach 1930, p. 796.

[37] London, BM 55306; hieroglyphic text: Jansen-Winkeln 2009, p. 285; translation: Gunn, Engelbach 1930, p. 812.

[38] Louvre, A 84; hieroglyphic text: Jansen-Winkeln 2009, p. 287; new publication of the statue: Perdu 2012, pp. 82–93; translation: Gunn, Engelbach 1930, pp. 806–807.

> The soul of the beneficent man is remembered because of his good deeds in his temple.[39]
>
> I went into Presence to loosen him who was bound, to relieve the virtuous man. I gave things to him who had none; I enriched the orphan in my city. And my recompense is that I be remembered because of my beneficence.[40]

These passages make it clear that the presentation of Kallimachos' merits is completely in line with the self-promotion of Egyptian priestly elites. The purpose of accomplishing these commendable actions is clear: Egyptian elites wanted to gain social prestige and a good fame which would last beyond their death.[41] According to the Karnak stela, Kallimachos not only acted in compliance with what was expected from him by the community in Thebes, but we may surmise that the style of his praise was shaped by the habits of self-representation and self-promotion of the Egyptian elites who authored the decree.[42]

## 4.2 The Epithets

In contrast to the deeds of Kallimachos, which correspond to the obligations of a good royal official, the epithets used to describe him are not always easy to explain against a traditional Egyptian background. The epithet Soter is at the same time the cult name of Ptolemy I and IX and an epiclesis of Greek gods who acted as saviours, like Zeus, Asklepios, etc. Translations of the royal title Soter show that the Egyptian language had two ways to translate and understand this concept, either as *ntj nd* or as *ntj nḥm*: that is, respectively, as "the one who rescues" or "the one who protects". It is worth noticing that in Egyptian autobiographies, as those mentioned above, the protection ensured by officials was expressed by these same verbs (*nd* or *nḥm*). Once again, therefore, from an Egyptian point of view, there is no compelling need to consider the choice of this epithet as a sign of insubordination against the central power. On the contrary, it is possible that the Egyptian issuers of the decree for Kallimachos saw the Greek word Soter as a good translation of the Egyptian expressions. Wanting to evoke the protective attitude of a member of the elite, they may have seen it as a fitting way to stress the

---

[39] Berlin ÄM 8163: hieroglyphic text: Jansen-Winkeln 2009, p. 289; translation: Gunn, Engelbach 1930, p. 807.
[40] Louvre, A 84: hieroglyphic text: Jansen-Winkeln 2009, p. 289; new publication and translation: Perdu 2012, pp. 82–93; translation: Gunn, Engelbach 1930, p. 809.
[41] See Jansen-Winkeln 2016, pp. 399–410.
[42] Cf. Otto 1954, pp. 74–79.

coherence between the deeds of the honoured royal official and the model of behaviour associated with the monarch.

Conversely, the description of Kallimachos as the Agathos Daimon of the city of Thebes more clearly points to the religious background of Theban theology. In a Theban context, Agathos Daimon is an *interpretatio Graeca* of the Egyptian god Shai, who was also called Aha or Wadjedj. This god was directly connected with the coming of the Nile flood. The pharaoh could be equated with him in Egyptian temple texts.[43] The close interrelation between the Nile flood and the Egyptian god translated in Greek as Agathos Daimon is, for instance, expressed at the so-called gate of Euergetes in Karnak, where Ptolemy III is called, with a *parallelismus membrorum*, "Hapy of Egypt, Agathos Daimon (Wadjedj) of those who live in it."[44] However, because of its clear symbolic value, the traditional link between the legitimate ruler and the Nile flood was also appropriated by royal officials in their autobiographical texts, as we have seen above in relation to the text of the priest Teos from Tanis.[45] The decree for Kallimachos seems to apply the same logic to the honorand by stating that he was the Agathos Daimon (that is, the Shai) and thereby the Nile, or Hapy, of the inhabitants of Thebes.[46]

Finally, the equivalence between Kallimachos and a bright star shining for the whole community is unusual in Greek tradition,[47] whereas in Egypt we know

---

**43** *LGG* II 266f.; cf. Quaegebeur 1975, p. 110–116. At the temple of Dendera, Ptolemy XV Kaisarion was called "Agathos Daimon (Wadjedj) of the land" (*Dend.* XII, 28,13–32,7).
**44** *Urk.* VIII, 69 a (= Clère 1961, pl. 5). See also Amun-Kematef as Agathos Daimon in Edfu, with a link to the Nile flood: Klotz 2012, pp. 40–41, 134–135.
**45** See also the aforementioned case of the 25th-dynasty notable Harwa. On this point, see Otto 1954, p. 77. This transfer from the royal to the elite sphere might respond to the desire of the upper-classes to appropriate the rhetoric of royal prestige for themselves. However, another, not necessarily contradictory, explanation points to the principle that the ideals of legitimate power radiate from the monarch throughout the various levels of the royal administration. For a similar argument concerning the Greek documentation, see Schubart 1937a and 1937b, stressing the point that the same values are referred to in Ptolemaic papyri, inscriptions and literary texts describing the profile of the good king and of the good official. On the ideology of the ideal monarch in the Ptolemaic kingdom, see now also Wyns 2018; Amendola 2018. On the Greek vocabulary of the good Ptolemaic official, see also Crawford 1978; Wyns 2018, pp. 153–157.
**46** One may notice that unlike in royal texts, neither the general benefactions of Kallimachos nor the more specific equation to the Agathos Daimon apply to the pan-Egyptian sphere of pharaonic rule.
**47** In Greek inscriptions, metaphorical references to a person as a star are scarcely documented in funerary texts, especially in poetic ones. This, however, is an entirely different domain from the honorific discourse of the decree for Kallimachos. The appearance of stars as the signs of supernatural events (e.g. the catasterism of the lock of Berenike II, the apotheosis of Caesar, the birth of Jesus) does not provide either a fitting term of comparison since in the case of Kallima-

of some examples from the Middle to the New Kingdom, where a close association between the king and a shining star is established in order to express the theme of the guidance of the pharaoh for his people.[48] Sesostris was the "perfect god, star of the two lands."[49] Moreover, a thousand years prior to Kallimachos, Ramesses II was called in Luxor "star of heaven, whom Re has elected for both lands."[50] In Egyptian traditions – and especially in the context of threatening famines in Kallimachos' times – one might relate the star to Sirius, whose heliacal rising indicated the beginning of the Nile flood on the 19th of July. However, this star was always identified with *female* deities: Sothis, Hathor-Tefnut or Isis. Another possibility is that, by naming Kallimachos "bright star", the priests thought of Orion – who also was compared with the pharaoh, who appears like Orion.[51] Orion was identified with Osiris and, as a consequence, he was also considered as a bringer of the Nile flood.[52] In ancient times, Orion was completely visible five days before the first appearance of Sirius, the 14th of July: following the calendar of Antiochos, "the whole Orion appears together with the sun and brings water and wind."[53] If this interpretation is correct, then the Egyptian community of Thebes discreetly elevated Kallimachos to a level of honour only comparable to the prestige of a pharaoh.

In this case too, however, one must notice that the metaphor of the pharaoh as a shining star was used by royal functionaries as well. For instance, in the Middle Kingdom, we know of an official describing himself in the following way: "I am a star for my peers, a leader for those greater than myself."[54] Another one praises himself as "single pillar, guiding star".[55] These texts can be compared with the account of Kallimachos' deeds in the Karnak stela also in another respect. Like Kallimachos, royal officials of the pharaonic past could claim, or be described with, royal epithets inasmuch as they fulfilled their duties as representatives of the pharaoh. Unlike the monarch, though, their euergetic initiatives and the prestige that derived from them applied to a purely local level, in contrast to the pharaoh whose sphere of intervention spanned the whole kingdom.

---

chos, the brightness of the star does not reveal a supernatural event but summarises the human deeds of the honorand.
48 Cf. Winkler 2013, pp. 238–240.
49 Firenze 2540/2 = Blumenthal 1970, p. 283.
50 *DZA* 29.088.330; see also Hutmacher 1965, p. 53, with further evidence.
51 E.g. *Urk.* IV, 1546, 13; *LGG* VI, 152b.
52 See Nagel 2017, pp. 85–86.
53 Boll 1910, 13; Merkelbach 1963, p. 29; Merkelbach 2001², p. 375.
54 Siut I, 264 = Grapow 1924, p. 36; see *Wb* IV, 83.3; Blumenthal 1970, p. 283.
55 Munich, Glyptothek 40, 9 = Grapow 1924, p. 36.

# 5 Kallimachos in the Light of Greek Honorific Inscriptions from Egypt and the Hellenistic World

Scholars arguing that the kind of euergetic interventions and honours documented for Kallimachos exceed the limits of Ptolemaic officials have particularly stressed the similarities between this decree and the priestly synodal decrees of the 3$^{rd}$ and 2$^{nd}$-cent.[56] However, this approach has also had the negative consequence of positioning Kallimachos' dossier apart from the more general developments of the honorific practice in Egypt and in the rest of the Hellenistic world. Conversely, we suggest that in order to fully understand the decree for Kallimachos, we must also keep in mind contemporaneous trends in the bestowal of honours upon non-royal benefactors both within and outside Egypt.[57]

## 5.1 Deeds and Epithets

Once we broaden up the scope of our analysis and search for synchronic Eastern Mediterranean parallels in addition to diachronic Egyptian ones, not only the deeds of Kallimachos, but also his honours as well as the rhetorical pathos employed by the Theban community find fitting parallels in 1$^{st}$-cent. honorific decrees for great civic benefactors. Western Asia Minor is particularly rich in comparable case studies. The most evident reason for this similarity lies in the fact that, during the 1$^{st}$ cent. BCE, Asia Minor was repeatedly ravaged by the Mithridatic and the Roman Civil Wars, exposing cities and communities to moments of extreme danger and uncertainty, which are to a certain extent comparable with, and even more dramatic than the situation in contemporaneous Thebaid. Honorific inscriptions from Asia Minor, together with literary sources, inform us about cities losing their autonomy, populations struggling for survival among violence, famine and abuses, and public buildings turning into ruins and becoming unusable for the inhabitants. Moreover, the disappearance of royal euergetism and the oppressive attitude of Rome in this period left the Asian *poleis* with but one source of salvation: the political and eco-

---

56 See for instance Blasius 2001, pp. 86–87; 92–93, on birthday celebrations as royal privilege.
57 See already Legras 2000 and 2012 for some methodological observations on the need to multiply comparative studies between late Ptolemaic Egypt and the contemporaneours political and social trends in the rest of the Hellenistic world. On this point, see also Bowman 2020, focusing on the life of Greek *poleis* in Ptolemaic Egypt.

nomic intervention of outstanding figures belonging to the highest-ranking families of the local communities.[58]

All the features of the honorific logic expressed in the Kallimachos decree are paralleled by the documentation from 1$^{st}$-cent. Asia Minor: mentions of the merits of the honorands' ancestors,[59] references to the desolation of the fatherland,[60] the bestowal of epithets loaded with religious connotation such as Soter, Euergetes, (New) Founder, and Father of the fatherland,[61] and, above all, the establishment of lavish cultic honours whose grandeur equated and often exceeded those for early-Hellenistic monarchs.[62] Similarly, the numerous virtues of Kallimachos – piety,

---

[58] On the ascension of a class of rich families controlling the political life of late-Hellenistic poleis for various generations, see, among others, Habicht 1995; Mann, Scholz 2012; Frölich 2013; Forster 2018.

[59] On this point, see in particular the case of the 1$^{st}$-cent. benefactor Diodoros Pasparos in Pergamon, who was honoured by his fellow citizens "for his euergetic attitude, which he has inherited from his ancestors, and because, by serving the city in a good way, he has caused the greatest [benefits] to the fatherland" (*IGR* IV 292, lines 22–24); cf. *MDAI(A)* 35 (1910), p. 407, no. 2, lines 5–7: "Diodoros Pasparos, son of Herodes, the chief priest and hereditary priest [of Zeus Megistos, who has given many demonstrations of his] goodwill and [has enhanced his virtue], inherited from his ancestors and maintained by his forefathers". On the honours for Diodoros, which testify to the most achieved case of cults granted to a civic benefactor in 1$^{st}$-cent. Asia Minor, see Chankowski 1998; Jones 2000; Forster 2018, pp. 233–243.

[60] See, for intance, the consequences of the Mithridatic war, as summarised by a section of a decree in honour of Diodoros Pasparos (*IGR* IV 292, lines 1–14). On the temporary suspension of a major civic festival due to war, cf. an earlier Pergamene decree concerning the double festival Soteria and Herakleia, which was suspended because of the war of Aristonikos (133–129 BCE) and later resumed thanks to personal euergetism: *MDAI(A)* 33 (1908), p. 406, no. 35. On the link between, on the one hand, military destructions and suspension of civic life, and, on the other hand, euergetism and personal power in the Hellenistic period, see Chaniotis 2005, pp. 36–43.

[61] For the accumulation of such epithets in 1$^{st}$-cent. honorific texts from Asia Minor, see Heller 2020. Among the relevant texts, see e.g. *SEG* LIV 1020 (decree for Hermogenes, one of the first citizens of Aphrodisias; second half of the 1$^{st}$ cent. BCE), lines 7–12: "he has been a good man in all respects, a lover of the fatherland, a founder and benefactor of the city, a saviour zealously and wisely committed to the people in its entirety and to every single citizen and showing the most pious disposition towards the gods and the fatherland". *TAM* V 2, 1098 (decree for Gaius Julius Xenon, *archiereus* of Caesar Augustus and of Goddess Rome; Thyateira, 27–2 BCE ?), lines 8–11: "in all respects a saviour and benefactor and founder and father of the fatherland, the first of the Greeks". See also the text of the dedications for the 'tyrant' Nikias in Cos, where the honorand is referred to as "Son of the *Dēmos*, hero loving the fatherland, benefactor of the city" (e.g. *IG* XII 4.2, 682, lines 5–9, with Buraselis 2004, pp. 30–65, and Stavrianopoulou 2017, pp. 288–289; 41–31 BCE).

[62] On the granting of *megistai timai* ("the greatest honours") to non-royal benefactors, see Strubbe 2004; Forster 2018, pp. 91–95, with previous refs. Civic rewards often included religious honours, labelled in epigraphic sources as *isotheoi timai* and consisting in the establishment of

kind-heartedness, honesty, generosity, love for truth and justice – as well as the positive effects of his conduct – general peace, old prosperity, abundance: in one word, salvation – is in line not only with the vocabulary defining the ideal official in the Ptolemaic evidence, but also with the language and ideals of contemporaneous honorific decrees for elite benefactors in the rest of the Hellenistic world.[63]

## 5.2 Honours

If we now focus on the honours granted to Kallimachos by the Theban priests, we may observe that during the Hellenistic period, and especially in the 1st cent. BCE, neither the erection of statues of a benefactor in a public space nor the introduction of an eponymous day for the celebration of his birthday can be considered as exclusive royal honours. Let us first deal with the case of statues. The proliferation of honorific and cultic statues of non-royal benefactors constitutes one of the most typical features of the landscape of Hellenistic cities. Sanctuaries, market places, gymnasia, and other types of public buildings and spaces provided a setting for the competitive display of the social prestige of both royal and non-royal benefactors, the latter category increasingly outnumbering the first one as a consequence of the fall of Hellenistic kingdoms and of the rise of local elites during the second half of the Hellenistic period. Important sanctuaries situated outside the cities were not different in this respect.[64]

A comparable dissemination of statues of elite members can be ascertained in late-Hellenistic Egypt. Here again, the premises of sanctuaries, cultic associations

---

statues and sacred spaces of the honorands and in the celebration of offerings and festivals commemorating their merits. See, for instance, *I.Kyme* 19 (decree for the gymnasiarch and benefactor L. Vaccius Labeo; Kyme, 2 BCE–14 CE), lines 5–10: "[the *dēmos*] decided to grant him the most magnificent honours and announced the plan to consecrate a temple in the gymnasium, in which the honours would be put in place, and to call him founder and benefactor and to erect portraits of gold of him, in compliance with what is established for the greatest benefactors of the *dēmos*, and for after his passing away from (the community of) humans, [the *dēmos* granted him] the (public) transferal, burial and placing of his body inside the gymnasium". See Strubbe 2004, pp. 328–330; Frölich 2013; Kuhn 2017.

63 Kallimachos' decree: piety (εὐσεβῶς), lines 6, 23; kind-heartedness ([φιλανθρωπί]αι), line 9; honesty (χρηστότητα), line 8; generosity (μεγαλοψύχως), line 11; love for truth and justice (ἀλή-θειαν μὲν καὶ δικαιοσύνην), line 8; peace (εἰρήνηι), line 6; old prosperity (τὴν ἀρχαίαν εὐδαιμο-νίαν), line 8; abundance (εὐθηνίας), line 13; salvation (σωτηρίαι), line 11 (cf. lines 21, 26). For a list of the virtues of the good official in the Ptolemaic documentary evidence, see Wyns 2018, p. 157. On the role of late-Hellenistic honorific decrees in the definition of an ideal model of conduct for politicians, see Forster 2018, pp. 269–326.

64 See esp. Ma 2013.

and gymnasia appear as suitable contexts for the display of statues of high-ranking citizens and royal officials. Portraits of public benefactors were erected in gymnasia situated both in Greek *poleis* and in the *chōra*. A decree from Ptolemais (104 BCE) informs us that the local gymnasium hosted royal portraits together with statues of gymnasiarchs.[65] The gymnasium of Kom Ombo had a statue of Boethos, the "founder of the gymnasium".[66] In Psenamosis, a village in the Western Delta (67–64 BCE), an association of landowners (*syngeōrgoi*) decreed the erection of portraits of their benefactor Paris, a royal *syngenēs*, who was the founder and life-long priest of the association.[67] The forecourt of Egyptian temples also hosted Egyptian-style portraits of high-ranking officials. Several examples of this practice are known from 2$^{nd}$ and 1$^{st}$-cent. Upper Egypt.[68]

Eponymous days for the birthday of non-royal benefactors are known both in the broader Eastern Mediterranean world and in Egypt since the 2$^{nd}$ cent. BCE. An inscription from the Carian city of Keramos mentions a yearly birthday sacrifice as part of the posthumous honours for a member (or a benefactor) of the local gymnasium.[69] Similarly, the gymnasiarchs of Cyrene were to make offerings to honour the deceased Barkaios, priest of Augustus and benefactor of the gymnasium, on the date of his birthday.[70] In Egypt, a mid-2$^{nd}$ cent. inscription from near Elephantine sheds light on the activities of an association of priests of Chnoubis and of the dynastic cult who met on the Setis Island to honour the royal family and Boethos, *archisōmatophylax*, *strategos* and founder of the settlements of Philometoris and Kleopatra in the Triakontaschoinos (Upper Thebaid, at the border with Nubia).[71]

---

65 *SB* V 8031 (*SEG* VIII 641); Legras 1999, pp. 224–227.
66 *I.Prose* 21 = *I.Varsovie* 42; see Pfeiffer 2020, no. 28.
67 *I.Prose* 40 = *CPI* I 113; see Paganini 2020 and Paganini 2022, with the previous refs.
68 See Moyer 2011a and 2011b. The texts accompanying the statues often list the general merits and achievements of the portrayed persons and, more specifically, those related to the life of the sanctuaries. On the euergetism of non-royal agents in Egyptian sanctuaries of the Hellenistic period, see Huß 1994, pp. 19–25, with the review by Colin 1994; Heinen 1994; Van Minnen 2000; Thiers 2006; Chauveau, Thiers 2006, pp. 397–399; Gorre 2009, pp. 492–495. For the precedents dating to the Persian occupation, see Meeks 1979, pp. 654–655; Quaegebeur 1979, pp. 714–715.
69 *I.Keramos* 9 (2$^{nd}$–1$^{st}$ cent. BCE), lines 14–18: "every year, on the 12$^{th}$ of the month Heraion, on his birthday, a ram shall be sacrificed to him by the *hieromnēmones* on the altar assigned to him and prizes shall be offered by them for the *paides* and the ephebes". The name of the honorand is lost in lacuna, but the presence of his father's name, Drakon, makes it possible to propose an identification with Aristokrates, son of Drakon, mentioned in *I.Keramos* 5b.
70 *SEG* IX 4 (Cyrene; 16/5 BCE), lines 28–30: "those who are gymnasiarchs each year shall burn incense to him and accomplish a sacrifice on the 5$^{th}$ of the month Pachon, which is his birthday". On incense in rituals addressed to human honorands, see Caneva forthcoming.
71 *I.Th.Sy.* 302 (150–145 BCE), lines 24–30: "those who have gathered in the Setis sanctuary to celebrate the yearly feasts in honour of King Ptolemy and the Queen and their children as well as

Boethos was still alive when he received this honour. Moreover, as a city founder, he had carried out a typically royal task. Evidently, the act of founding a city after the name of a member of the royal house could not be seen as a sign of usurpation of royal authority, and the same initiative had already been taken up by Ptolemaic officials as early as the 3$^{rd}$ century BCE.[72] Boethos surely was no secessionist, even though a local association in Upper Thebaid paid him special honours positioning him side by side with the ruling monarchs.

Boethos' career and rewards also prompt two more general considerations in relation to the broader background of the contemporaneous Hellenistic world. Firstly, leaving aside the Egyptian revolts, throughout its history, the Ptolemaic kingdom only knew few upper-ranking members of the royal administration who revolted with the intention of creating an autonomous personal dominion.[73] Therefore, one should not project on the Ptolemaic case the quite different situation of the Seleucid kingdom, which was physiologically characterised by the rise of semi-autonomous dynasts and overt secessionists in many of its peripheral regions. Secondly, the bestowal of great honours—even of cultic nature—upon high-standing Hellenistic royal collaborators cannot be seen *per se* as proof of an attempt to replace royal power. The analysis of the political conduct of local governors should not be evaluated by only taking into account its honorific footprint, since the nature and extent of honours largely depended on other factors, such as

---

the birthday of Boethos in compliance with the established royal law." The text is also published with commentary in *OGIS* 111; *I.Louvre* 14; *SB* V 8878; Pfeiffer 2020, no. 25. On the career of Boethos and the social composition of this association, see Heinen 2000, pp. 129–139 (esp. on Boethos as a founder); Fischer-Bovet 2014, pp. 322–323, 337–339; Caneva 2016, pp. 136–137; Paganini 2020.

72 See the case of the Ptolemaic *strategos* Aetos, who founded Arsinoe near Nadigos in Cilicia (*SEG* LII 1462; *PHRC* 010).

73 Unlike Seleucid renegades and secessionists, who have received growing attention in the recent scholarship (Chrubasik 2016; Engels 2017; Mittag 2017; Erickson 2018), the Ptolemaic evidence has not yet received a comprehensive treatment and typological analysis. The few known examples date to the 3$^{rd}$ cent. BCE and concern the periphery of the kingdom: Magas in Cyrene (mid-270s – late 250s BCE; Hölbl 2001, pp. 38–39, 45–46); Timarchos in Miletos (259–258 BCE; Hölbl 2001, p. 44); cf. Ptolemy the Son, if, as argued by Huß 1998, this figure is to be identified with the son of Lysimachos, who managed to establish a durable local dynasty in Lycia, with its centre in Telmessos. The situation changes in the 2$^{nd}$ cent. BCE, when tensions leading to the temporary dismemberment of the kingdom are related to dynastic wars between royal siblings, such as those opposing Ptolemy VI to Ptolemy VIII and, later, Ptolemy IX to Ptolemy X. A related topic concerns unrest and conflicts at court, with factions often fighting against each other and at times managing to steer revolts of the Alexandrian population, especially in moments when the royal power was weak. At the crossroads between court conflicts and indigenous revolts, the struggle between Ptolemy VI and Ptolemy VIII was temporarily exploited by the Egyptian courtier Dionysios Petosarapis, who led a big but unsuccessful revolt *ca.* 165/4 BCE (Hölbl 2001, p. 181).

the traditions of government in a certain region and the honorific habits of local communities, may they be *poleis* or other socio-political entities.

A few comparisons from Seleucid Asia Minor can better clarify this statement. In 267 BCE, a Seleucid local dynast, Achaios, was honoured together with two of his collaborators by a decree passed by the inhabitants of two villages in the Lykos valley, who intended to reward their benefactors for having ransomed several prisoners taken during the war with Celtic tribes.[74] In the second half of the same century, the honours bestowed by the city of Mylasa upon the local dynast Olympichos were in all respects similar to those for a sovereign, and indeed Olympichos operated as a local lord in his area of competence, taking advantage of the weakening of Seleucid power and of the short-lived extension of Antigonid hegemony on South-West Asia Minor.[75] Similarly to secessions, the rising of subordinate client dynasts with control over parts of the kingdom were more common in the Seleucid than in the Ptolemaic empire. Client dynasts could enjoy local autonomy in moments when the overarching power of Seleucid kings was made looser by wars and/or internal dynastic struggles. They might limit themselves to acting as brokers and mediators between the local and the kingdom level, or, as in the case of Attalid Pergamon, they could take advantage of an acute moment of crisis of the central power to establish themselves as fully autonomous dynasties.[76] Against this background, the fact that Achaios and Olympichos became recipients of cultic honours—a level of distinction that Ptolemaic local governors never achieved—may be seen as a consequence of the greater deal of autonomy that local holders of power could enjoy, in certain contexts, under the Seleucids, and as a reminder that until the end of the Ptolemaic kingdom, the only political figures who could be ritually equated to the gods were and remained the members of the royal house.

---

74 *CGRN* 143 (*IK Laodikeia am Lykos* 1; *PHRC* 060; January 267 BCE). On the status and honours of Achaios in the area, see McAuley 2018, pp. 38–39. Achaios was granted the yearly sacrifice of a bull in the sanctuary of Zeus at the village of Baba Kome, whereas his lower-ranking collaborators were honoured with less expensive animals, two rams, to be offered in the sanctuary of Apollo at Kiddiou Kome.

75 *CGRN* 150; *PHRC* 62 (240–200 BCE). The cultic honours for Olympichos comprised the erection of an altar of the benefactor, the celebration of a yearly procession and sacrifice accompanied by a *stephanēphoria*, and the singing of a hymn addressed to him as to a city founder. On Olympichos, see also Crampa 1969, pp. 89–96; Isager, Karlsson 2008; D'Agostini 2019, *passim*.

76 As seen above, this was not the case of Ptolemaic possessions, where even the most developed attempt at creating an independent state, in 3rd-cent. BCE Cyrenaica under Magas, did not survive one generation, as Magas' daughter Berenike II was betrothed to the future Ptolemy III in the 250s and thus brought Cyrenaica back to the Ptolemaic crown.

# 6 What Does the Decree for Kallimachos Tell Us About 1ˢᵗ-Cent. Thebaid?

The foregoing discussion has shown that the euergetic activity of Kallimachos was well rooted in the self-promotion strategies of his family and in line with the high standard set up for local elites in the Thebaid and, more generally, in the contemporaneous Hellenistic world. Neither his actions nor the way they were portrayed in the honorific decree found at Karnak can be interpreted as an overt provocation against the legitimate rulers or as the sign that a new secession was being planned in the Thebaid. As a consequence, the ideological significance of the empty cartouches of Kleopatra VII and Ptolemy XV on the stela bearing the decree should not be overstated.

In compliance with his official functions, Kallimachos' intervention secured peace and order far away from Alexandria, in a period of extreme emergency for the population. This could hardly have been seen in Alexandria as a violation of his mandate or as a lack of loyalty towards the queen Kleopatra and Ptolemaios Kaisar. When considered within its Egyptian context, the way the local community decided to express its gratitude towards Kallimachos is embedded in the tradition of values and actions characterising a good official and an honourable member of the elite. The decree certainly casts an "Egyptianising" light on the career of this Greek official. The priests and elders of Thebes made him a true Egyptian royal official, rewarding him with everlasting prestige in Thebes and, by doing this, they bound him to renew his euergetic attitude in future times. On the other hand, a detail is rather innovative in comparison to the situation of 2ⁿᵈ-century Ptolemaic Egypt (cf. the case of Boethos)[77]: Kallimachos did not become part of the priestly elite of Thebes. As far as we can see, he did not hold any priestly office, as had been the case with Ptolemaic high-ranking officials in earlier times.

The rhetoric of the decree is rich in imagery and epithets pushing the representation of Kallimachos as a benefactor to the furthest point reachable by a non-royal figure, yet without seemingly trespassing the limit of what could appear as a manifestation of open competition with the central power. Kallimachos became the saviour of Thebes thanks to the help of the Egyptian gods, who assisted him because he was a pious man, but the limited geographical scale of his action does not allow us to see an overlap with the pan-Egyptian scale defining the power of a pharaoh. Of course, in order to rescue the population from starvation, he used his own power and financial resources, possibly bypassing established royal rules

---

[77] On Boethos and other members of the Ptolemaic elite in 2ⁿᵈ-cent. Upper Egypt, such as Herodes, see e.g. Pfeiffer 2011.

concerning the import of food supplies – if a measure comparable to the *prostagma* of 50 BCE was still in force at all. This point, however, must remain a hypothesis. Be that as it may, clearly his family did not fall into disgrace because of his deeds, since later his brother Kronios also occupied a top-ranking place in the Ptolemaic administration of the Thebaid.

If we then look at the decree for Kallimachos from a broad late-Hellenistic perspective, we can observe that this high-ranking member of the regional elite of Ptolemais reached an outstanding success in relation to Ptolemaic Egypt, but did not achieve as great a status as some of his peers did in other regions of the Hellenistic world, such as Western Asia Minor. This leads us to our final observations about the specificity of the socio-political system of late-Hellenistic Thebaid.

On the one hand, remoteness and the unstable balance between regionalism and central control perhaps allowed the elites of the Thebaid to enjoy more autonomy than those of other Egyptian provinces. On the other hand, while all Egypt remained under Ptolemaic control till the very end of the kingdom, in Western Asia Minor the process of Roman provincialization after 133 BCE entirely liberated local elites from the interference of those interregional aggregators of power who had been the Seleucids and the Attalids. This new situation left top-ranking citizens in this area with the duty, but also with the privilege, of directly negotiating their cities' destiny with Rome. Another fundamental difference between Egypt and other regions of the Hellenistic world is the low number of cities in the Egyptian *chōra* and their limited political autonomy in relation to the royal power.[78] In order to reach the top of the social hierarchy of the Thebaid, Kallimachos and his family could not limit themselves to controlling the highest-ranking positions in the civic administration of Ptolemais Hermiou. They also had to hold key-positions in the royal administration of the Thebaid, while also establishing a

---

[78] For a (dated) discussion of the autonomy of Greek cities in Ptolemaic Egypt, see Schubart 1910. On Ptolemais Hermiou, see also Plaumann 1910, Abd el-Ghani 2001 and recently Kayser 2017; Bowman 2020, pp. 67–75. The limited autonomy of Greek *poleis* in Egypt is also confirmed by the analysis of the agents of the ruler cults, who can be primarily identified with Greek and Egyptian elite members, in addition to the monarchs themselves. A very little space is documented for cities, pointing to the absence of the dynamics of *do ut des* between monarchs and cities in other regions of the Hellenistic world (Caneva 2018). Two Oxyrhynchus papyri (*P.Oxy.* XXVII 2465, fr. 2 and *SB* VI 8993) shed light on Alexandrian civic decrees regulating divine honours for Ptolemaic rulers, respectively for Arsinoe Philadelphos (after 270 BCE) and for Ptolemy VI with Kleopatra II (175/4 BCE). For the rest, both non-cultic and cultic honours established for benefactors in Egypt stem from the initiative of semi-private social bodies such as professional and cultic associations, gymnasia, military groups, organised groups of clerouchs and members of Egyptian temple personnel. This statement holds true for honours addressed to non-royal recipients.

fruitful collaboration with the Egyptian elite, in the sanctuaries and in the city of Thebes, in order to ensure the success of their initiatives as royal officials. However, despite this plurality of regional settings in the construction of power and prestige, local powers could not grow to their utmost potential without associating themselves with the central source of legitimacy, which made their success ultimately depending on their good reputation in Alexandria.[79] This mutual advantage probably caused the durability of the *status quo* until the very end of the history of the Ptolemaic kingdom. A concurrent factor of these last decades of peace may have been the deterrent of a possible new internal war: this event would have worsened a situation that was already highly problematic for both the central power and the local economy.

In addition to the bonds that linked the members of Kallimachos' family with their *polis* and the court, the evidence shows them repeatedly engaged in euergetic initiatives towards the Egyptian temples in the region. This point highlights another fundamental feature of the elite's self-promotion in late-Ptolemaic Thebaid: its ethnic and cultural heterogeneity. If, as stated above, this feature contributed to the fragmentation of the sources of authority and power in comparison with other regions of the Hellenistic world, it also explains the hybrid nature of the honours and of the honorific rhetoric of the decree for Kallimachos. When considered from this broad perspective, the Karnak decree reveals complementary dynamics making the two main ethnic components of the regional elite, the Greek and the Egyptian, closer to each other and therefore able to establish a common ground for mutually fruitful negotiations. On the one side, we have the family of Kallimachos, a top-ranking Greek family of royal officials from Ptolemais, acting for at least three generations as the benefactors of a region mainly inhabited by Egyptians and repeatedly directing their euergetic initiatives in favour of the prominent sanctuary of Amun at Karnak. On the other side, the community of Thebes, led by the priests of Amun-Re and by the Egyptian-style council of elders, honoured Kallimachos in a Greek-style decree. In doing so, they even described themselves as a *polis*, thus fully embracing the logic of civic honorific decrees through which they carried out their interaction of *do ut des* with these Ptolemaic officials. Thus, the dual cultural background of the honours bestowed upon Kallimachos shows to what extent the social life of $1^{st}$-cent. Thebaid was hybrid rather than one-sidedly Hellenised or Egyptianised.

---

[79] In this respect, see Moyer 2011a and 2011b on the autobiographical texts of Egyptian *syngeneis* in Upper Egypt, stressing the point that they had received from the kings the symbol of their status, the *mitra*.

To conclude with, when we leave aside the common scholarly verdict that makes Kallimachos a secessionist, his peculiar profile may become more understandable and contribute to a refined assessment of the socio-political landscape of 1st-cent. Thebaid and of the close interaction between Greek and Egyptian elites, with their agendas and hierarchies. From case to case, such a concentration of stakeholders in one region could unleash violent competition or result into fruitful collaboration. The initiative of people like Kallimachos, with its balance of autonomous agency and loyalty to the central power, seems rather to belong to the second possibility. It may even be considered as the ultimate protection of the Thebaid against the political anarchy and military chaos that struck other regions of the Hellenistic world at the time of the Roman Civil Wars.

## Appendix: Text and Translation of the Kallimachos Decree from Karnak

The Greek text (based on *I.Prose* 46)

[βασιλευόντων Κλεοπ]άτρας θεᾶς [φ]ιλοπάτο[ρος καὶ Π]τολεμαίου τοῦ καὶ Καίσαρος θεοῦ φιλοπάτορος φιλο-

[μήτορος, ἔτους ιγ′, Ἀρτ]εμισίου ιη′ Φαμενὼθ ιη′, ἔδοξε τοῖς ἀπὸ Διοσπόλεως τῆς [μ]εγάλης ἱερεῦσι τοῦ

[μεγίστου θεοῦ Ἀμο]νρασωνθὴρ καὶ τοῖς πρεσβυτέροις καὶ τοῖς ἄλλοις πᾶσι· ἐπειδὴ Καλλίμαχος ὁ συγγενὴς

[καὶ στρατηγὸς καὶ ἐπ]ὶ τῶν προσόδων τοῦ Περιθήβας καὶ [γ]υμνασίαρχος καὶ ἱπ[πάρ]χης καὶ πρότερον παρα-

[5] [λαβὼν ὑπ' ἐπισφαλῶν] καὶ ποικίλων περιστάσεων κατεφθαρμένην τὴν πόλιν ἔθαλψε κηδεμονικῶς ἀνεπιβάρητο[ν]

[διατηρήσας αὐτὴν ἐν] τῆι πάσηι εἰρήνηι, τά τε τῶν μεγίστων καὶ πατρώιων θεῶν ἱερὰ εὐσεβῶς ἐξυπηρέτησε καὶ τοὺς βίους

[τῶν ἐν αὐτοῖς ἔσωσε] καὶ καθόλου πάντας, δαπανησάμενος ἀνὰ δαπά[ν]ας τοὺς ἄπαντας ἐποίησε νεα[νί]ζειν τε καὶ

[εἰς τὴν ἀρχαίαν εὐ]δαιμονίαν πάντα ἤγαγεν, ἀλήθειαν μὲν καὶ δικαιοσύνην [ἰ]σχ[υρ]ὰς [ποιήσας] καὶ δὴ καὶ χρηστότητα

[παρασχών, φιλανθρωπί]αι δὲ καὶ τοῖς κατ' εὐεργεσίαν ὑπε[ρ]βαλοῦ[σ]ι[ν] ἀεὶ π[αραγενό]μενος· ἔ[τι δὲ καὶ ν[ῦ]ν [····9····]

[10] [ἐπιγιγνομένης τῆς] σκληρᾶς σιτοδείας ἐκ τῆς γενομένης ἀνιστορήτου ἀπορίας καὶ σχεδὸ[ν] τὴν πόλιν τρ[ι]βούσης

[ἀνάγκης ἐπι]δοὺς μεγαλοψύχως ἑαυ[τ]ὸν αὐτόκλητο[ς] ἐπὶ τῆι ἑκάστου τῶν ἐντοπίων σωτηρίαι ἐσέφερε, πονήσας

[ὥσπερ πατὴρ ὑπὲρ] οἰκείας πατρίδος καὶ τέκνων γνησίων σὺν τῆι τῶν θεῶν εὐμενείαι ἀνενλιπεῖς μὲν διηνε[κ]ῶς
[σιτίων σχεδ]ὸν πάντας πάντων ἐ[τ]ήρησεν, ἀνεπαισθήτους δὲ τῆς περιστάσεως ἐξ ἧς παρέσχεν εὐθηνίας
[διεφύλαξε]· συσχούσης δὲ τὴν οὖσαν σιτοδείαν καὶ ἐν τῶι ἐνεστῶτι ἔτει σκληροτέρας καὶ [ἀτε]λευ[τ]ήου σιτο[δ]είας
[15] [παραμεν]ούσης μιᾶι μιᾶς ἀβ[ρ]ο[χ]ίας καὶ πολὺ μᾶλλον ὡς οὐδεπώποτε τοῦ δεινοῦ καθ' ὅλην ἐπιταθέντος
[τὴν χώραν, π]αντελῶς δὲ τῆς πόλεως κρινομένης καὶ οὐθενὸς οὐδεμίαν ἰδία[ν ἔτι] πρὸς τὸ ζῆ[ν τε]τραφότο[ς]
[ἐλπίδα, π]άντων δὲ διὰ τὴν ἀπορίαν λελιποψυ[χ]ηκότων καὶ συνεγγὺς ἑκάστου παραιτου[μ]έ[ν]ου πά[ντα, οὐ]-
[δενὸς δὲ συλλα]μβάνοντος, ἐπικαλεσάμενος τὸν καὶ τότε συμπαραστάντα αὐτῶι μέγιστον θεὸν
[Ἀμονρασωνθ]ὴρ καὶ εὐγενῶς μόνος ὑποστὰς τὸ βάρος πάλιν ὥσπερ λαμπρὸς ἀστὴρ καὶ δαίμων ἀγαθὸς
[20] [τοῖς ἅπασι]ν ἐπέλαμψε· τὸν γὰρ ἑαυτοῦ βίον ὁλοσχερῶς ἀνέθετο τοῖς χρῆσθαι βουλομένοις, ἐπιφ[αν]νέστα[τα δὲ]
[καλῶς ἐβοήθησεν] τοῖς κατοικοῦσι τὸν Περιθήβας καὶ διαθρέ[ψ]ας καὶ σώσας πάντας σὺν γυναιξὶ καὶ τέκνοις καθάπερ ἐ[κ]
[ζάλης καὶ ἀντι]πάλων χειμώνων εἰς εὐδινοὺς λιμένας ἤγαγεν· τὸ δὲ πάντων πρῶτον καὶ μέγιστον τῆς
[εὐσεβείας, ἔχω]ν ἐπιμελείας τῶν εἰς τὸ θεῖον ἀναπεμπομένων πάντων ὡς ἔνι κράτιστα εὐσεβῶς καὶ ἀγ[ρ]ύπνως
[ὑπὲρ τῶν ἱερῶν ἐφ]ρόντισεν, ὥστε ἀφ' ὅ<τ>ου ὁ πατὴρ τοῦ πατρὸς αὐτοῦ Καλλιμάχου τοῦ συγγενοῦς καὶ ἐπιστρατήγου
[25] [ἀνενεώσατο αὐτὰς ποι]ηθῆναι τὰς τῶν κυρίων θεῶν κωμασίας καὶ πανηγύρεις εὖ μάλα ὁσίως καὶ [κ]α[λ]ῶς ὥσπε[ρ] ἐπὶ τῶν
[ἀρχαίων χρόνων· ἀ]γαθῆι τύχηι· προσαγορεύεσθαι μὲν αὐτὸν σωτῆρα τῆς πόλεως, ἥ ἐστιν ἀρχεῖον, ὃ σταθ[μίο?]ν,
[ἀναθεῖναι δὲ αὐτοῦ ἐν] τῆι γενεσίωι ἡμέραι ἐν ἐπισήμοις τόποις τοῦ ἱεροῦ τοῦ μεγίστου θεοῦ Ἀμονρασωνθήρ
[τρεῖς εἰκόνας αὐτοῦ, μίαν] μὲν τοὺς ἱερεῖς ἐκ σκληροῦ λίθου, δύο δὲ τὴμ πόλιν, ἣν μὲν χαλκῆν, ἣν δὲ [ὁ]μοίως σκληρόλιθον,
[ἄγειν δὲ κατ' ἐνιαυτὸν ἐ]πώνυμον τὴν αὐτὴν ἡμέραν καὶ θύειν τοῖς κυρίοις θεοῖς καὶ στεφανη[φ]ορεῖν καὶ εὐωχεῖσθαι
[30] [καθάπερ νόμιμόν ἐστιν], τὸ δὲ ψήφισμα ἀναγράψαι εἰς στήλην λιθίνην τοῖς τε Ἑλληνικοῖς καὶ ἐγχωρίοις γράμμασι,
[καὶ ἀναθεῖναι αὐτὴν ἐπὶ] τῆς κρηπῖδος τοῦ αὐτοῦ ἱεροῦ, ὡς καὶ δημοσίαι τέτευχεν αὐτὸς τῆς παρὰ τοῦ μεγίστου θεοῦ

[Ἀμονρασωνθὴρ εὐμενείας, ὅ]πως εἰς τὸν αἰῶνα αἰείμνηστοι αὐτῶι ὦσιν αἱ εὐεργεσίαι.

Translation
[Under the reign of Kleop]atra Thea Philopator [and] of Ptolemy, also named Kaisarion, Theos Philopator Philo[metor, year 13, on 18 Art]emisios / 18 Phanemoth, it has been decreed by the priests [of the greatest god Amo]nrasonther from Diospolis Megale, by the (council of the) elders and by all the others.

Because Kallimachos, *syngenēs* [and *stratēgos* and] revenue officer for the Perithebas district, gymnasiarch and hipparch, received in the past (under his government) the city, which had lain in desolation as a result of manifold [disastrous] circumstances, and carefully set it upright [and maintained it] unburdened, [in] complete peace. He piously outfitted the sanctuaries of the greatest and ancestral gods and [saved] the lives [of those dwelling in them] and of all people in general. Thanks to all the expenses he made time after time, he caused all things to flourish once again and he brought them back [to their old] prosperity, [reinforcing] truth and justice and giving proof of his honesty, with kind-heartedness and always being among those who would stand out for their beneficent attitude. And further on, recently [. . .] since a severe famine caused by a crop-failure occurred, the like of which had never been recorded, and the city was almost consumed [by need], he devoted himself with generosity and contributed to the salvation of each of the local inhabitants. Working hard [as a father for] his own fatherland and legitimate children, with the favour of the gods he took care that practically all people would have abundance of food, regularly and with no interruption, and even kept them free from any concern about the sources of the supplies he offered to them. The lack of food, however, continued in the present year and, conceding no break, became even more severe, combining the effects of a failure of the inundation upon another, and these fearful conditions hit the whole [land] more than ever before, so that the situation of the city was extremely critical and nobody had any personal hope of survival. All people had become weak from want and almost everybody was in need of everything, but could get nothing. Then (Kallimachos), invoking the greatest god [Amonrasonth]er, who also in this situation stood at his side, and nobly carrying alone once again the burden of these circumstances, shone [upon everyone] like a bright star and a good *daimon*: for he has dedicated his whole properties to those who wished to make use of them, and most notably he [has brought help in a noble way] to the inhabitants of the Perithebas district, offering nourishment and salvation to all people together with their wives and children, as if he guided them away from [a storm and] contending winds into peaceful harbours. But the first and greatest sign of his piety (was that), having the supervision of everything concerning the divine, he took care [of the sacred rites] piously and sleeplessly to the greatest degree possible, so that, since the time when the father of his father Kallimachos, *syngenēs* and *epistratēgos*, had resumed them, the processions and festivals of the lord gods have been celebrated in a most holy and beautiful way, just as in [ancient time].

With good fortune. He shall be addressed as Saviour of the city, which is the seat of the government and the [garrison (?)]. On his birthday, [three portraits of his are to be set up] in the most conspicuous places of the sanctuary of the greatest god Amonrasonther; [one] (of them), made of hard stone, (is to be consecrated by) the priests; (the remaining) two (by) the city, of which one in bronze and one likewise in hard stone. [Every year] this same day [is to be celebrated] as his eponymous day and sacrifices are to be made to the lord gods, accompanied by the wearing of garlands and by a feast, in the way that is customary. The decree shall be inscribed on a stone stele in both Greek and native characters, [and shall be set up on] the terrace of this same sanctuary, in order that, since even in the public life he has obtained [the favour] of the greatest god [Amonrasonther], his benefactions may be remembered forever.

# Bibliography

Abd el-Ghani 2001
    Abd el-Ghani, M., "The Role of Ptolemais in Upper Egypt outside its Frontiers", in I. Andorlini, et al. (eds.), *Atti del XXII Congresso Internazionale di Papirologia. Firenze, 23-29 agosto 1998*, Florence, 2001, vol. I, pp. 17–33.

Amendola 2018
    Amendola, D., "A Ptolemaic 'Speculum Principis' in P. Berol. inv. 13045, A I–III?", in G. Roskam, S. Schorn (eds.), *Concepts of Ideal Rulership from Antiquity to the Renaissance*, Turnhout, 2018, pp. 123–154.

Assmann 2001
    Assmann, J., *Tod und Jenseits im Alten Ägypten*, Munich, 2001.

Birk 2020
    Birk, R., *Türöffner des Himmels: Prosopographische Studien zur thebanischen Hohepriesterschaft der Ptolemäerzeit*, ÄA 76, Wiesbaden, 2020.

Birk 2023
    Birk, R., "D'un monde à l'autre. Prophètes thébains et fonctionnaires lagides dans la statuaire privée à la fin de l'époque ptolémaïque", in R. Roure (ed.), *Le multilinguisme dans la Méditerranée antique*, Diglossi@ 1, Pessac, 2023, pp. 115–150.

Birk et al. forthcoming
    Birk, R., Hoffmann, F., Medini, L., "Texte zur hermopolitanischen Theologie aus dem Grab des Petosiris in Tuna el-Gebel", in M. Flossmann-Schütze et al. (eds.), *Weltentstehung und Theologie von Hermopolis Magna*, TeG 12, Vaterstetten, forthcoming.

Blasius 2001
   Blasius, A., "Army and Society in Ptolemaic Egypt: A Question of Loyalty", *AfP* 47, 2001, pp. 81–98.
Blasius 2015
   Blasius, A., "Die Familie der Kallimachoi: griechische Elite im ägyptischen Kontext", in L.D. Morenz, A. El Hawary (eds.), *Weitergabe. Festschrift für die Ägyptologin Ursula Rößler-Köhler zum 65. Geburtstag*, Wiesbaden, 2015, pp. 75–102.
Blumenthal 1970
   Blumenthal, E., *Untersuchungen zum ägyptischen Königtum des Mittleren Reiches – Teil 1: Die Phraseologie*, Berlin, 1970.
Boll 1910
   Boll, F., *Griechische Kalender: I. Das Kalendarium des Antiochos*, Heidelberg, 1910.
Bowman 2020
   Bowman, A., "The Epigraphy of the 'Greek Cities'", in A. Bowman, Ch. Crowther (eds.), *The Epigraphy of Ptolemaic Egypt*, Oxford, 2020, pp. 59–75.
Buraselis 2004
   Buraselis, K., "Kos between Hellenism and Rome: Studies on the Political, Institutional and Social History of Kos from ca. the Middle Second Century B.C. until Late Antiquity", *TAPhS* 90.4, 2004, pp. 1–189.
Burstein 1985
   Burstein, S.M., *The Hellenistic Age from the Battle of Ipsos to the Death of Kleopatra VII*, Cambridge, 1985.
Caneva 2016
   Caneva, S.G., "Ritual Intercession in the Ptolemaic Kingdom: A Survey of Grammar, Semantics and Agency", in S.G. Caneva (ed.), *Ruler Cults and the Hellenistic World: Studies in the Formulary, Ritual and Agency of Ruler Cults in Context*, Erga-Logoi 4, 2016, pp. 117–154.
Caneva 2018
   Caneva, S.G., "Ptolemy I: Politics, Religion, and the Transition to Hellenistic Egypt", in T. Howe (ed.), *Ptolemy I Soter: A Self-Made Man*, London, 2018, pp. 88–127.
Caneva forthcoming
   Caneva, S.G., "Incense in Hellenistic Ruler Cults", in M. Bradley et al. (eds.), *Incense and the Ancient Sensorium*, Cambridge, forthcoming.
CGRN
   J.-M. Carbon, S. Peels, V. Pirenne-Delforge (eds.), *Collection of Greek Ritual Norms*, Liège, 2016, <http://cgrn.ulg.ac.be>, accessed 30 August 2024.
Chaniotis 2005
   Chaniotis, A., *War in the Hellenistic World: A Social and Cultural History*, Malden, MA, Oxford, 2005.
Chankowski 1998
   Chankowski, A.S., "La procédure législative à Pergame au Ier siècle au J.-C. À propos de la chronologie relative des décrets en l'honneur de Diodoros Pasparos", *BCH* 122.1, 1998, pp. 159–199.
Chauveau, Thiers 2006
   Chauveau, M., Thiers, C., "L'Égypte en transition. Des Perses aux Macédoniens", in P. Briant, F. Joannès (eds.), *La transition entre l'empire achéménide et les royaumes hellénistiques (vers 350–300 av. J.-C.)*, Paris, 2006, pp. 375–404.

CPI
: A. Bowman, Ch. Crowther, R. Mairs, K. Savvopoulos (eds.), *Corpus of Ptolemaic Inscriptions from Egypt*, vols. I–III, Oxford, 2021 (vol. I), vols. II–III forthcoming.

Colin 1994
: Colin, F., "Review of W. Huß, *Der makedonische König und die ägyptischen Priester*, HistEinz 85, Stuttgart, 1994", *CdE* 69/138, 1994, pp. 374–378.

Chrubasik 2016
: Chrubasik, B., *Kings and Usurpers in the Seleukid Empire: The Men who Would Be King*, New York, Oxford, 2016.

Clère 1961
: Clère, P., *La porte d'Évergète à Karnak, 2ᵉ partie*, MIFAO 84, Cairo, 1961.

Crampa 1969
: Crampa, J., *Labraunda: Swedish Excavations and Researches. III/1 – The Greek Inscriptions: Part I: 1–12 (Period of Olympichus)*, Lund, 1969.

Crawford 1978
: Crawford, D., "The Good Official of Ptolemaic Egypt", in H. Maehler, V.M. Strocka (eds.), *Das Ptolemäische Ägypten: Berlin, 17.–29. September 1976*, Mainz, 1978, pp. 195–202.

D'Agostini 2019
: D'Agostini, M., *The Rise of Philip V: Kingship and Rule in the Hellenistic World*, Studi di Storia greca e romana 16, Alessandria, 2019.

Engels 2017
: Engels, D., *Studies on the Seleukid Empire between East and West*, StudHell 57, Leuven, 2017.

Erickson 2018
: Erickson, K. (ed.), *The Seleukid Empire, 281–222 BC: War Within the Family*, Swansea, 2018.

Fischer-Bovet 2014
: Fischer-Bovet, Ch., *Army and Society in Ptolemaic Egypt*, Cambridge, 2014.

Forster 2018
: Forster, F.R., *Die Polis im Wandel: Ehrendekrete für eigene Bürger im Kontext der hellenistischen Polisgesellschaft*, Die hellenistische Polis als Lebensform 9, Berlin, 2018.

Frood 2007
: Frood, E., *Biographical Texts from Ramessid Egypt*, Atlanta, 2007.

Frölich 2013
: Frölich, P., "Funérailles publiques et tombeaux monumentaux intra-muros dans les cités grecques à l'époque hellénistique", in M.-Cl. Ferriès et al. (eds.), *Forgerons, élites et voyageurs d'Homère à nos jours. Hommages en mémoire d'Isabelle Ratinaud-Lachkar*, Grenoble, 2013, pp. 227–309.

Gnirs 1996
: Gnirs, A.M., "Die ägyptische Autobiographie", in A. Loprieno (ed.), *Ancient Egyptian Literature: History and Forms*, ProbläG 10, Leiden, New York, Cologne, 1996, pp. 191–241.

Gorre 2009
: Gorre, G., *Les relations du clergé égyptien et des Lagides d'après les sources privées*, StudHell 45, Leuven, 2009.

Grapow 1924
: Grapow, H., *Die bildlichen Ausdrücke des Aegyptischen: Vom Denken und Dichten einer altorientalischen Sprache*, Leipzig, 1924.

Gunn, Engelbach 1930
: Gunn, B., Engelbach, R., "The Statues of Harwa", *BIFAO* 30, 1930, pp. 369–391.

Habicht 1995
: Habicht, Ch., "Ist ein 'Honoratiorenregime' das Kennzeichen der Stadt im späteren Hellenismus?", in M. Wörrle, P. Zanker (eds.), *Stadtbild und Bürgerbild im Hellenismus*, Vestigia 47, Munich, 1995, pp. 87–92.

Heinen 1994
: Heinen, H., "Ägyptische Tierkulte und ihre hellenistischen Protektoren: Überlegungen zum Asylieverfahren SB III 6154 (= IG Fay. II 135) aus dem Jahre 69 v. Chr.", in M. Minas, J. Zeidler (eds.), *Aspekte spätägyptischer Kultur: Festschrift für Erich Winter zum 65. Geburtstag*, AegTrev 7, Mainz, 1994, pp. 157–168.

Heinen 2000
: Heinen, H., "Boéthos, fondateur de poleis en Égypte ptolémaïque", in L. Mooren (ed.), *Politics, Administration and Society in the Hellenistic and Roman World: Proceedings of the International Colloquium, Bertinoro 19–24 July 1997*, StudHell 36, Leuven, 2000, pp. 123–153.

Heinen 2006
: Heinen, H., "Hunger, Not und Macht: Bemerkungen zur herrschenden Gesellschaft im ptolemäischen Ägypten", *AncSoc* 36, 2006, pp. 22–44.

Heise 2007
: Heise, J., *Erinnern und Gedenken: Aspekte der biographischen Inschriften der ägyptischen Spätzeit*, OBO 226, Fribourg, Göttingen, 2007.

Heller 2020
: Heller, A., *L'âge d'or des bienfaiteurs. Titres honorifiques et sociétés civiques dans l'Asie Mineure d'époque romaine ($I^{er}$ s. av. J.-C. – $III^e$ s. ap. J.-C.)*, Geneva, 2020.

Hölbl 2001
: Hölbl, G., *A History of the Ptolemaic Empire*, London, New York, 2001.

Huß 1994
: Huß, W., *Der makedonische König und die ägyptischen Priester: Studien zur Geschichte des ptolemaiischen Ägypten*, HistEinz 85, Stuttgart, 1994.

Huß 1998
: Huß, W., "Ptolemaios der Sohn", *ZPE* 121, 1998, pp. 229–250.

Hutmacher 1965
: Hutmacher, R., *Das Ehrendekret für den Strategen Kallimachos*, BKP 17, Meisenheim am Glan, 1965.

Isager, Karlsson 2008
: Isager, S., Karlsson, L., "A New Inscription from Labraunda – Honorary Decree for Olympichos: I.Labraunda no. 134 (and no. 49)", *Epigraphica Anatolica* 41, 2008, pp. 39–52.

Jansen-Winkeln 1998
: Jansen-Winkeln, K., "Die Inschrift der Porträtstatue des Hor", *MDAIK* 54, 1998, pp. 227–235.

Jansen-Winkeln 2001
: Jansen-Winkeln, K., *Biographische und religiöse Inschriften der Spätzeit aus dem Ägyptischen Museum Kairo – Teil 1: Übersetzungen und Kommentare; Teil 2: Texte und Tafeln*, ÄAT 45, Wiesbaden, 2001.

Jansen-Winkeln 2005
: Jansen-Winkeln, K., "Ein Priester als Restaurator: Zu einer ptolemäischen Inschrift am Luxortempel", *ZÄS* 132, 2005, pp. 35–39.

Jansen-Winkeln 2007
  Jansen-Winkeln, K., "Drei Statueninschriften einer Familie aus frühptolemäischer Zeit", *SAK* 36, 2007, pp. 49–79.
Jansen-Winkeln 2009
  Jansen-Winkeln, K., *Inschriften der Spätzeit – Teil III: Die 25. Dynastie*, Wiesbaden, 2009.
Jansen-Winkeln 2013
  Jansen-Winkeln, K., "Eine Bau- und Bittinschrift am Tempel von Luxor", *ZÄS* 140, 2013, pp. 1–12.
Jansen-Winkeln 2016
  Jansen-Winkeln, K., "Zu Kult und Funktion der Tempelstatue in der Spätzeit", in L. Coulon (ed.), *La Cachette de Karnak. Nouvelles perspectives sur les découvertes de Georges Legrain*, BdE 161, Cairo, 2016, pp. 399–410.
Jones 2000
  Jones, Ch.P., "Diodoros Pasparos Revisited", *Chiron* 30, 2000, pp. 1–14.
Kayser 2017
  Kayser, F., "Ptolémaïs de Haute-Égypte. Une cité grecque dans son environnement égyptien", in F. Kayser, L. Medini (eds.), *Communautés nouvelles en Égypte hellénistique et romaine*, Chambéry, 2017, pp. 15–68.
Kloth 2002
  Kloth, N., *Die (auto-)biographischen Inschriften des ägyptischen Alten Reiches: Untersuchungen zu Phraseologie und Entwicklung*, SAK-B 8, Hamburg, 2002.
Klotz 2012
  Klotz, D., *Caesar in the City of Amun: Egyptian Temple Construction and Theology in Roman Thebes*, MRE 15, Turnhout, 2012.
Kuhn 2017
  Kuhn, Ch.T., "The Refusal of the Highest Honours by Members of the Urban Elite in Roman Asia Minor", in A. Heller, O.M. van Nijf (eds.), *The Politics of Honour in the Greek Cities of the Roman Empire*, Leiden, Boston, 2017, pp. 199–219.
Legras 1999
  Legras, B., *Néotês. Recherches sur les jeunes Grecs dans l'Égypte ptolémaïque et romaine*, Hautes Études du monde gréco-romain 26, Paris, 1999.
Legras 2000
  Legras, B., "Réponse à Kostas Buraselis. Le culte royal ptolémaïque: Trois remarques", in G. Thür (ed.), *SYMPOSION 2009 – Vorträge zur griechischen und hellenistischen Rechtsgeschichte: Seggau, 25–30 August 2009*, Vienna, 2010, pp. 435–441.
Legras 2012
  Legras, B., "Le pouvoir des Ptolémées. Singularité égyptienne ou normalité hellénistique?", in E. Santinelli-Foltz, Ch.-G. Schwentzel (eds.), *La puissance royale. Image et pouvoir de l'Antiquité au Moyen Âge*, Rennes, 2012, pp. 73–83.
Lembke, Vittmann 1999
  Lembke, K., Vittmann, G., "Die Standfigur des Horos, Sohn des Thotoes (Berlin, Ägyptisches Museum SMPK 2271)", *MDAIK* 55, 1999, pp. 299–313.
Ma 2013
  Ma, J., *Statues and Cities: Honorific Portraits and Civic Identity in the Hellenistic World*, Oxford, 2013.
Mann, Scholz 2012
  Mann, C., Scholz, P. (eds.), *'Demokratie' im Hellenismus: Von der Herrschaft des Volkes zur Herrschaft der Honoratioren*, Mainz, 2012.

Manning 2003
> Manning, J.G., *Land and Power in Ptolemaic Egypt: The Structures of Land Tenure*, Cambridge, 2003.

Manning 2011
> Manning, J.G., "The Capture of the Thebaid", in P.F. Dorman, B.M. Bryan (eds.), *Perspectives on Ptolemaic Thebes*, SAOC 65, Chicago, 2011, pp. 1–16.

McAuley 2018
> McAuley, A., "The House of Achaios: Reconstructing an Early Client Dynasty of Seleucid Anatolia", in K. Erickson (ed.), *The Seleucid Empire, 281–222 BC: War Within the Family*, Swansea, 2018, pp. 37–58.

McGing 1997
> McGing, B.C., "Revolt Egyptian Style: Internal Opposition to Ptolemaic Rule", *AfP* 43, 1997, pp. 273–314.

McGing 2004
> McGing, B.C., "Ptolemaic Thebarchs", *AfP* 50, 2004, pp. 119–137.

Meeks 1979
> Meeks, D., "Les donations aux temples dans l'Égypte du I$^{er}$ millenaire avant J.-C.", in E. Lipiński (ed.), *State and Temple Economy in the Ancient Near East*, OLA 6, Leuven, 1979, vol. II, pp. 605–687.

Mekis 2016
> Mekis, T., "Quelques données nouvelles sur les stèles Budapest MBA inv. n° 51.1928 et Prague MN P 1636, et sur la famille de Iâhmès fils de Smendès, propriétaire de la statue Caire JE 37075", in L. Coulon (ed.), *La Cachette de Karnak. Nouvelles perspectives sur les découvertes de Georges Legrain*, BdE 161, Cairo, 2016, pp. 383–395.

Merkelbach 1963
> Merkelbach, R., *Isisfeste in griechisch-römischer Zeit: Daten und Riten*, Meisenheim am Glan, 1963.

Merkelbach 2001$^2$
> Merkelbach, R., *Isis regina – Zeus Sarapis: Die griechisch-ägyptische Religion nach den Quellen dargestellt*, Munich, 2001$^2$.

Mittag 2017
> Mittag, P.F., "Misconduct and Disloyalty in the Seleucid Court", in A. Erskine, Ll. Llewllyn-Jones, Sh. Wallace (eds.), *The Hellenistic Court: Monarchic Power and Elite Society from Alexander to Cleopatra*, Swansea, 2017, pp. 359–372.

Moyer 2011a
> Moyer, I., "Court, *Chora*, and Culture in Late-Ptolemaic Egypt", *AJP* 132, 2011, pp. 15–44.

Moyer 2011b
> Moyer, I., "Finding a Middle-Ground: Culture and Politics in the Ptolemaic Thebaid", in P.F. Dorman, B.M. Bryan (eds.), *Perspectives on Ptolemaic Thebes*, SAOC 65, Chicago, 2011, pp. 115–145.

Nagel 2017
> Nagel, S., "Mittelplatonische Konzepte der Göttin Isis bei Plutarch und Apuleius im Vergleich mit ägyptischen Quellen der griechisch-römischen Zeit", in M. Erler, M.A. Stadler (eds.), *Platonismus und spätägyptische Religion: Plutarch und die Ägyptenrezeption in der römischen Kaiserzeit*, BzA 364, Berlin, 2017, pp. 79–126.

Otto 1954
> Otto, E., *Die biographischen Inschriften der ägyptischen Spätzeit: ihre geistesgeschichtliche und literarische Bedeutung*, ProblÄg 2, Leiden, 1954.

Paganini 2020
    Paganini, M.C.D., "Cults for the Rulers in Private Settings: The Gymnasia and Associations of Hellenistic Egypt", in S.G. Caneva (ed.), *The Materiality of Hellenistic Ruler Cults*, Kernos Suppl. 36, Liège, 2020, pp. 125–145.
Paganini 2022
    Paganini, M.C.D., "Religion and Leisure: A Gentry Association of Hellenistic Egypt", in S. Skaltsa, A. Cazemier (eds.), *Associations and Religion in Context: The Hellenistic and Roman Eastern Mediterranean*, Kernos Suppl. 39, Liège, 2022, pp. 227–248.
Perdu 2012
    Perdu, O., *Les statues privées de la fin de l'Égypte pharaonique (1069 av. J.-C.–395 apr. J.-C.). Tome I: Hommes*, Paris, 2012.
Pfeiffer 2011
    Pfeiffer, S., "Die Politik Ptolemaios' VI. und VIII. im Kataraktgebiet: Die 'ruhigen' Jahre von 163 bis 136 v. Chr.", in A. Jördens, J.F. Quack (eds.), *Ägypten zwischen innerem Zwist und äußerem Druck: die Zeit Ptolemaios' VI. bis VIII. – Internationales Symposion Heidelberg 16.–19.9.2007*, Philippika 45, Wiesbaden, 2011, pp. 235–254.
Pfeiffer 2020
    Pfeiffer, S., *Griechische und lateinische Inschriften zum Ptolemäerreich und zur römischen Provinz Aegyptus*, EQÄ 9, Berlin, 2020.
PHRC
    S.G. Caneva (ed.), *The Practicalities of Hellenistic Ruler Cults*, Padua, Liège, 2018, <http://www.phrc.it>, accessed 30 August 2024.
Plaumann 1910
    Plaumann, G., *Ptolemais in Oberägypten: Ein Beitrag zur Geschichte des Hellenismus in Ägypten*, Leipzig, 1910.
Quaegebeur 1975.
    Quaegebeur, J., *Le dieu égyptien Shaï dans la religion et l'onomastique*, OLA 2, Leuven, 1975.
Quaegebeur 1979
    Quaegebeur, J., "Documents égyptiens et rôle économique du clergé en Egypte hellénistique", in E. Lipiński (ed.), *State and Temple Economy in the Ancient Near East*, OLA 5, Leuven, 1979, vol. II, pp. 707–729.
Quaegebeur 1989
    Quaegebeur, J., "La statue du général Pétimouthês, Turin, Museo Egizio cat. 3062 + Karnak, Karakol N° 258", in E. Van 't Dack et al. (eds.), *The Judean-Syrian-Egyptian Conflict of 103-101 B.C.: A Multilingual Dossier Concerning a "War of Sceptres"*, CollHell 1, Brussels, 1989, pp. 88–108.
Ricketts 1982
    Ricketts, L.M., "The Epistrategos Kallimachos and a Koptite Inscription: SB V 8036 Reconsidered", *AncSoc* 13/14, 1982, pp. 161–166.
Ricketts 1990
    Ricketts, L.M., "The Administration of Ptolemaic Egypt under Cleopatra VII", PhD Thesis, University of Minnesota, 1990.
Ritner 2011
    Ritner, R.K., "Ptolemy IX (Soter II) at Thebes", in P.F. Dorman, B.M. Bryan (eds.), *Perspectives on Ptolemaic Thebes*, SAOC 65, Chicago, 2011, pp. 97–114.

Rossini 2022
: Rossini, A., "Decreto onorario dei sacerdoti di Amon-Ra per lo stratego Callimaco dopo una carestia", *Axon* 6.1, 2022, pp. 113–181.

Schäfer 2011
: Schäfer, D., *Makedonische Pharaonen und hieroglyphische Stelen: Historische Untersuchungen zur Satrapenstele und verwandten Denkmälern*, StudHell 50, Leuven, 2011.

Schubart 1910
: Schubart, W., "Spuren politischer Autonomie in Aegypten unter den Ptolemäern", *Klio* 10, 1910, pp. 41–71.

Schubart 1937a
: Schubart, W., "Das hellenistische Königsideal nach Inschriften und Papyri", *AfP* 12, 1937, pp. 1–26.

Schubart 1937b
: Schubart, W., "Das Königsbild des Hellenismus", *Die Antike* 13, 1937, pp. 272–288.

Spier, Potts, Cole 2018
: Spier, J., Potts, T., Cole, S.E. (eds.), *Beyond the Nile. Egypt in the Classical World*, Los Angeles, 2018.

Stadler 2009
: Stadler, M.A., *Weiser und Wesir: Studien zu Vorkommen, Rolle und Wesen des Gottes Thot im ägyptischen Totenbuch*, ORA 1, Tübingen, 2009.

Stanwick 2002
: Stanwick, P.E., *Portraits of the Ptolemies: Greek Kings as Egyptian Pharaohs*, Austin, 2002.

Stavrianopoulou 2017
: Stavrianopoulou, E., "Altäre auf den Straßen für die 'Söhne des Volkes'", in H. Beck et al. (eds.), *Von Magna Graecia nach Asia Minor: Festschrift für Linda-Marie Günther zum 65. Geburtstag*, Philippika 116, Wiesbaden, 2017, pp. 281–297.

Strubbe 2004
: Strubbe, J.H.M., "Cultic Honours for Benefactors in the Cities of Asia Minor", in L. De Ligt et al. (eds.), *Roman Rule and Civic Life: Local and Regional Perspectives*, Amsterdam, 2004, pp. 315–330.

Thiers 2006
: Thiers, C., "Égyptiens et Grecs au service des cultes indigènes. Un aspect de l'évergétisme en Égypte ptolémaïque", in M. Molin (ed.), *Les régulations sociales dans l'Antiquité*, Rennes, 2006, pp. 275–301.

TM
: Trismegistos, online database, <http://www.trismegistos.org> accessed 30 August 2024.

Van Minnen 2000
: Van Minnen, P., "Euergetism in Graeco-Roman Egypt", in L. Mooren (ed.), *Politics, Administration and Society in the Hellenistic and Roman World*, StudHell 36, Leuven, 2000, pp. 437–469.

Van 't Dack et al. 1989
: Van 't Dack, E. et al., *The Judean-Syrian-Egyptian Conflict of 103–101 B.C.: A Multilingual Dossier Concerning a "War of Sceptres"*, CollHell 1, Brussels, 1989.

Vercoutter 1950
: Vercoutter, J., "Les statues du général Hor, gouverneur d'Heracleopolis, de Busiris et d'Héliopolis", *BIFAO* 49, 1950, pp. 85–114.

Veïsse 2004
: Veïsse, A.-E., *Les révoltes égyptiennes. Recherches sur les troubles intérieures en Égypte du règne de Ptolémée II à la conquête romaine*, StudHell 41, Leuven, Paris, 2004.

Vleeming 2015
> Vleeming, S.P., *Demotic Graffiti and Other Short Texts Gathered from Many Publications (Short Texts III 1201–2350)*, StudDem 12, Leuven, Paris, Bristol, CT, 2015.

Winkler 2013
> Winkler, A., "A Royal Star: On the 'Miracle of the Star' in Thutmoses III's Gebel Barkal Stela and a Note on the King as a Star in Personal Names", *RdE* 64, 2013, pp. 231–248.

Wyns 2018
> Wyns, V., "The State Ideology of the Ptolemies: Origins and Influences", *CdE* 183, 2018, pp. 137–174.

Zivie-Coche 2004
> Zivie-Coche, Chr., *Statues et autobiographies de dignitaires. Tanis à l'époque ptolémaïque*, TTR 3, Paris, 2004.

Marie-Pierre Chaufray
# *Lésôneis* en Thébaïde : avant et après les crises

Depuis l'époque saïte, le *lésônis* est, dans les temples égyptiens, le prêtre nommé à la tête de l'administration pour un an[1]. Le terme *lésônis* est la transcription phonétique en grec de l'égyptien *mr-šn* mais le titre est parfois également traduit par ἀρχιερεύς « grand-prêtre ». Il est souvent suivi du nom de la divinité principale du temple dans lequel le prêtre exerçait la fonction. Celui-ci était, semble-t-il, élu annuellement par ses pairs et il faisait la plupart du temps partie des prêtres de haut rang issus de familles aisées. Son rôle consistait à administrer les biens du temple, à en gérer les revenus et à en payer les impôts. En cas de problème, le *lésônis* devait rembourser sur ses biens propres le déficit du temple. Pour reprendre l'expression d'Andrew Monson, le *lésônis* était, à l'époque ptolémaïque, une sorte de fermier d'impôts pour les revenus du temple. Il devait garantir un minimum de revenus pour le temple et pour la Couronne (impôts) mais pouvait garder le surplus pour lui-même[2].

Dans la Thébaïde à l'époque ptolémaïque, les sources font connaître des *lésôneis* dans sept lieux : Nag el-Mesheikh (Lepidotôn Polis), Thèbes, Pathyris, Edfou, Eléphantine, Philae et/ou Syène. Les trois *lésôneis* de Nag el-Mesheikh sont attestés dans des documents encore inédits et qui ne sont pas précisément datés ; ils ne seront donc pas étudiés ici[3]. Pour les *lésôneis* d'Éléphantine, Syène ou Philae, ils sont mentionnés dans des lettres dont la plupart sont encore inédites, et, pour celles qui sont publiées, il n'est pas toujours aisé de savoir dans quel temple le *lésônis* mentionné travaillait. La chronologie de ces lettres est également très incertaine[4].

Cet article se limitera donc aux *lésôneis* de Thèbes, d'Edfou et de Pathyris. L'objectif est de voir si l'on peut suivre ces prêtres avant et après les crises qui ont touché la Thébaïde à l'époque ptolémaïque. Il s'agira ainsi de tenter de savoir si les différentes crises ont eu des conséquences sur le personnel du temple et si d'anciennes familles de prêtres ont été remplacées par de nouvelles familles.

---

[1] Pour plus de détails sur la fonction, voir Chaufray 2023.
[2] Monson 2012, p. 218.
[3] O. G. Michaelides 204 (TM 171854), inédit mais traduit en anglais par B. Muhs (2014, p. 160). Les autres documents sont O. G. Michaelides 206 (TM 738010) et ODL 133 (TM 92101) décrits par U. Kaplony-Heckel (2000, p. 108).
[4] Voir Pestman 1995, p. 135–136.

Pour Thèbes et Edfou, les sources mentionnant des *lésôneis* sont antérieures à la grande révolte thébaine de 206 av. J.-C., et aucune source immédiatement postérieure n'est conservée. Certains de ces *lésôneis* ont néanmoins vécu au début du règne de Ptolémée III, au moment de la troisième guerre de Syrie, quand, d'après certaines sources classiques, une *seditio domestica* se serait produite dans le pays, obligeant Ptolémée III à revenir en Égypte[5]. Cette crise n'a trouvé que peu d'échos dans les sources égyptiennes[6], mais peut-être l'action de certains *lésôneis* pourrait-elle s'expliquer dans un tel contexte. À Pathyris, des *lésôneis* sont attestés en activité pendant et après la grande révolte de 206–180, et jusqu'au début du $i^{er}$ s. av. J.-C., lorsque plusieurs crises se sont produites en Thébaïde.

## 1 Les *lésôneis* de Thèbes

Dix *lésôneis* sont attestés à Thèbes entre 276 et 118 av. J.-C. (Tab. 1). Cinq d'entre eux portent le titre de *lésônis* d'Amon indiquant qu'ils étaient en service dans le temple de ce dieu à Karnak (2, 4, 7, 8, 9). Le nom d'Amon doit certainement être restitué après le titre de *lésônis* pour Pétéharprès fils d'Esminis (3) et sous-entendu pour Pasomtous fils de Paninouthis (5) car ils apparaissent dans des reçus pour l'impôt du chef de la nécropole comme Pétémestous fils d'Onnôphris (2) et Pétémestous (4) : cet impôt était payé par les prêtres funéraires pour les défunts qu'ils transportaient dans la nécropole[7]. Le formulaire indique, de manière générale, que l'impôt est payé au chef de la nécropole, qui est l'agent du *lésônis* d'Amon dont le nom est également donné. Khaponchônsis, Marrès(?) et Harsièsis (7, 8, 9) sont mentionnés dans des reçus de concessions funéraires rédigés par des scribes également désignés comme des agents du *lésônis* d'Amon[8]. Hôros (6) apparaît également dans un reçu de concession funéraire mais il est le défunt pour qui l'impôt est versé. Il est simplement désigné comme *lésônis*, sans précision de la divinité pour laquelle il exerçait la fonction. Amasis (1), le premier *lésônis* dont on peut dater l'exercice à Thèbes, à l'époque ptolémaïque, est mentionné dans un reçu d'impôt lié à la vente de deux maisons. Une partie de l'impôt sur les ventes immobilières étant destinée au temple, la mention du *lésônis* dans

---

5 Veïsse 2004, p. 3–5.
6 El-Masry, Altenmüller, Thissen 2012, p. 161.
7 Voir Muhs 2005, p. 88–95.
8 Voir Muhs 2005, p. 95–98.

le reçu se justifie[9]. Étant donné que le reçu est rédigé par « le scribe des *phylai* » et que des reçus parallèles thébains sont rédigés par le premier prophète, le *lésônis* est certainement en fonction dans le grand temple d'Amon, même si la divinité n'est pas précisée[10]. Le dernier *lésônis* connu, en 118 av. J.-C., Psemminis fils de Phagônis (10), apparaît dans un serment de temple juré dans le temple de Djèmé. Comme pour Amasis, il est juste désigné comme « le *lésônis* ». Il pourrait s'agir du phylarque de la deuxième *phylè* mentionné dans un reçu thébain[11]. Dans ce cas, ce serait aussi un *lésônis* d'Amon, en service dans le temple du dieu à Karnak.

**Tab. 1:** Succession des *lésôneis* thébains.

| | Nom | Divinité | Sources | Date |
|---|---|---|---|---|
| 1 | Amasis | | *P.BM Glanville* 10529 (p. 43–44, TM 43769), v°, l. 3 | 276 av. J.-C. |
| 2 | Pétémestous fils d'Onnôphris | Amon | *P.BM Andrews* 1 (TM 310), D, l. 1 | 265/264 av. J.-C. |
| 3 | ? Pétéharprès fils d'Esminis | [Amon] | *O.TT 32* (TM 50968), l. 2 | 264/263 av. J.-C. |
| 4 | Pétémestous | Amon | *O.BM EA 5730* (TM 51738), l. 4 *O.Bodl. 371* (TM 51746), l. 5–6 *O.Taxes* II 117 (TM 130110), l. 2 | 261–259 av. J.-C. |
| 5 | Pasomtous fils de Paninouthis | (Amon) | *O.BM EA 5734* (TM 51740), l. 5 | 258/257 av. J.-C. |
| 6 | Hôros | | *O.Taxes* II 123 (TM 130116), l. 2 | *c.* 253 av. J.-C. |
| 7 | Khaponchônsis fils de Pétéharprès | Amon | *P.BM Andrews* 13 (TM 47615), l. 8–9 | 241 av. J.-C. |
| 8 | Marrès (?) fils d'Esminis | Amon | *O.Vleem.* 53 (TM 3050), l. 11 | 228/227 av. J.-C. |
| 9 | Harsièsis fils de Hôros | Amon | *P.Fam.Theb.* 24 (TM 2925), l. 3 | 227/226 av. J.-C. |
| 10 | Psemminis fils de Phagônis | | *P.Tor.Amen.* 11 (TM 44639), l. 19–20 | 118 av. J.-C. |

Pétémestous fils d'Onnôphris (2) est témoin dans un contrat où il énumère tous ses titres, dont différents titres de prophète et de scribe :

---

9 Voir Depauw 2000, p. 56–63.
10 Voir Depauw 2000, p. 57.
11 *O.Mattha* 272 (TM 49895), l. 1.

*jt-nṯr ḥm-nṯr Ỉmn-m-ỉp.t-sw.t ḥm Ḥḏ.t Ḥr ḥm-nṯr Bȝst.t ḥry- ỉb Wȝs.t ḥm-ntr Mw.t nḥm sḫ ḥw.t-nṯr ȝt Ỉmn ḥȝp n Ỉmn mr- šn n Ỉmn sḫ ḥtm.t-nṯr n Ỉmn ḥm-nṯr Ḥr-mn Ỉy.t-nfr nȝ nṯr.w n Ỉsw.t*

père divin, prophète d'Amon dans Karnak, serviteur de la Couronne Blanche et de Horus, prophète de Bastet qui réside à Thèbes, prophète de Mout salvatrice, scribe du temple, prêtre-*ȝt* d'Amon, prêtre-*ḥȝp* d'Amon, *lésônis* d'Amon, scribe du sceau divin d'Amon, prophète d'Hor-men et d'Iy-nefer, et des dieux d'Isout.

Le contrat conserve également le nom de sa mère, Eschônsis. Ce Pétémestous est-il identique à son homonyme mentionné sans patronyme dans trois reçus d'impôt (4) ? Difficile de savoir vu la fréquence du nom Pétémestous à Thèbes, mais c'est possible puisque la fonction de *lésônis* était réitérable, comme on peut le voir à Edfou[12]. S'il s'agit de la même personne, Pétémestous n'a alors pas été *lésônis* de façon continue de l'an 21 à l'an 26 de Ptolémée II (265 à 259 av. J.-C.), puisque Pétéharprès (3) semble avoir occupé la charge en l'an 22.

Ce Pétéharprès n'apparaît pas dans les sources avec le titre de *lésônis*, mais il est mentionné, en 264 av. J.-C., comme le supérieur du chef de la nécropole dans un reçu d'impôt du chef de la nécropole. Or, dans ces reçus, le supérieur est toujours le *lésônis* d'Amon. Pétéharprès était scribe du temple en 281 av. J.-C. et sur une statue dédiée à son père, la liste de ses titres montre qu'il détenait plusieurs charges scribales, comme Pétémestous[13].

De Meulenaere a pu reconstruire sa famille sur cinq générations (Fig. 1), mais Pétéharprès appartient à la dernière, et on ne peut plus suivre la famille par la suite, pendant les crises de la Thébaïde[14].

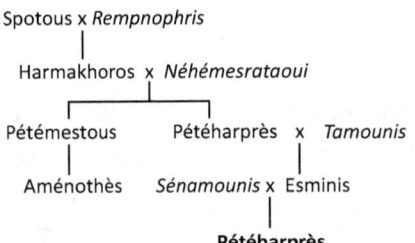

**Fig. 1:** Tableau généalogique de la famille de Pétéharprès.

---

**12** Voir infra, p. 76.
**13** *P.Ryl.Dem.* III 12–13 (TM 8540, 46175), r°, H, l. 1, v° l. 1, et Statue *CG* 680 : *ḥm Ḥr sš nsw sš Ỉmn sš Mnṯ nb Ḏrwt ḥm-nṯr 3-nw Mȝʿ.t nb.t ỉr.t Rʿ ḥry (jmyw) wnwt Ỉmn n sȝ 4-nw sš pr-ḥḏ n pr Ỉmn* : serviteur de Horus, scribe royal, scribe d'Amon, scribe de Montou maître de Tôd, troisième prophète de Maât maîtresse de l'œil de Ré, supérieur des astronomes d'Amon de la quatrième *phylè*, scribe du trésor du domaine d'Amon. Sur la correction du titre de scribe Montou maître de Tôd (au lieu de Médamoud), voir Birk 2020, p. 494 ; sur le titre *ḥry sbȝ* corrigé en *(jmyw) wnwt*, voir Birk 2014, p. 81, n. 13.
**14** De Meulenaere 1962, p. 69.

Les autres *lésôneis* thébains sont mentionnés dans des documents démotiques où les séquences de titres ne sont pas développées (5, 6) ou peu : le titre de « père divin » est conservé pour trois *lésôneis* (7, 8, 9), celui de « prophète d'Amonrasonther » pour un (7) et celui de scribe du livre divin pour un autre (9)[15].

Sept autres *lésôneis* thébains sont connus par des sources non datées, dont plusieurs statues où sont conservées de longues titulatures et de nombreuses informations généalogiques (Tab. 2). Deux d'entre eux (15, 16) sont *lésôneis* de Montou et pourraient avoir été en fonction dans le temple de ce dieu à Médamoud.

**Tab. 2:** *Lésôneis* non datés.

| | Nom | Titulature[16] | Source |
|---|---|---|---|
| 11 | Ioufâa fils de Nakhtefmout | *ỉt-nṯr ḥm-nṯr wn ḥm-nṯr n Ḏḥwty n pr Ỉmn w'b n wnmj tȝ ḥȝ.t n pȝ nṯr 'ȝ*[17] *ỉmỉ-ỉbd=f mr-šn sš ḥtm.t-nṯr ỉmỉ-st-' ỉry ps ỉry 'fd w'b tȝ ḥr(t)-ỉb 'ȝ-w'b n Wsỉr ḥry-ỉb Ỉp.t n pr Ỉmn-Ỉp.t ḥr sȝ tpy sš tȝ ḥry 'mr n pr Ỉmn-Ỉp.t n sȝ tp ỉdnw n pr Ỉmn-Ỉp.t sȝ 3-nw ḥm-nṯr Ỉmn-Ỉp.t ḥry s.t wr.t*[18] père divin, prophète de la lumière, prophète de Thôt dans le domaine d'Amon, prêtre-*ouâb* à la droite à l'avant du grand dieu, prêtre mensuel, *lésônis*, scribe du sceau divin, officiant, préposé à la flamme (?)[19], préposé au coffre, prêtre de la salle intermédiaire[20], grand-des-prêtres d'Osiris qui réside à Louxor du domaine d'Aménophis pour la première *phylè*, scribe-*tȝ*, supérieur de la boulangerie du domaine d'Aménophis pour la première *phylè*, substitut du domaine d'Aménophis pour la troisième *phylè*, prophète d'Aménophis, qui est sur son grand siège. | Statue Caire *CG* 48621 (TM 109415) |
| 12 | Iry-iry fils de Hôros | *mr-šn Ỉmn*, *lésônis* d'Amon | Statue Caire JE 38013 (TM 90663) |

---

**15** *P.BM Andrews* 13 (TM 47615), l. 8–9 ; *O.Vleem.* 53 (TM 3050), l. 11 ; *P.Fam.Theb.* 24 (TM 2925), l. 3.
**16** Seuls les titres inscrits dans la même séquence que le titre de *lésônis* sont indiqués ici.
**17** Sur ce titre renvoyant à la position du prêtre pour le portage de la barque, voir également la statue Caire JE 37448. Cf. Abdelrahman 2021, p. 197–199.
**18** Pour la titulature complète, voir Birk 2020, p. 512.
**19** Voir Jansen-Winkeln 2001, p. 56, n. 56.
**20** Sur la réalité correspondant à cette désignation, voir Spencer 1984, p. 85–87.

Tab. 2 (suite)

| Nom | Titulature | Source |
|---|---|---|
| 13 Pkorkhônsis fils d'Esbendétis | ỉt-nṯr ḥm-nṯr Ỉmn m Ỉp.t-s.wt ḥm-nṯr Ỉmn Wsr-ḥȝ.t ḥm-nṯr wʿb n Rʿ tp ḥw.t n pr-Ỉmn n sȝ tpy ỉmỉ-s.t-ʿ n Ỉmn n sȝ 3-nw mr-šn ʿȝ-wʿb ḥrỉ sštȝ n Mw.t wr.t nb(.t) Ỉšrw n sȝ 3.nw n sȝ 4.nw ḥrỉ sštȝ ʿb-nṯr<br>père divin, prophète d'Amon dans Karnak, prophète de la barque d'Amon, prophète et prêtre-*ouâb* de Ré sur le toit du temple du domaine d'Amon de la première *phylè*, officiant d'Amon de la troisième *phylè*, *lésônis*, grand-des-prêtres, supérieur des secrets de Mout, la grande, maîtresse d'Ishérou de la troisième *phylè*, de la quatrième *phylè*, supérieur des secrets, purificateur du dieu | Statue BM EA 48038 (inédite / TM 702194) |
| 14 Pétémestous fils d'Onnôphris | ỉt-nṯr ḥm-nṯr Ỉmn m Ỉp.t-s.wt ḥm-nṯr ḥḏ(.t) wʿb Ḥr m Nḫn n Ḫnsw-pȝ-ẖrd ʿȝ wr tpy n Ỉmn ḥry-mnḫ.t n Ỉmn r-šn n Ỉmn sš ḫtm.t-nṯr<br>père divin, prophète d'Amon dans Karnak, prophète de la (Couronne) Blanche, prêtre-*ouab* de Horus à Hiérakonpolis et de Khonsou l'enfant, l'aîné, le grand, premier né d'Amon, archistoliste d'Amon, *lésônis* d'Amon, scribe du sceau divin | Statue ex-Caire JE 37982 (TM 701947) |
| 15 Pétamounis | mr-šn Mnṯ ḥm-nṯr 2-nw<br>*lésônis* de Montou, deuxième prophète | O.Theb. p. 39 (D 51), (TM 92962) |
| 16 Nekhtmônthès fils d'Eshyris | mr-šn Mnṯ<br>*lésônis* de Montou | P.BrooklynDem. 153 (TM 89014), conc., l. 2 |
| 17 Har- ? fils de Psenpchered | mr-šn Ḏḥwty<br>*lésônis* de Thôt | ShortTexts III 1494 (TM 81155), l. 6 |

Pétémestous fils d'Onnôphris (14) est homonyme du *lésônis* en fonction en 265/264 av. J.-C. (Tab. 1, n° 2). Des similarités se trouvent dans leurs titres respectifs : ils sont tous les deux prophètes et *lésôneis* d'Amon, scribe du sceau divin, et ils portent des titres liés à la Couronne blanche et à Horus[21]. L'identification est tentante, mais le nom de leurs mères est différent. Les noms de Pétémestous et d'Onnôphris étant très répandus dans le clergé thébain, ce genre d'homonymie devait être fréquent.

Le dernier *lésônis* mentionné dans les sources thébaines est en fonction en 118 av. J.-C. L'écart de près d'un siècle avec les *lésôneis* du iiie s. rend impossible

---

21 Sur ce titre, voir Traunecker 1998, p. 1222–1225.

l'identification d'éventuels liens généalogiques. En l'état actuel des sources, il est donc difficile de suivre les *lésôneis* thébains à travers les crises qui ont secoué la Thébaïde. Peut-être des liens avec des statues encore inédites permettront d'aller plus loin.

## 2 Les *lésôneis* d'Edfou

Neuf *lésôneis* sont connus à Edfou, dont huit en service dans le temple de Horus entre 246 et 233 av. J.-C. (Tab. 3).

**Tab. 3:** Succession des *lésôneis* de Horus à Edfou.

| | Nom | Sources | Date |
|---|---|---|---|
| 1 | Bérénepthis fils d'Estphènis | *P.Eleph.Dem.* 8 (TM 44566), l. 9 | 246/245 av. J.-C. |
| 2 | Pétéharpochratès fils de Pétamounis | *P.Eleph.Dem.* 8 (TM 44566), l. 7 | 238/237 av. J.-C. |
| 3 | Thotmôsis le jeune fils de Pétéharsomtous | *P.Eleph.Dem.* 8 (TM 44566), l. 5 | 233/232 av. J.-C. |
| 4 | Pinyris fils d'Estphènis | *P.Bürgsch.* 14 (TM 43412), l. 3 | 232/231 av. J.-C. |
| 5 | Thotmôsis l'aîné fils de Harsièsis | *P.Eleph.Dem.* 8 (TM 44566), l. 14 | 230/229 av. J.-C. |
| 1 | Bérénepthis fils d'Estphènis | *P.Eleph.Dem.* 8 (TM 44566), l. 9 | 229/228 av. J.-C. |
| 2 | Pétéharpochratès fils de Pétamounis | *P.Eleph.Dem.* 8 (TM 44566), l. 7 | 228/227 av. J.-C. |
| 6 | Pétéharpochratès fils de Thotmôsis | *P.Eleph.Dem.* 8 (TM 44566), l. 12 | 226/225 av. J.-C. |
| 7 | Estphènis fils de Pinyris | *P.Bürgsch.* 13 (TM 5858), l. 5 | 225/224 av. J.-C. |
| 8 | Ptômphis fils d'Estphènis | *P.Eleph.Gr.* 25 (TM 5857), l. 5–6 | 231/230 av. J.-C. ? 227/226 av. J.-C. ? 224/223 av. J.-C. ? |
| 9 | Honès | *ShortTexts* III 2087 (TM 69165), col. 2, l. 3 | Sans date |

Cinq d'entre eux sont mentionnés dans un papyrus démotique conservé dans la collection de Berlin (1, 2, 3, 5, 6). La finalité exacte du document est difficile à comprendre. Il s'agit d'une liste écrite par les scribes du temple qui commence par : « Voici les biens (?) appartenant aux prêtres dont les noms sont donnés ci-dessous ». Au lieu de biens (*nkt*), on pourrait aussi lire « les parts » (*dnỉ.t*). La raison pour laquelle cette liste est dressée n'est pas donnée mais tous les prêtres nommés ont été *lésônis* entre 246 et 226, soit une période de vingt ans. Leurs biens ou parts sont exprimés en partie d'année, ce qui signifie qu'il devait s'agir de revenus sacerdotaux venant de différentes prébendes.

La liste fait partie des archives d'un fonctionnaire grec, Milon, qui était *praktor* des temples en grec, probablement une sorte d'huissier, envoyé pour récupérer l'argent des prêtres endettés[22]. La liste semble donc avoir été rédigée dans le contexte d'une crise dans le temple d'Edfou où plusieurs prêtres avaient contracté des dettes. Bérénepthis fils d'Estphènis (1) s'est, en effet, endetté alors qu'il était *lésônis* du temple en l'an 2 et en l'an 19[23]. Sa dette portait sur le *byssos*, lin précieux fabriqué uniquement dans les temples, qui devaient donner à la Couronne une partie de leur production[24]. Pinyris (4), le frère de Bérénepthis (1), a également contracté des dettes lorsqu'il était *lésônis* en l'an 16, et un autre membre de la famille, Estphènis (7), soit le fils de Pinyris, soit le père des deux frères (Fig. 2), a contracté une dette en l'an 23[25]. Il était alors probablement *lésônis* lui aussi, bien que son titre n'apparaisse pas.

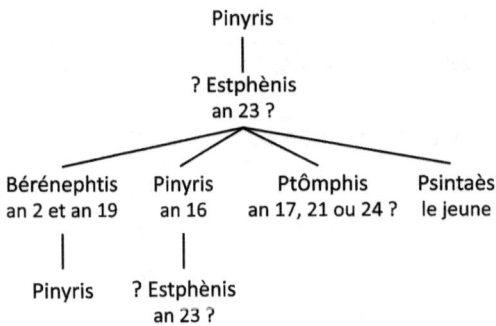

**Fig. 2:** Famille de Bérénepthis fils d'Estphènis.

Dans les années 23 à 25, la famille a dû vendre une partie de ses biens. Une enquête a probablement été déclenchée en l'an 23 parce que la situation était allée trop loin. Une offre d'achat pour la maison de Ptômphis, autre membre de la famille, est également conservée dans les archives de Milon[26]. Ptômphis y est désigné comme ὁ γενόμενος ἀρχιερεύς, « l'ancien *lésônis* ». Sans doute avait-il, lui

---

22 Clarysse 2003, p. 17–27. Manning 2003, p. 83–85. Monson 2012, p. 214, 217.
23 *P.Bürgsch.* 13 (TM 5858), l. 7, 16 et *P.Eleph.Gr.* 27a+*P.Eleph.Dem.* 10 (TM 44603), l. 15, 28.
24 Préaux 1939, p. 99–103.
25 *P.Bürgsch.* 14 (TM 43412), l. 3 ; *P.Bürgsch.* 13 (TM 5858), l. 5 et *P.Eleph.Gr.* 27a+*P.Eleph.Dem.* 10 (TM 44603), l. 11.
26 *P.Eleph.Gr.* 25 (TM 5857), l. 5–6.

aussi, contracté des dettes pendant sa charge, ou bien était-il simplement garant des membres de sa famille. Étant donné qu'on ne connaît pas le nom des *lésôneis* en fonction pour les ans 17, 21 et 24, Ptômphis a peut-être exercé la fonction l'une de ces années-là. L'exemple de cette famille dont plusieurs membres ont exercé une haute responsabilité dans le grand temple d'Edfou montre qu'il pouvait être difficile de respecter ses engagements vis-à-vis de la Couronne.

Ce qui reste obscur dans ce dossier est la liste des *lésôneis* transmise par les scribes des prêtres à Milon en l'an 24. Est-ce que les *lésôneis* mentionnés sont tous endettés comme Bérénepthis ? Si oui, pourquoi les autres membres de la famille de Bérénepthis, qui ont exercé la fonction de *lésônis*, n'y sont pas nommés ? Si tel était néanmoins le cas, cela signifierait qu'il était difficile, à cette époque, d'être à la tête d'un grand temple. La première année d'exercice de la fonction par Bérénepthis, l'an 2 de Ptolémée III, (246/245 av. J.-C.) se trouve correspondre à la date de la *seditio domestica* dont aucun détail n'est conservé. Peut-être qu'un contexte difficile a ouvert la voie à l'endettement successif des *lésôneis* d'Edfou devenus incapables, ou peu désireux, de respecter leurs obligations vis-à-vis de la Couronne. À la même époque, dans le village de Tebtynis (Fayoum), Pachès, « l'ancien *lésônis* de Soknebtynis en l'an 4 », ὁ γενό[μ]ενος ἀρχιγερεὺς [το]ῦ Σοκονοβτύνιος ἐν τῶι δ (ἔτει), est, lui aussi, comme Bérénepthis, endetté sur le *byssos*[27]. L'administration lui demande de payer sa dette, sans quoi ses biens seront confisqués.

Plus tard, au iie s. av. J.-C., des ordonnances royales contiennent des remises de dettes sur le *byssos*[28]. Le problème des arriérés de *byssos* semble donc avoir été récurrent. Par conséquent, la dette de Bérénepthis n'est peut-être pas liée à un contexte difficile.

## 3 Les *lésôneis* de Pathyris

Les cinq *lésôneis* connus à Pathyris sont attestés dans des documents qui appartenaient probablement aux archives du temple de Hathor[29] (Tab. 4).

Deux *lésôneis* sont contemporains de la grande révolte thébaine (1, 2). Pétéharoèris fils de Pétéharsomtous (1) était le 4e prophète de Hathor. Il est mentionné

---

27 *P.Petr.* III 53p (TM 7482).
28 Sous Ptolémée V, en 196 av. J.-C. : *OGIS* I 90, l. 17–18 ; sous Ptolémée VIII, Cléopâtre II et III, en 121–118 av. J.-C. : *P.Tebt.* I 5, l. 62–64.
29 Vandorpe, Waebens 2009, p. 100–101, §35.

**Tab. 4:** Succession des *lésôneis* de Hathor à Pathyris.

| | Nom | Sources | Date |
|---|---|---|---|
| 1 | Pétéharoèris fils de Pétéharsomtous | P. Berl. P. 9068 (TM 46901), inédit, r°, l. 2–3, v° | 208 ou 191 av. J.-C. |
| 2 | Nekhtminis fils d'Esminis | *P. Ryl. Dem.* 32 (TM 500), l. 2, 13 | 204 av. J.-C. |
| 3 | Thotortaios fils de Nekhtminis | O. BM EA 29719 (TM 51481), l. 6 | 157 av. J.-C. |
| 4 | Sesoôsis fils de Psemminis | T. Hess Dem. 1 (TM 90899), l. 11 | 148 av. J.-C. |
| 5 | Pétéharsomtous fils de Pakèbkis | T. Caire JE 51437 (TM 51160), l. 6 | 104 av. J.-C. |

dans un acte juridique daté de l'an 2 de Haronnophris (204 av. J.-C.)[30]. La date est certaine car le scribe de l'acte, Harpaèsis fils de Thotortaios, est connu dans un autre document écrit en l'an 1 du roi rebelle qui est nommé dans la formule de datation[31]. Ces documents montrent qu'à Pathyris, l'administration du temple avait reconnu le roi rebelle.

Pétéharoèris fils de Pétéharsomtous est également le destinataire de deux lettres inédites : l'une au British Museum, l'autre à Berlin, datées respectivement de l'an 10 et de l'an 14[32]. Il est impossible de décider si les années doivent être placées sous le règne de Ptolémée IV, avant la crise, ou sous le règne de Chaonnophris (pendant la rébellion) ou de Ptolémée V, si les Ptolémées avaient repris le pouvoir à Pathyris. Le contenu des lettres ne donne aucune indication sur le contexte historique.

Cependant, la famille de Pétéharoèris peut être reconstituée grâce à un acte juridique écrit par les prêtres de Hathor en 158/157 av. J.-C., où signe un 4ᵉ prophète de Hathor du nom de Harsièsis. Cet Harsièsis porte les titres de son grand-père et de son arrière-grand-père (Fig. 3). La famille était donc toujours active à cette époque, après la grande révolte, et elle occupait toujours une position élevée dans le clergé de Hathor. Le fait que le clergé de Pathyris ait accepté le roi rebelle et daté les actes rédigés à cette époque de son règne n'a apparemment pas eu de graves conséquences sur la famille.

Le deuxième *lésônis* contemporain de la révolte, Nekhtminis fils d'Esminis (2), signe juste après le 4ᵉ prophète de Hathor dans l'acte daté de 204 av. J.-C.[33] Étant donné la date du contrat, Nekhtminis fils d'Esminis ne peut être identifié à son homonyme qui signe un reçu de temple une cinquantaine d'années plus tard,

---

30 *P.Ryl.Dem.* 32 (TM 500).
31 P. BM EA 10486 (TM 620), l. 2.
32 P. BM EA 10555.5 A (TM 625), P. Berl. P. 9068 (TM 46901) : publication en cours par G. Baetens et moi-même.
33 *P.Ryl.Dem.* 32 (TM 500), l. 13.

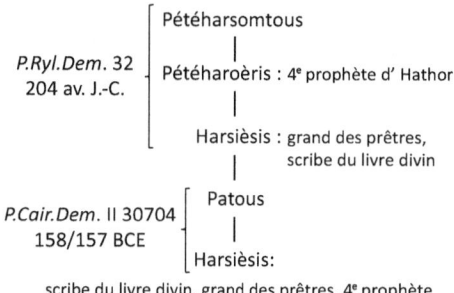

**Fig. 3:** Arbre généalogique de Pétéharoèris.

en 157 av. J.-C., et dont le titre avait été lu par erreur comme le supérieur du *lésônis* (*p3 ḥry mr-šn*)[34]. En fait, le titre doit être lu *p3 rmṯ nty šn*, qui correspond au titre grec « épistate du temple », un fonctionnaire chargé du contrôle des temples. Ce deuxième Nekhtminis, qui était épistate du temple au iie siècle, pourrait être l'un des descendants du *lésônis* de 204, mais je n'ai pas pu reconstituer d'arbre généalogique.

Le reçu du temple de 157 av. J.-C. est signé par trois prêtres : le premier est l'épistate, et le dernier, Phibis fils de Panechatès, est probablement un scribe du temple. Le deuxième signataire est le troisième *lésônis* connu à Pathyris : Thotortaios fils de Nekhtminis, peut-être l'épistate qui signe juste avant lui. Thotortaios pourrait être un descendant du scribe Harpaèsis fils de Thotortaios, rédacteur des deux actes susmentionnés sous le règne de Haronnôphris. Il s'agirait alors d'une deuxième famille de prêtres ayant gardé ses fonctions dans le temple de Hathor après la révolte. Il manque néanmoins, dans les sources, un Esminis fils de Harpaèsis qui pourrait faire la filiation (Fig. 4).

Le quatrième *lésônis* de Pathyris est Sesoôsis, fils de Psemminis, qui signe un autre reçu de temple en qualité de *lésônis*[35]. Il y a, comme dans le reçu précédent, trois signataires. Le premier, Harsièsis fils de Patous, qui ne porte pas de titre pourrait être le 4e prophète de Hathor mentionné dans l'acte de 158/157 av. J.-C.[36] La dernière signature est celle du scribe du temple Phibis fils de Panechatès. Il est plus difficile, pour ce *lésônis*, de trouver des ancêtres car le nom de Psemminis est commun.

Le dernier *lésônis* de Pathyris est connu grâce à ses archives[37]. Dans un acte juridique daté de 99 av. J.-C., une courte description physique nous apprend qu'il avait

---

[34] O. BM 29719 (TM 51481), l. 4.
[35] T. Hess Dem. 1 (TM 90899).
[36] *P.Cair.Dem.* II 30704, col. 2, l. 6–7.
[37] Vandorpe, Waebens 2009, p. 160–162, § 46.

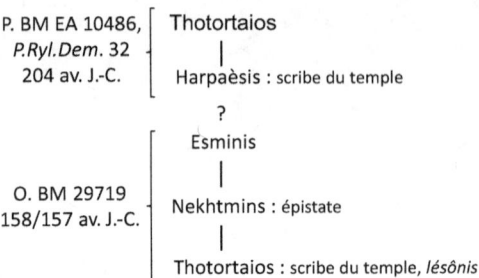

**Fig. 4:** Arbre généalogique de Thotortaios.

alors 40 ou 50 ans. Entre 95 et 90 av. J.-C., il signe des documents en qualité d'épistate, et, en parallèle, il continue à rédiger des documents en tant que scribe du temple. On perd sa trace en 89 av. J.-C. Pétéharsomtous a vécu pendant une période de troubles dans le nome Pathyrite. Ces troubles sont perceptibles par des années pendant lesquelles l'impôt sur la récolte (*épigraphè*) n'était plus versé au trésor, comme en témoigne l'absence de reçus de cet impôt : entre 107 et 103 ; 102 et 94/93 ; 91 et 88 av. J.-C.[38]. Les documents qui mentionnent Pétéharsomtous pendant ces périodes ne témoignent d'aucun trouble particulier. En 104, le reçu que signe Pétéharsomtous en tant que *lésônis* prouve que les rentrées d'argent avaient toujours lieu. Le reçu est même signé par l'épistate, le fonctionnaire en charge du contrôle du temple. En 95/94, Pétéharsomtous est lui-même épistate et atteste un versement pour le temple[39]. En 89, il signe également, en tant que scribe du temple, un reçu d'argent[40]. S'il y a des troubles à Pathyris, ils ne sont pas perceptibles dans la documentation du temple.

Pour conclure, il est difficile de savoir si les crises de la Thébaïde ont eu des conséquences sur les *lésôneis* d'Amon à Thèbes puisque nous n'avons pas de sources pendant les crises ni après. À Edfou, les problèmes rencontrés par les *lésôneis* au iiie s. av. J.-C. pourraient avoir commencé à l'époque de la *seditio domestica*, mais comme cette *seditio* n'est pas documentée, l'hypothèse ne peut être vérifiée. À Pathyris, au contraire, les sources permettent de voir que la grande révolte n'a pas eu de conséquences sur les familles de grands prêtres qui ont gardé leur place dans le temple de Hathor ; pour les crises qui ont suivi, elles n'ont pas laissé de traces dans la documentation du temple. Néanmoins, beaucoup de documents sont encore inédits et peut-être que cette vision changera quand les archives du temple seront publiées.

---

**38** Vandorpe 2000, p. 415, 433–436, Veïsse 2004, p. 68–69.
**39** O. Caire sans n° (TM 51237).
**40** O. Caire JE 51449 (TM 43399).

# Bibliographie

Abdelrahman 2021
Abdelrahman, A., « Two Unpublished Bases of Statues at the Egyptian Museum, Cairo (JE.37998, JE 37448) from Karnak Cachette », *EJARS* 11, 2021, p. 193–202.

Birk 2014
Birk, R., « Titel-Bilder: Zur amtsspezifischen Ikonographie thebanischer Priester der Ptolemäerzeit » in G. Neunert, A. Verbovsek, K. Gabler (éd.), *Bild: Ästhetik – Medium – Kommunikation – Beiträge des dritten Münchner Arbeitskreises Junge Ägyptologie*, GOF IV/58, Wiesbaden, 2014, p. 79–102.

Birk 2020
Birk, R., *Türöffner des Himmels: Prosopographische Studien zur thebanischen Hohepriesterschaft der Ptolemäerzeit*, ÄA 76, Wiesbaden, 2020.

Chaufray 2023
Chaufray, M.-P., *La fonction du lésônis de l'époque saïte à l'époque ptolémaïque*, StudHell 61, Louvain, 2023.

Clarysse 2003
Clarysse, W., « The Archive of the Praktor Milon » in K. Vandorpe, W. Clarysse (éd.), *Edfu: An Egyptian Provincial Capital in the Ptolemaic Period, Brussels, 3 September 2001*, Bruxelles, 2003, p. 17–27.

De Meulenaere 1962
De Meulenaere, H., « Prosopographia Ptolemaica. Deuxième série », *CdE* 37, 1962, p. 66–75.

Depauw 2000
Depauw, M., *The Archive of Teos and Thabis from Early Ptolemaic Thebes (P.Brux.dem.inv.E.8252-8256)*, MRE 8, Turnhout, 2000.

El-Masry, Altenmüller, Thissen 2012
El-Masry, Y., Altenmüller, H., Thissen, H.-J., *Das Synodaldekret von Alexandria aus dem Jahre 243 v. Chr.*, BSAK 11, Hambourg, 2012.

Jansen-Winkeln 2001
Jansen-Winkeln, K., *Biographische und religiöse Inschriften der Spätzeit aus dem Ägyptischen Museum Kairo*, vol. I-II, ÄAT 45, Wiesbaden, 2001.

Kaplony-Heckel 2000
Kaplony-Heckel, U., « Ein Weizen-Überweisungsauftrag zugunsten des (Tempel)-Wirtschafters Hor (das demotische Kalkstein-Ostrakon Leipzig ÄM 4789) », *JEA* 86, 2000, p. 99–109.

Manning 2003
Manning, J.G., *Land and Power in Ptolemaic Egypt: the Structure of Land Tenure*, Cambridge, 2003.

Monson 2012
Monson, A., *From the Ptolemies to the Romans: Political and Economic Change in Egypt*, Cambridge, 2012.

Muhs 2005
Muhs, B.P., *Tax Receipts, Taxpayers, and Taxes in Early Ptolemaic Thebes*, OIP 126, Chicago, 2005.

Muhs 2014
Muhs, B., « Temple Economy in the Nag' el-Mesheikh Ostraca » in M. Depauw, Y. Broux (éd.), *Acts of the Tenth International Congress of Demotic Studies: Leuven, 26–30 August 2008*, OLA 231, Louvain, 2014, p. 155–164.

Pestman 1995
: Pestman, P.W., « Haronnophris and Chaonnophris: Two Indigenous Pharaohs in Ptolemaic Egypt (205–186 B.C.) » in S.P. Vleeming (éd.), *Hundred-Gated Thebes: Acts of a Colloquium on Thebes and the Theban Area in the Graeco-Roman Period*, P.L.Bat. 27, Leyde, New York, Cologne, 1995, p. 101–137.

Préaux 1939
: Préaux, C., *L'Économie royale des Lagides*, Bruxelles, 1939.

Spencer 1984
: Spencer, P., *The Egyptian Temple: A Lexicographical Study*, Londres, 1984.

Traunecker 1998
: Traunecker, C., « Les graffiti des frères Horsaisis et Horemheb. Une famille de prêtres sous les derniers Ptolémées » in W. Clarysse, A. Schoors, H. Willems (éd.), *Egyptian Religion: The Last Thousand Years – Studies dedicated to the Memory of Jan Quaegebeur*, OLA 85, Louvain, 1998, vol. II, p. 1192–1229.

Vandorpe 2000
: Vandorpe, K., « Paying Taxes to the Thesauroi of the Pathyrites in a Century of Rebellion (186–88 BC) » in L. Mooren (éd.), *Politics, Administration and Society in the Hellenistic and Roman World: Proceedings of the International Colloquium, Bertinoro 19-24 July, 1997*, StudHell 36, Louvain, 2000, p. 405–436.

Vandorpe, Waebens 2009
: Vandorpe, K., Waebens, S., *Reconstructing Pathyris' Archives: A Multicultural Community in Hellenistic Egypt*, CollHell 3, Bruxelles, 2009.

Veïsse 2004
: Veïsse, A.-E., *Les « révoltes égyptiennes ». Recherches sur les troubles intérieurs en Égypte du règne de Ptolémée III à la conquête romaine*, StudHell 41, Louvain, 2004.

Laurent Coulon
# Les cimetières osiriens, témoins de la politique des Lagides et de ses aléas

Dans la continuité de l'avènement progressif du culte d'Osiris à l'échelle nationale dans le courant du I$^{er}$ millénaire av. J.-C., la dynastie lagide a massivement investi dans le développement de ce culte et de celui de sa parèdre Isis. Les Ptolémées, particulièrement à partir de Ptolémée III, ont en effet corrélé le culte de leur dynastie et celui de ces divinités, comme il le faisait parallèlement pour Sérapis et Dionysos[1]. Les nécropoles osiriennes, abritant les figurines enterrées rituellement à l'issue des rites de Khoiak, sont les témoins de cet investissement royal considérable[2].

Dans le cadre de ce colloque consacré aux relations conflictuelles qu'ont entretenues le pouvoir lagide et la Thébaïde, il s'agit d'explorer ici quel impact ont pu avoir ces crises politiques dans le développement des cimetières osiriens, sur la base des données nouvelles apparues ces dernières décennies. Appréhender la crise politique sous l'angle du culte d'Osiris se justifie d'autant plus que les leaders des révoltés thébains se sont revendiqués par leur nom d'une « légitimité osirienne ». La lutte autour des lieux de culte osirien et la maîtrise des cérémonies osiriennes deviennent à l'évidence enjeux de pouvoir.

Nous formulons donc ici l'hypothèse que l'association du culte osirien avec celui des Lagides amène un parallélisme entre les périodes de développement du culte osirien et celles pendant lesquelles le pouvoir lagide n'est pas ou moins contesté. Comme on va le voir, il s'agit davantage d'une piste d'interprétation que d'un fait démontrable dans la mesure où les données disponibles sont à ce jour encore très incomplètes. L'apport rapide de nouveaux éléments par l'archéologie offre néanmoins la perspective d'affiner à moyen terme les premières réponses qui peuvent être formulées.

---

[1] Coulon 2010 ; Preys 2015 ; Smith 2017, p. 356–358 (avec réf.) ; Caneva, Bricault 2019.
[2] Comme nous l'avons mis précédemment en évidence (Coulon 2008), le développement à l'époque ptolémaïque de la « Grande Place » de Karnak abritant l'abaton local peut être mis en relation avec l'importance acquise par le culte du souverain que prennent en charge certains membres éminents du clergé osirien.

# 1 Le développement des cimetières osiriens à l'époque ptolémaïque

Diodore de Sicile rendait compte de la multiplication des tombeaux d'Osiris dans les différentes régions d'Égypte en mettant en scène un accord passé entre la déesse Isis et les prêtres du pays, chaque clergé local se voyant confier, en échange de revenus, la charge de la sépulture d'Osiris dans son territoire, associé aux cultes des animaux sacrés[3]. Ce récit mythologique reflète assez largement la situation de l'Égypte tardive où chaque métropole religieuse aménage dans son temenos un tombeau du dieu Osiris dans sa forme locale. Cette multiplication des tombeaux n'empêche pas les souverains de créer une fiction nationale par le biais de la reconstitution rituelle du corps d'Osiris qui s'apparente à une unification politique du territoire sous la coupe du pharaon[4]. Si ce processus est déjà à l'œuvre antérieurement à l'époque ptolémaïque, les Lagides vont considérablement promouvoir cette vision géopolitique du culte osirien et faire des festivités de Khoiak, qui se déploient autour des tombeaux d'Osiris, un évènement central de l'année égyptienne.

Des témoignages archéologiques des rites de Khoiak, principalement des figurines d'« Osiris végétants », étaient connus anciennement par des fouilles et trouvailles du début du XXe siècle et avaient pu être mis en regard des « recettes » de fabrication décrites dans les textes relatifs aux mystères de Khoiak[5] ; mais l'essor des tombeaux osiriens au Ier millénaire av. J.-C. est beaucoup mieux connu depuis trois décennies grâce à la mise au jour de quatre cimetières, dont certains ont pu être fouillés assez précisément, à Giza (l'Osireion de Rô-Sétaou), Abousir (le cimetière de Sokar récemment découvert), Oxyrhynchos (l'Osireion de Per-khefa) et Karnak (la « Grande place » au nord-est du temple d'Amon-Rê). Ces sites viennent s'ajouter à ceux connus par des fouilles du début du XXe siècle (Tehné[6], Wadi Qubannet el-Qirud[7], el-Sheikh Fadl[8]) ou dont l'existence est simplement supposée à partir d'indices externes (un site aux alentours de Touna el-Gebel[9], l'autre près de Meïdoum[10]).

Mais, à la différence de ces derniers, pour lesquels seule l'analyse stylistique, épigraphique ou archéométrique des artefacts découverts offre une possibilité de datation, les premiers sites cités fournissent, quoique de manière partielle, des

---

3 Diodore de Sicile, Livre I, § XXI.
4 Assmann 2000.
5 Raven 1982 ; Centrone 2009.
6 Lefebvre 1903 ; Raven 1982, p. 21–24 ; Love 2023, p. 313–378.
7 Lilyquist 2003, p. 12–15 ; Centrone 2009, p. 81–91.
8 Centrone 2009, p. 42–46.
9 Centrone 2009, p. 46–57.
10 Centrone 2009, p. 36–41.

indices chronologiques qui permettent d'ancrer leur développement dans l'histoire de l'Égypte lagide et, dans certains cas, des périodes précédentes.

## Les catacombes osiriennes de Giza

Les catacombes osiriennes de Rô-Sétaou, d'abord fouillées illégalement en marge du chantier avorté du Ring road traversant la partie sud du plateau des Pyramides de Giza, ont longtemps été un fantôme archéologique. Néanmoins, un nombre suffisant de données peuvent être maintenant réunies pour en fixer certaines caractéristiques et plusieurs repères chronologiques.

De ce sanctuaire, c'est le mobilier rituel qui est le mieux connu, un grand nombre d'objets ayant afflué sur le marché de l'art durant les années 1990. Trois catégories d'artefacts sont représentées. La première consiste en des figurines osiriennes de 36 cm de long, en terre cuite, avec une perruque tripartite, une barbe divine et le phallus en érection ; elles étaient emmaillotées de lin et ornées d'amulettes. Maarten J. Raven en a le premier analysé un exemplaire conservé à Leyde[11]. Martina Minas a ensuite étudié un large ensemble de figurines du même type et de sarcophages en bois les contenant, apparus auparavant dans le commerce et dans certaines collections à travers le monde ; elle a pu mettre en évidence, au sein des inscriptions, l'association de la titulature de souverains lagides, de leurs ancêtres dynastiques et de Sokar-Osiris[12].

La deuxième catégorie d'objets représentée consiste en des vases, parfois dotés d'un couvercle, contenant des huiles et onguents divers, majoritairement en faïence, mais parfois en albâtre et inscrit au nom d'un pharaon dont le nom est suivi par « aimé d'Osiris / Sokar-Osiris » complété parfois par l'épithète « maître de Rô-Setaou ». L'inventaire de ces vases a été réalisé indépendamment par Klaus Koschel[13] et Eric Welvaert[14], ce dernier avançant un total de 258 vases et fragments, datables du Nouvel Empire jusqu'au début de l'époque ptolémaïque.

Enfin, en troisième lieu, un certain nombre de chaouabtis « extra-sépulcraux » semblent bien provenir de la même origine ; ils auraient été déposés au Nouvel Empire comme objets votifs auprès du sas vers la *douat* que constituait le sanctuaire de Rô-Setaou[15].

---

11 Raven 1998.
12 Minas 2006.
13 Koschel 2001 et 2009.
14 Welvaert 2008.
15 Pasquali 2008 ; Collombert 2021, p. 290–292. Des lots d'ouchebtis et des vases canopes sont aussi signalés en lien avec le site du cimetière osirien de Rô-Sétaou (Lehner, Hawass 2017, p. 496, fig. 20.4 et 20.5).

Un contexte archéologique a pu être heureusement déterminé pour ces trouvailles, lorsque le Service des Antiquités de l'Égypte fouilla partiellement la zone sud de Giza concernée par les fouilles clandestines, à environ 2,5 km des grandes pyramides[16]. Y furent découverts des sarcophages contenant des figurines osiriennes dans de petites tombes creusées dans le roc. L'information avait été succinctement évoquée par la presse égyptienne[17], puis par Zahi Hawass[18], s'appuyant sur les fouilles menées par les inspecteurs Ehab Amer et Mohamed Youssef. Les archéologues avaient notamment recueilli plusieurs sarcophages en bois contenant des figurines en terre cuite à l'apparence semblable à celle de Leyde, des vases en forme de calice, des godets plus plats, ainsi que des ensembles de dix petits vases montés sur une base rectangulaire[19]. D'après les indications des archéologues sur les documents préliminaires, certains vases portaient le nom « Sokar-Osiris » et une partie contenait des produits non identifiés. Ce mobilier provenait d'un secteur rocheux dans lequel avaient été creusées des niches.

Un premier compte rendu de cette trouvaille figure dans la thèse inédite d'Amal Samuel Isaac[20]. Le contexte de découverte des sarcophages d'époque ptolémaïque y est explicite, en l'occurrence des niches de 80 à 100 cm de profondeur. À l'extrémité ouest de ces niches se trouvait une petite chambre funéraire contenant le sarcophage en bois d'une cinquantaine de centimètres. C'est devant l'orifice de cette petite niche intérieure qu'étaient accumulés les vases rituels[21]. Il est par ailleurs signalé que les figurines sont faites d'argile mélangée à des graines.

On dispose depuis récemment d'une première publication « officielle » sur le site des catacombes de Giza dans un article paru en 2022[22], montrant l'aspect de la falaise semi-circulaire dans laquelle sont aménagées les niches et comportant la publication des inscriptions des sarcophages ptolémaïques. Malgré les avancées réalisées dans la publication des caractéristiques principales du site et des artefacts qu'il a livrés, il reste de très nombreuses zones d'ombre qui ne pourront commencer à se dissiper, si cela est encore possible, uniquement après une fouille complète et systématique du site. Dans l'état actuel de nos connaissances, les éléments datés

---

16 Je remercie les professeurs Hassan Ibrahim Amer et Abdelrahman Ali Abdelrahman pour les informations inédites qu'ils m'ont communiquées à différents stades de mon enquête.
17 Adly 1994, p. 87.
18 Hawass 2007, p. 392 et 396.
19 Sur ce type d'objets (signalé par Koschel 2001, p. 237–238, Taf. 13, et Welvaert 2008, p. 166–167), voir maintenant Grallert 2017.
20 Samuel Isaac 2010.
21 Samuel Isaac 2010, fig. 70 (environ 15 vases sont visibles).
22 Abdelrahman, Eissa 2022.

qui proviennent de manière assurée ou très probable du cimetière osirien de Giza se répartissent comme suit :

| Datation | | Vases inscrits datés[23] | Sarcophages inscrits datés[24] |
|---|---|---|---|
| XVIIIe dynastie | Amenhotep III | 6 vases | |
| | Aÿ | 2 vases | |
| | Horemheb | 7 vases | |
| XIXe dynastie | Ramsès Ier | 1 vase | |
| | Séthy Ier | 31 vases | |
| | Ramsès II | 62 vases | |
| | Mérenptah | 8 vases | |
| | Amenmesse | 2 vases[25] | |
| | Séthy II | 5 vases | |
| | Siptah | 3 vases | |
| | Taousert | 9 vases | |
| XXe dynastie | Sethnakht | 3 vases | |
| | Ramsès III | 21 vases | |
| | Ramsès IV | 7 vases | |
| | Ramsès VI | 5 vases | |
| | Ramsès VII | 2 vases | |
| TPI | — | | |
| XXVIe-XXIX[e] dyn. | — | | |
| XXXe dyn. | Néctanébo Ier | 1 vase[26] | |
| | Nectanébo II | 15 vases | |
| Époque ptolémaïque | Ptolémée Ier Ptolémée II | Plusieurs vases | Freiburg, Galerie Puhze (Ptol. I-III ?) |
| | Ptolémée III | | Freiburg, Galerie Puhze (Ptol. I-III ?) ; Londres, Charles Ede Limited |
| | Ptolémée IV | | El-Ahram Storerooms n°502 |
| | Ptolémée VI | | Vienne, KHM ÄS 10090[27] ; El-Ahram Storerooms n°503 |
| | Ptolémée VIII | | Barcelone, Museu Egipci, Inv. Nr. E 476. |

---

23 D'après Welvaert 2008 et Koschel 2001 et 2009.
24 D'après Minas 2006; Samuel Isaac 2010 et Abdelrahman, Eissa 2022.
25 Signalé par Koschel 2009, n°88–89, p. 138–139.
26 Signalé par Koschel 2009, p. 143, n°113.
27 *KHM Wien Objektdatenbank*, Ägyptische Sammlung, INV 10090.

Les vases datés sont attribuables à deux périodes : entre Amenhotep III et Ramsès VII d'une part, et entre Nectanébo Ier et Ptolémée II, d'autre part. Ils ne disparaissent pas du mobilier des tombes après le début de l'époque ptolémaïque mais les exemplaires associés ne comportent plus le cartouche du roi régnant.

Pour ce qui est des sarcophages, ils se répartissent chronologiquement entre le début de l'époque ptolémaïque, au minimum Ptolémée III‹, et le règne de Ptolémée VIII. Les exemplaires découverts lors des fouilles officielles entrent aussi dans cette délimitation chronologique.

Même s'il est donc difficile de tirer des conclusions définitives à partir de données si incomplètes, il apparaît clairement que les Ptolémées ont poursuivi dès le début de l'époque ptolémaïque les rites osiriens qui étaient pratiqués à Rô-Sétaou. À partir du IIIe siècle, culte dynastique et culte osirien y sont étroitement associés. Ces découvertes offrent un aperçu particulièrement intéressant sur la réalité archéologique du cimetière osirien de Rô-Sétaou à Memphis, endroit d'autant plus stratégique que son histoire remonte avant le Ier millénaire av. J.-C. et a donc pu jouer un rôle dans la diffusion du modèle du tombeau d'Osiris à travers le territoire égyptien[28].

## 2 Le cimetière de Sokar à Abousir

En 2018, une équipe égyptienne dirigée par Ayman Ashmawy Ali a fouillé un cimetière situé à 500 m au sud de la tombe d'Ioufâa à Abousir. D'après le rapport archéologique très documenté qui en a été publié[29], 26 tombes ont été découvertes, chacune consistant en un puits de 1 m sur 1,5 m, auquel on accède par un petit escalier à une profondeur d'environ 2 m et contenant une, deux ou trois niches, fermées par une dalle de calcaire ou un muret de briques. Parfois, les tombes se réduisent à de petits puits creusés dans la roche. D'après le décompte fourni, le total des niches est de 36. Chaque niche contient un sarcophage avec, à l'intérieur, une figurine « sokarienne ». Le fouilleur a noté que, bien que les tombes ne soient pas disposées à des distances régulières, elles semblaient être organisées en rangées. En outre, le matériel trouvé dans les tombes est très similaire à celui trouvé à Giza ou à Oxyrhynchos, par exemple les vases à onguent en faïence (montés par 10 sur un socle), les amulettes et les boules associées au rituel des 4 boules.

---

**28** Par comparaison, les premières inhumations (fin du Nouvel Empire, début TPI) dans le cimetière osirien de Karnak ne montrent pas de decorum royal particulier.
**29** Ashmawy Ali 2022.

La présence d'une indication de l'année sur l'un des sarcophages est particulièrement précieuse. Le texte mentionne l'an 11 de Ptolémée IV aimé de 'Sokar dans Tjenenet', une forme du dieu surtout attestée par les litanies de Sokar, intégrées aux cérémonies osiriennes, dans lesquelles elle figure en tant qu'une des nombreuses formes locales de cette divinité[30].

L'un des questionnements essentiels sur cette découverte récente concerne la nature même des figurines enterrées dans ce cimetière. Les fouilleurs affirment qu'il s'agit de momies de faucons, animaux qu'ils associent avec la mention de Sokar. Néanmoins, aucune radiographie n'a été effectuée et la présence d'ossements de ces animaux n'est pas explicitement mentionnée, ce qui laisse le lecteur dans le doute. La figurine publiée n'a pas l'apparence habituelle des momies de faucons : elle est dotée d'une couronne blanche, inhabituelle dans ce contexte. Par ailleurs, les sépultures montrent d'étonnantes similarités avec celles des cimetières de figurines osiriennes : les tombes creusées dans la roche rappellent celles trouvées à Tehné[31], l'aménagement intérieur celles de Giza ; s'apparentent également aux sépultures osiriennes les vases associés ainsi que les boules d'argile inscrites au nom des déesses présidant au rituel des 4 boules, qui comme le note le fouilleur, ne se rencontrent pas dans le cas de sépultures animales. Le lien entre Sokar et les figurines osiriennes semble d'ailleurs plus évident qu'avec les momies de faucon : certaines figurines de Khoiak étaient inhumées dans des sarcophages à tête du faucon de Sokar[32], notamment à Tehné et, dans les textes des chapelles osiriennes de Dendera, la fabrication d'une figurine de Sokar est détaillée.

Notre hypothèse serait donc qu'il s'agit ici non de momies animales mais de figurines de Khoiak. À l'évidence, seule une analyse plus détaillée des objets eux-mêmes pourra la conforter ; si, néanmoins, la présence d'os de rapaces était confirmée, nous serions en présence de sépultures d'un type mixte très particulier. La présence d'une date sur l'un des sarcophages rappelle en tout cas celles présentes au-dessus des niches ou sur les plaques d'obturation à Oxyrhynchos et confirmerait un rythme annuel pour les enterrements.

---

30 *LGG* VI, 675b.
31 Lefebvre 1903, p. 299 et pl. I (A).
32 Comme le note Raven 1982, p. 7, cela a induit déjà anciennement l'interprétation fautive de ces objets comme des momies de faucon.

## 3 Les catacombes osiriennes d'Oxyrhynchos

La découverte des catacombes osiriennes d'Oxyrhynchos par une équipe hispano-égyptienne en 2001 a considérablement affermi nos connaissances sur le fonctionnement de ce type de cimetière osirien, d'autant que la publication détaillée des découvertes est maintenant disponible[33]. Dans une des galeries souterraines composant la structure, les niches accueillant les figurines osiriennes sont surmontées chacune d'une inscription en hiératique (avec quelques signes en démotique) précisant le souverain lagide et l'année de règne correspondant au moment de l'enterrement rituel[34]. Des plaques d'obturation des niches provenant d'une autre galerie fournissent des dates plus détaillées, indiquant le jour de l'enterrement, qui correspond au 30ᵉ jour du mois de Khoiak, en accord avec les indications fournies par les textes des chapelles osiriennes de Dendera. Des séquences d'utilisation peuvent être déterminées, montrant que les niches étaient remplies d'une année sur l'autre, en alternant chaque côté du couloir et en progressant de l'ouest vers l'est.

Les datations fournies permettent de situer les enterrements entre le règne de Ptolémée VI et celui de Ptolémée XII, du milieu du IIᵉ s. au milieu du Iᵉʳ s. av. J.-C. L'existence de l'Osireion est néanmoins très probablement antérieure à cette période. Le nom du sanctuaire, *Per-khefa*, est attesté dès l'époque saïte dans des titulatures sacerdotales[35], et est mis à l'honneur dans un édifice datant du début de l'époque ptolémaïque, dont ne sont connus que quelques blocs portant les noms d'Alexandre IV Aegos, Ptolémée Iᵉʳ et Ptolémée II[36].

La nature partielle des données disponibles ne permet pas de cerner la totalité des évolutions subies par ces catacombes osiriennes, mais nous disposons ici néanmoins d'indices supplémentaires fournis par les séquences de remplissages des niches. Il est en effet possible de repérer des interruptions intervenant dans l'utilisation des loculi accueillant les figurines de Khoiak. Certaines ne reçoivent pas à ce jour d'explication évidente, comme l'absence d'inscription correspondant à l'an 34 sous le règne de Ptolémée VI (147 av. J.-C.). D'autres sont plus explicables. Ainsi, entre l'an 132 et l'an 113, depuis l'an 38 ou 39 de Ptolémée VIII jusqu'au règne conjoint de Cléopâtre III et Ptolémée IX Sôter II, soit une durée de près de 20 ans, la galerie cesse d'être utilisée. Le début de cet intervalle coïncide avec la crise qui éclate vers 131 avant J.-C. entre Ptolémée VIII Évergète II et Cléopâtre II, amenant la prise d'autonomie de cette dernière (entre 131 et 129), qui est suivie

---

33 Mascort (éd.) 2018.
34 Coulon, dans Mascort (éd.) 2018, I, p. 171–196.
35 Amer, Erroux-Morfin, Padró 2014, p. 60–61.
36 Töpfer 2015, p. 121–123 (avec réf.).

d'une période de troubles dans la *chôra*[37]. L'interruption du culte osirien est certainement l'une des conséquences de cette crise.

## 4 Les catacombes osiriennes de Karnak

Le dernier cimetière osirien considéré ici est celui de Karnak. Dans le secteur nord-est du temple d'Amon-Rê, des catacombes construites en brique cuite ont été aménagées sous Ptolémée IV[38]. Il s'agissait alors de l'extension d'un cimetière qui avait déjà connu au moins deux phases : un cimetière primitif, sous forme de niches indépendantes dont les plus anciennes sont antérieures au milieu de la XXIe dynastie, puis, à l'époque saïte, un bâtiment vouté dont certaines briques estampillées portent le cartouche de Néchao II[39]. Il convient aussi de prendre en compte les stèles royales ou laissées par des membres de l'élite[40] ainsi que les monuments appartenant au clergé osirien[41] qui confirment l'existence d'une activité continue dans la nécropole entre ces phases de développement attestées archéologiquement.

La reconstruction de l'histoire des catacombes osiriennes ptolémaïques de Karnak ne peut s'appuyer que sur des vestiges très partiels du bâtiment. Seule une partie d'un des quatre couloirs constituant cet édifice est partiellement conservée en élévation et son décor préservé pour un tiers environ. Ces vestiges se sont avérés être suffisants pour reconstituer le plan du bâtiment : trois couloirs parallèles surmontés d'une voûte et dont les parois latérales sont dotées de quatre rangées de niches superposées ; ces trois couloirs sont desservis par un couloir transversal. Le nombre total de niches aménagées peut être évalué à 720, ce qui correspond à une symbolique calendérique[42].

Au sein des vestiges, aucune niche n'a été retrouvée contenant une figurine osirienne. La présence des plaques d'obturation stockées à l'extrémité du couloir laisse penser que la galerie n'avait pas été entièrement utilisée. Aucune inscription n'a pu être retrouvée qui serait en lien avec la chronologie d'utilisation des niches. Contrairement à ce qui s'est produit à Oxyrhynchos, il n'est donc pas possible d'exploiter les niches pour estimer la durée d'utilisation du bâtiment.

---

37 Coulon, dans Mascort (éd.) 2018, I, p. 182 ; Lanciers 2020, p. 38–39.
38 Coulon, Leclère, Marchand 1995.
39 Leclère 2010 (avec réf.).
40 *E.g.* Coulon 2012.
41 *E.g.* Coulon 2001.
42 Coulon 2015, p. 311–313.

Les décors qui se sont effondrés en même temps que les vestiges de l'édifice portent uniformément le cartouche de Ptolémée IV et de la reine Arsinoé III. Un premier état du décor remployé dans le radier de fondation des couloirs laisse apparaître des cartouches qui sont eux aussi ceux de Ptolémée IV. Dans ces conditions, l'hypothèse la plus plausible est qu'un nouveau décor a été substitué au premier peu après sa réalisation, voire avant son achèvement. Au vu des cartouches présents, la construction des catacombes a dû intervenir après la bataille de Raphia et le mariage de Ptolémée IV et d'Arsinoé III en 217 av. J.-C. et bien sûr avant le début de la sécession de la Thébaïde en 205 av. J.-C., qui coïncide avec le décès du pharaon lagide.

Il n'est pas exclu que des cartouches d'autres pharaons aient été présents dans les couloirs du centre et du nord du bâtiment, ainsi que dans le couloir transversal, mais aucun vestige n'en a été retrouvé.

Le relief qui a été ajouté à l'époque tardive à l'angle nord-est du mur d'enceinte qui entoure la partie sacrée de Karnak, Ipet-sout, à l'arrière de l'Akhmenou, porte une inscription ajoutée sous Ptolémée V qui dit : « Restauration du monument effectuée par (Ptolémée V) et (Cléopâtre I) les dieux épiphanes, pour son père Osiris ».[43] Cette restauration ne peut être identifiée archéologiquement. L'hypothèse que le second état de décoration au nom de Ptolémée IV puisse avoir été l'œuvre de son successeur paraît douteuse.

Dans le voisinage immédiat des catacombes osiriennes, le temple d'Osiris de Coptos, que j'identifie au « sanctuaire de Chentayt », lieu de préparation et de conservation provisoire de la figurine fabriquée au mois de Khoiak, a été entièrement reconstruit sous Ptolémée XII et sa décoration a été achevée sous Tibère. Du fait de l'absence d'autres structures pour l'enterrement des figurines qui serait contemporaine de ces constructions, il apparaît très vraisemblable que les catacombes osiriennes construites sous Ptolémée IV étaient toujours utilisées pour accueillir les figurines qui avaient passé un an dans le « sanctuaire de Chentayt ».[44]

## 5 Approche transversale

Si l'on envisage maintenant de manière globale les témoignages archéologiques dont nous disposons à ce jour sur les tombeaux d'Osiris à l'époque ptolémaïque, nous pouvons tirer quelques constats généraux. En premier lieu, la multiplication récente des découvertes de cimetières osiriens conforte ce que nous apprenons

---

[43] Coulon, Leclère, Marchand 1995, p. 222–223 et pl. XII.
[44] Coulon 2003 ; Coulon 2016, p. 21–24.

les textes, aussi bien égyptiens que grecs, sur la présence systématique d'un tombeau d'Osiris dans les différentes régions d'Égypte. Nul doute que d'autres verront le jour dans un avenir proche. Il est notable que, dans l'état dans lequel ils nous parviennent, la phase ptolémaïque de leur développement soit particulièrement saillante, les vestiges monuments les plus importants qui soient conservés appartenant à cette période. Tout comme la dynastie lagide a, par le biais des décrets, imposé le culte dynastique et la manière dont celui-ci pouvait s'intégrer dans les décors des temples égyptiens[45], en bonne part à travers l'association au culte osirien[46], cette politique s'est étendue aux nécropoles divines. Néanmoins, si les Ptolémées ont donné une nouvelle envergure aux cimetières, ceux-ci connaissent déjà à cette époque une longue histoire pour certains, particulièrement à Giza, où dès le Nouvel Empire une forte activité cultuelle est attestée, à laquelle chaque pharaon est lié. C'est donc avant tout une forte continuité avec les cultes pharaoniques que les souverains lagides ont recherchée, l'accent étant mis sur l'Osiris local, sans traces d'une quelconque hellénisation. La diversité des traditions spécifiques à chaque métropole est préservée, ce qui explique la variété des « recettes » employées pour la confection des figurines. Cela n'empêche pas néanmoins la mise en œuvre d'un arsenal rituel commun (rite des 4 boules par exemple).

Si l'on cherche à évaluer maintenant l'existence de phases de développement des cimetières osiriens au sein de la période de domination lagide, il faut à l'évidence rappeler encore une fois le caractère très incomplet des données que nous possédons. Néanmoins, quelques traits saillants se font jour : les règnes de Ptolémée III[47] et Ptolémée IV, dans la seconde moitié du III$^e$ siècle av. J.-C., d'une part, et les règnes de Ptolémée VI jusqu'à Ptolémée XII, avec quelques interruptions, sont bien représentés. Cela correspond aussi aux périodes de mise en place et d'affirmation dans la *chôra* du culte royal et dynastique. Il ne peut être tout à fait dû au hasard que le règne de Ptolémée IV soit particulièrement bien attesté dans une bonne partie des sources. Il est possible que ce soit sous ce règne qu'ait été systématisée la politique osirienne des Lagides à l'échelle du territoire égyptien[48]. C'est aussi dans le même laps de temps qu'est située la construction du mammisi

---

[45] Preys 2022.
[46] Preys 2015.
[47] Rappelons aussi ici que l'Osireion de Canope est fondé sous ce règne. Cf. Bricault 2006, p. 32–33. Sur le développement du culte osirien dans cette région sous les Ptolémées, voir Yoyotte 2010.
[48] Sur la politique constructive de Ptolémée IV, voir dernièrement Minas-Nerpel, Preys 2023, p. 75–112.

de Coptos vénérant la figure du dieu enfant à travers le couple Harsiesis-Harpocrate, particulièrement mis à l'honneur également par Ptolémée IV[49].

L'une des caractéristiques marquantes de la documentation épigraphique des catacombes osiriennes consiste dans la manière dont les pharaons lagides ont établi un lien extrêmement étroit entre leur royauté et celle d'Osiris. Dans les inscriptions hiératiques surmontant les niches des catacombes d'Oxyrhynchos, une équivalence est établie entre l'année de règne du pharaon et celle du règne d'Osiris[50]. La date de l'an 11 de Ptolémée IV inscrite sur un des sarcophages d'Abousir participe de la même logique. Dans les inscriptions des sarcophages de Giza, la mention développée de la lignée des pharaons ancêtres constitue une proclamation manifeste de l'association qui est voulue entre la dynastie lagide et Sokar-Osiris.

Dans cette perspective, il convient de rappeler que le développement des tombeaux d'Osiris se fait en parallèle et selon une logique similaire de celui des nécropoles animales[51]. L'analogie architecturale entre les deux types de structures est évidente[52] et leur fonctionnement respectif présente des similitudes, notamment en ce qui concerne la solennité des cérémonies d'inhumation[53]. Comme l'a souligné Dieter Kessler, l'intérêt porté par les Ptolémées au développement des nécropoles animales était surtout motivé par l'association qu'il pouvait y établir avec le culte royal[54], et cet aspect est, on l'a vu, particulièrement saillant aussi pour les catacombes osiriennes.

---

49 Pantalacci 2014, p. 417–418 ; voir aussi Preys 2015, p. 190.
50 Coulon 2008, p. 24.
51 Coulon 2008, p. 22–23.
52 Dans certains cas, en l'absence de données suffisantes sur les artefacts inhumés, les fouilleurs ne peuvent trancher entre catacombes animales et catacombes osiriennes. Voir par exemple le cas des catacombes de Gournet Murai (Abou Zaid 2018).
53 Ainsi, même pour les animaux sacrés dont les momies étaient proposées aux pèlerins pendant toute l'année, les enterrements dans les galeries étaient des événements annuels. Voir Nicholson 2021, p. 248.
54 Kessler 1989, p. 243 : « Das Interesse der Ptolemäer an den Tierfriedhöfen war nicht der ägyptische Kult und die Befriedung der Einheimischen, sondern das Funktionieren des Herrscherkultes am Totentempel, der durch die offizielle Einführung des Gottes Serapis in griechischer Kultbildform und eine griechischen Vorstellungen angepaßte Form der Herrscherapotheose für die makedonische Oberschicht, die die ägyptischen Kultformen zwangsläufig ertragen müßte, akzeptabel gemacht wurde. »

## 6 Comment se reflètent les crises politiques dans les cimetières osiriens ?

À travers les différents cas énumérés, reflets d'une politique consciente des Ptolémées de développer les tombeaux osiriens tout à travers l'Égypte et d'y associer le culte dynastique, comment pouvons-nous tenter d'évaluer l'impact des crises politiques qui affectent la Thébaïde ? L'indice le plus évident est celui fourni par les interruptions du culte osirien causées par la mise à distance du pouvoir lagide. De telles interruptions sont illustrées par les ruptures dans les séquences de remplissage des catacombes d'Oxyrhynchos, consécutives notamment à l'instabilité causée par la prise d'autonomie de Cléopâtre II[55]. Une autre interruption qui peut être déterminée avec un certain degré de probabilité est celle qui est intervenue dans le fonctionnement des catacombes osiriennes de Ptolémée IV. Le graffito du mur d'enceinte d'Ipet-sout au nom de Ptolémée V mentionne une restauration de la butte osirienne, qui implique qu'il y a vraisemblablement eu une cessation du culte dans la « Grande Place » osirienne. Une hypothèse très plausible est que cette interruption se soit produite sous les révoltes thébaines menées par Horounnefer/Ânkhounnefer[56] et que la remise en route du culte ait eu lieu à la fin du règne de Ptolémée V, entre 185 et 180 av. J.C. — c'est là la seule trace de ce roi à Karnak[57]. Le programme théologico-politique exprimé par le nom pris par le(s) roitelet(s), fondé sur l'épithète osirienne Ounnefer, révèle à lui seul le positionnement idéologique du ou des chefs de la rébellion qui assument pleinement l'identification à Osiris[58], concurrençant donc directement celle qui était, on l'a vu, mise en exergue par les Lagides.

L'état de destruction quasi totale dans lequel ont été retrouvés les vestiges des catacombes de Karnak ne permet pas de définir si son utilisation en a été continue ou non. Aucune atteinte aux cartouches de Ptolémée IV n'est, en tous les cas, visible. Comme le constate aussi René Preys[59], « en étudiant les temples, on vient à la conclusion que Horounnefer et Ânkhounnefer n'étaient pas intéressés dans la construction ou décoration des temples, mais qu'ils n'avaient pas non plus de raison de s'attaquer aux temples ». Il est notable par ailleurs que dans le cas du culte du taureau Bouchis, à Ermant, dans lequel un fort investissement la-

---

55 Voir *supra*.
56 Voir dernièrement sur cette période et l'identité du/des leaders de la révolte : Veïsse 2022.
57 Lanciers 1986, p. 90–92.
58 Veïsse 2013, p. 508.
59 Voir sa contribution « Révoltes, meurtres et intrigues : L'histoire des Ptolémées d'après les parois des temples égyptiens », dans ce volume, § 4a.

gide est attesté, aucune trace de la prise de pouvoir des roitelets thébains ne soit décelable et que la succession des Bouchis semble se faire sans discontinuité aucune[60].

Un seul cas de « traitement violent » d'un monument pourrait être cité, celui infligé à la statue de Takhybiat, découverte dans la Cachette de Karnak (Caire JE 37452)[61]. L'inscription qu'elle porte assure qu'elle était initialement installée dans le temple d'Osiris de Coptos à Karnak, fonctionnant en lien étroit avec le cimetière osirien. Les recoupements prosopographiques permettent de situer l'activité de cette prêtresse sous Ptolémée III ou Ptolémée IV. Takhybiat étant la fille d'un certain Ânkhpakhered, dont on sait par ailleurs qu'il portait le titre de « prophète des dieux [Évergètes] », qui a vécu les répercussions du Décret de Canope, j'avais supposé que Takhybiat ait pu faire partie de ces « filles de prêtres » chargées de rendre le culte et de chanter des hymnes pour la princesse Bérénice au mois de Khoiak[62]. Or la statue de la prêtresse montre des signes de destruction qui semblent volontaires, sa tête ayant été brisée d'une manière qui peut difficilement être accidentelle. Il est dès lors légitime de se demander si l'implication de la prêtresse dans les cultes dynastiques, en lien direct avec un édifice osirien à proximité des catacombes de Ptolémée IV, pourrait avoir conduit les révoltés thébains à la viser spécifiquement jusqu'à briser son effigie. De manière plus large, nous sommes amenés à nous demander si les véritables transformations qui affectent les cultes thébains durant la période de la révolte ne concerneraient pas surtout les personnes — certains acteurs au service des Lagides étant ciblés[63] — plutôt que les structures cultuelles elles-mêmes.

# 7 Conclusion

La masse croissante des données disponibles sur les nécropoles osiriennes en Égypte confirme les liens étroits entre un programme généralisé de développement de ces structures cultuelles et la politique des Lagides visant à intégrer le culte royal et dynastique au culte osirien. Tout en s'inscrivant dans une tradition religieuse souvent ancienne et en respectant la personnalité de l'Osiris de chaque localité, le pouvoir ptolémaïque imbrique très étroitement, surtout à partir du IIIe

---

60 Goldbrunner 2004, p. 290–291.
61 B-CK 931.
62 Coulon 2008, p. 31–32.
63 Voir la contribution de R. Birk dans ce volume.

s. av. J.-C., la personnalité du pharaon régnant et la lignée de ses ancêtres avec la figure du dieu des morts célébrée comme modèle de royauté.

Naturellement, en période de crise politique, ce lien étroit proclamé entre la figure d'Osiris et la dynastie des Ptolémées a conduit une défiance envers les lieux de culte « officiels » consacrés au dieu. Tout au moins peut-on parfois discerner le changement induit par cette période dans l'interruption des cultes associant dieux thébains et souverains lagides, comme certains indices, malheureusement encore fort ténus, le laissent penser. Ce à quoi ressemblaient les cultes dans la Thébaïde sous la férule de roitelets révoltés n'est pas aisé à caractériser. En dehors de l'affirmation d'un lien étroit avec Osiris par leur nom de règne, nous n'avons pas à ce jour une quelconque idée de la manière dont ce dieu était célébré à cette période. La richesse de l'apport des fouilles archéologiques de ces dernières décennies laisse espérer que le tableau que nous avons pu dresser soit largement complété au gré des découvertes futures.

# Bibliographie

Abdelrahman, Eissa 2022
 Abdelrahman, A. A., Eissa, M., « Remains of Two Ptolemaic Coffins for Osiris Mummies-corn (sic) from the Giza Plateau », *Shedet* 9, 2022, p. 10–17.

Abou Zaid 2018
 Abou Zaid, O., « A New Discovery of Catacomb in Qurnet Murai at Thebes », *BIFAO* 117, 2018, p. 9–27.

Adly 1994
 Adly, E., Revue de presse, *Bulletin d'Information Archéologique* 9–10, janvier-décembre 1994.

Amer, Erroux-Morfin, Padró 2014
 Amer, H. I., Erroux-Morfin, M., Padró, J., avec la collaboration de J.-C. Goyon, « 4. Inscriptions murales de la chapelle funéraire de Heret » in J. Padró *et al.* (éd.), *La Tombe N°1 à la Nécropole Haute, Oxyrhynchos IV*, Nova Studia Aegyptiaca 8, Barcelone, 2014, p. 57–68.

Ashmawy Ali 2022
 Ashmawy Ali, A., « The Cemetery of Sokar: A Report on the Excavations of the SCA at Abusir (Season 2018) » in F. Coppens, J. Janák, K. Smoláriková (éd.), *Knowledge and Memory: Festschrift in Honour of Ladislav Bareš*, Prague, 2022, p. 53–64.

Assmann 2000
 Assmann, J., « Re-membering Osiris: From the Death Cult to Cultural Memory », in G. Brandstetter, H. Völckers (éd.), *Membra disiecta: Einbalsamierung und Anatomie in Ägypten und Europa – Teil 1, ReMembering the Body: Körper-Bilder in Bewegung*, Ostfildern-Ruit, 2000, p. 44–78.

Bricault 2006
 Bricault, L., *Isis, Dame des flots*, AegLeod 7, Liège, 2006.

Caneva, Bricault 2019
 Caneva, S. G., Bricault, L., « Sarapis, Isis et la continuité dynastique lagide. À propos de deux dédicaces ptolémaïques d'Halicarnasse et de Kaunos », *Chiron* 49, 2019, p. 1–22.

Centrone 2009
- Centrone, M. C., *Egyptian Corn-Mummies: A Class of Religious Artefacts Catalogued and Systematically Analysed*, Saarbrücken, 2009.

Collombert 2021
- Collombert, P., « La formule de Khâemouaset » in P. Collombert, L. Coulon, I. Guermeur, C. Thiers (éd.), *Questionner le sphinx. Mélanges offerts à Chr. Zivie-Coche*, BdE 178, Le Caire, 2021, p. 231–292.

Coulon 2001
- Coulon, L., « Un serviteur du sanctuaire de Chentayt à Karnak. La statue Caire JE 37134 », *BIFAO* 101, 2001, p. 137–152.

Coulon 2003
- Coulon, L., « Le sanctuaire de Chentayt à Karnak » in Z. Hawass (éd.), *Egyptology at the Dawn of the 21st Century: Proceedings of the Eighth International Congress of Egyptologists, Cairo, 2000*, Le Caire, vol. I., 2003, p. 138–146.

Coulon 2008
- Coulon, L., « La nécropole osirienne de Karnak sous les Ptolémées » in A. Delattre, P. Heilporn (éd.), *« Et maintenant ce ne sont plus que des villages . . . »: Thèbes et sa région aux époques hellénistique, romaine et byzantine. Actes du colloque tenu à Bruxelles les 2 et 3 décembre 2005*, PapBrux 34, Bruxelles, 2008, p. 17–31 et pl. IV-V.

Coulon 2010
- Coulon, L., « Le culte osirien au $I^{er}$ millénaire av. J.-C. Une mise en perspective(s) » in L. Coulon (éd.), *Le culte d'Osiris au $I^{er}$ millénaire av. J.-C. Découvertes et travaux récents*, BdE 153, Le Caire, 2010, p. 1–19.

Coulon 2012
- Coulon, L., « Une stèle déposée par un grand chef libyen près de la butte osirienne de Karnak » in Chr. Zivie-Coche, I. Guermeur (éd.), *« Parcourir l'éternité ». Hommages à Jean Yoyotte*, I, BEHE-SR 156, Turnhout, 2012, p. 375–386.

Coulon 2015
- Coulon, L., « Du périssable au cyclique. Les effigies annuelles d'Osiris » in S. Estienne, V. Huet, Fr. Lissarague, Fr. Prost (éd.), *Figures de dieux. Construire le divin en images*, coll. Histoire, série Histoire ancienne, Rennes, 2015, p. 295–318, pl. XXIII–XXIV.

Coulon 2016
- Coulon, L., « Les chapelles osiriennes de Karnak. Aperçu des travaux récents », *BSFE* 195-196, juin-octobre 2016, p. 16–35.

Coulon, Leclère, Marchand 1995
- Coulon, L., Leclère, F., Marchand, S., « "Catacombes" osiriennes de Ptolémée IV à Karnak. Rapport préliminaire de la campagne de fouilles 1993 », *CahKarn* 10, 1995, p. 205–256.

Goldbrunner 2004
- Goldbrunner, L., *Buchis: Eine Untersuchung zur Theologie des heiligen Stieres in Theben zur griechisch-römischen Zeit*, MRE 11, Turnhout, 2004.

Grallert 2017
- Grallert, S., « Szépművészeti Múzeum Budapest 51.2523 und 51.2534: auf der Suche nach Kontext und Funktion von Modellgefäßgruppen auf gemeinsamer Basisplatte » in K.A. Kóthay (ed.), *Burial and Mortuary Practices in Late Period and Graeco-Roman Egypt: Proceedings of the International Conference held at Museum of Fine Arts, Budapest, 17–19 July 2014*, Budapest, 2017, p. 51–60.

Hawass 2007
> Hawass, Z. A., « The Discovery of the Osiris Shaft at Giza » in Z.A. Hawass, J. Richards (éd.), *The Archaeology and Art of Ancient Egypt: Essays in Honour of David B. O' Connor*, vol. I, CASAE 36, 2007, p. 379–397.

Kessler 1989
> Kessler, D., *Die heiligen Tiere und der König – Teil I: Beiträge zu Organisation, Kult und Theologie der spätzeitlichen Tierfriedhöfe*, ÄAT 16, Wiesbaden, 1989.

KHM Wien Objektdatenbank *KHM Wien Objektdatenbank*, online database, https://www.khm.at/de/object/316252, consulté le 30 août 2024.

Koschel 2001
> Koschel, K., « Königliche Miniatursalbgefäße eines undokumentierten Fundkomplexes », *SAK* 29, 2001, p. 235–249.

Koschel 2009
> Koschel, K., « Salbgefäße ohne Ende? Königliche Miniatursalbgefäße eines undokumentierten Fundkomplexes: Teil II », *SAK* 38, 2009, p. 131–150.

Lanciers 1986
> Lanciers, E., « Die ägyptischen Tempelbauten zur Zeit des Ptolemaios V. Epiphanes (204–180 v. Chr.): Teil 1 », *MDAIK* 42, 1986, p. 81–98.

Lanciers 2020
> Lanciers, E., « The Civil War between Ptolemy VIII and Cleopatra II, (132–124): Possible Causes and Key Events » in G. Gorre, S. Wackenier (éd.), *Quand la fortune du royaume ne dépend pas de la vertu du prince. Un renforcement de la monarchie lagide de Ptolémée VI à Ptolémée X (169–88 av. J.-C.) ?*, StudHell 59, Leuven, 2020, p. 21–54.

Leclère 2010
> Leclère, F., « Le quartier de l'Osireion de Karnak. Analyse du contexte topographique » in L. Coulon (éd.), *Le culte d'Osiris au I$^{er}$ millénaire av. J.-C. Découvertes et travaux récents*, BdE 153, Le Caire, 2010, p. 239–268.

Lefebvre 1903
> Lefebvre, G., « Sarcophages égyptiens trouvés dans une nécropole gréco-romaine à Tehneh », *ASAE* 4, 1903, p. 227–231.

Lehner, Hawass 2017
> Lehner, M., Hawass, Z., *Giza and the Pyramids*, Londres, 2017.

Lilyquist 2003
> Lilyquist, C., *The Tomb of Three Foreign Wives of Tuthmosis III*, New Haven, Londres, 2003.

Love 2023
> Love, E.O.D., *Petitioning Osiris: The Old Coptic Schmidt Papyrus and Curse of Artemisia in Context among the Letters to Gods from Egypt*, ZÄS-B 11, Berlin, Boston, 2023.

Mascort (éd.) 2018
> Mascort M., (éd.), *L'Osireion d'Oxirrinc. Oxyrhynchos IV*, Nova Studia Aegyptiaca X, Barcelone, 2018.

Minas 2006
> Minas, M., « Die ptolemäischen Sokar-Osiris-Mumien: Neue Erkenntnisse zum ägyptischen Dynastiekult der Ptolemäer », *MDAIK* 62, 2006, p. 197–213.

Minas-Nerpel, Preys 2023
> Minas-Nerpel, M., Preys, R., *The Kiosk of Taharqa – Volume II: The Ptolemaic Decoration (TahKiosk nos. E1–24, F1–4)*, Travaux du CFEETK, BiGen 72, Le Caire, 2023.

Nicholson 2021
: Nicholson, P.T., *The Catacombs of Anubis at North Saqqara. An Archaeological Perspective*, BMPES 12, Louvain, 2021.

Pantalacci 2014
: Pantalacci, L., « Les sept Hathors, leurs bas et Ptolémée IV Philopator au mammisi de Coptos », *BIFAO* 114, 2014, p. 397–418.

Pasquali 2008
: Pasquali, S., « Le dépôt extra-sépulcral trouvé par Fl. Petrie à Gîza-Sud », *RdE* 59, 2008, p. 357–368.

Preys 2015
: Preys, R., « La royauté lagide et le culte d'Osiris d'après les portes monumentales de Karnak » in Chr. Thiers (éd.), *Documents de théologies thébaines tardives 3*, CENiM 13, Montpellier, 2015, p. 159–215.

Preys 2022
: Preys, R., « Le culte des Ptolémées dans les temples égyptiens. Les décrets royaux et la décoration des temples » in G. Lenzo, C. Nihan, M. Pellet (éd.), *Les cultes aux rois et aux héros à l'époque hellénistique. Continuités et changements*, ORA 44, Tübingen, 2022, p. 171–194.

Raven 1982
: Raven, M. J., « Corn-Mummies », *OMRO* 63, 1982, p. 7–38, pl. 1–4.

Raven 1998
: Raven, M. J., « A New Type of Osiris Burials » in W. Clarysse, A. Schoors, H. Willems (éd.), *Egyptian Religion: The Last Thousand Years*, I, OLA 84, Louvain, 1998, p. 227–239.

Samuel Isaac 2010
: Samuel Isaac, A., [*Traces of Osiris Myth in Religious, Funerary Beliefs, and his Worshiping Centers, in the Light of Recent Archeological Discoveries until the End of the Late Period*] in arabic, Diss. Faculté d'archéologie, Département des antiquités égyptiennes, Université du Caire, 2010.

Smith 2017
: Smith, M., *Following Osiris: Perspectives on the Osirian Afterlife from Four Millennia*, Oxford, 2017.

Töpfer 2015
: Töpfer, S., *Fragmente des sog. « Sothisrituals » von Oxyrhynchos aus Tebtynis*, The Carlsberg Papyri 12, CNIP 40, Copenhague, 2015.

Veïsse 2013
: Veïsse, A.-E., « Retour sur les « "révoltes égyptiennes" » in G. Charpentier, V. Puech (éd.), *Villes et campagnes aux rives de la Méditerranée ancienne. Hommages à Georges Tate*, Topoi. Orient-Occident. Supplément 12, 2013, p. 507–516.

Veïsse 2022
: Veïsse, A.-E., « The 'Great Theban Revolt', 206–186 BCE » in P.J. Kosmin. I.S. Moyer (éd.), *Cultures of Resistance in the Hellenistic East*, Oxford, 2022, p. 57–74.

Welvaert 2008
: Welvaert, E., « Les petits vases de Sokar-Osiris, seigneur de Ro-Setaou. Traces d'un temple inconnu sur le marché de l'art: Rapport provisoire » in M. Broze, F. Doyen, C. Cannuyer (éd.), *Interprétation, mythes, croyances et images au risque de la réalité. Roland Tefnin in memoriam*, Acta Orientalia Belgica 21, Bruxelles, 2008, p. 165–182.

Yoyotte 2010
: Yoyotte, J., « Osiris dans la région d'Alexandrie » in L. Coulon (éd.), *Le culte d'Osiris au $I^{er}$ millénaire av. J.-C. Découvertes et travaux récents*, BdE 153, Le Caire, 2010, p. 33–38.

Thomas Faucher
# How Did Coins Survive the Theban Crises in the Ptolemaic Period?

## 1 Introduction

Archaeological evidence and material culture in general have to be part of the debate when discussing political and sociological changes. It may not be as precise as texts but it can prove to be helpful. Therefore, this chapter on the numismatic evidence of this period brings up another way of looking at this specific episode of crises.

The evidence presented here is part of a larger study on the monetisation of Egypt in the Ptolemaic and the early Roman periods undertaken by the author. These data should contribute to understand the broader context and to examine whether the monetisation of the Thebaid as a region significantly differed from that of other areas of Egypt.

## 2 The Corpus

Before presenting the coins found in the Thebaid and the city of Thebes, it is worth trying to appreciate to which extent they can be considered representative of the coins that once circulated.

The corpus is rather limited if we take into account the dozens of millions of coins formerly circulating in Ptolemaic Egypt. In general, the survival rate of coins can be estimated, contrary to many other artefacts. Naturally, such figures can hardly claim to be precise, because they depend mainly on our ability to quantify the productivity of the dies which are used for striking coins. But it is unlikely that this rate may be as low as 1: 1,000, as opposed to 1: 5,000, 1: 10,000 or even 1: 20,000 (i.e. that among 20,000 coins, only one would have reached modern collections).[1] It is therefore plausible that the same rates also apply to the coins unearthed from sites, which is not much. Of course, considering this paucity, it would be highly fortunate if all coins were lost at the same rate. In the city of

---

[1] See Callataÿ 2000. Some exceptional cases exist like the coinages of cities that struck coins and for which we have extensive city excavations. See for example the case of Thasos in Greece (for which each die is represented by an elevated number of coins, meaning a very high survival rate).

ə Open Access. © 2025 the author(s), published by De Gruyter. [CC BY-NC-ND] This work is licensed under the Creative Commons Attribution-NonCommercial-NoDerivatives 4.0 International License.
https://doi.org/10.1515/9783111608051-006

Thebes, at least until the end of the 3$^{rd}$ century BCE, gold, silver, and bronze coins were circulating and used for all purposes, whether it was trade, taxes, or religion; every part of daily life that was monetised. However, for the Ptolemaic period, no gold coin has so far been found at Luxor or Karnak, and ones of silver are found very rarely, if at all. To date, only two late Ptolemaic silver hoards as well as only one tetradrachm dating to the 3$^{rd}$ century BCE are known. We are subsequently left with a vast majority of bronze coins (it would be more accurate to classify them as copper alloys, since the metal contents of these coins differ greatly among the periods).

The discovered coins separate in two find categories: hoards and stray finds. Hoards can represent a large part of the discovered coins, even in regular excavations, which are the main source of the corpus. If nine hoards are so far known from Ptolemaic Thebes (representing more than half of all discovered coins), it is sometimes difficult to establish whether or not a group of coins may be considered as a hoard, when coins were not found in a container. This was the case for a group of late Ptolemaic bronze coins recently found in the excavations of the Osirian chapels on the pathway of Ptah, and for a number of groups of late Ptolemaic bronze coins from the Egyptian excavations in front of the first pylon of Karnak. In any case, these hoards need to be taken under closer scrutiny. The main reason is that bronze coins are not usually hoarded as a reserve of value; this is usually only the case for coins of precious metal which had been deposited by their owners together with other metal objects.[2] We then have to try to understand why these coins have been buried, and more precisely, why they have gone lost and not recovered by their owners.

On the other hand, we might assume that the rest of the coins has been lost randomly, thus providing a better representation of the actual circulation. Not even this is the case. Small coins were lost in greater numbers than large and better-quality coins. In other words, high-quality alloy coins were less likely to be lost than poor-quality ones. It would of course be possible to refine these categories but it is just a cautionary measure not to consider the numismatic evidence as flawless.

The corpus is composed of published coins and ones that the author had the chance to study or see at Luxor and Karnak. Some coins are also being kept at the Egyptian Museum of Antiquities in Cairo (Tab. 1):

---

[2] See for instance the P. Ryl. Gr. 2 125, a petition to Serapion, chief of police, from Oursenouphis, who describes the content of a hoard hidden by his grandmother in the early days of the Roman Empire in Euhemeria.

**Tab. 1:** Single finds and hoards from Karnak and Luxor.

| Single finds from excavations | Hoards |
|---|---|
| Karnak (1) | EH I, 194, Nectanebo wall, 687AE |
| Achoris chapel (34) | EH I, 197, Bubastide door, 12AE |
| Osirian chapels (108) | EH I, 211, Ptolemaic baths, 316AE |
| Ptah temple (2) | EH I, 240, Achoris chapel, 64AR |
| Chabaka treasury (3) | EH I, 251, Karnak 1924/5, ?AE |
| Karnak north (1) | EH I, 183, Luxor Birabi, 1907–1911, 47AE |
| Ptolemaic and Roman baths (218) | EH I, 190, Ramesseum, Thebes, 1896, 68AE |
| Luxor, sphinx alley (1) | EH I, 193, Luxor Birabi, 1915/6 |
| Luxor, 1$^{st}$ pylon (12) | EH I, 215, Luxor, sphinx alley, 16AR |

The list of the different stray finds and hoards found at Karnak and Luxor clearly shows that the numbers are not impressive and that the coins were mostly gathered in certain areas. The hoards complement quite well the distribution of stray finds and are very useful for understanding storage and hoarding practices of coins in this period.

Hoards have been presented earlier in the first volume of *Egyptian Hoards*.[3]

**Tab. 2:** Single finds and hoards from the Thebaid (without Karnak and Luxor).

| Single finds from excavations | Hoards |
|---|---|
| Abbad (7) | EH I, 151, Kuft, 1874/5, 438+AR |
| Abydos (68) | EH I, 168, Upper Egypt, before 1905, 112AV |
| Aswan (6) | EH I, 172, Elephantine, before 1993, 679AE |
| Berenike (7) | EH I, 175, Philae, before 1980, 4AE |
| Bi'r Samut (16) | EH I, 191, Nag Hammadi, 1937, 80AE |
| Coptos (1) | EH I, 209, Keneh, 1923, 45+AV, 200AR |
| Edfu (10) | EH I, 216, Dendera, 1918, 3AR |
| Erment (20) | EH I, 248 Abydos, before 1940, 72AE |

The numbers are hardly more impressive on the regional level of the Thebaid (Tab. 2), as only a limited number of sites have yielded information, and if so only with restricted amounts of data. Yet again, the hoards contribute to a better understanding of the monetary processes.

On a more general level of Ptolemaic Egypt, it is important to look at the quality of the data from Upper Egypt. Whereas Fig. 1 reveals the distribution of the sites with numismatic data from the Ptolemaic period, Fig. 2 shows the distribu-

---

3 Faucher, Meadows, Lorber 2017, pp. 9–14.

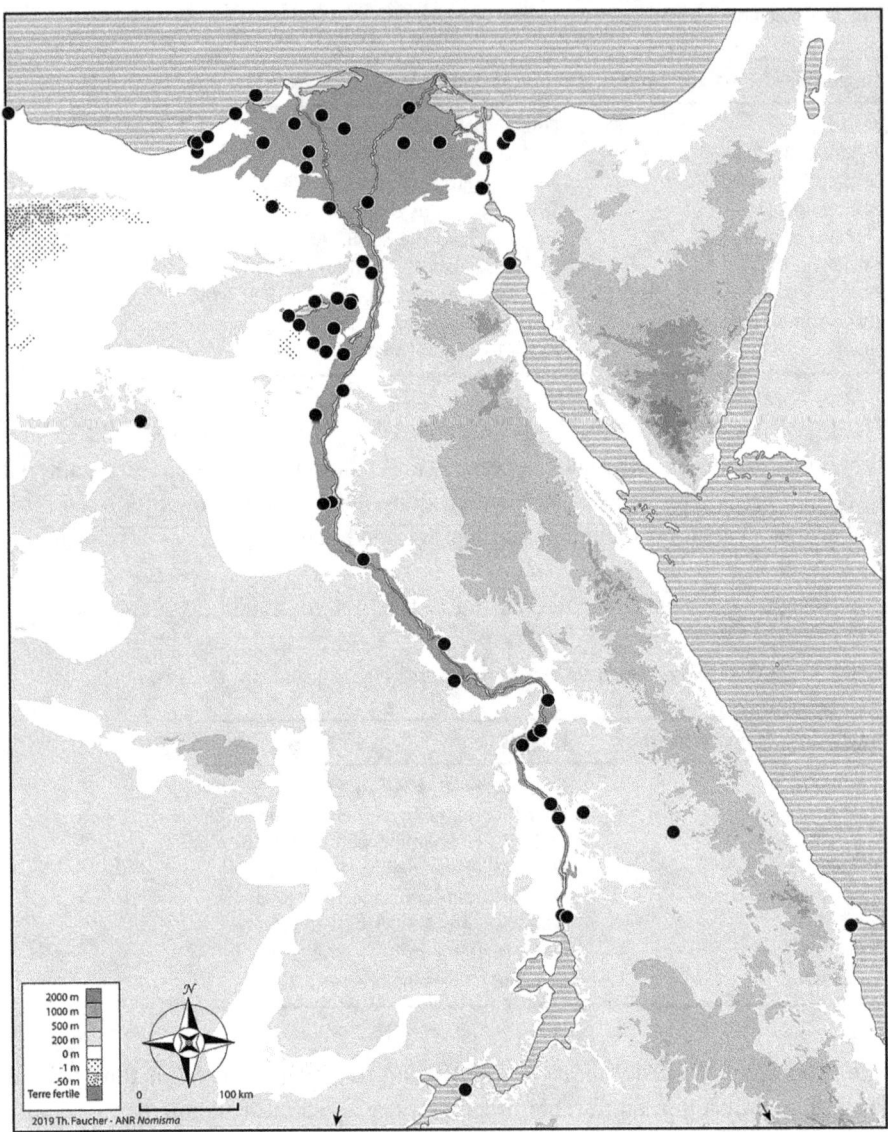

**Fig. 1:** Location of sites with numismatic information (© Thomas Faucher).

tion of hoards during the same period. Even if the Thebaid may be slightly underrepresented on this map, it is likely that the sample may be representative.

Nevertheless, there is a slight proportion of hoards containing Ptolemaic coins in Upper Egypt, 18 in total, whilst 112 are known from Egypt as a whole. The

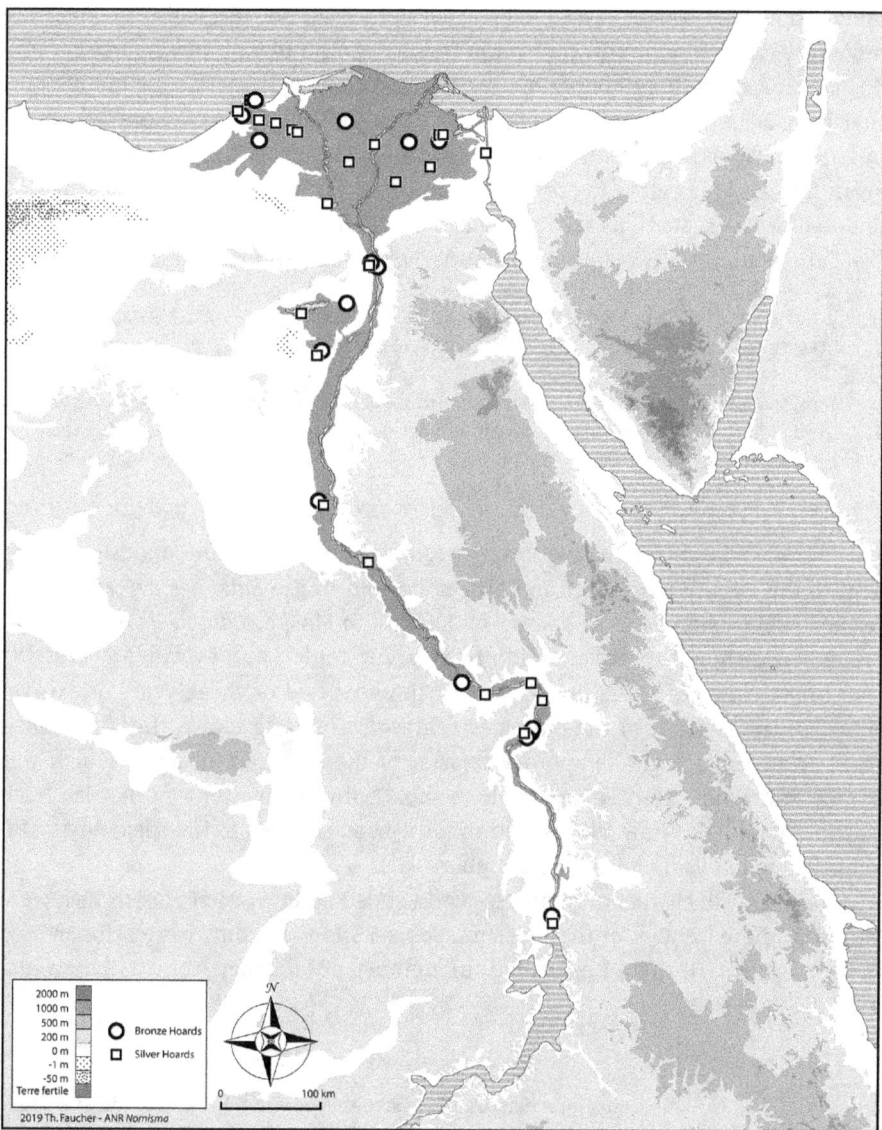

**Fig. 2:** Location of Ptolemaic silver and bronze hoards (© Thomas Faucher).

tables show that Karnak and Luxor are a very good starting point to study the monetary circulation in the Thebaid in terms of both number and diversity.

Of course, these numbers are very low, considering the large amount of coins that have been unearthed in the region since the 19$^{th}$ century. Here and there published reports do mention Ptolemaic coins, especially at Karnak, where Legrain for example refers to two Ptolemaic coins found in the so-called *Cachette*[4], and Redford's excavations record coins in the temple of Akhenaten[5].

Other excavations mention coin finds, here are some examples:

> Il n'a pas fourni d'autres découvertes que celles de deux vases en terre, remplis de nombreuses pièces de bronze à l'effigie de divers Ptolémées.[6]

> Nous y avons découvert deux trésors superposés . . . ils étaient constitués comme tous les trésors que nous découvrons, de jarres remplies de monnaies ptolémaïques et romaines . . . Un autre trésor fut découvert à l'ouest de l'angle sud-ouest de l'enceinte, mais il ne comporte que des grosses pièces d'un seul type.[7]

In older excavations coins were not specifically recorded but supposedly were sent to the Egyptian Museum in Cairo to be sold in the *Salle des ventes*. This, at least, is what emerges from a letter by Legrain to Maspero dated 3$^{rd}$ March 1905, which was brought to my attention by Laurent Coulon and in which it is stated that the latest discoveries would pay for the next two or three years of excavations.[8] If the records of the *Salle des ventes* are missing today, there is indeed mention of coins in the temporary register of the Egyptian Museum, which was begun somewhat later. For example, a "box full of coins, sent by Baraize from Karnak" dated 17$^{th}$ June 1919 is said to have been shipped to the Alexandria Museum, some ten years later (30 December 1931).

It is highly likely that most of these coins ended up in wooden boxes which were stored in the basement of the museum. Some 1.3 tons of coins were rediscovered there recently.[9] Of them I estimated the number of Ptolemaic coins to be around 40,000.

---

4 Legrain 1905, p. 8: ". . . ainsi que deux monnaies, viennent dater la cachette de la période ptolémaïque."
5 Redford 1977, p. 36: "The whole of this level, both in A and B, represents part of the eastern quarter of the city of Thebes, dated on the basis of pottery and coins, between approximately the 7$^{th}$ and the early 2$^{nd}$ century BC." Redford et al. 1991, p. 81: "Thereafter there is evidence (pottery, one coin), of squatter occupation in Ptolemaic times."
6 Pillet 1925.
7 Chevrier 1949.
8 Faucher et al. 2012, n. 28.
9 Faucher, Rerolle, Everett 2019.

# 3 Discussions

Searching for the effects of the Theban crises on the coinage of the Ptolemaic period is to search for differences between stable, or at least normal periods, and those of crisis. It therefore seems relevant to first present the different finds made in Thebes throughout the Ptolemaic period.[10] Then, there is also the need to better acknowledge the coinage process. One of the keys to elucidate phenomena of crises through the presence or absence of coins in certain locations on a both local, regional, or even countrywide scale, is to understand the global mechanisms of a monetary system, from how the coins entered the system, who diffused them into the market, to how they ended up in the ground.

## 3.1 Coin Finds in Diospolis Magna

### 3.1.1 The Stray Finds

An overview of the material found at Karnak and the Thebaid shows that, except for some cases of hoard finds, it was only the excavations after the 1970s that brought to light preserved material and hence opened prospects of quantifying the coin distribution throughout the temples (Fig. 3).

The diversity of locations certainly offers a good and varied sample which, to some extent, may be viewed as representative of the entire material buried at the site. As previously mentioned, the gathered material is mostly restricted to bronze coins. The distribution of precious metal coins (gold and silver) is therefore omitted here, except for the late Ptolemaic silver, for reasons that will be given below.

A closer look at the distribution of coins is possible by separating the series (Fig. 4). The Ptolemaic bronze coinage recently has been reassigned to a number of series, subdivided into ten, to which all numismatists now adhere.[11] The dates of the series refer to the time spans during which the coins were struck. The dates themselves, however, are still being debated.[12] This is not the place to discuss the details of these series. Here, they shall just be mentioned as part of a more specific analysis, especially on the Great Revolt.

The absence of series 1 (under Ptolemy I) is the first characteristic of this corpus, followed by a limited number of coins from series 2 (310 – *ca.* 261). The intro-

---

10 For a preliminary study, see Faucher 2016.
11 Picard, Faucher 2012; Lorber 2018.
12 See Lorber 2018, 2024.

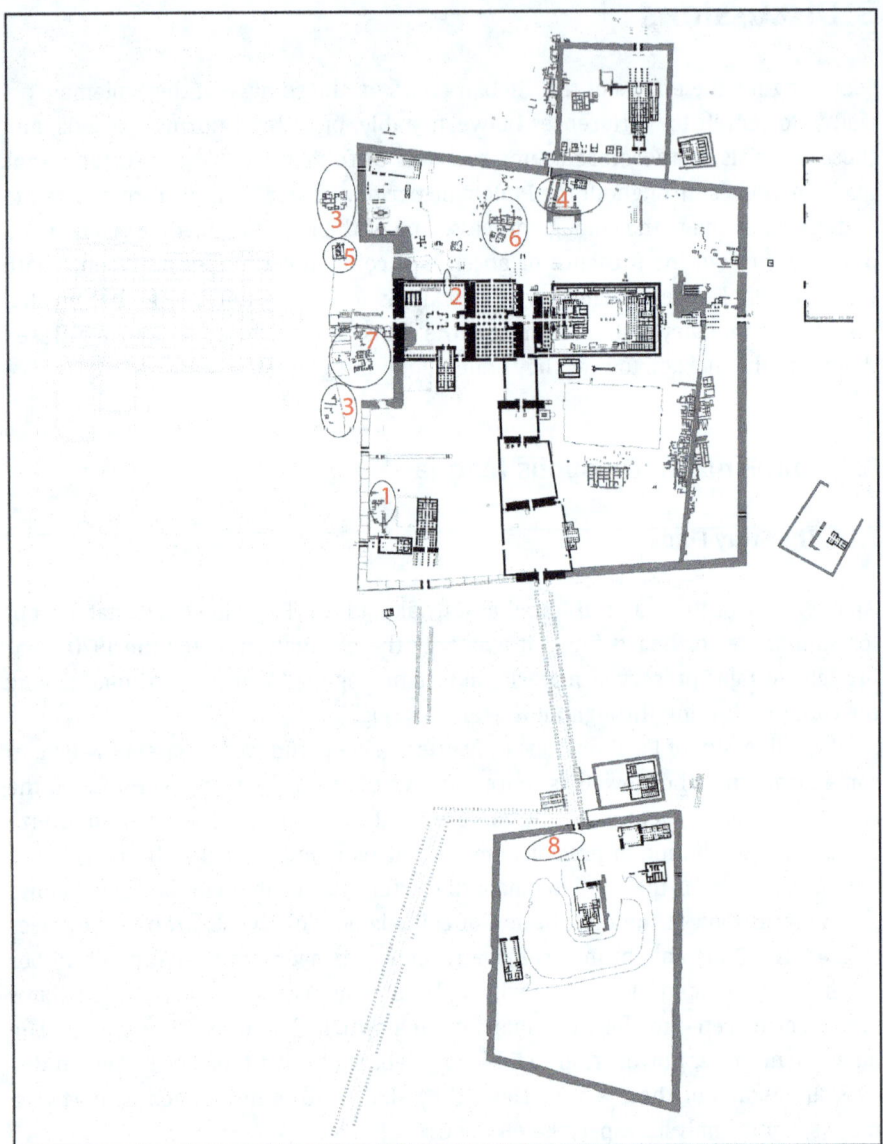

**Fig. 3:** Plan of the Karnak temples with the coin finds. Courtesy of the CFEETK for the base plan (© Thomas Faucher).

duction of the third series in 261 BCE or before, under Ptolemy II, represents a clear change concerning the coins at Karnak and Luxor. After this date, the coin occurrences are relatively stable until the second half of the $2^{nd}$ century, through

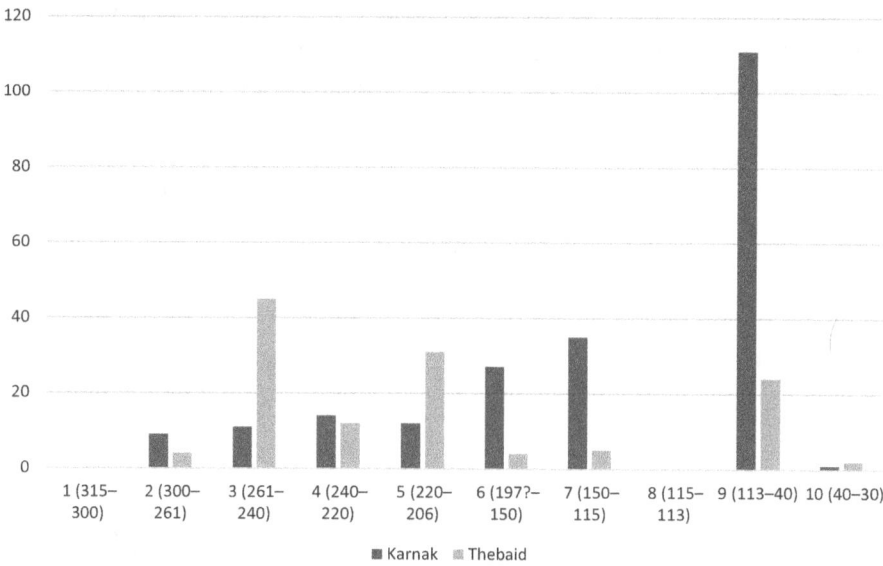

**Fig. 4:** Coin distribution of stray finds by series in Karnak and the Thebaid in the Ptolemaic period (© Thomas Faucher).

series 4 to 7. The gap for series 8 is normal since it was very limited and so far exclusively restricted to the area around Alexandria. Series 9 (113–40 BCE) is the best-represented group, which is not surprising, considering the length of its timespan. Coins ascribed to Cleopatra VII are barely known at Thebes.

As for the Thebaid data, the general impression remains unchanged, in spite of slight differences for some series. The frequencies within series 1 and 2 are yet again low, whereas a surge appears at the onset of series 3. The subsequent series are characterised by more moderate occurrences, especially during series 6 and 7. The same impression as for Karnak and Luxor is noticeable with the coins of Cleopatra VII. The main difference is the relatively low incidence of series 9 coins. In fact, this unfortunately is less related to the number of finds than to their readability. Most of the series 9 coins are poorly or very poorly preserved, which hence increases the efforts and the necessary time for their restoration.

A number of these series 9 coins originate from the excavations in front of the first pylon. Many went unnoticed, and it is only recently that increased interest led to their proper registration. The discrepancies in the numbers for series 9 are due mainly to the fact that the data from the Thebaid are based on published material, whilst most of that from Karnak was directly accessible to me. For instance, a hoard found at Karnak by J. Lauffray was thought to contain anciently forged series 9 coins and thus fell short of being submitted to orderly registration and conservation. Only some specimens were cut in order to analyse their alloys, since such coins often contain high percentages of lead.[13]

It needs to be kept in mind that the series endured over several periods. If the number of coins for each series is divided by the number of its respective years of duration, the distribution clearly levels out. This also puts in perspective the figures for series 9 and at the same time stresses the surge at the introduction of series 3.

Naturally, the specificity of the region can only be grasped if the data are compared to a larger sample from a different region.

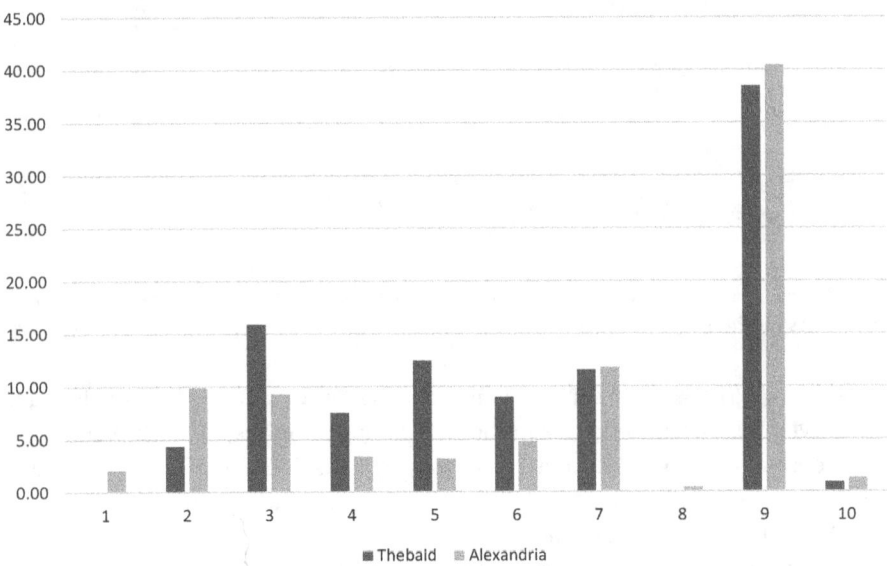

**Fig. 5:** Coin distribution of stray finds by series in the Thebaid and Alexandria (© Thomas Faucher).

Data from Alexandria and the Thebaid show clear differences and provide insights on how the coins were used in the Thebaid in comparison to the capital (Fig. 5). The two main differences consist of the earlier introduction of coins in Alexandria, as represented by a relatively large number of finds for the series 2 coins (and series 1), but also a high number of coins attributed to Cleopatra VII here.

Besides the stray finds from archaeological excavations, the various hoards from the Ptolemaic period found in Karnak offer a different and maybe more

---

13 Lauffray 1995.

vivid picture of the coin circulation. They are not numerous but nonetheless shed light on the hoarding pattern in the region during this period.

### 3.1.2 Hoards

The period's earliest hoard is also the largest one yet known from Karnak (at least as far as we are aware of). It was found during the excavations of the Opet temple in 1968.[14]

**Fig. 6:** Hoard *EH* I, 194 at its discovery (© CFEETK, n° 1691).

It weighs 40 kg and consists of 687 large bronze coins from series 4 and 5 which probably had been buried during or just before the Great Revolt (Fig. 6). The content has not yet been fully recorded, owing to its incomplete restoration.[15] Its discovery was recently reassessed by C. Traunecker, who was part of the archaeological team when the hoard was found. According to Traunecker, the hoard was found within

---

**14** *EH* I, 190; Lorber 2018, p. 149.
**15** A first cleaning was undertaken after the hoard was discovered. A total of 250 coins were then cleaned. Now the lot is in the storeroom of the Ministry of Tourism and Antiquities of Abu Jud in Luxor.

the "pure" storeroom, a place dedicated to the reception of the offerings for the venerated god.[16] The premises would then have served as a safe. Whether the hoard had been part of the temple's revenues, or destined as tax payments, or even as disbursements for priests remains unclear, but it is interesting to note that it had been left where it was. The fact that there are no traces of destruction reveal that the coins had been put aside or discarded rather than lost.

Towards the end of series 5, which corresponds with the beginning or slightly before the Great Revolt, most coins were withdrawn from circulation. Two denominations, the tetrobols and diobols, were maintained, though countermarked by the issuing authority. This was the case of the 12 coins in a hoard found during excavations in 1970–2 below the pavement of the Bubastite portal, inside a trench dug out in preparation of a Sound and Light show.[17] The date of its deposition is uncertain. The restoration work carried out on the floor of the Bubastite portal may possibly be part of those attributed to Ptolemy IV inside the courtyard of the second pylon. Several features date them to the second part of Philopator's reign.[18] If we consider that the hoard had been buried below the doorway as a sort of votive offering, this would mean that the countermarking of the coins predates the revolt and that there had been sufficient time for them to circulate before the restoration work had begun.[19]

Interestingly, one of the coins of the hoard displays a homemade countermark. Instead of the usual cornucopia countermark which typically was stamped by the approved *officinae*, this particular coin shows a triangle which had been engraved by hand. Its execution was careful, and it had been neatly placed on the left side of the eagle, just like on the regular coins. There is sufficient reason to believe its owner had been unable to obtain an official countermark and that he made it himself, so as to assure it remained in circulation.

Though not from hoards, two Ptolemaic coins of series 6 from the excavations near the temple of Ptah may have been put into circulation after the beginning of the Great Revolt. Being the earliest of the series 6 coins, it is very likely that they were lost before the revolt's end in 186 BCE, thus indicating that the coin circulation did not entirely stop during these long years of insecurity, despite the scarce evidence of these coins.

---

16 Traunecker 2020, p. 50.
17 *EH* 197. Lauffray, Sa'ad, Sauneron 1975, pp. 14, 22.
18 Minas-Nerpel, Preys 2023. I would like to thank the authors for providing me with the text before its publication.
19 This dating is advocated lately by Gorre, Lorber 2020, p. 168.

One of the most interesting hoards at Karnak was discovered in front of the first pylon during the Egyptian excavations in the Ptolemaic baths.[20] The hoard consisted of 316 bronze coins from series 7 in two denominations, one large one of 30 mm displaying the head of Zeus Ammon, and a smaller one depicting the head of Isis. The interest of this hoard lay mostly in the prospect of obtaining more precise classifications with regard to $2^{nd}$ century denominations.[21] It sheds much light on the coins stored and used in this part of the site during the second half of the $2^{nd}$ century BCE.

We further know that imitative coins too were in circulation inside the temple during the same period. It has been known that these imitations were produced in the region, though this has remained so far unconfirmed by the archaeological evidence. The latter came to light during the excavations by Laurent Coulon just outside the walls of the chapel of Osiris Wennefer Neb-Djefau, where an artisanal mint had once struck imitations of Ptolemaic coins.[22]

In this specific area were found both regular coins minted in Alexandria as well as imitative coins. The discovery of a chapelet of blanks, a preliminary state of the coin, before it is cut and struck, confirms indeed that the workshop had actually been operating at this exact location. This is the only monetary workshop known so far from Ptolemaic Egypt, though, certainly not an official one, since all the coins struck by the Ptolemies and the Romans were struck in Alexandria.

Later on, coins belonging to the series 9 which were produced from the very end of the $2^{nd}$ century until 40 BCE mostly circulated within this area. We have multiple examples of them but only few pot hoards. Nevertheless, the excavations at the north of the Taharqa gate undertaken by R. Fazzini around the Mut temple recorded an empty hoard in 2010.[23] The pot was found empty, though some coins, a total of 13 coins of series 9, were dropped next to the pot by their owner when he recovered the pot content.

Since there are no other known pots, it is more than likely that most of the groups of series 9 coins were buried together and that they should be considered hoards, as a number of them were found by the Egyptian excavators in front of the first pylon and another group of 198 coins near the Achoris chapel.[24]

---

20 Boraik, Faucher 2010.
21 Faucher, Lorber 2010.
22 Faucher *et al.* 2012.
23 Fazzini 2010, p. 4, figs. 10a–d.
24 Lauffray 1995.

The latest known Ptolemaic coins to be hoarded consist of a group of silver coins of Cleopatra VII unearthed in a pot during the excavations near Achoris chapel.[25]

## 3.2 Why Were these Coins Found There, and what Can We Say about the Circulation of Coins in Thebes during the Ptolemaic Period and more Precisely, during Times of Crisis?

As stated above, the finds reveal only little about the gold and silver coins. An early hoard containing silver coins of Ptolemy I was found in Kuft (*EH* I, 151); a hoard of gold coins struck under Ptolemy II is said to come from Upper Egypt (*EH* I, 168); the most interesting is certainly the hoard found in Qena in 1923, consisting of a minimum of 45 gold coins and 200 silver coins attributed to Ptolemy VI and Ptolemy VIII and buried in or around 145 BCE (*EH* I, 209). Nothing more than a guess can be made as to whether gold or silver coins were in circulation in Southern Egypt during the Ptolemaic period, and especially during the periods of crisis. An exception are the very late silver coins which will be discussed further below.

Bronze coins by and large began to circulate in the Thebaid at the introduction of the series 3 coins, which coincides with an extensive reform on taxation under Ptolemy II, and commonly known as the Revenue Laws.[26] The date of the introduction of the series 3 is estimated at 261 BCE or slightly earlier.[27] By year 22 of Ptolemy II the yoke tax, which was paid in kind, was replaced by the salt tax paid in cash,[28] just like the reformed *apomoira*.[29] This must have had a significant impact on the use of coinage, and the fact that its archaeological frequency increases after this event seems to confirm this. Large bronze coins from that period are found recurrently in excavations. This is surprising because, due to their substantial weight, sometimes reaching almost 100 g, these coins would seem very hard to lose. This consequently represents another indication that coins were used extensively, and that they circulated both in the city and inside the temples.[30]

---

25 Lauffray 1995.
26 Grenfell 1896.
27 Picard, Faucher 2012 propose a date of *ca.* 261 BCE while Gorre, Lorber 2020 offer the date of 264 BCE.
28 Muhs 2005, p. 7.
29 Clarysse, Vandorpe 2007.
30 Few of these large Ptolemaic coins of the 3$^{rd}$ century were found during the excavations of the chapel of Osiris Wennefer Neb-Djefau, led by Laurent Coulon and Cyril Giorgi.

By the end of the 3rd century BCE, it is quite likely that bronze coins had been integrated to the normal taxation procedures, if not also regular trade exchange. Their presence in the fortresses of the Eastern Desert also show that they were used there.

The year 207/6 BCE saw the outbreak of the Great Revolt.

To understand how the circulation of coins could be affected by the revolt, one needs to better understand the mechanisms that had brought the coins into circulation, so as to determine the impact on the different money networks.

In a recent article, Gilles Gorre argued that the priests were an essential part in the supply of coins to the secular population.[31] Mentioning the *apomoira* and diverse payments from the crown to priests, Gorre argues that their networking would make them the best agents to disseminate coinage within the society.

Another possible access way to coinage may have been provided by the military personnel. *Opsoniôn* or *misthos* could be paid in cash, and coins could therefore have entered the market in this way. Several pieces of evidence attest to the presence of soldiers in front of the first pylon at Karnak, if not a garrison, then at least a series of individuals of certainly Greek origin.[32]

**Fig. 7:** Hemiobol of Ioppe found at the site of Abbad, near Edfu (© Thomas Faucher).

Two coins struck in Ioppe (Jaffa, Fig. 7) equivalent to the Alexandrian series 5 and dated prior to the Revolt originate from the excavations in front of the first pylon. Typically, foreign Ptolemaic bronze coins did not circulate inside Egypt, even if they theoretically could do so. The fact that such coins have been found inside fortresses of the Eastern Desert as well as in regions secured by garrisons, like

---

31 Gorre 2014.
32 Redon, Faucher 2016.

Edfu, is firm evidence that they had been brought there by soldiers from Palestine, probably as part of their local pay, most likely after the battle of Raphia.[33] The occurrence of coins in the ground in front of the first pylon testifies to the presence of soldiers there during this period. Later on, in the 2$^{nd}$ century BCE, the public as well as private baths cleared in the mound against the first pylon yet again point to the presence of Greeks here, again, most likely related to the army.[34]

The hoard next to the wall of Nectanebo and the Opet temple containing large bronze coins of series 5 which had been discarded by the priests may indeed witness to the Revolt. The excavations in front of the first pylon lead to suggest that the houses here had been devastated by fire.[35] Similarly, the apparent haste by the military to evacuate the fortresses in the Eastern Desert illustrates the suddenness and the vehemence of this episode.[36] This hoard contained several hundred drachms on the silver standard and hence represented a substantial sum. It is surprising, to say the least, that these coins were left behind considering that even their value in raw metal made them subject to trade.

What happened after the beginning of the Revolt? We know that receipts for tax payments ceased to be issued[37] and that the use of bronze coinage plummeted, as for instance demonstrated by two demotic marriage contracts in which silver only was used to estimate sums.[38] If, according to some papyrologists, the introduction of the bronze standard and the devaluation of bronze coinage was linked to the secession of the Thebaid, this would clearly have represented a major change in the monetary system.

The hoard found under the floor of the Bubastite portal shows that the coins countermarked by the official *officinae* had arrived at Karnak slightly prior to or just after the beginning of the Revolt. Of course, it cannot be excluded that these coins had been deposited there as ex-votos only after the decrease of their value or even their obsolescence, but at least one other countermarked coin (found in the excavations of the Roman baths, in front of the first pylon) still made its way to Karnak.

We are left with very little evidence for that period, and it is impossible to say if series 6 coins which were found in relatively large numbers in both Karnak

---

33 Redon, Faucher 2023.
34 The discovery of a Doric capital at the northern end of the sphinx alley at Karnak indicates the former existence of a "Greek" temple there and, together with the baths, hence also of a Greek community, most probably military personnel (Chevrier 1947, pp. 162–163, pl. XXI).
35 Lauffray 1995.
36 Redon, Faucher 2017.
37 The last receipt dates to 207 BCE; see Pestman 1995, pp. 103, 105. Moreover, no banker is mentioned between 207 and 186 BCE; cf. Bogaert 1998, p. 188.
38 Gorre 2014, p. 92, n. 5.

and the Thebaid entered the market before or after the end of the revolt, or with the recapture of the city of Thebes by the Ptolemies. We can nonetheless ascertain that the coinage circulated already early in the $2^{nd}$ century BCE. And by the mid-century, this circulation had regained levels that are also observed elsewhere in Egypt. This emerges clearly from the coins found in Karnak, in the hoard of the Ptolemaic baths. But could the loss of this hoard constitute a sign of an episode of turmoil in the city? To date, there is no other evidence to corroborate this assumption. Another clear sign of the monetary activity is the workshop excavated next to the chapel of Osiris Neb Djefau. Its existence allows the following conclusions. The first is that the craftsman was an experienced minter, which is unusual in view of the fact that the official mint was located in Alexandria, some 900 km away. The second is that the inhabitants of the temple (priests) either were in desperate need for cash or that the coins were used for other purposes. Could they for instance have served as ex-voto offerings? We have the example of the Bubastite portal. One other imitative coin was found next to a foundation deposit in *Karnak North*. Coins found outside and inside the chapel of Osiris Neb Djefau may also be taken as votive deposits[39] even if the more canonical deposits apparently lacked coins.[40]

Linking any of the evidence to the known episodes remains problematic. For example, even if certainly not massive, the presence of Seleucid or Israelite soldiers at Thebes during the capture of Egypt by Antiochus IV in 169 BCE has left no numismatic traces.[41]

Finally, the evidence from the $1^{st}$ century reveals a significant and maybe continuous use of coins, mainly of poor quality. The highly protracted lifespan of series 9 makes it very hard to distinguish the different episodes of upheaval in the Thebaid and at Karnak in this period.

Next to bronze coins, silver now begins to be attested towards the end of the period, but not in the same hoards.

This shift in the hoarding pattern is linked to a major change in the issuing of silver coins around 50 BCE. Since the beginning of the Ptolemaic period, silver coins had very high silver contents close to 100%. Though they declined in the second and at the beginning of the first centuries, they nonetheless stayed above 90%.[42] In and around 50 BCE, however, the silver proportion plummeted to 30%, the rest being copper. This prompted the newly minted coins to be used and considered differently, and the fact that they from now on are found in archaeo-

---

39 Cyril Giorgi records six material groups in which one or more coins had been deposited and qualified as hoards.
40 Schmitt 2017.
41 See Thiers 1995.
42 See Olivier 2012; Faucher, Olivier 2020.

logical deposits is a sign that were treated more like bronze coins than like ones of silver.

What can we draw from this evidence? The answer to the question as to how coins can survive crises is therefore: fairly well. It still is difficult to understand the monetisation processes just after the Great Revolt. The impact of the latter on coinage itself must have been significant, not only in the Thebaid, but all over Egypt too. A recall of millions of coins was undertaken and the introduction of the new series 6 was a complex task, especially in the south with the disappearance of taxes and royal offices. But the coins nevertheless arrived. The presence of the royal bank at Thebes and the abundant evidence of coin circulation in the second and throughout the first centuries show that coins had become part of everyday life and that they survived all crises. The poor alloy qualities in the coins after the second half of the $2^{nd}$ century BCE and the evidence of their use in the city itself is additional evidence for the complete adoption of coins by the population, whatever the political situation may have been.

## Bibliography

Bogaert 1998
    Bogaert, R., "Liste géographique des banques et des banquiers de l'Égypte ptolémaïque", *ZPE* 120, pp. 165–202.

Boraik, Faucher 2010
    Boraik, M., Faucher, T., "Le trésor des bains de Karnak", *CahKarn* 13, 2010, pp. 79–100.

Callataÿ 2000
    Callataÿ, F. de, "Les taux de survie des émissions monétaires antiques, médiévales et modernes. Essai de mise en perspective et conséquences quant à la productivité des coins dans l'antiquité", *RevNum* 155, 2000, pp. 83–109.

Chevrier 1947
    Chevrier, H., "Rapport sur les travaux de Karnak, 1947–1948 [sic 1946–1947]", *ASAE* 47, 1947, pp. 161–183.

Chevrier 1949
    Chevrier, H., "Rapport sur les travaux de Karnak, 1948–1949", *ASAE* 49, 1949, pp. 241–267.

Clarysse, Vandorpe 2007
    Clarysse, W., Vandorpe, K., "The Ptolemaic Apomoira", in H. Melaerts (ed.), *Le culte du souverain dans l'Égypte ptolémaïque au IIIe siècle avant notre ère. Actes du colloque international, Bruxelles, 10 mai 1995*, StudHell 34, 2007, pp. 5–42.

Faucher 2016
    Faucher, T., "Des monnaies grecques en Thébaïde. Trouvailles monétaires dans Karnak ptolémaïque", in G. Gorre, A. Marangou (eds.), *La présence grecque dans la vallée de Thèbes*, Archéologie et Culture, Rennes, 2016, pp. 141–146.

Faucher, Lorber 2010
Faucher, T., Lorber, C.C., "Ptolemaic Bronze Coinage in the Second Century BC", *AJN* 4, 2010, pp. 35–80.
Faucher, Meadows, Lorber 2017
Faucher, T., Meadows, A.R., Lorber, C., *Egyptian Hoards I: The Ptolemies*, BiEtud 168, Cairo, 2017.
Faucher, Olivier 2020
Faucher, T., Olivier, J., "From Owls to Eagles: Metallic Composition of Egyptian Coinage (fifth–first Centuries BC)", in K. Butcher (ed.), *Debasement: Manipulation of Coin Standards in Premodern Monetary Systems*, Warwick, 2020, pp. 97–109.
Faucher, Rerolle, Everett 2019
Faucher, T., Rerolle, C., Everett, D., "Saving the money", *Scribe. The Magazine of the American Research Center in Egypt*, Spring 2019/3, pp. 8–13.
Faucher et al. 2012
Faucher, T., Coulon, L., Frangin, E., Giorgi, C., "Un atelier monétaire à Karnak au ii$^e$ s. av. J.-C.", *BIFAO* 111, 2012, pp. 143–165.
Fazzini 2010
Fazzini, R., "The Brooklyn Museum's 2010 Season of Fieldwork at the Precinct of the Goddess Mut at South Karnak: Preliminary Report", pp. 1–38, <https://d1lfxha3ugu3d4.cloudfront.net/features/docs/Preliminary_Report_2010.pdf>, accessed 30 August 2024.
Gorre 2014
Gorre, G., "La monnaie de bronze lagide et les temples égyptiens. La diffusion de la monnaie de bronze en Thébaïde au III$^e$ siècle av. J.-C.", *Annales. Histoire, Sciences Sociales* 69/1, 2014, pp. 91–113.
Grenfell 1896
Grenfell, B.P., *Revenue Laws of Ptolemy Philadelphus*, Oxford, 1896.
Gorre, Lorber 2020
Gorre, G., Lorber, C., "The Survival of the Silver Standard after the Grand Mutation", in T. Faucher (ed.), *Money Rules! The Monetary Economy of Egypt, from Persians until the Beginning of Islam*, BiEtud 176, Cairo, 2020, pp. 149–170.
Lauffray 1995
Lauffray, J., *La chapelle d'Achôris à Karnak* I, Paris, 1995.
Lauffray, Sa'ad, Sauneron 1975
Lauffray, J., Sa'ad, R., Sauneron, S., "Rapport sur les travaux de Karnak. Activités du Centre franco-égyptien en 1970–1972", *Karnak* 5, 1975, pp. 1–42.
Legrain 1905
Legrain, G., *Les recentes découvertes de Karnak*, Cairo, 1905.
Lorber 2018
Lorber, C.C., *Coins of the Ptolemaic Empire, Part I: Ptolemy I through Ptolemy IV*, Numismatic Studies 35, 2 vols., New York, 2018.
Lorber 2024
Lorber, C.C., *Coins of the Ptolemaic Empire, Part II: Ptolemy V through Cleopatra VII*, Numismatic Studies 46, 3 vols., New York, 2024.
Minas-Nerpel, Preys 2023
Minas-Nerpel, M., Preys, R., *The Kiosk of Taharqa* II: *The Ptolemaic Decoration (TahKiosk nos. E1–24, F1–4)*, BiGen 72, Cairo, 2023.
Muhs 2005
Muhs, B.P., *Tax Receipts, Taxpayers, and Taxes in Early Ptolemaic Thebes*, Chicago, 2005.

Olivier 2012
>Olivier, O., *Archè et Chrèmata en Égypte au IIe siècle avant J.-C. (204–81 av. J.-C.). Étude numismatique et d'histoire*, PhD Thesis, Université d'Orléans, 2012.

Pestman 1995
>Pestman, P.W., "Haronnophris and Chaonnophris: two Indigenous Pharaohs in Ptolemaic Egypt (205–186 BC)", in S.P. Vleeming (ed.), *Hundred-Gated Thebes: Acts of a Colloquium on Thebes and the Theban Area in the Greco-Roman Period*, P.L.Bat. 27, Leiden, New York, Cologne, 1995, pp. 101–137.

Pillet 1925
>Pillet, M., "Rapport sur les travaux de Karnak (1924–1925)", *ASAE* 25, 1925, pp. 1–24.

Picard, Faucher 2012
>Picard, O., Faucher, T., "Les monnaies lagides", in O. Picard, C. Bresc, T. Faucher, G. Gorre, M.-C. Marcellesi, C. Morrisson (eds.), *Les monnaies des fouilles du Centre d'Études Alexandrines*, EtudAlex 25, Cairo, 2012, pp. 17–108.

Redford 1977
>Redford, D., "The Excavations of the University Museum Akhenaten Temple Project at Karnak", *Expedition* 19/4, 1977, pp. 33–38.

Redford *et al.* 1991
>Redford, D., Orel, S., Redford, S., Shubert, S., "East Karnak Excavations, 1987–1989", *JARCE* 28, 1991, pp. 75–106.

Redon, Faucher 2016
>Redon, R., Faucher, T., "Les Grecs aux portes d'Amon. Les bains de Karnak et l'occupation ptolémaïque du parvis ouest du temple de Karnak", in G. Gorre, A. Marangou (eds.), *La présence grecque dans la vallée de Thèbes*, Archéologie et Culture, Rennes, 2016, pp. 121–134.

Redon, Faucher 2017
>Redon, R., Faucher, T., "Forts et mines d'or du désert Oriental d'Égypte. Découvertes récentes dans le district de Samut", *Revue archéologique* 1, 2017, pp. 101–109.

Redon, Faucher 2023
>Redon, R., Faucher, T., "Recent Discoveries of BE Arrowheads and Joppa Coins in the Eastern Desert of Egypt: In the Footsteps of Soldiers of the Ptolemaic Army", *BASOR*, 2023, pp. 1–29.

Schmitt 2017
>Schmitt, F., "Les dépôts de fondation à Karnak, actes rituels de piété et de pouvoir", *CahKarn* 16, 2017, pp. 351–371.

Thiers 1995
>Thiers, C., "Civils et militaires dans les temples. Occupation illicite et expulsion", *BIFAO* 95, 1995, pp. 493–516.

Traunecker 2020
>Traunecker, C., "Varia autour du temple d'Opet à Karnak, Partie I", *Pharaon Magazine* 41, 2020, pp. 44–52.

Joseph G. Manning
# Volcanoes, Floods, and Social Unrest: The Theban Unrest in Its Social and Environmental Context

Social unrest under the Ptolemies has received considerable attention in recent years. While some new evidence has appeared, the basic outline of the events discussed by Anne-Emmanuelle Veïsse and Brian McGing remain good guides to most of the evidence and provide sound historical sketches of events (see Tab. 1).[1]

**Tab. 1:** Basic chronology of rural unrest in the Ptolemaic period (adapted from Veïsse 2004, pp. 78–79). In some cases, unrest is inferred by the absence of tax receipts in certain years in Upper Egypt, e.g. after 157–133 BCE and after 146 (or 142) – 131 BCE, Veïsse 2004, p. 46.

| Dates of documented social unrest | Location |
|---|---|
| *ca. 245–238 BCE | Probably throughout Egypt |
| 217 BCE | Revolt of demobilized soldiers after Raphia |
| *207–186 BCE | Throughout Egypt |
| 168–164 BCE | Throughout Egypt |
| after 157–133 BCE | Pathyris (Upper Egypt) |
| after 146/2–131 BCE | Edfu (Upper Egypt) |
| *131–122 BCE | Throughout Egypt |
| 107–84 BCE | Upper Egypt |
| 84/83 BCE | Middle Egypt |

Explanations for the unrest have tended to concentrate either on economic or "anti-Greek nationalism" as the principal cause of the unrest.[2] In both cases, the unrest appears to come in direct reaction or response to Ptolemaic state building and its attendant pressures, including resource requirements for military mobilization and monetary inflation. But I suggest that the situation is more complex than either a causal model centered on the new fiscal regime or ethnic tensions alone. This is not to mention, of course, the internal dynastic conflicts that generated opposing factions that could also turn violent, or the individual violence in the countryside that, one has the impression, was endemic. Both of these may have been additional factors in understanding the wider unrest of the period. It is

---

1 McGing 1997; Veïsse 2004. See also Pestman 1995; Johstono 2016.
2 Johstono 2016, p. 185.

difficult not to associate the Alexandrian riots in 203 BCE as in some way connected to the great Theban revolt.[3]

The concept of an ancient Egyptian "nationalism" has frequently been invoked in the context of the Ptolemaic unrest, but I am not convinced that it is useful.[4] There were surely symptoms of cultural unity, in language, religious, and funerary practice, festivals, and even "shared myths." But this does not amount to a nation-state or to a sense of unity between elite and non-elite groups; there was too much cultural differentiation between the relatively small number of elites and the vast bulk of the population, the primary agrarian producers. Most of the evidence for an Egyptian ideology that unified the entire polity around a concept of "state" derives from the context of Egyptian temples and their priesthoods and the scribal class who can hardly be understood as acting in concert with the bulk of the Egyptian population.[5] The basic debate hinges on an often unstated issue, namely, how were people (and how many?) mobilized against the state? How coordinated was the violence? This is of particular, and perhaps even unique, relevance for the historical understanding of the great Theban revolt (205–186 BCE) because of its spatial and temporal dimensions, but I suspect that the periods that have (*) in Tab. 1 were all times of serious social distress related to poor Nile flooding.

# 1 What Were these Events?

Typically, the unrest outside of the major cities of Alexandria and Ptolemais are referred to as "revolts" in the literature, occasionally even rather dramatically as "revolutions," and are generally thought of as separate and distinct phenomena from the urban riots in Alexandria.[6] We are, as so often, hampered by the nature of our sources for the events, almost all of which give us a perspective from the Ptolemaic state. The most common term in Greek texts is *tarache*. Other kinds of texts, the Oracle of the Potter treated briefly below for example, couch resistance in terms of good kingship deploying historico-religious language. These periods of social instability are understood, usually, as part of the decline of internal Ptole-

---

3 On Alexandria, see Barry 1993.
4 See, for example, for ancient Egypt: Wilkinson 2010.
5 Here I can only give a nod to an enormous literature on nation-states and nationalism. I follow Gellner's (2009) basic views. See Moreno García 2019, esp. pp. 96–107.
6 Barry 1993. On "revolution," see Peremans 1978.

maic power, coinciding, more or less, to the loss of its Mediterranean power and to the increasing dominance of Rome in the eastern Mediterranean after 200 BCE.

Clearly, over the three centuries of Ptolemaic rule the "revolts" we are dealing with were different kinds of events, some very local, others widespread. We should not assume that the causes were the same. The longest and widest-occurring event was the great Theban revolt. It was violent, it was sustained, there was land abandonment throughout the Thebaid, it took some doing for Ptolemaic forces to put the revolt down, and it had serious consequences for the Ptolemaic state as well as for the "rebels".[7] There are some parallels to state formation processes originating from Thebes that are well known from pharaonic history. This ancient history echoed in the throne names of the rebel kings.[8]

The Theban revolt was by far the most serious internal political crisis for the Ptolemaic state in its history. Much of the Nile valley broke away from Ptolemaic control for twenty years. Two rulers, Haronnophris and Chaonnophris, established a dynasty of sorts in the Thebaid. Some notarial contracts are dated using their names as if they were the legitimate rulers, or at least held political control over the Thebaid. Their throne names are evocative of messianism.[9] The messianic elements as a means of mobilizing a group against the state have interesting parallels in the First Slave Revolt in Sicily in the 130s BCE.[10] Clearly, a political strategy was involved in the Theban revolt.

However we understand the nature of the unrest, though, there are two areas that I think require more thought. The first is the understanding of what Jean Bingen referred to as the "structural tensions" of Ptolemaic society between on one hand ruling coalitions, the rulers and the royal court, and other interest groups including the "aristocratic" class and on the other hand the majority of the population.[11] Improving our understanding of the events requires us to have a more complex social model in mind, but we also require a more theoretically informed framework, something that I am only able to moot here. The historical social sciences offer a rich corpus of material with which to think. We might ask who the "rebels" were for example. Were they, as Tilly has suggested in his study of collective violence, "specialists in inflicting physical damage (such as police, soldiers, guards, thugs, and gangs) . . ."[12]? The great Theban revolt certainly in-

---

7 *SB* 20.14659, a decree dealing with the enslavement of rebels during the great Theban revolt.
8 Clarysse 1978.
9 Vandorpe 1995.
10 Engels 2017, pp. 385–408.
11 Bingen 2007. Recently the point is well made by Strootman 2017, p. 44. On the Ptolemaic aristocracy, see the important study by Rowlandson 2007.
12 Tilly 2003, pp. 4–5.

volved soldiers.[13] To what extent were non-elites involved? We might posit also that environmental and demographic pressures, combined with the new fiscal system, put more pressure on local societies than in the past. All of this points the way for a much more complex social model of Ptolemaic society. Part of developing a more complex model of Ptolemaic society must include the force that united the entire territory, the Nile river itself and the environmental constraints that it imposed on Ptolemaic society.

## 2 Volcanoes and Nile Flood Variability

The annual flood of the Nile river was the lifeblood of agriculture and thus of Egyptian civilization throughout its history. The variability of the flood is a notable feature of the river. Despite this inter-annual variability, the flood came gradually, and it normally flooded most of the agrarian land in the valley. A modern study of the Nilometer recordings of flood heights in the Islamic period suggests that roughly 70% of flood years were sufficient.[14] It is likely that on average this was also the case in antiquity. But on the other hand, 22% of the Islamic period flood heights were low. Low flood heights of course would not have uniformly affected the whole of Egyptian agriculture, and a single year of poor flooding, given grain storage and a means of distribution, would normally not spell disaster. But several years of poor flooding could expose the society to serious stress, and it is these periods that should be examined carefully.

The early work by Barbara Bell and Karl Butzer established the relationship between long-term inter-annual variability of the Nile flood and political "discontinuity." Both were concerned with periods of centralized power decline, namely the end of the Old, Middle and New Kingdoms. But the historical and environmental data was not chronologically precise enough to be certain of any causal link between flood variability and political instability.[15] To be sure, the explanation of the fall of dynasties of centralized political control that marked the end of the Old, Middle and New Kingdoms had more to them than simply a series of Nile flood failures. In one of his last studies, Butzer proposed a far more complex, coupled natural-human system model of human – environment interaction.[16] It is

---

13 *OGIS* 90.19–20.
14 Said 1993, p. 96.
15 Bell 1975; Butzer 1984.
16 Butzer 2012.

this more complex understanding of the interactions between human society and the environment, and the feedbacks to both systems, that must be further developed for pre-modern Egyptian history, including of course the Ptolemaic and Roman periods.

We now know that there were several natural drivers of long- and short-term flood variability. These include the El-Nino-Southern Oscillation (ENSO). Another driver of Nile flooding, via the East African Monsoon, were explosive volcanic eruptions. Large eruptions inject sulfates into the stratosphere, which produces cooling by reduction in solar radiation that in turn perturbs the annual East African Monsoonal rains around Lake Tana, the source of the Blue Nile and the most important source of the annual Summer flood of the Egyptian Nile.[17]

Francis Ludlow and I published a preliminary paper in 2017 laying out the hypothesis that Nile flood suppression and social unrest were coincident.[18] Despite the news coverage that has over-dramatized the causal connection between large eruptions and monsoon failure, poor flooding and social unrest, we have established the link in a statistically robust time series between volcanic eruptions documented and dated in ice cores, inferred Nile flooding suppression and three types of social data that we have suggested might be related to societal stress – unrest, termination of war, the priestly decrees, and land sales (Fig. 1). In each case, our work shows that there was a high degree of correlation. Of course, as the saying goes, correlation is not causation. But we have argued that the high degree of correlation here is telling us something significant about the connection between poor flooding and social distress.

We were careful not to simply propose a deterministic relationship. But as we noted in the paper, the high-resolution climate records that have been published in the past few years do allow us to examine social instability inter-coupled with environmental change in far greater detail. The coupling of poor Nile flooding and social unrest are well attested in later historical sources.[19] Poor flooding could induce a range of societal responses, from apocalyptic interpretations of flood failure, to fear and panic (as noted in the Canopus decree), to crop failure leading to food distress, and in some extreme cases, famine.

One of the interesting results of this kind of work is that it allows us to rethink the context of social unrest even if we only have laconic information. For example, the famous "sedition" mentioned by Justin, which was the cause of Ptolemy III's returning prematurely from military campaign against the Seleu-

---

[17] Manning et al. 2017; Williams 2019.
[18] Ludlow, Manning 2016.
[19] E.g. 'Abd al- Laṭīf al-Baghdādī 2021, p. 137.

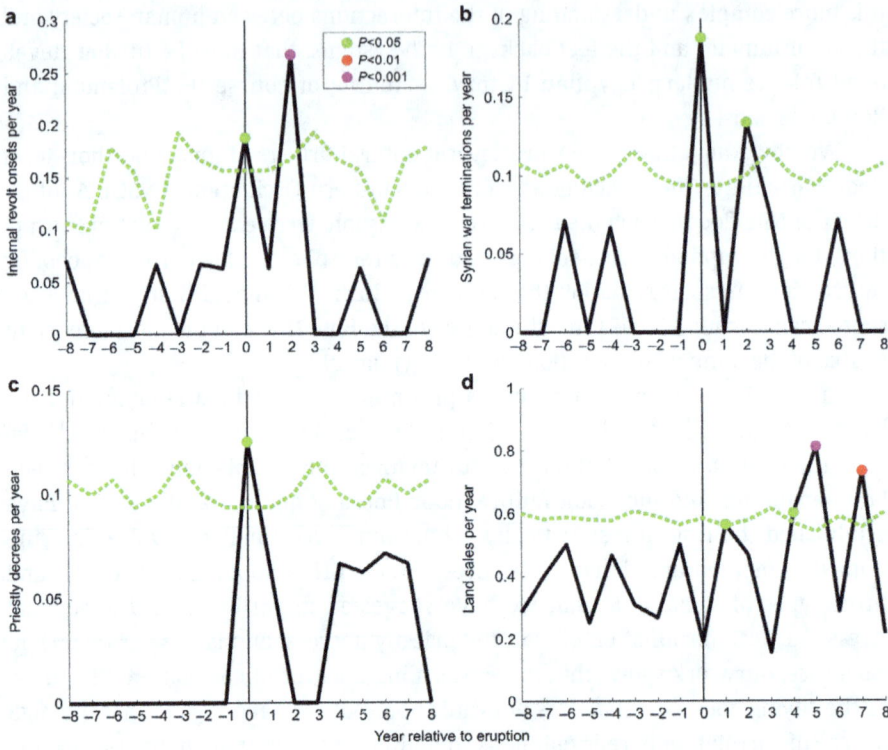

**Fig. 1:** Response to volcanism in Egyptian social indexes (reproduced from Manning et al. 2017, fig. 3). **a** Dates of the initiation of internal revolts against Ptolemaic rule composited relative to the dates of 16 volcanic eruptions (represented at year 0 on the horizontal axes; years 1–8 then represent the first to eighth years after these eruptions, and years −1 to −8 the first to eighth years before), excluding an 8-year buffer at the start and end of our 305–30 BCE period. Dots indicates statistically significant values estimated using Barnard's exact test (green: $P < 0.05$, red: $P < 0.01$, magenta: $P < 0.001$). Green dashed lines give the 95% confidence threshold also estimated using Barnard's exact test. Data associated with any secondary eruptions within the compositing window are excluded, and remaining data expressed as a fraction of all records to prevent bias. **b** Same as a, but for the dates of terminations of the "Syrian Wars", i.e., wars between the Ptolemaic and Seleukid states. **c** Same as a, but for priestly decrees. **d** Same as a, but for Demotic language land sales with significance estimated using the 2-sample student's t-test. Revolt onset dates N = 10; Syrian Wars N = 9; decrees N = 9; land sales N = 84. Eruption years N = 18, and non-eruption years N = 258 (305–30 BCE).

kids, probably refers to the same "event" as mentioned in the Canopus Decree that highlights what must have been a rather dramatic series of events about which we know very little.[20] Nonetheless, the importation of grain by Ptolemy III to solve a looming food crisis (if not widespread famine) in the 240s BCE looks like a very serious event triggered by very low Nile flooding.[21] *P. Edfu* 8, the petition of Philotas to the king detailing a severe multi-year Nile flood, although undated, fits perfectly in this historical context as well.[22] The volcanic record would strongly suggest that there well might have been Nile flood problems in the 240s BCE. The same can be said of the late third century BCE, the early second century BCE and the 160s BCE.

The so-called priestly decrees from the Ptolemaic period, clustered (at least based on the surviving evidence) around the end of the third and early second centuries BCE (specifically 243 – ca. 180 BCE), are extremely valuable for shedding light on the political and cultural relationships between the priesthoods throughout Egypt and the dynasty.[23] These decrees were the result of "national" assemblies of priests from the temples throughout Egypt.[24] The text of the decrees were erected in front of every temple and written in two languages (Greek and Egyptian, and three scripts, Greek, demotic and hieroglyphic). As such, this was a new feature of the Ptolemaic state. Various arguments have been made about both the purpose of these texts and their apparent disappearance by the middle of the second century BCE.[25]

## 3 Literary Reflections

There is also a large corpus of literary texts that have never been brought into a conversation about social responses to climatic change. Consider, for example, the famous prophetic text known as the "Oracle of the Potter," certainly among

---

**20** Justin, *Epitome*, 27.1.9; Porphyry, *FGrHist*, 260 F43.
**21** McGing has concluded that there was no real unrest event, at least there is no event documented, around 245 BCE that would lead to a conclusion of something very serious happening in the Egyptian countryside.
**22** Manning 2018, pp. 162–167.
**23** For doubtful later examples, see Gorre, Veïsse 2020, pp. 116–118.
**24** Hölbl 2001, pp. 105–106; Gorre, Veïsse 2020, pp. 113–139. See also the most recent study of these decrees by Recklinghausen 2018. For the most recently discovered decree, which is also the earliest (243 BCE), see El-Masry, Altenmüller, Thissen 2012.
**25** Gorre, Veïsse 2020, p. 114 suggest that the purpose of these synods was to enforce loyalty of the priesthoods to the dynasty, which was fulfilled by 180 BCE. At this point, they argue, the need for synods no longer existed.

the more interesting papyrus texts in the Austrian National Library in Vienna. Whenever the original date of composition, the core of the text's content suggests a second century BCE historical context. The surviving copies that we have are dated to the Roman period (2$^{nd}$ and 3$^{rd}$ century CE), attesting to the text's continued resonance in later periods.

The text, written in the crabbed and very cursive hand of that time, describes a devastated Egyptian landscape and prophesies the coming of a savior king who will restore Egypt and its life-giving river:

> The river, [since it will not have] sufficient water, [will flood], but (only) a little so that scorched will be [the land . . .] but unnaturally. [For] in the [time] of the Typhonians [people will say] 'wretched Egypt [you have been maltreated] by the [terrible] malefactors who have committed evil against you.' And the sun will darken as it will not be willing to observe the evils in Egypt. The earth will not respond to seeds. These will be part of its blight. {The} farmer will be <du>nned for taxes <for> wh<at> he did not plant. There will be fighting in Egypt because people will be in need of food. What one plants, [another] will reap and carry off. When this happens, there will be [war and slaughter] which [will kill] brothers and wives. For [these things will happen] when the great god Hephaistos will desire to return to the [city], and the Girdleweavers[26] will kill each other as they [are Typhonians. —] evil will be done . . . . Men will die at the hands of each other; two of them will come to the same place to aid one. Among women who are pregnant death will also be common. The Girdleweavers will kill themselves as they also are Typhonians. . . . . Finally, the leaves will fall. The Nile, which had lacked water, will be full and winter, which had changed its orderly ways, will run its proper course and then summer will resume its own track, and normal will be the wind's breezes which previously had been weak. For in the <time> of the Typhonians the sun will darken to highlight the character of the evils <and> to reveal the greed of the Girdleweavers. . . . .[27]

Reading *Oracle* against the backdrop of explosive volcanism that can now be shown to have significantly impacted the Nile in and beyond the mid-second century BCE, the prophecy becomes equally prominent as a description of the material and psychological stresses associated with Nile failure and how these stresses are interwoven with and interpreted via the prism of contemporary political concerns and religious worldviews. The text thus details the failure of the Nile flood, reduced agricultural production, dust and landscape degradation, land abandonment, the inevitable coming of the collector of the harvest tax despite the dire conditions, and social unrest. All of this resonates with the expected consequen-

---

26 The title "girdleweavers" is generally thought to refer to Greco-Macedonian military dress, while "Typhonians", also a reference to Greeks, is a mythological gloss on the Egyptian god Seth, a god of chaos and outside/foreign influence on Egypt.
27 Trans. Burstein 1985, pp. 136–137.

ces of volcanically induced Nile failure during the period.[28] *Oracle* is often understood as an anti-Greek text in the form of prophesying the coming of a legitimate king in the context of chaos and a deeply disturbed world.[29] Even if not explicit, the text clearly alludes to the Seleukid invasion of Egypt by Antiochus IV, 170–168 BCE, an event that had major repercussions in the Mediterranean world, not least in triggering Roman intervention to prevent Seleukid domination of Egypt. It is possible that the timing of the invasion could be associated, in part, with poor Nile flooding. But despite its important historical context, the primary scholarly focus has been on the religious aspects of the prophecy, less on imperial dynamics, and even less on the climatic and environmental conditions that it literally recounts in vivid detail.

The results of Nile flood failure and environmental stress are turned into a commentary on legitimate kingship and "weaponized" against the Ptolemaic kings. This is not nationalism *per se*. Rather, it is very clever propaganda joined with the widely held belief system that connected legitimate kingship and the Nile flood. The text, then, can be read as a literal description of the impact of an explosive volcanic eruption: dust veils obscuring the sun, failure of the Nile flood, reduced agricultural production, dust, and landscape degradation, the inevitable coming of the collector of the harvest tax despite the dire conditions, and social unrest. Since the text of the *Oracle* had a long editorial history, there would be little point in trying to establish a precise historical context, but it would certainly fit the middle of the second century BCE very well.

Paleoclimatology was in its infancy when Bell and Butzer published their important work on Nile flooding and political instability. Climate sciences have advanced remarkably in the last thirty years. Climate proxy records now are on decadal, annual and in some cases now sub-annual time scales. This changes how we can understand the interaction of human societies and their environments potentially on an annual scale, allowing us to integrate historical and climate data on the same scale for the first time. Ptolemaic Egypt provides rich historical evidence with which to work, and with new climate data we can begin to build a more dynamic understanding of Egyptian history at a pivotal moment.

---

**28** Manning et al. 2017.
**29** For comments on the text, see *inter alia* Eddy 1961; Koenen 1968; Burstein 1985, pp. 136–139; Collins 1994; Gozzoli 2006, pp. 297–301; Beyerle 2017.

# Bibliography

ʿAbd al- Laṭīf al-Baghdādī ʿAbd al- Laṭīf al-Baghdādī, *A Physician on the Nile: A Description of Egypt and Journal of the Famine Years*, T. Mackintosh-Smith (trans.), New York, 2021.

Barry 1993
: Barry, W.D., "The Crowd of Ptolemaic Alexandria and the Riot of 203 B.C.", *EMC* 37/3, 1993, pp. 415–431.

Bell 1975
: Bell, B., "Climate and the History of Egypt: The Middle Kingdom", *AJA* 79/3, 1975, pp. 223–269.

Beyerle 2017
: Beyerle, S., "Authority and Propaganda: The Case of the *Potter's Oracle*", in J. Baden, H. Naiman, E. J.C. Tigchelaar (eds.), *Sibyls, Scriptures, and Scrolls: John Collins at Seventy*, Supplements to the Journal for the Study of Judaism 175, Leiden, Boston, 2017, pp. 167–184.

Bingen 2007
: Bingen, J., *Hellenistic Egypt: Monarchy, Society, Economy, Culture – Edited with an Introduction by Roger S. Bagnall*, Edinburgh, 2007.

Burstein 1985
: Burstein, S.M., *The Hellenistic Age from the Battle of Ipsos to the Death of Kleopatra VII*, Cambridge, 1985.

Butzer 1984
: Butzer, K.W., "Long-term Nile Flood Variation and Political Discontinuities in Pharaonic Egypt", in J.D. Clark, S.A. Brandt (eds.), *From Hunters to Farmers: The Causes and Consequences of Food Production in Africa*, Berkeley, 1984, pp. 102–112.

Butzer 2012
: Butzer, K.W., "Collapse, Environment, Society", *Proceedings of the National Academy of Sciences of the United States of America* 109/10, 2012, pp. 3632–3639.

Clarysse 1978
: Clarysse, W., "Hurgonaphor et Chaonnophris, les derniers pharaons indigènes", *CdE* 53, 1978, pp. 243–253.

Collins 1994
: Collins, J.J., "The Sibyl and the Potter: Political Propaganda in Ptolemaic Egypt", in L. Bormann, K. Del Tredici, A. Standhartinger (eds.), *Religious Propaganda and Missionary Competition in the New Testament World: Essays Honoring Dieter Georgi*, NovTest-Suppl. 74, Leiden, New York, Cologne, 1994, pp. 57–69.

Eddy 1961
: Eddy, S.K., The King is Dead: Studies in the Near Eastern Resistance to Hellenism 334–31 BC, Lincoln, 1961.

El-Masry, Altenmüller, Thissen 2012
: El-Masry, Y., Altenmüller, H., Thissen, H.-J., *Das Synodaldekret von Alexandria aus dem Jahre 243 v. Chr.*, BSAK 11, Hamburg, 2012.

Engels 2017
: Engels, D., *Benefactors, Kings, Rulers: Studies on the Seleukid Empire between East and West*, StudHell 57, Leuven, Paris, Bristol, CT, 2017.

Gellner 2009
: Gellner, E., *Nations and Nationalism*, Ithaca, 2009.

Gorre, Veïsse 2020
> Gorre, G., Veïsse, A.-E., "Birth and Disappearance of the Priestly Synods in the Time of the Ptolemies", in G. Gorre, S. Wackenier (eds.), *Quand la fortune du royaume ne dépend pas de la vertu du prince. Un renforcement de la monarchie lagide de Ptolémée VI à Ptolémée X (169–88 av. J.-C.)?*, StudHell 59, Leuven, Paris, Bristol, CT, 2020, pp. 113–139.

Gozzoli 2006
> Gozzoli, R.B., *The Writing of History in Ancient Egypt during the First Millennium BC (ca. 1070–180 BC): Trends and Perspectives*, GHP Egyptology 5, London, 2006.

Hölbl 2001
> Hölbl, G., *A History of the Ptolemaic Empire*, London, 2001.

Johstono 2016
> Johstono, P., "Insurgency in Ptolemaic Egypt", in T. Howe, L.L. Brice (eds.), *Brill's Companion to Insurgency and Terrorism in the Ancient Mediterranean*, Leiden, Boston, 2016, pp. 183–215.

Koenen 1968
> Koenen, L., "Die Prophezeiungen des 'Töpfers'", *ZPE* 2, 1968, pp. 178–209.

Ludlow, Manning 2016
> Ludlow, F., Manning, J.G., "Revolts under the Ptolemies: A Paleoclimatological Perspective", in J.J. Collins, J.G. Manning (eds.), *Revolt and Resistance in the Ancient Classical World and the Near East: In the Crucible of Empire*, CHANE 85, Leiden, Boston, pp. 154–171.

Manning 2018
> Manning, J.G., *The Open Sea: The Economic Life of the Ancient Mediterranean World from the Iron Age to the Rise of Rome*, Princeton, 2018.

Manning et al. 2017
> Manning, J.G., Ludlow, F., Stine, A.R., Boos, W.R., Sigl, M., Marlon, J.R., "Volcanic Suppression of Nile Summer Flooding Triggers Revolt and Constrains Interstate Conflict in Ancient Egypt", *Nature Communications* 8:900, 2017, DOI: 10.1038/s41467-017-00957-y.

McGing 1997
> McGing, B.G., "Revolt Egyptian Style: Internal Opposition to Ptolemaic Rule", *AfP* 43, 1997, pp. 274–314.

Moreno García 2019
> Moreno García, J.C., *The State in Ancient Egypt: Power, Challenges and Dynamics*, Debates in Archaeology, London, New York, 2019.

Peremans 1978
> Peremans, W., "Les révolutions égyptiennes sous les Lagides", in H. Maehler, V.M. Strocka (eds.), *Das ptolemäische Ägypten: Akten des internationalen Symposions 27.–29. September 1976 in Berlin*, Mainz, 1978, pp. 39–50.

Pestman 1995
> Pestman, P.W., "Haronnophris and Chaonnophris: Two Indigenous Pharaohs in Ptolemaic Egypt (205–186 BC)", in S.P. Vleeming (ed.), *Hundred-Gated Thebes: Acts of a Colloquium on Thebes and the Theban Area in the Graeco-Roman Period*, P.L.Bat. 27, Leiden, New York, Cologne, 1995, pp. 101–137.

Recklinghausen 2018
> Recklinghausen, D. von, *Die Philensis-Dekrete: Untersuchungen über zwei Synodaldekrete aus der Zeit Ptolemaios' V. und ihre geschichtliche und religiöse Bedeutung*, ÄA 73, Wiesbaden, 2018.

Rowlandson 2007
> Rowlandson, J., "The Character of Ptolemaic Aristocracy: Problems of Definition and Evidence", in T. Rajak, S. Pearce, J. Aitken, J. Dines (eds.), *Jewish Perspectives on Hellenistic Rulers*, HCS 50, Berkeley, Los Angeles, London, 2007, pp. 29–49.

Said 1993
> Said, R., *The River Nile: Geology, Hydrology, Utilization*, Oxford, 1993.

Strootman 2017
> Strootman, R., *The Birdcage of the Muses: Patronage of the Arts and Sciences at the Ptolemaic Imperial Court, 305–222 BCE*, Interdisciplinary Studies in Ancient Culture and Religion 17, Leuven, Paris, Bristol, CT, 2017.

Tilly 2003
> Tilly, C., *The Politics of Collective Violence*, Cambridge, 2003.

Vandorpe 1995
> Vandorpe, K., "City of Many a Gate, Harbour for Many a Rebel: Historical and Topographical Outline of Greco-Roman Thebes", in S.P. Vleeming (ed.), *Hundred Gated Thebes: Acts of a Colloquium on Thebes and the Theban Area in the Graeco-Roman Period*, P.L.Bat. 27, Leiden, New York, Cologne, 1995, pp. 203–239.

Veïsse 2004
> Veïsse, A.-E., *Les "révoltes égyptiennes". Recherches sur les troubles intérieurs en Égypte du règne de Ptolémée III à la conquête romaine*, StudHell 41, Leuven, Paris, Dudley, MA, 2004.

Wilkinson 2010
> Wilkinson, T., *The Rise and Fall of Ancient Egypt: The History of a Civilisation from 3000 BC to Cleopatra*, London, 2010.

Williams 2019
> Williams, M., *The Nile Basin: Quaternary Geology, Geomorphology and Prehistoric Environments*, Cambridge, 2019.

Martina Minas-Nerpel
# Arsinoe, Berenice, and Cleopatra: The 'ABC' of the Ptolemaic Ruler Cult in the Times of Crisis

In his article "Ruler, court, and power: the king and institutions in early Egypt", John Baines states that "Kings cannot rule alone. They rule through other people, through rituals, through institutions, and especially through expectations that are set up and manipulated".[1] This is true for all periods of ancient Egypt, and especially so under foreign domination. For the early Hellenistic rulers of Egypt, the use of the diverse traditions was crucial to form Ptolemaic Egypt, but this also raised diverse expectations. The Ptolemies faced an immense task in constructing an identity for their country and reign, for which they used the ancient Egyptian past and concepts, which go back several thousands of years, to create a successful social imaginary. It became vital to emphasise the divine status of the royal couple and dynastic unity, for which the queen was instrumental. This led to the creation of various forms of ruler and dynastic cults, which were expanded, adjusted, and manipulated over almost three hundred years of Ptolemaic history. The ruler cult, as much as that of Sarapis which was launched under Ptolemy I Soter, extended under Ptolemy II Philadelphos, and linked to the ruler cult,[2] created a means of connection and shared identification for Egypt's various ethnic groups from diverse cultural backgrounds. This paper investigates, with a particular focus on the powerful queens, some of the rituals, institutions, and expectations that were set up under Ptolemaic rule before, during, and after the times of crisis in the Thebaid.

---

1 Baines 2019, p. 239.
2 See Pfeiffer 2008b, pp. 387–408.

---

**Note:** I am very grateful Ralph Birk and Laurent Coulon for inviting me to Berlin for a very stimulating conference in May 2019, to Kenneth Griffin and René Preys for reading a draft of this chapter.

# 1 Setting the Scene: the Ptolemaic Ruler and Dynastic Cults

The Ptolemaic ruler and dynastic cults had different forms and components, depending on the context.[3] On the Greek side, there were two forms. Firstly, the ruler cult, which had its roots outside Egypt;[4] it is not the focus of this contribution. Secondly, the eponymous or dynastic cult, which started as a cult for Alexander the Great. From Ptolemy II onwards, the Ptolemaic couples were added to Alexander's cult, and some of the queens received priesthoods of their own.[5] Thirdly, the Egyptian ruler cult of the Ptolemies, which was, at least partly, based on age-old Egyptian traditions and understandings, with innovative components added. The Ptolemies as deified rulers turned into mortal gods,[6] received or shared temples with the immortal gods, Greek and Egyptian, they owned altars on which they received offerings, they were revered during religious and royal festivals and in related rituals, in which they were bestowed with the same honours as the immortal gods.

Alexander and the Ptolemies used the sacral legitimation of the Egyptian kingship. By ensuring the divine support for them, the Egyptian priests implied their own strong position. The institution of ancient Egyptian kingship, so central to Egyptian culture, was long-lived. It dominated Egyptian society for several thousands of years and survived numerous foreign conquests, in part because of the divine status with which the ruler was credited. In all periods the pharaoh depended on the gods. The ruler was regarded and presented as the living manifestation of Horus. The kingship, assumed by a mortal ruler who needed divine legitimation, was a demonstration of the power of the creator god. According to the *Myth of the Divine Birth*, attested from the Old Kingdom onwards,[7] the pharaoh was the bodily offspring of the gods and thus their deputy. Such myths were mobilised politically and used to establish and reinforce the king's and the dynasty's claim to the throne.[8]

This contribution focuses on the question of how the times of crisis affected the Ptolemaic ruler cult and how much we can actually grasp of it in the sources available. These sources include, for the purpose of this paper, hieroglyphic tem-

---

3 For a summary of the cult forms, see Pfeiffer 2008a.
4 For a summary, see Pfeiffer 2019, pp. 430–431.
5 Clarysse, van der Veken 1983; Minas 2000; Caneva 2016, chapters 4–5.
6 For this definition of deified rulers as mortal gods, see Pfeiffer 2019, p. 429.
7 Megahed, Vymazalová 2015, pp. 155–164. A full version of the myth is known from the reign of Hatshepsut in the Eighteenth Dynasty, see Brunner 1991.
8 For the context, see Goebs, Baines 2018, pp. 653–657.

ple inscriptions and Egyptian ritual scenes on the one hand, and the eponymous priesthoods as recorded in the praescripts of Greek and Demotic papyri on the other hand. The absence of evidence does not necessarily mean, of course, that established cult rituals were not continued or priests were not appointed, although it can mean exactly that. Very occasionally, we find direct references in this respect, for example in *P. dem. Tor. Botti* from Deir el-Medina, which dates to the month of Phamenoth (7 April to 6 May) 187 BCE. It is also dated according to the eponymous priests in Alexandria. Instead of the name of the priest serving in the eponymous cult of Ptolemy I Soter and the living king in Ptolemais follows the remark *jrm p3 ntj jw(?) pr-ꜥ3 r ḥn-s r jr⸗f wꜥb Ptlwmjs p3 s3wtr*, "and (at the time of) the one whom Pharaoh will appoint as priest of Ptolemy Soter".[9] The situation in the Thebaid was obviously still unstable, so the eponymous priest of Alexander was not yet appointed and Ptolemy V Epiphanes was not yet included in the cult. *P. dem. BM Reich 10226* from Thebes, dating to the 18 Phamenoth of Epiphanes' twentieth regnal year (23 February 185 BCE), is the first papyrus after the uprising to be dated to both the eponymous priests in Alexandria and Ptolemais.[10]

For the construction of a Ptolemaic ruler ideology, with its Egyptian and Greek components and cults, the creation and presentation of a specific Hellenistic queenship was instrumental.[11] This paper will concentrate on the powerful Ptolemaic queens, starting with Arsinoe II, the sister-wife of Ptolemy II Philadelphos. She was the first queen to be venerated in the eponymous cult, not only as part of the deified royal couple, but also in her own right by her own priestess. And it was with Arsinoe II, introduced as a *synnaos thea* (co-templar or temple-sharing) goddess, that the Ptolemaic ruler cult found its starting point in the Egyptian temples. It then developed and was manipulated for more than two centuries, not only by the kings, but also decisively by the queens. This paper is thus structured in three main parts: in the first step (section 2), the beginnings and developments of the cults before the times of crisis in the Thebaid are investigated, in the second (section 3), those during the times of crisis. The third step (section 4) intends to shed light on the question of how the cults were affected and changed after the times of crisis.

---

[9] Zauzich 1971, p. 44, improved the original reading of Botti 1967, p. 25.
[10] For the details and the context, see Minas 2000, p. 127.
[11] See, for example, Winter 1978; Quaegebeur 1978; Minas 2000; Pfeiffer 2008a; Minas-Nerpel 2019a; Minas-Nerpel 2019b.

## 2 The Dynastic Cult and Ruler Cult before the Times of Crisis

### 2.1 Ptolemy I Soter

In 290/289 BCE, Ptolemy I introduced an eponymous cult for Alexander the Great as *ktistes* (city founder) in Alexandria.[12] Although Ptolemy I received divine honours outside Egypt,[13] he did not associate himself with Alexander's eponymous cult in Egypt's new capital city. Hence, he was not seeking the same honours as Alexander, but he clearly linked Ptolemaic power to the great Macedonian king.

### 2.2 Ptolemy II Philadelphos and Arsinoe II

Ptolemy II changed this framework lastingly by several measures on different levels. On the one hand, he took Alexander's eponymous cult a step further by associating himself and his sister-wife Arsinoe II with it, thus seeking in 272/271 BCE divinity for the *Theoi Adelphoi*. By adding the subsequent ruling Ptolemaic couples during their lifetime from Ptolemy IV Philopator onwards and the retrospective inclusion of the first Ptolemaic couple from 214 BCE,[14] this cult consequently developed into a dynastic cult. In its Hellenistic expression, the Ptolemaic self-presentation was thus clearly anchored in the cult of Alexander.

The epithet *Theoi Adelphoi* referred to the sibling marriage, meant to be understood as a *hieros gamos* or holy union of Osiris and Isis or Zeus and Hera. The *Theoi Adelphoi* thus absorbed both Egyptian and Greek mythologies and transformed them into historic reality.[15] This also resulted in a new and enhanced role of the queen. Already during her lifetime Arsinoe II became critical to the projection of the image of the Ptolemaic dynasty. Her importance increased after her death in 270 BCE, also by receiving her own eponymous cult in Alexandria. It was performed by a *kanephoros*, a 'basket bearer',[16] and mentioned in the prescripts

---

12 Minas 2000, pp. 87–89 (with references to the evidence).
13 According to Pausanias, *Hellados Periegesis*, 1.8.6, and Diodorus Siculus, *Bibliotheca historica*, 20.99–100, Ptolemy son of Lagus was venerated as a god in a *polis* cult after having saved Rhodes from being conquered by Demetrius Poliorcetes in 305 BCE. See Hölbl 2001, p. 22; Caneva 2018, pp. 108–109 (with further references).
14 See Minas 2000, pp. 112–114.
15 Lembke 2012, pp. 209–211; Carney 2013, pp. 49–64. More generally on close-kin marriages in Egypt, see Frandsen 2009, esp. pp. 48–60 (Graeco-Roman Egypt).
16 See Minas 1998, pp. 43–60; Bailey 1999, pp. 156–160.

of Greek and Demotic papyri directly after the Alexander priest. This priestess of Arsinoe II was only the first in a long list of personal priesthoods for Ptolemaic queens, but it set, in many respects, the example or goal to which subsequent female rulers tried to live up.

New features of the ruler cult were introduced to the Egyptian temples. The starting point was established by decreeing that the deceased Arsinoe II was to be venerated as a *synnaos thea* in all Egyptian temples, as attested on the Mendes Stela, which records not only the installation of a new sacred ram in the Delta city, but also the introduction of Arsinoe's cult to all temples of Egypt, with her statues being placed beside those of the main deities.[17] Arsinoe II thus became a goddess in her own right, not only as a part of the royal couple. This is also emphasised by private dedications such as the stela of Totoes (Fig. 1), a *pastophoros* (priest) and *nautes* (sailor) of Arsinoe II.[18] The stela shows the deified Arsinoe II with her distinctive personal crown,[19] facing a figure of an Egyptian god, now lost except for his lunar crown, with whom she is worshipped as his *synnaos thea*.

In the Hellenic environment, one of the most extraordinary images of Arsinoe must have been planned for her sanctuary at Cape Zephyrium east of Alexandria, where the queen, probably already before her death in 270 BCE, was worshipped as Aphrodite. According to Pliny, her statue suspended by magnetic fields was to be positioned in the temple's centre, but this project was never completed.[20] Two epigrams of the Hellenistic poet Posidippus, generally placed before Arsinoe's death in 270 BCE,[21] celebrate this sanctuary, which is now completely destroyed. It was dedicated by Callicrates of Samos, the supreme commander of the royal navy from the 270s to the 250s, who had a specific interest in promoting this aspect of Arsinoe during her life-time.[22] As a loyal supporter of the Ptolemaic rulers and brilliant strategist, Callicrates' obvious intention was to mediate with novel approaches between the Greek traditions and the new policies of Ptolemaic Egypt. By many Classical scholars the sanctuary at Cape Zephyrium is regarded as

---

17 The Mendes Stela is housed in the Egyptian Museum Cairo, CG 22181, see Kamal 1904, vol. II, pls. LIV–LV. For the specific part of the inscription, see Urk. II, 41.11; Schäfer 2011, pp. 262–263.
18 For the publication of the stela, now in a private collection, see Albersmeier, Minas 1998, pp. 3–29. For the office of a *pastophoros*, see Hoffmann, Quack 2014, pp. 127–156.
19 Nilsson 2012; for additional information, see Minas-Nerpel 2019a, pp. 157–160.
20 Pliny, *Naturalis historia* 34, 148. Strabo, *Geographica*, 17.800 (XVII.1.16), described the location. For the reconstruction of the temple and its cult statue, see Pfrommer 2002, pp. 61–69.
21 Posidippus, *Epigrams* 116 and 119: Nisetich 2005, pp. 43–44; see Fraser 1972, vol. I: p. 239, vol. II: p. 389 (n. 393); Stephens 2003, pp. 181–182; Minas-Nerpel 2019b, pp. 199–200.
22 See Hauben 1970, pp. 41–46 (with further references), and Bing 2002–2003, pp. 243–266.

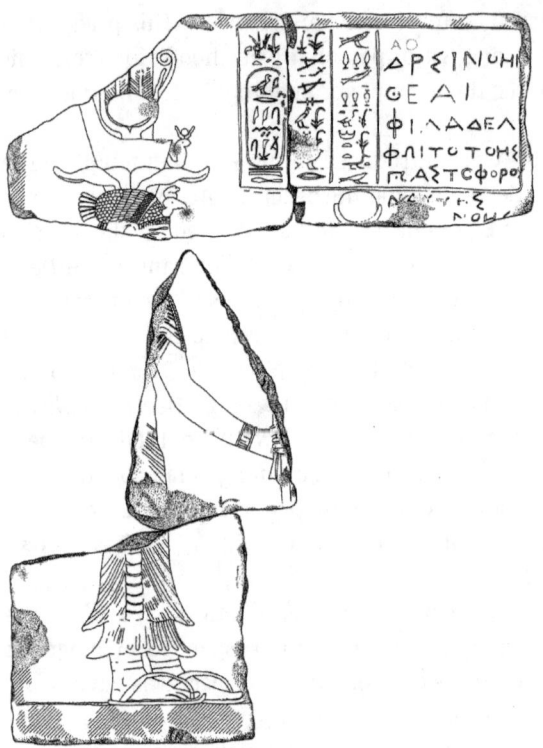

**Fig. 1:** Stela of Totoes (Albersmeier, Minas 1998, p. 8, Fig. 2).

the most important of the Ptolemaic temples to Arsinoe,[23] but Posidippus' poetic references are almost the only source. Susan Stephens therefore questions the real significance of this cult and wonders whether it might simply have been the subject for poetic promotion. She points out that in modern discussions, there is a tendency to construct rites and prerogatives for the temple based only on the evidence of the few poems preserved. She therefore assumes that Posidippus' promotion might have acted as a magnet to draw other events or poems into its orbit.[24] We are not able to solve this question about this specific cult of Arsinoe II, but its impact was substantial, because it spread rather swiftly in the Mediterranean, to harbours and cities, which were Ptolemaic possessions or influenced by

---

**23** For references and a short discussion of the different poetic sources, see Stephens 2005, pp. 245–248; Müller 2009, pp. 215–216.
**24** Stephens 2005, pp. 246–247.

the Ptolemaic navy.[25] Egypt was a power at sea, and the sphere of influence of the Ptolemaic navy throughout the Mediterranean was expanded by using the figure of the queen, now Aphrodite Euploia ("She of fair sailing"), as patroness of the maritime empire.

In ancient Egypt, Isis was not connected to the sea or worshipped with an epiclesis such as *Euploia, Pelagia*, or their Egyptian equivalents; she was rather connected with the wind and the fluvial navigation.[26] Laurent Bricault suggests a transfer of the epithet *Euploia* from Aphrodite to Isis via Arsinoe.[27] The evolution of Arsinoe's marine aspects, essentially Greek in origin, were largely promoted by the actions of the admiral Callicrates by founding her sanctuary and cult on Cape Zephyrium. We can trace such cultic transfers also with the help of an Egyptian epithet of Arsinoe II, *wḏꜣ(.t) bꜣ*, attested for her on the aforementioned Mendes Stela, where Arsinoe is praised with various epithets.[28] Directly after being designated as *mrj(.t) bꜣ* "beloved by the ram", she is called *wḏꜣ(.t) bꜣ*,[29] "the whole one of the ram", meaning "the perfect one of the ram", creating a parallelism with the preceding epithet *mrj(.t) bꜣ*.

The epithet *wḏꜣ.t bꜣ* is very rarely attested, usually only as a designation of Isis,[30] to be found in hymns to this goddess in the Graeco-Roman period, for the first time in her temple at Aswan, dating to the time of Ptolemy IV Philopator, which is two generations after Arsinoe II was first praised with it.[31] An almost verbatim copy of the Aswan hymn is preserved in the temple at Kalabsha, dating to the time of Augustus.[32] In the temple of Hathor at Dendera, the epithet is re-

---

25 Carney 2013, p. 98.
26 See Barbanti 2005, p. 151; Merkelbach 1995, p. 66.
27 See Bricault 2006, especially pp. 18, 26–29, 33, 101–103, 177–178.
28 Urk. II, 40, 1–2 (line 11). For a detailed discussion of this epithet *wḏꜣ.t bꜣ*, see Minas-Nerpel 2019a, pp. 151–157.
29 Roeder 1959, p. 181, translated "die den Bock pflegt". According to Schäfer 2011, pp. 248, 261 (ns. 204–205), it is a title of a priestess. Thiers 2007, p. 65, n. 11, translates the epithets as "aimée du bélier, celui qui est sain (?)", viewing *wḏꜣ* as an adjective describing the ram rather than the queen. In contrast, I see the epithets as a whole characterise Arsinoe II. Nilsson 2012, pp. 142, 157, renders the epithet as "She who is the high priestess of Ba-neb-djedet", wishing to see the queen as "the earthly wife of the local ram god of Mendes—that is, a God's wife" (p. 116). For Arsinoe as a god's wife, see Minas-Nerpel 2019a, pp. 161–165.
30 *LGG* II, p. 649b, s.v. *wḏꜣ.t bꜣ* "Die Pflegerin (?) des Ba", notes the epithet for Isis only, not for Arsinoe II.
31 Bresciani, Pernigotti 1978, pp. 80–81: C11; Minas-Nerpel 2019a, p. 152 (with n. 55); Nagel 2019, p. 122, n. 566.
32 Gauthier 1911, pp. 15–16; Minas-Nerpel 2019a, p. 152 (with n. 56); Nagel 2019, p. 122, n. 566: the ram headed Khnum replaces the ram god Ba in this epithet.

peated in slightly different form twice, dating to the time of Cleopatra VII.[33] It hence appears, on present evidence, as if Arsinoe II received this title first. It is not until the reign of Ptolemy IV that Isis is attested with this title in her temple at Aswan. The use for Isis was then probably meant to strengthen the goddess' role as a queen by assigning her an epithet of Arsinoe,[34] the dynastically powerful queen *par excellence*, rather than the other way around.

As is discussed in section 3 below, major changes were introduced under Ptolemy IV in the dynastic cults, and it seems that this transfer of the Mendes epithet from the deified queen Arsinoe II to the immortal goddess Isis has been part of a greater concept, developed shortly before the uprising in the Thebaid that resulted in a major crisis of the Ptolemaic kingdom. These changes under Philopator were made possible by the initiatives introduced under and for his parents Ptolemy III and Berenice II. The visual results manifest themselves specifically in Thebes in temple reliefs, as is demonstrated in the next sub-section (2.3).

## 2.3 Ptolemy III Euergetes I and Berenice II

When in 243 BCE Ptolemy III and his wife Berenice II were associated as *Theoi Euergetai* to the eponymous cult of Alexander and the *Theoi Adelphoi*, their legitimacy and hereditary connection to their direct predecessors, ancestral in nature, and the great Macedonian king, political in nature, was emphasised.[35] It was not yet a full dynastic cult since the first Ptolemaic couple was still excluded, which would only change under the next Ptolemaic ruler (see below, section 3).

From the early Ptolemaic Period onwards, the Egyptian priests met regularly in assemblies, mainly in or around Alexandria and Memphis, establishing Egyptian forms of ruler and dynastic cults. The resulting honorific decrees were published in Greek, hieroglyphic Egyptian, and Demotic. The first attested example of such a synodal decree is that of Alexandria, dating to 3 December 243 BCE,[36] the same year in which the ruling couple was added to the Alexander cult. This synod of 243 met in the capital in the temple of Isis and the *Theoi Adelphoi*,[37] not only

---

[33] *Dend.* XII, 2, 6; *Dend.* XIV, 146, 8; Minas-Nerpel 2019a, pp. 152–153 (with ns. 57–58): the ram headed Khnum replaces again the ram god Ba in both epithets.
[34] For Isis and other goddesses as queens, see Hoffmann 2015, pp. 146–147.
[35] See Minas 2000, p. 102: *PSI IV* 389 from August–September 243 BCE is the earliest papyrus to attest this.
[36] El-Masry, Altenmüller, Thissen 2012. See Huss 1991, pp. 201–203, and Gorre, Veïsse 2020, pp. 115–125, for a list of the known seventeen synods.
[37] Line 19: El-Masry, Altenmüller, Thissen 2012, pp. 78, 81–82, 201.

demonstrating the dynastic connection but also the importance of Isis, which was further emphasised under Ptolemy IV (see below, section 3). The synod in Alexandria resulted in Ptolemy III and his wife Berenice II being henceforth venerated as *synnaoi theoi* of the immortal gods.

Already under Ptolemy II, the Egyptian priests seemed to have met in synods, but no decrees survive, although the years before and after the death of Arsinoe II (270 BCE) were marked by intense exchanges between the king and the Egyptian priesthoods.[38] We might therefore assume that already in the time of the second Ptolemy, the native priests developed their own forms of ruler cults by transforming the king into an Egyptian god. This would have been consistent with the Greek approach, as attested, for example, by Posidippus, who stated that Ptolemy II was "god and king at once".[39] Originally from Pella in Macedon, this court poet lived and worked in Alexandria between 300 and 250 BCE, probably with the support of Ptolemy II.[40] Ptolemaic propaganda developed the Hellenistic ruler into a god king who was accorded a divine cult together with his consort. The Egyptian pharaoh, though his office was divine, had never been the object of such a cult.[41] This demonstrates the innovative thought processes in Ptolemaic Egypt and the need to present the rulers with newly constructed identities.

Likewise from the reign of Ptolemy III onwards, a new medium of the ruler cult was used in the Egyptian environment: the dynastic ancestors could be listed, characterised as *synnaoi theoi*, in hieroglyphic inscriptions right after the cartouches of the ruling king and queen. The dynasty was thus further established in the Egyptian temples. At the same time, it was highlighted that its power depended on divine and ancestral legitimation. So far, only one example is attested for the time of Ptolemy III on a fragment of a coffin for an Osiris figurine:[42] the reigning couple is not only beloved by Sokar Osiris, but also by the *Theoi Adelphoi*. As the dynasty grew, the lists became increasingly longer.[43] The last of these specific ancestor enumerations dates to the time of Ptolemy XII Neos Dionysos.[44] Alexander and the first Ptolemaic couple never appear in those, so Ptolemy II and Arsinoe II are the first rulers to be mentioned. Two facts are obvious: firstly, the great conqueror was thus not the source of legitimation in the Egyptian ruler

---

[38] See Huss 1991, pp. 189–190, referring to the synods in Sais in 266/265 and in Mendes in 264/263. See also Gorre, Veïsse 2020, pp. 115–121.
[39] Posidippus, AB 63.9: Nisetich 2005, p. 31.
[40] Thompson 2005, p. 272.
[41] For the ancient Egyptian king's divinity see, for example, Baines 1995, pp. 4–11.
[42] Minas 2006, pp. 202–204, Dok. 12.
[43] Minas 2000, pp. 3–79.
[44] Minas 2000, pp. 20–23: Dok. 44–48, pp. 27–28: Dok. 54.

cult, in contrast to the eponymous cult in Alexandria; and secondly, the starting point was not the first Ptolemaic couple, who are depicted, for example, in the lunette of the Kom el-Hisn Stela, which attests the Canopus Decree (238 BCE).[45] The starting point was in fact the second Ptolemaic couple, thus emphasising that it was Arsinoe II with whom this worship started in the Egyptian temples.

The iconographic expression of the Ptolemaic ruler cult, and thus the emphasis of legitimate rule, is first attested in Egyptian temples in a ritual scene on the propylon of the Khonsu Temple in Karnak, in which Ptolemy III is shown burning incense for his parents, the deceased Ptolemy II and Arsinoe II (Fig. 2).[46] This motif might have been influenced by a type of ritual scene attested on stela and on temple walls, in which Ptolemy II is depicted worshipping his deceased and deified sister-wife Arsinoe II.[47] In the axially corresponding scene of the Khonsu gate, Ptolemy III and Berenice II receive the divine rulership from Khonsu:[48] by composing the *jmj.t-pr* (testament), he performs a notarial act, by which he hands over to the king the possession of everything that exists (Fig. 3). This ritual thus legitimises the Ptolemaic reign. Two details of these two corresponding scenes are particularly important for this contribution. Firstly, Berenice II, as the ruling queen, is not included in the ritual action of venerating the deceased royal couple, despite the fact that she receives divine rulership from Khonsu in the corresponding scene, and secondly, Berenice II is described with a Horus name in the latter scene.

As for the first point, no *living* queen is ever included in such a ritual scene, in which the Ptolemaic ancestors are venerated from the time of Ptolemy III onwards,[49] apart from a single and highly unusual scene, which is located in the temple of Month at Tod: Ptolemy VIII, accompanied by his sister-wife Cleopatra II, burns incense and pours libations for several of their dynastic ancestors.[50] In the Ptolemaic Period divine and dynastic legitimation were very important, and the

---

**45** The Kom el-Hisn Stela is housed in the Egyptian Museum Cairo, CG 22186; see Kamal 1904–05, pls. 59–61; Pfeiffer 2004, pp. 28–38, Figs. 2–3.
**46** Clère 1961, pl. 61; Urk. VIII, 78–79 (= no. 93). For the royal cult expressions in the Ptolemaic ritual scenes from Ptolemy III onwards, see Preys 2015a, p. 204, and his contribution in this volume.
**47** See Quaegebeur 1971a, pp. 239–270; Quaegebeur 1971b, pp. 191–217; Quaegebeur 1978, pp. 245–262; Quaegebeur 1988, pp. 73–108; Caneva 2016, pp. 181–182; Minas-Nerpel 2021, pp. 117–146.
**48** Clère 1961, pl. 43.
**49** See Minas 2000, pp. 61–73, for a compilation and discussion of these ritual scenes, with references to Winter 1978, pp. 147–160, and Quaegebeur 1989, pp. 93–116.
**50** Thiers 2003, pp. 272–275: no. 318; see also Minas 2000, pp. 24–25: Dok. 51 (with further references): this specific scene at Tod should be understood as a visualised list of dynastic ancestors.

**Fig. 2:** Karnak, Temple of Khonsu, propylon: Ptolemy III burns incense for his parents, Ptolemy II and Arsinoe II (Clère 1961, pl. 61).

Egyptian priests and designers were familiar with the birth legends. The traditional divine triad in the Khonsu Temple consisted of Amun, Mut, and Khonsu, but in a transferred sense it could also comprise the *Theoi Adelphoi* and Ptolemy III: the ruling king as the divine child worships his parents. This identification would explain why the ruling queen was always excluded from Ptolemaic ancestor worship scenes and only three figures are depicted: the father and the mother on one side of the ritual scene and the child on the other. In a triad, there was no place for the living queen, an obvious limitation in the patterns of queenship.

The second point of interest in this context is the fact that Berenice II received a Horus name when her husband's and her own divine rule is established and confirmed by Khonsu. She is called ḥr.t sꜣ.t ḥqꜣ jrj(.t) n ḥqꜣ.t, "the female Horus: daughter of a ruler, born by a female ruler".[51] Before the Ptolemaic Period, the title of a female Horus is attested for some powerful queens in the Middle and

---

[51] Urk. VIII, 83, 7 (= no. 98a). For Berenice's Horus name, see also Eldamaty 2015, pp. 24–29; Cassor-Pfeiffer, Pfeiffer 2019, pp. 206–207.

**Fig. 3:** Karnak, Temple of Khonsu, propylon: Khonsu composes the *jmj.t-pr* (testament) for Ptolemy III and Berenice II (Clère 1961, pl. 43).

New Kingdoms, such as Sobekneferu of the Twelfth Dynasty, Hatshepsut of the Eighteenth Dynasty, and Tauseret of the Nineteenth Dynasty.[52] The God's Wives of Amun of the Third Intermediate Period were also designated as a female Horus.[53] Being a female Horus was a considerable advance in Berenice's status over Arsinoe II, but she was still defined via her relationship to Arsinoe II in order to strengthen her dynastic power. In other places, Berenice II received further epithets which are partially attested for queens in the Old Kingdom and for the God's Wives of Amun of the Late Period.[54] Only one is highlighted here as an example, since it refers back to a point made earlier: like the epithet *wḏꜣ.t bꜣ* of Arsinoe II (see above, section 2.2), the epithet "female vizier, Thoth's daughter", first attested for Berenice II, is transferred to Isis under Ptolemy IV in her temple in Aswan.[55] The use for Isis was again probably meant to strengthen the goddess'

---

[52] Troy 1986, pp. 139–143.
[53] See Eldamaty 2011, pp. 72–76; Koch 2012, p. 67; Aufderhaar 2016, pp. 143–144.
[54] Payraudeau 2015, pp. 209–225. See also Cassor-Pfeiffer, Pfeiffer 2019, pp. 199–238.
[55] Stadler 2009, p. 154; Cassor-Pfeiffer, Pfeiffer 2019, p. 211. For the context, see Nagel 2019, p. 539.

role as a queen, especially since the goddess could also be called, later on, a female Horus.[56]

The meaning of both corresponding scenes on the Khonsu propylon – the confirmation of the Ptolemaic rulers by immortal gods and the divine ancestors – was probably obvious to the ancient Egyptians, even to those who could not read the inscriptions. For people entering the sacred precinct of Khonsu through this gate, both scenes were just above the height of their heads, that is in the second register from the bottom on both the inner sides of the gate. Viewers could recognise the ruling king venerating his divine dynastic ancestors, and Arsinoe II could be identified by her distinctive crown, which was shown not only in temple decoration and on statues, but also on private monuments such as the aforementioned stela of Totoes (see Fig. 1). This private monument demonstrates that alongside the official cult instigated by the royal court there was popular devotion to Arsinoe II in the Egyptian environment.

These two scenes on the Khonsu propylon were an integral part of the decoration programme that was developed for the monumental gateways in Karnak.[57] The Khonsu gate, decorated under Ptolemy III, was the first of the Ptolemaic Period to be completed and thus contains the oldest scene so far known. Two further gateways in Karnak were embellished with these dynastic legitimation scenes, the gate of the Second Pylon[58] and the Montu gate.[59] It is, however, reasonable to suggest that ancestor worship scenes were present, and probably first created, in the north.[60] Except for the temple of Behbeit el-Hagar, temples north of Athribis are almost completely lost, but the Delta was of great importance to the Ptolemies and much closer to them than the Thebaid. The Alexandria Decree of 243[61] and the Kom el-Hisn Stela with the Canopus Decree of 238 BCE,[62] for ex-

---

56 *LGG* V, 297c; Nagel 2019, pp. 549–550.
57 Preys 2015a, pp. 159–215, esp. 160–169; Preys 2015b, pp. 149–184, esp. Fig. 1.
58 Preys 2015a, pp. 160–169, Figs. 3–4: Seshat inscribes the annals for Ptolemy VI and Cleopatra II, with the corresponding scene showing Ptolemy VI worshiping his ancestral deities, Ptolemy V and Cleopatra I. See Broze, Preys 2021, pp. 118–120, 133–135: Ka2Pyl 20 (*jmj.t-pr*) and Ka2Pyl 24 (ancestors).
59 Aufrère 2000, pp. 233–241, no. 13a. The Montu gate was completed under Ptolemy IV; Khonsu-Thoth confirms the rule of and the *jmj.t-pr* for Ptolemy III and Berenice II.
60 J. Yoyotte discussed this issue on the basis of other examples in his Collège de France courses 'Égyptologie' (*Annuaire du Collège de France* 92, 94, 95 of 1991–1995), edited and reprinted by Guermeur (ed.) 2013, pp. 497–607.
61 El-Masry, Altenmüller, Thissen 2012, p. 27 (with fig.), pp. 32–34 (with figs.), Taf. 3: the figure of Ptolemy I is almost erased and that of Berenice I entirely perished.
62 Egyptian Museum Cairo, CG 22186; see Pfeiffer 2004, pp. 28–38, Figs. 2–3.

ample, show the Ptolemaic ancestors in the lunette, including the first Ptolemaic couple, as discussed above.

Both Arsinoe II and Berenice II could be considered, in many ways, as prototypes for the powerful Ptolemaic queens who succeeded them. Berenice II, on the one hand, was the first Ptolemaic queen to be designated as a female Horus. Four of the Cleopatras followed her example: Cleopatra I, her daughter Cleopatra II, her grand-daughter Cleopatra III, and Cleopatra VII.[63] Berenice II thus surpassed Arsinoe II, but she was not the first queen in ancient Egypt to be designated as such. With Arsinoe II, on the other hand, the ruler cult started in the Egyptian temples. Ptolemy II successfully projected onto her the dynastic needs, and the deceased queen was as important for him as the living one. Through adoption Berenice II claimed her legitimacy and divine ancestry from the formidable Arsinoe II.[64] Had Ptolemy II tried to explain the consanguinity as a Zeus–Hera or Osiris–Isis union, his son even forced the impression of a feigned sibling marriage. Berenice II and Ptolemy III thus emulated the second Ptolemaic couple.[65] In a poem honouring the queen, Callimachus praised Berenice's devotion to the king.[66] She vowed to offer a lock of her hair in exchange for his safe return from the war. This lock was dedicated in the sanctuary at Cape Zephyrium, where Arsinoe II was worshipped as Aphrodite and Isis. Berenice II thus linked herself in cultic terms too with her immediate predecessor.

Berenice II also continued another aspect of her predecessor: the maritime connection of a Ptolemaic queen that was established for Arsinoe II was resumed under her direct successor, as is attested, for example, by the so called Sophilos mosaic in Alexandria.[67] It shows queen Berenice II in a *chlamys* and a suit of armour made of silver. In recognising her military power, the queen is crowned by the bow of a war ship, marking her as the mistress of the sea. This attribute em-

---

[63] See Eldamaty 2011, pp. 54–55, for an overview of their Horus names.

[64] See Huss 2001, p. 354; van Oppen 2015, p. 36, describes the adoption and devotion to Arsinoe II as the "full-scale absorption of Berenice II in the Lagide house".

[65] Nilsson 2012, p. 144, sees the adoption as supporting her interpretation of Arsinoe II as God's Wife, but one should note that the adoption process was not continued in the Ptolemaic dynasty, since the couples following Ptolemy III and Berenice II were mostly siblings or otherwise closely related, except for Ptolemy V and Cleopatra I.

[66] The poem survives in Catullus' translation (C. 66) and two papyri (*PSI* 1092 and *pOxy*. 2258C). For the evidence and a discussion, see Gutzwiller 1992, pp. 359–385, and Llewellyn-Jones, Winder 2016, pp. 139–162.

[67] Alexandria, Graeco-Roman Museum, inv. no. 21739. See Grimm 1999, pp. 80–81, fig. 81c; Pfrommer 2002, pp. 89–90, figs. 78a–b.

phasises her connection to Isis Pelagia, who was worshipped by the Greek population in this role.[68]

## 3 The Dynastic Cult and Ruler Cults Shortly before and during the Times of Crisis

Ptolemy IV became king of Egypt in 221 BCE and married his sister Arsinoe III within his first regnal year.[69] In 216/215 BCE, less than two years after the battle of Raphia in 217 BCE, the couple was introduced as *Theoi Philopatores* to the Alexander cult.[70] In the following year (215/214 BCE), far-reaching changes were set up in the dynastic cult: firstly, the first Ptolemaic couple was now included in the Alexander cult. Secondly, an additional eponymous cult was created, this time in Upper Egypt, and the emphasis was clearly not on Alexander: in Ptolemais Hermiu, its *ktistes* (city founder) Ptolemy I and his wife Berenice I as well as the ruling couple were now worshipped, copying in the Greek city of Upper Egypt the system that Ptolemy II once implemented in Alexandria.[71] The southern eponymous cults never developed as elaborately as those in the capital city.

Another three years later, in the twelfth regnal year of Ptolemy IV (211/210 BCE), a further eponymous priesthood was created posthumously for the king's mother, Berenice II,[72] who had been murdered after her son's ascension to the throne at the behest of Sosibios, the king's advisor.[73] Like her immediate predecessor, Arsinoe II, she was now honoured as a single queen by her own priestess, the *athlophoros* ("contest-prize bearer") – a fact that highlights the importance of both queens for the dynasty. Berenice II even gained priority over her adopted mother in the eponymous cult in Alexandria: in the dating formulae of documentary texts, the *athlophoros* was not just added to the dynastic priest of Alexander and the Ptolemies and Arsinoe's *kanephoros*, but was placed right before the *kanephoros*. Thus, the younger queen gained precedence over the older one, which was also demonstrated by the fact that the eponymous priestesses in Alexandria first served Berenice II and only in the

---

[68] Merkelbach 1995, p. 66, § 116 (Isis Pelagia), p. 116, § 212 (15).
[69] Hölbl 2001, pp. 127–128.
[70] Minas 2000, pp. 107–112.
[71] Minas 2000, pp. 112–116; Caneva 2016, p. 179.
[72] Minas 2000, pp. 116–119.
[73] Hölbl 2001, p. 128.

following year Arsinoe II.[74] In processions and cultic rituals, the *athlophoros* must have come first, too. Other queens, such as Cleopatra III, would try to surpass earlier queens by receiving more than one eponymous priesthood and by taking on the role of the Alexander priest herself, thus making the eponymous cult meaningless in the end.[75] It seems that from Berenice II onwards the queens, or perhaps the advisors around them, wanted to surpass the prestige gained so far, almost outplaying the earlier dynastic predecessors.

These drastic developments in the dynastic cult must have been carefully devised in Alexandria by elevating the first Ptolemaic couple, thus further legitimising and strengthening the Ptolemaic dynasty by developing the cult of Alexander the Great into a full dynastic cult. The emphasis of the eponymous cult in Alexandria was now on Alexander and all Ptolemaic couples. In addition, two queens, Arsinoe II and Berenice II, were singled out by separate priesthoods, reflecting their powerful status within the dynasty. Arsinoe III also received her own priestess in Alexandria, but only from the seventh year of her son Ptolemy V Epiphanes

**Fig. 4:** Karnak, Kiosk of Taharqa (photograph: M. Minas-Nerpel).

---

74 Minas 2000, pp. 117–118; Caneva 2016, p. 181.
75 Minas 2000, pp. 147–150, 157–161.

(199/198 BCE) onwards, when this priesthood was introduced during a further reorganisation of the eponymous cults in the middle of the Thebaid uprising.[76]

Under Ptolemy IV, the Egyptian temples also saw important changes in regard to the visual and textual display of divine and Ptolemaic interaction and the royal cult. As discussed above (see *supra*, sections 2.2–2.3), the royal epithets of Arsinoe II and Berenice II were transferred to Isis, thus enhancing the goddess' role as a ruler. A further detail is of immediate interest in this context, not only because of the divine legitimation of the Ptolemaic rulers, but also because it is directly connected with the times of crisis in the Thebaid and located in the heart of this area, in the temple of Amun-Ra in Karnak. During the 7$^{th}$ century BCE, under the Kushite king Taharqa, a kiosk was built in the temple of Amun-Ra on the central axis in the middle of the first courtyard (Fig. 4).[77] It comprised originally two rows of five columns, of which only one remains standing at full height.[78] The columns are connected by screen walls, which were restored under Ptolemy IV Philopator.[79] These intercolumnar walls were decorated on the exterior and interior, divided in each case into two parts, a *soubassement* and an upper register. The *soubassement* comprised processions of nomes. The ritual scenes of the upper register are destroyed in most cases, but parts of the scenes on the northern walls are preserved up to a height of around 20 cm, displaying the feet of the divine and royal actors. In one of these ritual scenes, TahKiosk E4 (Figs. 5a–b) on panel 4 on the exterior of the northern walls, this is sufficient to determine the type of scene: the king and queen are turning their backs to the sanctuary and hold in their hands the divine sceptres, the king the *wꜣs*-sceptre and the queen the *wꜣḏ*-sceptre. The king wears sandals and the so-called 'Macedonian mantle',[80] of which only the fringes are preserved. Before him, two divinities

---

[76] Minas 2000, pp. 120–131, esp. 125.
[77] PM II, pp. 24–25 (14)–(24). Barguet 1962a, pp. 47, 50–51; Lauffray 1970; Lauffray 1975. For the history of the kiosk before the Ptolemaic Period, see Hourdin 2018 and Hourdin in preparation.
[78] The Taharqa Kiosk is often connected with the other colonnades erected under this king, but their layout is different, see Leclant 1965, pp. 56–58 (East colonnade), p. 84 (South colonnade), pp. 85–86 (North colonnade).
[79] For the Ptolemaic renovations of the Taharqa Kiosk, see Minas-Nerpel, Preys 2023.
[80] From at least the time of Ptolemy III onwards, this mantle is attested in the royal representation, for example, in the aforementioned scene dedicated to the divine legitimation of the ruling couple on the gate of the Khonsu Temple in Karnak (see Fig. 3 above). Warda 2012, pp. 75–79, suggests that this can be understood as an extension to a foreign ruler of the representational scheme used by the Egyptian priestly class for the purpose of self-definition. For a discussion of the mantle, see also Bianchi 1978, pp. 65–102. Preys (2015b) argues that the fact that it was used for the king indicated that he was also a human being and not only a god. For this garment in a non-royal iconography, see Coulon 2001, p. 87, and Perdu 2012, pp. 50–53. A voluminous fringed

conduct for him the ritual of producing and presenting the *jmj.t-pr* (testament). During the reign of Ptolemy IV Philopator, this scene, which was introduced to the temples under his father Ptolemy III Euergetes I, as attested on the Khonsu propylon discussed above (see *supra*, section 2.2 and Fig. 3),[81] was transformed into a ritual of presenting the sword of victory to the king. This is, for example, attested in the temple of Sobek and Haroeris at Kom Ombo, where Haroeris presents Ptolemy VIII, accompanied by Cleopatra II and Cleopatra III, with the sword of victory (Fig. 6).[82] This exact type of scene, the presentation of the sword of victory, was engraved on the panel of the Kiosk of Taharqa, combined with the composition of the *jmj.t-pr*: the lower parts of a reed with frogs attached are visible above the feet of the second figure, a goddess, who was probably depicted writing the text of the *jmj.t-pr* on it. Such parts of a reed were not present above the feet of the first god (see Figs. 5a–b). This means that the god was probably stretching his arm towards the king to present him the sword of victory, which is destroyed. The versions of this cult scene dating to the reign of Ptolemy IV always combine the presentation of the *jmj.t-pr* or the sword of victory with a corresponding ritual scene dedicated to the royal ancestors.[83] It is therefore possible that such an ancestor veneration scene was engraved on the corresponding panel of the southern walls of the Kiosk (TahKiosk E10 on panel 10), which is now completely destroyed.

Several of the panels of the Kiosk's intercolumnar walls were left undecorated. It seems that under Ptolemy IV the Taharqa Kiosk needed drastic restoration and new intercolumnar walls were erected.[84] While they were in the process of decoration, a major crisis broke out in the Thebaid in 207/206 BCE. All construction and decoration works were stopped in the area of unrest, as is attested in the

---

mantle is also depicted in the tomb of Petosiris at Tuna el-Gebel, where he, his male family members, and officials are represented with this garment; see, for example, Cherpion et al. 2007, pp. 33, 36–38, 56, 80. The tomb's pronaos shows strong Hellenistic influence, presenting a mixed Hellenising art style with Egyptian and Greek elements, demonstrating that the native elite engaged with the new Hellenistic rulers and their style.

**81** For the origin of this scene and the changes throughout the Ptolemaic Period, see Preys 2016, Preys 2020, and the contribution by René Preys in this volume. For the historical implications and the importance for the history of the Kiosk of Taharqa, see Chapter 4 of Minas-Nerpel, Preys 2023.

**82** *Kom Ombos* I, 462; PM VI, p. 189 (74). For the ritual of presenting the sword of victory to the king and the ideological traditions and implications, see also Recklinghausen 2018, pp. 319–331.

**83** Preys 2016, pp. 395–402.

**84** For a detailed discussion, see Minas-Nerpel, Preys 2023.

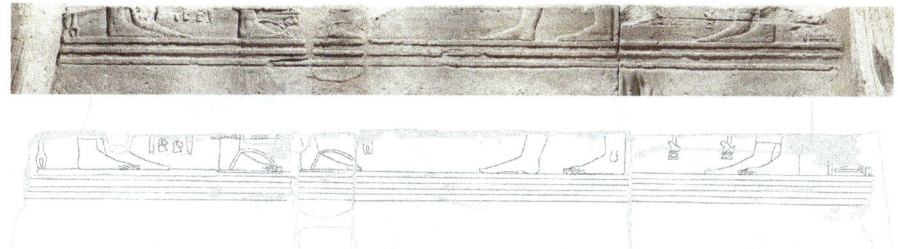

**Fig. 5a–b:** Karnak, Kiosk of Taharqa, panel 4: TahKiosk E4 (photograph and copyright: CFEETK; drawing: R. Preys; copyright: The Belgian-German Epigraphic Mission to Karnak).

dedication inscription of the temple of Horus at Edfu.[85] This is also the case for the temple of Amun-Ra at Karnak, where work was not resumed until the times of Ptolemy VI Philometor, whose name can be found on the Second Pylon and elsewhere in Karnak.[86] Under Ptolemy V, whose reign was dominated in the major part by the rebellion, no building work was conducted in Karnak; only one scene on the enclosure wall of Ramesses II refers to Epiphanes, but the date is problematic.[87] The Second Decree of Philae, dating to 6 September 186 BCE, attests to the recapture of the Thebaid, the termination of the uprising, and the continuation of construction work in Upper Egypt under Ptolemy V Epiphanes.[88] Building and decoration work at Egyptian temples would reach a peak under his two sons, Ptolemy VI Philometor and Ptolemy VIII Euergetes II.[89] Their answer to their own times of crisis – external and increasingly domestic – was to concentrate on the

---

[85] Under Ptolemy X Alexander I, the dedication inscription of the temple of Horus at Edfu was engraved relating the building's history. The revolt in the Thebaid (207/206–187/186 BCE) is described as part of this, see *Edfou* IV, 8, 4–5 (exterior of the naos) and *Edfou* VII, 6, 6–8 (exterior of the enclosure wall); see Cauville, Devauchelle 1984, pp. 35–36, and Kurth 2004, p. 50: "Its main gates and the double doors of its chambers were completed by year 16 of his majesty (Ptolemy IV Philopator). Then trouble broke out. There was an uprising of rebels in Upper Egypt, and work on the 'Throne Seat of the Gods' [Edfu] was suspended. The rebellion in the south lasted until year 19 of the king of Upper and Lower Egypt, the heir of the Father-loving Gods, son of Ra, Ptolemy, beloved by Ptah, justified, the God who Appears, the strong one, the king who put an end to the trouble completely, and his name was recorded [in the temple]."
[86] For the Second Pylon at Karnak, see Broze, Preys 2021; for the general building activity in Karnak under Ptolemy VI Philometor, see Minas 1996, pp. 60–66. See also Veïsse 2004, pp. 14–16.
[87] See Lanciers 1986, pp. 91–92 (with nn. 68–74), with further references to this relief and its problematic date. For more recent comments, see Coulon, Leclère, Marchand 1995, p. 222, pl. XII; Coulon 2009, pp. 8–9; Winand, Broze, Preys 2012, p. 98 and the contribution by L. Coulon in this volume.
[88] See Recklinghausen 2018, pp. 29, 61–81.
[89] See Minas 1996; Minas 1997.

**Fig. 6:** Kom Ombo, Temple of Sobek and Haroeris: Ptolemy VIII, accompanied by Cleopatra II and Cleopatra III, receives the sword of victory from Haroeris (*Kom Ombo* I 462).

native temples and to dedicate large amounts of money for the construction and embellishments of Egyptian sanctuaries.

When the construction work of Ptolemy IV Philopator was obviously disrupted in Karnak due to the uprising (and probably never taken up again under this king), the recently created eponymous cult in Ptolemais succumbed as well. In Philopator's fifteenth regnal year (208/207 BCE) the last eponymous priest was nominated in Ptolemais for the next twenty-two years until year 20 of Ptolemy V Epiphanes (186/185 BCE), with one single exception, that of Kleitomachos, son of Dikaiarchos in year seven of Ptolemy V (199/198 BCE).[90] This singular occurrence might be due to the fact that in this specific year a large reorganisation of the eponymous cults in both Alexandria and Ptolemais was undertaken, with the exclusion of the *Theoi Soteres* from the Alexander cult in Alexandria, the inclusion of Ptolemy V Epiphanes to this cult, the creation of a priesthood for his murdered mother Arsinoe III, to be mentioned after the *athlophoros* of Berenice II and the

---

90 Clarysse, van der Veken 1983, pp. 40–41.

*kanephoros* of Arsinoe II.⁹¹ It seems that despite the uprising in the Thebaid, those in Upper Egypt loyal to the king in Alexandria were able to appoint a priest and use his name in the dating formula of several documentary papyri.⁹²

In contrast to Alexandria, the dynastic cult in Ptolemais was not properly eponymous in the literal sense since one priest served several successive years, so the years could not be distinguished by different priests' names. For example, Nikanor, son of Bakchios, served five years under Ptolemy IV (215/214–211/210 BCE), and Heniochos, son of Lusanias, two years (209/208–208/207 BCE) until the cult was disrupted.⁹³ When it was reinstated on a regular basis, Hippalos, son of Sosos, served for fifteen years, from 186/185 until 170/169 BCE.⁹⁴

# 4 The Dynastic and Ruler Cults after the Times of Crisis until Cleopatra III

In the winter of 194/193 BCE, Ptolemy V married Cleopatra I, a Seleucid princess, and a new chapter of the powerful status of Ptolemaic queens was heralded, which is only obvious in the Egyptian temples from the reign of her two sons, Ptolemy VI and VIII, onwards, since few were extended and decorated under the fifth Ptolemy due to the uprising. It is worth mentioning in this context the only two contemporary inscriptions in the temple of Horus at Edfu were put down in 186 BCE, that is after the rebellion. In the southern *bandeau du soubassement* in room V, Ptolemy V is mentioned with his full five-fold titulature, in the corresponding northern section of the *bandeau du soubassement* his wife Cleopatra I with her full protocol, including her Horus name.⁹⁵ The same division and designation of the king and queen appears also in the second case, that is on the two door jambs of the vestibule of the treasury: the southern one bears the full titulature of Ptolemy V, the northern one Cleopatra's, again including her Horus name.⁹⁶ This separation of royal names is exceptional and underlines the queen's increased status, since she is not just mentioned after the king's name but singled out as a co-ruler in the corresponding section of the room.

---

**91** Minas 2000, pp. 120–131.
**92** Minas 2000, p. 126.
**93** Clarysse, van der Veken 1983, pp. 40–41.
**94** Clarysse, van der Veken 1983, pp. 40–45.
**95** *Edfou* I, 517; PM VI, p. 142 (166); see Lanciers 1986, p. 94; Eldamaty 2011, p. 31; Bielman Sánchez, Lenzo 2015, p. 462.
**96** *Edfou* II, 158–159; PM VI, p. 139 (139 a–b); see Lanciers 1986, p. 94; Eldamaty 2011, pp. 32–33.

After her husband's death in spring 180 BCE, Cleopatra I demonstrated her resilience and reigned on behalf of her minor son Ptolemy VI,[97] who received, very suitably, the epithet Philometor. For the first time in Ptolemaic history, it was a queen who ruled and was named first in the dating formulae of documentary papyri and inscriptions.[98] In this respect, she was more successful than her mother-in-law, Arsinoe III. After Philopator's death, the latter had intended to reign on behalf of her young son Ptolemy V, but was killed instead.[99] In contrast to her, Cleopatra I survived her husband's death and laid the foundation for the increasing prestige of the Ptolemaic queen, which her daughter Cleopatra II and granddaughter Cleopatra III sought and received. Cleopatra III especially manipulated the dynastic cult by creating several eponymous priesthoods for herself. Cleopatra II and Cleopatra III surpassed any other Ptolemaic queen in the ritual scenes in which they appeared.[100] This is a notable difference to Cleopatra I and all their successors, except for Cleopatra VII. The first Cleopatra had changed the status of a Ptolemaic female ruler considerably, but she was never *depicted* as a *living* queen on any Egyptian temple wall, mostly due to the fact that her husband Ptolemy V faced the uprising in Upper Egypt, which dominated the major part of his reign. As a result, not many temples were extended or decorated.[101] Cleopatra I must still have been visible in the temples, but in a different form: in both the First (185 BCE) and Second (186 BCE) Decrees of Philae, it was proclaimed that the queen's statues should be placed in the temples right next to those of the king and the respective local gods,[102] with the latter presenting the king with a sword of victory to emphasis the king's military success against real and imagined enemies. In addition, the lunette of the Nobaira copy of the Memphis decree of 196 BCE also shows Cleopatra I behind her husband Ptolemy V.[103] This specific copy dates to year 23 of Ptolemy V (182 BCE), that is fourteen years after the Memphis decree was promulgated, as attested on the Rosetta Stone. The text underwent

---

[97] Bielman Sánchez, Lenzo 2015, pp. 9–17.
[98] *P. Freib. III* 12–33: in the prescript, Cleopatra I is called "the goddess Epiphanes", whereas her son is only called Ptolemaios; see Hazzard 2000, pp. 125–126, and Minas 2000, pp. 133–134.
[99] See Grimm 1997, pp. 233–249.
[100] Minas-Nerpel 2011, pp. 58–76; Minas-Nerpel 2014, pp. 143–166; Minas-Nerpel 2015, pp. 809–821.
[101] Lanciers 1986, pp. 81–98; Lanciers 1987, pp. 173–180.
[102] Recklinghausen 2018, pp. 84–90; 135–139; 308–331; see also Thiers 2002, pp. 396–399, for the specific decree instructions, and pp. 389–404, for the discussion of three-dimensional examples of Ptolemy VI Philometor and Cleopatra II in Karnak.
[103] CGC 22188; Kamal 1904–1905: pp. 183–187, pl. LXII; Hoffmann, Pfeiffer 2021, pp. 37–43, esp. Fig. 5.

several changes in these years,[104] and the iconography in the lunette was also adapted in regard to the queen: in 196 Ptolemy V had not yet been married to the Seleucid princess, but in 182 he was, so the royal side of the lunette was extended by the *living* queen.

Because Egyptian temples were abundantly constructed, extended, and/or decorated under Ptolemy VI and Ptolemy VIII, it is only logically consistent that their queens – Cleopatra II and her daughter Cleopatra III – were depicted more often than any other Ptolemaic queen. However, this was not the only reason for the queens' salience: they also played a very active role in the dynasty, and they were essential to its survival. The powerful status of both mother and daughter, which is evident in some features of the Egyptian temple reliefs, relates directly to the increased emphasis on the dynasty through the ancestral lists after the cartouches of the reigning king and queen(s).[105] This emphasis on the queen and the dynasty was important for the continuation of the Ptolemaic ruler and became an essential part of temple decoration under Ptolemy VI and Ptolemy VIII.

Towards the end of the second century BCE, the eponymous cult was further used to express the position of the ruling king and queen and to emphasise their importance rather than that of the entire dynasty. At first, Ptolemy IX and Ptolemy X took over the office of the Alexander-priest themselves, and finally even the queen, Cleopatra III, although the office had originally been male.[106] Various eponymous priesthoods had been created for this specific queen, which rendered not only the year dating, but also the dynastic idea and emphasis of important members almost obsolete. After 84/83 BCE, the dynastic cult seemed to have lost its significance since priestly names are no longer attested in demotic papyri.[107]

# 5 Conclusion

The Ptolemies, as rulers of a multicultural country, used different identities in different circumstances, connecting themselves to existing traditions, modifying them, or creating new ones. For example, even if Alexander the Great was never

---

**104** Simpson 1996, p. 5.
**105** Minas 2000, pp. 186–192; Minas-Nerpel 2011.
**106** Minas 2000, pp. 160–161 (with references to the evidence).
**107** *P. dem. Hamb. ined. 2* (= *Urk. dem. Hawara XXIa–b*, see Lüddeckens 1998, pp. 221–230), dating to 83 BCE, is so far the last papyrus to attest the name of an eponymous priests; see Clarysse, van der Veken 1983, no. 207. See also Minas 2000, pp. 161–162. The last Greek papyrus that named an eponymous priest is P. Ashm. 22, dated to May/June 106 BCE, see Minas 2000, p. 162.

introduced to the ancestor lists in the Egyptian environment, some similarities of the ancestor veneration in the Egyptian temples with the purely Hellenistic eponymous cult are obvious, at least until Ptolemy I and Berenice I were introduced to the latter under Ptolemy IV; in this regard, they varied, since the hieroglyphic ancestor lines never connected the ruling king and queen with Alexander the Great or Ptolemy I and Berenice I. In the Hellenistic environment, Alexander was the one force, with whom the Ptolemies wanted to be connected, at least in Alexandria. In Ptolemais, Alexander did not form this all-important anchor. The emphasis was on the founder of the city and the dynasty himself.

In the Egyptian temples, the tradition of adding the ancestors in a list started with Ptolemy III naming his deified parents Ptolemy II and Arsinoe II (as his adopted mother). This found its iconographic expression in the first ancestor veneration scene on the gate of Khonsu in Karnak (see Fig. 2), which axially corresponds with a scene in which Ptolemaic rule is confirmed (see Fig. 3). This type of scene is expanded by the presentation of the sword of victory under Ptolemy IV, who also put more emphasis on the entire dynasty by including the first Ptolemaic couple to the cult of Alexander and the Ptolemies. The *Theoi Soteres* were never retrospectively included in these hieroglyphic ancestor lines, despite the fact that they could feature in ritual scenes, in which they received offerings,[108] or they were depicted on the copies of the synodal decrees.[109] Although there were plenty of similarities and cross-influences, there remained subtle differences in the mode of expression. However, the Thebaid crisis affected all royal cults equally: during the uprising, the building and decoration activities of the Ptolemies in Upper Egypt were interrupted, and in Ptolemais, no priest was appointed, except for one single exception. In Alexandria, far removed from provincial Thebes, the eponymous cults continued to function.

With the worship of Arsinoe II the ruler cult started to develop in the Egyptian temples. She was also the first queen to be specifically venerated by a single eponymous priesthood in the dynastic cult. Arsinoe was a vital image of the dynasty, which provided, through various iconographic and textual means, legitimacy for herself, her brother-husband, and their successors. She received temples of her own and even a festival, the *Arsinoeia*. Arsinoe II set the example for her female successors, and her iconographic and cultic details were used by

---

**108** See the ritual scene in Edfu in the room of the western staircase: PM VI, p. 142 (165); *Edfou* I, 526–527, pl. 36a; Winter 1978, p. 152, Dok. 28: Ptolemy IV offers food to Horus, Hathor, and Harsomtus, followed by three royal couples: Ptolemy I and Berenice II (called Arsinoe), Ptolemy II and Arsinoe II, Ptolemy I and Berenice I.
**109** For the Kom el-Hisn Stela, see nn. 45 and 62 above.

later queens, her epithets even for goddesses such as Isis. The transfer of epithets from Arsinoe II and Berenice II to Isis under Ptolemy IV was probably meant to stress the goddess' royal character. It could possibly resonate in the adaptation of a royal iconographic solution on the tetradrachms of Ptolemy IV, the jugate busts of the ruling couple to represent Sarapis and Isis, the divine couple.[110] Berenice II surpassed Arsinoe II with being awarded a Horus name, but some of the following queens gained other signs of status by, for example, being named in the dating *formulae* of the documentary papyri first, because they ruled for or with their (still minor) sons. The cults, both the dynastic and the ruler cults, reacted to the political shifts and demands. Egyptian temples attest not only to the continuation and elaboration of theological traditions but also to the creative thought of the Egyptian priests on many levels. This resulted in sophisticated modes of expressions, both in textual and artistic regards.

Other conceptual changes were more subtle and not (easily) recognisable for the ancient public, such as the addition, and finally replacement, of the presentation of the *jmj.t-pr* through the sword of victory under Ptolemy IV, which is handed by gods to the ruling couple, as attested, for example, on the intercolumnar walls of the Taharqa Kiosk at Karnak (see Figs. 4–5 and Fig. 6 for Kom Ombo). In the Egyptian temples, the ancestor veneration had already been established a generation earlier, as the ritual scenes of Ptolemy III on the Khonsu gate (see Figs. 2–3) demonstrate. In the temple inscription, these scenes find their equivalent in the new practice of adding the ancestors after the royal cartouches, a practice vastly extended almost until the very end of the Ptolemaic dynasty. It was also under the fourth Ptolemy that major changes were introduced to the eponymous cult, on the one hand by adding the first Ptolemaic couple to the Alexander cult in Alexandria, thus creating a real dynastic cult, and on the other hand by establishing an additional eponymous priesthood in Ptolemais, thus binding the Greek speaking population of Upper Egypt further to the Ptolemies.

The royal court in Alexandria used the Egyptian traditions to create a social and cultic discourse that lasted several centuries, binding the population and priests to the dynasty as much as they could, also in or after times of crisis. The court and the queens themselves used the circumstances to enhance the queens' status, as reflected through the development of the ruler cult. The Ptolemies and their queens as well as their advisors were highly successful in constructing an identity for their dynasty, expressed in visual and textual sources. They created not only a textual repertory, but also an iconographic one for the diverse ethnic groups in their kingdom, with a strong emphasis on the queens. "Multilingualism"

---

**110** On this numismatic series, see Landvatter 2012, pp. 61–90.

was thus not only expressed in texts such as the trilingual decrees or the bilingual papyri, but also – in a manner of speaking – in the artistic sense.

## Bibliography

Albersmeier, Minas 1998
    Albersmeier, S., Minas, M., "Ein Weihrelief für die vergöttlichte Arsinoe II. Philadelphos", in W. Clarysse, A. Schoors, H. Willems (eds.), *Egyptian Religion: The Last Thousand Years – Studies Dedicated to the Memory of Jan Quaegebeur* I, OLA 84, Leuven, 1998, pp. 3–29.

Aufderhaar 2016
    Aufderhaar, W., "The Sphinxes of Shepenwepet II", in M. Becker, A.I. Blöbaum, A. Lohwasser (eds.), "Prayer and Power": Proceedings of the Conference on the God's Wives of Amun in Egypt during the First Millenium BC, ÄAT 84, Münster 2016, pp. 137–153.

Aufrère 2000
    Aufrère, S.H., *Le propylône d'Amon-Rê-Montou à Karnak-Nord*, MIFAO 117, Cairo, 2000.

Bailey 1999
    Bailey, D.M., "The Canephore of Arsinoe Philadelphos: What Did She Look Like", *CdE* 74, 1999, pp. 156–160.

Baines 1995
    Baines, J., "Kingship, Definition of Culture, and Legitimation", in D. O'Connor, D.P. Silverman (eds.), *Ancient Egyptian Kingship*, ProblÄg 9, Leiden, New York, 1995, pp. 3–47.

Baines 2019
    Baines, J., "Ruler, Court, and Power: the King and Institutions in Early Egypt", in M. Albert, E. Brüggen, K. Klaus (eds.), *Die Macht des Herrschers: personale und transpersonale Aspekte*, Macht und Herrschaft 4, Göttingen, 2019, pp. 239–276.

Barbantani 2005
    Barbantani, S., "Goddess of Love and Mistress of the Sea: Notes on a Hellenistic Hymn to Arsinoe-Aphrodite (P. Lit. Goodsp. 2, I–IV)", *AncSoc* 35, 2005, pp. 135–165.

Barguet 1962
    Barguet, P., *Le temple d'Amon-Rê à Karnak. Essai d'exégèse*, RAPH 21, Cairo, 1962.

Bielman Sánchez, Lenzo 2015
    Bielman Sánchez, A., Lenzo, G., *Inventer le pouvoir féminin. Cléopâtre I et Cléopâtre II, reines d'Egypte au II$^e$ s. av. J.-C.*, Echo 12, Bern et al., 2015.

Bing 2002–2003
    Bing, P., "Posidippus and the Admiral: Kallikrates of Samos in the Milan Epigrams", *Greek, Roman and Byzantine Studies* 43, 2002–2003, pp. 243–266.

Botti 1967
    Botti, G., *L'archivio demotico da Deir el-Medineh. Catalogo del Museo Egizio di Torino*, Serie 1, 1: Monumenti e testi, Florence, 1967.

Bresciani, Pernigotti 1978
    Bresciani, E., Pernigotti, S., *Assuan*, Biblioteca di studi antichi 16, Pisa, 1978.

Bricault 2006
    Bricault, L., *Isis, dame des flots*, AegLeod 7, Liège, 2006.

Broze, Preys 2021
 Broze, M., Preys, R., *La porte d'Amon. Le deuxième pylône de Karnak* I: *Etudes et relevé épigraphique*, BiGen 63, Cairo, 2021.
Brunner 1991
 Brunner, H., *Die Geburt des Gottkönigs: Studien zur Überlieferung eines altägyptischen Mythos*, ÄgAbh 10, Wiesbaden, 1991.
Caneva 2016
 Caneva, S.G., *From Alexander to the Theoi Adelphoi: Foundation and Legitimation of a Dynasty*, StudHell 56, Leuven, 2016.
Caneva 2018
 Caneva, S.G., "Ptolemy I: Politics, Religion and Transition to Hellenistic Egypt", in T. Howe (ed.), *Ptolemy I Soter, a Self-made Man*, Oxford, Philadelphia, 2018.
Carney 2013
 Carney, E.D., *Arsinoë of Egypt and Macedon: A Royal Life*, Oxford, New York, 2013.
Cassor-Pfeiffer, Pfeiffer 2019
 Cassor-Pfeiffer, S., Pfeiffer, S. "Pharaonin Berenike II.: Bemerkungen zur ägyptischen Titulatur einer frühptolemäischen Königin", in M. Brose, P. Dils, F. Naether, L. Popko, D. Raue (eds.), *En détail – Philologie und Archäologie im Diskurs: Festschrift für Hans-Werner Fischer-Elfert*, ZÄS Beiheft 7, Berlin, Boston, 2019, pp. 199–238.
Cauville, Devauchelle 1984
 Cauville, S., Devauchelle, D., "Le temple d'Edfou: étapes de la construction. Nouvelles données historiques", *RdE* 35, 1984, pp. 31–55.
Cherpion et al. 2007
 Cherpion, N., Corteggiani, J.-P., Gout, J.-F., *Le tombeau de Pétosiris à Touna el-Gebel, relevé photographique*, BiGen 27, Le Caire, 2007.
Clarysse, van der Veken 1983
 Clarysse, W., van der Veken, G., *The Eponymous Priests of Ptolemaic Egypt: Chronological Lists of the Priests of Alexandria and Ptolemais with a Study of the Demotic Transcriptions of Their Names*, P.L.Bat. 24, Leiden, 1983.
Clère 1961
 Clère, P., *La porte d'Évergète à Karnak*, 2$^e$ partie, MIFAO 84, Cairo, 1961.
Coulon 2001
 Coulon, L., "Quand Amon parle à Platon (La statue Caire JE 38033)", *RdE* 52, 2001, pp. 85–125.
Coulon 2009
 Coulon, L., "Une trinité d'Osiris thébains sur un relief découvert à Karnak", in C. Thiers (ed.), *Documents de théologies thébaines tardives (D3T 1)*, CENiM 3, Montpellier, 2009, pp. 1–18.
Coulon, Leclère, Marchand 1995
 Coulon, L., Leclère, F., Marchand, S., "Catacombes osiriennes de Ptolémée IV à Karnak", *CahKarn* 10, 1995, pp. 205–257.
Eldamaty 2011
 Eldamaty, M., "Die ptolemäische Königin als weiblicher Horus", in A. Jördens, J.F. Quack (eds.), *Ägypten zwischen innerem Zwist und äußerem Druck: die Zeit Ptolemaios' VI. bis VIII. – Internationales Symposion Heidelberg 16.–19.9.2007*, Philippika 45, Wiesbaden, 2011, pp. 24–57.
Eldamaty 2015
 Eldamaty, M., "Die Gottesgemahlin des Amun", in M. Eldamaty, F. Hoffmann, M. Minas-Nerpel (eds.), *Ägyptische Königinnen vom Neuen Reich bis in die islamische Zeit: Beiträge zur Konferenz in

der Kulturabteilung der Botschaft der Arabischen Republik Ägypten in Berlin am 19.01.2013, Vaterstetten, 2015, pp. 67–85.

El-Masry, Altenmüller, Thissen 2012
El-Masry, Y., Altenmüller, H., Thissen, H.-J., *Das Synodaldekret von Alexandria aus dem Jahre 243 v. Chr.*, SAK Beiheft 11, Hamburg, 2012.

Frandsen 2009
Frandsen, P.J., *Incestuous and Close-kin Marriage in Ancient Egypt & Persia: An Examination of the Evidence*, CNIP 34, Copenhagen, 2009.

Fraser 1972
Fraser, P.M., *Ptolemaic Alexandria*, 3 vols., Oxford, 1972.

Gauthier 1911
Gauthier, H., *Le temple de Kalabchah* I. *Texte*, Les temples immergés de la Nubie, Cairo, 1911.

Goebs, Baines 2018 Goebs, K., Baines, J., "Functions and Uses of Egyptian Myth", *RHR* 235/4, 2018, pp. 645–681.

Gorre, Veïsse 2020
Gorre, G., Veïsse, A.-E., "Birth and Disappearance of the Priestly Synods in the Time of the Ptolemies", in G. Gorre, S. Wackenier (eds.), *Quand la fortune du royaume ne dépend pas de la vertu du prince. Un renforcement de la monarchie lagide de Ptolémée VI à Ptolémée X (169–88 av. J.-C.)?*. StudHell 59, Leuven, 2020, pp. 113–140.

Grimm 1997
Grimm, G., "Verbrannte Pharaonen: Die Feuerbestattung Ptolemaios' IV. Philopator und ein gescheiterter Staatsstreich in Alexandria", *AntWelt* 3, 1997, pp. 233–249.

Grimm 1999
Grimm, G., *Alexandria: Die erste Königsstadt der hellenistischen Welt*, Mainz, 1999.

Guermeur (ed.) 2013
Guermeur, I. (ed.), *Histoire, géographie et religion de l'Égypte ancienne. Opera selecta par Jean Yoyotte*, OLA 224, Leuven, 2013.

Gutzwiller 1992
Gutzwiller, K., "Callimachus' Lock of Berenice: Fantasy, Romance, and Propaganda", *AJP* 113, 1992, pp. 359–385.

Hauben 1970
Hauben, H., *Callicrates of Samos: A Contribution to the Study of the Ptolemaic Admiralty – with a Samian Inscription Published in Appendix by Günter Dunst*, StudHell 18, Leuven, 1970.

Hazzard 2000
Hazzard, R.A., *Imagination of a Monarchy*. Phœnix (T) Suppl. Vol. 37, Toronto, 2000.

Herklotz 2000
Herklotz, F., "Berenike II. – Königin und Göttin", in A. Lohwasser (ed.), *Geschlechterforschung in der Ägyptologie und Sudanarchäologie: Beiträge eines Kolloquiums am Seminar für Sudanarchäologie und Ägyptologie der Humboldt-Universität zu Berlin, 8.5. und 19.6.1999*, IBAES 2, Berlin, pp. 43–61, <http://www2.rz.hu-berlin.de/nilus/net-publications/ibaes2/Herklotz/text.pdf>, accessed 30 August 2024.

Hölbl 2001
Hölbl, G., *A History of the Ptolemaic Empire*, London, 2001.

Hoffmann 2015
Hoffmann, F., "Königinnen in ägyptischen Quellen der römischen Zeit", in M. Eldamaty, F. Hoffmann, M. Minas-Nerpel (eds.), *Ägyptische Königinnen vom Neuen Reich bis in die islamische*

*Zeit: Beiträge zur Konferenz in der Kulturabteilung der Botschaft der Arabischen Republik Ägypten in Berlin am 19.01.2013*, Vaterstetten, 2015, pp. 139–156.

Hoffmann, Quack 2014
Hoffmann, F., Quack, J.F., "Pastophoros", in A.M. Dodson, J.J. Johnston, W. Monkhouse (eds.), *A Good Scribe and an Exceedingly Wise Man: Studies in Honour of W. J. Tait*, London, 2014, pp. 127–156.

Hoffmann, Pfeiffer 2021
Hoffmann, F., Pfeiffer, S., *Der Stein von Rosetta*, Ditzingen, 2021.

Hourdin 2018
Hourdin, J., "The Kushite Kiosks of Karnak and Luxor: a Cross-over Study", in E. Pischikova, J. Budka, K. Griffin (eds.), *Thebes in the First Millennium BC: Art and Archaeology of the Kushite Period and Beyond*, GHP Egyptology 27, London, 2018, pp. 255–270.

Hourdin in preparation
Hourdin, J., *The Kiosk of Taharqa* I: *the Kushite Building and Decoration*, BiGen, Cairo, in preparation.

Huss 1991
Huss, W., "Die in ptolemaiischer Zeit verfaßten Synodal-Dekrete der ägyptischen Priester", *ZPE* 88, 1991, pp. 189–208.

Huss 2001
Huss, W., *Ägypten in hellenistischer Zeit, 332–30 v. Chr.*, Munich, 2001.

Kamal 1904–05 Kamal, A., *Stèles ptolémaïques et romaines*, CGC 22001–22208, Cairo, 1904–05.

Koch 2012
Koch, C., *"Die den Amun mit ihrer Stimme zufriedenstellen": Gottesgemahlinnen und Musikerinnen im thebanischen Amunstaat von der 22. bis zur 26. Dynastie*, SRaT 27, Dettelbach, 2012.

Kurth 2004
Kurth, D., *The Temple of Edfu: A Guide by an Ancient Egyptian Priest*, Cairo, New York, 2004.

Lanciers 1986
Lanciers, E., "Die ägyptischen Tempelbauten zur Zeit des Ptolemaios V. Epiphanes (204–180 v. Chr.): Teil 1", *MDAIK* 42, 1986, pp. 81–98.

Lanciers 1987
Lanciers, E., "Die ägyptischen Tempelbauten zur Zeit des Ptolemaios V. Epiphanes (204–180 v. Chr.) – Teil 2: Irrtümlich Ptolemaios V. zugeschriebene Denkmäler", *MDAIK* 43, 1987, pp. 173–180.

Landvatter 2012
Landvatter, T., "The Serapis and Isis Coinage of Ptolemy IV", *AJN* 24, 2012, pp. 61–90.

Lauffray 1970
Lauffray, J., "La colonnade-propylée occidentale de Karnak dite 'Kiosque de Taharqa' et ses abords. Rapport provisoire des fouilles de 1969 et commentaire architectural", *Kêmi* 20, 1970, pp. 111–64.

Lauffray 1975
Lauffray, J., "La colonnade propylée occidentale de Taharqa à Karnak et les mâts à emblème (compte rendu de la seconde campagne de fouilles 1970–1971)", *CahKarn* 5, 1975, pp. 77–92.

Leclant 1965
Leclant, J., *Recherches sur les monuments thébains de la XXVe dynastie dite éthiopienne*, BdE 36, Cairo, 1965.

Lembke 2012
 Lembke, K., "Interpretatio aegyptiaca vs. interpretatio graeca? Der ägyptische Staat und seine Denkmäler in der Ptolemäerzeit", *Mediterraneo Antico* 15, 2012, pp. 199–216.

Llewellyn-Jones, Winder 2016
 Llewellyn-Jones, L., Winder, S., "The Hathoric Model of Queenship in Early Ptolemaic Egypt. The Case of Berenike's Lock", in I. Rutherford (ed.), *Greco-Egyptian Interactions: Literature, Translation, and Culture, 500 BCE–300 CE*, Oxford, 2016, pp. 139–162.

Lüddeckens 1998
 Lüddeckens, E., *Demotische Urkunden aus Hawara: Umschrift, Übersetzung und Kommentar von E. Lüddeckens unter Mitarbeit von R. Wassermann nach Vorarbeiten von W. Erichsen und Ch. F. Nims, Bearbeitung der griechischen Registratur-Vermerke von R. W. Daniel*, Verzeichnis der orientalischen Handschriften in Deutschland, Suppl.-Band 28, Stuttgart, 1998.

Megahed, Vymazalová 2015
 Megahed, M., Vymazalová, H., "The South-Saqqara Circumcision Scene: a Fragment of an Old Kingdom Birth legend", in F. Coppens, J. Janák, H. Vymazalová (eds.), *Royal versus Divine Authority: Acquisition, Legitimization and Renewal of Power – Prague, June 26–28, 2013*: 7. Symposion zur ägyptischen Königsideologie, Wiesbaden, 2015, pp. 275–287.

Merkelbach 1995
 Merkelbach, R., *Isis regina – Zeus Sarapis: Die griechisch-ägyptische Religion nach den Quellen dargestellt*, Stuttgart, 1995.

Minas 1996
 Minas, M., "Die Dekorationstätigkeit von Ptolemaios VI. Philometor und Ptolemaios VIII. Euergetes II. an ägyptischen Tempeln, 1. Teil", *OLP* 27, 1996, pp. 51–78.

Minas 1997
 Minas, M., "Die Dekorationstätigkeit von Ptolemaios VI. Philometor und Ptolemaios VIII. Euergetes II. an ägyptischen Tempeln, 2. Teil", *OLP* 28, 1997, pp. 87–121.

Minas 1998
 Minas, M., "Die Kanephoros: Aspekte des Ptolemäischen Dynastiekults", in H. Melaerts (ed.), *Le culte du souverain dans l'Égypte ptolémaïque au III$^e$ siècle avant notre ère. Actes du colloque international, Bruxelles 10 mai 1995*, StudHell 34, Leuven, 1998, pp. 43–60.

Minas 2000
 Minas, M., *Die hieroglyphischen Ahnenreihen der ptolemäischen Könige: ein Vergleich mit den Titeln der eponymen Priester in den demotischen und griechischen Papyri*, AegTrev 9, Mainz, 2000.

Minas 2005
 Minas, M., "Macht und Ohnmacht: Die Repräsentation ptolemäischer Königinnen in ägyptischen Tempeln", *AfP* 51, 2005, pp. 127–154.

Minas 2006
 Minas, M., "Die ptolemäischen Sokar-Osiris-Mumien: Neue Erkenntnisse zum ägyptischen Dynastiekult der Ptolemäer", *MDAIK* 62, pp. 197–215.

Minas-Nerpel 2011
 Minas-Nerpel, M., "Cleopatra II and III: The Queens of Ptolemy VI and VIII as Guarantor of Kingship and Rivals for Power", in A. Jördens, J.F. Quack (eds.), *Ägypten zwischen innerem Zwist und äußerem Druck: die Zeit Ptolemaios' VI. bis VIII. – Internationales Symposion Heidelberg 16.–19.9.2007*, Philippika 45, Wiesbaden, pp. 58–76.

Minas-Nerpel 2014
 Minas-Nerpel, M., "Koregentschaft und Thronfolge: Legitimation ptolemäischer Machtstrukturen in den ägyptischen Tempeln der Ptolemärzeit", in F. Hoffmann, K.S. Schmidt

(eds.), *Orient und Okzident in hellenistischer Zeit: Beiträge zur Tagung 'Orient und Okzident – Antagonismus oder Konstrukt? Machtstrukturen, Ideologien und Kulturtransfer in hellenistischer Zeit', Würzburg 10.-13. April 2008*, Vaterstetten, 2014, pp. 143–166.

Minas-Nerpel 2015

Minas-Nerpel, M., "Ptolemaic Queens in the Egyptian Temple Reliefs: Inter-cultural Reflections of Political Authority, or Religious Imperatives?", in P. Kousoulis (ed.), *Proceedings of the Tenth International Congress of Egyptologists, University of the Aegean, Rhodes, 22–29 May 2008*, OLA 241, Leuven, 2015, pp. 809–821.

Minas-Nerpel 2019a

Minas-Nerpel, M., "Ptolemaic Queens as Ritualists and Recipients of Cults: the Cases of Arsinoe II and Berenike II", *AncSoc* 49, 2019, pp. 141–183.

Minas-Nerpel 2019b

Minas-Nerpel, M., "'Seeing Double': Intercultural Dimensions of the Royal Ideology in Ptolemaic Egypt", in J. Budka (ed.), *Egyptian Royal Ideology and Kingship under Periods of Foreign Rulers – Case Studies from the First Millennium BCE: 9th Symposium on Egyptian Royal Ideology, Munich, May 31–June 2, 2018*, KSG 4.6, Wiesbaden, 2019.

Minas-Nerpel 2021

Minas-Nerpel, M., "Beyond Boundaries: the Roles of the Queens in the Ptolemaic Ruler Cult", in G. Lenzo et al. (eds.), *Les cultes aux rois et aux héros dans l'Antiquité. Continuités et changements à l'époque hellénistique*, ORA, Tübingen, pp. 117–146.

Minas-Nerpel, Preys 2023

Minas-Nerpel, M., Preys, R., *The Kiosk of Taharqa* II: *the Ptolemaic Decoration*, BiGen 73, Cairo, 2023.

Müller 2009

Müller, S., *Das hellenistische Königspaar in der medialen Repräsentation: Ptolemaios II. und Arsinoe II.*, Beiträge zur Altertumskunde 263, Berlin, 2009.

Nilsson 2012

Nilsson, M., *The Crown of Arsinoë II: the Creation of an Imagery of Authority*, Oxford, 2012.

Nisetich 2005

Nisetich, F., "The Poems of Posidippus", in K. Gutzwiller (ed.), *The New Posidippus: a Hellenistic Poetry Book*, Oxford, 2005, pp. 17–64.

van Oppen 2015

van Oppen, B., *Berenice II Euergetis: Essays in Early Hellenistic Queenship*, Basingstoke, 2015.

Payraudeau 2015

Payraudeau, F., "Considérations sur quelques titres des reines de l'Ancien Empire à l'époque ptolémaïque", in R. Legros (ed.), *Cinquante ans d'éternité. Jubilé de la Mission archéologique française de Saqqâra*, BdE 162, Cairo, 2015, pp. 209–225.

Perdu 2012

Perdu, O., *Les statues privées de la fin de l'Egypte pharaonique (1069 av. J.-C. – 395 apr. J.-C.) – t. I: Hommes*, Paris, 2012.

Pfeiffer 2004

Pfeiffer, S., *Das Dekret von Kanopos (238 v. Chr.): Kommentar und historische Auswertung eines dreisprachigen Synodaldekretes der ägyptischen Priester zu Ehren Ptolemaios' III. und seiner Familie*, AfP Beihefte 18, Munich, 2004.

Pfeiffer 2008a

Pfeiffer, S., *Herrscher- und Dynastiekulte im Ptolemäerreich*, MBPF 98, Munich, 2008.

Pfeiffer 2008b
Pfeiffer, S., "The God Serapis, His Cult and the Beginnings of the Ruler Cult in Ptolemaic Egypt", in P. McKechnie, P. Guillaume (eds.), *Ptolemy II Philadelphus and His World*, Mnemosyne 300, Leiden, 2008, pp. 387–408.

Pfeiffer 2019
Pfeiffer, S., "A Successful Ruler and Imperial Cult", in K. Vandorpe (ed.), *A Companion to Greco-Roman and Late Antique Egypt*, Blackwell Companions to the Ancient World, Oxford, 2019, pp. 533–549.

Pfrommer 2002
Pfrommer, M., *Königinnen vom Nil*, Mainz, 2002.

Preys 2015a
Preys, R., "La royauté lagide et le culte d'Osiris d'après les portes monumentales de Karnak", in C. Thiers (ed.), *Documents de théologies thébaines tardives (D3T 3)*, CENiM 13, Montpellier, 2015, pp. 159–215.

Preys 2015b
Preys, R., "Roi vivant et roi ancêtre. Iconographie et idéologie royale sous les Ptolémées", in C. Zivie-Coche (ed.), *Offrandes, rites et rituels dans les temples d'époques ptolémaïque et romaine. Actes de la journée d'études de l'équipe EPHE (EA 4519) 'Égypte ancienne: Archéologie, Langue, Religion'*, Paris, 27 juin 2013, CENiM 10, Montpellier, 2015, pp. 149–184.

Preys, Dégremont 2013
Preys, R., Dégremont, A., "Cléopâtre I et la couronne d'Arsinoé. À propos des scènes de culte royal sur la porte ptolémaïque du 2$^e$ pylône de Karnak", in C. Thiers (ed.), *Documents de théologies thébaines tardives (D3T 2)*, CENiM 8, Montpellier, 2013, pp. 95–109.

Quaegebeur 1971a
Quaegebeur, J., "Documents Concerning a Cult of Arsinoe Philadelphos at Memphis", *JNES* 30, 1971, pp. 239–270.

Quaegebeur 1971b
Quaegebeur, J., "Ptolemée II devant Arsinoé divinisée", *BIFAO* 69, 1971, pp. 191–217.

Quaegebeur 1978
Quaegebeur, J., "Reines ptolémaïques et traditions égyptiennes", in H. Maehler, V.M. Strocka (eds.), *Das ptolemäische Ägypten: Akten des Int. Symposions, 27.–29. September 1976 in Berlin*, Mainz, 1978, pp. 245–262.

Quaegebeur 1985
Quaegebeur, J., "Arsinoé Philadelphe, reine, 'roi' et déesse, à Hildesheim", *GM* 87, 1985, pp. 73–78.

Quaegebeur 1989
Quaegebeur, J., "The Egyptian Clergy and the Cult of the Ptolemaic Dynasty", *AncSoc* 20, 1989, pp. 93–116.

Quaegebeur 1998
Quaegebeur, J., "Documents égyptiens anciens et nouveaux relatifs à Arsinoé Philadelphe", in H. Melaerts (ed.), *Le culte du souverain dans l'Égypte ptolémaïque au III$^e$ siècle avant notre ère. Actes du colloque international, Bruxelles 10 Mai 1995*, StudHell 34, Leuven, 1998, pp. 73–108.

Recklinghausen 2018
Recklinghausen, D. von, *Die Philensis-Dekrete: Untersuchungen über zwei Synodaldekrete aus der Zeit Ptolemaios' V. und ihre geschichtliche und religiöse Bedeutung*, ÄA 73, Wiesbaden, 2018.

Roeder 1959
Roeder, G., *Die ägyptische Götterwelt*, Die ägyptische Religion in Texten und Bildern 1, Zurich, 1959.

Schäfer 2011
Schäfer, D., *Makedonische Pharaonen und hieroglyphische Stelen*, StudHell 50, Leuven, 2011.

Simpson 1996
: Simpson, R.S., *Demotic Grammar in the Ptolemaic Sacerdotal Decrees*, Griffith Institute Monographs, Oxford, 1996.

Stadler 2009
: Stadler, M., *Weiser und Wesir: Studien zu Vorkommen, Rolle und Wesen des Gottes Thot im ägyptischen Totenbuch*, ORA 1, Tübingen, 2009.

Stephens 2003
: Stephens, S.A., *Seeing Double: Intercultural Poetics in Ptolemaic Alexandria*, HCS 37, Berkeley, 2003.

Stephens 2005
: Stephens, S.A., "Battle of the Books", in K. Gutzwiller (ed.), *The New Posidippus: A Hellenistic Poetry Book*, Oxford, 2005, pp. 229–248.

Thiers 2002
: Thiers, C., "Deux statues des dieux Philométors à Karnak (Karnak Caracol R177 + Cheikh Labib 94CL1421 et Caire JE 41218)", *BIFAO* 102, 2002, pp. 389–404.

Thiers 2003
: Thiers, C., *Tôd. Les inscriptions du temple ptolémaïque et romain* II: *Textes et scènes nos 173–329*, FIFAO 18,2, Cairo, 2003.

Thiers 2007
: Thiers, C., "Le mariage divin des dieux Adelphes dans la stèle de Mendès (Caire CG 22181)", *ZÄS* 134, 2007, pp. 64–65.

Thompson 2005
: Thompson, D., "Posidippus, Poet of the Ptolemies", in K. Gutzwiller (ed.), *The New Posidippus: A Hellenistic Poetry Book*, Oxford, 2005, pp. 269–283.

Troy 1986
: Troy, L., *Patterns of Queenship in Ancient Egyptian Myth and History*, Boreas 14, Uppsala, 1986.

Urk. II
: Sethe, K., *Hieroglyphische Urkunden der griechisch-römischen Zeit*, Urk. II, Leipzig, 1904.

Urk. VIII
: Firchow, O. (ed.), *Thebanische Tempelinschriften aus griechisch-römischer Zeit aus dem Nachlass von Kurt Sethe*, Urk. VIII, 1, Berlin, 1957.

Veïsse 2004
: Veïsse, A.-E., *Les "révoltes égyptiennes". Recherches sur les troubles intérieurs en Égypte du règne du Ptolémée III à la conquête romaine*, StudHell 41, Leuven, Paris, Dudley, MA, 2004.

Warda 2012
: Warda, A., *Egyptian Draped Male Figures – Inscriptions and Context: 1st Century BC–1st Century AD*, Doctoral Dissertation, Faculty of Oriental Studies, University of Oxford, 2012.

Winand, Broze, Preys 2012
: Winand, J., Broze, M., Preys, R., "L'activité épigraphique belge dans le temple de Karnak", in *Ceci n'est pas une pyramide . . . Un siècle de recherche archéologique belge en Egypte*, Leuven, 2012, pp. 92–105.

Winter 1978
: Winter, E., "Der Herrscherkult in den ägyptischen Ptolemäertempeln", in H. Maehler, V. M. Strocka (eds.), *Das ptolemäische Ägypten*: *Akten des internationalen Symposions, 27.–29. 9.1976 in Berlin*, Mainz, 1978, pp. 147–160.

Zauzich 1971
: Zauzich, K.-T., "Korrekturvorschläge zur Publikation des demotischen Archivs von Deir el-Medineh", *Enchoria* 1, 1971, pp. 43–56.

Jan Moje
# The Great Revolt 206–186 BCE in the Demotic Sources from Elephantine

## 1 Introduction

Even though ancient evidence for the Great Revolt (206–186 BCE) originates mostly from Thebes and other regions in the Thebaid, the southern border of Egypt, Elephantine, was not spared from civil war – even if the city had no active role in the revolt, for example as a basis for rebel troops or residence of persons active in the rebellion.[1] Sources in this question from Elephantine are rare, but some noteworthy pieces of information on the Great Revolt can be found within the Demotic corpus from Elephantine.

The great Upper Egyptian revolt against Ptolemaios IV Philopator and his successor Ptolemaios V Epiphanes caused decade-long (political) turmoil throughout the entire country.[2] For example, the work on the doors for the Edfu temple had to be stopped,[3] and many sacred animal mummies could not be transported to their final resting places, as seen in the Demotic ibis coffins from Tuna el-Gebel.[4]

The majority of sources show that the revolt had bases in Thebes and the Thebaid, where the usurper was officially accepted as the legitimate ruler, even if it is known that the rebellion did not start in Thebes itself.[5] Besides the relevant Greek texts, several Demotic papyri date after both Theban rebel-kings Haronnophris and Chaonnophris.[6] The first attestation of the rebel ruler dates from the 10 November 205 BCE.[7] The latest document from Thebes mentioning the second rebel ruler Chaonnophris dates to his 14$^{th}$ regnal year (191 BCE). Five years later, in 186 BCE, he was defeated.

---

1 Already stated by Pestman 1995, pp. 134–146, see also Locher 1999, p. 25. I would like to express my thanks to the organisers for inviting me to this inspiring conference.
2 For an actual overview and the mention of the revolt within the sacerdotal decrees from Philae cf. Recklinghausen 2018, pp. 286–302.
3 Pestman 1995, p. 103, with further literature. See also Moje 2020b.
4 Thissen†, Moje in press. Regarding the question of individual mobility throughout the country during the rebellion see also the contribution of R. Birk in this volume.
5 See Veïsse 2004, pp. 240–242.
6 Depauw et al. 2008, pp. 80–84; Pestman 1995. For the names cf. Zauzich 1978a.
7 Regnal year 1, 29th of Pachons: Tabl. Cairo EM JdE 38258, ed. Vleeming 2015, no. 2098 and Depauw 2006. For the history cf. also Hölbl 1994 and Huß 2001.

Even though Elephantine was supposedly not a part of the rebellion, it felt the effects of the civil war, as for example, nearby Philae was beyond the control of the Ptolemaic state, even if only for a short period of time.[8] Documents related to the unrest are few, but the corpus of the Demotic sources can offer some – albeit limited – insight into the revolt and its effects. A Demotic graffito from the Isis temple in Aswan was supposed to be proof of a Meroitic occupation of Aswan between 196 and 189 BCE.[9] Locher showed that this interpretation was wrong, and in fact, the graffito states the presence of refugees from Nubia in the region of Aswan.[10] Even a connection with the Great Revolt is uncertain, as the dating could also refer to Ptolemaios III, IV, or XII.

## 2 The Statistical Evidence

A general overview of the chronological development of the Demotic sources from Elephantine (Fig. 1) shows that, after a slow start in the Late Period in the early Ptolemaic Period, during the reigns of Ptolemaios I Soter to Ptolemaios III Euergetes, the number of sources decline at the time of Ptolemaios IV. In the middle and late Ptolemaic Period, only a few sources in Demotic are attested. Then, from the beginning of Roman rule onwards, Demotic was used widely again.

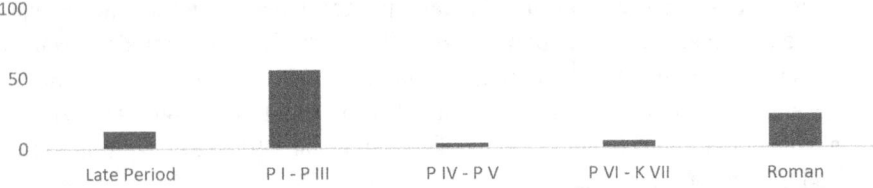

**Fig. 1:** General chronological development of all Elephantine sources in Demotic (in % of all attested Demotic sources from the Late to Roman Period).

A detailed look at these sources (Figs. 2–3) shows a partially modified picture. The use of Demotic tax receipts declined rapidly and was nearly absent from the middle Ptolemaic Period onwards (Fig. 2). In Thebes, tax payments to the bank were interrupted between 207–192/1 BCE.[11] Only at the beginning of Roman rule, De-

---

8 Recklinghausen 2018, pp. 232–233, with further literature.
9 Locher 1999, pp. 72–74; Recklinghausen 2018, p. 286.
10 Locher 1999, pp. 72–74; Recklinghausen 2018, p. 286.
11 McGing 1997, p. 285.

motic was used for these receipts once again, but not for long; during the reign of successive Roman emperors, Demotic was again increasingly replaced by Greek. Also, the system of Demotic countersigning and tax payment declaration came to a complete end during the reign of Ptolemaios IV.

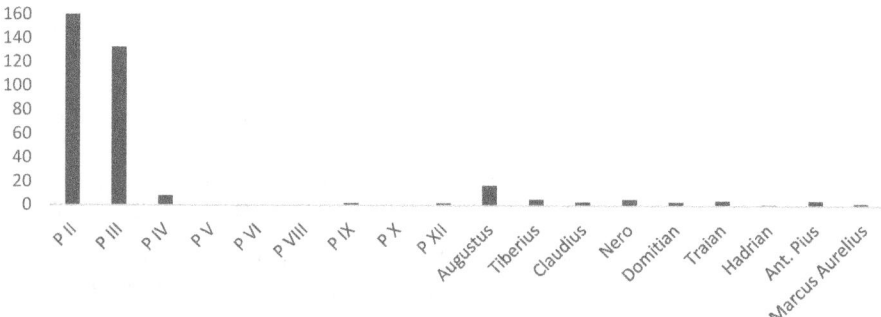

**Fig. 2:** Chronological development of the Demotic tax receipts from Elephantine (absolute amounts).

On the other hand, private Demotic sources (letters, accounts, delivery and sale documents or marriage contracts etc.) as well as religious documents (for example oracular inquiries or documents from the Khnoum temple administrative archive like lists of priests on duty) only slightly decreased from the middle Ptolemaic Period onwards (beginning with Ptolemaios IV Philopator). These types of documents are attested throughout the entire period of Elephantine Demotica. Admittedly, the use of Demotic letters themselves was less attested from the middle Ptolemaic Period onwards.[12] The last Demotic document from the island is a bilingual receipt from the 14th regnal year of Marcus Aurelius, dated 1 April 174 CE.

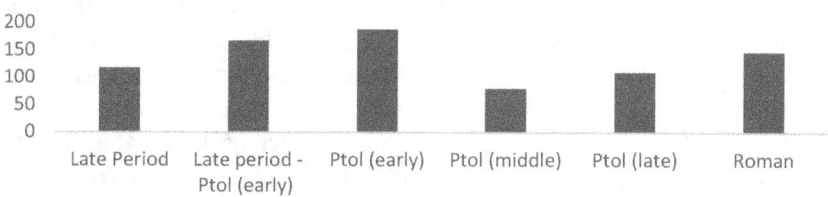

**Fig. 3:** Chronological development of the private and religious Demotica from Elephantine (absolute amounts).

---

12 See already Zauzich 1978b, p. VIII.

The Greek sources show a comparable development (Fig. 4). After the early Ptolemaic Period a small decline can be detected, with a renewed increase in Greek sources starting from the later middle Ptolemaic Period. In general, the time of Ptolemaios VI/VIII can be considered the the peak of Hellenization.[13]

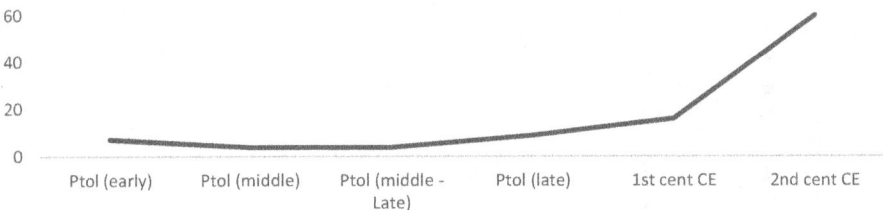

**Fig. 4:** Preliminary chronological development of the Greek sources from Elephantine (dating by R. Duttenhöfer) (in % of all currently known Elephantine sources dating to the Ptolemaic and Roman periods).

The statistical evidence suggests that during the reign of Ptolemaios IV Philopator, something caused a large decline in the usage of official documents in Demotic, but less so in that of private documents. This trigger event could be, the Upper Egyptian Great Revolt against Ptolemaios IV and his successor. The above-mentioned riots would have impacted many aspects of life and thus be traceable in the development of the sources over time.[14] One would expect an increase in Demotic documents in Elephantine again after the revolt, but this happened only partially and primarily with the private documents, as life and trade in Elephantine resumed. Peculiarly, the official documents in Demotic, especially tax receipts, never resumed; instead, the Greek receipts increased in the record.

In my opinion, this pattern can be explained by the lasting effects of the revolt. As Pestman has already shown,[15] Elephantine itself was not on the side of the rebels but remained loyal to the Ptolemaic dynasty. The Ptolemaic army was present on the island even during 197–194 BCE when they had lost Thebes and were forced upstream. At that time, the connection to the northern part of the country and the capital Alexandria was interrupted, which was, eventually, restored between 194 and 191 BCE.[16] The ongoing presence of the royal army also results in the continuous use of Greek for official documents. The marriage contract Pap. Berlin P 13593 of 12 October 198 BCE mentions an Egyptian soldier from

---

13 Vandorpe 2011, p. 292.
14 See also Moje 2019, pp. 488–489; for Thebes see Arlt 2011, pp. 25–28.
15 Pestman 1995, pp. 134–136, also for the following section. See also Locher 1999, p. 25.
16 See also McGing 1997, pp. 285–289.

the Ptolemaic military camp *ꜥfnṱ*.¹⁷ It can be located in the vicinity of Syene, as Pap. Berlin P 13596–7 confirms.¹⁸

According to the Rosetta decree from 196 BCE, attested also in Elephantine, from the reign of Ptolemaios V, the king lightened some taxes and abolished others.¹⁹ But with Pfeiffer (2010), these measures can be found in nearly all decrees.²⁰

Therefore, these activities cannot be the cause for the missing middle Ptolemaic Demotic tax receipts. Instead, another event may have been responsible. Since the restoration of the integrity of the Ptolemaic state, authorities in Upper Egypt may have distrusted Egyptian locals much more than they previously had. If so, local agents who previously held positions such as tax farmers or officials would have been dismissed and replaced by (allegedly) trustworthy Greeks, who then wrote Greek — not Demotic – or by other locals who were trained as Greek writing scribes.²¹

This change from Egyptian to Greek after the later reign of Ptolemaios V can be noticed in further written domains as well. One indicator of this development is a change in language use in multilingual sources. Concerning epigraphical sources, Egyptian Hieroglyphic-Demotic texts peaked in the early middle Ptolemaic Period, while their quantity decreased in favour of sources with Greek parts.²² Concomitantly, a Greek subscription under Egyptian documents was ordered to be mandatory²³ during the reign of Ptolemaios VI in 145 BCE, which again reduced the status of written Egyptian.

Apart from three Greek tax receipts with Demotic subscription from the late Ptolemaic Period,²⁴ no tax receipts from the middle and late Ptolemaic Periods are attested. Not until the reign of Augustus, which can be considered a caesura with the political and administrative system of the Ptolemies,²⁵ were Egyptians again influential in the administration. Then, these receipts were again written in Demotic,²⁶ even if the taxes were now collected by state institutions (with their

---

17 Erichsen 1939. See also Pestman 1995, pp. 107, 115.
18 Publication in preparation by K.-T. Zauzich. But for the section on the camp see already Erichsen 1939, p. 4: *gl-šr n ꜥfnṱ iw=f ip r Swn* "soldier from Afentj, which is assigned to Syene".
19 See Devauchelle 1986, pp. 45–47.
20 Pfeiffer 2010, pp. 87–88.
21 Vandorpe 2011, p. 297.
22 Cf. Moje 2019, see also Moje 2020.
23 Papyrus Salt 5 (Pap. Louvre gr. 2390): Pestman 1985; Lippert 2012, p. 212.
24 Ptolemaios IX: Pap. Berlin P 21690; Ptolemaios XII: Ostr. Berlin P 9389 and Ostr. Cambr Fitzw GR.P.47.
25 Pfeiffer 2010b and Pfeiffer 2010c.
26 Cf. Depauw 2012, especially pp. 494–495.

Egyptian personnel).[27] After the peak in Augustus' reign, the use of Demotic declined again and is paralleled by an increase in Greek receipts.

# 3 The Textual Evidence

Even if the Demotic texts from Elephantine never mention the revolt explicitly, there are a few references to the rebellion. This survey will critically evaluate the attestations that have been brought forward and will proceed from uncertain to certain evidence.

## 3.1 Pap. Berlin P 13564 (Uncertain Evidence)

The letter Pap. Berlin P 13564 from a unknown man to *Pa-rṯ sꜣ Ir.t-ḥr-r.r=w* deals first with the purchase of doors. A second part of the letter mentions two men, former employees of the sender, from a town *Pr-w-qr* who were brought to the south (*in=w st r pr-rsy*) and guarded (local dialectal *ḥrꜣḥ* for regular *ḥrḥ*). The sender demands to know where they will be brought to.

> (. . .) wn rmṯ Pr-w-qr ¹⁷| 2 in=w st r pr-rsy ḥn ¹⁸| nꜣ rmṯ.w Pr-w-rq iw=w tꜣy r w' ḥm (n) kꜣm (. . .) iw bw-ir-rḫ=n pꜣ mꜣ' ²¹| nty iw=w tꜣy n.im=w r.r=f iw=w ḏd n=w ²²| ḥrꜣḥ n pꜣ s 2 my ḥn=w s ²³| iw ir pꜣ šn n pꜣ mꜣ' nty iw=w tꜣy.t=w r.r=f (. . .)

> (. . .) There are two men from Philae ¹⁷| who were brought to the south among ¹⁸| the men from Philae, who belong to a small garden (. . .) We do not know the place ²¹| to which they are brought, while it is said to them: ²²| "Guard the two men!" May it be ordered ²³| to ask for the place to which they will be brought! (. . .)

The papyrus can be dated to the 3ʳᵈ regnal year of Ptolemaios IV Philopator (219 BCE) or Ptolemaios V Epiphanes (202 BCE). The two men's place of origin is written *Pr-w-qr* in l. 16 and *Pr-w-rq* in l. 18 (⟨…⟩, ⟨…⟩). Zauzich suggested that these may represent otherwise unknown variants of *Pr-iw-rq* "Philae".[28] Recently, Effland and Effland have surmised that these toponyms refer to the Osiris tomb in Abydos, a toponym which is mentioned in l. 2–3 (*ꜣbḏw*),[29] and where the letter's sender supposedly wrote from. They date the papyrus to 202 BCE and suppose

---

27 Cf. Vandorpe 2011, p. 302, already for the middle Ptolemaic Period onwards.
28 Zauzich 1971, cat. 34; Zauzich 1993, *sub* P 13564.
29 Effland, Effland 2013, p. 115.

that the two men were imprisoned in Elephantine during the Great Revolt. The authors do not explicitly justify this reading, although hieroglyphic *Pqr*[30] or *Ww-pqr* ("Peqer-district" as the sacred precinct at Abydos),[31] also attested in Demotic as *W-pkr*[32], are likely candidates for their identification. However, the orthography in Pap. Berlin P 13564 is hard to reconcile with *W-pkr*, as the initial *p* in *pkr* is coherently present in Demotic attestations.[33] On Elephantine, a variant of *Pr-iw-rq* is attested as *Pr-rq* (.[facsimile]).[34] Another full variant with a special form for *iw* from Elephantine in Pap. Berlin P 15609 has the following form: [facsimile]. In view of these attestations, the toponyms *Pr-w-qr* (l. 16) and *Pr-w-rq* (l. 18) are translated as "Philae", assuming that the "*iw*" [facsimile] (as in the Elephantine parallel P 15609) was reduced to a "*w*". Likewise, the first writing can be explained as a letter-mixing by inattention. Thus, "Philae" appears to be the origin of the arrested men. In my opinion, neither the date can be fixed to 202 BCE nor a connection with the Great Revolt can be made with any certainty. Besides, the imprisonment of two men from Abydos far south in Elephantine is hard to explain – a local quarrel between Philae and Elephantine is a much more straightforward solution.

## 3.2 Pap. Berlin P 15802 (Possible Evidence)

The unpublished and very fragmentary Ptolemaic letter Pap. Berlin P 15802 mentions previous correspondence with Thebes regarding the arrival of 200 Nubians (*[i]kš 200*) in – possibly – Elephantine. Whether this event relates to the Great Revolt needs to be discussed in the final publication. The priestly decree Philensis II attests that Nubian soldiers supported Chaonnophris in the final battle against the Ptolemaic general Komanos near the southern border of Egypt in 186 BCE, where the rebel-king fled after his expulsion from the Thebaid.[35] Military expeditions occupied the Dodekaschoinos during the time of Ptolemaios VI, and the Nubians were no longer considered a serious threat.

---

30 *Wb* I, p. 561:6–9.
31 *Wb* I, p. 243:7; Erichsen 1954, p. 87.
32 Erichsen 1954, p. 141.
33 See *CDD w*, pp. 1–2.
34 Pap. Berlin P 15515, x+11 and P 15527 v, 10. Facsimile of the reference in the latter from *CDD p*, p. 66.
35 Philensis II: Eldamaty 2005, pp. 20, 44. See Recklinghausen 2018, pp. 34, 61–62.

## 3.3 Pap. Berlin P 23625 (Possible Evidence)

The unpublished and fragmentary Ptolemaic letter Pap. Berlin P 23625 dates to an 18$^{th}$ regnal year. According to Zauzich,[36] it mentions that *Pa-rṯ* and *N3-nfr-ỉb-Rʿ* had intended to travel to the sender but returned to the south due to (incorrect?) news about a revolt in Elephantine and Syene. This letter may be connected to the Great Revolt, but the full publication is needed for a thorough analysis.

## 3.4 Pap. Berlin P 13567 (Possible Evidence)

Pap. Berlin P 13567 is a middle Ptolemaic draft of a *mqmq*-petition, followed by a list of disconnected notes.

> ¹| *p3 ꜥb3k mq¹mq* ²| *ḏi.t wṯ=w ṯ=y m-s3 p3 mšʿ* ³| *n hrw 2 r T3-št-rsy* ⁴| *gr ḏi.t w[ṯ=w ///]* ⁵| *r ḫpr n.ỉm=w* ⁶⁻⁷| *(r-)db3 p3 ḥq3 nty-ỉw=y n.ỉm=f* ⁸| *Ḥr p3 ḥr n Pa-š3 r* ⁹| *ḏi.t šm=w m-s3=f* ¹⁰| *P3-hb s3 Ḏḥwtỉ-ỉw* ¹¹| *p3 rmṯ Nḫb* ¹²| *T3-ḏỉ-Ỉy-m-ḥtp t3 ḥr(j.t) T3y-nfr* ¹³| *p3 3ḥ k3m nty (n) Swn* ¹⁴| *t3 ḥr.t (n-)ḏr.t Pa-mn-n-s*

> ¹| The memorandum. ²| Causing to send me behind the army ³| within two days to the Southern Land, ⁴| or causing to send [someone else?] [///], ⁵| to be there(?).³⁷ ⁶⁻⁷| Because of hunger in which I am. ⁸| Horos, the servant of Pasis, to ⁹| cause to come for him. ¹⁰| Phibis, son of Thoteus, ¹¹| the man from Elkab. ¹²| Teteimouthes, the handmaid of Thanouphis. ¹³| The garden area, which is located in Syene. ¹⁴| The handmaid. By Pamonasis.

Following Zauzich, the content can be reconstructed as follows:[38] Pamonasis was ordered to follow the army to the southern nome, but he tries to convince the intended addressee to assign another man because he is affected by hunger.

Since this text dates to the middle Ptolemaic Period, one may tentatively suppose that the participation in military activities and the hunger mentioned in the text could be contextualised in the setting of the revolt and/or its aftermaths. For example, Greek texts from the sitologos archive in Syene[39] mention extensive grain deliveries in the 18$^{th}$ year of Ptolemaios V (187 BCE) from several areas to the granary in Syene for the soldiers stationed there. Besides, the – undated – report Pap. Berlin P 23571 mentions that the sender has placed 3400 artabas of emmer at a third person's disposal "for the people of Syene".[40]

---

36 Zauzich 1971, cat. 252.
37 Suggestion made by Zauzich 1993, *sub* P 13567.
38 Zauzich 1993, *sub* P 13567.
39 Edited in *SB VI*, 9367.
40 Zauzich 1971, cat. 198; Zauzich in press, *sub* P 23571.

## 3.5 Pap. Berlin P 15527 (Clear Evidence)

The letter Pap. Berlin P 15527 of Horos, son of Kolluthos, to three wab-priests of Khnoum-Haroeris informs them that he intended to visit them in Philae. But at the time of his visit, all three were absent, and Horos was told that "they went south to the land of Nubia" (šm=w n=w r rsy r p3 t3 nḥs). He was worried about them and asks them twice to return to their temple and to not consider himself an enemy. Due to my attribution of the mentioned events to the Great Revolt, the text dates to the 18th regnal year of Ptolemaios V, 187 BCE.[41]

(. . .) ḫpr ỉbd 3 pr.t sw 17 [5|] tw=y ỉw.w[42] r Pr-ỉw-rq [6|] ỉrm Gm=w-Ḥp s3 Pa-rṭ Pa-t3.wỉ [7|] s3 Pa-ḥy Pa-nfr s3 Gm=w-Ḥp [8|] ḏd ỉw=n wšd ỉw=n [9|] ʿḥʿ ỉrm=tn ḏd=w n=n [10|] šm=w n=w r rsy r p3 t3 nḥs [11|] ỉn šm=s r ḥ3.ṯ=tn [12|] ḏd bn-ỉw=n ỉr p3 rwš [13|] t3 nty ỉw=tn ḫn=s ḥw [14|] r-ḥr=tn ỉw=n snt n Ḫnm [15|] n ḥw r-ḥr=tn ʿn s.t-db3 [16|] nb r.šp=n n p3 ỉwn [17|] ỉ.ỉr=n ỉr=w (r-)db3 n3 md.wt [18|] rn=w r ḏi.t wḏ3 n3y=n nṯr.w [19|] ỉ.ỉr p3y bk pḥ r.r=k[43] [20|] ỉ.mn r p3y=tn ỉrpy [21|] p3y=tn ṯ3w my wḏ3=f [22|] m-ỉr ỉr wš n ỉy r Pr-wʿb [23|] n p3 grḥ m-ỉr ḏi.t [Vso 1|] ḥtb ṯ p3 nṯr [Vso 2|] r wʿ gy šn=y [Vso 3|] N3-nfr-ỉb-Rʿ p3 ḥm-nṯr Ḫnm (r-)db3 [Vso 4|] p3 wḏ3y n3 ỉrpy.w [Vso 5|] mn ḏ3 nb (. . .) [Vso 8|] bn-pw=y srf r ỉy r ʿḥʿ [Vso 9|] ỉrm=tn ỉw=y ḥrp [Vso 10|] r ỉy r Pr-(ỉw-)rq n p3 hrw ḏd [Vso 11|] ỉw=y (r) ʿḥʿ ỉrm=tn ỉw=s [Vso 12|] (n) ḥ3.ṯ=y ỉ.ỉr=tn ỉp [Vso 13|] n.ỉm=n r ḫyr [Vso 14|] n3-wḏ3[44] ḥ3.ṯ=n ỉ.ỉr [Vso 15|] p3 nṯr (n) ḥw r-ḥr=tn ỉ.ỉr=tn [Vso 16|] nw r p3y bk m-ỉr wrr [Vso 17|] r p3y=tn ỉrpy (. . .)

(. . .) When the 17th of Phamenoth arrived, [5|] I came to Philae [6|] with Komoapis, son of Parates, (with) Patous, [7|] son of Pachois, (and with) Panouphis, son of Komoapis, [8|] to worship you (and) [9|] to visit you. We were told: [10|] "They travelled south to the land of Nubia." [11|] Did you not realise, [12|] that we worry [13|] about the (situation) in which you are much more [14|] than you (by yourself?)? We fear Khnoum [15|] even more than you! Every calamity [16|] which we received on the voyage, [17|] it was on account of the matters [18|] in question, in order to keep our gods safe. [19|] Once this letter reaches you, [20|] come (back) to your temple! [21|] Your breath: May it be thriving! [22|] Do not stop coming to the Abaton [23|] in the night! Do not let [Vso 1|] the god penalise[45] me [Vso 2|] in some manner! I have queried [Vso 3|] Nepherpres, the priest of Khnoum, about [Vso 4|] the well-being of the temples. [Vso 5|] There is no disadvantage. (. . .) [Vso 8|] I did not waste time to come and meet [Vso 9|] with you, rising early, [Vso 10|] to come to Philae today [Vso 11|] and to meet with you, as [Vso 12|] it was close to my heart. (But) you consider [Vso 13|] us to be enemies! [Vso 14|] Our heart is more open towards [Vso 15|] the god than towards you. Once you [Vso 16|] see this letter, do not delay [Vso 17|] to come (back) to your temple! (. . .)

---

41 Martin 2011, cat. C15, see also Pfeiffer 2021, pp. 114–115 and already Veïsse 2004, pp. 227–228.
42 Cf. Den Brinker, Muhs, Vleeming 2005, p. 51.
43 Reading variant Zauzich 1978b: {r-r=k} <r-ḥr-tn>.
44 Cf. Den Brinker, Muhs, Vleeming 2005, p. 51. Reading variant Zauzich 1978b: n3-nfr.
45 For a translation, cf. Den Brinker, Muhs, Vleeming 2005, p. 51.

This flight of a group of priests and the described circumstances – their sudden departure, the peril and danger in travelling – suggest that these priests were somehow affected or even involved in the revolt and decided to flee to Nubia, while neglecting the required religious service. In year 18 the revolt was nearly over, after the defeat of Chaonnophris and his Nubian auxiliary troops at the southern Egyptian border. Would it be possible that these three priests had been on the side of the rebels and fled south over the border, fearing retaliatory measures from the victorious Ptolemaic troops? Zauzich points out that the sender asks about possible damages to the temple (which had not happened),[46] which also points to a violent context.[47] Likewise, the sender claims that the addressees' life will be spared and the state will be merciful to them.[48]

## 3.6 Pap. Berlin P 23641 (Clear Evidence)

The unpublished and very fragmentary letter Pap. Berlin P 23641 was sent to a certain *Ns-Ḫnm-pꜣ-mtr*;[49] the name of the sender is lost. Two lines contain information which may reflect the rebellion (see Fig. 5).

⁵⁾ [///] *Ḥr-Wn-nfr* ⸢*pꜣ*⸣ *nty ir iy rs* ⁶⁾ [///] ⸢..?..⸣ *iw=f b[g]s Yb*

⁵⁾ [///] Haronnophris is the one who came to the south ⁶⁾ [///] ⸢..?..⸣ to rebel (against) Elephantine . . .

In his first edition in 1971, Zauzich assumed *b[k]i* "to suffer shipwreck".[50] But this word ends clearly with an "*s*", with a haplography of the determinative 𓏴 which is the same as the last element of the "*s*". The "*g*" is still partially visible within the destroyed passage, so that *b⸢g⸣s* is a very probable reading.[51] Zauzich's and Pestman's readings as "he rebels *in* Elephantine" should therefore be

---

46 Zauzich 1978b, *sub* P 15527. See also Martin 2011, pp. 319–320.
47 Destruction of temples during the revolt is mentioned in Philensis II: Recklinghausen 2018, pp. 61–62.
48 Zauzich 1983, p. 424.
49 This variant of the name given in Zauzich 1971, cat. 268 will be preferred here, against the other version *Ns-Ḫnm pꜣ mr-šn* suggested there.
50 Erichsen 1954, p. 125; *CDD b*, p. 92 has no further attestations.
51 For this correction see Den Brinker, Muhs, Vleeming 2005, p. 17. Erichsen 1954, p. 125; *CDD b*, p. 92 has no further attestations. *bgs* is the normal term connected in later attestations of the rebel-kings. For the Greek termini for "revolt" see Veïsse 2007.

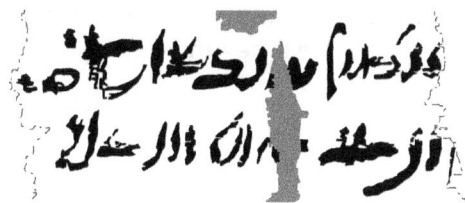

**Fig. 5:** Pap. Berlin P 23641, l. 5–6 (facsimile J. Moje).

modified.[52] As stated above, the area of Elephantine/Syene was loyal to the Ptolemies during the entire time of the Great Revolt. Thus, "he rebels *against* Elephantine" is to be preferred here. Furthermore, it is less probable that a new sentence begins with the lemma *Yb* "Elephantine".

In this text, the supposed name of the rebel-king Haronnophris is neither written in a cartouche, nor followed by ꜥnḫ wḏꜣ snb "life, peace, health", nor does it use other royal prerogatives.[53] But rendering the names of rebel-kings as if they were those of private persons is already attested in other documents.[54] On Elephantine, rendering Haronnophris' name in a royal manner would have meant a formal acceptance of his rule.

Unfortunately, it remains unclear when this letter was written: Does it reflect the actual ongoing rebellion, or does the sender refer to past events?

## 4 Summary

This brief study intended to exemplify from the perspective of the Demotic sources, how Elephantine was affected by the Great Revolt, even if its "territory" was loyal to the Ptolemaic state and had never been occupied by rebel troops. Most of the evidence is indirect, such as the decline of official Egyptian documents etc., but the few relevant texts show the effects of the revolt on a local scale, with individuals being affected in their daily life. In general, most of these private sources never mention the rebellion directly. For the locals writing Demotic letters the revolt was an impressive experience and part of their cultural memory, it could also affect

---

[52] Zauzich 1983, p. 424; Pestman 1995, p. 135.
[53] This form for Haronnophris' name is attested in the Demotic Theban documents dated to him.
[54] Pestman 1995, pp. 135, 125–126.

their personal life, so it can be found in such letters, but mainly not as a main topic. Official texts regarding the revolt will be expected to be written in Greek.

# Bibliography

Arlt 2011
    Arlt, C., "Scribal Offices and Scribal Families in Ptolemaic Thebes", in P.F. Dorman, B. M. Bryan (eds.), *Perspectives on Ptolemaic Thebes*, SAOC 65, Chicago, 2011, pp. 17–34.

Ashton 2001
    Ashton, S.-A., *Ptolemaic Royal Sculpture from Egypt: The Interaction between Greek and Egyptian Traditions*, BARIS 923, Oxford, 2001.

Den Brinker, Muhs, Vleeming 2005
    Den Brinker, A.A., Muhs, B., Vleeming, S.P., *A Berichtigungsliste of Demotic Documents*, StudDem 7, Leuven, 2005.

Depauw 2006
    Depauw, M., "Egyptianizing the Chancellery during the Great Theban Revolt (205–186 BC): A New Study of the Limestone Tablet Cairo 38258", *SAK* 34, 2006, pp. 97–105.

Depauw 2012 Depauw, M., "Language Use, Literacy, and Bilingualism", in C. Riggs (ed.), *The Oxford Handbook of Roman Egypt*, Oxford, 2012, pp. 493–506.

Depauw et al. 2008
    Depauw, M., Arlt, C., Elebaut, M., Georgila, A., Gülden, S., Knuf, H., Naether, F., Verreth, H., *A Chronological Survey of Precisely Dated Demotic and Abnormal Hieratic Sources, Version 1.0 February 2007*, Trismegistos Online Publications 1, Cologne, Leuven, 2008.

Devauchelle 1986
    Devauchelle, D., "Fragments de décrets ptolémaïques en langue égyptienne conserves au Musée du Louvre", *RdE* 37, 1986, pp. 45–51.

Effland, Effland 2013
    Effland, U., Effland, A., *Abydos: Tor zur ägyptischen Unterwelt*, Darmstadt, Mainz, 2013.

Eldamaty 2005
    Eldamaty, M., *Ein ptolemäisches Priesterdekret aus dem Jahr 186 v. Chr.: Eine neue Version von Philensis II in Kairo*, AfP Beihefte 20, Munich, Leipzig, 2005.

Erichsen 1939
    Erichsen, W., *Ein demotischer Ehevertrag aus Elephantine*, Berlin, 1939.

Erichsen 1954
    Erichsen, W., *Demotisches Glossar*, Copenhagen, 1954.

Hölbl 1994
    Hölbl, G., *Geschichte des Ptolemäerreiches: Politik, Ideologie und religiöse Kultur von Alexander dem Großen bis zur römischen Eroberung*, Darmstadt, 1994.

Huß 2001
    Huß, W., *Ägypten in hellenistischer Zeit. 332–30 v. Chr.*, Munich, 2001.

Lippert 2012
    Lippert, S.L., *Einführung in die altägyptische Rechtsgeschichte*, EQÄ 5, Berlin², 2012.

Locher 1999
    Locher, J., *Topographie und Geschichte der Region am Ersten Nilkatarakt in griechisch-römischer Zeit*, AfP Beihefte 5, Stuttgart, Leipzig, 1999.

Martin 2011
: Martin, C.J., "The Demotic Texts", in B. Porten (ed.), *The Elephantine Papyri in English: Three Millennia of Cross-cultural Continuity and Change*, Leiden, 1996, pp. 277–385.

McGing 1997
: McGing, B.C., "Revolt Egyptian Style: Internal Opposition to Ptolemaic Rule", *AfP* 43, 1997, pp. 273–314.

Moje 2019
: Moje, J., "Bemerkungen zur Entwicklungsgeschichte der demotischen Epigraphik im kulturgeschichtlichen Kontext des späten Ägypten", in M. Brose, P. Dils, F. Naether, L. Popko, D. Raue (eds.), *Én détail: Philologie und Archäologie im Diskurs*, ZÄS Bf 7, Berlin, 2019, pp. 733–756.

Moje 2020
: Moje, J., "History of Recording Demotic Epigraphy", in V. Davies, D. Laboury (eds.), *The Oxford Handbook of Egyptian Epigraphy and Palaeography*, New York, 2020, pp. 492–507.

Moje 2020b
: Moje, J., "Verwaltung oder Praxis: Die demotischen Aufschriften der Ibis-Bestattungen in Tuna el-Gebel und ihre Aussagekraft für den lokalen Ibis-Kult", in M. Flossmann-Schütze, F. Hoffmann, A. Schütze (eds.), *Tuna el Gebel: Eine ferne Welt – Tagungsband zur Konferenz der Graduate School 'Distant Worlds' vom 16. bis 19.1.2014 in München*, Tuna el Gebel 8, Vaterstetten, 2020, pp. 375–391.

Pestman 1985
: Pestman, P.W., "Registration of Demotic Contracts in Egypt. P. Par. 65; 2nd cent. B.C.", in R. Feenstra (ed.), *Satura Roberto Feenstra sexagesimum quintum annum aetatis complenti ab alumnis collegis amicis oblata*, Fribourg, 1985, pp. 17–25.

Pestman 1995
: Pestman, P.W., "Haronnophris and Chaonnophris: Two Indigenous Pharaohs in Ptolemaic Egypt (205–186 B.C.)", in S.P. Vleeming (ed.), *Hundred-Gated Thebes: Acts of a Colloquium on Thebes and the Theban Area in the Graeco-Roman Period*, P.L.Bat. 27, Leiden, New York, Cologne, 1995, pp. 101–137.

Pfeiffer 2010
: Pfeiffer, S., "Das Dekret von Rosette: Die ägyptischen Priester und der Herrscherkult", in G. Weber (ed.), *Alexandreia und das ptolemäische Ägypten: Kulturbegegnungen in hellenistischer Zeit*, Berlin, 2010, pp. 84–108.

Pfeiffer 2010b
: Pfeiffer, S., *Der römische Kaiser und das Land am Nil: Kaiserverehrung und Kaiserkult in Alexandria und Ägypten von Augustus bis Caracalla (30 v. Chr.–217 n. Chr.)*, Historia Einzelschriften 212, Stuttgart, 2010.

Pfeiffer 2010c
: Pfeiffer, S., "Octavian-Augustus und Ägypten", in A. Coşkun, H. Heinen, S. Pfeiffer (eds.), *Identität und Zugehörigkeit im Osten der griechisch-römischen Welt: Aspekte ihrer Repräsentation in Städten, Provinzen und Reichen*, Bern, 2010, pp. 55–79.

Pfeiffer 2011
: Pfeiffer, S., "Die Politik Ptolemaios' VI. und VIII. im Kataraktgebiet: Die 'ruhigen' Jahre von 163 bis 136 v. Chr.", in A. Jördens, J.F. Quack (eds.), *Ägypten zwischen innerem Zwist und äußerem Druck: die Zeit Ptolemaios' VI. bis VIII. – Internationales Symposion Heidelberg 16.–19.9.2007*, Philippika 45, Wiesbaden, 2011, pp. 235–254.

Pfeiffer 2021
Pfeiffer, S., "Innere Konflikte und herrschaftliche Versöhnungsstrategien im ptolemäischen Ägypten (3.-2. Jh. v. Chr.)", in S. Pfeiffer, G. Weber (eds.), *Gesellschaftliche Spaltungen im Zeitalter des Hellenismus (4. bis 1. Jahrhundert v. Chr.)*, Oriens et Occidens 35, Stuttgart, 2021, pp. 107–128.

Recklinghausen 2018
Recklinghausen, D. von, *Die Philensis-Dekrete: Untersuchungen über zwei Synodaldekrete aus der Zeit Ptolemaios' V. und ihre geschichtliche und religiöse Bedeutung*, ÄA 73, Wiesbaden, 2018.

Thissen, Moje in press
Thissen†, H.J., Moje, J., *Demotische Texte aus den Ibis-Galerien von Tuna el-Gebel*, Tuna el Gebel, Vaterstetten, in press.

Vandorpe 2011
Vandorpe, K., "A Successful, but Fragile Biculturalism: The Hellenization Process in the Upper Egyptian Town of Pathyris under Ptolemy VI and VIII", in A. Jördens, J.F. Quack (eds.), *Ägypten zwischen innerem Zwist und äußerem Druck: die Zeit Ptolemaios' VI. bis VIII. – Internationales Symposion Heidelberg 16.–19.9.2007*, Philippika 45, Wiesbaden, 2011, pp. 292–308.

Veïsse 2004
Veïsse, A.-E., *Les "révoltes égyptiennes". Recherches sur les troubles du règne de Ptolémée III à la conquête romaine*, StudHell 41, Leuven, Paris, Dudley, M., 2004.

Veïsse 2007
Veïsse, A.-E., "Le vocabulaire de la révolte dans l'Egypte ptolémaïque: *tarachè, apostasis, amixia*", in B. Palme (ed.), *Akten des 23. Internationalen Papyrologen-Kongresses*, PapVind 1, Vienna, 2007, pp. 715–718.

Vleeming 2015
Vleeming, S.P., *Demotic Graffiti and Other Short Texts Collected from Many Publications: Short Texts III 1201–2350*, StudDem 12, Leuven, 2015.

Zauzich 1971
Zauzich, K.-Th., *Ägyptische Handschriften Teil 2*, Verzeichnis der Orientalischen Handschriften in Deutschland 19,2, Wiesbaden, 1971.

Zauzich 1978a
Zauzich, K.-Th., "Neue Namen für die Könige Harmachis und Anchmachis", *GM* 29, 1978, pp. 157–158.

Zauzich 1978b
Zauzich, K.-Th., *Papyri von der Insel Elephantine 1*, DPB 1, East-Berlin, 1978.

Zauzich 1983
Zauzich, K.-Th., "Die demotischen Papyri von der Insel Elephantine", in E. van't Dack, P. van Dessel, W. van Gucht (eds.), *Egypt and the Hellenistic World: Proceedings of the International Colloquium Leuven 24–26 May 1982*, StudHell 27, Leuven, 1983, pp. 421–435.

Zauzich 1993
Zauzich, K.-Th., *Papyri von der Insel Elephantine 2*, Demotische Papyri aus den Staatlichen Museen zu Berlin 3, Berlin, 1993

Zauzich in press
Zauzich, K.-Th., *Papyri von der Insel Elephantine 3*, Demotische Papyri aus den Staatlichen Museen zu Berlin, in press.

Alexandra Nespoulous-Phalippou
# Native Revolts from South Thebes to North Thebes: Historical Facts and Royal Ideology According to the Priestly Decrees from Ptolemy V Epiphanes' reign (204–180 BCE)

Ptolemy V Epiphanes' reign (204–180 BCE) was very turbulent.[1] The kingdom was divided when he accessed the throne at the age of five.[2] Indeed, Upper Egypt had entered secession in 206 BCE during the reign of his father, Ptolemy IV Philopator.[3] When the latter and the queen were murdered two years later, the orphan heir was too young to govern, and so the rule was assigned to regent courtiers in anticipation of his eligibility to reign. In addition to Upper Egypt, several sporadic centres of disturbance had broken out under Epiphanes' reign.[4]

The corpus of documents relating to these conflicts, which are the priestly decrees,[5] is relatively large. Their number is truly greater under Ptolemy V Epiphanes than any other Ptolemaic king: five are attested with certainty.[6] From a diachronic standpoint, their study may help to discern historical facts and to perceive the Ptolemaic king through the eyes of the Egyptian priesthood.

Indeed, these official epigraphic documents so specific to the Ptolemaic period give valuable insight into the political events of the reign of Ptolemy V Epiphanes. The comprehension of the evolving relationship between the Alexandrian crown and the local clergies depends on two issues. On the one hand, the heterogeneity of the corpus of these synodal decrees, and on the other, a paradox specific to this reign involving the decline of the Alexandrian authority (in Egypt and the Eastern Mediterranean) whilst numerous decrees were issued stating the

---

1 Bouché-Leclercq 1903, I, pp. 341–401; Huß 2001, pp. 473–536; Hölbl 2001, pp. 125–178; Veïsse 2004, pp. 5–20; Pfeiffer 2017, pp. 119–135.
2 Bikerman 1940, pp. 124–131.
3 About that conflict: Alliot 1951, pp. 421–443; Alliot 1952, pp. 18–26; Vandorpe 1986, pp. 294–302; Beckerath 2000, pp. 43–46; Huß 2001, p. 447–449 and pp. 506–513; Hölbl 2001, pp. 153–159; Veïsse 2004, pp. 11–20; O'Neil 2012, pp. 133–149; Pfeiffer 2017, pp. 123–125; Recklinghausen 2018, I, pp. 286–288.
4 Veïsse 2004, pp. 7–14. About the foreign policy of Epiphanes: Huß 2001, pp. 514–523; Hölbl 2001, pp. 134–143.
5 Chauveau 1997, pp. 51–53; Hoffmann 2000, pp. 153–175; Veïsse 2004, p. 203; Quack 2008, pp. 275–289; Gozzoli 2009, pp. 145–152.
6 Clarysse 1999, p. 43.

king's euergetism towards the divinities and the Egyptian population. The phraseology of these decrees reveals an evolution in the way the ideological image of the king was depicted by the Egyptian priests.

# 1 Priestly Decrees from the Reign of Ptolemy V Epiphanes

## 1.1 Features of the Priestly Decrees (Also Called Synodal Decrees)

The priestly decrees are quite original in their hybrid nature and thus reflect "cultural crossroads" between Greek and Egyptian traditions, as outlined by Willy Clarysse. Whilst their iconography and topics stem more from Egyptian culture, their composition and structure reflect Greek influence.[7] Their composition in fact complies with euergetism decrees from Greek cities, and their layout has a very precise form, as they are canonically divided into five parts. Such decrees first present a triple dating (Macedonian, Egyptian, and the Greek way of noting eponymous priests of the current Macedonian year). Next, a preamble gives the synod's location, the reason for the meeting, and the respective sacerdotal titles of the attending priests. Also stated is an enumeration of the king's decisions taken in honour of the Egyptian gods, their servants, and the people. In return for these benefits, the priests then record their own decisions, taken collectively to honour the king. As a reward for royal euergetism, the decrees were intended to determine the rules of dynastic worship within the realm of native temples for the king or the royal couple as *synnaoi theoi*.[8] The publication requirements of these decrees typically conclude these documents. They furnish information on the political program of a reign and the methods of religious life related to dynastic worship. Notably, these texts often relate contemporaneous events from the Lagids in the form of historical accounts. These narratives usually serve as eulogies to the glory of the ruling king.

Attention needs to be drawn to the issuing authority of these decrees.[9] Unlike the commemorative stelae, it is more the priest's decisions that are registered

---

7 Clarysse 1999, pp. 41–65; Cole 2019, pp. 231–258; for an analysis of synodal decrees (with previous bibliography), see Recklinghausen 2018, I, pp. 1–8 and pp. 181–234.
8 Lanciers 1991, pp. 117–145; Pfeiffer 2004, pp. 235–237; Pfeiffer 2011, pp. 116–141.
9 Clarysse 1999, p. 51.

here than those by the king; the first purpose, as mentioned, is to define the methods of dynastic worship and the clergy's organisation within the native temples.[10]

This process of erecting stelae displaying decrees of euergetism considerably differs from traditional Egyptian practices, whilst the thereon-contained texts are usually in hieroglyphic, Demotic and Greek script. The native vernacular language, Demotic, was usually used for administrative texts, and thence also here.[11] The use of a foreign language such as Greek within the domain of the temple – then considered the preserver of native traditions – is one of the innovative features of these stelae. However, given the systematic presence of the hieroglyphic version (the other versions are sometimes missing) in the synodal decrees, it is worth analysing them on a diachronic scale.[12]

## 1.2 Presentation of the Priestly Decrees Under the Reign of Ptolemy V Epiphanes

A comprehensive and diachronic study of this official epigraphic documentation brings new insights into synodal practice, which constitutes a major aspect of the relationship between the priests and the Ptolemaic kings.[13] As mentioned, five decrees are attested with certainty to the rule of Ptolemy V Epiphanes (204–180 BCE). The main feature of this reign consists of the fact that the synodal decrees are the most numerous to be attested. The state of the documentation doesn't seem to be due to chances of discoveries nor to preservation but is rather the reflection of reality. Without being able to observe a multiplication of the synods under this reign, it is at least a multiplication of published priestly decrees that can be observed.

Presented in chronological order, each decree is named after its provenience and the date years according to the Julian calendar. Let us also present the synods which led to the drafting of decrees and also the reasons.

---

[10] For a comparison between the corpus of commemorative stelae and those of synodal decrees and their respective features: Nespoulous-Phalippou 2015a, II, pp. 254–258.
[11] Daumas 1972, pp. 41–45; for Demotic in synodal decrees: Devauchelle 1999, pp. 11–23; Chauveau 1999, pp. 25–39.
[12] For the composition and the publication of the acts of synodal decrees: Nespoulous-Phalippou 2015a, II, pp. 243–253; Recklinghausen 2018, I, pp. 181–234.
[13] Huß 1994; Huß 1999, pp. 117–126; Pfeiffer 2010, pp. 84–108.

**1) A priestly decree dated to the reign of Ptolemy V Epiphanes (199–194[?] BCE).** It is known only in the form of five fragments from a single stela discovered on the island of Elephantine (Louvre, AF 10077–10078, 1–4).[14] We are indebted to D. Devauchelle (1986, pp. 45–51) for having recognised a copy of a synodal decree from Elephantine preserved in five fragments dated to Ptolemy Epiphanes, thanks to the presence of the epithet *nb nfrw* "possessor of perfection" or "master of beauty". This one is characteristic of this reign but was temporary in its protocol. It is generally agreed that this epithet is dated between 199/198 BCE, the year of the establishment of the king's cult, and the winter of 194/193 BCE, that of his marriage with Queen Cleopatra I. The too-small fragments of preserved text reveal neither the circumstances under which a synod was organised nor the content of the decree.[15] Maybe the synod was held on the occasion of the Egyptian coronation of the king and/or the setting up of the Macedonian dynastic cult, which could be dated to the reign's year 7.[16]

**2) The Memphis Decree (196 BCE).** Dated to the 9$^{th}$ year of the reign of Ptolemy V (27 March 196 BCE), this decree is known from the Rosetta Stone (British Museum, EA 24),[17] a stela from Nobareh (Cairo, CG 31088),[18] a stela from Noub Taha (Alexandria 21352),[19] and three fragments of a stela from Elephantine (Louvre E 12677 + AF 10006-7).[20] The Rosetta Stone is the best preserved. The Nobareh stela is particular because it is a late copy re-edited in the 23$^{rd}$ year.[21] The synod of the Memphis Decree (196 BCE) was held on the occasion of the king's coronation anni-

---

14 Devauchelle 1986, pp. 46–47 and pl. 9; Nespoulous-Phalippou 2015a, II, pp. 281–282.
15 Nespoulous-Phalippou 2015a, II, p. 259.
16 For the dating of the dynastic cult: Minas 2000, p. 123. For a translation of this synodal decree, see: Nespoulous-Phalippou 2015a, II, pp. 259–260.
17 Bibliography: Sethe 1904 (*Urk.* II), pp. 166–198; Gauthier 1916 (*LdR* IV), p. 277; Daumas 1952, *passim*; Roeder 1959, pp. 167–190; Quirke, Andrews 1988, pp. 8–9; Huß 1991, p. 195 and n. 39; Clarysse 1999, p. 43; Leclant 1999, pp. 12–13, n. 3; Huß 2001, pp. 504–505, n. 30; Hölbl 2001, p. 165, pp. 174–175, n. 38; Veïsse 2004, p. 206; Thompson 2012, pp. 111–112. For the Demotic version: Spiegelberg 1922, pp. 38–65; Devauchelle 1990; Simpson 1996, pp. 258–271; and also: Spiegelberg 1917, pp. 117–118; Farid 1995, p. 75. For the Greek text: *SB* V, n° 8299; Dittenberger 1903–1905 (OGIS 90); Bernand 1992, pp. 44–49; Burnet 2003, pp. 43–46; *TM*, 8809; Nespoulous-Phalippou 2015a, II, pp. 283–301.
18 Gauthier 1916 (*LdR* IV), p. 282; PM IV, 50; Bouriant 1885, pp. 1–20; Kamal 1904, pp. 183–187, pl. 62–63; Sethe 1916, pp. 284–297; Daumas 1952, pp. 6–7; Huß 1991, p. 195, n. 39; Yoyotte 1993–1994, pp. 690–692; Clarysse 1999, p. 43; Veïsse 2004, p. 206.
19 Daumas 1952, p. 284; Fraser 1956, pp. 57–62; Huß 1991, p. 195, n. 39; Clarysse 1999, p. 43; Veïsse 2004, p. 206.
20 Devauchelle 1986, pp. 46–47, pl. 9; cf. Bernand 1982, pp. 24–25, n° 90.
21 Yoyotte 1993–1994, pp. 690–692; Nespoulous-Phalippou 2015a, I, pp. 8–9.

versary ceremony in the Egyptian manner.²² It had several political goals, in particular, the pacification of the kingdom following the repression of the Lykopolite revolt in the Delta²³ and the implementation of a whole series of economic measures, thus establishing a genuine political programme.

**3) The Alexandria Decree (186 BCE).** This decree is known as the *Philensis II* Inscription at Philae,²⁴ on top of the west wall of the Birthhouse, and also by the Cairo Stela TR 27/11/58/4.²⁵ The Alexandria Decree (186 BCE) is an extraordinary synod since it is the result of a particular political event of major importance, namely the repression of the revolt in Upper Egypt which had broken out 20 years earlier under the reign of his father, Ptolemy IV Philopator.

**4) The Memphis Decree (185 BCE).** It is known by the *Philensis I* Inscription at Philae, on the wall of the Birthhouse, close to *Philensis II*.²⁶ There is also a fairly large fragment from Dendara²⁷ as well as a similar one from Taposiris Magna.²⁸ One year after the Alexandria Decree (186 BCE), the Memphis Decree from 185 BCE resulted from a synod on the occasion of a religious ceremony, namely the installation of the living Apis bull. The main part of the text is dedicated to Cleopatra I, following her euergetism. Although not alluded to in the text, this may have had to do with the recent birth of Ptolemy VI Philometor, referred to later in his titles as "the twin of the living Apis", with which the priests chose specifically to honour the queen.²⁹

---

22 After a first nomination when he was five (Polybius, *History*, XV, 25,3; Bernand 1992, pp. 47–48; Veïsse 2004, p. 189), and a second when he was an adult of 14 years of age (during the Greek ceremony of *anakleteria*) which would have been when he took up his office: Polybius, *History*, XVIII, 55,3; Bernand 1992, p. 58; Veïsse 2004, pp. 187–188. For the dating of this ceremony: Veïsse 2004, p. 191.
23 Huß 2001, pp. 507–509; Hölbl 2001, pp. 155–156 and p. 166; Veïsse 2004, pp. 7–9.
24 Sethe 1904, pp. 214–230; Müller 1920, pp. 57–88, pl. 21–40; Pierce et al. (eds.) 1996, pp. 600–605, n° 134; Nespoulous-Phalippou 2015a, II, pp. 302–317; Recklinghausen 2018, I, pp. 10–13 (for the location of the text).
25 Eldamaty 2005.
26 Sethe 1904, pp. 198–214; Müller 1920, pp. 21–56, pl. 1–20; now see the complete and full publication of both the Alexandria (186 BCE) and Memphis decrees (185 BCE): Recklinghausen 2018.
27 Daumas 1958, pp. 73–82.
28 Discovered in 2015, the stela is being studied by D. von Recklinghausen and K. Martinez: Recklinghausen 2018, I, pp. 17–18.
29 About the dating of the birth of Ptolemy VI Philometor: Ray 1978, pp. 113–120. For the epithet *ḥtr ḥp ʿnḫ m sḫnt=sn* "the twin of the living Apis on their *meskhenet*", as symbolic twinning: Arnette 2017, p. 50.

**5) The Memphis Decree (182 BCE).** Until 2018 this decree was known from two hieroglyphic stelae preserved at the Egyptian Museum. The first one is the Cairo stela TR 2/3/25/7 and the second one the Cairo stela JE 44901.[30] In 2015 I did finish the publication of my PhD thesis with the following words: "Enfin, avec l'espoir que les sables d'Égypte nous livrent un jour une meilleure copie de ce décret nous conclurons avec Daressy: 'Nous avons là des feuillets mutilés de l'histoire des Lagides, il est grandement à souhaiter qu'on arrive à les compléter'".[31] Three years later, this wish came true with the discovery of two well-preserved stelae from Kom Ombo. Both are dated to Epiphanes's reign, and one is a new copy of the Memphis decree (182 BCE). The publication of the stelae has been announced by Dr. Shafia Badier and Dr. Ali Abdelhalim Ali who both are part of the Kom Ombo team.[32] The discovery of a new copy of this decree allows us to identify its correct date which until now has been problematic. A photograph published on a web blog[33] permits to read the text's beginning and to resolve the dating problem.

ḥ3.t-sp 23 qrpy3ys (sw) 24 nty jr 3bd jmy.w T3-mry 3bd 4 pr.t (sw) 24

Year 23, qerpiaos-month, day 24 that corresponds to these who are in Egypt, 4th month of peret-season, day 24.

This date is the same as that of the Nobareh stela, the late copy of the decree of the 9th year of the reign. Thus, according to the Egyptian calendar, the Memphis Decree (182 BCE) is dated to 29 May 182 BCE.[34]

The Memphis Decree, being the last of the reign (182 BCE), shows that the synod had taken place on the occasion of another religious ceremony: the Mnevis bull's induction. Its content differs markedly from the other decrees because it is truncated from the usual priestly and publication requirements. It is exclusively known from hieroglyphic stelae, which is why it is difficult to identify the real

---

**30** Daressy 1911, pp. 1–8 (Cairo RT 2/3/25/7); Daressy 1916–1917, pp. 175–179; (Cairo JE 44901); Nespoulous-Phalippou 2015a.
**31** Nespoulous-Phalippou 2015a, II, p. 280.
**32** https://www.ifao.egnet.net/recherche/archeologie/kom-ombo/ accessed 30 August 2024.
**33** https://djedmedu.wordpress.com/2018/08/17/kom-ombo-scoperte-due-stele-di-tolomeo-xii/ accessed 30 August 2024.
**34** Dating the synod was problematic, because of the divergence between both stelae of the Memphis Decree (182 BCE) (TR 2/3/25/7: ḥ3.t-sp 23 qrpy3ys sw 24 nty jr 3bd n jmy.w T3-mry sw 24 and JE 44901: ḥ3.t-sp 23 ỉply3s sw 22 nty jr 3bd n jmy.w T3-mry) and between the Cairo stela TR 2/3/25/7 and the Nobareh stela (ḥ3.t-sp 23 qrpy3ys sw 24 nty jr 3bd n jmy.w T3-mry 3bd 4 pr.t sw 24) too. For the whole discussion: Nespoulous-Phalippou 2015a, II, pp. 157–160.

purpose of this text. However, its publication seems to be related to a very important repression of a trouble centre in the Delta, in the area of northern Thebes, as will be seen below.

## 2 Conflicts in South Thebes

The priestly decree by the synod in Alexandria in year 19 of Ptolemy V Epiphanes (186 BCE) mentions an important conflict in the Thebaid. It is the first Egyptian artefact mentioning Aristonikos, son of Aristonikos,[35] an eminent general who played a major role in the events under Epiphanes. Aristonikos is reported to arrive before the king as a herald to announce victory over Ankhunnefer, the rebel of Upper Egypt and illegitimate king known as Chaonnophris in Greek sources.[36]

Aristonikos's official proclamation is the main subject at the beginning of the decree issued by the Alexandria synod (*Philensis II*, ll. 3-4):[37]

ḥft smj s(.t) n ḥm=f m rʒ mḥ-jb n ḥm[=f] mry nsw ḥry ḥrp-nfr.w
Jwrsdʒny<k>ws pʒ Jwrs[dʒ]nyg[w]s m s.t
[Q]ʒmꜥnws [n]ty jmytw jmy-[jb].w tpy(.w) n.w ḥm=f m-ḏd
ꜥḥʒ~n=f m [4] Tʒ-šmꜥw m ww n Wʒs.t ḥnꜥ sbj ḫftj nṯr.w
[bṯ]nw(?) Ḫ[r-wn-nf(r)] ḥnꜥ [ts]y.w nty(.w) nḥsy.w
dmḏ=sn ḥnꜥ=f smʒ~n=f sn ʒmm [snṯ(w)] pn [ꜥnḫ]

[The priests gathered in Alexandria] (. . .) after this was related to his majesty from the mouth of [his] majesty's trusted man, the king's beloved, the commander-in-chief of the cavalry, Aristoni<k>os, son of Aris[to]nik[o]s, about [K]omanos who is among the king's first friends, saying: 'He (= Komanos) fought in [4] Upper Egypt in the territory of Thebes against

---

35 Carrez-Maratray 2014, pp. 81–105; Nespoulous-Phalippou 2015b, pp. 151–183.
36 Clarysse, De Meulenaere 1978, pp. 243–253; Vandorpe 1986, pp. 294–302; Pestman 1995, pp. 101–137; McGing 1997, pp. 285–289; Veïsse 2004, pp. 11–26; Coulon 2008, pp. 17–32.
37 For the commentary of the whole passage: Recklinghausen 2018, I, pp. 34–46 (and in this volume); for the features of this preamble: Recklinghausen 2018, I, p. 46.

the enemy, the rebel against the gods, the [reb]el [Ankhunnefer], with the [troop]s of Nubians who rallied behind him. He slaughtered them (and) this [coward] had been seized [alive]'.

After the usual canonic part in the text referring to several measures of royal euergetism appears an inserted transitional sentence concerning the returned rewards to the king or the royal couple by the Egyptian gods.[38] Placed between the two major parts of these decrees, it introduces a list of decisions by the Egyptian priests representing the native gods.[39] This list aims to establish dynastic worship and its methods in the temple precinct, as seen above.

Nevertheless, the framework of this decree is slightly different, since it exceptionally contains an elaborate narrative interjected between the above sentence and the priestly measures.[40] It furnishes detailed information about alleged exactions committed by rebels in Upper Egypt[41] and the subsequent countermeasures commanded by the sovereign.[42] The latter involved the raising of troops, mainly Greeks, and their supplies.[43] To this end, the monarch supplied large sums of gold and silver,[44] and as a corollary to these material and logistical measures, ground operations were carried out by the generals and their troops, which led to victory and the capture of the enemy.[45] The outcome of the conflict is presented in a phraseology similar to that of the preamble but in more detail. Last but not least, the narrative ends with the king's consequences for all dissidents, in order to pacify the country.[46]

An extract of this part is recalled here because of its relevance, despite the many gaps (*Philensis II*, ll. 7–8):[47]

---

[38] For the part on royal euergetism: Recklinghausen 2018, II, pp. 8–11 (*Philensis II*, ll. 4–7; Cairo stela TR 27/11/58/4, ll. 12–22). For the transition sentence: Recklinghausen 2018, II, p. 11 (*Philensis II*, l. 7; Cairo stela TR 27/11/58/4, ll. 22–23).

[39] For the part relating to the priestly measures on royal worship: Recklinghausen 2018, II, p. 17 (*Philensis II*, ll. 12–16).

[40] For the whole narrative: Recklinghausen 2018, II, pp. 12–17 (*Philensis II*, ll. 7–12; Cairo stela TR 27/11/58/4, ll. 23–34). See his article in these proceedings too.

[41] Recklinghausen 2018, II, pp. 12–13 (*Philensis II*, ll. 8–9; Cairo stela TR 27/11/58/4, ll. 23–27).

[42] Recklinghausen 2018, II, p. 13 (*Philensis II*, l. 9; Cairo stela TR 27/11/58/4, l. 26).

[43] Recklinghausen 2018, II, pp. 13–14 (*Philensis II*, ll. 9–10; Cairo stela TR 27/11/58/4, ll. 27–29).

[44] Recklinghausen 2018, II, p. 14 (*Philensis II*, l. 10; Cairo stela TR 27/11/58/4, ll. 29–30).

[45] Recklinghausen 2018, II, pp. 15–16 (*Philensis II*, ll. 10–11; Cairo stela TR 27/11/58/4, ll. 30–34).

[46] Recklinghausen 2018, I, pp. 69–70; II, p. 16 (*Philensis II*, l. 11; Cairo stela TR 27/11/58/4, ll. 34–35).

[47] Recklinghausen 2018, II, pp. 11–12 (*Philensis II*, ll. 7–8; Cairo stela TR 27/11/58/4, ll. 22–25) and I, pp. 61–62 (translation) and pp. 61–69 (commentary).

𓈖𓏏𓂋𓅱𓇾𓈀𓈁𓇾𓄿𓏏𓏥 [hieroglyphs]

*rdj.t~n nṯr.w B3q.t [m]j-qd=sn ḥnʿ [nṯr].wt r-ḏr[8]=sn*
*jr.[t~n] [nsw bjty s3 Rʿ] Pt[w]lm[y]s ʿnḥ(w) ḏ.t mry Ptḥ [nṯr] pr(w) nb n (p3) ḫftj*
*n nṯr[.w] Ḥr-wn-n[f](r) š3 bʾl jmytw B3q.t*
*twt ʿwny.w stnm w.w nb(.w) [n.w] B3q.t j(w)=f [sḥp(r)] tw3w ḥr*
*shm=sn t3š njwty [ḥr] sk [ḥm.w ḥr npḏ wʾb.w]=sn ḥnʿ wn[wty].w ḥw.t-nṯr=sn*
*jt ḫ3w.w(t)=sn stp [dbḥ.w]=sn sprw-ʿ=sn r g3j.t=sn ḥnʿ 3 j[sk] [sḥm].w n.w nṯr.w*

> The gods of Egypt in their totality and all the [goddess]es caused everything [8] that the [king in Upper and Lower Egypt, son of Ra], Pt[o]lem[y] living forever, beloved of Ptah, the [god] Epiphanes, has done[48] against the enemy of the god[s], Ankhunne[f](er), who had begun the fight in Egypt. The looters had gathered (to) disrupt all districts [of] Egypt because he [brought about] evil due to their power on the province of Thebes [by] destroying [the sanctuaries, massacring] their [priests] and the cler[gies] of their temples, (by) seizing their altars and their [liturgical material]; they thus attacked their naos as well as the [statue]s of the gods.

Whilst the preamble clearly states Komanos[49] to be the author of this victory, the plural suffix pronoun which systematically appears throughout the entire account reported to the king certainly seems to refer to both generals. Aristonikos is undeniably integrated into this conflict, as he obviously had fought alongside Komanos. This is attested by his military title and by the fact that he is an eyewitness to the victory.[50] Whereas Komanos no longer is given a mention in the subsequent synodal decrees, Aristonikos makes a new appearance in the last decree of the reign, and not the least.

---

**48** The syntactic construction is difficult: Recklinghausen 2018, I, p. 62, n. b; I have also proposed before to read the word *nb.t* "lordship, authority (of the king)" in the sense of "domination (over an enemy)" but without certainty: Nespoulous-Phalippou 2015a, II, p. 310 and n. 695.
**49** *PP* VI 14611 and 15892; Westermann 1939, pp. 1–12; Peremans, Van't Dack 1953, pp. 21–33; Welles 1965, pp. 93–104; Clarysse 1981, pp. 347–349; Hauben 1988, pp. 207–211; Mooren 1977, pp. 74–84; Hölbl 2001, p. 145 and pp. 156–157; Huß 2001, pp. 510–511, 517, 525 and 549–552; McKechnie 2011, pp. 219–234; on the reading in *Philensis II*: Recklinghausen 2018, I, p. 40, n. o and pp. 40–41, n. p (with bibliography on this character).
**50** Nespoulous-Phalippou 2015b, p. 162; on the hieroglyphic and demotic military titles of Aristonikos: Recklinghausen 2018, I, pp. 37–38, n. l.

## 3 Conflicts in North Thebes

The historical account in the priestly decree of Ptolemy V (published in year 23) contains many interesting facts for our knowledge about the political events at the end of his reign. A new edition of the text moreover allows a review of some points pertaining either directly or indirectly to Aristonikos. The general's activities have been known previously, thanks to Daressy who submitted two studies about the respective stela of the Memphis Decree (182 BCE). The first from 1911 was devoted to Cairo stela TR 2/3/25/7[51] and the second from 1917 to Cairo stela JE 44901.[52] The earlier article included a hieroglyphic copy, an up-to-date translation, and a very short commentary (due to lack of time) which already highlighted the interest of these documents. The second contains only a standardised copy of the hieroglyphic text. In addition to Aristonikos's intervention at Diospolis Mikra – or Northern Thebes – where a native revolt had occurred, Daressy interpreted in particular two maritime expeditions led by this general. The destination of the first was Apameia on the Orontes, near the outskirts of the Seleucid Kingdom, the second was Arados, on the Phoenician coast.[53] However, the purpose of these expeditions raised some concern among scholars, owing to its *editio princeps* and the lack of other references in literary sources.[54]

However, a new draw-up of the text through a synoptic frame and an in-depth study led to the dismissal of the previously privileged hypothesis of the Syro-Palestinian expedition.[55] This allowed to redefine all the events mentioned in the context of a native revolt in North Thebes and its area.[56] This ancient city which was a "chapel" of South Thebes[57] was located at the Mediterranean coastline and is identical to present Tell el-Balamun.[58] It is thus exclusively within this troubled historical context of interior politics that the military actions of Aristonikos need to be reassessed.[59]

---

[51] Daressy 1911, pp. 1–8.
[52] Daressy 1916–1917, pp. 175–179.
[53] Daressy 1911, pp. 6–8.
[54] Veïsse 2004, p. 10, n. 29.
[55] Nespoulous-Phalippou 2015a, II, pp. 228–230.
[56] Nespoulous-Phalippou 2015a, II, pp. 217–218.
[57] Guermeur 2011, pp. 171–172.
[58] Gauthier 1925, p. 178; Guermeur 2005, pp. 117–125 and pp. 265–266; Leclère 2008, I, p. 279; Thiers 2009, p. 26; Nespoulous-Phalippou 2015a, I, p. 100, n. 98; p. 106, n. 107.
[59] For the commentary of the whole historical account: Nespoulous-Phalippou 2015a, II, pp. 205–241.

The narrative begins with the mention of the revolt that broke out in North Thebes and then continues with a royal action after the king's arrival at the place of conflict (JE 44901, ll. 12-13):[60]

*jw=f jr~n=f ḫꜣj.t (m) ṯtf(?) bṯꜣ.w(?) šꜣ ḥm=f r Wꜣs.t mḥ(.t)*
*n(?) [ḫsf sḫ(.t) n(.t)] [13] [jt]nw(?) n nṯr.w qn~n=f sbj bʾl m-ʿb sky.w*
*wn dmḏ ḫnʿ=sn (sic) m bw nb [šm{.tw}=sn jm=w jw=sn] m sḫ.t n(.t) Smꜣ-Bḥd.t*

He (= the enemy) fomented a revolt (*ḫꜣj.t*) displaying (?) the crimes (?); thus his Majesty came to North Thebes (*Wꜣs.t mḥ(.t)*) in order to [drive back the attack of the [13] opponent (?)] of the gods. He has defeated the fighting enemy with armed troops who were with him in every place that [they reached, while they were] in the province of Sema-Behdet.

After a first confrontation, the text goes on to mention the repression of rebels by royal troops in the Sema-Behdet province during the Nile's flood.[61] The next passage mentions a war fleet ordered to surround enemies in the conflict area.[62] Another passage evokes a supply of money and cereals to the royal troops by the king.[63] An important observation is that in this version of the decree's narrative, the king is thereafter no longer mentioned.

The historical account then focuses on every move of Aristonikos as the commander-in-chief of the cavalry.[64] His first notable action consists of an expedition outside Egypt with a large fleet to recruit soldiers and increase the army's ranks, involving mainly horsemen and foot soldiers for the royal fleet based at Lake Borollos.[65] Analogous to Daressy, it is very tempting to draw parallels between this episode and the account by Polybius (*History*, XXII, 17) who evokes military action in the delta during Epiphanes's reign and also mentions the recruitment of mercenaries in Greece by the general himself:

---

60 For the text commentary: Nespoulous-Phalippou 2015a, I, pp. 96–106.
61 RT 2/3/25/7, ll. 24–25; JE 44901, ll. 13–14: Nespoulous-Phalippou 2015a, I, pp. 107–113.
62 This passage is quite obscure (RT 2/3/25/7, ll. 25–26; JE 44901, l. 14): Nespoulous-Phalippou 2015a, I, pp. 114–117.
63 RT 2/3/25/7, ll. 26–27; JE 44901, l. 14: Nespoulous-Phalippou 2015a, I, pp. 118–119.
64 RT 2/3/25/7, l. 27; JE 44901, ll. 14–15: Nespoulous-Phalippou 2015a, I, pp. 120–124.
65 RT 2/3/25/7, ll. 27–29; JE 44901, l. 15: Nespoulous-Phalippou 2015a, I, pp. 125–131. For the toponym *Pꜣ-ym-sꜣy* identified as the Borollos Lake: Nespoulous-Phalippou 2015a, I, pp. 130–131.

He (i.e. Ptolemy Epiphanes) then came to Naukratis with his army. Aristonikos having brought back here the mercenaries who were raised by him in Greece.[66]

After Aristonikos's return with his backup troops, the decree mentions several trips to the delta in order to supply the army in the conflict area. Several military operations are reported to be associated with a stronghold located in the Behdet province, but the identification of its nature and precise location remain problematic.[67]

The last sentences of the Memphis Decree (182 BCE) mention the safety of the Egyptian people under Aristonikos and his heroic actions in the war zone. It seems that Aristonikos had brought water and food to the people following a swamp pestilence in the Behdet province.[68] He is then presented as the one who himself had defended the mentioned bastion and who had won over the rebels in the area of Northern Thebes.[69]

# 4 The Evolution of Royal Ideology According to the Priestly Decrees Under the Reign of Ptolemy V Epiphanes

The data collected from both the Alexandria (186 BCE) and the Memphis decrees (182 BCE) need to be relocated within their political contexts and considered according to the ideological stances of these official sources. As a result, an ideological evolution may indeed emerge from the corpus of the synodal decrees. Spread over the entire reign of Epiphanes, they show a diachronic evolution.

The synodal decree of Alexandria (186 BCE) contains some peculiarities which have already been mentioned above. The country's military and political security were the king's prerogatives. This is why historical narratives usually occur in the part that, following the king's euergetism, enumerates several measures concerning the Egyptian gods, the priests and their representatives, and the people. This is especially the case for the priestly decree of year 9, or the Memphis Decree (196 BCE), in which the king is presented as the one who had prevailed in the Lykopolite revolt. Ten years later, in the synodal decree of Alexandria (186 BCE), the king is no longer described as a participant in the victory (see below).

---

66 Cf. Polybe, *Histoire*, pp. 956–957.
67 RT 2/3/25/7, ll. 29–31; JE 44901, ll. 15–16: Nespoulous-Phalippou 2015a, I, pp. 132–140.
68 RT 2/3/25/7, ll. 31–32; JE 44901, ll. 16–17: Nespoulous-Phalippou 2015a, I, pp. 141–147.
69 RT 2/3/25/7, ll. 33–35; JE 44901, l. 17: Nespoulous-Phalippou 2015a, I, pp. 148–155.

Moreover, the historical narrative relating to actions led by Komanos with numerous details is very developed and is located in the second part of the decree pertaining to the priestly decisions. A new fact was that the victory was granted to the sovereign in his name by the gods because of the king's euergetism. But this euergetism is generic and impersonal; it consists of a list enumerating an ideal ideological programme or even current economic measures. The text further mentions the king issuing directives for the enemy's repression without being personally engaged in combat. Although he held the decision-making power, it was the priests who took care of naming the people who actually fought and won.

There is hence a major ideological evolution in relation to the Memphis Decree of the 9th year (196 BCE), where the sovereign himself is presented as the one who acted for the defence and security of the country (Nobareh Stela, ll. 22-23; Urk. II, 182,3–183,6):[70]

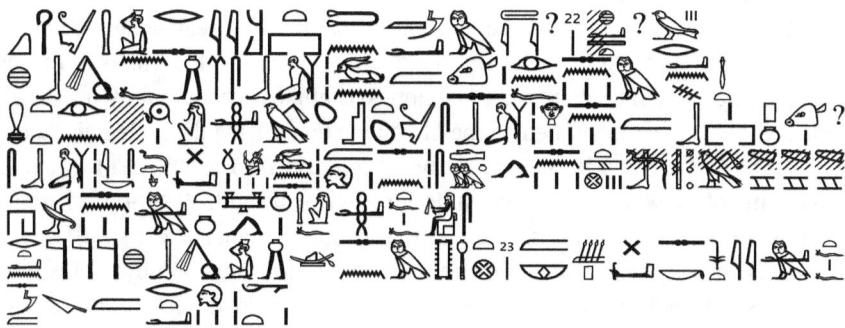

ḥꜣq~n ḥm=f rsy.t tn mꜣꜥ m pḥry.t(?) [22] nḫt(?) wr.w
ḥb~n=f jn(y.w) m sbj.w wn m-ḫnt=s jr~n=f sn mꜥn(w.w) ꜥꜣ.t
mjt.t jr~n [pꜣ?] Rꜥ ḥnꜥ Ḥr sꜣ ꜣs.t n sbj.w ḥr=sn m bw pn ḫnt.t(?)
sbj.w jsk ḏdb.w mšꜥ wn=sn m tp=sn stnm=sn tš.w [jw] ḫꜣb.t [m jdb.w-Ḥr][71]
th=sn mtn.w n.w ḥm=f ḥnꜥ jt=f špś
rdj.t~n nṯr.w ḥb=f jn(w) jm=sn m Jnb-ḥḏ [23] m ḥb šsp sk nsy.t m-ꜥ jt=f
smꜣ(=tw sn) m rdj.t tp.w-ḫt

His Majesty (i.e. Ptolemy Epiphanes) seized this fort (i.e. that of Lykopolis) truly by circling (?) [22] it(?) (. . . ? . . .). He slaughtered the ones who came from the rebels, who were at their forefront. He gave them a severe beating as Ra and Horus, son of Isis, had done for those who rebelled against them in this place before (?). As for the enemies who had gathered

---

70 Nespoulous-Phalippou 2015a, II, pp. 292–293. For a translation of both demotic and hieroglyphic versions of the narrative from the Memphis Decree (196 BCE): Recklinghausen 2018, I, p. 63.
71 For a new establishment of this sentence: see Birk 2021, pp. 10–22, who has convincingly read: "[indem] Unrecht [in] den [Ufern] des [Horus] (= den Tempeln) war".

their troops under their aegis, who had disturbed the provinces and damaged [Egypt], and who had transgressed the right path of his majesty and his august father, the gods let him execute those who were brought of them to Memphis [23] during the feast of the reception of kingship from his father. (They) shall be killed by being impaled.

Wanting to reinforce royal legitimacy, the priests who wrote this text thus embedded the image of the king in the ever-present native tradition of the pharaoh slaying his enemies. The Macedonian ruler is furthermore compared to the gods Ra and Horus, according to the pharaonic tradition. Nevertheless, this ideological fiction is clearly revealed by the age of the sovereign, then a young adolescent. This is confirmed by Polybius who states that Ptolemy Epiphanes will not participate in combat before his 25$^{th}$ year (*History*, XXII, 17).[72]

The ten years separating the decrees of Memphis (196 BCE) and Alexandria (186 BCE) resulted in a phraseological progression that provides a more just vision of the sovereign, more faithful to reality and to political events. In counterpoint, the Egyptian priests for the first time had chosen to honour the Greek generals who were the main actors of the moment and the genuine heroes of the Thebaid. In this respect, Komanos comes first, and after him Aristonikos who certainly fought alongside the latter. This constituted a tangible innovation during the Ptolemaic rule.

An additional step is taken with the Alexandria Decree (186 BCE) which, from this point of view, has a considerable ideological weight. For the first time, the names of both generals are included in the section on dynastic worship, which otherwise is reserved exclusively for the members of the royal family.[73] This integration is established indirectly through the commemoration's content. In addition to the mention of a series of priestly measures, including the erection of a king's statue accompanied by the deity of the city holding up the victory scimitar, comes an original passage concerning the setting up of festivals in the Egyptian temples to memorialise the victory over the rebels in Upper Egypt (*Philensis II*, ll. 14–15):[74]

---

72 Nespoulous-Phalippou 2015a, II, p. 207.
73 See the passage in the Canopus decree relating the princess's death: Pfeiffer 2004, pp. 144–193.
74 Recklinghausen 2018, I, pp. 92–101.

*m-tw=tw jr 3bd 4 šmw (sw) 3 n smj=s(.t) r [ḥm=f] [. . .] mry n nsw [ḥry ḥrp-nfr.w]
[Jwrsd3ny]<g>w[s] [p3] [Jwr]s[d3]nygw[s]
m-dd ndrjw sbj {n} btnw ḥn' 3bd 3 šmw [sw 23 hrw] [r]d[~n(?)] Q3m'nws
nty jmj[tw] jmy-jb[15][.w] [. . .] ḥm=f 3m(m)=tw jm=f
m ḥb wr m-[ḫnt(?)] qbḥ.wy r tp-rnp.t nb r tr [nb]
jw=sn w3ḥ 'ḫ sqr wdn.w [ḥn' ḥ.t nb.t twt] n jr(w)
m-[tw]=tw rdj.t w3ḥ ḥr tp=sn [m] ḥb.w jpn*

Let the third day of the 4th month of *shemu* (i.e. Mesore) be celebrated, the day when it (i.e. the victory) was announced to [his majesty by the mouth of his majesty's trusted man], the beloved of the king, [the commander-in-chief of the cavalry], [Aristonik]o[s] [son of Aristo] ni[kos], saying: 'the enemy, the rebel has been defeated' and that [the 23rd day] of the 3rd month of *shemu* (i.e. Epiphi) is celebrated on the day, when Komanos, who is among the first friends [15] (. . .) of his majesty, had them seize him (i.e. Ankhunnefer), (namely) as a great festival in Egypt every year and [every] season. They (i.e. the priests) will set up altars, and make libations [with everything that needs] to be done. Let wreaths be worn on their heads at these festivals.

The passage then becomes relatively lacunar but clearly refers to the processional appearances of the royal couple's statues on the occasion of these festivities (*Philensis II*, ll. 15–16):[75]

*š3'=s(n) {r} (sic) ḥb(.w)] [. . .] ['3.w dsr].w
m-tw[=tw] [. . .] [ḥn'] jsk sw rdj=t(w) ḫ' sšm.t n.t ḥq3.t
rdj=t(w) sḫ'=f ḥn'=f m hrw.w jpn m-tw=tw jgr [. . .] nb.t T3.wy m hrw.w jpn tp-rnp.t nb
ḥn' šp{.t}(?) [16] [. . .] [dd(.t) w3s] m-tw=tw jr p3 grḥ nty ḫ3.t hrw.w ḥr db' ḥtm [. . .] rd.wy m jtr.ty
ḥ.t nb.t jr ḥb.w jpn sšm(.w) [jw s nb jr(w) wnw.t]=sn m ḥw.t-nṯr*

(Then) they will begin the celebrations [. . .] [greatly and exceptionally]. One should [. . .], moreover, the statue of the queen shall appear; its appearance in procession will be celebrated with him (i.e. the king) during these days. May also be (?) [. . .] the mistress of the two

---

75 Recklinghausen 2018, I, pp. 92–101.

lands during these days, each year, and the price of victory (?) [16] [. . .] [stability, power]. And let the night preceding (these) days be celebrated by (un)sealing (?) [. . .] (. . .?. . .)[76] in the temples; all the rites [celebrating] these festivals will be led [by each man on duty] in the temple.[77]

Thus, in the official framework of the dynastic worship, the establishment in year 19 of two national and annual feasts is observed: one marking the cessation of the conflict in Upper Egypt and its announcement by Aristonikos, the other celebrating the effective date of the victory of Komanos. Through this source, Komanos and Aristonikos officially enter history.

Besides the fact that the establishment of these feasts for dynastic worship represented an economic interest for the priests, their celebration, which partly took place outside the temple walls, reinforced the monarchic propaganda and royal approval among the people.[78] Since year 19 (6 September 186 BCE),[79] the feasts of the third shemu-month thus allowed to widely commemorate each year the names and the participation of both generals in the pacification of the kingdom, and even the reunification of the so-called Two Lands, according to the native tradition. By associating the names of these Greek generals with dynastic worship and festivals, the priests displayed their efforts to integrate them deeply into the kingdom's history thus forging the framework of a new political vision from an ideological standpoint.[80]

It is noteworthy that the Memphis Decree (182 BCE), the reign's last known decree, uses the singular suffix pronoun for every move of Aristonikos, which, as opposed to the Alexandria Decree (186 BCE) using the plural in all war deeds, distinctly places the emphasis on this latter general. According to the text, the pacification of the Delta by Aristonikos seems to have focussed on this last centre of turmoil (*supra*), and thus he is presented as the true hero. The efforts by the priests to honour the magnificence and memory of this singular historical character are particularly evident in the decree's final sentence (TR 2/3/25/7, l. 35):

---

76 Recklinghausen 2018, I, p. 92, translates: "Und man soll in der Nacht vor d(ies)en Tagen verbringen, indem die Siegel von (ihren) Stand[orten] in den beiden Heiligtümern (= die Tempel Ägyptens) lösen (?)" (see pp. 95–96, n. q., too). On seals and stamps: Vandorpe 2014b, pp. 141–151.

77 This passage could mention an evening or nocturnal rite but the content is not clear: might we understand a feast similar to that evoked by Herodotus in Papremis (*History*, II, 63) where the priests deny the worshippers access to the temples? Might we consider a feast like the rite of lighting the lamps (λυχναψία)? On this topic: Perpillou-Thomas 1993, pp. 221–222; Aubert 2004, p. 319.

78 On this kind of processions: Thiers 2003, pp. 23–30.

79 For the date: Recklinghausen 2018, I, p. 8 and pp. 30–31.

80 For a commentary on these feasts and their meaning, see also: Recklinghausen 2018, I, pp. 353–355.

𓈖𓈖𓏏𓏤𓂋𓏺𓂝𓏏𓈎𓈖𓌞𓏏𓇾𓏏𓇿𓏥

*jw[=f] jr qn m-stwt jty*

[He] (i.e. Aristonikos) won (*jr qn*) the victory like (*m-stwt*) a/the sovereign.

This end is indeed surprising because a synodal decree typically enumerates the priestly measures, which aim to define the dynastic worship in the Egyptian temples, as was the case for the earlier decrees under Epiphanes's reign. Hence, this last decree reflects a new step which much resembles a commemorative document in tribute to Aristonikos. As a matter of fact, the king is considered the official guarantor of the decision-making power. Though he may have partly participated in the repression of the conflict, thus corroborating with Polybius' account (*History*, XXII, 17), his presence is nevertheless demoted to the background before entirely disappearing in the rest of the historical account which also concludes the last part of the decree. The decree's original form therefore reflects the deliberate will of the priests who in a synodal gathering had celebrated the installation of the new Mnevis bull. It was they who pragmatically recorded the political currents to appropriately honour the one who had truly helped the people of Egypt.

By pacifying the country, Aristonikos takes in the role otherwise reserved for the pharaoh, as shown by the last sentence. One would have expected the priests to update the measures of the dynastic cult by indirectly honouring Aristonikos through the establishment of a feast, as in the case of the Alexandria decree. The inherent difficulties in this absence of dynastic cult may perhaps be solved by assuming the king's absence during the synod and/or that the monarchic legitimacy had diminished in the eyes of the priests.[81]

The frequency of the decrees under Epiphanes's reign may possibly suggest that the priests deemed it unnecessary to update the taken measures to the dynastic worship if a recent decree noted them already. But this explanation hardly satisfies. A loss of legitimacy from an ideological point of view can be upheld if the monarch played the role of an economic guarantor only, as attested in the first part, by updating the concrete measures. Despite his repeated proclamations of amnesties and boasts of magnanimity, the king seems to have been a diffident character in the eyes of his subjects. Greek literary sources agree with scorning his laziness, cruelty, and desiring investment in the kingdom's affairs. Several anecdotes let slip the sovereign's indifference and catnaps at official meetings.[82]

---

[81] On the ideological evolution during the reign with several hypotheses which could explain the particular form of the Memphis Decree (182 BCE): Nespoulous-Phalippou 2015a, II, pp. 261–272.
[82] About the personality of Epiphanes: Bouché-Leclercq 1903, I, pp. 388–389 and p. 396; For a cross profile of both Aristonikos and Epiphanes: Nespoulous-Phalippou 2015b, pp. 171–172.

Royal unpopularity may have increased during his reign, which may be in accord with the periods when Ptolemy remained under the responsibility of his benefactor and tutor Aristomenes before his access to the throne and when he still was at the mercy of pernicious and unscrupulous courtiers.[83] The ideology of these decrees evolves to the point that the royal euergetism is increasingly reduced to a cliché, while the mythological allusions to "Horus son of Isis and Osiris" in the 9$^{th}$ year of his reign entirely disappear to highlight a more accurate and nuanced vision of Epiphanes's real participation in the kingdom's affairs and events. Through the ideological and phraseological evolution of these decrees, it seems that the priests gradually began to express a certain reserve with regard to the king's politics and behaviour.

Conversely, the Egyptian priests and moreover the Memphite priests who probably had written up the synod proceedings, in particular, chose to honour Aristonikos who was both the hero (in the classical sense) of South Thebes and North Thebes.

Soon after my paper on Aristonikos was published (2015b), Willy Clarysse reached out to me and I thank him for drawing my attention to a papyrus from the Sijpesteijn collection which is a petition addressed to "Aristonikos eunouchos". Ptolemaic petitions are often addressed to the king, the royal couple, or sometimes a very important character.[84] The mention of *eunouchos* probably refers to our character and may signify that Aristonikos was the king's representative.[85]

This would corroborate the increasing importance of Aristonikos under the reign of Ptolemy V Epiphanes as he took forward to become the king's favourite delegate and more privileged interlocutor before the priests and people, both Egyptian and Greek.

The synodal decree of the 23$^{rd}$ year is exceptional in that the methods of the dynastic worship as *synnaos theos* in honour of the king are not present. Despite the last decree of Epiphanes' reign, royal legitimacy apparently once again was defied in Alexandria when Ptolemy was murdered at barely 30 years of age, probably poisoned by courtiers, in the 25$^{th}$ year of his reign, two years after the publication of the Memphis Decree (182 BCE).

---

[83] For the major role played by Aristomenes: Hölbl 2001, pp. 138–139; Huß 2001, pp. 484–486, pp. 502–504 and pp. 524–525; Bouché-Leclercq 1903, I, pp. 363–364, pp. 388–390. He next was supplanted by Polycrates.

[84] Veïsse 2013, pp. 81–89.

[85] On this title which could have a literal sense or a derived meaning regarding his political function, see: Carrez-Maratray 2014, pp. 81–105; Nespoulous-Phalippou 2015b, pp. 152–157.

## 5 Conclusion

The interior politics under Ptolemy V Epiphanes (204–180 BCE) suffered a series of turbulences. The remoteness of the capital Alexandria on the Mediterranean coast, far off from Upper Egypt recurrently became problematic when it came to warranting control over the latter. Some peculiarities of the priestly decrees issued under the reign of Epiphanes can be explained by rebellious disturbances in native temples. The end of the Great Revolt in Upper Egypt was proclaimed in Epiphanes's 19th year of rule, 20 years after its separation from the kingdom, while the insurgencies in Lower Egypt under his reign were probably quelled in year 21.[86] The mobilisation of garrisons, like for instance the one at Bir-Sammut, to pacify the Thebaid partly explains the recruitment of mercenaries in Greece to quash the revolt in North Thebes and its area in the delta.[87] The 21st year is pivotal, owing to the drastic measures taken for the country's pacification. The priestly decree of year 23 and Greek papyri testify to an amnesty of country-wide importance announced in year 21. These philanthropa were part of a royal policy aimed at pacifying the kingdom after the unrest which disturbed the inner safety. The same year in Upper Egypt the cult of Arsinoe II benefited from renewed popularity with the settlement of a priesthood of canephorus in the city of Ptolemais, next to that of Ptolemy and the rulers in power.[88] The enforcement of the peace terms was seemingly problematic, as is shown by two royal epistolary ordinances addressed to the epistates of each Egyptian province in year 22. Both recall the importance of the law and the need to implement it. The recalling of the amnesty proclaimed in year 21 in the decree of year 23 testifies to the updating of the paragraph on royal measures by the priests of the native temples with respect to earlier decrees, including the Alexandria (186 BCE) and the Memphis decrees (185 BCE). Nevertheless, the disturbed context and the weakness of edicts that seem to have characterised the Ptolemaic policy justified the repetition of law and order from one ordinance to another. This is probably why the priests chose to consign the decree of year 21 to stone, two years after its proclamation.[89]

As we have seen, Komanos and Aristonikos were key figures during the reign of Epiphanes. The inauguration of a nationwide feast commemorating their high

---

**86** On the hypothesis about the dating of those events: Nespoulous-Phalippou 2015a, II, pp. 208–216.
**87** Dietze 2000, pp. 77–89; Vandorpe 2014, pp. 105–135; Fischer-Bovet 2014a; Fischer-Bovet 2014b, pp. 137–170; Brun et al. 2013, p. 115; Redon 2014, pp. 45–80. Cf. Dunand 1979, pp. 77–97; Thiers 1995, pp. 493–516.
**88** Cf. Minas 1998, p. 56.
**89** Nespoulous-Phalippou 2012, pp. 151–165.

feats of arms is a testimony to the importance of the reunification of the Two Lands after the defection of the Thebaid. Moreover, the priests would have honoured the true heroes of Egypt. Reflecting the importance of Aristonikos' role, the decree of year 23 is crucial in the sense that it is more an honorary decree for the man who had won all the victories under the kingship, from South Thebes to North Thebes, according to the meaning of his name "the victory-bearer".

## Bibliography

Alliot 1951
> Alliot, M., "La Thébaïde en lutte contre les rois d'Alexandrie sous Philopator et Épiphane (216–184)", *RBPH* 29/2-3, 1951, pp. 121–143.

Alliot 1952
> Alliot, M., "La fin de la résistance égyptienne dans le Sud sous Épiphane", *REA* 54, 1952, pp. 18–26.

Arnette 2017
> Arnette, M.-L., "La gémellité biologique dans l'Égypte ancienne. Synthèse des cas potentiels", *BIFAO* 117, 2017, pp. 29–75.

Aubert 2017
> Aubert, M.-Fr., "Torches et candélabres dans les terres cuites de l'Égypte gréco-romaine", *CdE* 79/157-158, 2004, pp. 305–319.

Beckerath 2000
> Beckerath, J. von, "Zum zweiten Philae-Dekret Ptolemaios' V", in K.M. Cialowicz, J.A. Ostrowski (eds.), *Les civilisations du bassin méditerranéen. Hommages à Joachim Sliwa*, Krakow, 2000, pp. 43–46.

Bernand 1992
> Bernand, A., *La prose sur pierre dans l'Égypte hellénistique et romaine*, 2 vols., Paris, 1992.

Bernand 1982
> Bernand, Ét., *Inscriptions grecques d'Égypte et de Nubie. Répertoire bibliographique des OGIS*, ALUB 272, Centre de recherche d'histoire ancienne 45, Paris, 1982.

Bikerman 1940
> Bikerman, E., "L'avènement de Ptolémée V Épiphane", *CdE* 15/29, 1940, pp. 124–131.

Birk 2021
> Birk, R., "Der Rand des Rosettasteins: Eine Neulesung von Z.1 des hieroglyphischen Texts", *CdE* 96/191, 2021, pp. 10–22.

Bouché-Leclercq 1904
> Bouché-Leclercq, H., *Histoire des Lagides*, vol. I, Paris, 1903.

Bouriant 1885
> Bouriant, U., "La stèle 5576 du musée de Boulaq et l'inscription de Rosette", *RecTrav* 6, 1885, pp. 1–20.

Brun et al. 2013
> Brun, J.-P., Deroin, J.-P., Faucher, Th., Redon, B., Téreygeol, F., "Les mines d'or ptolémaïques. Résultats des prospections dans le district minier de Samut (désert oriental)", *BIFAO* 113, 2013, pp. 111–142.

Burnet 2003
  Burnet, R., *L'Égypte ancienne à travers les papyrus. Vie quotidienne*, Paris, 2003.
Carrez-Maratray 2014
  Carrez-Maratray, J.-Y., "L'armée lagide sur le front du Delta, intervenants et champs d'opération (encore le syngénès Aristonikos Caire JE 85743)", in A.-E. Veïsse, St. Wackenier (eds.), *L'armée en Égypte aux époques perse, ptolémaïque et romaine. École Pratique des Hautes Études, IV$^e$ section, Sciences historiques et philologiques III : Hautes études du monde gréco-romain* 51, CahAigyptos 2, Geneva, 2014, pp. 81–105.
Chauveau 1997
  Chauveau, M., *L'Égypte au temps de Cléopâtre*, Paris, 1997.
Chauveau 1999
  Chauveau, M., "Bilinguisme et traductions", in D. Valbelle, J. Leclant (eds.), *Le Décret de Memphis. Colloque de la Fondation Singer-Polignac à l'occasion du bicentenaire de la découverte de la pierre de Rosette, Paris, 1$^{er}$ juin 1999*, Paris, 1999, pp. 25–39.
Clarysse, De Meulenaere 1978
  Clarysse, W., De Meulenaere, H., "Notes de prosopographie thébaine 7. Hurgonaphor et Chaonnophris, les derniers pharaons indigènes", *CdE* 53/106, 1978, pp. 243–253.
Clarysse 1981
  Clarysse, W., "Aristomenes, Brother of Komanos", *CdE* 56/112, 1981, pp. 347–349.
Clarysse 1999
  Clarysse, W., "Ptolémée et temples", in J. Leclant, D. Valbelle (eds.), *Le Décret de Memphis. Colloque de la fondation Singer-Polignac à l'occasion du bicentenaire de la découverte de la pierre de Rosette, Paris, 1$^{er}$ juin 1999*, Paris, 1999, pp. 41–65.
Cole 2019
  Cole, E., "Negotiating Elite Identity through Linguistic Display in Ptolemaic and early Roman Egypt", *AncSoc* 49, 2019, pp. 231–258.
Coulon 2008
  Coulon, L., "La nécropole osirienne de Karnak sous les Ptolémées", in A. Delattre, P. Heilporn (eds.), « *Et maintenant ce ne sont plus que des villages . . .*». *Thèbes et sa région aux époques hellénistique, romaine et byzantine. Actes du colloque tenu à Bruxelles les 2 et 3 décembre 2005*, PapBrux 34, Brussels, 2008, pp. 17–32.
Daressy 1911
  Daressy, G., "Un décret de l'an XXIII de Ptolémée Épiphane", *RecTrav* 33, 1911, pp. 1–8.
Daressy 1916–1917
  Daressy, G., "Un second exemplaire du décret de l'an XXIII de Ptolémée Épiphane", *RecTrav* 38, 1916–1917, pp. 175–179
Daumas 1952
  Daumas, Fr., *Les moyens d'expression du grec et de l'égyptien comparés dans les décrets de Canope et de Memphis*, CASAE 16, Cairo, 1952.
Daumas 1958
  Daumas, Fr., "Un duplicata du Premier Décret ptolémaïque de Philae", in *Festschrift zum 80. Geburtstag von Professor Dr. Hermann Junker*, MDAIK 16/2, 1958, pp. 73–82.
Daumas 1972
  Daumas, Fr., "Les textes bilingues et trilingues", in *Textes et Langages de l'Égypte pharaonique III. Hommages à Jean-François Champollion*, BdE 64/3, Cairo, 1972, pp. 41–45.

Devauchelle 1986
    Devauchelle, D., "Fragments de décrets ptolémaïques en langue égyptienne conservés au Musée du Louvre", *RdE* 37, 1986, pp. 45-51.
Devauchelle 1990
    Devauchelle, D., *La pierre de Rosette. Présentation et traduction*, Paris, 1990.
Devauchelle 1999
    Devauchelle, D., "Le démotique et le déchiffrement de la pierre de Rosette", in D. Valbelle, J. Leclant (eds.), *Le Décret de Memphis. Colloque de la Fondation Singer-Polignac à l'occasion du bicentenaire de la découverte de la pierre de Rosette*, Paris, 1999, pp. 11-23.
Dietze 2000
    Dietze, G., "Temples and Soldiers in Southern Ptolemaic Egypt: Some Epigraphic Evidence", in L. Mooren (ed.), *Politics, Administration and Society in the Hellenistic and Roman World: Proceedings of the International Colloquium, Bertinoro, 19-24 July 1997*, StudHell 36, Leuven, pp. 77-89.
Dittenberger 1903-1905
    Dittenberger, W., *Orientis Graeci inscriptiones selectae (OGIS)*, 2 vols., Leipzig, 1903-1905.
Dunand 1979
    Dunand, Fr., "Droit d'asile et refuge dans les temples en Égypte lagide", in J. Vercoutter (ed.), *Hommages à la mémoire de Serge Sauneron*. II, *Égypte post-pharaonique*, Cairo, 1979, pp. 77-97.
Eldamaty 2005
    Eldamaty, M., *Ein ptolemäisches Priesterdekret aus dem Jahr 186 v. Chr.: Eine neue Version von Philensis II in Kairo*, AfP Beihefte 20, Leipzig, 2005.
Farid 1995
    Farid, A., *Fünf demotische Stelen aus Berlin, Chicago, Durham, London und Oxford mit zwei demotischen Türinschriften aus Paris und einer Bibliographie der demotischen Inschriften*, Berlin, 1995.
Fischer-Bovet 2014a
    Fischer-Bovet, Chr., *Army and Society in Ptolemaic Egypt*, Cambridge, 2014.
Fischer-Bovet 2014b
    Fischer-Bovet, Chr., "Un aspect des conséquences des réformes de l'armée lagide. Soldats, temples égyptiens et inviolabilité (asylia)", in A.-E. Veïsse, St. Wackenier (eds.), *L'armée en Égypte aux époques perse, ptolémaïque et romaine*, CahAigyptos 2, Paris, 2014, pp. 137-170.
Fraser 1956
    Fraser, P., "An Unpublished Fragment of the Memphian Decree of 196 B.C.", *BSAA* 41, 1956, pp. 57-62.
Gauthier 1916
    Gauthier, H., *Le livre des rois d'Égypte IV. Recueil de titres et protocoles royaux, noms propres de rois, reines, princes et princesses, noms de pyramides et de temples solaires, suivi d'un index alphabétique*, MIFAO 20, Cairo, 1916.
Gauthier 1925
    Gauthier, H., *Dictionnaire des noms géographiques contenus dans les textes hiéroglyphiques* I, Cairo, 1925.
Gozzoli 2009
    Gozzoli, R.B., *The Writing of History in Ancient Egypt during the First Millenium BC (ca 1070-180 BC). Trends and Perspectives*, GHP 5, London, 2009.
Guermeur 2005
    Guermeur, I., *Les cultes d'Amon hors de Thèbes. Recherches de géographie religieuse*, BEPHE – Sciences religieuses 123, Turnhout, 2005.

Guermeur 2011
> Guermeur, I., "Saïs et les Thèbes du Nord", in D. Devauchelle (ed.), *La XXVIe dynastie : continuités et ruptures. Actes du colloque international organisé à Lille les 26 et 27 novembre 2004 à l'Université Charles-de-Gaulle – Lille 3*, Paris, 2011, pp. 165–174.

Hauben 1988
> Hauben, H., "The Barges of the Komanos Family", *AncSoc* 19, 1988, pp. 207–211.

Hoffmann 2000
> Hoffmann, Fr., *Ägypten – Kultur und Lebenswelt in griechisch-römischer Zeit: Eine Darstellung nach den demotischen Quellen*, SGKAW, Berlin, 2000.

Hölbl 2001
> Hölbl, G., *A History of the Ptolemaic Empire*, London, 2001.

Huß 1991
> Huß, W., "Die in ptolemäischer Zeit verfassten Synodal-Dekrete der ägyptischen Priester", *ZPE* 88, 1991, pp. 198–208.

Huß 1994
> Huß, W., *Der makedonische König und die ägyptischen Priester: Studien zur Geschichte des ptolemäischen Ägypten*, HistEinz 85, Stuttgart, 1994.

Huß 1999
> Huß, W., "Le basileus et les prêtres égyptiens", in D. Valbelle, J. Leclant (eds.), *Le Décret de Memphis. Colloque de la Fondation Singer-Polignac à l'occasion du bicentenaire de la découverte de la pierre de Rosette, Paris, 1er juin 1999*, Paris, 1999, pp. 117–126.

Huß 2001
> Huß, W., *Ägypten in hellenistischer Zeit: 332–30 v.Chr*, Munich, 2001.

Kamal 1904
> Kamal, A., *Stèles ptolémaïques et romaines. Catalogue général du Caire, n° 22001–22208*, 2 vols., Cairo, 1904–1905.

Lanciers 1991
> Lanciers, E., "Die ägyptischen Priester des ptolemäischen Königskultes", *RdE* 42, 1991, pp. 117–145.

Leclant 1999
> Leclant, J., "Le lieutenant Bouchard, l'Institut d'Égypte et la pierre de Rosette", *BSFE* 146, 1999, pp. 6–24.

Leclère 2008
> Leclère, Fr., *Les villes de Basse-Égypte au Ier millénaire avant J.-C. Analyse archéologique et historique de la topographie urbaine*, BdE 144, 2 vols., Cairo, 2008.

McGing 1997
> McGing, Br.C., "Revolt Egyptian Style: Internal Opposition to Ptolemaic rule", *AfP* 43/2, 1997, pp. 273–314.

McKechnie 2011
> McKechnie, P., "Who were the Alexandrians? Palace and City, Aristarchus and Comanus, 170–145 BC", in A. Jördens, J.Fr. Quack (eds.), *Ägypten zwischen innerem Zwist und äußerem Druck: die Zeit Ptolemaios' VI. bis VIII. – Internationales Symposion Heidelberg 16.–19.9.2007*, Philippika 45, Wiesbaden, 2011, pp. 219–234.

Minas 1998
> Minas, M., "Die ΚΑΝΗΦΟΡΟΣ: Aspekte des ptolemäischen Dynastiekults", in H. Melaerts (ed.), *Le culte du souverain dans l'Égypte ptolémaïque du IIIe siècle avant notre ère. Actes du colloque international, Bruxelles, 10 mai 1995*, StudHell 34, Leuven, 1998, pp. 43–60.

Minas 2000
> Minas, M., *Die hieroglyphischen Ahnenreihen der ptolemäischen Könige: Ein Vergleich mit den Titeln der eponymen Priester in den demotischen und griechischen Papyri*, AegTrev 9, Mainz, 2000.

Mooren 1977
> Mooren, L., *La hiérarchie de cour ptolémaïque. Contribution à l'étude des institutions et des classes dirigeantes à l'époque hellénistique*, StudHell 23, Leuven, 1977.

Müller 1920
> Müller, W.M., *Egyptological Researches III: The Bilingual Decrees of Philae*, Carnegie Institution of Washington 53 (3), Washington, 1920.

Nespoulous-Phalippou 2012
> Nespoulous-Phalippou, A., "L'amnistie décrétée en l'an 21 de Ptolémée Épiphane (185/184 a. C.)", *ENiM* 5, 2012, pp. 151–165.

Nespoulous-Phalippou 2015a
> Nespoulous-Phalippou, A., *Ptolémée Épiphane, Aristonikos et les prêtres d'Égypte. Le décret de Memphis (182 a.C.) : Édition commentée des stèles Caire RT 2/3/25/7 et JE 44901*, CENiM 12, 2 vols., Montpellier, 2015.

Nespoulous-Phalippou 2015b
> Nespoulous-Phalippou, A., "Aristonikos fils d'Aristonikos. *Floruit* d'un eunuque et commandant en chef de la cavalerie sous le règne de Ptolémée Épiphane", *RdE* 66, 2015, pp. 151–183.

O'Neil 2012
> O'Neil, J.L., "The Native Revolt against the Ptolemies (206–185 BC): Achievements and Limitations", *CdE* 87/173, 2012, pp. 133–149.

Peremans, Van't Dack 1953
> Peremans, W., Van't Dack, E., "Komanos des premiers amis", in W. Peremans, E. Van't Dack (eds.), *Prosopographica*, StudHell 9, Leuven, Leiden, 1953, pp. 21–33.

Perpillou-Thomas 1993
> Perpillou-Thomas, Fr., *Fêtes d'Égypte ptolémaïque et romaine d'après la documentation papyrologique grecque*, StudHell 31, Leuven, 1993.

Pestman 1995
> Pestman, P.W., "Haronnophris and Chaonnophris: Two Indigenous Pharaohs in Ptolemaic Egypt (205–186 B.C.)", in S.P. Vleeming (eds.), *Hundred-Gated Thebes: Acts of a Colloquium on Thebes and the Theban Area in the Graeco-Roman Period*, P.L.Bat. 27, Leiden, New York, Cologne, 1995, pp. 101–137.

Pfeiffer 2004
> Pfeiffer, S., *Das Dekret von Kanopos (238 v.Chr.): Kommentar und historische Auswertung eines dreisprachigen Synodaldekretes der ägyptischen Priester zu Ehren Ptolemaios' III. und seiner Familie*, AfP Beihefte, Leipzig, 2004.

Pfeiffer 2010
> Pfeiffer, S., "Das Dekret von Rosette: Die ägyptischen Priester und der Herrscherkult", in G. Weber (ed.), *Alexandreia und das ptolemäische Ägypten: Kulturbegegnungen in hellenistischer Zeit*, Berlin, 2010, pp. 84–108.

Pfeiffer 2011
> Pfeiffer, S., "Herrscherlegitimität und Herrscherkult in den ägyptischen Tempeln griechisch-römischer Zeit", in D. von Recklinghausen, M.A. Stadler (eds.), *KultOrte: Mythen, Wissenschaft und Alltag in den Tempeln Ägyptens*, Berlin, 2011, pp. 116–141.

Pfeiffer 2017
> Pfeiffer, S., *Die Ptolemäer. Im Reich der Kleopatra*, Stuttgart, 2017.

Pierce et al. (eds.) 1996
> Pierce, R.H., Eide, T., Hägg, T., Török, L. (eds.), *Fontes Historiae Nubiorum* II – *From the Mid-Fifth to the First Century BC: Textual Sources for the Middle Nile Between the 8th Century BC to the 6th AD*, Bergen, 1996.

PM IV
> Porter, B., Moss, R.L.B., *Topographical Bibliography of Ancient Egyptian Hieroglyphic Texts, Reliefs, and Paintings*: IV. *Lower and Middle Egypt (Delta to Cairo to Asyût)*, Oxford, 1934.

Polybe, *Histoire*
> Polybe, *Histoire*, D. Roussel (trans.), Bruges, 1970.

*PP* VI
> Peremans, W., Van't Dack, E., *Prosopographia Ptolemaica* VI. *La cour, les relations internationales et les possessions extérieures, la vie culturelle, Nos 14479–17250*, StudHell 17, Leuven, 1968.

Quack 2008
> Quack, J.F., "Innovations in Ancient Garb? Hieroglyphic Texts from the Time of Ptolemy Philadelphus", in P. McKechnie, Ph. Guillaume (eds.), *Ptolemy II Philadelphus and His World*, Mnemosyne Supplements 300, Leiden, Boston, 2008, pp. 275–289.

Quirke, Andrews 1988
> Quirke, St., Andrews, C.A., *The Rosetta Stone: Facsimile Drawing, with an Introduction and Translations*, London, 1988.

Ray 1978
> Ray, J.D., "Observations on the Archive of Hor", *JEA* 64, 1978, pp. 113–120.

Recklinghausen 2018
> Recklinghausen, D. von, *Die Philensis-Dekrete: Untersuchungen über zwei Synodaldekrete aus der Zeit Ptolemaios' V. und ihre geschichtliche und religiöse Bedeutung*, ÄA 73, 2 vols., Wiesbaden, 2018.

Redon 2014
> Redon, B., "Le maillage militaire du Delta égyptien sous les Lagides", in A.-E. Veïsse, St. Wackenier (eds.), *L'armée en Égypte aux époques perse, ptolémaïque et romaine*, CahAigyptos 2, Paris, 2014, pp. 45–80.

Roeder 1959
> Roeder, G., *Die ägyptische Götterwelt: Die ägyptische Religion in Texten und Bildern*, Die Bibliothek der alten Welt 5/1, Zurich, 1959.

*SB* V
> Preisigke, Fr., Bilabel, Fr., Kiessling, E., Rupprecht, H.A., *Sammelbuch griechischer Urkunden aus Ägypten* V, Strasbourg, 1915–2016.

Sethe 1904
> Sethe, K., *Hieroglyphische Urkunden der griechisch-römischen Zeit*, Urkunden des ägyptischen Altertums II, Leipzig, 1904.

Sethe 1916
> Sethe, K., "Zur Geschichte und Erklärung der Rosettana", *NGWG* 1916/2, 1916, pp. 284–297.

Simpson 1996
> Simpson, R.S., *Demotic Grammar in the Ptolemaic Sacerdotal Decrees*, Oxford, 1996.

Spiegelberg 1917
> Spiegelberg, W., "Weitere Bemerkungen zu dem demotischen Text der Rosettana", *ZÄS* 53, 1917, pp. 117–118.

Spiegelberg 1922
> Spiegelberg, W., *Der demotische Text der Priesterdekrete von Kanopus und Memphis (Rosettana)*, Heidelberg, 1922.

Thiers 1995
  Thiers, Chr., "Civils et militaires dans les temples. Occupation illicite et expulsion", *BIFAO* 95, 1995, pp. 493–516.

Thiers 2003
  Thiers, Chr., "Fêtes et propagande sous les Lagides. Les sorties processionnelles des statues du Pharaon-Basileus", *Egypte* 32, 2003, pp. 23–30.

Thiers 2009
  Thiers, Chr., *La stele de Ptolémée VIII Évergète II à Héracléion*, The Underwater Archaeology in the Canopic Region in Egypt, Oxford Center of Archaeology – Monograph 4, Oxford, 2009.

Thompson 2012
  Thompson, D.J., *Memphis under the Ptolemies*, Princeton, Oxford, 2012.

*TM Trismegistos*, online database, <https://www.trismegistos.org> accessed 30 August 2024.

Vandorpe 1986
  Vandorpe, K., "The Chronology of the Reigns of Hurgonaphor and Chaonnophris", *CdE* 51/122, 1986, pp. 294–302.

Vandorpe 2014a
  Vandorpe, K., "The Ptolemaic Army in Upper Egypt ($2^{nd}$–$1^{st}$ centuries BC)", in A.-E. Veïsse, S. Wackenier (eds.), *L'armée en Égypte aux époques perse, ptolémaïque et romaine*, Cahiers de l'atelier Aigyptos 2, Geneva, 2014, pp. 105–135.

Vandorpe 2014b
  Vandorpe, K., "Seals and Stamps as Identifiers in Daily Life in Greco-Roman Egypt", in M. Depauw, S. Coussement (eds.), *Identifiers and Identification Methods in the Ancient World*, OLA 229, Leuven, Paris, Walpole, 2014, pp. 141–151.

Veïsse 2004
  Veïsse, A.-E., *Les "révoltes égyptiennes". Recherches sur les troubles intérieurs en Égypte du règne de Ptolémée III à la conquête romaine*, StudHell 41, Leuven, 2004.

Veïsse 2013
  Veïsse, A.-E., "L'expression de l'identité dans les pétitions d'époque ptolémaïque. Étude préliminaire", in S. Bussi (ed.), *Egitto dai Faraoni agli Arabi : atti del convegno Egitto: amministrazione, economia, società, cultura dai Faraoni agli Arabi*, Milano, Università degli Studi, 7–9 gennaio 2013, Pisa, Rome, 2013, pp. 81–89.

Welles 1965
  Welles, C.B., "The Problem of Comanus", *BASP* 2, 1965, pp. 93–104.

Westermann 1939
  Westermann, W.L., "Komanos of the First Friends (187 [?]-161 BC)", *AfP* 13, 1939, pp. 1–12.

Yoyotte 1993–1994
  Yoyotte, J., "La 'stèle de Nébireh'", ACF $94^e$ année, Paris, 1993–1994, pp. 690–692.

René Preys
# Révoltes, meurtres et intrigues : L'histoire des Ptolémées d'après les parois des temples égyptiens

## 1 Introduction

Parmi toutes les dynasties qui succédèrent à Alexandre le Grand, la dynastie ptolémaïque se distingue indéniablement par sa longévité. Si le succès est en partie dû au savoir-faire sur le terrain de certains de ses membres, il réside aussi en la capacité à créer une image de soi qui allait perdurer, même quand cette compétence faisait cruellement défaut. Pendant près de trois siècles, la machine de l'État a dû générer en même temps une représentation de *Basileus* grec et de Pharaon égyptien, mais également une conception qui allait fusionner les deux en une unité cohérente. C'est dire que, si les deux pensées se sont développées chacune de leur côté, elles se sont également influencées[1].

La théorie de Pharaon fut évidemment conçue dans le milieu des prêtres dont les Ptolémées ont immédiatement sollicité la collaboration. La Stèle du Satrape érigée sous le nom d'Alexandre IV, mais développant la politique de Ptolémée fils de Lagos, démontre que ce fut la stratégie choisie bien avant l'instauration officielle de la dynastie[2]. Le désir des Ptolémées était dès lors d'être acceptés par les dieux comme pharaons légitimes[3], réalité dont découlerait le consentement des prêtres. Cette collaboration était à coup sûr financièrement bénéfique pour les deux parties, puisqu'un pays en paix est productif et taxable aussi bien pour le roi que pour les temples[4]. Il n'est pas nécessaire d'y sous-entendre une hypocrisie de la part des protagonistes. D'une part, la relation entre les prêtres et le roi a toujours été basée sur les mêmes principes, et ceux-ci avaient depuis longtemps démontré que la nationalité du pharaon ne faisait guère de différence. D'autre part, rien n'interdit l'idée que les Ptolémées accordaient du crédit à l'efficacité du rituel dans le temple d'Ho-

---

[1] Moyer 2011, p. 115–116.
[2] Pour la stèle du Satrape, voir Schäfer 2011, p. 200, 282–284.
[3] Pour la légitimité de Ptolémée I exprimée à l'aide de sa titulature : Abd el Gawad 2012, p. 5.
[4] Thiers 1999, p. 439–440 ; Schäfer 2011, p. 283 ; Caneva 2016, p. 65–66 ; Gorre 2009, p. 489–495, Manning 2011, p. 3–4. Voir particulièrement l'idée du '*middle ground*' dans Moyer 2011.

rus à Apollonopolis, de la même manière qu'ils croyaient à leur identification à Apollon ou à Harpocrate[5].

L'instrument de travail par excellence des prêtres était les hiéroglyphes grâce auxquels ils écrivaient des textes afin de communiquer avec les dieux, le lieu de cette communication étant le temple. Il n'est dès lors pas surprenant de constater que l'époque ptolémaïque fut parmi les époques les plus productives en matière de construction de temples, à laquelle il faut ajouter une réflexion profonde sur le système hiéroglyphique. Le résultat fut une multiplication de ses moyens d'expression, allant de pair avec une intensification de la pensée théologique. Les parois des temples de cette époque sont couvertes de textes et d'images qui sont en grande partie basés sur une tradition de plusieurs siècles, mais dont la teneur est largement amplifiée. Il ne s'agissait nullement de conserver la connaissance du passé, mais bien d'activement développer la pensée « moderne » en tenant compte de la situation politique actuelle contemporaine[6].

Or, l'histoire des Ptolémées en Égypte présente pour le moins une succession d'événements mouvementés. La grande révolte thébaine n'est qu'une des difficultés auxquelles furent confrontés ces rois. Des mésaventures familiales aux invasions étrangères, les prêtres, à la fois politiciens et théologiens[7], ont dû ménager le pouvoir en place et s'adapter à des modifications parfois précipitées de la situation. Les cartouches laissés vides témoignent probablement de leur embarras, mais surtout aussi de leur incapacité à suivre le déroulement des événements[8] ; en dépit de l'incertitude politique, il fallait bien poursuivre le travail de gravure du décor des parois. Pourtant, ce même décor témoigne de changements parfois radicaux et brusques durant ces trois cents ans, non seulement quant à la théologie, à l'utilisation des principes de décoration (la « grammaire du temple ») et du système hiéroglyphique – en somme du monde du temple –, mais également quant à l'adéquation aux idées politiques, c'est-à-dire au monde extérieur au temple. Le schéma décoratif que nous avons appelé le schéma du culte royal est un exemple parmi d'autres où l'on peut suivre le parcours parfois contrarié des Ptolémées.

---

5 Schäfer 2011, p. 285–286. Pour la relation entre le roi et le clergé dans le cadre des synodes : Recklinghausen 2018, p. 191–193 ; Preys 2022.
6 Pour la relation entre les synodes et la décoration des temples égyptiens : Preys 2022.
7 Moyer 2011, p. 123–124.
8 Eldamaty 2007.

## 2 Le schéma du culte royal

Le schéma décoratif du culte royal offre une composition combinant images et textes qui fut utilisée par les prêtres dans la décoration des temples. Comme on le retrouve déployé de la même manière dans un grand nombre de temples[9], cela indique qu'il s'agit d'un schéma dont les règles étaient bien établies et devaient impérativement être suivies. Ceci ne signifie nullement que le schéma fut copié servilement durant les trois cents ans d'histoire ptolémaïque. La création et l'évolution du schéma démontrent au contraire le dynamisme de la pensée théologique en conformité avec la politique de cette période.

Le schéma du culte royal est composé de deux scènes qui mettent en avant le couple royal dans sa relation avec les dieux et avec ses ancêtres[10]. La première scène que nous avons appelée « la scène de la transmission de l'*jmj.t-pr* » figure le roi et la reine pour lesquels un dieu de l'écriture, le plus souvent Thot ou Sechat, inscrit l'*jmj.t-pr*. Ce document consiste en un inventaire de tout ce qui existe dans le temps et l'espace et qui est placé sous la domination du roi. Ce document est rédigé sur l'ordre du créateur incarné par la divinité principale du temple et, de ce fait, garantit la légitimité du couple royal. Le fait que la divinité agissante s'adresse au pluriel au couple démontre parfaitement que c'est bien le pouvoir en tant que couple royal qui est envisagé dans ce schéma. Ceci constitue une différence fondamentale avec la conception du pharaon des périodes précédentes. Même si les idées et le vocabulaire peuvent être retracés au moins jusqu'au Nouvel Empire[11], la conception du schéma du culte royal est indéniablement une innovation de l'époque ptolémaïque. Ce constat est corroboré par l'iconographie du couple qui souligne aussi bien l'aspect humain que divin du roi. Le roi est en effet habillé tel un humain : il porte un long manteau à franges sur lequel est jeté un châle qui couvre une épaule. Ce type d'habit n'a rien de royal et, contrairement à ce qui a été proposé, il n'a rien de commun avec le manteau du jubilé connu depuis les premières dynasties[12]. Ce sont les statues de privés de l'époque ptolémaïque qui illustrent au contraire l'usage de cet habit[13]. Le roi est chaussé de sandales, un autre élément renvoyant à la nature humaine du roi. La double couronne atteste toutefois qu'il ne s'agit pas d'un simple mortel, mais qu'il appartient à la sphère royale. La couronne est souvent entourée d'un diadème qui pourrait

---

9 Pour une liste des attestations et une étude diachronique du schéma, voir Preys 2017.
10 Pour l'iconographie du schéma : Preys 2015b.
11 Pfeiffer 2008, p. 19–24 ; Minas 2005, p. 128–133 ; Minas 2015, p. 91–98.
12 L'habit du jubilé est bien connu au début de l'époque ptolémaïque puisqu'il est encore utilisé sur une porte de Médamoud (Sambin, Carlotti 1995).
13 Bianchi 1978 ; Coulon 2001, p. 87 ; Zivie-Coche 2004, p. 206 (n. 54), Cafici 2021, p. 82–86.

évoquer le diadème grec, si ce n'était qu'un uraeus y est joint. À l'inverse, le couple royal tient en main des sceptres qui les mettent en relation avec la sphère divine : le roi se voit octroyé le sceptre-*ouas* des dieux, la reine le sceptre-*ouadj* des déesses. Plus important encore, est le fait que le couple tourne le dos au sanctuaire du temple. En effet, les principes de la décoration des temples consistent à montrer le roi entrant dans le temple, et donc tournant le dos à la porte d'entrée, tandis que les divinités habitant le sanctuaire tournent le dos à l'arrière du temple. Le schéma du culte royal applique donc la règle des divinités au couple royal, renforçant ainsi l'idée du couple en tant que *theoi sunnaoi*.

La seconde scène du schéma, appelée « la scène du culte des ancêtres », est toujours placée à proximité ; il peut s'agir du mur parallèle ou d'un registre supérieur. Le roi régnant y figure adorant le couple royal défunt. Si le roi régnant apparaît ici seul, et non pas en couple, cela montre que ce n'est pas lui qui est au centre de l'attention ; il n'est que celui qui « agit envers ». Les ancêtres, par contre, se définissent en couple ; ce dernier constitue ainsi le pendant du couple royal de la première scène. Mais tandis que le couple royal vivant est caractérisé par une iconographie qui fusionne l'aspect humain et divin, le couple des ancêtres ne se distingue nullement des autres dieux. Seuls les cartouches indiquent qu'il s'agit, à l'origine, d'humains. Le roi vivant dans cette scène apparaît dans son costume habituel de ritualiste.

Le schéma met donc en complémentarité le couple royal régnant et le couple royal défunt/les ancêtres. Dans chaque version, les deux couples seront donc identifiés individuellement. Par exemple, sur la porte d'Amon à Karnak[14], dans la première scène le roi et la reine seront identifiés comme Ptolémée VI et Cléopâtre II, tandis que le couple de la deuxième scène porte les noms de Ptolémée V et Cléopâtre I. Le schéma peut toutefois être interprété de deux points de vue. Le premier identifie les deux couples de manière synchronique ; les deux couples ne peuvent dès lors pas incarner les mêmes personnes. Le couple ancêtre de la deuxième scène doit nécessairement représenter les parents du couple régnant de la première scène. C'est ce qui est indiqué par le nom inscrit dans les cartouches. Le deuxième point de vue considère les deux scènes de manière diachronique[15] en identifiant les deux couples. Le schéma décrit ainsi la transformation que subira chaque couple royal : de couple vivant, il deviendra couple ancêtre, laissant la place à une autre couple vivant qui, à son tour, deviendra le couple ancêtre, et ainsi de suite. Le schéma illustre ainsi le cycle royal, c'est-à-dire la succession d'un couple royal par un autre ; il garantit en outre pour chaque couple aussi

---

14 Broze, Preys 2021 : *Ka2Pyl* 20 et 24.
15 On pourrait aussi opposer l'interprétation historique à l'interprétation théologique.

bien sa légitimité sur terre que son culte post mortem, ce culte qui par essence garantit la légitimité de leur successeur.

## 3 Le début

Au début de l'histoire des Ptolémées, les prêtres ont conçu ce schéma pour le roi. Si le milieu des prêtres nous est relativement bien connu par les nombreuses statues qu'ils nous ont léguées[16], on sait moins la manière dont la connaissance était transmise d'une génération à l'autre, et comment une génération maniait cette connaissance. Il ne sera jamais possible de mettre un nom sur les auteurs, mais heureusement dans le cas du schéma du culte royal, nous disposons d'une source d'information qui nous donne au moins une idée de l'origine du schéma du culte royal.

La relation et, en particulier, la communication entre les prêtres et le roi sont vaguement connues, mais les détails nous échappent en grande partie. Ainsi, nous savons que les prêtres de Ptah étaient proches du pouvoir[17], mais il est plus difficile d'appréhender comment cela se traduisait en pratique. Nous avons toutefois connaissance d'un instrument mis en place par le pouvoir pour établir la communication[18] ; il s'agit des synodes[19] dont les décisions sont connues grâce aux décrets, lisibles sur des stèles dans tous les temples de l'Égypte[20]. La stèle de Kom el-Hisn qui porte le texte du décret de Canope[21] datant de l'an 9 de Ptolémée III Évergète figure dans son cintre tous les protagonistes du schéma du culte royal. Le couple royal, reprenant les caractéristiques iconographiques que l'on connaît des parois de temples, est suivi des deux divinités de l'écriture, Thot et Sechat, et finalement des ancêtres en couple. Ici encore, le pouvoir royal, qu'il soit vivant ou défunt, est défini en tant que couple. Il y a donc peu de doute que la scène de la stèle applique les mêmes principes que dans les scènes sur les parois des temples. Le décret ne mentionne pas les aspects iconographiques, et

---

16 Pour une étude des documents privés : Gorre 2009.
17 Gorre 2009, p. 605–622.
18 Concernant les décrets en tant que communication entre pouvoir et clergé : Moyer 2011, p. 123 qui critique les anciennes théories qui « exclude the possibility that this decree ... was part of a process of mutual recognition (or misrecognition) and invention in which the priests played a significant role ».
19 Pour le peu d'information que nous possédons sur l'organisation de ces synodes, voir Recklinghausen 2018, p. 181–185.
20 Pour la relation entre les décrets et la décoration des temples : Preys 2022.
21 Pour une étude approfondie du décret de Canope, voir Pfeiffer 2004.

aucun lien ne peut être établi entre le texte et la scène du cintre. Il est toutefois fort probable que le décret de Canope qui met en place le culte royal dans les temples égyptiens sous Évergète était accompagné d'indications quant à la figuration de ce culte royal sur les parois des temples. La création du schéma décoratif ou, au moins ses composants, auraient donc fait l'objet de discussion pendant le synode[22]. De quelle manière cela s'est-il réalisé, et quels prêtres ont pris les décisions, nous ne saurons jamais.

À Kom el-Hisn, ces suggestions ont été transposées dans la scène du cintre de la stèle, mais à Karnak, elles se retrouvent sous la forme du schéma du culte royal sur la porte de Khonsou érigée au nom d'Évergète[23]. Ainsi, pour la première fois, on voit apparaître les décisions du synode sur les parois des temples. L'étude de la porte de Khonsou[24] montre, de plus, que le schéma du culte royal prend place dans un contexte plus large exposant le culte d'Osiris. Ainsi le couple royal passant du statut de vivant, régnant sur l'Égypte, au statut de défunt, ancêtre légitimant le successeur, traverse les mêmes phases que celles d'Osiris, roi d'Égypte mis au monde par Ipet-ouret/Nout[25], et devenant le dieu défunt légitimant son fils et successeur Horus. Les scènes entourant le schéma du culte royal sont dédiées à ces deux aspects d'Osiris et confirment ce que nous savons de l'organisation du culte royal grâce aux statues de leurs prêtres, à savoir que le culte royal et le culte osirien étaient fortement liés, et souvent aux mains des mêmes personnes[26].

Que les indications pratiques concernant le culte royal du décret de Canope aient pu être prolongées par des précisions concernant la « grammaire du temple » est indubitablement prouvé par le décret de Raphia daté de l'an 6 de Ptolémée IV Philopator[27]. Ce décret qui clarifie l'organisation du culte des *theoi Philopatores* décrit avec moult détails l'image qui doit être utilisée dans le contexte de ce culte, ainsi que celle qui doit figurer dans le cintre de la stèle : le roi doit être représenté terrassant son ennemi, tandis que le dieu du temple lui offre l'épée de la victoire[28]. Cette mention explicite et détaillée de l'image royale était impérative, en ce qu'elle imposait un changement du schéma décoratif du culte royal instauré par le décret de Canope. Suite à la victoire de Ptolémée IV à

---

22 Preys 2022, p. 174–177.
23 Clère 1961, pl. 43 et 61.
24 Preys 2015a, p. 169–184.
25 La proximité du temple d'Opet par rapport à la porte de Khonsou était particulièrement propice au développement de ce thème, puisque le temple est considéré comme le lieu de naissance d'Osiris.
26 Preys 2015a, p. 203–209.
27 Gauthier, Sottas 1925 ; Thissen 1966.
28 Image décrite dans la version démotique : Gauthier, Sottas 1925, p. 9–10 (2), 39, 60–61 ; Thissen 1966, p. 23, 71.

Raphia, les prêtres ont voulu mettre l'accent sur l'aspect invincible du roi[29]. Pour les prêtres connaissant la mythologie d'Horus protecteur de son père Osiris, ceci coulait de source. Dans la partie historique du texte, l'action du roi est explicitement comparée à celle d'Harsiesis, tandis que l'image du roi destinée au temple fut appelée « Ptolémée protecteur de son père dont la victoire est belle » (*ptwlmjs nḏ-jt=f n₃-ˁn p₃j=f qn*) ; dans la version grecque, ce fut traduit par καλλινικου. La prédilection de Philopator pour Harpocrates est bien connue et suit la même tendance, tout comme l'idée de l'intervention de Serapis durant la bataille de Raphia[30].

L'utilisation du schéma du culte royal par Philopator à Edfou illustre parfaitement les répercussions du décret de Raphia. Le texte historique d'Edfou[31] nous apprend que le travail au temple qui débuta sous Évergète fut, dans une première phase, continué par Philopator. Toutefois, en l'an 10, la corde fut à nouveau tendue, c'est-à-dire les travaux reprirent, et la salle hypostyle fut ajoutée. Or, il se trouve que le sanctuaire, décoré lors de la première phase, et la salle hypostyle, gravée après l'an 10, contiennent chacun une version du schéma du culte royal. Alors que la version du sanctuaire[32] suit parfaitement les règles instaurées par le décret de Canope, celle de la salle hypostyle illustre les changements suite au décret de Raphia. En effet, la première scène ne figure plus le dieu de l'écriture écrivant l'*jmjt-pr*, mais le dieu du temple offrant au roi l'épée de la victoire[33].

La confrontation entre les décrets de Canope et de Raphia et la décoration pariétale des temples nous apprennent que les décisions prises par les prêtres en délibération avec le pouvoir durant les synodes étaient respectées, et donc que ces synodes constituaient une autorité reconnue à travers du pays. Elles témoignent également de la connexion entre le centre du pouvoir à Alexandrie et l'administration des temples, ces derniers étant bien au courant des changements décidés et imposés par le pouvoir central. Tout comme le décret de Raphia a changé la conception du schéma du culte royal, il n'est pas inconcevable que d'autres événements, parfois moins paisibles, aient eu un impact sur le schéma.

---

[29] Ceci ne signifie nullement que cet aspect était absent de l'idéologie royale avant Philopator. Voir pour cela la stèle érigée à Saïs en l'honneur de Philadelphe (Thiers 1999, p. 437 ; pour la possibilité de la tenue d'un synode, voir n. 44)

[30] Preys 2015a, p. 197. Pour l'activité architecturale de Philopator, liée aux dieux enfants, voir Minas-Nerpel, Preys 2023, p. 75–112.

[31] Cauville, Devauchelle 1984, p. 32–35.

[32] *Edfou* I, 26, 17–28, 4. Pour une comparaison entre la version du sanctuaire d'Edfou et celle de la porte de Khonsou : Preys 2017, p. 391–395.

[33] *Edfou* II, 40, 2–12. Pour cette scène : Preys 2017, p. 400–403 ; pour la relation avec le décret de Raphia, Preys 2022, p. 182–184.

# 4 Les tribulations ptolémaïques

## 4.1 La révolte thébaine

La fin du règne de Ptolémée IV voit apparaître la plus grande menace interne à laquelle les Ptolémées ont dû faire face. La grande révolte thébaine et la scission de la Thébaïde pendant près de vingt ans ont eu une grande incidence sur le schéma du culte royal : il ne fut plus utilisé. Pourtant les noms des rois Horounnefer et Ankhounnefer[34] témoignent d'une connexion théologique avec Horus et Osiris[35], auxquels il faut ajouter Isis et Amon dont il se dit aimé. Or, l'interaction entre la théologie d'Amon et d'Osiris est bien au centre du développement du schéma tel qu'on peut le constater sur les portes monumentales de Karnak datant des règnes d'Évergète et de Philopator. D'autre part, le lien entre Horus et Osiris est également reconnaissable dans l'utilisation du schéma dans le temple d'Horus à Edfou sous Philopator[36]. Les noms du roi indigène et le lien qu'ils établissent avec plusieurs divinités rendent improbable l'idée que le pouvoir de ce roi ne possédait pas un fondement religieux. Il est dès lors remarquable de constater que ces vingt ans d'interruption du pouvoir ptolémaïque n'ont produit aucune décoration de temple. En fait, Horounnefer et Ankhounnefer mêmes n'ont pas laissé de traces ; ils sont seulement mentionnés dans les textes des autres rois, et principalement dans les papyrus[37]. Cependant, cette situation pourrait s'expliquer de différentes manières.

Il est possible qu'il ait bien eu de l'activité, si pas de construction au moins de décoration. On peut, par exemple, penser aux parois extérieures du naos d'Edfou qui sont restées non décorées jusqu'au règne d'Évergète II. Une période de vingt ans est amplement suffisante pour graver une telle surface.[38] Les traces de cette activité auraient toutefois complètement été éradiquées, après la restauration du pouvoir ptolémaïque. D'autres exemples de l'histoire égyptienne montrent à quel point il est difficile d'éliminer complètement ce type de traces. Il est donc plus probable qu'il n'y ait, en effet, pas eu d'activités.

---

34 Pour ces personnages, voir Veïsse 2004, p. 94–99.
35 Pour la connexion entre les rois indigènes et le culte d'Osiris, voir la contribution de Laurent Coulon dans ce volume.
36 Preys 2021.
37 Pour les sources mentionnant le roi, Veïsse 2004, p. 12–13.
38 La façade de la porte du deuxième pylône de Karnak fut gravée en quelques années entre 180 et 175 (voir Preys 2018, p. 340). Il faut toutefois remarquer que si les surfaces sont disponibles, cela ne constitue pas une raison pour les décorer. Les faces extérieures du naos de Philae construit par Évergète I, par exemple, ne furent gravées que sous Auguste.

S'il n'y a pas eu d'activités, ceci peut s'expliquer par le manque de moyens financiers et la difficulté d'accès aux matériaux et à la main-d'œuvre. Investir dans les temples exige de l'argent. Or, nous savons très peu sur la situation financière du royaume thébain durant ces vingt années. La seule certitude est que la révolte n'a pas émis ses propres monnaies. Il n'est pas certain si Horounnefer et Ankhounnefer ont continué à utiliser la monnaie ptolémaïque, ou s'ils sont retournés à une économie de paiement en nature[39]. Peut-être, toutes les ressources étaient-elles détournées vers le financement de l'activité militaire. Certaines sources pointent vers une taxation des temples durant cette période qui aurait pu servir à soutenir l'effort militaire[40]. Pourtant, investir dans les temples ne pouvait qu'être bénéfique à celui au pouvoir. Une manière économique aurait été d'usurper de la décoration existante. Quand on se rappelle les efforts du premier Ptolémée pour s'attirer la collaboration des prêtres, on peine à s'imaginer que le roi indigène aurait pu concevoir une révolte menée à bon terme sans le soutien des temples.

Il est toutefois difficile d'apprécier la situation de la Thébaïde sous le règne de Horounnefer et d'Ankhounnefer, et en particulier la position qu'adoptent les temples par rapport à la révolte[41]. Si les activités architecturales dans un temple reflètent l'investissement économique, alors les nombreuses constructions sous les premiers Ptolémées et sous Ptolémée IV Philopator en particulier[42], suggèrent que les temples se portaient relativement bien sous ces règnes. Mais qui profitaient de ces avantages financiers ? Certainement les hautes sphères du clergé, qui auraient dès lors peu de raison de se soulever contre le pouvoir ptolémaïque[43]. Est-il envisageable qu'une partie du clergé ne jouît pas de ces avantages et ait choisi le parti de la révolte[44] ? La destruction de certains temples et leur reconstruction durant les règnes de Philométor et d'Évergète II ont parfois été liées aux événements durant la révolte, mais aucune preuve décisive n'a jamais pu être livrée que les « rebelles »

---

**39** Pour une étude des monnaies lors de la révolte thébaine, voir notre étude du lot de monnaies trouvé sous la porte boubastide nord à Karnak dans Minas-Nerpel, Preys 2023, p. 83–88. Voir aussi la contribution de Thomas Faucher dans ce volume.
**40** De nouveau l'accusation provient des décrets : Veïsse 2004, p. 98, 135.
**41** Pour un état de la question concernant la relation entre le pouvoir ptolémaïque et le clergé, Gorre 2009, p. XXVI–XXXII. Voir aussi les remarques de Moyer 2011, p. 124 concernant la mutilation des stèles portant les décrets.
**42** Pour un résumé de l'activité architecturale de Ptolémée IV, Minas-Nerpel, Preys 2023, p. 75–112.
**43** Vandorpe 1995, p. 232–233 ; Gorre 2009, p. 557–582. Voir aussi Horpakhepech (Klotz, LeBlanc 2012) qui pacifie la chôra pour le roi ou Hakoris qui choisit le camp des Ptolémées (Clarysse 1991).
**44** Veïsse 2004, p. 220–222.

se sont attaqués aux temples dans leur aspect matériel[45]. Si la situation était précaire et que certains débordements[46] ont pu être à l'origine d'attaque contre ou même la destruction de temples[47], il n'est pas question d'une politique systématique contre les temples qui n'auraient pas soutenu la révolte, comme, par exemple, la destruction des reliefs. Les parois du temple d'Edfou étaient couvertes de reliefs clamant la légitimité de Ptolémée Philopator, entre autres grâce au schéma du culte royal.

En somme, en étudiant les temples, on vient à la conclusion que Horounnefer et Ankhounnefer n'étaient pas intéressés dans la construction ou décoration des temples, mais qu'il n'avait pas non plus de raison de s'attaquer aux temples. Les deux attitudes ont de quoi nous laisser perplexes, mais elles semblent exclure l'aspect nationaliste dont certains ont voulu teinter la révolte[48]. Les sources qui prétendent le contraire, c'est-à-dire principalement les différents décrets édités en faveur d'Épiphane ont été écrits par les vainqueurs[49]. Si certains temples de la Thébaïde ont activement soutenu la révolte, ils n'ont probablement pas participé à la rédaction de l'histoire de la révolte. Si d'autres sont restés, dans le meilleur des cas, neutres[50], leur « histoire » a été intégrée dans la version officielle[51] : les rebelles identifiés aux ennemis d'Osiris étaient responsables de tous les actes exécrables contre les temples et furent détruits par le roi légitime Épiphane identifié à Harendotes.

Ainsi le cercle se referme. Tandis que l'identification de Philopator à Harendotes était basée sur sa victoire sur les ennemis étrangers, celle d'Épiphane l'est sur sa victoire sur les ennemis internes[52]. L'érection de statues en faveur d'Épi-

---

[45] Voir entre autres, le temple de Médamoud (Sambin 1992, p. 172 ; Vandorpe 1995, p. 222) et l'article de F. Relats Montserrat dans ce volume.

[46] Plusieurs cas sont connus de personnes qui ont profité de la situation pour s'octroyer des biens qui ne leur appartenaient pas (Veïsse 2004, p. 140).

[47] Il faut toutefois remarquer que les références à la destruction des temples pour la révolte thébaine proviennent principalement des décrets royaux et ne peuvent que rarement être corroborées par d'autres documents: Veïsse 2004, p. 135–136. Les preuves de destruction de temple semblent plus fondées pour la révolte de 160 (Veïsse 2004, p. 138). Voir toutefois McGing 1997.

[48] Pour les différentes théories concernant l'aspect nationaliste de la révolte, voir Moyer 2011, p. 119.

[49] Pour les décrets du règne de Ptolémée V, voir Nespoulous-Phalippou 2015; Recklinghausen 2018 ; Veïsse 2004, p. 13–14. Voir aussi le texte historique d'Edfou, Cauville, Devauchelle 1984, p. 35–36 ; Veïsse 2004, p. 14–15.

[50] Voir le « pragmatisme » des prêtres thébains : Veïsse 2004, p. 235–237.

[51] Veïsse 2004, p. 207.

[52] Veïsse 2004, p. 210. Pour l'aspect mythologique dans les décrets de Philensis I et II, Recklinghausen 2018, p. 294–298. Cette identification sera encore utilisée sous Évergète II (Thiers 2009, p. 32). On peut également évoquer le prêtre Horpakhepech (« Horus est l'épée ») rattaché au culte royal sous le règne de Ptolémée V : Klotz, LeBlanc 2012, p. 681.

phane est copiée sur celle de Philopator. Tout ceci est mis en place par les synodes qui ont multiplié les honneurs pour Épiphane. Ceux-ci sont en partie copiés sur les décisions du décret de Raphia, en particulier concernant la statue érigée pour le roi. Dans le décret de Memphis de 196 (an 9), la statue du roi porte le nom de « Ptolémée protecteur de l'Égypte » (*ptwlmjs nḏ n bȝq.t*) et sera accompagnée d'une statue du dieu lui offrant l'épée de la victoire[53]. Aucune indication n'est offerte pour la décoration de la stèle. Pourtant, sur la stèle de Nobareh[54], le roi, accompagné de la reine tenant dans sa main le sceptre-*wȝḏ*, transperce un ennemi de sa lance. Le cheval si caractéristique de la stèle du décret de Raphia a toutefois disparu, mais le dieu de la ville présente l'épée au roi. Derrière le couple divin suivent les trois couples d'ancêtres. Cet aspect égyptien sera encore plus accentué dans le décret de 186 (an 19). La statue est maintenant appelée « Ptolémée, détenteur de victoire » (*ptwlmjs nb qn*). Une statue du dieu offrant l'épée de la victoire accompagnera également cette statue. Le sujet de la scène du cintre de la stèle est cette fois précisé ; il s'agira d'une image du roi frappant un ennemi (*smȝ sbj*) devant le dieu présentant l'épée de la victoire. Aucune attestation du décret n'a conservé son cintre, mais les deux stèles portant le décret de 182 (an 23) figurent le roi dans la pose traditionnelle de frapper les ennemis. À chaque fois, le roi est accompagné de sa reine levant le bras droit dans le dos du roi. Sur la stèle Caire RT 2 /3 /25 /7, la triade locale est suivie des dieux Philopatores[55].

Le lien entre les décrets et le schéma décoratif sous Épiphane semble confirmé par les deux stèles trilingues trouvées récemment à Kom Ombo et datées de l'an 23 de ce roi[56]. Sur chaque stèle, le roi frappant les ennemis et la reine se trouvent en présence d'une triade dont le dieu présente l'épée de la victoire. Sur la première stèle, le couple royal des Philopatores prend la suite du couple régnant. Sur la deuxième stèle, Sechat est en train d'inscrire l'*jmj.t-pr*. Les deux stèles combinent ainsi la première et la seconde version du schéma du culte royal.

Cette réutilisation par Épiphane montre à quel point le schéma du culte royal était intégré à part entière au vocabulaire royal ptolémaïque. D'une part, si une décoration de temple au nom de Horounnefer ou d'Ankhounnefer décrivant leur idéologie royale avait survécu, il est peu vraisemblable qu'elle aurait utilisé le schéma du culte royal. D'autre part, si l'activité décorative du règne d'Épiphane

---

53 *Urk.* II, 189, 8.
54 Kamal 1904–1905, p. 183–187, pl. LXII-LXIII ; Nespoulous-Phalippou 2015, p. 8–9.
55 Le cintre de la stèle Caire JE 44901 est inachevé : Nespoulous-Phalippou 2015, p. 7–12. Pour les statues décrites dans les décrets de Ptolémée V, voir aussi Recklinghausen 2018, p. 310–319.
56 *Newsletter of the Egyptian Ministry of Antiquities* 27, 2018, p. 1. Contrairement aux premières annonces lors de la découverte, ces stèles ne datent pas du règne de Ptolémée XII (ainsi faussement repris par Panov, Lanciers 2023, p. 61–62).

avait été plus abondante, il est probable qu'elle aurait utilisé la deuxième version du schéma impliquant la présentation de l'épée de la victoire.

### 4.1.1 Philométor et Évergète II

Le règne de Ptolémée VI Philométor fut riche en rebondissements. Après avoir régné sous la tutelle de sa mère Cléopâtre I, il forme un couple avec sa sœur Cléopâtre II[57]. Suite à des menaces étrangères, le couple s'associe à leur frère cadet, le futur Ptolémée VIII. Cette union ne survit que quelques années après lesquelles le plus jeune Ptolémée prend le pouvoir et oblige Ptolémée VI à l'exil. Celui-ci peut toutefois reprendre le contrôle en 163, après quoi il régnera ensemble avec son épouse jusqu'à sa mort en 145.

Ces phases du règne se reflètent dans les textes hiéroglyphiques par les différentes formes que prend l'épithète Philométor[58]. Celle de la quatrième phase *nṯr.wj mrj.wj mw.t=snj* est particulièrement intéressante en mettant doublement l'accent sur le couple royal : d'une part, grâce à l'utilisation du duel de *nṯr* et, d'autre part, en adoptant le duel du suffixe de la troisième personne. Après une période où le pouvoir était géré par trois personnes, l'orthographe de l'épithète veut clairement mettre en avant la reprise en main du pouvoir par le couple royal. Seule l'écriture hiéroglyphique était capable de rendre ce message aussi visuel : deux signes *nṯr* (au lieu de trois) et deux traits (au lieu de trois). Il n'est dès lors pas étonnant que le schéma du culte royal, construit sur le principe du couple, réapparaisse au nom de Philométor exactement au même moment. On relève quatre attestations sur les monuments de ce roi.

Le premier, sans surprise, est directement connecté avec le synode rassemblé en l'an 20. La stèle du décret[59], en mauvais état, nécessiterait une étude épigraphique approfondie. Toutefois, on en comprend pour le moment que les prêtres se sont réunis, et qu'il y est question de statues royales et du couronnement du roi. Le paragraphe décrivant les circonstances qui ont donné lieu à la réunion n'est malheureusement pas identifié, mais la date laisse peu de doute sur un lien avec le retour du couple. Le cintre montre dès lors le dieu présentant l'épée de la victoire au roi accompagné de la reine tenant le sceptre-*wꜣḏ* en présence des ancêtres[60].

---

57 Pour cette période, voir aussi Habachy 2023b.
58 Preys 2018.
59 Le Caire CG 22184 : Kamal 1904–1905, p. 178–181, pl. LVIII ; Lanciers 1987 ; Recklinghausen 2018, p. 8; Panov, Lanciers 2023.
60 Contra Panov, Lanciers 2023, p. 35 qui identifie le sceptre comme un sceptre-*wꜣs*.

En l'an 24, le roi est encore victorieux sur un autre champ de bataille, la Nubie, qui lui permet d'offrir le Dodekaschoinos à Isis. La stèle gravée sur un bloc de granit dans le temple de Philae présente une double scène. À gauche, la déesse Isis présente l'épée de la victoire que le roi accepte de la main droite. La déesse est accompagnée d'Harendotes, le dieu auquel aussi bien Philopator qu'Épiphane s'identifient dans leurs décrets respectifs. Dans la main gauche, le roi tient un objet non identifié[61]. Il est habillé du manteau à franges caractéristique de la scène du schéma du culte royal, et est accompagné de la reine qui lève le bras dans le dos du roi. Les ancêtres sont toutefois absents[62]. Dans la scène parallèle, le roi et la reine offrent le champ à Osiris et Isis, image évoquant la donation du Dodecaschoinos.

Pourtant deux attestations sur les parois des temples ne choisissent pas la présentation de l'épée, mais bien la présentation de l'*jmj.t-pr*. Sur la porte d'Amon à Karnak, le schéma du culte royal apparaît sur les épaisseurs des montants. Sechat y inscrit le document pour Ptolémée VI et Cléopâtre II, les *theoi Philometores*, tandis que Philométor exécute le culte pour les dieux Épiphanes. À Kom Ombo, la scène apparaît sur la façade du sanctuaire[63] où la scène des ancêtres n'est pas conservée. Le dieu Khonsou-Thot y agit au nom des deux dieux du temple qui se tiennent derrière lui. Le choix de la présentation de l'*jmj.t-pr* pourrait suggérer que la décoration de ces temples ne date pas de la période suivant directement le retour du roi, mais que quelques années ont passé avant que l'activité de construction et de décoration de Philométor se soit mise en route. En ce sens, le lien avec la « victoire » se serait affaibli[64].

Ptolémée VIII Évergète II après avoir épousé la veuve de son frère Cléopâtre II, épousa également sa fille Cléopâtre III. Ces deux reines n'ont pas seulement créé de nombreux problèmes dans ce ménage à trois avec Évergète II, mais également durant les deux règnes suivants.

---

61 *LD*. IV, 27. Le dessin de Lepsius doit clairement être modifié. Ni le gobelet d'encensement ni l'aiguière pas plus que la table d'offrandes devant le roi ne sont visibles. Des traces de cartouches sont par contre visibles devant la tête du roi. Il est possible de comparer la position du roi avec celle de la porte monumentale de Qous datant de l'époque de Ptolémée X Alexandre. Voir Preys 2015b, p. 162.

62 Le schéma du culte royal n'est pas complet. Il est donc possible que la victoire du roi ait justifié l'utilisation de la scène de l'épée de victoire, sans toutefois qu'il s'agisse du schéma du culte royal. Dans cette scène, l'habillement du roi aurait été « contaminé » par le schéma. En effet, la scène de la présentation de l'épée au roi ne portant pas le manteau à franges apparaît en dehors du schéma. Voir par exemple à Edfou : Recklinghausen 2018, p. 319–331.

63 *KO* I, 14.

64 La présence de la quatrième forme de l'épithète de culte Philométor assure que la gravure du décor est bien postérieure au retour de Ptolémée VI (Preys 2017, p. 238).

Comme nous l'avons démontré, le règne d'Évergète II constitue une période charnière dans l'utilisation du schéma du culte royal. Les scènes gravées sur les parois extérieures du naos d'Edfou sont particulièrement intéressantes pour plusieurs raisons. Elles démontrent que le schéma décoratif du culte royal n'était pas un carcan rigide, mais au contraire une structure autorisant de multiples variations souplement modulables suivant les circonstances – dans ce cas-ci les particularités historiques du règne d'Évergète II. Le schéma témoigne ainsi de la virtuosité théologique des hiérogrammates de cette période.

Pour la disposition des scènes du schéma, les décorateurs étaient confrontés à une première difficulté. Le nombre de scènes de culte des ancêtres avait grandement augmenté. Lors de la création du schéma sous Évergète I, il n'était question que d'une scène de culte des ancêtres dédiée aux Philadelphes. Sous Évergète II, les Philadelphes, Évergètes, Philopatores et Épiphanes recevaient chacun leurs propres scènes. Ceci constitue le nombre maximum de scènes qui seront dédiées aux ancêtres[65]. Ces quatre scènes furent placées en symétrie sur les deux murs extérieurs du naos, aux troisième et quatrième registres[66]. On peut se demander pourquoi il était nécessaire de multiplier les scènes dédiées aux ancêtres. Quand Ptolémée VI Philométor, dont les ancêtres étaient aussi nombreux que ceux d'Évergète II puisqu'ils étaient frères, fit décorer la porte d'Amon du deuxième pylône de Karnak, il se limita à une scène figurant ses ancêtres directs, c'est-à-dire ses parents. Ainsi, sous Évergète II, une scène dédiée au couple vivant aurait pu être placée sur la paroi ouest du naos et une scène dédiée aux Épiphanes sur la paroi est du naos.

Cette solution est sans compter que le « couple » des *theoi Evergetes* était actuellement composé de trois personnes. Une telle disposition aurait donc créé une asymétrie inacceptable entre la scène ouest (dédiée à trois figures) et la scène est (dédié à deux figures). La solution logique dans l'ensemble des principes de la grammaire du temple était de dédoubler l'image du roi. Le « couple » royal fut donc distribué sur deux scènes : Ptolémée avec Cléopâtre II, et Ptolémée avec Cléopâtre III.

Pour arriver à ce procédé, les décorateurs ont scindé la scène de la transmission de l'*jmj.t-pr* en deux étapes. La première scène montre Thot écrivant le docu-

---

65 Seule la fameuse scène du temple de *Tôd* II, 318, datant également d'Évergète II comporte, en plus des quatre couples, l'image de Ptolémée VI Philométor et de Ptolémée Eupator (Minas 1996, p. 75).

66 Sur les parois extérieures du naos, on trouve Épiphane et Évergète au troisième registre et Philadelphe et Philopator au quatrième registre. Le même principe fut appliqué sur les parois intérieures du pronaos (*Edfou* III, 130, 13–131, 11 (Épiphane) ; 140, 9–141, 8 (Philopator) ; 181, 12–182, 10 (Évergète) ; 191, 9–192, 5 (Philadelphe) ).

ment pour Ptolémée et Cléopâtre III (paroi ouest) tandis que, dans la seconde scène, il le transmet à Ptolémée et Cléopâtre II (paroi est). Cette division n'est en soi pas innovatrice, car elle avait déjà été utilisée sous Philopator pour correspondre aux deux scènes dédiées aux ancêtres Philadelphes et Évergètes. Dans le sanctuaire d'Edfou, les deux scènes impliquant l'*jmj.t-pr* sont placées sur la paroi ouest, l'une au-dessus de l'autre en symétrie avec les deux scènes dédiées aux ancêtres sur la paroi est. Ainsi, la paroi ouest est dédiée au couple vivant Philométor[67], et la paroi est aux couples défunts Philadelphes et Évergètes.

Les décorateurs d'Évergète II ont fait un autre choix pour les parois extérieures du naos. Dans tous les exemples précédents du schéma du culte royal, les deux scènes du schéma étaient visibles d'un point de vue commun[68]. Les deux parois extérieures du naos ne permettaient pas ce jeu visuel. Si les scènes du couple vivant étaient placées sur une paroi et celles du couple des ancêtres sur l'autre paroi, le schéma du culte royal ne pouvait pas être appréhendé en même temps. C'est ici que le dédoublement de la scène de la transmission de l'*jmj.t-pr* offrait de nouvelles possibilités au décorateur. Au lieu de placer les deux scènes sur la même paroi comme dans le sanctuaire d'Edfou, les décorateurs les ont distribuées sur les deux parois, en plaçant les scènes du culte des ancêtres dans les registres supérieurs. Ceci dispose les trois couples royaux verticalement l'un au-dessus de l'autre, créant ainsi visuellement une connexion entre les vivants et les ancêtres. De plus, il n'était pas nécessaire, pour ainsi dire, de se déplacer de la paroi ouest à la paroi est pour contempler le schéma, puisque chaque paroi en possédait sa propre version. Les parois extérieures du naos ne possèdent donc non pas une attestation du schéma, mais bien deux, chacune avec sa scène de l'*jmj.t-pr* et ses scènes des ancêtres.

Ce stratagème ouvrait à nouveau un nombre de possibilités inédites. Le dédoublement de la scène de la transmission de l'*jmj.t-pr* permettait de distribuer les deux reines sur les deux scènes, créant un principe de symétrie que l'on retrouve dans d'autres temples[69] : à la figure de Cléopâtre III, en tant que *ḥm.t-nswt* sur la paroi ouest, correspond l'image de Cléopâtre II, en tant que *sn.t-nswt* sur la paroi est. Toutefois, seuls les textes hiéroglyphiques permettent de faire la différence. En dupliquant les figures féminines, tout comme on duplique le roi, le temple donne l'impression que tout est « normal », et qu'il y a un couple royal

---

67 Dans ces cas, les deux scènes de la transmission de l'*jmj.t-pr* sont dédiées au même couple : Ptolémée et Arsinoé Philopator.
68 Par exemple, sur la porte de Khonsou, l'observateur se tenant entre les deux montants peut voir les deux scènes à sa droite et à sa gauche. De même dans le sanctuaire d'Edfou, un point de vue unique au centre de la salle suffit à voir les deux scènes.
69 Voir Minas 1996, 1997.

« normal » au pouvoir. Visuellement, on peut donc « lire », sur la paroi ouest, Thot écrivant l'*jmj.t-pr* pour Ptolémée et Cléopâtre, surmonté des scènes dédiées aux ancêtres, tandis que, sur la paroi est, c'est Thot qui offre l'*jmj.t-pr* à Ptolémée et Cléopâtre, surmonté des scènes dédiées aux ancêtres. Ce n'est que textuellement que l'on peut ajouter *II* et *III* aux Cléopâtres, ou *Philadelphe, Évergète, Philopator, Épiphane* aux ancêtres. En somme : deux scènes pour trois détenteurs du pouvoir qui donnent l'impression de n'être qu'à deux.

Et pourtant, ils sont bien à trois et les textes ne laissent aucun doute à ce sujet. La sœur Cléopâtre possède une titulature bien plus développée : « Fille royale, sœur royale, épouse royale, mère royale, souveraine, dame du double pays Cléopâtre, sœur et épouse du fils de Rê, Ptolémée vivant éternellement, aimé de Ptah, les deux dieux Évergètes »[70]. Cléopâtre III, quant à elle, n'est qualifiée que de « souveraine, dame du double pays Cléopâtre, épouse royale du fils de Rê, Ptolémée vivant éternellement, aimé de Ptah »[71].

Ces titulatures véhiculent deux informations essentielles. Non seulement la titulature de Cléopâtre II est plus développée, mais en outre, cette reine est la seule à être mère royale. Elle doit donc être considérée comme la mère du fils Ptolémée représenté devant elle. Le texte accompagnant « Ptolémée fils de Ptolémée vivant éternellement, aimé de Ptah », en reprenant la formule de la titulature grecque, ne laisse aucun doute ; il est « l'héritier du roi, celui que la souveraine a mis au monde (i.e. d'une fille royale), successeur du seigneur unique »[72]. Rien de tel ne définit Cléopâtre III, pourtant aussi fille royale, ou le fils Ptolémée placé devant elle qui est le « ka royal ». En un sens, on pourrait dire que cette image est un *space filler*. Ensuite, la titulature de Cléopâtre II épouse de Ptolémée est suivie de l'épithète *nṯr.wj mnḫ.wj*. Elle forme donc un couple avec Ptolémée VIII. Le texte au-dessus du couple les définit à nouveau comme *nṯr.wj mnḫ.wj*, suivi de la précision : « le souverain et la souveraine avec leur fils »[73]. Par contre, dans la scène figurant Cléopâtre III, l'épithète de culte est au pluriel *nṯr.w mnḫ.w*[74] comme si le couple Ptolémée VIII-Cléopâtre III ne pouvait pas être envisagé sans la présence de Cléopâtre II.

Il semble ainsi que les parois extérieures reflètent astucieusement une situation historique qui éclaire la relation entre les trois personnages. Dater cette si-

---

70 *s3.t nswt sn.t nswt ḥm.t nswt mw.t nswt ḥq3.t nb.t t3.wj qljw3p3dr3 sn.t ḥm.t n.t s3 rꜥ ptwlmjs ꜥnḫ ḏ.t mrj ptḥ nṯr.wj mnḫ.wj* (*Edfou* IV, 249, 5–6).
71 *ḥq3.t nb.t t3.wj qljw3p3dr3 ḥm.t nswt n.t s3 rꜥ ptwlmjs ꜥnḫ ḏ.t mrj ptḥ* (*Edfou* IV, 93, 1–2).
72 *Edfou* IV, 249, 3.
73 *ḥq3 ḥq3.t ḥnꜥ s3=sn* : *Edfou* IV, 248, 15–17. La colonne latérale divine mentionne encore l'épithète de culte au duel (*Edfou* IV, 249, 8).
74 *Edfou* IV, 92, 8 ; 93, 4.

tuation est plus difficile. Si Cléopâtre II est bien la mère de « Ptolémée fils de Ptolémée » alors celui-ci ne peut être que Ptolémée Memphites. Cela peut dès lors suggérer que la décoration du naos décrit le moment où Cléopâtre II avait le dessus sur Cléopâtre III parce qu'elle avait produit l'héritier. La décoration doit donc être postérieure à la naissance de Ptolémée Memphites, et postérieure au mariage d'Évergète II avec sa nièce, tout en étant antérieure à la naissance du futur Ptolémée IX, et antérieure à la mort de Memphites[75]. Malheureusement, de tous ces événements, seule la date de la mort de Memphites semble certaine.

Le schéma du culte royal sur les parois du naos du temple d'Edfou utilise la scène de la transmission de l'*jmj.t-pr*. Toutefois, la scène de la transmission de l'épée de victoire apparaît également pendant le règne d'Évergète II. Dans la salle hypostyle du temple de Kom Ombo, Haroëris présente le glaive à Ptolémée VIII accompagné des deux Cléopâtres. La scène symétrique n'est pas conservée ; il est donc difficile d'affirmer que nous avons affaire, dans ce cas, au schéma du culte royal. Bien que l'image du roi présente toutes les caractéristiques iconographiques du schéma, il ne tourne pas le dos au sanctuaire. Malheureusement, bien qu'il soit tentant de relier cette scène aux troubles survenus entre 130 et 124, ou avec la grande entente de 118, rien ne permet actuellement de dater cette scène avec précision.

### 4.1.2 Sôter II et Alexandre I

Avec la mort d'Évergète II, l'importance des deux Cléopâtres ne fit qu'augmenter et les problèmes ne s'atténuèrent pas. Le schéma décoratif en est encore le témoin.

À Edfou, sur la paroi extérieure ouest du naos, le dieu Montou transmet l'épée de la victoire à Ptolémée IX Sôter II. Le cartouche de Ptolémée IX, ainsi que l'épithète Philométor, confirme que la scène reflète la situation lors du premier règne de ce roi entre 116 et 107[76]. L'intérêt de la scène ne réside pas tant dans l'interaction entre le dieu et le roi qui reprend les idées mises en place depuis Philopator, mais bien dans le personnage féminin qui accompagne le roi. En effet,

---

[75] La naissance des deux princes est toutefois problématique et repose principalement sur l'interprétation de leur nom d'Horus qui semble associer leur naissance à celle du taureau Apis. Il est toutefois improbable qu'aussi bien Ptolémée VI que Ptolémée Memphites et Ptolémée IX soient nés au même moment qu'un Apis. Une étude plus approfondie des parois pourra peut-être apporter de nouvelles données.
[76] Pour les titulatures de Ptolémée IX durant ses deux règnes, voir Caßor-Pfeiffer 2008a, Habachy 2023a.

pour la première fois, il ne s'agit pas de l'épouse du roi, mais bien de la mère du roi. Elle reprend une titulature qui ressemble fortement à celle que Cléopâtre II avait affichée sur les parois extérieures du naos : « mère royale, sœur royale, épouse royale, fille royale, maîtresse du sud et du nord, souveraine, dame du double pays, Cléopâtre, mère divine du fils de Rê Ptolémée, vivant éternellement, aimé de Ptah »[77]. Il faut toutefois remarquer plusieurs divergences. D'une part, elle ajoute le titre de « maîtresse du sud et du nord » (ḥnw.t šmˁ mḥw) qui met en avant l'importance de la reine. D'autre part, la suite des épithètes n'est pas identique, puisque le titre de mère royale est placé en premier lieu. Ces deux éléments montrent clairement que Cléopâtre est, de fait, la personne qui détient le pouvoir, et que son statut de mère est à la base de cette prétention.

L'identification de la mère de Ptolémée IX est problématique et est un dossier qu'on n'ouvrira pas dans ce contexte. Rappelons seulement que les écrits classiques tendent à identifier Cléopâtre III comme mère utérine, ce que la plupart des égyptologues ont accepté, mais que la théorie a été mise en doute par Devauchelle et Cauville[78]. Carrez-Maratray quant à lui tout en suivant la théorie de Devauchelle et Cauville[79], propose que les deux Cléopâtres auraient été la mère du roi, l'une étant la vraie mère, l'autre l'ayant adopté[80].

Mais l'identification de la reine en question n'est que le premier problème que pose l'image de la reine dans la scène de la transmission de l'épée ; cette image a bel et bien été violemment attaquée[81]. Le moment et les raisons de cette attaque peuvent dépendre de l'identification de la reine. Dans le cas de Cléopâtre III, deux moments pourraient correspondre à cette destruction. Soit, en premier lieu, l'image de la reine fut attaquée après sa dispute avec son second fils. En 107, en effet, la reine chasse son fils Ptolémée IX dans le but de régner avec son second fils Ptolémée X Alexandre. Celui-ci la remercia en l'éliminant en 101, et en la remplaçant par Bérénice III. Les raisons de la dispute entre le fils et sa mère ne sont pas claires, mais elles furent assez sérieuses pour que le fils l'assassine. Ce déchaînement de violence aurait pu se propager aux images de la

---

77 mw.t nswt sn.t nswt ḥm.t nswt s3.t nswt ḥnw.t šmˁ mḥw ḥq3.t nb.t t3.wj qljw3p3dr3 mw.t nṯr n.t [s3] Rˁ ptwlmjs ˁnḫ ḏ.t mrj ptḥ : Edfou IV, 340, 11–12.
78 Cauville, Devauchelle 1984, p. 47–50.
79 Pour les différentes théories : Pro Cléopâtre II : Cauville, Devauchelle 1984, p. 47–52 ; Egberts 1987, Egberts 1995 ; Carrez-Maratray 2002 ; Eldamaty 2011, p. 34 ;
Pro Cléopâtre III : Minas 2005, p. 141 ; Caßor-Pfeiffer 2008a, p. 22 ; Caßor-Pfeiffer 2008b, p. 236–242; Ritner 2011, p. 97. Hölbl 2001, p. 205 ; Traunecker 2013, p. 178–179 ; Bielman Sanchez, Lenzo 2015, p. 394–395; Pfeiffer 2017, p. 169, 175, 238 (n. 3).
80 Carrez-Maratray 2002.
81 Les photos montrent clairement qu'il s'agit d'une destruction totalement différente des attaques post-pharaoniques dont le roi, dans la même scène, fut la victime.

reine. Il est étonnant de voir que seule l'image de la reine de la scène de la transmission du pouvoir a été attaquée, et non pas d'autres images sur le pronaos ou sur le mur d'enceinte. Ceci démontre, à notre avis, l'importance de cette scène, une expression puissante de la légitimité du roi. De plus, dans le cas de la scène du pronaos d'Edfou, la reine Cléopâtre III se présente comme la source de cette légitimité. Si Ptolémée X s'est retourné contre sa mère, c'était peut-être parce qu'elle tenait trop au pouvoir aux dépens du fils aspirant à une certaine indépendance. Il faut toutefois remarquer que la destruction ne s'est pas propagée à l'image du roi Ptolémée IX[82]. En deuxième lieu, nous entrevoyons une autre possibilité au moment du retour au pouvoir de Ptolémée IX. Celui-ci aurait voulu dissocier sa légitimité de la figure de sa mère qui, de plus, l'avait chassé en faveur de son jeune frère[83]. À nouveau, le fait que la scène soit fortement liée à l'idée de légitimité royale peut expliquer que les autres figures de la reine n'aient pas attiré l'attention. Pour revenir une dernière fois à Cléopâtre II, on voit mal dans quelles circonstances, son image aurait pu devenir problématique. Si elle a soutenu Ptolémée IX après la mort d'Évergète II, elle était morte depuis longtemps quand Ptolémée X est placé sur le trône par Cléopâtre III.

Ptolémée X Alexandre nous a laissé sa propre version du schéma du culte royal sur la porte monumentale du temple de Qous. Cette version entérine une évolution que l'on voit apparaître dès le règne d'Évergète II, mais se confirme avec la scène de Sôter II sur le pronaos d'Edfou et celle d'Alexandre sur la porte de Qous, où le schéma se détache de plus en plus de la scène du culte des ancêtres. D'une part, la présence du fils Ptolémée dans les scènes d'Évergète indique une nouvelle vision tournée vers le futur (le successeur) plutôt que vers le passé (les ancêtres). D'autre part, un autre changement est la mise en symétrie de la scène royale avec des scènes exprimant la royauté du dieu. Ainsi sur la porte de Qous, qui permettait parfaitement d'appliquer le schéma tel qu'il existe depuis le règne d'Évergète I, la scène de la transmission de l'épée est placée symétriquement à une scène dédiée à Osiris. Toutefois, cette évolution est moins importante pour notre propos que la présence, une fois encore, d'une reine non identifiable en raison de la destruction de la partie supérieure de la scène. Si la décoration de la porte date d'avant le meurtre de la mère, alors cette reine est Cléopâtre III. Dans le cas contraire, il pourrait s'agir de Bérénice III associée au pouvoir par

---

[82] Malgré les disputes entre Ptolémée IX et X, il n'y a pas, à ma connaissance, de *damnatio memoriae* détectable sur les parois des temples de cette époque. Le cas de l'image de la reine est peut-être une indication que ce « jeu » se jouait par l'intermédiaire des images des reines, constituant la base de légitimité pour les deux rois.
[83] L'élimination de l'épithète de culte Philométor en est probablement un signe : Caßor-Pfeiffer 2008a, p. 25.

Alexandre I. Le fait que le roi est appelé le dieu Philométor (*p3 nṯr mrj mw.t=f*) pourrait faire pencher la balance en faveur de la première théorie.

Ainsi, quand Sôter II revient en 88 sur le trône d'Égypte, exactement en l'an 30 de son règne – juste à temps pour célébrer son jubilé – Cléopâtre II et Cléopâtre III avaient disparues; il nous laisse alors la dernière version du schéma du culte royal. Ici encore, cette scène révèle des surprises. Si durant son premier règne, Ptolémée IX Sôter II se fait représenter avec sa mère, pendant le deuxième règne, il apparaît tout à fait tout seul[84], comble de l'ironie pour un discours idéologique basé sur le concept du couple. La scène est, de surcroît, surmontée de la scène du culte des ancêtres où apparaît Évergète II en couple avec son épouse Cléopâtre. Le cartouche qui identifie cette Cléopâtre se lit : « épouse royale mère royale Cléopâtre » *ḥm.t nswt mw.t nswt qljw3pdr*. Le titre de *ḥm.t nswt* de Cléopâtre III s'est transformé en nom propre. Elle n'est plus Cléopâtre ; elle est Épouse-Cléopâtre, mère de Sôter II. Il se pourrait que cette scène nous offre la dernière pièce du puzzle concernant la mère de Ptolémée IX. Accompagnant son mari dans cette scène d'adoration des ancêtres, Cléopâtre semble bien avoir été considérée comme la mère de Sôter II[85]. Cette scène présente, néanmoins, un dernier problème : comment accorder sa présence dans la scène des ancêtres à la violence avec laquelle l'image du pronaos fut attaquée ? Est-ce que le roi a eu un changement d'attitude par rapport à sa mère, ou doit-on quand même attribuer la destruction de l'image du pronaos à Alexandre ?

Quoi qu'il en soit, l'asymétrie entre le roi vivant seul et le couple d'ancêtres au-dessus ne peut être plus poignante. Clairement, le schéma décoratif du culte royal avait joué son rôle, d'Évergète I à Sôter II. Tant l'image du roi dans son manteau à frange tenant le sceptre-*w3s* que les textes sur la paroi de l'enceinte d'Edfou proclament encore plus ou moins les mêmes idées[86], mais elles ont perdu toute conviction. Ptolémée XII y renoncera.

# 5 Conclusions

Mis en place au début de l'époque ptolémaïque, le schéma du culte royal établit la légitimité du pharaon. Il s'adapte non seulement à la réalité ptolémaïque qui met en avant le couple royal, mais également aux changements continus de la poli-

---

84 *Edfou* VI, 277, 2–11.
85 Voir également l'opinion de Chauveau 1998, p. 1264, n. 6.
86 Pour l'étude des textes du schéma décoratif et leur évolution d'Evergète I à Soter II, voir Preys 2017.

tique lagide. À peine un « couple » à trois ou la primauté d'une reine, les révoltes et les meurtres ont-ils posé de problème majeur. Ce schéma offre ainsi un exemple supplémentaire de la flexibilité du « langage » du temple égyptien combinant texte et image.

La lecture « politique » du schéma du culte royal dans le temple d'Edfou montre bien à quel point les prêtres des temples étaient des protagonistes actifs dans la politique des Lagides. Loin d'être retranchés dans leur temple, ils jouaient le jeu, choisissaient leur camp et le communiquaient, entre autres, par un moyen qui leur est propre et qu'ils contrôlaient parfaitement : les parois des temples. En dépit de toutes les tribulations des Ptolémées, les hiérogrammates ont réussi à maintenir la communication avec les dieux, et à les convaincre qu'il y avait véritablement un pharaon légitime, garant de la Maât.

## Bibliographie

Abd El Gawad 2012
    Abd El Gawad, H., « Tell Me Your Name and I Can Tell You how Your Kingship was: The Royal Names of the first three Ptolemies (332–222 BC) » in H. Abd El Gawad, N. Andrews, M. Correas-Amador, V. Tamori, J. Taylor (éd.), *Current Research in Egyptology 2011: Proceedings of the Twelfth Annual Symposium, CRE 12*, Oxford 2012, p. 1–14.

Bianchi 1978
    Bianchi, R., « The Striding Draped Male Figure of Ptolemaic Egypt » in H. Maehler, V.M. Strocka (éd.), *Das ptolemäische Ägypten*, Mayence, 1978, p. 95–102.

Bielman Sánchez, Lenzo 2015
    Bielman Sánchez, A., Lenzo, G., *Inventer le pouvoir féminin. Cléopâtre I et Cléopâtre II, reines d'Égypte au II$^e$ s. av. J.-C.*, ECHO 12, Berne, 2015.

Broze, Preys 2021
    Broze, M., Preys, R., *La porte d'Amon. Le deuxième pylône de Karnak I: Etudes et relevé épigraphique*, BiGen 63, Le Caire, 2021.

Cafici 2021
    Cafici, G., *The Egyptian Elite as Roman Citizens: Looking at Ptolemaic Private Portraiture*, HES 14, Leyde, Boston, 2021.

Carrez-Maratray 2002
    Carrez-Maratray, J.-Y., « L'épithète Philometor et la réconciliation lagide de 124–116 », *RdE* 53, 2002, p. 61–74.

Caneva 2016
    Caneva, S.G., *From Alexander to the Theoi Adelphoi: Foundation and Legitimation of a Dynasty*, StudHell 56, Louvain, 2016.

Caßor-Pfeiffer 2008a
    Caßor-Pfeiffer, S., « Zur Reflexion ptolemäischer Geschichte in den ägyptischen Tempeln unter Ptolemaios IX. Philometor II./Soter II. und Ptolemaios X. Alexander I. (116–80 v. Chr.) – Teil 1: Die Bau- und Dekorationstätigkeit », *JEH* 1.1, 2008, p. 21–77.

Caßor-Pfeiffer 2008b
　　Caßor-Pfeiffer, S., « Zur Reflexion ptolemäischer Geschichte in den ägyptischen Tempeln unter Ptolemaios IX. Philometor II./Soter II. und Ptolemaios X. Alexander I. (116–80 v. Chr.) – Teil 2: Kleopatra III. und Kleopatra Berenike III. im Spiegel der Tempelreliefs », *JEH* 1.2, 2008, p. 235–265.

Cauville, Devauchelle 1984
　　Cauville, S., Devauchelle, D., « Le temple d'Edfou : Étapes de la construction. Nouvelles données historiques », *RdE* 35, 1984, p. 31–55.

Chauveau 1998
　　Chauveau, M., « Une nouvelle déesse Philadelphe » in W. Clarysse, A. Schoors, H. Willems (éd.), *Egyptian Religion – The Last Thousand Years, II: Studies Dedicated to the Memory of Jan Quaegebeur*, OLA 85, Louvain, 1998, p. 1263–1275.

Clarysse 1991
　　Clarysse, W., « Hakoris, an Egyptian Nobleman and His Family », *AncSoc* 22, 1991, p. 235–243.

Clère 1961
　　Clère, P., *La porte d'Évergète à Karnak, 2ᵉ partie : Planches*, MIFAO 84, Le Caire, 1961.

Coulon 2001
　　Coulon, L., « Quand Amon parle à Platon (La statue Caire JE 38033) », *RdE* 53, 2001, p. 85–112.

Egberts 1987
　　Egberts, A., « A Note on the Building History of the Temple of Edfu », *RdE* 38, 1987, p. 55–61.

Egberts 1995
　　Egberts, A., « A Note on "A Note on the Building History of the temple of Edfu" », *RdE* 46, 1995, p. 208–209.

Eldamaty 2007
　　Eldamaty, M., « Die leeren Kartuschen aus der Regierungszeit von Kleopatra VII. im Tempel von Dendera » in J.-C. Goyon, C. Cardin (éd.), *Proceedings of the Ninth International Congress of Egyptologists*, OLA 150, Louvain, 2007, p. 501–534.

Eldamaty 2011
　　Eldamaty, M., « Die ptolemäische Königin als weiblicher Horus » in A. Jördens, J.F. Quack (éd.), *Ägypten zwischen innerem Zwist und äußerem Druck: die Zeit Ptolemaios' VI. bis VIII. – Internationales Symposion Heidelberg 16.–19.9.2007*, Philippika 45, Wiesbaden, 2011, p. 24–57.

Gauthier, Sottas 1925
　　Gauthier, H., Sottas, H., *Un décret trilingue en l'honneur de Ptolémée IV*, Le Caire, 1925.

Gorre 2009
　　Gorre, G., *Les relations du clergé égyptien et des Lagides d'après les sources privées*, StudHell 45, Louvain, 2009.

Habachy 2023a
　　M. Habachy, « L'épithète de culte comme indice de datation. A quel moment les inscriptions hiéroglyphiques ont-elles qualifié Ptolémée IX de "dieu Sôter" ? », *JEH* 16, 2023, p. 219–249.

Habachy 2023b
　　Habachy, M., « Le "dieu" Philométor et une hypothèse sur le couronnement de quelques rois lagides » in M. Habachy, F. Servajean (éd.), *A Wise Man for the Beloved Land. Recueil d'études dédiées au professeur Aly Omar Abdalla par ses amis, collègues et étudiants*, CENiM 34, 2023, p. 111–133.

Hölbl 2001
　　Hölbl, G., *A History of the Ptolemaic History*, London, New York, 2001.

Kamal 1904–1905
> Kamal, A. B., *Catalogue général des antiquités égyptiennes du Musée du Caire, N° 22001–22208, Stèles ptolémaïques et romaines*, T.1-2, Le Caire, 1904–1905.

Klotz, LeBlanc 2012
> Klotz, D., Leblanc, M., « An Egyptian Priest in the Ptolemaic court, Yale Peabody Museum 264191 » in C. Zivie-Coche, I. Guermeur (éd.), *« Parcourir l'éternité ». Hommages à Jean Yoyotte*, BEHE sc. hist. et philol. 156, Turnhout, 2012, p. 645-698.

Lanciers 1987
> Lanciers, E., « Die Stele CG 22184: Ein Priesterdekret aus der Regierungszeit des Ptolemaios VI. Philometor », *GM* 95, 1987, p. 53-61.

Manning 2011
> Manning, J. G., « The Capture of the Thebaid » in P.F. Dorman, B.M. Bryan (éd.), *Perspectives on Ptolemaic Thebes*, SAOC 65, Chicago, 2011, p. 1–15.

McGing 1997
> McGing, B.C., « Revolt Egyptian Style: International Opposition to Ptolemaic Rule », *AfP* 43, 1997, p. 273-314.

Minas 1996
> Minas M., « Die Dekorationstätigkeit von Ptolemaios VI. Philometor und Ptolemaios VIII. Euergetes II. an ägyptischen Tempeln (Teil 1) », *OLP* 27, 1996, p. 52-78.

Minas 1997
> Minas, M., « Die Dekorationstätigkeit von Ptolemaios VI. Philometor und Ptolemaios VIII. Euergetes II. an ägyptischen Tempeln (Teil 2) », *OLP* 28, 1997, p. 87-121.

Minas 2005
> Minas, M., « Macht und Ohnmacht: Die Repräsentation ptolemäischer Königinnen in der ägyptischen Tempeln », *AfP* 51/1, 2005, p. 127-154.

Minas-Nerpel 2015
> Minas-Nerpel, M., « Arsinoe II. und Berenike II.: frühptolemäische Königinnen im Spannungsfeld zweier Kulturen » in M. Eldamaty, F. Hoffmann, M. Minas-Nerpel (éd.), *Ägyptische Königinnen vom Neuen Reich bis in die islamische Zeit: Beiträge zur Konferenz in der Kulturabteilung der Botschaft der Arabischen Republik Ägypten in Berlin am 19.01.2013*, Vaterstetten, 2015, p. 87-114.

Minas-Nerpel, Preys 2023
> Minas-Nerpel, M., Preys, R., *The Kiosk of Taharqa II: the Ptolemaic Decoration (TahKiosk nos. E1–24, F1–4)*, BiGen 72, Le Caire, 2023.

Moyer 2011
> Moyer, I., « Finding a Middle Ground: Culture and Politics in the Ptolemaic Thebaid », in P.F. Dorman, B.M. Bryan (éd.), *Perspectives on Ptolemaic Thebes*, SAOC 65, Chicago, 2011, p. 1–15.

Nespoulous-Phalippou 2015
> Nespoulous-Phalippou, A., *Ptolémée Épiphane, Aristonikos et les prêtres d'Égypte : Le décret de Memphis (182 a.C.). Édition commentée des stèles Caire RT 2/3/25/7 et JE 44901*, CENiM 12, Montpellier, 2015.

Panov, Lanciers 2023
> Panov, M., Lanciers, E., « The Memphite Sacerdotal Decree of 161 BCE », *JEH* 16, 2023, p. 30–82.

Pfeiffer 2004
> Pfeiffer, S., *Das Dekret von Kanopos (238 v. Chr.): Kommentar und historische Auswertung eines dreisprachigen Synodaldekretes der ägyptischen Priester zu Ehren Ptolemaios' III. und seiner Familie*, AfP Beihefte 18, Munich, 2004.

Pfeiffer 2008
: Pfeiffer, S., *Herrscher- und Dynastiekulte im Ptolemäerreich: Systematik und Einordnung der Kultformen*, MBPF 98, Munich, 2008.

Pfeiffer 2017
: Pfeiffer, S., *Die Ptolemäer: Im Reich der Kleopatra*, Stuttgart, 2017.

Preys 2015a
: Preys, R., « La royauté lagide et le culte d'Osiris d'après les portes monumentales de Karnak » in C. Thiers (éd.), *Documents de théologies thébaines tardives (D3T 3)*, CENiM 13, Montpellier, 2015, p. 159–215.

Preys 2015b
: Preys, R., « Roi vivant et roi ancêtre. Iconographie et idéologie royale sous les Ptolémées » in C. Zivie-Coche (éd.), *Offrandes, rites et rituels dans les temples d'époques ptolémaïque et romaine. Actes de la journée d'études de l'équipe EPHE (EA 4519) « Égypte ancienne : Archéologie, langue, religion »*, Paris, 27 juin 2013, CENiM 10, Montpellier, 2015, p. 149–184.

Preys 2017
: Preys, R., « Les scènes du culte royal à Edfou. Pour une étude diachronique des scènes rituelles des temples de l'époque gréco-romaine » in S. Baumann et H. Kockelmann (éd.), *Der ägyptische Tempel als ritueller Raum: Theologie und Kult in ihrer architektonischen und ideellen Dimension – Akten der internationalen Tagung, Haus der Heidelberger Akademie des Wissenschaften, 9.–12. Juni 2015*, SSR 17, Wiesbaden, 2017, p. 389–418.

Preys 2018
: Preys, R., « Le cas "Philométor" dans les temples égyptiens », *BIFAO* 117, 2018, p. 329–356.

Preys 2021
: Preys, R., « Une image de l'hippopotame ... 3000 ans plus tard » in W. Claes, M. De Meyer, M. Eyckerman, D. Huyge (éd.), *Remove that Pyramid ! Studies on the Archaeology and History of Predynastic and Pharaonic Egypt in Honour of Stan Hendrickx*, OLA 305, Louvain, 2021, p. 899–910.

Preys 2022
: Preys, R., « Le culte des Ptolémées dans les temples égyptiens. Les décrets royaux et la décoration des temples », in G. Lenzo, C. Nihan, M. Pellet (éd.), *Les cultes aux rois et aux héros à l'époque hellénistique. Continuités et changements*, ORA 44, Tübingen, 2022, p. 171–194.

Recklinghausen 2018
: Recklinghausen, D. von, *Die Philensis-Dekrete. Untersuchungen über zwei Synodaldekrete aus der Zeit Ptolemaios' V. und ihre geschichtliche und religiöse Bedeutung*, ÄA 73, Wiesbaden, 2018.

Ritner 2011
: Ritner, R.K., « Ptolemy IX (Soter II) at Thebes » in P. F. Dorman, B. M. Bryan (éd.), *Perspectives on Ptolemaic Thebes*, SAOC 65, Chicago, 2011, p. 97–114.

Sambin 1992,
: Sambin, C., « Les portes de Médamoud du Musée de Lyon », *BIFAO* 92, 1992, p. 147–184.

Sambin, Carlotti 1995
: Sambin, C., Carlotti, J.-F., « Une porte de fête-sed de Ptolémée II remployée dans le temple de Montou à Médamoud », *BIFAO* 95, 1995, p. 383–457.

Schäfer 2011
: Schäfer, D., *Makedonische Pharaonen und hieroglyphische Stelen: historische Untersuchungen zur Satrapenstele und verwandten Denkmälern*, StudHell 50, Louvain, 2011.

Thiers 1999
: Thiers, C. « Les jardins de temple aux époques tardives » in S. Aufrère (éd.), *Encyclopédie religieuse de l'univers végétal : croyances phytoreligieuses de l'Égypte ancienne* 1, Montpellier, 1999, p. 107–120.

Thiers 2009
    Thiers, C., *La stèle de Ptolémée VIII Évergète II à Héracléion: The Underwater Archaeology in the Canopic Region in Egypt*, Oxford, 2009.

Thissen 1966
    Thissen, H.-J., *Studien zum Raphiadekret*, Beiträge zur Klassischen Philologie 23, Meisenheim am Glan, 1966.

Traunecker 2013
    Traunecker, C., « Thèbes, été 115 avant J.-C. Les travaux de Ptolémée IX Sôter II et son prétendu "Château de l'Or" à Karnak » in C. Thiers (éd.), *Documents de théologies thébaines tardives (D3T 2)*, CENiM 8, Montpellier, 2013, p. 177–226.

Vandorpe 1995
    Vandorpe, K., « City of Many a Gate, Harbour for Many a Rebel » in S. P. Vleeming (éd.), *Hundred-Gated Thebes: Acts of a Colloquium on Thebes and the Theban Area in the Graeco-Roman Period*, P.L.Bat. 27, Leyde, New York, Cologne, 1995, p. 203–240.

Veïsse 2004
    Veïsse, A.-E., *Les « révoltes égyptiennes ». Recherches sur les troubles intérieurs en Égypte du règne de Ptolémée III à la conquête romaine*, StudHell 41, Louvain, 2004.

Zivie-Coche 2004
    Zivie-Coche, C., *Tanis. Statues et autobiographies de dignitaires. Tanis à l'époque ptolémaïque*, TTR 3, Paris, 2004.

Felix Relats Montserrat

# La destruction des temples pendant les révoltes : un état de la question à partir de l'exemple de Médamoud

Situé au Nord-Est de Karnak, le village moderne de Médamoud est en partie implanté sur le *kôm* de l'antique *M3dw*, la plus septentrionale des villes dédiées au culte de Montou. Son temple, connu depuis le XVIIIe siècle, fut dégagé au début du XXe siècle par deux équipes de l'Ifao dirigées respectivement par F. Bisson de la Roque (1924–1932) et Cl. Robichon (1933–1940)[1]. À partir de leurs fouilles, le monument est habituellement décrit comme une fondation de Ptolémée V Épiphane dont la décoration se serait poursuivie jusqu'au règne de Trajan[2]. Cependant, l'exploration des fondations de l'entrée du temple (secteur appelé le « mur-pylône » par les premiers fouilleurs) mit au jour le remploi de nombreux blocs du début de l'époque ptolémaïque. Ceux-ci sont datés entre les règnes de Ptolémée II Philadelphe et IV Philopator, signe de l'activité architecturale du début de l'époque lagide sur le site. Leur remploi témoignait, aux yeux de Bisson de la Roque, de la destruction d'un premier monument – construit sous les premiers lagides – lors de la grande révolte de 206 av. J.-C. comme il le résuma à la fin des fouilles :

> Il y a lieu de distinguer, dans les constructions de Médamoud, deux époques ptolémaïques, que je suppose séparées par la révolte de l'an 206 sous Ptolémée IV (…) : le dernier temple subsistant, commencé sans doute par Ptolémée VII [sic], et un petit temple construit par Ptolémée III, entièrement détruit.[3]

L'Histoire évènementielle trouvait ici une matérialisation concrète dans les données de terrain et le site fut désormais considéré comme l'exemple paradigmatique des effets des révoltes en Thébaïde au même titre que l'arrêt des travaux des temples de Deir el-Médina et d'Edfou[4]. Il illustrait ainsi le tableau sombre

---

[1] Pour une histoire des fouilles, se reporter à Relats Montserrat 2024 p. 13–112.
[2] Lanciers 1986, p. 89–90. L'auteur reprend une hypothèse déjà formulée par F. Bisson de la Roque (1926, p. 123).
[3] Bisson de la Roque 1946, p. 42. Ptolémée VII désigne probablement Ptolémée VIII Évergète II car Bisson de la Roque suivait la numérotation établie par H. Gauthier (*LdR* IV/2, p. 307). Le fouilleur avait auparavant attribué la fondation du temple à Ptolémée V Épiphane (*infra* p. 208).
[4] « The consequences of the rebel holding Thebes were perceptible at Medamud, where the Ptolemaic temple was destroyed, as well as in Hathor's temple at Deir el-Medina, where the decora-

dressé par les synodes sacerdotaux qui précisent que les rebelles avaient « causé du tort aux temples » (τὰ ἱερὰ ἀδικήσαντας) pour citer la formule retenue par le décret de Memphis[5].

Le point de vue de Bisson de la Roque a été repris, avec plus ou moins de nuances, dans la littérature égyptologique[6]. Pourtant, il est exclusivement fondé sur la documentation textuelle : le fouilleur datait les maçonneries uniquement par des critères épigraphiques et accordait une grande importance aux sources littéraires extérieures au site. Or depuis les années 1920 non seulement l'archéologie a profondément modifié ses méthodes, mais la documentation s'est aussi étoffée. Dans le cas de Médamoud, le principal problème est posé par le difficile accès à la documentation des fouilles. Certes F. Bisson de la Roque a publié des rapports annuels résumant l'avancée de ses travaux mais sans offrir de synthèse globale ; Cl. Robichon, de son côté, n'a jamais détaillé les recherches menées sur le site[7]. Récemment J.-Fr. Carlotti et Ch. Sambin ont publié une partie des remplois du début de l'époque ptolémaïque et ont prouvé qu'une partie des maçonneries actuellement visibles sur le site remontent au Nouvel Empire. Leurs réflexions se fondent cependant sur une partie de la documentation uniquement et ils n'ont pas clarifié le lien entre les différentes politiques architecturales lagides et la révolte de 206 av. J.-C.[8]. L'examen exhaustif de la documentation issue des fouilles sur le site permet désormais de repenser la façon dont l'histoire du temple doit être replacée dans les évènements qui ont perturbé la Thébaïde sous la domination lagide. Il s'agira également de distinguer les effets collatéraux des évènements politiques sur les monuments pharaoniques des destructions mentionnées dans le discours synodal officiel.

---

tion started under Ptolemy IV was halted during the rebellion and only continuated several years later by Ptolemy VI » (Vandorpe 1995, p. 232).

5 Cité d'après Veïsse 2004, p. 135. Sur les synodes de l'époque ptolémaïque, outre les contributions au présent volume, se référer à Clarysse 2000, p. 41–65.

6 Revez 1999 ; Sambin 2001 ; Larcher 2013 ; voir aussi *supra* n. 4. Pour une vision plus circonspecte : Veïsse 2004, p. 141, n. 83.

7 Relats Montserrat 2024, p. 1–11.

8 Sambin-Nivet, Carlotti 2016. Un article de synthèse paru par J.-Fr. Carlotti (2015) propose une contextualisation historique de l'évolution du temple mais ne tient compte que d'une partie de la documentation issue des fouilles du site. Il est à signaler que cette dernière publication s'est faite sans l'accord de la mission que l'Ifao mène à Médamoud. Plus globalement, le recours systématique à l'expression des « premiers Ptolémées » place toujours Ptolémée V comme une rupture de l'histoire du site sans que celle-ci ne soit réellement explicitée.

# 1 Peut-on parler d'un « temple des premiers Ptolémées » à Médamoud ?

Bisson de la Roque regroupait derrière l'expression « les premiers Ptolémées » les souverains ayant régné avant la révolte de 206 av. J.-C (Ptolémée II à Ptolémée IV). Les conséquences de cet évènement expliqueraient l'existence de deux monuments : un temple latéral attribué à ce premier groupe de rois et le sanctuaire principal, que nous appellerons le temple de Montou, construit après la révolte.

## 1.1 Autopsie d'une théorie : destructions et reconstructions à Médamoud

Un des principaux résultats des fouilles françaises fut la découverte d'un riche corpus épigraphique témoignant de l'occupation du site sur un temps long[9]. En effet dès la fin de la première campagne en 1925, Bisson de la Roque avait déjà mis au jour des blocs du Moyen Empire et de la Deuxième Période intermédiaire (XIIe, XIIIe et XVIIe dynasties), du Nouvel Empire (XVIIIe et XIXe dynasties), de l'Époque tardive (XXVIe dynastie) ainsi que de l'époque ptolémaïque et romaine[10]. Pour expliquer une telle diachronie, le fouilleur formula l'hypothèse, reprise par la plupart des auteurs, que le temple de Montou aurait connu plusieurs fondations : une première sous Sésostris III, puis sous Thoutmosis III et enfin au milieu de l'époque ptolémaïque[11]. Ces différentes fondations auraient entraîné l'arasement des bâtiments antérieurs, seule la dernière phase architecturale étant visible de nos jours.

Méthodologiquement, Bisson de la Roque fondait sa réflexion sur la lecture des cartouches conservés sur le monument. Or, les maçonneries visibles dans le cas de Médamoud ne sont pas en très bon état de conservation, le temple de Mon-

---

9 Comme la plupart des temples thébains, l'occupation de Médamoud remonte au tout début du Moyen Empire, sous la XIe dynastie. Si les vestiges en pierre de cette période sont inexistants, à l'exception d'une table d'offrande en grès au nom de Montouhotep II, c'est sûrement de ce même règne que date le premier bâtiment en brique crue, connu sous le nom de temple primitif. Son arasement complet avant le règne de Sésostris III explique qu'il ne soit pas ici pris en considération dans notre réflexion en raison du décalage stratigraphique qui le sépare du reste des constructions du site. Pour une publication du temple primitif, Relats Montserrat 2024, p. 161–202.
10 Pour une présentation des résultats de la première campagne : Bisson de la Roque 1926, p. 30–63.
11 L'exposé des différents temples successifs est détaillé dans : Bisson de la Roque, Clère 1929, p. 16–18 et dans Bisson de la Roque 1946, p. 33–44. Pour les reprises de cette restitution architecturale, voir *supra* n. 6.

tou étant préservé sur 1,40 m d'élévation en moyenne[12]. À l'exception de deux portes en granit inscrites aux noms de Sésostris III et d'Aménophis II, il identifia les cartouches des souverains compris entre les règnes de Ptolémée VI Philométor et d'Antonin le Pieux[13]. Cette datation put être précisée grâce à la découverte d'un éclat de grès lors du dégagement du sanctuaire de la barque – provenant vraisemblablement de la destruction de son élévation – gravé avec le cartouche de Ptolémée V Épiphane ▒▒▒▒ (Inv. 1431)[14]. L'observation de ces données convainquit le fouilleur que la construction du monument fut débutée par Épiphane qui aurait fait réinstaller à leur emplacement actuel les deux portes en granit des Moyen et Nouvel Empires. Les travaux se seraient ensuite poursuivis pendant toute la fin de l'époque ptolémaïque et la décoration aurait été achevée à l'époque romaine[15].

Le fait que le fouilleur n'ait reconnu aucun cartouche des souverains antérieurs à la grande révolte de 206 av. J.-C. sur les maçonneries du temple de Montou confirmait une telle restitution. En revanche Ptolémée III Évergète était attesté sur le montant d'une porte découverte hors contexte au sud du téménos[16]. Aux yeux de Bisson de la Roque, elle ne pouvait pas appartenir au temple de Montou (commencé par Ptolémée V) ni à sa phase antérieure (remontant à Thoutmosis III) ; elle fut donc interprétée comme les restes d'un « petit temple au sud du grand temple »[17]. L'avancement des fouilles offrit à Bisson de la Roque de nouveaux arguments grâce à la découverte d'un lot de 197 blocs décorés entre les règnes de Ptolémée II et Ptolé-

---

[12] Seules 4 colonnes du portique sont préservées, le reste du monument étant arasé entre son assise de réglage et la première ou deuxième assise d'élévation.
[13] Sont attestés : Ptolémée VI, Ptolémée VIII Évergète II, Ptolémée X Alexandre et Ptolémée XII Néos Dionysos ; Néron, Vespasien, Domitien, Trajan et Antonin le Pieux.
[14] Bisson de la Roque, Clère, 1929, p. 6. Pour Inv. 1431 : Bisson de la Roque 1926, p. 58. La transcription proposée par Bisson de la Roque est à corriger en prenant en considération la cassure de l'éclat : [...] jw' nṯr mry-jt stp(~n) Ptḥ [...] (Bisson de la Roque 1926, p. 123 ; Lanciers 1986, p. 90 et n. 59). Un deuxième éclat (Inv. 1496) , portant aussi le cartouche du même souverain, fut découvert lors du déblaiement du temple mais n'a pas été mentionné par Bisson de la Roque ▒▒▒▒ ([...] jw' [nṯr] mr-[jt] stp~n Ptḥ wsr-k3 [...]) : Registre 1925–1928, p. 116.
[15] Au fur et à mesure de l'avancement des campagnes, le point de vue de Bisson de la Roque a évolué sur la datation proposée pour certaines maçonneries. Ainsi le mur péribole (appelé par le fouilleur le mur d'enceinte) est d'abord attribué à l'époque romaine avant d'être attribué à Ptolémée XII Néos Dionysos (Bisson de la Roque 1927, p. 121).
[16] Le fouilleur précise que la porte se trouvait hors contexte au-dessus d'une butte au sud du temple. Les trois blocs formant le montant furent remontés par Bisson de la Roque (1927, p. 8). Son emplacement, sans rapport avec le reste des vestiges découverts dans le secteur illustre qu'elle fut sûrement déplacée lors de l'exploitation du site par les *sebakhin*.
[17] Bisson de la Roque 1926, p. 8.

mée IV provenant de 6 portes différentes[18]. Ils furent réutilisés ensemble dans les deux assises inférieures des fondations du mur-pylône et de la partie ouest du mur péribole. Comme cette documentation était remployée dans les fondations du temple de Montou, ils devaient provenir du même temple latéral. La cohérence chronologique de ce lot offrit un indice à Bisson de la Roque pour considérer que le temple latéral aurait été détruit lors de la grande révolte. À cette occasion le temple de Montou, remontant au Nouvel Empire, aurait aussi été endommagé, ce qui justifierait sa reconstruction par Ptolémée V Épiphane.

Derrière cette analyse, plusieurs présupposés guidaient la réflexion du fouilleur : le premier était que le graveur d'une inscription était aussi le bâtisseur de la maçonnerie qui en était le support. Il accordait aussi une grande importance à l'épigraphie, ce qui explique aussi que, pour Bisson de la Roque, les murs anépigraphes ne pouvaient pas être datés. Enfin, il associait le remploi des blocs avec la destruction des monuments auxquels ils appartenaient en mettant un place un schéma selon lequel seul un épisode violent justifiait une modification architecturale. Bisson de la Roque reprenait ici un argumentaire antérieur aux fouilles de l'Ifao, formulé pour la première fois par Georges Legrain dans un article faisant le point sur la documentation épigraphique disponible au début du XXe siècle. Selon ce dernier, le temple aurait été endommagé une première fois par l'invasion assyrienne, aurait été restauré par Montouemhat, puis aurait de nouveau été endommagé par Cambyse avant d'être reconstruit à l'époque ptolémaïque[19]. Même si Bisson de la Roque ne fit jamais directement référence aux théories de Legrain et garda un certain flou sur les effets des attaques assyrienne et perse, il reprit à son compte l'importance des guerres dans l'évolution architecturale du temple. D'ailleurs, dans de nombreuses synthèses sur Médamoud la restitution de Bisson de la Roque et celle de Legrain sont tout simplement fusionnées[20].

## 1.2 La question du « petit temple latéral »

La théorie de Bisson de la Roque supposait donc l'existence d'un petit temple annexe où il proposait de replacer toute la documentation du début de l'époque pto-

---

[18] Bisson de la Roque 1933, p. 38. À cette documentation il faut rajouter les dalles qui fermaient la crypte. En 1926 une seule fut sortie (Inv. 2469 : Bisson de la Roque 1927, p. 13 et Fig. 9). Les deux autres le furent en 1929 (Inv. 4476 et 4477 : Bisson de la Roque 1930, p. 119). J.-Fr. Carlotti a reconnu dans ces blocs les linteaux de deux des portes remployées dans le mur-pylône (Sambin-Nivet, Carlotti 2016, p. 409–419).
[19] Legrain 1916, p. 85 et 95.
[20] Voir supra n. 11.

lémaïque avant son remploi. Pour confirmer sa localisation, il décida d'explorer en profondeur le secteur sud du grand temple, là où avait été découverte la porte de Ptolémée III. En 1931, fut mis au jour un caisson de briques associé à des dépôts de fondation attribués au même souverain[21]. C'est ce monument qui fut interprété comme les restes du « temple des premiers Ptolémées » détruit par la révolte de 206 av. J.-C.[22].

Toutefois la restitution proposée par le fouilleur soulève de nombreuses interrogations. En effet les vestiges se présentaient sous la forme d'un rectangle de 27 x 16 m dont les murs étaient construits avec un appareil simple en briques disposées en parpaings[23]. 1,90 m d'élévation étaient préservés, correspondant probablement aux fondations du monument ce qui expliquerait son remplissage par une couche de sable de même épaisseur que la hauteur subsistante des murs[24]. Seuls quatre dépôts de fondation furent découverts dans cette couche à proximité de l'intérieur des angles du caisson en briques[25]. Ils étaient composés chacun d'un mortier en grès à deux anses, d'un mortier en granite rose, d'un pilon triangulaire en granite rose et de petites briques en bronze, en terre émaillée, en albâtre et en cornaline[26]. Bisson de la Roque les attribua sans hésitation à Ptolémée III en raison de la présence du cartouche d'un Ptolémée-vivant-éternellement-aimé-de-Ptah (*Ptwlmys-'nḫ-ḏ.t-mry-Ptḥ*) sur les briquettes émaillées. Cependant aucun argument ne permet d'être aussi catégorique car une telle titulature pourrait aussi bien correspondre à celle de Ptolémée V Éphiphane, de Philométor, d'Evergète II, de Sôter II ou de Ptolémée XII Néos Dyonysos[27]. Du point de vue typologique, ils correspondent au groupe I établi par J.M Weinstein qui réunit tous les dépôts de fondations de l'époque ptolémaïque trouvés dans des temples égyptiens

---

21 Bisson de la Roque 1933, p. 37–41.
22 Bisson de la Roque (1933, p. 38) interprète le mur comme faisant « barrage » du sable dont il était rempli, signe qu'il y voyait une sorte de caisson de fondations. Pour la présentation de ce monument dans la littérature égyptologique, voir *supra* n. 11.
23 Bisson de la Roque 1933, pl. V.
24 L'assise supérieure des murs se trouvait à -1,35 m et le mur s'enfonçait jusqu'à -3,25 m par rapport au niveau de référence pris par Bisson de la Roque qui correspondait au niveau de circulation du seuil du portique du temple. Bisson de la Roque avait déjà fait cette observation, voir *supra* n. 22.
25 D'après la description des fouilleurs, les objets étaient regroupés dans la couche de sable, sans aucun puits (Bisson de la Roque 1933, fig. 29 et planche V).
26 Inv. 5859 pour l'angle nord-est ; Inv. 5860 pour l'angle nord-ouest ; Inv. 5861 pour l'angle sud-ouest et Inv. 5862 pour le sud-est (Bisson de la Roque 1933, p. 40–41, fig. 29–30).
27 Beckerath 1999, p. 235–245. Cette liste doit désormais être complétée par : Hallof 2010, p. 46–49 (P.3/E.1–E.16), p. 76–77 (P.5/E.3–E.4), p. 95–101 (P6/E.3–23, 25–30, 32, 34), p. 141–153 (P.8/E.3–8, 12–15, 18–36, 38–42), p. 188–196 (P.9/E.1–4, 14–17, 24–27, 30–31, 35–7) et p. 251–262 (P.12/E.9, 19, 33, 60).

entre les règnes de Ptolémée I Sôter à Ptolémée X Alexandre par opposition au groupe II (de culture gréco-égyptienne)[28]. Les dépôts de Médamoud étaient enfin accompagnés de neuf tessons en céramique qui servaient à isoler le matériel du sable, mais qui ne furent pas publiés. Le registre d'inventaire précise qu'ils avaient une décoration florale proche des jarres ptolémaïques habituellement datées entre le III$^e$ et II$^e$ siècle av. J.-C. (Inv. 5860)[29].

Aucune autre structure ne put être rattachée à ce caisson en briques. Toutefois, dans leur inventaire, les fouilleurs mentionnèrent plusieurs objets trouvés « dans le remblai au-dessus du sable », sans que leur niveau ne fût précisé[30]. Bisson de la Roque signala en particulier la présence d'une monnaie en bronze de 30 mm de diamètre portant un profil de Sérapis avec corne sur le droit (Inv. 6395)[31]. Sur son revers est représenté un aigle sur un foudre, ailes fermées, tête non tournée, avec une corne d'abondance et l'inscription ΠΤΟΛΕΜΑΙΟΥ ΒΑΣΙΛΕΩΣ. Un poinçon se trouve au centre de la pièce sur ses deux faces. Elle fut datée de Ptolémée IV, confirmant ainsi la datation haute attribuée au caisson en briques[32]. La description livrée de la pièce peut toutefois être remise en doute. En effet, il est peu probable qu'il s'agisse d'une figuration de Sérapis puisque les profils de cette divinité sont normalement reconnaissables par le port de la couronne *atef* ou du *calathos* non mentionnés dans la description[33]. Ce type de monnaie occupe par ailleurs une place secondaire dans le monnayage lagide et il faut attendre l'époque impériale pour voir son développement[34]. La présence d'une corne est en revanche un des attributs traditionnels de la figure de Zeus-Ammon et pourrait correspondre à un type courant de frappe à l'époque lagide représentant le dieu sur le droit et un aigle sur le revers[35]. Dans ce cas, sa datation ne peut plus être attribuée au seul règne de Ptolémée IV Philopator, d'autant que la nouvelle classification des pièces en bronze

---

28 Weinstein 1973, p. 352–363.
29 Inv. 5860 = *Registre 1929–1931*, p. 518. Ces neufs tessons furent découverts sous le dépôt de l'angle nord-ouest. La céramique a été étudiée par Z. Barahona Mendieta (2016b, p. 214) qui renvoie à : Schreiber 2003, Fig. 135.
30 La description publiée par F. Bisson de la Roque (1933, p. 66) doit être complétée par ses notes : *Registre 1932–1939*, p. 573.
31 Bisson de la Roque 1933, p. 66. Inv. 6395.
32 Avis suivi par Carlotti 2015, p. 106–107 et note 98.
33 Pour les critères de représentation des figures de Sérapis dans le monnayage égyptien : Bricault (éd.) 2008, p. 41.
34 Bricault (éd.) 2008, p. 239.
35 Pour l'iconographie des Zeus : Faucher 2013, p. 157. Nous laissons de côté le monnayage à l'effigie d'Alexandre, datant de Ptolémée II, avec une corne d'Amon qui pourrait aussi correspondre à la description donnée mais n'a pas d'aigle sur le revers (Faucher 2013, p. 155).

insiste sur la nécessité de ne plus considérer les règnes comme une césure[36]. Au vu de la description offerte, la monnaie doit appartenir à un stade antérieur à la grande réforme des bronzes lagides du IIe siècle qui vit l'apparition de la comptabilité décimale et du motif du double aigle sur le revers[37]. Elle pourrait correspondre ainsi à la Série 05 des monnaies Alexandrines (tête de Zeus, aigle sur foudre, avec corne d'abondance à gauche) en cours entre 220 à 197 av. J.-C. et qui couvre les règnes de Ptolémée IV Philopator et d'Épiphane[38]. Surtout, rien ne prouve que le remblai où fut découverte la monnaie puisse être associé au caisson en briques précédemment évoqué. Au contraire le reste du matériel contenu dans ce remblai est assez hétérogène et mélange des éclats de calcaire[39], de granodiorite[40] et de grès[41]. Si peu d'éléments sont datables, ils pourraient provenir de la destruction du

---

[36] Pour une nouvelle classification des monnaies en bronze : Lorber 2015, p. 135–158 ; Faucher, Lorber 2010, p. 35–80. Voir également les remarques d'O. Picard et de Th. Faucher (2012, p. 17) : « Les monnayages lagides ont toujours été jusqu'à présent classés par règnes [...] mais ce mode de classement ne correspond pas à la logique de la politique monétaire des Ptolémées pendant les quelques trois siècles de la production des monnayages lagides. Le choix même du nom Ptolemaios pour les rois successifs [...] ne permet jamais de reconnaître par ce moyen le souverain régnant ».

[37] Pour le développement du motif de la double aigle sur le revers (Faucher 2010, p. 104). Il est également à noter que les pièces figurant Zeus avec un seul aigle deviennent plus petites, autour de 22 mm à partir de cette date.

[38] Picard, Faucher, 2012, p. 48–49, 53 et pl. 10–11. Faute d'avoir accès à une photographie de la pièce, cette identification reste conjoncturelle. En effet le traitement stylistique d'un même motif peut ainsi modifier une datation. Les principaux critères pour en fixer les évolutions sont les marques de l'atelier, la disposition de la corne d'abondance par rapport à l'aigle, les cheveux du dieu et la précision du dessin. Par exemple le motif de l'aigle est beaucoup moins soigné à la fin du IIe siècle (Faucher 2013, p. 176). La qualité du monnayage a aussi été un des critères de réflexion dans le cadre d'ateliers de faux-monnayeurs (Faucher *et al.* 2011, p. 160 et Fig. 14 – avec des monnaies allant jusqu'au règne de Ptolémée VIII Évergète II). La présence de deux aigles par exemple classerait la monnaie après la réforme du IIe siècle.

[39] Il s'agit d'éclats très petits et non rattachables à un monument connu, mais qui peuvent être probablement attribués aux monuments du Moyen ou du Nouvel Empire : Inv. 6389, 6390, 6391, 6392, 6394 (*Registre 1932–1939*, p. 574). Inv. 6394 présente un martelage du nom d'Amon probablement attribuable à l'épisode amarnien.

[40] Inv. 6399 dont la taille (20 x 16 x 17 cm) correspondrait au type de statues de Sésostris III qui avaient été préservées dans le temple ptolémaïque. Pour ce fragment de statue : *Registre 1932–1939*, p. 574.

[41] Deux autres fragments en grès qui présentent le décor papyriforme des soubassements des temples ptolémaïques : Inv. 6396–6397. Fut également découvert un sphinx en grès Inv. 6393 de petite taille (H : 20 cm, L : 40 cm) : *Registre 1932–1939*, p. 574. Il est difficile d'attribuer une datation à ces pièces qui pourraient, au moins pour les deux reliefs, appartenir au temple ptolémaïque.

temple de Montou et avoir été charriés lors de la construction des structures byzantines construites à cet emplacement[42].

Enfin, plus globalement, la restitution de Bisson de la Roque ne répond pas à toutes les interrogations soulevées par la documentation. En effet, pourquoi le soi-disant temple latéral aurait-il des dépôts de fondation aux noms de Ptolémée III alors que la plus ancienne porte remployée dans le mur-pylône date de Ptolémée II ? En outre, si le monument avait été détruit, des traces de cendres auraient dû être signalées à proximité du caisson[43]. Enfin, J.-Fr. Carlotti a fait remarquer que les blocs du début de l'époque ptolémaïque remployés dans le mur-pylône ne s'adaptaient pas au caisson en briques découvert en 1931[44]. Ils s'assemblent pour former 6 portes et ne constituent en aucun cas des maçonneries d'un temple à part entière. De ce fait, le caisson en briques découvert en 1931 ne correspond pas au « temple des premiers Ptolémées », même s'il est difficile d'aller plus loin dans l'interprétation de la nature de cette construction. J.Fr. Carlotti a proposé d'y voir les fondations d'un monument qui ne fut jamais terminé[45]. La présence de dépôts de fondation royaux plaide en faveur d'une structure cultuelle et, au vu de sa localisation en périphérie du temple, il pourrait s'agir d'un projet avorté de mammisi. Une autre possibilité serait de relier ledit caisson avec des dépôts de terre limoneuse de forme circulaire découverts dans le même secteur. Il s'agirait alors de l'enclos d'un jardin de temple[46].

---

[42] Tant les blocs en grès (structures ptolémaïques), en calcaire (structures Nouvel Empire) que le fragment de statue (les statues en granit encore en place dans le temple ptolémaïque). Pour une étude des matériaux du temple : Relats Montserrat, Karlshausen, De Putter 2021.

[43] La fouille, menée par Robichon, documenta les dépôts limoneux, signe qu'elle fut faite avec suffisamment de précision pour noter la présence de cendre. Celle-ci fut par exemple notée lors de la fouille des fours à potiers du début du Nouvel Empire localisés au niveau du parvis de l'époque romaine (Bisson de la Roque 1931, p. 21). Pour la datation de ces fours : Barahona Mendieta, Relats Montserrat, Séguier 2019.

[44] Carlotti 2015, p. 107.

[45] Carlotti 2015, p. 107 renvoyant au caisson construit pour le pylône encadrant les môles de la porte d'Évergète (Zignani 2003, p. 712–713).

[46] Relats Montserrat 2024, p. 293–294. Pour les jardins des temples : Thiers 1999. D'après les fouilleurs, ces bassins furent installés à l'époque romaine à l'emplacement du caisson en briques. Leur datation repose uniquement sur l'emploi de la brique cuite, dont l'usage se généralise certes à l'époque romaine mais qui est déjà attestée au Nouvel Empire et surtout à partir de la Basse Époque. Il serait tentant d'associer le caisson de briques à ces arbres pour en faire une sorte d'enclos les ceinturant, mais aucune preuve ne peut être avancée. Nous n'avons trouvé aucun parallèle de dépôt de fondation pour de tels aménagements, mais cette hypothèse aurait le mérite de ne pas supposer deux phases d'aménagement distinctes pour la zone. La présence de plantations d'arbres a récemment été mise en lumière à Médamoud au niveau du parvis du temple : Relats Montserrat, Barahona Mendieta, Séguier 2019.

## 1.3 Le temple de Montou a-t-il été fondé par Épiphane ?

Aucun argument archéologique n'assure donc l'existence d'un monument latéral à Médamoud, pas plus que sa destruction pendant la révolte de 206 av. J.-C. Reste donc à vérifier le deuxième argument sous-tendant la restitution de Bisson de la Roque, à savoir l'attribution de la construction du temple de Montou au règne de Ptolémée V Épiphane. Celle-ci repose uniquement sur les cartouches identifiés, alors que toutes les maçonneries intérieures (appelées « avant-temple » par le fouilleur) sont anépigraphes. Elles ont été datées de l'époque ptolémaïque en référence aux autres élévations inscrites les entourant. Or depuis les années 1920, les critères de datation architecturaux se sont développés à la suite des premiers travaux de J.-Cl. Golvin. Ainsi le mur péribole, la grande cour et les porches présentent un traitement de surface des lits d'attente typique de l'époque ptolémaïque avec des cadres d'anathyrose et un piquetage formant de larges rainures pour le mortier[47]. Deux autres types de traitements sont toutefois attestés, illustrant que le monument actuel est le résultat de phases architecturales d'époques différentes. Le premier, typique du Nouvel Empire, est préservé au niveau des murs de pourtour de l'avant-temple[48]. Le deuxième, visible sur les murs de la partie sud des salles XVI à XVIII, se rapproche des constructions de l'Époque tardive[49].

Ainsi, il apparaît que le temple n'est pas une fondation du milieu de l'époque ptolémaïque. Au contraire, une partie des maçonneries actuellement préservées remontent au Nouvel Empire. Ces dernières peuvent être attribuées à Thoutmosis III qui installa le radier sur lequel elles reposaient. Plusieurs éclats au nom de ce souverain (ainsi que d'Aménophis II et Thoutmosis IV) furent d'ailleurs découverts lors du dégagement du temple, signe que leurs cartouches décoraient encore ses élévations du monument lors de son débitage. Ensuite, à l'Époque tardive – probablement à la XXX$^e$ dynastie, trois salles furent érigées dans l'arrière-temple (XVI-XVIII)[50]. Enfin l'époque ptolémaïque a visiblement modifié la disposition intérieure du temple du Nou-

---

47 Golvin, Larronde 1982 ; Golvin, Larronde, Maarouf 1985 ; Niederberger 1999, p. 101 ; Carlotti 2015, p. 86. Pour le décalage entre l'érection d'une maçonnerie et sa décoration: Golvin, Vergnieux 1985, p. 335–338.
48 Carlotti 2015, p. 80–88 ; Relats Montserrat 2024, p. 216.
49 Les maçonneries des trois salles de l'arrière-temple (XVI, XVII et XVIII) présentent deux types de traitement de surface. Sur leur mur nord, le lit d'attente est similaire à celui du reste des maçonneries ptolémaïques du temple. En revanche le mur sud et ses retours d'angle respectifs (mur ouest de XVI, mur ouest de XVII et mur est de XVIII) ne possèdent aucun canal pour le mortier, mais se distinguent par la présence systématique de mortaises en queue d'aronde, par un piquetage répandu sur toute la surface des lits d'attente, l'absence de décrochements et la construction en assises horizontales régularisées. Pour la description précise : Relats Montserrat 2024, p. 246–252.
50 Relats Montserrat 2024, p. 280–281.

vel Empire avec l'installation d'un nouveau sanctuaire de barque. Une inscription au niveau du mur sud-ouest de cette chambre porte la fin d'un cartouche terminant par *[...]-ʿnḫ-ḏt-mry-Ptḥ* ⟦...⟧ qui peut être attribué à Ptolémée III, V, VI, VIII ou IX[51]. La politique lagide étendit également le temple thoutmoside vers l'ouest (avec l'hypostyle, le portique, la grande cour et porches) et l'entoura d'un péribole[52].

Ces observations architecturales peuvent être également confirmées par la relecture d'un groupe de cartouches présents dans le temple qui ne furent pas correctement identifiés par Bisson de la Roque. Il s'agit de la procession de soubassement qui couvre les salles XVI et XVII gravée au nom d'un Ptolémée ⟦...⟧, ⟦...⟧, ⟦...⟧ (*Ptlmys* / *Ptlwmys*)[53]. L'absence de l'épithète *ʿnḫ ḏt*, qui devient systématique à partir de Ptolémée III, assure leur attribution au règne de Ptolémée II[54]. Du début de l'époque ptolémaïque date aussi la gravure des jambages de la porte de la salle XXI. Celle-ci est communément appelée « la chambre d'Arsinoé », même si le

---

51 L'inscription ne fut pas relevée par les fouilleurs. A ce jour elle porte le numéro 48b, en attendant la nouvelle publication des inscriptions du temple par L. Medini et F. Relats Montserrat.
52 Pour un survol de l'histoire du temple : Relats Montserrat, Karlshausen, De Putter 2021.
53 Drioton 1927, p. 36–40 (num. 69–91). La datation de Ptolémée II de la procession de soubassement avait été remarquée par J. Yoyotte (1961, p. 86, n. 1 et p. 138, n. 1). Ch. Sambin et J.-Fr. Carlotti, au regard de ces cartouches, datent ces salles de Ptolémée II sans prendre en considération le traitement du lit d'attente des blocs : Sambin-Nivet, 2015b ; Carlotti 2015, p. 93–96.
54 Sur l'épithète *ʿnḫ-ḏt* : Felber 2004, p. 137–140. À Edfou, les soubassements du mur extérieur du naos ont été seulement partiellement gravés, signe des hésitations sur le nom du souverain régnant en période de guerre civile. Les scribes ont gravé *Ptwlmys-ʿnḫ-ḏt* en laissant un espace vide derrière, signe que l'épithète était considérée comme constitutive du nom des souverains à cette époque. Il existe aussi des cas où les cartouches de Ptolémée III, IV, V, VI, VIII et XII sont dépourvus d'épithètes mais il s'agit toujours de scènes d'hommages aux ancêtres. Pour une liste des attestations : Hallof 2010, p. 46 (P.3/E.2), p. 62 (P.4/E.1), p. 76 (P.5/E.1, P.5/E.5), p. 94 (P.6/E.1), p. 147 (P.8/E.16), p. 252 (P.12/E.2). À Tôd, Ptolémée VIII Évergète II rend hommage à Ptolémée II, III, IV, V, VI et à Eupator : *Tôd* II, 318 (Grenier 1992, fig. 1, p. 33 ; Minas 2000, p. 24–25). Au Kasr el-Agouz, Ptolémée VIII Évergète II rend hommage à Ptolémée II, III, IV (Mallet 1909, p. 69, fig. 31 ; Minas 2000, p. 29), à Ptolémée V (Mallet 1909, p. 91, fig. 48), et à Ptolémée IV (Mallet 1909, p. 92, fig. 49). À Dakka, Ptolémée IV Philopator rend hommage à Ptolémée II et III (Minas 2000, p. 3–5, pl. 1). Au deuxième pylône de Karnak, Ptolémée VI rend hommage à Ptolémée V (*Urk.* VIII, 120, num. 150). À Esna, Ptolémée VI rend hommage à Ptolémée V (*Esna* II, 13, l. 7). Dans tous ces exemples, les cartouches des rois ancêtres sont dépourvus d'épithètes, mais les rois sont identifiables par la suite du texte. Enfin, deux autres attestations présentent la graphie *Ptlmys* pour Ptolémée VIII et XII, mais il s'agit de montants de portes où les graveurs ont manifestement manqué de place. Ainsi à Edfou un cartouche de Ptolémée XII est situé sous le linteau de la porte du pylône avec une très petite surface (*Edfou* VIII, 22 ; Bartels 2009, pl. 5). Le deuxième cartouche qui n'est pas présent dans une scène d'hommage aux ancêtres se trouve sur la porte de la chapelle de barque à Dendera. Elle fut décorée par Ptolémée VIII, qui a toujours ses cartouches développés, sauf dans la colonne marginale d'un tableau du montant sud de la porte. Les registres font 49 cm de haut, laissant peu d'espace pour une gravure complète du nom de naissance du roi (Cauville 1993, p. 91, pl. 5 et fig. 4).

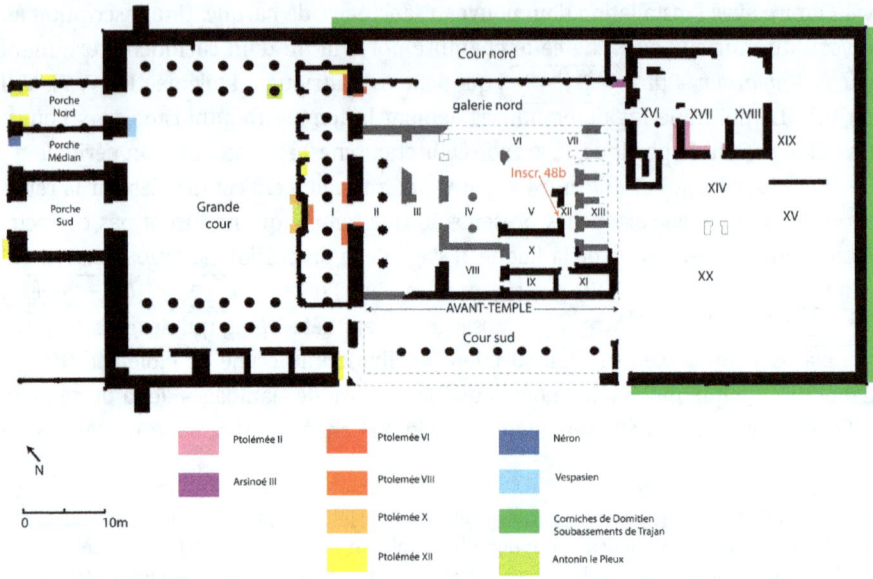

**Fig. 1:** Cartouches préservés dans le temple de Montou lors de son dégagement (© Felix Relats Montserrat).

texte fait référence au couple royal : [hieroglyphs] *[...] 3rsjn3t nṯr.wy mr(y) jt=w* (« [Ptolémée IV et] Arsinoé, les dieux *Philopators* »)[55]. Bisson de la Roque proposa d'y voir une chapelle tardive consacrée à la mémoire d'Arsinoé III, car la mention de cette reine ne s'adapte pas à la restitution architecturale qu'il proposait[56]. Or dans la mesure où le nom de Ptolémée II est préservé dans les inscriptions du temple, il est plus probable que la mention des dieux *Philopators* soit aussi contemporaine de leur règne. De ce fait, des cartouches des souverains antérieurs à 206 av. J.-C. sont présents sur les murs du temple, signe que ce dernier n'a pas été arasé après la grande révolte (Fig. 1). Leur nombre devait être plus important si on compte aussi les éclats aux noms de Ptolémée II et III découverts lors du déblaiement du temple, provenant vraisemblablement du débitage de ses élévations[57]. L'ensemble de cette documentation prouve, par conséquent, que ce monument ne peut plus être

---

[55] Drioton 1926, p. 35 (num. 67).
[56] Il proposa d'abord de l'attribuer à Arsinoé IV, fille de Ptolémée XII Néos Dionysos (Bisson de la Roque 1926, p. 110). Dans son rapport, le fouilleur suit la numérotation d'H. Gauthier et parle de Ptolémée XIII (*LdR* IV/2, p. 409). Il rectifia ensuite au profit d'Arsinoé III mais considérant qu'il s'agissait d'une « chapelle qui lui est certainement très postérieure » (Bisson de la Roque, Clère 1929, p. 6).
[57] Plusieurs éclats ont gardé le cartouche de Ptolémée II : Inv. 1146 [hieroglyphs] (*Registre 1925–1928*, p. 88) ; Inv. 1619 [hieroglyphs](*Registre 1925–1928*, p. 125) ; Inv. 2259 [hieroglyphs](*Registre 1925–1928*, p. 181). Un

considéré comme « le second temple ptolémaïque ». Au contraire, le temple de Médamoud connut des phases successives d'agrandissement et de modifications depuis le Moyen Empire, suivant un modèle similaire à celui d'autres temples thébains[58].

## 2 Restituer l'activité architecturale du début de l'époque ptolémaïque à Médamoud

Il apparaît que l'hypothèse d'une série de destructions successives, héritée des travaux de Legrain et de Bisson de la Roque, ne peut plus être retenue : d'une part, l'existence d'un temple latéral, construit et détruit avant la grande révolte, doit être abandonnée ; d'autre part, Ptolémée V Épiphane n'a pas fondé le temple de Montou au vu de la présence de maçonneries du Nouvel Empire et du début de l'époque ptolémaïque. Il est donc nécessaire de revenir sur l'évolution architecturale du site au iiie siècle.

### 2.1 Inventaire de la documentation antérieure à la grande révolte

Lors de la conquête macédonienne à la fin du IVe siècle, Médamoud devait présenter les restes d'un temple thoutmoside, modifié à l'époque ramesside[59]. Par la suite, les souverains kouchites et la XXVIe dynastie laissèrent également leur

---

éclat portait le cartouche de Ptolémée III : Inv. 1446 (jw' n ntr.wy-sw.wy – *Registre 1925–1928*, p. 112). Pour les éclats au nom de Ptolémée V (Inv. 1431 et 1496) voir *supra* note 14. Le plus probable est que l'ensemble de cette documentation décorait le temple lui-même et que sa présence dans le remblai du monument témoigne de son débitage.

58 La porte en granit de Sésostris III avait été préservée à son emplacement d'origine jusqu'à l'époque ptolémaïque : Relats Montserrat 2017, p. 132. Pour d'autres maçonneries de cette époque préservées au Nouvel Empire : Relats Montserrat, Karlshausen, De Putter 2021.

59 La question de l'activité des souverains ramessides dépasse l'objet du présent article. Des blocs de Séthy Ier, Ramsès II, Mérenptah, Séthy II, Ramsès III et IV ont été découverts aussi bien remployés dans des fondations établies à l'époque ptolémaïque que dans des maisons ultérieures. La porte de Tibère a également livré une série de blocs ramessides remployés dans le cœur de sa maçonnerie. P. Brand a proposé de les attribuer au temple funéraire de Séthy Ier à Gourna qui aurait servi de carrière pour alimenter la construction du propylône de Médamoud (Brand 2000, p. 191). Si le style de la gravure ainsi que la mention du nom du temple dans la légende de deux scènes sont de solides arguments en faveur de son hypothèse, d'autres blocs issus du même lot ne s'adaptent pas au plan de Gourna. La question sera traitée par l'auteur dans l'édition de cette documentation.

marque sur le site même si leur œuvre architecturale ne peut pas être localisée[60]. C'est dans ce contexte architectural qu'il faut insérer la politique architecturale lagide antérieure à 206 av. J.-C. Cette dernière est habituellement résumée aux blocs remployés dans le mur-pylône qui ont focalisé l'attention de la littérature égyptologique, d'autant que leur remploi était considéré comme un signe de la destruction du monument. Or la documentation est beaucoup plus diverse[61]. En prenant en considération l'ensemble du matériel de Médamoud, plusieurs ensembles se dégagent en fonction de leur contexte archéologique de découverte (Tab. 1).

Le premier groupe est formé par la documentation épigraphique encore en place sur les murs du temple lors de son dégagement[62]. Il s'agit des salles XVI-XVIII décorées par Ptolémée II, ainsi que la chapelle aux noms de Ptolémée IV et d'Arsinoé III précédemment évoquées qui témoignent de l'activité du début de l'époque ptolémaïque dans le téménos (Tab. 1 – groupe 1).

Le deuxième groupe concerne les différents éclats découverts lors du déblaiement du site qui proviennent, vraisemblablement, du débitage des élévations du temple (Tab. 1 – groupe 2). Les cartouches de Ptolémée II, III et V sont attestés, confirmant ainsi que leurs noms décoraient encore le temple lors de son abandon[63]. Il est à signaler qu'un de ces blocs est en calcaire alors que le reste de la documentation est en grès (MAG/O/116)[64]. À ce même groupe il faut rajouter les blocs rem-

---

**60** La documentation de la Troisième Période intermédiaire et de la Basse Époque est uniquement connue par des blocs épars remployés soit dans les fondations ptolémaïques soit dans les habitations tardives installées dans le dromos. Leur emplacement d'origine ainsi que leur liaison avec les maçonneries antérieures ne peuvent donc pas être établis. Voir : Relats Montserrat 2018.
**61** Les articles de Ch. Sambin (1988, 1992, 2001 et Sambin, Carlotti 1995) ont porté exclusivement sur les portes remployées dans le mur pylône. Seul l'article de J.-Fr. Carlotti (2015) a pris en considération une documentation plus étendue même s'il fonde son propos majoritairement sur les rapports publiés par Bisson de la Roque qui ne rendent compte que des principaux résultats de chaque campagne.
**62** La quasi-totalité de ces maçonneries ont été démontées par Bisson de la Roque ou Robichon et ne furent pas remontées. Les blocs sont toutefois encore dans le musée lapidaire du site.
**63** Pour les blocs découverts lors du déblaiement du temple, voir *supra* note 57. Lors de la fouille du secteur sud du temple fut découvert un autre cartouche de Ptolémée II (Inv. 2629 : Bisson de la Roque, Clère, Drioton 1928, p. 53) et un relief de Ptolémée IV représentant un arbre (Inv. 3072 : Bisson de la Roque, Clère, Drioton 1928, p. 54 ; Sambin-Nivet 2015a, p. 282–283).
**64** Le bloc en calcaire MAG/O/116 porte le cartouche de Ptolémée II. Il n'a pas été mentionné dans le registre d'inventaire de Bisson de la Roque, mais est conservé dans le musée lapidaire du site. Il a probablement été découvert par A. Varille et Cl. Robichon quand ils ont repris l'exploration du site et que le registre d'inventaire n'a pas été systématiquement été rempli. Sur ce bloc : Relats Montserrat, Karlhausen, De Putter 2021.

**Tab. 1:** Bilan de la documentation ptolémaïque de Médamoud antérieure à la révolte de 206 av. J.-C.

| Groupe | Contexte archéologique | Monuments | Datation |
|---|---|---|---|
| 1 | Blocs *in situ* dans le temple | Salles XVI-XVIII de l'arrière-temple | Ptolémée II |
| | | Chapelle d'Arsinoé | Ptolémée IV |
| 2 | Blocs hors contexte | Déblais issus du débitage du temple | Ptolémée II |
| | | | Ptolémée III |
| | | | Ptolémée V |
| | | Remplois dans les structures tardives | Ptolémée III |
| | | | Ptolémée V |
| 3 | Autres monuments du site | Pylône de la tribune | Ptolémée II |
| | | Mur de 5 m | Ptolémée III (?) |
| 4 | Blocs remployés à l'époque lagide ou impériale | Remplois dans le mur-pylône | Ptolémée II à Ptolémée IV |
| | | Autel de la grande cour | Ptolémée III |
| | | Remploi dans les fondations de l'hypostyle | Ptolémée II |
| | | Remploi dans le dallage de la salle XVII | Ptolémée III (?) |
| | | Remploi dans la porte de Tibère | Ptolémée II |
| | | | Ptolémée VI |
| | | Remplois dans le dallage du porche nord | Ptolémée XII |

ployés dans les structures postérieures à l'abandon des cultes dont l'origine ne peut pas être précisée. La documentation couvre les règnes de Ptolémée III[65] et de Ptolé-

---

**65** Le bloc Inv. 4507, gravé aux noms de Ptolémée III et Bérénice II, fut remployé dans une maison installée au nord-ouest du lac (Bisson de la Roque 1930, p. 49 ; *Registre 1929–1931*, p. 391). Il faut peut-être associer cette « maison » dont parle Bisson de la Roque avec le pavement en briques cuite fouillé dans le même secteur en 1927 et en 1930 (« installation 10 »). Ce dernier peut être daté entre les V$^e$ et VII$^e$ siècles ap. J.-C. grâce aux céramiques découvertes (Barahona Mendieta 2016b, p. 97 et p. 180–183 ; Bisson de la Roque, Clère, Drioton 1928, p. 29). Du même règne date le haut d'une stèle cintrée (Inv. 3172) représentant le roi et la reine devant Montou. Elle fut découverte lors de la fouille des fondations d'une maison moderne détruite pour construire le magasin (Bisson de la Roque, Clère 1929, p. 27 ; Relats Montserrat 2024, p. 69). Un autre bloc, aujourd'hui préservé dans le musée en plein air du site (MAG/O/72 = Inv. 5435) porte la titulature de Bérénice II (*Registre 1929–1931*, p. 482). Il appartenait à l'origine à une scène d'offrande représen-

mée IV[66]. Enfin, c'est dans cette catégorie qu'il faut aussi classer la porte de Ptolémée III découverte lors du déblaiement du site au sud du temple, ainsi que quelques blocs de Ptolémée II, III et IV extraits des maisons du village moderne[67]. Manifestement, le temple offrait une source de matériaux de construction suffisamment importante pour supposer une origine locale pour cette documentation, même si l'existence d'autres constructions de la même époque sur le site ne peut pas être exclue. En ce sens, au moins deux autres monuments peuvent être datés d'une phase antérieure à la grande révolte[68]. Le premier est d'un petit pylône construit à proximité de la tribune (Tab. 1 – groupe 3)[69]. Il est daté de Ptolémée II et devait occuper une position similaire à celui découvert à Tôd[70]. Le deuxième est une enceinte, édifiée probablement par Ptolémée III qui marquait l'entrée du téménos[71].

Le dernier groupe (Tab. 1 – groupe 4) est formé par la documentation remployée pendant l'époque ptolémaïque et romaine à l'intérieur même du téménos. Le lot principal est celui situé dans les fondations du mur-pylône (Ptolémée II-IV) ainsi que dans l'autel de la grande cour formé avec des blocs du règne de Ptolé-

---

tant la reine face au Pakaouraâshespses. Il fut découvert lors de la fouille du secteur sud-ouest, dans les déblais.

66 Lors de la fouille du dromos, deux blocs portant une dédicace au nom de Ptolémée IV (Inv. 6239–6240) furent découverts à 41m de la porte de Tibère dans un mur d'une maison située à l'est du socle du 15$^e$ sphinx de la rangée nord du dromos (Bisson de la Roque 1933, p. 66). La datation du remploi ne peut être assurée car aucune céramique n'est associée à ladite maison.

67 En 1936, Ahmed Fakry, inspecteur du service des Antiquités à Louqsor apporta à Cl. Robichon et à A. Varille une série de blocs « provenant du village de Médamoud » (*Registre 1932–1939*, p. 625). Ils portaient les cartouches de Ptolémée II (Inv. 8730), Ptolémée III (Inv. 8731), Ptolémée IV (Inv. 8729) .

68 Nous laissons de côté le « magasin pur » (šnʿ wʿb) attribué habituellement à Ptolémée III en référence avec la porte au nom de ce roi découverte dans le secteur qui n'entretient cependant aucun lien avec le bâtiment en briques (*contra* Traunecker 1987, p. 154–155). La fourchette chronologique de ce type de constructions couvre la Basse Époque et l'époque ptolémaïque et ne peut être précisée d'avantage (Leclère 2008, p. 630–636).

69 Le monument est formé des blocs Inv. 5901, 5959, 5960, 5961, 6025 et 6027 (Bisson de la Roque 1933, p. 66). Les blocs furent perturbés à l'époque chrétienne mais furent assemblés par Bisson de la Roque qui proposa de les replacer au pied de la rampe conduisant à la tribune, suivant un dispositif similaire à celui ultérieurement découvert à Tôd. Le fouilleur affirma que ces blocs sont gravés avec le cartouche de Ptolémée III, mais sur les photographies apparait la titulature de Ptolémée II [Ḥr] ḥwnw-qnj, Nbtj [wr-pḥtj], Ḥr-nbw sḫʿ-n sw jt[=f]. D'autres blocs, sans cartouches préservés, ont quant à eux été identifiés comme le parapet de la tribune qui peut avec toute vraisemblance être attribuée à la même phase architecturale (Bisson de la Roque 1933, p. 66).

70 Pierrat 1995, p. 450 ; Bisson de la Roque 1941, p. 36–42.

71 Relats Montserrat, Barahona Mendieta, Séguier 2019, p. 298–301 et p. 315–316.

**Fig. 2:** Remploi d'un bloc de Ptolémée II dans la maçonnerie de la porte de Tibère (BP6) (© Mission Médamoud Ifao/G. Polin nu_2018_06470).

mée III[72]. D'autres parties du temple ont cependant également livré des remplois de la même époque : ainsi, la porte entre la salle hypostyle et la salle III était fondée sur 3 assises de fondations, dont l'intermédiaire remployait un montant au nom de Ptolémée II (Inv. 4885)[73]. Ensuite, le dallage des salles XVI à XVIII livra trois morceaux de grès probablement attribuables à Ptolémée III (Inv. 5252)[74].

---

[72] Sur la documentation du mur-pylône, *supra* n. 18. Pour l'autel : Bisson de la Roque 1927, p. 25–29 ; Varille 1942, p. 40–42 ; Ernst 2002, p. 15–17.

[73] Sur Inv. 4885 : Bisson de la Roque 1931, p. 80 et Bisson de la Roque 1933, Fig. 27. Il s'agit de l'assise d'un jambage droit d'une porte gravée d'un texte de dédicace au nom de Ptolémée II « ¹[... le maître] des couronnes, Ptolémées, il a fait [comme son monument] (...) ²[une porte en] grès [...] » (¹[... nb] ḫʿ.w, Ptlwmys jr [n=f m mn=f] (...) ²[sbȝ m] jnr ḥḏ nfr n rwḏ.t [...]), sur le tableau intérieur est gravée une scène de purification représentant le souverain encadré de deux divinités (wʿb sp-4). Pour la traduction de l'expression jnr ḥḏ nfr n rwḏ.t : Harris 1961, p. 71.

[74] Sur Inv. 5252 : Bisson de la Roque 1931, p. 80. Le journal de fouille précise que ces blocs furent « trouvés séparément dans un des dallages démontés dans les chambres XVI à XVIII » (Bisson de la Roque 1930–1932, p. 41). J.-Fr. Carlotti et Ch. Sambin ont proposé de l'attribuer à une des portes remployées dans le mur-pylône (Porte F, dite « des dieux ancêtres ») suivant la datation stylistique déjà soulignée par Bisson de la Roque : Bisson de la Roque 1931, p. 80 ; Sambin, Carlotti 2015, p. 410 et pl. 9.

Enfin, les fondations de la porte de Tibère réutilisaient aussi deux blocs datés Ptolémée II (Inv. 5548 et 5549)[75] et un de Ptolémée VI (Inv. 4359)[76]. Le volume de remplois dans ce monument est cependant bien plus important comme l'a prouvé une fenêtre réalisée dans le montant sud qui a mis au jour un nouveau bloc présentant une frise de cartouches de Ptolémée II probablement issue d'une porte (BP. 6 – Fig. 2).

## 2.2 Les projets architecturaux de la monarchie lagide à Médamoud au iiie siècle

Au vu de cet inventaire, l'activité menée sur le site de Médamoud est beaucoup plus diversifiée que ne le présentaient les anciens fouilleurs. Il est toutefois impossible, dans l'état actuel de la documentation, de restituer le programme architectural précis règne par règne, pas plus que de déterminer l'emplacement originel de chacun de ces blocs (Tab. 2)[77]. Néanmoins 6 projets architecturaux se dessinent (a-f) :

**a) Les modifications du temple du Nouvel Empire.** Les différents éclats découverts lors du dégagement du temple témoignent des premières modifications apportées à l'édifice du Nouvel Empire dès le règne de Ptolémée II[78]. La preuve de ces travaux est fournie par le bloc MAG/O/116 en calcaire de Tourah portant le cartouche du souverain[79]. Même si son emplacement originel n'est pas connu, l'usage extrêmement rare de ce matériau à l'époque ptolémaïque en région thébaine est un indice fort pour considérer qu'il s'agit d'une maçonnerie érigée au Moyen ou au Nouvel Empires, laissée anépigraphe et encore en place sous Ptolémée II[80].

---

[75] Bisson de la Roque 1933, p. 66. La lecture de Bisson de la Roque, qui y voyait un cartouche de Ptolémée Ier, doit être sûrement corrigée au profit de Ptolémée II : (𓍢𓏏) et (𓍢𓏏).

[76] Bisson de la Roque 1930, p. 3, fig. 3.

[77] Carlotti 2015. Nous ne suivons cependant pas l'auteur dans les « campagnes » proposées qui sous-entendent une succession de travaux qui ne peut être vérifiée au vu de la documentation. Par exemple, il place la construction de la chambre d'Arsinoé après celle du péribole (*infra* n. 87), ce qui amène l'auteur à restituer trois campagnes au sein du règne de Ptolémée II. Or si plusieurs projets architecturaux peuvent être distingués, rien n'empêche qu'ils aient été lancés en même temps.

[78] Pour la liste des éclats, voir *supra* n. 57.

[79] *Supra* n. 64.

[80] Pour le bloc MAG/O/116, voir *supra* n. 64. Pour l'utilisation de matériaux de construction du temple de Médamoud : Relats Montserrat, Karlshausen, De Putter 2021. L'usage du calcaire de Tourah en région thébaine disparaît après le Moyen Empire à l'exception de Médamoud où il est encore en usage au Nouvel Empire. Le bloc MAG/O/116 ainsi qu'un autre éclat portant le nom d'un Ptolémée non identifiable sont les seuls exemples de l'usage du calcaire à Thèbes à cette époque, alors que le reste de la documentation de l'époque est en grès même à Médamoud. Le

C'est sûrement dans le même secteur qu'il faut placer la porte érigée par le même souverain ultérieurement remployée (Inv. 4885). Ces travaux se sont poursuivis encore sous Ptolémée III, IV et V comme l'illustrent les éclats découverts lors du dégagement du temple. Il est probable que les travaux aient été complétés jusqu'au règne de Ptolémée VI Philométor dont les cartouches décorent la façade de l'avant-temple (façade de l'hypostyle et la porte ouest de la cour nord).

**b) Les travaux dans l'arrière-temple** (entre Ptolémée II et Ptolémée IV).

**b.1) La décoration de trois salles de l'arrière-temple.** Les murs sud et est des salles XVI-XVIII furent probablement érigés à la fin de la Basse-Époque comme le prouve le traitement de leur lit d'attente. Elles furent cependant décorées par Ptolémée II qui y grava une procession géographique[81].

**b.2) Le massif au nord des salles XVI-XVIII.** Au nord des trois salles, séparé par un coup de sabre, apparaît sur les plans un massif de maçonnerie restitué par les fouilleurs comme un escalier[82]. Cet espace présente un traitement de surface du lit d'attente typique de l'époque ptolémaïque et constitue donc d'un ajout postérieur aux salles XVI à XVIII. Il doit être antérieure à la fin du règne de Ptolémée IV, date à laquelle fut décorée la chapelle d'Arsinoé, elle-même reposant sur le massif en question[83].

**b.3) L'entrecolonnement nord.** Il longe le côté nord de l'avant temple et présente un traitement de surface de son lit d'attente typique de l'époque ptolémaïque. En raison de la présence de la chambre d'Arsinoé à son extrémité est, il doit être antérieur à la décoration de cette chambre[84].

---

plus probable est donc que ces blocs aient été érigés au Moyen ou au Nouvel Empires, mais qu'ils soient restés anépigraphes jusqu'à l'époque lagide.
81 Pour le traitement de surface du lit d'attente des murs sud de ces trois salles, *supra* p. 7. La procession géographique a été étudiée par Fr. Ghiringhelli (2019). Il est probable qu'Inv. 1146 (*supra* n. 57) provienne du même lot car il représente la partie inférieure d'une entité géographique portant un plateau d'offrandes.
82 Bisson de la Roque 1927, p. 94 ; Carlotti 2015, p. 97 et Fig. 4.
83 *Supra* n. 49.
84 Bisson de la Roque qualifie la chambre de « construction ajoutée » à l'entrecolonnement (1926, p. 109). J.-Fr. Carlotti a proposé d'attribuer à cette colonnade le bloc Inv. 4507 aux noms de Ptolémée III et de Bérénice II (2015, p. 93 et *supra* n. 65). Cependant les mesures du bloc ne correspondent pas à celles de l'entrecolonnement : l'Inv. 4507 est composé de trois fragments auxquels il faut associer l'Inv. 4508 pour former la titulature royale. L'ensemble mesure 1,67 m sans compter la lacune qui couvre le cartouche de Bérénice II alors que l'entrecolonnement mesure 1,70 m. Par ailleurs, plutôt qu'une architrave, le bloc pourrait également correspondre à un linteau ou à un fragment d'un plafond.

**b.4) La chambre d'Arsinoé.** Son érection peut être attribuée au plus tard au règne de Ptolémée IV, date de sa décoration. En raison de sa situation elle est antérieure à la construction du péribole, de l'adjonction du massif au nord des salles XVI-XVIII et de la colonnade nord. Il est cependant impossible d'attribuer à un règne précis chacun de ces travaux à l'exception du terminus *ante quem* qu'offre la gravure de la chapelle.

**c) La construction du pylône près de la tribune.** La présence d'un monument inscrit aux noms de Ptolémée II à proximité de la tribune est un argument de plus pour dater le dromos d'une date haute. L'analyse stylistique des sphinx permet en effet de les attribuer à une fourchette comprise entre le règne de Nectanébo I$^{er}$ et le début de l'époque ptolémaïque[85]

**d) La construction du péribole.** Contrairement à la vision de Bisson de la Roque, le péribole tel qu'il est visible aujourd'hui correspond à deux phases architecturales distinctes séparées par un coup de sabre dans sa maçonnerie au niveau de la grande cour[86]. La partie est, qui enserre le cœur du temple, est la plus ancienne et est antérieure au règne de Ptolémée IV en raison de la présence de la chambre d'Arsinoé qui repose sur la face intérieure du péribole nord[87]. Les travaux de construction du péribole ont peut-être commencé dès le règne de Ptolémée II, mais sa décoration fut réalisée à l'époque impériale[88].

**e) La mise en place d'une série de porches.** En étudiant la documentation remployée dans le mur-pylône, J.-Fr. Carlotti a fait remarquer que les blocs s'assemblaient pour former 6 portes, dont 2 à linteau brisé à l'origine incluses dans un mur d'entrecolonnement[89]. Or, une telle disposition rappelle celle des porches actuels ouverts sur le mur-pylône qui datent quant à eux de la fin de l'époque ptolémaïque (la gravure des textes au nom de Ptolémée XII offre le *terminus ante quem* pour leur érection)[90]. Les porches actuels seraient dans ce cas une refondation de

---

[85] Cabrol 2001, p. 183, n. 29 ; Relats Montserrat 2024, p. 304–307.
[86] Carlotti 2015, p. 99 ; Relats Montserrat 2024, p. 219 et 255.
[87] Contra Carlotti 2015, p. 97. Les assises de la chambre d'Arsinoé sont visibles dans Bisson de la Roque 1926, Fig. 51. Pour la démonstration complète, voir Relats Montserrat 2024, p. 252.
[88] Si on accepte que le mur péribole était fermé à l'ouest par un mur-pylône où replacer les portes remployées.
[89] Porte A dite « de Djêmê » (Ptolémée IV), porte B dite « de la course à la rame » (Ptolémée III), porte C dite « de fête sed » (Ptolémée II), porte D dite « des seigneurs aux formes mystérieuses » (Ptolémée II), porte E et porte F dite « des dieux ancêtres » (Ptolémée III) : Sambin-Nivet, Carlotti 2016, p. 382–383 et pl. 14.
[90] *Contra* Sambin-Nivet, Carlotti 2016, p. 383 qui évoquent le règne de Ptolémée VI mais cela n'affecte que le portique et non pas les porches.

l'entrée originelle du temple. Le remploi de ces portes à l'ouest du coup de sabre au niveau de la cour sud témoigne d'un agrandissement du temple après Ptolémée IV et offre un indice pour supposer que la documentation provenait du même secteur où elle fut remployée.

**f) La construction d'une enceinte** (« le mur de 5 mètres »). La fouille menée en 2018–2019 sur le secteur du parvis du temple a permis d'apporter une nouvelle datation pour les maçonneries en briques qui y furent découvertes. L'une d'entre elles, appelée « mur de 5 m » par Bisson de la Roque, peut désormais être attribuée à l'époque ptolémaïque en raison de l'usage de la technique à assises courbes et des céramiques découvertes dans sa tranchée de fondation (datées entre la deuxième moitié du III$^e$ s. au début du I$^{er}$ s. av. J.-C.). Une hypothèse pour préciser cette fourchette chronologique, serait de la relier à la stèle Caire TN 2/4/80/1 dédiée par Ptolémée III Évergète, qui commémore l'érection d'une enceinte en l'honneur de « Montou-Rê, taureau qui réside à Médamoud ». Or, le règne de ce souverain (246–222 av. J.-C.) correspond à la fourchette chronologique donnée par les céramiques découvertes dans la tranchée de fondation du mur de 5 m.

**Tab. 2:** restitution chronologique des travaux à Médamoud.

| Règne | Monument | Remarques |
|---|---|---|
| Ptolémée II | Décoration des chambres de l'arrière-temple XVI-XVIII | Terminus *ante quem* pour leur construction |
| | Début modifications internes au temple du Moyen et du Nouvel Empires | Poursuivies jusqu'à Ptolémée VI |
| | Construction d'une nouvelle entrée du temple : porte de « fête-sed » et des « seigneurs mystérieux » | Remployées dans le mur-pylône |
| | Construction du pylône près de la tribune | Terminus *ante quem* pour le dromos |
| Ptolémée III | Nouvelle enceinte (mur de 5 m) | Datation céramique |
| | Porte de « la course à la rame » et des « dieux ancêtres » (portes de porches ?) | Remployées dans le mur-pylône |
| | Autel de la grande cour | Remployé *in situ* |
| Ptolémée IV | Chambre d'Arsinoé | Terminus *ante quem* pour la construction du mur-péribole |
| | Porte de Djêmé | Remployée dans le mur-pylône |

**Tab. 2** (suite)

| Règne | Monument | Remarques |
|---|---|---|
| Ptolémée VI | Décoration de la façade de l'avant-temple | Terminus *ante quem* pour leur construction |
| Ptolémée VIII | Début de la décoration du portique | |
| Ptolémée XII | Décoration des porches et du mur pylône | |

Cette classification ne couvre certes pas tous les blocs, dont la localisation originelle reste pour une partie incertaine. Ainsi la documentation remployée dans la porte de Tibère pourrait provenir de plusieurs portes ou de reliefs muraux du temple dans la mesure où ils sont gravés de scènes d'offrande représentant le roi face à une divinité (Haroéris de Qous sur Inv. 5548, Khnoum d'Éléphantine sur Inv. 5549 et Montou seigneur de Médamoud sur Inv. 4359)[91]. Néanmoins, au terme de cet inventaire, une continuité de travaux apparait à Médamoud pendant tout le long du IIIe siècle av. J.-C, même s'il n'est pas toujours possible d'estimer la politique architecturale de chacun des souverains individuellement. Par ailleurs, plusieurs travaux, particulièrement à l'intérieur du temple, se sont poursuivis pendant les IIe et Ier siècles, voir même jusqu'à l'époque impériale (comme pour la décoration du péribole).

## 2.3 L'occupation urbaine à Médamoud

Pour compléter le portrait de l'activité sur le site au IIIe siècle, il faudrait également considérer l'évolution de la ville de Médamoud qui entourait le temple. Celle-ci nous échappe cependant en grande partie dans la mesure où Bisson de la Roque et Robichon concentrèrent leur intérêt sur les maçonneries en pierre du téménos[92]. Le reste du site, désigné comme le *kôm* de Médamoud, fut uniquement exploré en 1928 quand un petit sondage fut réalisé à son extrémité sud-ouest. Fu-

---

[91] L'analyse de cette documentation est complexifiée par le fait que les blocs sont encore dans les fondations du monument, ce qui empêche de vérifier leurs caractéristiques. Ainsi Bisson de la Roque se contredit dans la description du matériau des deux blocs au nom de Ptolémée II (Inv. 5548 et 5549). Dans son registre d'inventaire, il précise qu'ils sont en calcaire – ce qui permettrait de les attribuer aux maçonneries du Moyen ou Nouvel Empire – mais dans le rapport publié il les classe parmi les blocs en grès. Comparer : *Registre 1929–1931*, p. 491 et Bisson de la Roque 1933, p. 66.

[92] Relats Montserrat 2020a. Pour une présentation complète des recherches menées entre 1925 et 1940 sur le *kôm* : Relats Montserrat 2024, p. 48–112.

rent découverts à cette occasion une série de 8 fours datés par Bisson de la Roque d'époque byzantine[93]. Le réexamen de cette documentation par Z. Barahona Mendieta a pu corriger cette attribution et a montré que les céramiques issues de la fouille de ces fours datent d'une fourchette couvrant la toute fin de la Troisième Période intermédiaire jusqu'à l'époque romaine avec un pic de production à l'Époque tardive[94]. Leur fonctionnement aux IV$^e$ et III$^e$ siècles av. J.-C. est toutefois assuré[95]. La présence de ce secteur pourrait être un nouvel indice du déplacement progressif de l'occupation urbaine vers le sud *kôm*, phénomène que la mission Ifao qui a repris l'exploration du site depuis 2011 a mis en exergue[96].

Outre ces quartiers artisanaux, les fouilles du début du xx$^e$ siècle avaient livré du matériel, certes hors contexte, mais qui illustre l'intégration de Médamoud dans les réseaux commerciaux du début de l'époque ptolémaïque. Ainsi au moins un bol attique à vernis noir datant du début du IV$^e$ siècle av. J.-C., un masque de théâtre gréco-italique polychrome (Inv. 5310) daté entre le III$^e$ et le II$^e$ siècle av. J.-C. et un timbre amphorique au nom de Ἀπολλοδώρου apposé sur une anse rhodienne daté vers 127 av. J.-C (Inv. 6105) furent découverts par Bisson de la Roque[97]. À cette documentation, il faut également ajouter une production locale d'amphores d'imitation égéenne pendant le III$^e$ siècle av. J.-C., dont les fours n'ont pas encore été découverts. Ces exemplaires furent découverts lors d'une prospection pédestre réalisée en 2014 et dans le remblai de surface recouvrant la zone J9/K9 en cours de fouille depuis 2020, mais leur grand nombre et la présence de surcuits et de scories vitrifiées sont des forts arguments pour supposer que production était réalisée à Médamoud[98]. Si le contexte stratigraphique de l'ensemble de ce matériel n'est pas établi, leur présence sur le site témoigne de la pénétration en Thébaïde des productions méditerranéennes et de leur influence sur les productions de la région thébaine. L'identité des consommateurs et des commanditaires nous échappe cependant et l'installation de communautés grec-

---

**93** Bisson de la Roque 1933, p. 35–36 et Bisson de la Roque 1931 p. 85 et fig. 73 (« Inv. 4827. – Un fragment de vase à décor floral violet sur fond rouge que je considère comme nous donnant le type de la poterie faite à Médamoud dans les fours d'époque byzantine trouvés en 1928 »).
**94** Barahona Mendieta 2014, fig. 7–9 et 12–16.
**95** Barahona Mendieta 2016a, p. 28 et 37 (céramique du Groupe 1).
**96** Relats Montserrat 2019, p. 195.
**97** Barahona Mendieta 2015. Nous pouvons considérer que ces pièces proviennent des déblais issus de la destruction du site et qu'il est impossible de définir leur localisation initiale. Leur origine locale ne fait cependant aucun doute.
**98** Barahona Mendieta 2016a, p. 35–36. Une tranchée diagnostique de 32 m de longueur et de 10 m de largeur a été ouverte en 2019 dans la zone J9/K9. Plusieurs fours de la XXV$^e$ dynastie ont été retrouvés. Toutefois, le remblai recouvrant la zone a livré de nombreux surcuits d'amphores du III$^e$ siècle av. J.-C. signe de la production à proximité de ce matériel (Relats Montserrat 2020b).

ques à Médamoud n'est confirmée par l'épigraphie qu'à partir du milieu du IIe siècle av. J.-C[99]. Ainsi deux stèles en grec furent découvertes lors du déblaiement du temple, la première portant une prière à Héraclès dédiée par des prêtres de Tôd en visite à Médamoud, datée du 29 mars 105 av J.-C. (Inv. 1720 = Louvre E 12929)[100]. La deuxième est une inscription dédicatoire adressée par les habitants de Thèbes et de Kéramiké (Κεραμεῶται) au dieu local datée stylistiquement du IIe s.[101]. Il s'agit d'un des arguments pour faire de τὰ Κεραμεῖα le nom grec de Médamoud, signe de la présence grecque sur le site[102]. Celle-ci s'est par la suite poursuivie à l'époque impériale avec l'installation d'un temple isiaque au sud-ouest du téménos daté probablement du IIe s. apr. J.-C., confirmant l'intégration du site dans les dynamiques culturelles hellénistiques[103].

## 3 La place des révoltes dans le programme architectural de Médamoud

La politique architecturale de la monarchie lagide à Médamoud pendant le IIIe s. av. J.-C. ne peut donc plus être limitée à la construction d'un monument secondaire. Au contraire, les souverains ont œuvré de manière continue dans le temple de Montou et ont lancé plusieurs projets, poursuivis ou étendus jusqu'à l'époque impériale. Dans la restitution de Bisson de la Roque, la révolte de 206 av. J.-C. était un moteur architectural en raison des destructions qu'elle occasionna et qui entraînèrent une réponse du pouvoir royal. C'est ce lien entre les révoltes et la politique architecturale lagide qui doit être revisité dans le cas de Médamoud.

---

**99** Pour la présence des Grecs à Thèbes d'après les sources épigraphiques : Clarysse 1995. Pour les précautions à prendre dans l'interprétation du matériel céramique, voir les différentes contributions de l'ouvrage collectif : Gorre, Marangou (éd.) 2015.
**100** SB 5 8202 : Drioton 1927, p. 72–77 (num. 412) ; Bernand 1992, p. 57–59 (num. 18). La stèle fut découverte posée à plat sur le dallage de la colonnade sud de la grande cour.
**101** SB 5 8201 : Bisson de la Roque 1933, p. 73–74.
**102** Les discussions autour des Κεραμεῖα thébains ont été résumés dans : Bataille 1946. Un des principaux arguments pour confirmer son identification reste l'importance de la production céramique à Médamoud. Pour un exposé synthétique de celle-ci : Relats Montserrat 2019, p. 190–195.
**103** Ce monument avait été appelé « la maison carrée » par Bisson de la Roque : Saragoza 2012 ; Relats Montserrat 2024.

## 3.1 Remplois, destructions de monuments et décrets synodaux

Le principal argument de Bisson de la Roque pour supposer les dégradations des monuments était le remploi de la documentation du III$^e$ siècle étant donné que le démontage d'un monument impliquait automatiquement – aux yeux du fouilleur – sa destruction. Or pour vérifier une telle assomption, il faudrait encore que les blocs aient été endommagés et que le remploi puisse être relié à un évènement politique précis. En outre, il n'est pas dit qu'un monument ait été démonté pour son remploi, cette première opération pouvant être antérieure et les blocs avoir été laissés de côté jusqu'à leur enfouissement[104]. L'ensemble de ces paramètres rendent la datation de ces différentes opérations difficiles à estimer (Tab. 3).

**Tab. 3:** Remplois dans le téménos.

| | Documents | Datation estimée du remploi |
|---|---|---|
| A | Bloc de Ptolémée II remployé dans les fondations de la porte entre les salles II et III (Inv. 4885) | Entre Ptolémée III et Ptolémée VI |
| B | 6 portes de Ptolémée II à Ptolémée IV remployées dans le mur-pylône | Entre Ptolémée IV et Ptolémée XII (probablement après Ptolémée VIII) |
| C | Autel de Ptolémée III remployé dans le nouvel autel de la grande cour | |
| D | Au moins 3 blocs de Ptolémée II (Inv. 5548, 5549 et BP. 6) et un de Ptolémée VI dans les fondations et les élévations de la porte de Tibère (Inv. 4359) | Auguste |
| E | Bloc de Ptolémée XII Néos Dionysos remployé dans le dallage du porche nord (Inv. 4552) | Époque romaine |

Ainsi dans certains cas, il est même possible que le démontage soit antérieur à la révolte de 206 av. J.-C, comme le bloc Inv. 4885 gravé sous Ptolémée II et remployé au plus tard sous Ptolémée VI, dernier roi dont le nom est attesté dans l'avant-temple (Tab. 3.A et Fig. 1). Étant donné qu'il s'agit d'un bloc isolé, son remploi pourrait témoigner d'une réfection architecturale ponctuelle (peut-être liée à l'élargissement des portes du temple) plutôt que d'une conséquence de la grande révolte. Pour le cas des monuments découverts dans les fondations du mur-

---

[104] Voir les réflexions de Chr. Wallet-Lebrun (2009, p. 32) qui parle d'une « sorte de cimetière des pierres sacralisées ».

pylône (Tab. 3.B), les blocs furent remployés de manière cohérente lors d'une extension du mur péribole et ont, en ce sens, été installés à l'ouest d'un coup de sabre qui marque l'extension originelle du péribole (Fig. 3). Leur remploi doit être situé entre les règnes de Ptolémée IV (dernier roi attesté sur les portes réemployées) et Ptolémée XII (date du décor des porches). Il est cependant peu probable qu'il ait eu lieu avant le règne de Ptolémée VIII Évergète II qui a lancé la décoration du portique (Fig. 1 et Tab. 2)[105]. Une datation similaire vaut pour l'autel de la grande cour (Tab. 3.C). Or, même si ces trois exemples (Tab. 3.A, B, C) ont été démontés après la révolte de 206 av. J.-C, aucun des blocs n'a été dégradé et il est donc difficile de justifier leur remploi comme une preuve des troubles de la période.

D'autres remplois présentent des caractéristiques différentes comme ceux découverts dans les fondations et les élévations de la porte de Tibère qui réunissent des blocs de Ptolémée II et de Ptolémée VI, remployés à l'époque augustéenne lors de la construction du monument[106]. De la même façon, le dallage des porches nord livra un bloc au nom de Ptolémée XII Néos Dionysos « *Ptwlmys-ꜥnḫ-ḏt-mry-Ptḥ-ꜣs.t* » (Inv. 4552)[107]. Il témoigne forcément d'une réfection de ce dallage à l'époque romaine car les maçonneries environnantes datent du même souverain[108]. Dans ces deux exemples, la révolte de 206 av. J.-C. ne peut clairement pas être considérée comme responsable de leur remploi. En outre, ils illustrent que la documentation du début de l'époque ptolémaïque n'est pas la seule à avoir été remployée.

Par conséquent, les remplois ne peuvent pas être considérés intrinsèquement comme la preuve des exactions commises par les rebelles au vu de l'absence de traces de dégradations et de leur datation s'échelonnant pendant toute l'époque ptolémaïque. Ce dernier critère montre aussi qu'il faut abandonner l'insistance portée à la seule révolte de 206 av. J-C. et prendre également en compte les autres épisodes ayant perturbé le pouvoir royal (troubles dynastiques, guerres extérieures

---

[105] Il est peu probable que l'installation du portique soit antérieure au remploi de cette documentation dans la mesure où un contre-mur fut installé le long du péribole nord pour pouvoir soutenir le plafond reliant le portique au péribole nord. Or l'épaisseur du péribole et du contre-mur est la même que celle de la partie ouest du péribole (à l'ouest du coup de sabre marquant son extension). Voir Relats Montserrat 2024, p. 271.

[106] L'érection de la porte de Tibère sous Auguste est connue par sa stèle de fondation même si le monument fut essentiellement décoré par son successeur : Revez 2004.

[107] Outre ce bloc, le dallage du porche nord livra deux lots de blocs. Le premier lot est formé par des blocs gravés au nom de la divine adoratrice Shépénoupet II et témoigne sûrement de l'existence de chapelles de parvis érigées à l'Époque tardive devant se situer originellement sur le parvis du temple. Le deuxième lot est formé par une série de blocs de style ptolémaïque, même s'ils ne peuvent pas être attribués à un règne précis. Pour Inv. 4552 : Bisson de la Roque 1930, p. 49.

[108] Pour la gravure des porches : Sambin 1999, p. 398 et Thiers 2000.

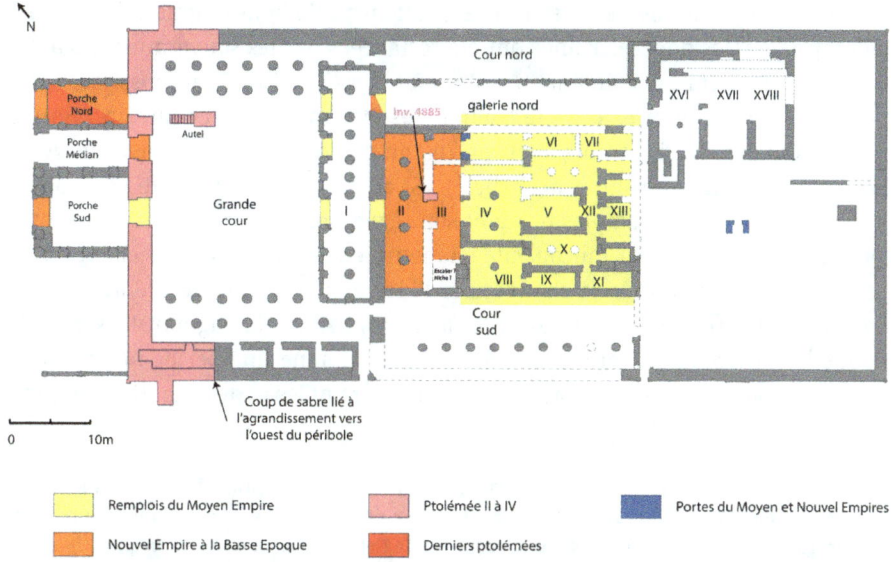

**Fig. 3:** Localisation des remplois découverts dans le temple de Montou (© Felix Relats Montserrat).

etc.). Si Bisson de la Roque avait seulement prêté attention au premier de ces évènements c'est parce qu'il suivait le discours des décrets synodaux décrivant les exactions des rebelles contre les sanctuaires. Or, depuis les années 1920, ce point de vue été remis en cause par l'historiographie[109]. D'une part, les dégradations décrites par ces sources reprennent un *topos* présent déjà dans les inscriptions pharaoniques[110]. En ce sens, certaines formules des versions hiéroglyphiques des décrets du règne de Ptolémée V remontent à un vocabulaire utilisé dès les Moyen et Nouvel Empires comme *gm wš* (« (les temples ou les statues des dieux) qui furent trouvées endommagé(e)s »)[111] ou *sk ḥm.w* (« (les rebelles) détruisant les tem-

---

[109] Voir la version démotique du décret de Memphis de 196 « les chefs rebelles qui avaient rassemblé une armée pour semer le désordre dans les provinces, qui avaient fait du tort aux temples » (cité d'après Veïsse 2004, p. 135).

[110] Pour une recension des formules exprimant l'idée de surpassement : Vernus 1992, p. 54–90. Le discours royal face aux révoltes rejoint ici le discours anti-Perse pointant les destructions réalisées par les souverains achéménides sur les temples égyptiens qu'elle qu'ait été leur réalité (Posener 1936 ; Devauchelle 1995 ; Forgeau 2018, p. 144 ; Klotz 2010, p. 152–156). Les décrets antérieurs à Ptolémée V ne développent pas les destructions des temples mais le retour des statues volées par les Perses : Thiers 2007, p. 100–106 ; Pfeiffer 2004, p. 85 (pour la version du décret de Canope).

[111] *Wb.* I, 368, 9. L'expression est employée dans le décret *Philensis II*, 6 (*sḫm.w n(y).w nṯr.w nty. w m gm wš m ḥm.w* « les statues des dieux qui furent trouvées endommagées dans les sanctuaires » – Recklinghausen 2018, I, p. 55). Un parallèle exact est utilisé dans le décret de Memphis de 182 (Nes-

ples »)¹¹². Plus généralement ces termes participent de la description du délabrement des temples dont les ruines ont été restaurées par les souverains¹¹³. D'autre part, ces textes sont des émanations du haut clergé, qui exerçait aussi des fonctions civiles ou militaires pour le compte des Ptolémées¹¹⁴. Au contraire, Haronnophris/Chaonnophris semble avoir entretenu de bonnes relations avec le clergé local et s'être fait couronner à Thèbes¹¹⁵. Si aucune trace d'atteinte généralisée n'a été relevée sur les temples pendant son règne, son nom n'a pas été inscrit sur leurs murs (peut-être par l'incapacité de mettre en œuvre de grands chantiers de construction)¹¹⁶. Il faut donc abandonner l'idée que la révolte de 206 av. J.-C. entraina des destructions massives de sanctuaires comme l'imaginait Bisson de la Roque¹¹⁷. En revanche, cet épisode doit être vu comme une période de troubles politiques ayant perturbé le fonctionnement des temples et des chantiers de cons-

---

poulous-Phalippou 2015, p. 72–73). Pour l'expression *gm wš* dans la phraséologie depuis le Moyen Empire : Blumenthal 1970, p. 118–119 (C. 1.27). L'emploi de *wš* se retrouve dans la littérature pour exprimer le chaos du pays, comme dans la prophétie de Néferty : *ḥḏd m jry.t, wš.t m gmy[.t]* « ce qui est détruit est à la place de ce qui a été réalisé, ce qui manque est à la place de ce dont la présence était manifeste » (trad. Vernus 2012, p. 402 ; Quack 1993, p. 78)

112   L'expression est utilisée dans le récit de la révolte dans *Philensis II*, 8 (Recklinghausen 2018, I, p. 55 et Nespoulous-Phalippou 2015, p. 309). La tournure *sk ḥm.w* est l'antithèse de l'expression utilisée par Hatshepsout dans la chapelle rouge *srwḏ=t ḥm.w nṯr.w* « pour que tu restaures les temples des dieux » (Lacau, Chevrier 1977, § 166, p. 107, l. 6 ; Larché, Burgos, Grimal, 2008, pl. 33). Des expressions proches se retrouvent dans les textes du Nouvel Empire. Ainsi la stèle de la restauration de Toutankhamon décrit le délabrement des temples : *jw r3.w-pr.w n(y).w nṯr.w nṯr.wt (...) w3(.w) r stp ḥm.wt=sn w3(.w) r mrḥ ḫpr(w) m j33* « les temples des dieux et des déesses (...) étaient tombés en ruine, leurs chapelles (*ḥm*) avaient été laissées se dégrader et devenir des ruines » (*Urk.* IV, 2027, 6; Biston-Moulin 2015, p. 26).

113   L'inscription de Sésostris I^er à Tôd évoque les décombres (*ḥm*) qui se trouvaient à l'emplacement du temple avant l'arrivée du roi (Barbotin, Clère 1991, p. 9 et 18). Des expressions similaires se trouvent à Éléphantine (sur l'inscription de Sésostris I^er et sur une stèle du sanctuaire d'Héqaib : Helck 1978, p. 70, col. 19 et Habachi 1985, p. 36, n°9, l. 6–7). Hatshepsout dans la grande inscription du Spéos Artémidos affirme « j'ai relevé ce qui était auparavant en ruine » (*jw ts~n=j stp(w).t ḥ3t-ʿ* : *Urk.* IV, 390, 7). Pour la traduction de *ḥ3t-ʿ* « au début » sans préposition : *AnLex* I, 236 (77.2575). Les rebelles deviennent des manifestations du chaos d'où leur désignation comme ennemis des dieux (*inter alia* « *ḥfty.w nṯr.w* ») : Vittmann 2005 (avec une discussion sur le lien avec l'expression grecque θεοῖσιν ἐχθρός) ; Veïsse 2004, p. 116–120.

114   Voir notamment Huss 1994, vol. 1, p. 74–88 ; Chevereau 1985, p. 187–200 ; Clarysse 2000, p. 54–58.

115   Pestman 1995 ; Veïsse 2004. Haronnophris et Chaonnophris doivent sûrement être désormais considérés comme une seule personne : Veïsse 2013.

116   Thiers 2009, p. 236. Pour le *P. Tebt.* III 781 souvent versé au dossier, voir *infra* n. 118.

117   Derrière l'interprétation de Bisson de la Roque se dessine aussi l'interprétation « nationaliste » des révoltes développée par P. Jouguet (directeur de l'Ifao à l'époque des fouilles de Médamoud) qui voyait les révoltes comme l'expression de la résistance nationale égyptienne face à l'occupation étrangère : Jouguet 1923, p. 419–445. Pour un aperçu historiographique : Veïsse 2004, p. I-XVI.

truction. À cette occasion certaines maçonneries ont pu être endommagées, d'autant que les temples étaient, pendant toutes les crises du pouvoir royal en Égypte ancienne, l'objet de convoitises diverses ou d'occupations[118]. Cependant la documentation à notre disposition pour Médamoud permet surtout de voir la reprise du pouvoir par les Lagides une fois leur autorité restaurée. Ces réflexions valent pour la crise des années 206–180 av. J.-C., mais également pour les autres tensions ayant troublé le pouvoir ptolémaïque dans la *chôra* qu'il faut intégrer à l'histoire du site.

## 3.2 Les effets indirects des révoltes et la perturbation des travaux

En ce sens, les modifications architecturales visibles dans la documentation dessinent une chronologie similaire à celle des autres temples thébains qui correspond aux phases de reprise en main de la Thébaïde par le pouvoir royal[119].

En ce qui concerne la révolte de 206–180 av. J.-C., aucune inscription de Médamoud n'en fait mention, aucun monument ne semble avoir été détruit et aucune trace d'incendie généralisé n'a été notée par Bisson de la Roque. La sécession de la Haute-Égypte a pu, en revanche, avoir une incidence indirecte à travers l'arrêt des chantiers royaux. Si l'exemple paradigmatique est celui du temple d'Edfou, la documentation de Médamoud pourrait également témoigner d'un phénomène similaire[120]. Ainsi au moins la décoration de deux monuments n'a pas été achevée peut-être en raison de la sécession de la Haute-Égypte : tout d'abord la gravure du montant gauche de la porte de Djémê, érigée par Ptolémée IV, n'a pas été terminée[121]. De même le péribole, dont la construction a été lancée dès le début de l'époque ptolémaïque (Tab. 2), n'a été décoré qu'entre les règnes de Domitien et de Trajan.

Si Ptolémée V est attesté sur le site, signe de la reprise en main du pouvoir royal, les tensions dynastiques qui ont suivi son règne semblent aussi avoir per-

---

118 Pour l'occupation des temples : Thiers 1995. Pour les violences au quotidien à l'encontre du personnel du temple : Dunand 1979. Une source documentaire grecque (*P. Tebt.* III 781) offre un exemple des violences perpétrées en 164 av. J.-C. Le papyrus rapporte le témoignage du responsable de l'Ammonieion, un petit temple égyptien dédié à Amon et situé à Moéris. Il évoque l'assaut que des troupes d'Antiochos ont fait subir au sanctuaire qui ont « fendu les ouvrages de pierre ; ils ont aussi endommagé les portes d'entrée » et même « fait tomber une partie de la toiture » (Veïsse 2004, p. 136). Cette source est souvent citée comme confirmation des violences perpétrées lors des révoltes mais est plutôt à comprendre dans le contexte de la sixième guerre de Syrie.
119 Thiers 2009, 2010, 2013, 2015.
120 Cauville, Devauchelle 1984, p. 35–36.
121 Sambin 1992, p. 162.

turbé le fonctionnement du temple[122]. Ptolémée VI Philométor a ainsi gravé plusieurs inscriptions du temple, mais son action à Médamoud semble dater de la fin de son règne. Par exemple sur le mur ouest de la galerie nord, Philométor rend hommage à ses ancêtres et à son fils Eupator, ce qui prouve que cette scène est postérieure au décès de ce dernier en 152 av. J.-C.[123]. De même sur le bloc Inv. 4359, la titulature du souverain présente la version D dans la typologie proposée par R. Preys (*nṯr.wy mr.wy mw.t=snj* 𓏏𓏏𓄿𓅓𓏏 « les deux dieux qui aiment leur mère ») datée entre 163 et 145 av. J.-C.[124]. D'après ces quelques indices, il serait possible que le chantier de Médamoud n'ait repris qu'à la fin du règne du souverain, après la crise l'opposant à son frère Ptolémée VIII Évergète II[125]. Ce dernier a, à son tour, lancé un grand chantier avec la construction du portique qui constitue le principal tournant, du point de vue architectural, dans la physionomie du temple. Sa décoration fut cependant essentiellement réalisée par Ptolémée X Alexandre et Ptolémée XII Néos Dionysos (Fig. 1) signe soit de l'interruption des travaux, soit de leur lancement à la fin du règne d'Évergète II[126]. Ainsi, majoritairement Médamoud semble avoir subi des effets collatéraux des révoltes de l'époque ptolémaïque, essentiellement visibles en négatif par la perturbation des chantiers royaux et par la reprise en main ultérieure de la monarchie. Celle-ci se manifeste par le lancement de travaux qui peuvent être interprétés à la fois comme une affirmation de leur pouvoir, mais aussi comme un geste de conciliation avec la population et les clergés thébains[127].

---

[122] Pour les cartouches de Ptolémée V Épiphane, voir *supra* p. 208.

[123] *jy~n nswt-bjty (jwʿ-n(y) nṯr.wy-pr(.wy) ḫprw-Ptḥ jr(w)-m3ʿ.t-Rʿ stp~n-Jmn) ḫr=k Jmn, nṯr.wy sn.wy, nṯr.wy mnḫ.wy, nṯr.wy mr.wy jt=w, nṯr.wy pr(.wy), p(3) nṯr r tnj jt=f, jn=f n=tn ḥ3py* – « Le roi de Haute- et Basse-Égypte (Ptolémée VI) vient vers toi Amon, (ainsi que vers) les dieux Philadelphes, les dieux Évergètes, les dieux Philopators, les Dieux Épiphanes et le dieu Eupator, afin de vous apporter le Nil » – Drioton 1926, p. 32 (Inscr. 58) ; Minas 2000, p. 37, doc. 74 (qui corrige la lecture de Drioton qui faisait de Eupator le sujet de *jn=f* ; il s'agit plutôt d'un prospectif dont le sujet renvoie au roi). Sur l'intégration d'Eupator dans le culte dynastique : Bielman-Sanchez, Lenzo 2015, p. 167.

[124] Sur le bloc Inv. 4359 (Bisson de la Roque 1930, p. 3). M. Minas (1996, p. 59 ; 1997, p. 111) datait le bloc du mariage de Philométor et Cléopâtre II, car elle n'avait pas eu accès au détail de la titulature. Nous suivons l'interprétation de R. Preys (2017) qui distingue deux versions des épithètes au duel pendant le règne : *nṯr.wj mr.wy mw.t=w* (175–170 av. J.-C.) et *nṯr.wy mr.wy mw.t=snj* (163 et 145 av. J.-C.), séparées par l'époque où le futur Ptolémée VIII fut associé au pouvoir aux côtés de Philométor et de Cléopâtre II.

[125] Bielman, Lenzo 2015, p. 92–110.

[126] Peut-être en raison des tensions opposant Cléopâtre II et Ptolémée VIII qui ont touché la ville de Thèbes dans les années 132–130 av. J.-C. (Veïsse 2004, p. 53–63).

[127] Sur les dons faits par les Ptolémées aux temples égyptiens après les révoltes : Veïsse 2004, p. 213–220.

Pour l'époque romaine, au contraire, un faisceau d'indices soulignent l'existence de dégradations ponctuelles ayant affecté les porches à l'occasion d'un incendie. Ce dernier est reconnaissable à différentes traces de feu au niveau du mur sud-ouest du porche sud, dont le cœur des maçonneries est rubéfié. Celui-ci expliquerait tout d'abord la réfection du dallage du porche nord où fut remployé un bloc au nom de Ptolémée XII Néos Dionysos (Inv. 4552 – Tab. 3.E). Ensuite, le porche sud présente un dispositif particulier pour ses décors qui ont été gravés sur des petites dalles collées à la maçonnerie intérieure de ses murs sud-ouest et sud. Les reliefs en question représentent des musiciens, stylistiquement datables de l'époque romaine[128]. Ils auraient ainsi remplacé un décor original endommagé pendant l'incendie. Il est cependant difficile de dater cet évènement, mais une hypothèse serait de le relier à la répression de la révolte de 29 av. J.-C., à laquelle Médamoud (*Kéramiké*) participa, d'après le décret trilingue de Philae 143, et qui fut matée par le préfet Cornelius Gallus[129]. Le texte évoque la prise de cinq villes par la force (*V urbium expugnator* « le preneur de 5 villes » / πέν[τε τε πόλεις, τὰς μὲν ἐξ ἐφόδου, τὰς δὲ ἐκ πολιορκία[ς] καταλαβόμενος « celui qui a pris 5 villes, les unes dès le premier assaut, les autres par le siège »)[130]. S'il est peu probable que la révolte ait affecté directement le temple à grande échelle au vu du manque de traces archéologiques d'un tel évènement, des combats auraient pu en endommager l'entrée qui constitue naturellement l'interface entre l'extérieur et le téménos[131]. L'absence de critères pour préciser la datation de cet incendie illustre toutefois la difficulté de faire correspondre les données historiques et archéologiques car cet évènement pourrait être beaucoup plus tardif, la décoration des porches s'échelonnant jusqu'aux règnes de Néron et de Vespasien (Fig. 1). Indépendamment de l'interprétation proposée pour cet incen-

---

[128] Drioton 1927, p. 27 (num. 328) ; Darnell 1995. En raison de la finesse du trait, Bisson de la Roque (1927, p. 33–34) et J.-Fr. Carlotti (2015, p. 112–113) les ont datés du début de l'époque ptolémaïque. Cependant cette datation ne repose sur aucun critère précis. Bisson de la Roque considère uniquement la datation des reliefs en fonction de leur beauté esthétique en associant la finesse du trait aux époques les plus anciennes. Au contraire, les instruments représentés dans la procession de musiciens rapprochent les reliefs de ceux des temples d'Edfou et de Dendera plus que des parallèles de l'époque ptolémaïque : Emerit 2020 et Relats Montserrat 2024, p. 278.
[129] Veïsse 2004, p. 74–76 ; Hoffmann, Minas-Nerpel, Pfeiffer 2009, p. 120–121 et p. 139–140 ; Klotz 2012, p. 227. Il est représentatif que la version hiéroglyphique ne corresponde pas aux versions latine et grecque et présente le préfet en position traditionnelle de combat face aux ennemis de l'Égypte et de constructeur de temples (Hoffmann, Minas-Nerpel, Pfeiffer 2009, p. 76–90). Les ennemis sont soit extérieurs (Nubiens, Libyens ...), soit qualifiés de *ḫfty.w*, qualificatif traditionnel pour désigner les opposants de la maât (*supra* n. 113).
[130] Hoffmann, Minas-Nerpel, Pfeiffer 2009, p. 138.
[131] Les parvis des temples accueillaient une agglomération importante. Voir l'étude consacrée à l'occupation de celui de Karnak : Redon, Faucher 2015.

die, le règne d'Auguste vit aussi l'érection d'une nouvelle enceinte et d'un nouveau propylône (la porte dite de Tibère). Ce programme architectural entraîna l'arasement du pylône thoutmoside et son remplacement par un parvis agrémenté de fosses de plantation pour des arbres[132]. Si aucun lien formel ne peut être identifié avec les tensions en Thébaïde mentionnées par l'épigraphie, un tel programme architectural doit, tout du moins, correspondre à un geste de conciliation envers les populations locales[133].

## 3.3 Le culte dynastique à Médamoud, une réponse à la situation politique ?

La documentation à notre disposition – essentiellement épigraphique et issue des maçonneries du temple – permet surtout de restituer l'activité architecturale de la monarchie lagide, plus que les révoltes elles-mêmes. Néanmoins, celle-ci est aussi à comprendre comme un moyen de reconquérir la légitimité des souverains face à la perte de leur autorité en Haute-Égypte dans une période de troubles multiples. Il est en ce sens illustratif qu'à chaque fois que le pouvoir royal est reconnu à Thèbes, les constructions reprennent à Médamoud (tous les souverains étant attestés sur le site depuis Ptolémée II à l'exception de Ptolémée IX Sôter II)[134]. Si cette observation vaut pour de nombreux temples thébains, Médamoud reste un temple d'importance secondaire. Or l'intérêt porté pour le site s'explique peut-être par l'importance du culte dynastique dans l'histoire du monument[135]. L'exemple paradigmatique est offert par la liste des ancêtres, gravée par Ptolémée VI, qui regroupe Ptolémée II, III, IV, V et son fils décédé Eupator. Comme le constate M. Minas, Ptolémée VI accomplit un acte cultuel adressé à Amon et à ses prédécesseurs honorés dans le temple à l'égal des dieux (Θεοὶ σύνναοι)[136].

Cette tradition remonte cependant à Sésostris III qui fit construire à Médamoud son principal sanctuaire de Haute-Égypte et accorda une grande place au culte monarchique dans le programme iconographique de son sanctuaire. Montou fut élevé au rang de dieu dynastique qui accorde la royauté. Le souverain se

---

132 L'arasement du pylône thoutmoside est régulier mais n'a gardé aucune trace de dégradations. Pour une description archéologique actualisée : Relats Montserrat, Barahona Mendieta, Séguier 2019.
133 Klotz 2012, p. 242.
134 Caßor-Pfeiffer 2008, p. 53. On laisse de côté évidemment les souverains qui ne sont pas attestés dans les temples : Ptolémées VII et XI. Pour la possible présence de Cléopâtre VII : Sambin 1999.
135 Relats Montserrat 2017, p. 132–8 ; Sambin-Nivet 2015b (pour la seule époque ptolémaïque).
136 Voir *supra* n. 123.

présenta ainsi comme l'héritier des Montouhotep, en rendant hommage au dieu thébain. La mention de la fête *sed* (encore présente sur le site à l'époque lagide avec la porte de Ptolémée II) contribuent également à construire l'image de Médamoud comme un sanctuaire monarchique[137]. Cet aspect du programme théologique, mis en place par Sésostris III, a durablement marqué le site. Par la suite, Médamoud a toujours été associé au culte royal et la mémoire de Sésostris III, exalté comme l'ancêtre fondateur, n'a jamais cessé d'être mise en valeur. En ce sens, les statues de ce souverain furent conservées probablement jusqu'à l'époque ptolémaïque dans le sanctuaire[138]. La préservation d'une partie du temple thoutmoside devait aussi contribuer à l'intérêt que la monarchie portait au site et explique sûrement le choix de ne pas refonder le sanctuaire mais de le modifier. De ce fait, l'action des Lagides permettait de les placer comme les héritiers de ces illustres prédécesseurs.

# 4 Conclusion

La politique architecturale de la monarchie lagide à Médamoud pendant le $III^e$ siècle av. J.-C. est donc continue : plusieurs projets lancés à cette époque (modifications du temple thoutmoside, péribole, enceintes, dromos) ont été poursuivis ou étendus jusqu'à l'époque impériale. C'est dans ce contexte qu'il faut insérer les effets de la révolte de 206 av. J.-C. ainsi que des autres conflits ayant secoué la *chôra* entre le $III^e$ et le $I^{er}$ siècle av. J.-C., qui n'avaient pas été retenus par les fouilleurs. Si l'hypothèse de Bisson de la Roque doit être abandonnée, il n'est pas pour autant question de nier les effets des révoltes. La documentation de Médamoud livre cependant plutôt une trace indirecte de leurs effets par l'arrêt des chantiers royaux et leur reprise à l'occasion du retour de l'autorité royale. Il s'agit donc de changer le regard que l'historiographie portait sur ces dégradations encore trop souvent analysées en termes de luttes « nationales ». En outre il faut reconnaitre la difficulté à faire correspondre les données historiques, souvent tirées de sources littéraires, et les faits archéologiques plus ou moins datables en fonction de l'état de la documentation. Au vu de ces remarques, il faut enfin arrêter de considérer le règne de Ptolémée IV comme un tournant dans l'histoire du site. L'expression les « premiers Ptolémées », couramment employée à Médamoud, est l'héritière d'une vision qui faisait de ce règne le dernier de l'âge d'or de la dynastie[139]. Or si la

---

[137] Relats Montserrat 2017.
[138] Relats Montserrat 2024, p. 245–247.
[139] Son règne correspond certes à la fin de la thalassocratie lagide en Méditerranée et au début du repli sur la vallée dans le contexte des guerres de Syrie. Voir la présentation d'E. Will (1967, p. 106).

perte des territoires extérieurs et les problèmes dynastiques sont indéniables, les Lagides ont développé une riche politique en Thébaïde. Architecturalement parlant à Médamoud, ce sont les constructions lancées par Ptolémée VI Philométor et surtout Ptolémée VIII Évergète II qui ont changé la physionomie du temple. Leur action correspond certes à une réponse face aux révoltes, par la matérialisation de l'autorité royale en Thébaïde, mais ces dernières ne peuvent plus être utilisées comme le seul moteur explicatif à l'évolution architecturale du temple.

# Bibliographie

Barahona Mendieta 2014
    Barahona Mendieta, Z., « La producción de cerámica en Medamud. Estudio preliminar de la cerámica procedente de los hornos del Reino Nuevo, Baja Época y Época Ptolemaica », *BCE* 24, 2014, p. 267–280.

Barahona Mendieta 2015
    Barahona Mendieta, Z., « Note préliminaire sur quelques céramiques grecques trouvées à Médamoud » in G. Gorre, A. Marangou (éd.), *La présence grecque dans la vallée de Thèbes*, Rennes, 2015, p. 113–117.

Barahona Mendieta 2016a
    Barahona Mendieta, Z., « La producción cerámica en época ptolemaica en Medamud, hasta comienzos de la dominación romana » in R. David (éd.), *Céramiques ptolémaïques de la région thébaine. Actes de la table ronde de Karnak les 28 et 29 septembre 2014*, CCE 10, Le Caire, 2016, p. 21–42.

Barahona Mendieta 2016b
    Barahona Mendieta, Z., *Contribución a la historia de medamud: Estudio histórico y caracterización diacrónica de la cerámica descubierta en Medamud en las excavaciones del IFAO. Contribución a la historia de la cerámica del Alto Egipto*, Thèse inédite soutenue à l'université autonome de Barcelone, Barcelone, 2016.

Barahona Mendieta, Relats Montserrat, Séguier 2019
    Barahona Mendieta, Z., Relats Montserrat, F., Séguier, R., « Nouvelles données sur un four à céramiques des XVII$^e$-XVIII$^e$ dynasties à Médamoud. Contexte archéologique, comparaison architecturale et étude céramologique », *BCE* 29, 2019, p. 165–229.

Barbotin, Clère 1991
    Barbotin, Chr., Clère, J.-J., « L'inscription de Sésostris Ier à Tod », *BIFAO* 91, 1991, p. 1–32

Bartels 2009
    Bartels, U., *Edfu : Die Darstellungen auf den Außenseiten der Umfassungsmauer und auf den Pylonen – Strichzeichnungen und Photographien, Die Inschriften des Tempels von Edfu* II, Dokumentationen I, Wiesbaden, 2009.

Bataille 1946
    Bataille, A., « L'emplacement des Kerameia Thébains », *CdE* XXI, fasc. 42, juillet 1946, p. 237–244.

Beckerath 1999
    Beckerath, J. von, *Handbuch der ägyptischen Königsnamen*, MÄS 49, Mayence, 1999.

Bernand 1992
    Bernand, É., *Inscriptions grecques d'Égypte et de Nubie au Musée du Louvre*, Paris, 1992.

Bielman-Sanchez, Lenzo 2015
    Bielman-Sanchez, A., Lenzo, G., *Inventer le pouvoir féminin. Cléopâtre I et Cléopâtre II, reines d'Égypte au IIe s. av. J.-C.*, ECHO 12, Berne, 2015
Bisson de la Roque 1926
    Bisson de la Roque, F., *Rapport sur les fouilles de Médamoud (1925)*, FIFAO III/1, Le Caire, 1926.
Bisson de la Roque 1927
    Bisson de la Roque, F., *Rapport sur les fouilles de Médamoud (1926)*, FIFAO IV/1, Le Caire, 1927.
Bisson de la Roque 1930
    Bisson de la Roque, F., *Rapport sur les fouilles de Médamoud (1929)*, FIFAO VII/1, Le Caire, 1930.
Bisson de la Roque 1931
    Bisson de la Roque, F., *Rapport sur les fouilles de Médamoud (1930)*, FIFAO VIII/1, Le Caire, 1931.
Bisson de la Roque 1930-1932
    Bisson de la Roque, F., « Journal de fouilles », carnet de fouilles, manuscrit, conservé aux archives de l'Ifao (ms_2004_06, ms_2004_07 et ms_2004_08), couvrant les campagnes de 1930, 1931 et de 1932.
Bisson de la Roque 1933
    Bisson de la Roque, F., *Rapport sur les fouilles de Médamoud (1931 et 1932)*, FIFAO IX/3, Le Caire, 1933.
Bisson de la Roque 1941
    Bisson de la Roque, F., « Notes sur le dieu Montou », *BIFAO* 40, 1941, p. 1-49.
Bisson de la Roque 1946
    Bisson de la Roque, F., « Les fouilles de l'institut français à Médamoud de 1925 à 1938 », *RdE* 5, 1946, p. 25-44.
Bisson de la Roque, Clère, Drioton 1928
    Bisson de la Roque, F., Clère, J.J., Drioton, É., *Rapport sur les fouilles de Médamoud (1927)*, FIFAO V/1, Le Caire, 1928.
Bisson de la Roque, Clère 1929
    Bisson de la Roque, F., Clère, J.J., *Rapport sur les fouilles de Médamoud (1928)*, FIFAO VI/1, Le Caire, 1929.
Biston-Moulin 2015
    Biston-Moulin, S., « Un nouvel exemplaire de la *Stèle de la restauration* de Toutânkhamon à Karnak », *Karnak* 15, 2015, p. 23-38.
Blumenthal 1970
    Blumenthal, E., *Untersuchungen zum ägyptischen Königtum des Mittleren Reiches* I, AAWL 61, Berlin, 1970.
Brand 2000
    Brand, P.J., *The Monuments of Sethi I : Epigraphic, Historical and Art Historical Analysis*, ProblÄg 16, Leyde, Boston, Cologne, 2000.
Bricault (éd.) 2008
    Bricault (éd.), L., *Sylloge nummorum religionis isiacae et sarapiacae (SNRIS)*, MAIBL 38, Paris, 2008.
Cabrol 2001
    Cabrol, A., *Les voies processionnelles de Thèbes*, OLA 97, Louvain, 2001.
Carlotti 2015
    Carlotti, J.-Fr., « Le programme architectural des premiers Ptolémées à Médamoud », *Memnonia* 26, 2015, p. 79-113

Caßor-Pfeiffer 2008
: Caßor-Pfeiffer, S., « Zur Reflexion ptolemäischer Geschichte in den ägyptischen Tempeln unter Ptolemaios IX. Philometor II./Soter II. und Ptolemaios X. Alexander I. (116–80 v. Chr.). Teil 1: Die Bau- und Dekorationstätigkeit », *JEH* 1/1, 2008, p. 21–77

Cauville 1993
: Cauville, S., « La chapelle de la barque à Dendera », *BIFAO* 93, 1993, p. 79–172.

Cauville, Devauchelle 1984
: Cauville, S., Devauchelle, D., « Le temple d'Edfou. Étapes de la construction. Nouvelles données historiques », *RdE* 35, 1984, p. 31–55.

Chevereau 1985
: Chevereau, P.-M., *Prosopographie des cadres militaires égyptiens de la Basse Époque. Carrières militaires et carrières sacerdotales en Égypte du XI$^e$ au II$^e$ siècle avant J.-C.*, Paris, 1985.

Clarysse 1995
: Clarysse, W., « Greeks in Ptolemaic Thebes » in S.P. Vleeming (éd.), *Hundred-Gated Thebes: Acts of a Colloquium on Thebes and the Theban Area in the Graeco-Roman Period*, P.L.Bat. 27, Leyde, New York, Cologne, 1995, p. 1–19.

Clarysse 2000
: Clarysse, W., « Ptolémées et temples » in D. Valbelle, J. Leclant (dir.) *Le décret de Memphis*, Paris, 2000, p. 41–65.

Darnell 1995
: Darnell, J.C., « Hathor Returns to Medamûd », *SAK* 22, 1995, p. 47–94.

Devauchelle 1995
: Devauchelle, D., « Le sentiment anti-perse chez les anciens Égyptiens », *Transeuphratène* 9, Paris, 1995, p. 67–80.

Drioton 1926
: Drioton, É., *Rapport sur les fouilles de Médamoud (1925), Les inscriptions*, FIFAO III/2, Le Caire, 1926.

Drioton 1927
: Drioton, É., *Rapport sur les fouilles de Médamoud (1926), Les inscriptions*, FIFAO IV/2, Le Caire, 1927.

Dunand 1979
: Dunand, F., « Droit d'asile et refuge dans les temples de l'Égypte lagide » in J. Vercoutter (dir.), *Hommages à la mémoire de S. Sauneron*, BdE 82/2, Le Caire, 1979, p. 77–97.

Emerit 2020
: Emerit, S., « Musiciens et processions dans le temple d'Hathor à Dendera. Iconographie et espace rituel », *Musiques, images, instruments* 18, 2020, p. 188–230.

Ernst 2002
: Ernst, H., « Der Opferkult in den Vorhöfen der Tempel in Edfu, Medamud, und Kom Ombo », *ZÄS* 129/1, 2002, p. 12–19.

Faucher 2010
: Faucher, Th., « Gravure et composition métallique des monnaies lagides », *RN* 166, 2010, p. 95–108.

Faucher 2013
: Faucher, Th., *Frapper monnaie. La fabrication des monnaies de bronze à Alexandrie sous les Ptolémées*, EtudAlex 27, Le Caire, 2013.

Faucher, Lorber 2010
    Faucher, Th., Lorber, C., « Bronze Coinage of Ptolemaic Egypt in the Second Century BC », *AJN* 22, 2010, p. 35–80.
Faucher *et al.* 2011
    Faucher, Th., Coulon, L., Frangin, E., Giorgi, C., « Un atelier monétaire à Karnak au II$^e$ s. av. J.-C. », *BIFAO* 111, 2011, p. 143–165.
Felber 2004
    Felber, H., « Von Söhnen, Vätern und Müttern. Ägyptische und griechische Aspekte frühptolemäischer Königstheologie » in D. Budde, S. Sandri, U. Verhoeven (éd.), *Kindgötter im Ägypten der griechisch-römischen Zeit. Zeugnisse aus Stadt und Tempel als Spiegel des interkulturellen Kontakts*, OLA 128, Louvain, 2004, p. 113–146.
Forgeau 2018
    Forgeau, A., *Nectanébo. La dernière dynastie égyptienne*, Paris, 2018.
Ghiringhelli 2019
    Ghiringhelli, Fr., « Rituel pour la présentation des territoires, un formulaire pré-ptolémaïque de processions des provinces d'Égypte » in A. Ashmawy, D. Raue, D. von Recklinghausen (éds.), *Von Elephantine bis zu den Küsten des Meeres*, SSR 24, Wiesbaden, 2019, p. 71–265.
Golvin, Larronde 1982
    Golvin, J.-Cl., Larronde, J., « Étude des procédés de construction dans l'Égypte ancienne I. L'édification des murs de grès en grand appareil à l'époque romaine », *ASAE* 68, 1982, p. 165–190.
Golvin, Larronde, Maarouf 1985
    Golvin, J.-Cl., Larronde, J., Maarouf, A. El-H., « Étude des procédés de construction dans l'Égypte ancienne II. L'édification des murs de grès en grand appareil à l'époque ptolémaïque », *ASAE* 70, 1985, p. 371–381.
Golvin, Vergnieux 1985
    Golvin, J.-Cl., Vergnieux, R., « Étude des procédés de construction dans l'Égypte ancienne III. La décoration des parois » in *Mélanges Gamal Eddin Mokhtar*, BdE 97/1, Le Caire, 1985, p. 325–381.
Gorre, Marangou (éd.) 2015
    Gorre, G., Marangou, A., (éd.), *La présence grecque dans la vallée de Thèbes*, Rennes, 2015.
Grenier 1992
    Grenier, J.-Cl., « Ptolémée Évergète II et Cléopâtre II d'après les textes du temple de Tôd » in N. Bonacasa, A. Di Vita (éd.), *Alessandria e il mondo ellenistico-romano. Studi in onore di Achille Adriani* I, StudMat 4, Rome, 1992, p. 32–37.
Habachi 1985
    Habachi, L., *Elephantine IV : The sanctuary of Heqaib*, AV 33, 2 vol., Mayence, 1985.
Hallof 2010
    Hallof, J., *Schreibungen der Pharaonennamen in den Ritualszenen der Tempel der griechisch-römischen Zeit Ägyptens*, SRaT 4, Dettelbach, 2010.
Harris 1961
    Harris, J.R., *Lexicographical Studies in Ancient Egyptian Materials*, VIO 54, Berlin, 1961.
Helck 1978
    Helck, W., « Die Weihinschrift Sesostris' I. am Satet-Tempel von Elephantine », *MDAIK* 34, 1978, p. 69–78.
Hoffmann, Minas-Nerpel, Pfeiffer 2009
    Hoffmann, F., Minas-Nerpel, M., Pfeiffer, S., *Die dreisprachige Stele des C. Cornelius Gallus : Übersetzung und Kommentar*, AfP Beihefte 9, Berlin, New York, 2009.

Huss, 1994
　　Huss, W., *Der makedonische König und die ägyptischen Priester*, HistEinz 85, Stuttgart, 1994.
Jouguet 1923
　　Jouguet, P., « Les Lagides et les Indigènes Egyptiens », *RBPH* 2/3, 1923, p. 419–445.
Klotz 2010
　　Klotz, D., « Two Studies on the Late Period Temples at Abydos », *BIFAO* 110, 2010, p. 127–163.
Klotz 2012
　　Klotz, D., *Caesar in the City of Amun: Egyptian Temple Construction and Theology in Roman Thebes*, MRE 15, Turnhout, 2012.
Lacau, Chevrier 1977
　　Lacau, P., Chevrier, H., avec la collaboration de M.-A. Bonhême et M. Gitton, *Une chapelle d'Hatshepsout à Karnak* I, Le Caire, 1977.
Lanciers 1986
　　Lanciers, E., « Die ägyptischen Tempelbauten zur Zeit des Ptolemaios V. Epiphanes (204–180 v. Chr.) : Teil 1 », *MDAIK* 42, 1986, p. 81–98.
Larché, Burgos, Grimal 2008
　　Larché, Fr., Burgos, Fr., Grimal, N., *La chapelle Rouge. Le sanctuaire de barque d'Hatshepsout*, 2 vol., Paris, 2008.
Larcher 2013
　　Larcher, C., s.v. « Médamoud » in R. S. Bagnall *et al.* (éd.), *The Encyclopedia of Ancient History*, Oxford, 2013, p. 4374.
Leclère 2008
　　Leclère, Fr., *Les villes de Basse Égypte au $I^{er}$ millénaire av. J.-C. Analyse archéologique et historique de la topographie urbaine*, BdE 144, Le Caire, 2008.
Legrain 1916
　　Legrain, G., « Notes sur le dieu Montou », *BIFAO* 12, 1916, p. 75–124.
Lorber 2015
　　Lorber, C.C., « Development of Ptolemaic Bronze Coinage in Egypt » in F. Duyrat, O. Picard (éd.), *L'exception égyptienne ? Production et échanges monétaires en Égypte hellénistique et romaine. Actes du colloque d'Alexandrie, 13–15 avril 2002*, EtudAlex 10, Le Caire, 2005, p. 135–158.
Mallet 1909
　　Mallet, D., *Le Kasr El-Agoûz*, MIFAO 11, Le Caire, 1909.
Minas 1996
　　Minas, M., « Die Dekorationstätigkeit von Ptolemaios VI. Philometor und Ptolemaios VIII. Euergetes II. an ägyptischen Tempeln (Teil 1) », *OLP* 27, 1996, p. 51–78.
Minas 1997
　　Minas, M., « Die Dekorationstätigkeit von Ptolemaios VI. Philometor und Ptolemaios VIII. Euergetes II. an ägyptischen Tempeln (Teil 2) », *OLP* 28, 1997, p. 87–121.
Minas 2000
　　Minas, M., *Die hieroglyphischen Ahnenreihen der ptolemäischen Könige: Ein Vergleich mit den Titeln der eponymen Preister in den demotischen und griechischen Papyri*, AegTrev 9, Mayence, 2000.
Nespoulous-Phalippou 2015
　　Nespoulous-Phalippou, A., *Ptolémée Épiphane, Aristonikos et les prêtres d'Égypte. Le Décret de Memphis (182 a.C.). - Édition commentée des stèles Caire RT 2/3/25/7 et JE 44901*, CENiM 12, Montpellier, 2015.

Niederberger 1999

    Niederberger, W.E., *Elephantine XX – der Chnumtempel Nektanebos' II.: Architektur und baugeschichtliche Einordnung*, AV 96, Mayence, 1999.

Pestman 1995

    P.W. Pestman, « Haronnophris and Chaonnophris: Two Indigenous Pharaohs in Ptolemaic Egypt (205–186 B.C.) » in S.P. Vleeming (éd.), *Hundred-Gated Thebes: Acts of a Colloquium on Thebes and the Theban Area in the Graeco-roman Period*, P.L.Bat. 27, Leyde, New York, Cologne, 1995, p. 101–138.

Pfeiffer 2004

    Pfeiffer, S., *Das Dekret von Kanopos (238 v. Chr.): Kommentar und historische Auswertung eines dreisprachigen Synodaldekretes der ägyptischen Priester zu Ehren Ptolemaios' III und seiner Familie*, AfP Beihefte 18, Munich, Leipzig, 2004.

Picard, Faucher 2012

    Picard, O., Faucher, Th., « Les monnaies lagides » in O. Picard, C. Bresc, Th. Faucher, G. Gorre, M.-Chr. Marcellesi, C. Morrisson (éd.), *Les monnaies de fouilles du Centre d'Études Alexandrines. Les monnayages de bronze à Alexandrie de la conquête d'Alexandre à l'Égypte moderne*, EtudAlex 26, Le Caire, 2012, p. 17–124.

Pierrat et al. 1995

    Pierrat G. et al., « Fouilles du Musée du Louvre à Tod, 1988–1991 », *CahKarn* 10, 1995, p. 405–503.

Posener 1936

    Posener, G., *La première domination perse en Égypte. Recueil d'inscriptions hiéroglyphiques*, BdE 11, Le Caire, 1936.

Preys 2017

    Preys, R., « Le cas "Philométor" dans les temples égyptiens », *BIFAO* 117, 2017, p. 329–356.

Quack 1993

    Quack, J., « Beiträge zur Textkritik der Prophezeihung des Neferti », *GM* 135, 1993, p. 77–79.

Recklinghausen 2018

    Recklinghausen, D. von, *Die Philensis-Dekrete: Untersuchungen über zwei Synodaldekrete aus der Zeit Ptolemaios' V. und ihre geschichtilche und religiöse Bedeutung*, ÄA 73, Wiesbaden, 2018.

Redon, Faucher 2015

    Redon, B., Faucher, Th., « Les Grecs aux portes d'Amon. Les bains de Karnak et l'occupation ptolémaïque du parvis ouest du temple de Karnak » in G. Gorre, A. Marangou (éd.), *La présence grecque dans la vallée de Thèbes*, Rennes, 2015, p. 121–134.

*Registre 1925–1928*

    « Médamoud (1925–1928) », registre d'inventaire, manuscrit, conservé aux archives de l'Ifao (ms_2004_09, ms_2004_10, ms_2004_11 et ms_2004_12), couvrant les campagnes de 1925, 1926, 1927 et de 1928 (sans auteur, plusieurs mains).

*Registre 1929–1931*

    « Médamoud (1929–1931) », registre d'inventaire, manuscrit, conservé aux archives de l'Ifao (ms_2004_13, ms_2004_14 et ms_2004_15), couvrant les campagnes de 1929, 1930 et de 1931 (sans auteur, plusieurs mains).

*Registre 1932–1939*

    « Médamoud (1932–1939) », registre d'inventaire, manuscrit, conservé aux archives de l'Ifao (ms_2004_16), couvrant les campagnes de 1932, 1933, 1934, 1936, 1938 et de 1939 (sans auteur, plusieurs mains).

Relats Montserrat 2017
   Relats Montserrat, F., « Sésostris III à Médamoud. Un état de la question » in G. Andreu-Lanoë, Fl. Morfoisse (éd.), *Sésostris III et la fin du Moyen Empire. Actes du colloque des 12-13 décembre 2014 Louvre-Lens et Palais des Beaux-Arts de Lille*, CRIPEL 31, Villeneuve d'Ascq, 2017, p. 119-139.

Relats Montserrat 2018
   Relats Montserrat, F., « Le chantier de Médamoud et la table d'offrande de Nitocris (Inv. 4314) », *BSFE* 198, 2018, p. 77-94.

Relats Montserrat 2019
   Relats Montserrat, « Médamoud » in L. Coulon, M. Cressent (éd.), *Archéologie française en Égypte*, BiGen 59, Le Caire, 2019, p. 190-195.

Relats Montserrat 2020a
   Relats Montserrat, F., « De la fouille au musée. Les partages des antiquités égyptiennes au début du XX$^e$ siècle à travers l'exemple de Médamoud » in M. Volait, A. Dalachanis (éd.), *BCH - moderne et contemporaine* 3, 2020, https://doi.org/10.4000/bchmc.614, consulté le 30 août 2024.

Relats Montserrat 2020b
   Relats Montserrat, F., « Médamoud (2019) », *Bulletin Archéologique des Écoles Françaises à l'Étranger* 1, 2020, https://doi.org/10.4000/baefe.1044, consulté le 30 août 2024.

Relats Montserrat 2024
   Relats Montserrat, F., *Médamoud I. L'histoire d'une fouille (1924-1940)*, FIFAO 96, Le Caire, 2024.

Relats Montserrat, Barahona Mendieta, Séguier 2019
   Relats Montserrat, F., Barahona Mendieta, Z., Séguier, R., « Un pylône thoutmoside à Médamoud. Résultats des fouilles de 2017-2018 autour du "mur de 9 mètres" », *BIFAO* 119, 2019, p. 273-329.

Relats Montserrat, Karlshausen, De Putter 2021
   Relats Montserrat, F., Karlshausen, Chr., De Putter, Th., « L'usage du calcaire dans l'architecture du temple de Médamoud à la lumière des autres temples thébains », *BIFAO* 121, 2021, p. 413-439.

Revez 1999
   Revez, J., *s.v.* « Médamoud » in K. A. Bard (éd.), *Encyclopedia of the Archeology of Ancient Egypt*, Londres, 1999, p. 571-578.

Revez 2004
   Revez, J., « Une stèle commémorant la construction par l'empereur Auguste du mur d'enceinte du temple de Montou-Rê à Médamoud », *BIFAO* 104, 2004, p. 495-510.

Sambin 1988
   Sambin, Ch., « Les portes de Médamoud », *BMML* 3, 1988, p. 4-45.

Sambin 1992
   Sambin, Ch., « Les portes de Médamoud du musée de Lyon », *BIFAO* 92, 1992, p. 147-184.

Sambin 1999
   Sambin, Ch., « Cléopâtre VII à Médamoud », *BIFAO* 99, 1999, p. 397-409.

Sambin 2001
   Sambin, Ch., *s.v.* « Médamoud » in D. Redford (éd.), *The Oxford Encyclopedia of Ancient Egypt*, Oxford, 2001, p. 351-352.

Sambin-Nivet 2015a
   Sambin-Nivet, Ch., « Médamoud. Le sanctuaire Djêmê de Montou », in Chr. Thiers (éd.), *D3T* 3, CENiM 13, Montpellier, 2015, p. 273-294.

Sambin-Nivet 2015b
  Sambin-Nivet, Ch., « Médamoud. Lieu de légitimation royale des Ptolémées », *Memnonia* 26, 2015, p. 115-127.
Sambin, Carlotti 1995
  Sambin, Ch., Carlotti, J.-Fr., « Une porte de fête-sed de Ptolémée II remployée dans le temple de Montou à Médamoud », *BIFAO* 95, 1995, p. 385-457.
Sambin-Nivet, Carlotti 2016
  Sambin-Nivet, Ch., Carlotti, J.-Fr., « Trois autres portes des premiers Ptolémées à Médamoud », *BIFAO* 115, 2016, p. 373-454.
Saragoza 2012
  Saragoza, Fl., « La "maison à double-carré" de Médamoud et les sanctuaires isiaques d'Égypte », *BIFAO* 112, 2012, p. 349-370.
Schreiber 2003
  Schreiber, G., *Late Dynastic and Ptolemaic Painted Pottery from Thebes (4th-2nd c. BC)*, DissPan III/6, Budapest, 2003.
Thiers 1999
  Thiers, Chr., « Les jardins de temple aux époques tardives », *ERUV* I, 1999, p. 107-120.
Thiers 2000
  Thiers, Chr., « Un protocole pharaonique d'Antonin le Pieux ? (Médamoud, Inscr. N° 1, C-D) », *RdE* 50, 2000, p. 266-270.
Thiers 1995
  Thiers, Chr., « Civils et militaires dans les temples. Occupation illicite et expulsion », *BIFAO* 95, 1995, p. 493-516.
Thiers 2007
  Thiers, Chr., *Ptolémée Philadelphe et les prêtres d'Atoum de Tjékou. Nouvelle édition commentée de la « stèle de Pithom » (CGC 22183)*, OrMonsp 17, Montpellier, 2007.
Thiers 2009
  Thiers, Chr., « Observations sur le financement des chantiers de construction des temples à l'époque ptolémaïque » in R. Preys (éd.), *7. Ägyptologische Tempeltagung : Structuring Religion, Leuven 28. September-1. Oktober 2005*, KSG 3.2, Wiesbaden, 2009, p. 231-244.
Thiers 2010
  Thiers, Chr., « Membra disiecta ptolemaica (I) », *CahKarn* 13, 2010, p. 373-399.
Thiers 2013
  Thiers, Chr., « Membra disiecta ptolemaica (II) », *CahKarn* 14, 2013, p. 467-491.
Thiers 2015
  Thiers, Chr., « Membra disiecta ptolemaica (III) », *CahKarn* 15, 2015, p. 347-356.
Tôd II
  Thiers, Chr., *Tôd : Les inscriptions du temple ptolémaïque et romain II – Textes et scénes Nos 173-239*, FIFAO 18/2, Le Caire, 2003.
Traunecker 1987
  Traunecker, Cl., « Les "temples hauts" de Basse Époque. Un aspect du fonctionnement économique des temples », *RdE* 38, 1987, p. 147-162.
Vandorpe 1995
  Vandorpe, K., « City of Many a Gate, Harbour for Many a Rebel » in S.P. Vleeming (éd.), *Hundred-Gated Thebes: Acts of a Colloquium on Thebes and the Theban Area in the Graeco-roman Period*, P.L.Bat. 27, Leyde, New York, Cologne, 1995, p. 203-240.

Varille 1942
:   Varille, A., « L'autel de Ptolémée III à Médamoud », *BIFAO* 41, 1942, p. 39–42.

Veïsse 2004
:   Veïsse, A.-E., *Les « révoltes égyptiennes ». Recherches sur les troubles intérieurs en Égypte du règne de Ptolémée III à la conquête romaine*, StudHell 41, Louvain, 2004.

Veïsse 2005
:   Veïsse, A.-E., « Le discours sur les violences dans l'Egypte hellénistique. Le clergé face aux révoltes » in J.-M. Bertrand (éd.), *La violence dans les mondes grec et romain*, Histoire ancienne et médiévale 80, Paris, 2005, p. 213–223.

Veïsse 2013
:   Veïsse, A.-E., « Retour sur les "révoltes égyptiennes" », Topoi (L.) – suppl. 12, 2013, p. 507–516.

Vernus 1992
:   Vernus, P., *Essai sur la conscience de l'histoire dans l'Égypte pharaonique*, Paris, 1992.

Vernus 2012
:   Vernus, P., « Le verbe gm(j). Essai de sémantique léxicale » In E. Grossman, St. Polis, J. Winand (éd.), *Lexical Semantics in Ancient Egypt*, LingAeg-StudMon 9, Hambourg, 2012, p. 387–438.

Vittmann 2005
:   Vittmann, G., « "Feinde" in den ptolemäischen Synodaldekreten – Mit einem Anhang: Demotische Termini für "Feind", "Rebell", "rebellieren" » in H. Felber (éd.). *Feinde und Aufrührer, Konzepte von Gegnerschaft in ägyptischen Texten besonders des Mittleren Reiches*, AAWL 78/5, Stuttgart, Leipzig, 2005, p. 198–220.

Wallet-Lebrun 2009
:   Wallet-Lebrun, Chr., *Le grand livre de pierre*, MAIBL 41, EtudEg 9, Paris, 2009.

Weinstein 1973
:   Weinstein, J.M., *Foundation Deposits in Ancient Egypt*, PhD, Pennsylvania University, UMI, 1973.

Will 1967
:   Will, E., *Histoire politique du monde hellénistique, 323-30 av. J.-C., t. II : Des avènements d'Antiochos III et de Philippe V à la fin des Lagides*, Nancy, 1967.

Yoyotte 1961
:   Yoyotte, J., « Processions géographiques mentionnant le Fayoum et ses localités », *BIFAO* 61, 1961, p. 79–138.

Zignani 2003
:   Zignani, P., « Observations architecturales sur la porte d'Évergète », *CahKarn* 11, 2003, p. 711–736.

Anne-Emmanuelle Veïsse
# De la « Grande Révolte de la Thébaïde » aux événements de 88 : un siècle d'insurrection thébaine ?

Entre la fin du III$^e$ siècle et le début du I$^{er}$ siècle av. nè, la région correspondant à la Haute-Égypte, que les Grecs nommaient Thébaïde, a connu plusieurs périodes de troubles. Le plus célèbre et le plus sérieux de ces épisodes fut la « Grande Révolte » des années 206–186, au cours de laquelle un ou deux meneurs – selon que l'on considère Haronnophris et Chaonnophris comme identiques ou distincts – se donnèrent le titre de pharaon et entreprirent de construire un nouvel État en se référant à un passé idéal, pré-ptolémaïque[1]. Presque exactement un siècle après l'écrasement de cette révolte par les forces lagides, des troubles naquirent à nouveau en Thébaïde en 88, à l'époque de la lutte pour le pouvoir entre les deux frères Ptolémée IX Sôter II et Ptolémée X Alexandre I[2]. Dans l'historiographie, ces événements n'ont pas suscité un intérêt débordant, sans doute pour deux raisons principales : d'une part, ils appartiennent à une période mal aimée de l'histoire de l'Égypte, coincée entre l'exubérance baroque du règne de Ptolémée VIII et le passage du pays dans l'orbite romaine ; d'autre part, ils ne sont connus qu'au travers de sources disparates et d'interprétation plutôt difficile. Il a ainsi été généralement admis, comme allant de soi, que les Thébains se révoltèrent une nouvelle fois contre la domination ptolémaïque, comme ils l'avaient fait cent ans plus tôt au temps d'Haronnophris. L'objet de cet article est de proposer une interprétation différente, selon laquelle il n'existe que peu de continuité, voire aucune, entre la Grande Révolte et les événements de 88. Il s'agira en somme de présenter différents arguments en faveur de la brève, mais lumineuse interprétation des faits déjà livrée par D. Agut et J.-C. Moreno-García : « La révolte de 88–85 ne visait pas à rétablir un pouvoir pharaonique, aussi fantasmatique soit-il. Un siècle après la reprise en main de la Thébaïde par Ptolémée VI, les insurgés thébains du premier

---

1 Pour un dernier bilan concernant la « Grande Révolte », voir Veïsse 2022a.
2 Sur les événements de 88, voir notamment Collart 1922 ; Préaux 1936, p. 548–550 ; Samuel 1965 ; Vant'Dack *et al.* 1989, p. 146–149 ; Huss 2001, p. 664–667 ; Veïsse 2004, p. 64–73, 225–226, 237–239 (analyses révisées dans cet article) ; Vandorpe, Waebens 2009, p. 49–50 et p. 95–97 ; Ritner 2011.

**Note:** Cet article a bénéficié de la lecture attentive de Michel Chauveau et de ses séminaires tenus à l'École Pratique des Hautes Études autour de la « Guerre des Sceptres » en 2019 : je l'en remercie vivement, toutes les erreurs restant de mon fait.

siècle av. J.-C. inscrivaient désormais leur action dans un conflit dynastique interne au pouvoir lagide (...) ; (ils) ne se réclamaient plus, comme leurs devanciers de la grande révolte un siècle plus tôt, d'un pharaon thébain, mais prenaient parti au sein d'un conflit dynastique entre prétendants macédoniens »[3].

# 1 État des sources

Les sources qui se rapportent directement aux troubles de l'année 88 sont à la fois bien connues et assez peu nombreuses. Elles relèvent de deux catégories bien différentes : d'un côté, les historiens peuvent s'appuyer sur un ensemble documentaire contemporain des événements, que l'on désignera ici comme « dossier pathyrite » ; de l'autre, sur un témoignage littéraire du IIe siècle de notre ère, celui de l'auteur grec Pausanias.

## 1.1 Le dossier pathyrite

Peu de choses sont connues de l'histoire de la petite ville de Pathyris, située à une trentaine de km au sud de Thèbes, avant le règne de Ptolémée VI. Au début de la Grande Révolte, l'autorité du pharaon « rebelle » (du point de vue du pouvoir lagide) Haronnophris y avait été reconnue : deux papyrus furent rédigés selon le comput de ses années régnales en 204[4]. Après la fin de cette révolte, Pathyris devint partie intégrante du dispositif de renforcement du contrôle ptolémaïque en Haute-Égypte. Entre 165 et 161, un camp militaire (*ochurôma*), subordonné au camp principal (*hupaithron*) implanté dans la ville voisine de Crocodilopolis, y fut établi et de nombreux Égyptiens recrutés en tant que *misthophoroi*, soldats recevant une solde, cette vitalité nouvelle se traduisant par un accroissement spectaculaire de la documentation papyrologique conservée[5].

Au cours de l'année 88, cinq lettres grecques furent adressées à divers destinataires pathyrites par un certain Platon, que l'on s'accorde à identifier comme

---

3 Agut, Moreno-García 2016, p. 725. Cette hypothèse avait déjà été envisagée par B. McGing (1997, p. 297–298 : « Events in the Thebaid around the year 88, however, do seem to constitute a revolt rather than just another outbreak of civil war – although there may be room for doubt about this » (...) « we might surmise in the Thebaid a mixture of local rivalry, different dynastic loyalties and straightforward revolt against the whole Ptolemaic administration »).
4 Voir Chaufray, Wegner 2016 : P. BM EA 10486 et *P. Ryl. Dem.* 32, respectivement datés de l'an 1 et de l'an 2 d'Haronnophris (27 septembre 204 ; entre le 12 novembre et le 11 décembre 204).
5 Pestman 1965 ; Vandorpe 2008 et 2014 ; Vandorpe, Waebens 2009.

stratège de Thébaïde[6]. Les deux premières (*SB* III 6300 et *P. Bour.* 10) ont été écrites par Platon le 28 mars 88 et datées selon le comput régnal de Ptolémée X (an 26, 16 Phamenoth). L'une a été adressée aux habitants de Pathyris, l'autre à un dénommé Nechthyris, exerçant des fonctions de commandement. Dans les deux cas, Platon informe ses correspondants qu'il vient de quitter Latopolis/Esna pour Pathyris, afin de parer à une situation critique dans la ville et/ou dans ses environs. Il intime en outre aux habitants de Pathyris d'assister Nechthyris jusqu'à ce que lui-même arrive sur les lieux. Il informe par ailleurs Nechthyris de l'envoi de ce courrier et lui enjoint de garder la place et les environs, tout en le mettant en garde contre ceux qui pourraient lui désobéir et s'engager dans une nouvelle sédition (*stasis*) :

***SB* III 6300**
Platon aux habitants de Pathyris ([τοῖς ἐν] Παθύρει [κ]ατοικ[οῦσι]), salut et bonne santé. Étant partis en toute hâte ([ἐξωρμη]κότες) de Latopolis pour parer à la situation présente, conformément aux intérêts de l'État ([κα]τὰ τὸ συμφ[έρον] τοῖς πράγμασι), nous avons jugé bon de vous le faire savoir, et de vous exhorter à garder vous-mêmes votre sang-froid (παρακαλέσαι εὐψυχο[τ]έρους ὑπάρχοντας ἐφ' ἑαυτῶν εἶνα[ι]) et à assister Nechthyris qui a été placé à votre tête (καὶ συγγίνεσθαι Νεχθύρει τῶι ἐφ' ὑμῶν τεταγμένωι) jusqu'à ce que nous soyons arrivés, aussi vite que possible (ὅτι τάχο[ς]), sur les lieux. [An 26], 16 [Pha]menoth.
*Verso* : Aux habitants de Pathyris.

***P. Bour.* 10**
Platon à Nechthyris, salut. Nous sommes partis en toute hâte (ἐξωρμήκα[μεν]) de Latopolis pour parer à la situation présente, conformément aux intérêts de l'État, et nous avons écrit aux habitants de t'assister. Tu feras bien de surveiller le lieu et d'être vigilant (καλῶς ποιήσεις συντηρῶν τὸν τόπον καὶ προϊστάμενος). Et quant à ceux qui s'aviseraient de ne pas t'obéir en s'engageant (?) dans une nouvelle (?)[7] sédition, de les mettre en sûreté ([το]ὺς

---

6 TM Arch 484 « Platon-correspondance » = Vandorpe, Waebens 2009, § 34a, p. 95–97. Voir Collart 1922 ; Van't Dack 1949 ; Mooren 1975, n°059 ; Mooren, Van't Dack 1981 ; Thomas 1975, p. 117–118 ; McGing, 1997, p. 298. Pour B. Laudenbach en revanche (Laudenbach 2024, p. 151–152), il est plus vraisemblable que l'auteur des lettres soit Platon le Jeune, sur lequel voir *infra*. Le stratège Platon (TM Per 12487) était probablement un descendant du Platon membre d'une grande famille alexandrine au IIe siècle : voir Coulon 2001, p. 99. Il est difficile de savoir si c'est lui, ou bien son fils (voir *infra*), qui se trouve mentionné dans le P. Heidelberg D 665 récemment publié par J. F. Quack (Quack 2022) et je remercie sincèrement Ralph Birk pour ses remarques à propos de ce document. Venue au jour via le marché des antiquités, « the Platon correspondence is not a private correspondence and was most probably kept in the archive of Pathyris' fortress or in another official archive of the town » (Vandorpe, Waebens 2009, p. 96). Faut-il rattacher à cette correspondance la mobilisation (πα[ράγ] γελμα) des soldats « qui sont avec Platon, parent et stratège », évoquée dans la quittance d'origine thébaine *O. Wilck.* 1535 ? (voir O. Krüger, *P. Ross. Georg.* II 10, p. 27–32). En l'absence d'une datation précise, il reste impossible de saisir le contexte dans lequel s'inscrit la mobilisation.
7 [δε]υτέραι στάσει ou [ὀξ]υτέραι στάσει : Laudenbach 2023.

δ' ἐπιχει[ροῦ]γτας μὴ [ὑπ]ακούειν σου [ . .]ҳτέραι στάσει [ . .] . ομένους [ἀσ]φαλισάμενος), jusqu'à ce que nous ayons accouru, aussi vite que possible, auprès de toi (ὅτι τάχος [ἐπι]βαλεῖν πρὸς σέ). Porte-toi bien. An 26, 16 Phamenoth.
*Verso* : À l'épistate (?) du Pathyrite[8] Nechthyris.

Une autre lettre fut écrite à Nechthyris deux jours plus tard seulement, le 30 mars (*P. Bour.* 11) , alors que Platon se trouvait vraisemblablement déjà en route vers Pathyris. Bien que son état très fragmentaire ne permette pas une traduction suivie, elle concerne à l'évidence des mesures d'approvisionnement :

**P. Bour. 11**
... Veille à ce que chacun de ceux qui sont auprès de toi (φρόντισον ὡς ἕ[κα]στος τῶν παρὰ [σο]ὶ[9]) ... une artabe de farine de blé à disposition (πυροῦ ἀρτάβην μ[ί]αν ἐν ἑτοίμωι) ... le pain (ὁ ἄρτος) ... l'orge (κριθή) ... [An 2]6, 18 Phamenoth.
Verso : À Nechthyris.

Une quatrième lettre (*P. Bad.* II 16) été adressée aux « prêtres » ainsi qu'aux autres gens à Pathyris. Ni le nom de l'expéditeur ni la date n'ont été conservées, mais, dans la mesure où le contenu est tout à fait similaire aux deux premières lettres écrites par Platon, il est vraisemblable qu'elle date de la même époque, et que le « seigneur roi » (*kurios basileus*) dont il y est question est toujours Ptolémée X Alexandre. Platon engage dans tous les cas ses correspondants à redoubler d'efforts afin d'assurer la sécurité de la place :

**P. Bad. II 16[10]**
... [j'approuve ?] ce que vous avez décidé ([τὰ] ὑφ' ὑμῶν κεχειροτογημένα). Vous ferez bien d'assister <Nechthyris qui a été placé à votre tête ?> (καλῶς ποιήσετε συγγεινόμενοι <Νεχθύρει τῶι ἐφ' ὑμῶν τεταγμένωι ?>) afin que la place reste sûre pour le seigneur roi (εἰς <τὸ> τὸν τόπον ἐν ἀσφαλείαι ὑπάρχοντα συντηρῆ<σαι> τοῦτον τῶι κυρίωι βασιλεῖ). Car en agissant ainsi, et en maintenant avec soin votre loyauté vis-à-vis des affaires de l'État (τὴν πρὸς τὰ πράγμα[τα εὔ]γοιαν δ[ι]ατηροῦντες) ... vous recevrez une gratitude appropriée (?) de

---

**8** ἐπισ(τάτῃ? τοῦ) Παθυ(ρίτου) Νεχθύρει : Laudenbach 2023 et Laudenbach 2024 (prev. ed. ἀπό-δ(ος) Νεχθύρει). Je remercie vivement Benoît Laudenbach pour m'avoir communiqué sa nouvelle lecture, ainsi que pour ses autres remarques concernant cet article. Pour les fonctions exercées par Nechthyris, voir Laudenbach 2024, p. 145–151.
**9** Selon la nouvelle lecture de B. Laudenbach, à paraître.
**10** Les premières lignes conservées de ce papyrus posent d'ardus problèmes de grammaire et de compréhension. Nous avons ici repris les corrections d'U. Wilcken (1924, p. 304), qui permettent de donner un sens satisfaisant à l'ensemble mais n'ont pas été introduites dans la *DDBDP*, sans doute en raison des remarques de F. Bilabel, *BL* II 173–174 (lequel ne propose cependant pas d'alternative) : restitution du groupe oublié <Νεχθύρει τῶι ἐφ' ὑμῶν τεταγμένωι> ; correction de εἰς τῶτον τόπον en εἰς <τὸ> τὸν τόπον ; correction de συντηρηθῆναι en συντηρῆσαι, le τοῦτον qui suit se rapportant à Nechthyris. Manifestement, plusieurs constructions grammaticales se sont télescopées, ce qui peut refléter l'urgence dans laquelle la lettre a été écrite.

la part de ceux qui sont au-dessus (de nous) (παρὰ τῶν [ἐ]πάνω [χάριτος πρεπ]ρύσης ἐπι [τεύξεσθε]).
Verso : Aux prêtres[11] et aux autres (gens) à Pathyris (τοῖς ἐν Παθύρει ἱ[ερεῦσι] καὶ τοῖς ἄλλο[ις]).

La cinquième lettre enfin (*P. Bour.* 12) 12 a été écrite le 1er novembre 88 et datée cette fois selon les années régnales de Ptolémée IX (an 30, 19 Phaophi). Platon, qui a désormais changé de camp, informe les « prêtres et les habitants de Pathyris » que Ptolémée IX est arrivé à Memphis et qu'il a désigné Hiérax pour subjuguer la Thébaïde « avec de très grandes forces » :

**P. Bour. 12**
Platon, aux prêtres et aux autres habitants de Pathyris (τοῖς ἐν Παθύρει ἱερεῦσι καὶ τοῖς ἄλλοις τοῖς κατοικοῦσι), salut. Notre frère Philoxénos nous a écrit, dans une lettre que nous a apportée Orsès, que le très grand roi Dieu Sôter (τὸν μέγιστον Θεὸν Σωτῆρα βασιλέα) est arrivé à Memphis, et que Hiérax a été chargé de soumettre la Thébaïde avec de très grandes forces (Ἱέρακα δὲ προκεχειρίσθαι μετὰ δυνάμεων μυρίων ἐπὶ καταστολὴν τῆς Θηβαίδος). Nous avons jugé bon de vous en informer afin que, sachant cela, vous gardiez bon courage (εὐθαρσεῖς ὑπάρχητε). An 30, le 19 Phaophi.
Verso : Aux prêtres et aux autres (gens) à Pathyris.

Nous ignorons à quand remonte le changement d'allégeance de Platon[12], mais la manière dont ce dernier désigne Ptolémée IX dans sa dernière lettre nous semble bien en tout cas refléter son insécurité personnelle : lui qui qualifiait Ptolémée X (pensons-nous) de « seigneur roi » (τῶι κυρίωι βασιλεῖ) dans le *P. Bad.* II 16 présente désormais le nouveau détenteur du trône comme « le très grand roi Dieu

---

[11] Le premier éditeur du papyrus, F. Bilabel (*P. Bad.* II, p. 24), avait estimé que la lettre était adressée à des prêtres thébains loyaux réfugiés dans la ville de Pathyris. Cependant, le texte ne donne aucun indice allant en ce sens, et le reste de la documentation indique que la situation à Thèbes était normale au moins jusqu'à juin 88 (voir *infra*). À vrai dire, le terme même ἱ[ερεῦσι] est réduit à un iota, mais la restitution est assurée par le prescrit du papyrus.

[12] Le Nechthyris commandant de place à Pathyris (voire de tout le nome pathyrite, cf. note 8 *supra*), TM Per 10672, doit-il être identifié au Nechthyris, fils de Psenmonthes (TM Per 57245) qui apparaît dans le *P. Conflict* 5 = TM 160, à l'époque du conflit syro-judéo-égyptien de 103–101 (voir Van't Dack *et al.* 1989, p. 66) et/ou au Nechthyris mentionné dans le *ZÄS* 42 (1905), p. 52–53 (P. Heidelberg Dem. 750a = TM 224 ; TM Per 16132) ? Ce dernier document est une lettre fragmentaire probablement trouvée à Pathyris et adressée au « premier *mr mšꜥ* d'Égypte » et « au /au fils du ? *mr mšꜥ* Nechthyris » à une date correspondant au 7 juillet 88 selon U. Kaplony-Heckel : [an 2?]9, 27 Pauni (voir Van't Dack *et al.* 1989, p. 145 ; *DBL*, 2005, p. 735 ; Vandorpe, Waebens 2009, p. 97). L'incertitude concernant la décennie régnale rend cependant son interprétation délicate. Dans tous les cas, si le basculement en faveur de Ptolémée IX avait eu lieu avant l'été à Pathyris, il est difficile de comprendre comment les documents pathyrites ont pu continuer à être datés selon les années de règne de Ptolémée X en août et jusqu'au début de septembre (*Forschungen und Berichte* 10 (1968), p. 145, n° 9 = TM 389 ; *P. Amh.* II 51 : voir tableau *infra*).

Sôter » (τὸν μέγιστον Θεὸν Σωτῆρα βασιλέα), en une surenchère de loyauté[13]. On notera aussi que Platon n'a été informé du retour du roi qu'indirectement, par son « frère » Philoxénos, et qu'il n'est pas chargé des opérations ni même associé à elles[14]. Son fils, « Platon le jeune », a pourtant réussi à poursuivre sa carrière sous Ptolémée IX, au moins jusqu'en septembre 87[15] : faut-il en déduire que Platon père a échappé à la disgrâce ?

Ce Platon le jeune a aussi adressé aux *presbuteroi* de Pathyris une lettre datée selon le règne du nouveau roi le 27 novembre 88 (*P. Ross. Georg.* II 10 : an 30, 15 Hathyr). À en juger par le contenu de cette dernière, qui concerne une affaire d'importance mineure, la situation semble avoir été calme à cette date dans la ville, de même que dans le nome (ou le district) Eileithyiaspolite, situé plus au sud[16]. Une toute autre impression se dégage pourtant des dernières pièces composant le « dossier pathyrite ». Le *P. Ross. Georg.* II 10 est en effet l'un des tout derniers papyrus à avoir été trouvés à Pathyris ; après lui, la documentation, si riche depuis l'établissement de la garnison dans les années 160, s'interrompt quasi-totalement[17]. Au cours des années qui suivirent, le nome pathyrite disparut même en tant qu'entité administrative et le territoire correspondant fut intégré dans le nouveau nome hermonthite[18]. Des blocs provenant du temple de Sobek à Crocodilopolis, la ville abritant la garnison-mère de celle de Pathyris, furent également réutilisés pour construire les fondations du lac sacré de Tôd[19]. La quasi-disparition de la documentation papyrologique à Pathyris et le démantèlement du temple de Crocodilopolis forment donc un tout cohérent, indiquant que les deux villes se vidèrent de l'essentiel de leurs habitants après 88[20].

---

[13] Peut-être faut-il d'ailleurs comprendre μέγιστος plutôt comme un superlatif relatif de supériorité : « le plus grand roi », Ptolémée X étant le moins grand.

[14] Voir Collart 1922, p. 281.

[15] Sur ce personnage (TM Per 81167), né d'un mariage contracté par le stratège Platon avec une Égyptienne, voir Coulon 2001 ; Birk 2020, p. 445–447 ; Birk 2023, p. 120–128. Platon le jeune supervisait encore le paiement des taxes dues par les temples d'Eileithyaspolis/Elkab le 8 septembre 87, un an donc après la restauration de Ptolémée IX : *BGU* XIV 2378 (an 30, 30 Mésorè, cf. *BL* XI 32).

[16] L'affaire concerne la restitution d'une ânesse et de son petit, illégalement saisis par l'épistate de l'Eileithyiaspolite et amenés à Pathyris : voir Vandorpe, Waebens 2009, p. 96.

[17] Pestman 1965, p. 51 ; Vandorpe 1995, p. 235 ; Vandorpe, Waebens 2009, p. 50. Seuls un à deux papyrus de provenance pathyrite pourraient dater du règne de Ptolémée XII : le *P. Cairo* II 30768 + *P. Cairo* II 30771 = TM 460 et possiblement le *P. Cairo* II 30670 = TM 402.

[18] Calderini 1973–1977 (vol. II), p. 177 et 1983–1986 (vol. IV), p. 17–18. Voir Devauchelle, Grenier 1982, p. 165 ; Vandorpe, Waebens 2009, p. 50; Eller 2022, p. 92–96.

[19] Voir Devauchelle, Grenier 1982.

[20] Cf. Devauchelle, Grenier 1982, p. 162, n. 1 : « Il n'est pas besoin d'insister sur le rôle administratif et, surtout, économique que le temple a dans sa ville pour se rendre compte que la disparition matérielle de celui-là est la preuve la plus évidente du déclin de celle-ci ». Pour les deux

## 1.2 Pausanias

L'autre source majeure sur les événements de Haute-Égypte/Thébaïde est Pausanias, dont la *Description de la Grèce* a été composée au IIe siècle de notre ère. Parmi les réflexions que lui ont inspiré les statues des rois lagides élevées devant l'Odéon à Athènes, il dit quelques mots de la fuite de Ptolémée X et la restauration de Ptolémée IX sur le trône d'Égypte en 88 :

> Cléopâtre (III) subit le châtiment de l'exil qu'elle avait imposé à Ptolémée (IX), elle fut tuée (ἀποθανοῦσαν) par Alexandre qu'elle avait elle-même fait roi d'Égypte. Mais, l'acte ayant été découvert, et Alexandre s'étant enfui par peur des Alexandrins[21] (καὶ Ἀλεξάνδρου φόβῳ τῶν πολιτῶν φεύγοντος), Ptolémée revint et tint l'Égypte pour la seconde fois. Il fit la guerre aux Thébains révoltés (Θηβαίοις ἐπολέμησεν ἀποστᾶσι) et, les ayant soumis la troisième année après la défection (ἔτει τρίτῳ μετὰ τὴν ἀπόστασιν), il les châtia au point de ne leur laisser aucun vestige de leur prospérité de jadis (ἐκάκωσεν, ὡς μηδὲ ὑπόμνημα λειφθῆναι Θηβαίοις τῆς ποτε εὐδαιμονίας), prospérité telle pourtant que cette ville dépassa en richesse les Grecs les plus riches, le sanctuaire de Delphes, et les Orchoméniens. Ptolémée subit peu de temps après le destin qui convenait, mais les Athéniens qui avaient reçu de lui tant de bienfaits, qu'il n'est pas nécessaire de rappeler, lui consacrèrent une statue en bronze, ainsi qu'à Bérénice, le seul enfant légitime qu'il eut. (*Périégèse*, I, 9, 3)[22]

La manière dont Pausanias présente ici les conditions du retour de Ptolémée IX en Égypte incite immédiatement à considérer ce passage avec prudence. D'une part, le fait que Ptolémée X ait assassiné sa mère Cléopâtre III (avec laquelle il régnait en association depuis 107) reste à prouver. Les papyrus et les monnaies permettent de placer la disparition de la reine en septembre 101[23] : elle était alors âgée et aurait somme toute très bien pu mourir de mort naturelle[24], d'autant

---

auteurs, il est possible que le temple de Pathyris ait subi le même sort que celui de Crocodilopolis (p. 160 et 168).

21 Pausanias dit « *politai* » : veut-il parler des habitants d'Alexandrie en général ou des citoyens de manière spécifique ? Nous avons préféré rendre le terme par « Alexandrins ».

22 Trad. adaptée de J. Pouilloux (CUF).

23 La première attestation d'un protocole mentionnant Ptolémée X et son épouse Cléopâtre Bérénice III est le *P. Adler. Gr.* 12, datant du 26 octobre 101. Le document étant d'origine pathyrite, il faut néanmoins prendre en compte les délais de communication depuis Alexandrie. D'après le témoignage des monnaies, la reine était probablement déjà morte au 16 septembre 101 : Mørkholm 1975, p. 12–13.

24 Voir Cuénod 2021, p. 201–202. Ptolémée IX étant vraisemblablement né aux environs de 142 (voir Bennett 2013, « Ptolemy IX », n. 5), Cléopâtre III approchait de la soixantaine. On pourra objecter que l'assassinat de la reine par son fils est également rapporté par Athénée (XII 73) et par Justin (XXXIX, 4) mais l'argument ne nous semble pas déterminant : comme l'a écrit A. E. Samuel (Samuel 1965, p. 381), « (it) might have been contemporary propaganda, or could even have later crept into the account ». L'assassinat de Cléopâtre Bérénice III par Ptolémée XI en 80 pour-

qu'elle venait de mener une campagne éprouvante en Syrie[25]. D'autre part et surtout, il est encore moins vraisemblable que ce meurtre ait pu être l'élément déclencheur d'un soulèvement des Alexandrins contre le roi treize ans plus tard[26]. De fait, Porphyre de Tyr livre une version des faits différente, sur laquelle nous reviendrons ci-après[27].

Une autre difficulté concerne les indications chronologiques données par Pausanias à propos cette fois de la guerre que Ptolémée IX, une fois de retour en Égypte, eut à mener « contre les Thébains révoltés ». Ces dernières ne sont pas, en effet, faciles à articuler, ni avec les lettres de Platon, ni avec le reste de la documentation thébaine. Selon Pausanias, la révolte a duré plus de deux ans, s'éteignant « la troisième année après la défection » (ἔτει τρίτῳ μετὰ τὴν ἀπόστασιν). Dans les lettres écrites par Platon en mars 88 (*SB* III 6300, *P. Bour.* 10, *P. Bour.* 11 et vraisemblablement aussi *P. Bad.* II 16), il n'était pas encore question d'un soulèvement général en Haute-Égypte ; de fait, au vu de l'empressement que Platon manifeste à venir de Latopolis à Pathyris[28], il est probable qu'il se serait déplacé plus tôt dans le cas contraire[29]. La Thébaïde était bien en révolte en revanche au 1ᵉʳ novembre 88, quand Hiérax fut chargé de soumettre la région avec une grande armée (*P. Bour.* 12). À Thèbes même, la situation semble avoir été normale au moins jusqu'au 5 juin 88, quand un dernier reçu bancaire a été daté selon le règne de Ptolémée X (*O. Bodl.* I 199) . Il semble donc que le soulèvement toucha la ville au début de l'automne 88, mais la date à laquelle il fut écrasé est plus difficile à établir.

---

rait avoir contribué à donner du crédit à la thèse d'un assassinat préalable de Cléopâtre III par Ptolémée X.
25 La présence de Cléopâtre III en Syrie lors du conflit syro-judéo-égyptien est rapportée par Flavius Josèphe, *Antiquités Juives* XIII 348–355, et confirmée par la statue du général Petimouthes (Van't Dack *et al.* 1989, p. 88–108).
26 Cf. Van't Dack *et al.* 1989, p. 140.
27 L'ouvrage dans lequel Porphyre traitait des monarchies hellénistiques est connu par la *Chronique* d'Eusèbe, dont on possède des fragments grecs (*Eusebi Chronicorum liber prior*, éd. A. Schoene, Berlin, 1875 : https://archive.org/details/EusebiusChroniconEd.SchoenePetermann/mode/2up, consulté le 30 août 2024) et une version arménienne complète (traduction latine de H. Petermann dans l'éd. Schoene ; traduction allemande de J. Karst reprise par F. Jacoby, *FGrHist*. II B 260 F2 8–9 ; traduction française d'A. Ouzounian, Les Belles Lettres, 2020). Voir Van't Dack *et al.* 1989, p. 138–143.
28 Cf. [ἐξωρμη]κότες / ἐξωρμήκα[μεν] [ἐ]κ Λάτων πόλ[εως] : « nous sommes partis en toute hâte (litt. nous nous sommes élancés) de Latopolis » ; μέχρι τοῦ [καὶ ἡμᾶ]ς ὅτι τάχο[ς παρεῖ]ναι τοῖς τόπο[ις] / [μέ]χρι τοῦ καὶ [ἡμᾶ]ς ὅτι τάχος [ἐπι]βαλεῖν πρὸς σέ : « jusqu'à ce que nous soyons arrivés, aussi vite que possible sur les lieux » / « jusqu'à ce que nous ayons accouru, aussi vite que possible, auprès de toi ».
29 En ce sens Collart 1922, p. 278 ; McGing 1997, p. 298.

Si l'on suit Pausanias, ce soulèvement aurait duré au moins jusqu'à la fin de l'année 86 ou le début de l'année 85 (deux années pleines + un nombre de mois indéterminé). Deux éléments amènent cependant à s'interroger sur la validité de cette information. Sont à considérer en premier lieu deux proscynèmes gravés sur les murs du temple d'Amon à Louxor, datés d'un « an 30 » que Jean Bingen a réattribué au règne de Ptolémée IX, sur des critères paléographiques[30] : ces inscriptions témoigneraient donc d'une restauration de l'autorité du roi dans la ville au plus tard à l'été 87, le premier datant en ce cas d'une période comprise entre le 11 juin et le 10 juillet (*SB* XVIII 13678 : [...] Pauni de l'an 30), le second du 26 juillet 87 (*SB* XVIII 13675 : 16 Epeiph de l'an 30)[31]. L'autre élément à verser au dossier est la possible célébration d'une fête-*sed* pour Ptolémée IX après son rétablissement en Égypte, antique cérémonie par laquelle la puissance royale conférée par le rite d'intronisation se trouvait renouvelée au terme d'une période de trente ans. Pourraient en effet être interprétées en ce sens certaines des nouvelles formulations du protocole du pharaon[32], un passage du texte historique du temple d'Edfou[33] et une stèle démotique du Sérapeum datée du 24 mars 86 (12 Phamenoth de l'an 31)[34]. Si l'on admet la réalité de cette célébration[35], on supposera aussi qu'elle fut motivée par le fait que la restauration définitive du roi sur son trône eut lieu la trentième année de son règne, débuté en 116 : coïncidence heureuse avec la durée séparant (en théorie du moins) le couronnement pharaonique et la tenue d'une fête-*sed*[36]. Mais cette cérémonie implique aussi, à notre sens, que la paix ait été précédemment rétablie sur

---

30 Bingen 1986, p. 332. Cf. Cowey 2000, p. 244.
31 Le *BGU* XVIII.1 2747 (86) peut être écarté du débat : voir Armoni 2001. Si le reçu *O. Theb. Gr.* 30 date bien lui aussi du règne de Ptolémée IX, la restauration de l'autorité du roi à Thèbes serait même antérieure au mois de mars 87 (an 30 ?, 1 Phamenoth).
32 Voir Traunecker 2013, p. 180–182 : « qui renouvelle (*wḥm*) les apparitions » (nom d'Horus ; précédemment « saint d'apparitions ») ; « Seigneur des très nombreuses fêtes-*sed* comme Ptah-Tatenen (nom d'Horus d'or ; précédemment « seigneur des fêtes-*sed* de Ptah-Tatenen »).
33 *Edfou* VII, 9, 8 : « Puis il (Ptolémée X) s'enfuit vers le pays d'Opôné et son frère aîné prit possession de l'Égypte et apparut de nouveau comme roi » (trad. De Wit 1961, p. 294) ; « Il s'enfuit vers Pount, et son frère aîné prit possession de l'Égypte et fut couronné à nouveau comme roi » (trad. Cauville, Devauchelle 1984, p. 52). Voir également Traunecker 1979, p. 429–430.
34 Brugsch 1886, p. 32–33 (n° 50*b*) (TM 99568) : « Im Jahre 31 des Königs Ptolemäus, welcher den Beinamen führt : der 'Sieger, welcher zum zweitenmale die königliche Herrschaft und das Diadem der Isis und des Osiris übernahm im Jahre 11 des lebenden Apis (...)' ».
35 Ainsi Bergman 1968, p. 110 ; Van't Dack *et al.* 1989, p. 150 ; Hölbl 2001, p. 212 ; Thompson 2012, p. 116; Habachy 2023, p. 231 et p. 234.
36 Cf. Bergman 1968, p. 114, n. 3.

l'ensemble du territoire égyptien[37] et donc, à nouveau, que la révolte thébaine ait été terminée avant les deux ans et quelques évoqués par Pausanias[38]. Selon l'éclairante hypothèse de M. Chauveau[39], Pausanias pourrait bien avoir été trompé par le fait que la révolte commença dans la 27e année du règne de Ptolémée X (débutant officiellement le 14 septembre 88, alors que le roi était déjà en exil, voir *infra*) et se termina la 30e année de Ptolémée IX (14 septembre 88 – 13 septembre 87), c'est-à-dire dans la « troisième année », mais d'un règne différent[40]. On ignore tout des sources auxquelles Pausanias, bien éloigné dans le temps et dans l'espace des événements qu'il rapporte, a puisé pour son récit. Sa confusion s'expliquerait d'autant mieux si, comme le fait n'est pas invraisemblable, il a utilisé des données similaires à celles utilisées par Porphyre / Eusèbe, dans lesquelles les faits marquants de l'histoire ptolémaïque étaient consignés en fonction des années de règne des souverains[41].

Un troisième problème enfin concerne l'importance de la répression à laquelle a été soumise la ville de Thèbes. Pour Pausanias, « aucun vestige de la prospérité de jadis » n'aurait été laissé à ses habitants par Ptolémée IX. Comme l'ont relevé plusieurs auteurs, cette affirmation doit cependant être nuancée[42]. Tout d'abord, des travaux furent menés au nom de Ptolémée IX après sa restauration sur le trône d'Égypte, aussi bien à Medinet Habou qu'à Karnak même[43], et d'autres furent par la suite effectués sous Ptolémée XII[44]. D'autre part, quoique la documentation papyrologique thébaine diminue effectivement de manière significative après 88[45], le décret passé par les prêtres d'Amon en l'honneur du stratège Kallimachos vers 39

---

[37] Nous révisons donc sur ce point notre opinion de 2004.
[38] On pourrait objecter que le couronnement de Ptolémée V à Memphis en 196 a également eu lieu à une période de révolte. Cependant, le contexte était tout à fait différent et le couronnement nécessité par le fait que le jeune roi venait d'accéder à la majorité.
[39] Nous remercions sincèrement Michel Chauveau, qui nous a autorisé à présenter ici cette hypothèse inédite.
[40] Dans cette hypothèse, le soulèvement de grande ampleur destiné à être réprimé par Hiérax aurait donc débuté entre le 14 septembre (début de la 27e année de règne théorique de Ptolémée X) et le 1er novembre 88 (date du *P. Bour.* 12) .
[41] Le passage dans lequel Porphyre , cité par Eusèbe, décompte les années régnales de Ptolémée IX et Ptolémée X montre à quel point l'imbrication complexe des computs des deux souverains était susceptible de créer de la confusion chez des observateurs extérieurs : voir Porphyre / Eusèbe, éd. Schoene, p. 166 pour la version grecque et Ouzounian 2020, p. 153, § 4 pour la version arménienne.
[42] Ainsi Vandorpe 1995, p. 235 ; Ritner 2011, p. 104–107 ; Traunecker 2013, p. 225 ; Thiers 2015, p. 351–352.
[43] La datation des monuments repose sur l'évolution de la titulature officielle entre le premier et le second règne de Ptolémée IX : voir Cassor-Pfeiffer 2008 ; Ritner 2011 ; Traunecker 2013 ; Thiers 2015 ; Habachy 2023.
[44] Hölbl 2001, p. 276.
[45] Cf. Clarysse 1984, p. 25 ; Vandorpe 1995, p. 235 ; Arlt 2011, p. 25–28.

(*OGIS* I 194 ; *I. Prose* 46) témoigne d'une certaine vitalité de la cité encore à cette date[46].

On retiendra à tout le moins le fait que, tandis que dans sa cinquième lettre Platon mentionnait en termes généraux une campagne contre « la Thébaïde », susceptible de concerner différents lieux de Haute-Égypte, Pausanias se réfère explicitement à une révolte survenue à Thèbes en particulier. Reste à tenter de déterminer les causes de cette révolte, sur lesquelles lui-même ne s'exprime pas.

## 2 Quelles furent les causes des troubles dans le Pathyrite et à Thèbes ?

Il ne fait guère de doute que le « dossier pathyrite » – dans lequel nous incluons aussi la disparition de la documentation papyrologique après 88 – doit être interprété dans le contexte de la lutte pour le pouvoir entre Ptolémée IX et Ptolémée X. Nous commencerons donc par en rapporter les principales étapes, en faisant débuter notre exposé à la mort de Ptolémée VIII en 116.

### 2.1 Le conflit dynastique entre Ptolémée IX et Ptolémée X

Phase 1 – les prémices de la guerre fratricide : les années 116 à 107
En 116, Ptolémée IX, l'aîné des enfants de Ptolémée VIII et Cléopâtre III, avait succédé à son père dans le cadre d'un règne conjoint avec sa mère[47], la reine exerçant

---

[46] Voir Hutmacher 1965, Heinen 2006 et Caneva, Pfeiffer dans le présent volume. Les prêtres d'Amon sont en effet en mesure de promulguer un décret, de le faire inscrire sur pierre en grec et en démotique, et de décider l'érection de trois statues en l'honneur du stratège, deux en pierre et une en bronze. Ils louent par ailleurs la générosité et la piété manifestées par Kallimachos à l'occasion de famines successives, et rappellent également les actions bienfaisantes déjà accomplies par son grand-père (« depuis que le père de son père Kallimachos, parent du roi et épistratège, [a restauré] les processions des dieux souverains ainsi que les panégyries, de très belle et sainte manière, comme dans les temps passés », l. 24–25). Le fait que cette restauration des fêtes religieuses ait elle-même été une conséquence, directe ou indirecte, de la révolte de 88 est une hypothèse tentante. Elle reste cependant fragile dans l'impossibilité où nous sommes de dater précisément la période d'activité du grand-père en question.

[47] Il est possible que Ptolémée IX ait régné durant quelques mois en association avec sa mère Cléopâtre III et sa grand-mère Cléopâtre II, jusqu'à la disparition de cette dernière : voir Chauveau 1998, p. 1273, n. 32 ; Bielman Sánchez, Lenzo 2015, p. 395–396 ; Cuénod 2021, p. 129–132. On admet généralement, en suivant Pausanias (I, 9,1) et Justin (XXXIX, 3), que Cléopâtre III n'accepta qu'à

une position de prééminence comme le montrent les protocoles officiels ; quant au cadet, Ptolémée X, il fut d'abord envoyé gouverner Chypre en qualité de stratège puis il s'y proclama roi en 114/3 – sans susciter apparemment d'opposition de la part d'Alexandrie[48]. Au début de l'automne 107, l'association entre mère et fils tourna à la rupture. Pausanias et Justin en attribuent la responsabilité à la seule Cléopâtre III : la reine souleva les Alexandrins contre Ptolémée IX (en leur faisant croire qu'elle avait fait l'objet d'une tentative de meurtre d'après le récit de Pausanias)[49]. Porphyre lui aussi évoque une déposition orchestrée par Cléopâtre III, mais précise qu'elle fit suite à l'assassinat, par Ptolémée IX, « des amis de ses parents » (cf. τοὺς φίλους τῶν γονέων ἀπέσφαξεν) en l'an 10 de son règne (108/107)[50]. Une inscription trouvée à Cyrène (*IGCyr* 011100) apporte du crédit à cette version des faits : elle porte en effet une lettre adressée aux Cyrénéens le 8 avril 108 par Ptolémée IX et son épouse Cléopâtre (col. B II), ainsi qu'un *prostagma* de portée générale émis par les mêmes souverains (col. B III) : l'absence de Cléopâtre III dans ces deux documents laisse penser que Ptolémée IX s'efforçait à cette époque d'évincer sa mère du pouvoir[51]. Le rapport de force finit néanmoins par tourner à son désavantage et il fut contraint de quitter Alexandrie à l'automne 107[52]. L'épisode donna lieu à un chassé-croisé entre les deux frères : Ptolémée X partit de Chypre, via Péluse[53], pour régner avec sa mère en Égypte ; Ptolémée IX réussit, sans doute après un passage

---

contre-cœur l'accession de son fils aîné au pouvoir, sous la pression des Alexandrins, après avoir tenté d'imposer son fils cadet ; pour Porphyre cependant (*apud* Eusèbe, éd. Schoene, p. 163–164), Cléopâtre III désigna elle-même Ptolémée IX comme associé au trône et le favorisa pendant un temps.

48 Voir Graslin-Thomé, Veïsse 2021, p. 419.
49 Pausanias, I, 9, 1–2 ; Justin, XXXIX, 4, 1–2.
50 Porphyre *apud* Eusèbe, éd. Schoene, p. 164, version grecque : « Vers l'an 10 de son règne il tua les amis de ses parents et fut, à cause de sa conduite cruelle, renversé du pouvoir sur ordre de sa mère et contraint de se réfugier à Chypre ».
51 Le *prostagma*, qui porte sur le sort des biens vacants ou objets d'un litige, vaut en effet pour l'ensemble du royaume et pas seulement pour Cyrène. On pourra également mentionner le fait que, selon Flavius Josèphe, Ptolémée IX envoya au début de l'année 109 des troupes à Antiochos IX « malgré sa mère, qui faillit le détrôner » (*Antiquités juives*, XIII, 10, 2). Voir Graslin-Thomé, Veïsse 2021, p. 419–420 et Veïsse 2022b, p. 141–142.
52 Le premier témoignage du règne conjoint de Cléopâtre III et Ptolémée X date du 30 octobre ou du 2 novembre 107 (*P. Dion.* 18 = *Pap. Lugd. Bat.* XXII 18). À en juger par les monnaies, le changement de souverain pourrait avoir eu lieu avant le 19 septembre 107 : Mørkholm 1975, p. 12.
53 D'après Porphyre, *apud* Eusèbe, éd. Schoene, p. 163–164, Cléopâtre III fit venir son fils cadet de la ville de Péluse et l'établit comme roi avec elle. À l'époque de la guerre contre Cléopâtre II, c'est aussi à Péluse que Ptolémée VIII avait débarqué pour mener la lutte contre sa sœur après avoir été contraint de se réfugier à Chypre : voir Cuénod, Olivier 2020, p. 212–213 et n. 70 ; Lanciers 2020, p. 48–49.

par la Syrie, à conquérir l'île pour son propre compte tout en maintenant aussi pendant quelques années (sans doute jusqu'à 101) la souveraineté sur Cyrène[54].

Phase 2 – les tentatives de Ptolémée IX pour se rétablir en Égypte entre 107 et 88
Après son expulsion d'Alexandrie en 107, Ptolémée IX ne se résigna pas à son sort. Bien au contraire, il tenta de se rétablir par la force en Égypte, une première fois à l'époque du conflit syro-judéo-égyptien des années 103–101 (« Guerre des Sceptres »)[55], puis probablement à nouveau dans les années 90.

À propos du premier de ces épisodes, Flavius Josèphe rapporte que Ptolémée IX réussit à franchir la frontière égyptienne après sa campagne en Judée, avant d'être chassé du pays par la contre-offensive de Cléopâtre III et de s'en retourner hiverner à Gaza[56]. En 1991, un papyrus démotique publié par E.-H. Zaghloul est venu éclairer d'un autre jour la politique égyptienne du roi en exil[57] : ce contrat de vente provenant de Hout Nesout, au nord de Mallawi, est en effet daté de l'« An 16, 2 Tybi, du roi Ptolémée, le dieu qui sauve, avec ceux qui sont sur le registre du prince (*wr*) d'Alexandrie (Rhakotis)[58] » (P. Mallawi inv. 602/7, TM 47353). A cette date, correspondant au 17 janvier 101, l'autorité de Ptolémée IX était donc reconnue en ce lieu au moins de Moyenne-Égypte, tandis que sa mère et son frère tenaient toujours l'essentiel du pays. Alors que le récit de Flavius Josèphe pouvait laisser penser à une simple incursion limitée aux environs de Péluse, le P. Mallawi montre donc que le roi a réussi à pénétrer plus avant dans la *chôra*, ou tout au moins à y dépêcher des troupes[59].

---

54 Voir Van't Dack *et al.* 1989, p. 24 et p. 33. La date exacte de la reconquête de Chypre doit probablement se situer à l'été 105 d'après Bennett 2013, « Ptolemy IX », n. 13. Pour Cyrène, voir Bagnall 1972, p. 363–368 ; Veïsse 2022b, p. 142–143
55 Sur ce conflit, voir Van't Dack *et al.* 1989 et l'étude à venir de M. Chauveau.
56 *Antiquités juives* XIII, 351–352 : « Ptolémée, partant de Syrie, se dirigea en toute hâte sur l'Égypte, pensant la trouver dégarnie de troupes et s'en emparer par surprise. Mais son espoir fut déçu. Vers le même temps, Chelkias, l'un des deux généraux de Cléopâtre, mourut en Coelé-Syrie en poursuivant Ptolémée. Cléopâtre, à la nouvelle de la tentative de son fils et de la déconvenue qu'il avait éprouvée en Égypte, envoya une partie de ses troupes pour le chasser du pays. Ptolémée, se retirant d'Égypte, passa l'hiver à Gaza, Cléopâtre, pendant ce temps, s'empara, après un siège en règle, de la garnison de Ptolémaïs et de la ville elle-même » (trad. J. Chamonard).
57 Zaghloul 1991.
58 Selon la relecture du protocole par M. Chauveau.
59 Plus problématique est l'interprétation du *P. Lüdd. Hawara* XIX a-b (TM 41474), un contrat démotique pourvu d'une souscription grecque (*SB* XXIV 16161), daté du 22 Phaophi de l'an 15 de Ptolémée IX (« le dieu qui sauve »). S'il s'agit bien du 8 novembre 103 (ainsi Huss 2006), le document indiquerait que l'autorité du roi avait également été reconnue un an et demi plus tôt à l'entrée du Fayoum. Pour E. Lüddeckens cependant (Lüddeckens *et al.* 1998, p. 208–209), le document doit être daté de l'année 85 : le scribe aurait considéré l'année du retour de Ptolémée IX en Égypte (88), comme l'an 12 de son règne, en faisant omission de la période de son exil à partir de

On peut à ce propos se demander si le pillage du sarcophage d'Alexandre, rapporté par Strabon, ne devrait pas être mis à l'actif de Ptolémée IX plutôt que de Ptolémée X, et rattaché à ces mêmes événements[60]. Dans un passage de sa description d'Alexandrie, Strabon affirme en effet que le « Ptolémée appelé *Kokkès* et *Pareisactos* (ὁ Κόκκης καὶ Παρείσακτος ἐπικληθεὶς Πτολεμαῖος), ayant fait marche depuis la Syrie (ἐκ τῆς Συρίας ἐπελθών), s'en empara, mais fut aussitôt chassé, si bien qu'il ne tira pas profit de son pillage » (XVII, 1, 8). Quoiqu'elle soit communément admise, l'identification de ce roi pillard à Ptolémée X est en effet loin d'être certaine. À première vue, elle semble trouver confirmation dans un passage de la *Chronique Pascale*, chronique byzantine rédigée au VIIe siècle et qui présente, à la manière de Porphyre / Eusèbe mais sous une forme plus abrégée encore, les règnes des souverains hellénistiques[61]. Ptolémée X y est effectivement présenté comme « le fils de Ptolémée, le second Évergète, et de mère *Kokkè* »[62]. Cependant, puisque le surnom *Kokkè* se rapporte ici clairement à Cléopâtre III, Ptolémée IX pourrait, tout aussi bien que son frère, avoir été affublé du surnom (moqueur et probablement injurieux) de « *Kokkès* »[63]. On peut même voir en lui un meilleur candidat, dans la mesure où il est bien difficile de situer dans le

---

107 (an 11). Il s'agirait néanmoins d'une pratique bien exceptionnelle, dans la mesure où tous les documents émis sous le second règne de Ptolémée IX ont été datés dans la continuité du premier (88 = an 29), y compris à Hawara (cf. *P. Lüdd. Hawara* XX : 84 = an 33). Les archives des embaumeurs d'Hawara, auxquelles le document appartient (TM Arch 359, voir Uytterhoeven 2009, p. 340–347) semblent pourtant rendre une datation dans les années 80 plus probable qu'une datation en 103 (cf. TM 41474), mais elles n'excluent pas non plus totalement cette dernière.

60 Cette hypothèse, déjà avancée par M. L. Strack (1897, p. 221), a été à nouveau considérée par M. Chauveau lors de ses séminaires tenus à l'EPHE en 2019.

61 Ed. L. Dindorf, 1832 : https://archive.org/details/chroniconpascha00dindgoog, consulté le 30 août 2024 ; éd. J. P. Migne, *Patrologia Graeca* 92, 1865 : https://archive.org/stream/PatrologiaGraeca/Patrologia%20Graeca%20Vol.%20092, consulté le 30 août 2024. On trouvera une traduction anglaise sur le site Attalus.org : http://www.attalus.org/translate/paschal.html, consulté le 30 août 2024.

62 P. 449 de l'édition Migne : « Ptolémée, appelé aussi Alexandre, fils de Ptolémée, le second Évergète, et de mère *Kokkè* (υἱὸς Πτολεμαίου τοῦ δευτέρου Εὐεργέτου καὶ Κοκκῆς μητρός) fut chassé de son royaume et tué à Myra en Lycie ».

63 Pour les sens possibles des surnoms *Kokkè* et *Kokkès*, voir Bennett 2013, « Ptolemy X », n. 2. D'après le grammairien Hésychios, le terme *kokkos* peut être employé pour désigner une couleur (pourpre, écarlate), mais aussi à propos des parties génitales de la femme (Hésychios, *Lexikon*, éd. H. Dufft, 1867, p. 894 : https://archive.org/details/hesychiialexand00schmgoog, consulté le 30 août 2024 ; cf. Green, 1990, p. 877 n. 4). Appliqué à Cléopâtre III, *Kokkè* pourrait donc signifier la « Rougeaude » ou bien désigner la souveraine au moyen d'une synecdoque obscène ; de la même manière, Ptolémée *Kokkès* serait soit « Ptolémée, (le) Rougeaud », soit « Ptolémée, (le) fils de *Kokkè* », au second sens du terme (pour une opinion différente, voir Whitehorne 1995, qui rattache *Kokkès* au *kokkux*, le coucou). L'autre surnom accolé au profanateur du sarcophage d'Alexandre par Strabon, *Pareisactos*, signifie « l'intrus », « celui qui a été secrètement introduit » (cf. Whitehorne 1995, p. 55 et 59). Nous ne

temps une expédition menée par Ptolémée X contre Alexandrie depuis la Syrie[64]. Quoi qu'il en soit, le caractère très éphémère du rétablissement de Ptolémée IX en Égypte se reflète dans la manière dont sont désignés les prêtres éponymes dans le protocole du contrat de Mallawi : les prêtres « qui sont sur le registre du prince d'Alexandrie » sont manifestement les prêtres éponymes nommés par Cléopâtre III et Ptolémée X, ce qui signifie que Ptolémée IX n'avait pas eu le temps de désigner ses propres prêtres éponymes[65].

Ptolémée IX pourrait avoir tenté une nouvelle fois de se rétablir en Égypte au cours des années 90, à en juger par la correspondance du soldat pathyrite Petesouchos, fils de Panebchounis, laquelle appartient à l'archive de Peteharsemtheus son frère[66]. Entre octobre 96 et janvier 94, Petesouchos a adressé à ce dernier, et à d'autres personnes à Pathyris, cinq lettres (trois rédigées en démotique, deux en grec) qui témoignent d'opérations militaires menées dans la région de Diospolis Mikra. Dans la première[67], expédiée depuis cette ville même, Petesouchos mentionne des « hommes de Crocodilopolis » sur lesquels il est chargé de veiller : le fait qu'il s'agisse de soldats, mobilisés depuis le camp de Crocodilopolis, est d'autant plus assuré que les hommes en question sont, comme il le précise lui-même, déchargés de toute tâche agricole[68]. Les trois lettres rédigées dans le courant de l'année 95 se rapportent elles aussi clairement à un contexte militaire : Petesouchos fait mention de pertes humaines[69], rassure néanmoins ses correspondants

---

voyons pas non plus d'impossibilité à rattacher ce second surnom à Ptolémée IX qui, d'après Flavius Josèphe, pensait s'emparer de l'Égypte « par surprise ».

64 Voir sur ce point Van't Dack et al. 1989, p. 143. Une incursion de Ptolémée IX jusqu'à Alexandrie expliquerait bien aussi le fait que Cléopâtre III ait décidé de mettre ses petits-fils en sécurité à Cos (Flavius Josèphe, *Antiquités juives* XIII, 348).

65 On notera la différence avec Ptolémée VIII qui, à l'époque de sa guerre contre Cléopâtre II, avait nommé ses propres prêtres éponymes alors qu'il n'avait pas encore repris Alexandrie (*BGU* III 993 et *P. Ehev.* 37, cf. Veïsse 2004, p. 57).

66 Les archives de Peteharsemtheus, fils de Panebchounis, rassemblent 113 à 115 documents, datés entre 174 et 88 : voir TM Arch 183 = Vandorpe, Waebens 2009, §47, p. 163–189, les lettres de Petesouchos correspondant aux n[os] 83, 86, 87, 88, 91 (p. 172). Pour l'analyse de cette correspondance et sa portée historique, voir Chauveau 1997, p. 222, Chauveau 2002 et Chauveau 2008.

67 Vandorpe, Waebens 2009 § 47, n° 83 = P. Phil. E 16743 = TM 102127 (démotique) : première édition Farid 2005, n°2, réédition Chauveau 2008, p. 28–33. La lettre date du 29 octobre 96.

68 Voir Chauveau 2008, p. 33 à propos des lignes 8 à 10 du papyrus (« Ce que j'ai fait a été de veiller sur les hommes de Crocodilopolis qui sont ici, alors qu'ils n'ont pas le souci de travailler la terre ! »).

69 Vandorpe, Waebens 2009 § 47, n° 87 = *P. Grenf.* II 36 (grec) (21 mai 95), en partic. l. 9–11 : « Ne soyez pas affligés pas à cause de ceux qui ont péri, ils s'attendaient à être tués ».

sur le fait que lui-même et les « jeunes (recrues) » (τὰ παιδία) se trouvent en bonne santé, sous la protection du stratège Ptolion[70], et rapporte la récompense accordée par ce dernier à l'officier égyptien Horos[71]. Par contraste, la dernière lettre, datée du 7 janvier 94[72], ne concerne que des affaires domestiques, ce qui laisse penser que les troubles étaient désormais terminés et la démobilisation imminente[73]. Quoique dans aucun de ces documents Petesouchos ne donne d'informations précises sur la nature des opérations militaires auxquelles il a participé, trois indices laissent se profiler l'ombre de Ptolémée IX. Le premier concerne le regain d'activité de ce dernier sur la scène syrienne à la même époque : d'après Flavius Josèphe, le roi poussa le prétendant séleucide Démétrios III contre son frère Philippe I et lui permit de s'établir à Damas (*Antiquités juives*, XIII 369–371), épisode que les modernes placent – indépendamment du dossier égyptien – aux alentours de 97/96 d'après le témoignage des monnaies[74] ; or, entre 103 et 101, c'était déjà depuis la Syrie que Ptolémée IX avait tenté de reprendre pied en Égypte. Le second élément à prendre en considération est l'augmentation massive de la frappe de tétradrachmes alexandrins entre 96/95 et 94/93, sachant qu'au IIe siècle les phases d'émissions les plus importantes coïncident avec les conflits extérieurs et/ou dynastiques[75]. Le troisième indice est à chercher dans la première lettre composée par Petesouchos (29 octobre 96), dans laquelle il évoque la gestion de champs dont il ne peut s'occuper directement, en raison de son éloignement. Il donne à ce propos à ses correspondants de curieuses instructions que M. Chauveau a proposé de rendre de la manière suivante : « Celui qui viendra contre vous à ce sujet, vous l'enverrez auprès de Sôter (*Swtr*) ! » (l. 20–21). Selon M. Chauveau : « On peut dès lors se demander s'il ne s'agit pas là d'une plaisanterie en rapport avec le contexte politique de l'époque : (…) Petesouchos recommanderait à ses correspondants d'envoyer un éventuel importun 'chez Sôter', c'est-à-dire auprès de Ptolémée IX Sôter II, le frère-ennemi de leur propre maître, manière de dire : envoyez-le au diable ! »[76]. Le détail des opérations nous échappe et plusieurs hypothèses sont envisageables : le roi a-t-il fait en personne une nouvelle incursion en territoire égyp-

---

70 Vandorpe, Waebens 2009 § 47, n° 88 = *P. Lips*. I 104 (grec) (30 juin 95), l. 10–11 et 22–27 : « Je suis en bonne santé ainsi que les jeunes recrues » / « Le stratège Ptolion nous protège grandement, et nous lui en sommes énormément reconnaissants » (trad. J.-L. Fournet).
71 Vandorpe, Waebens 2009 § 47, n° 86 = P. Claude 2 (TM 44928), éd. Chauveau 2002, p. 50 (démotique) (avril-août 95) : « Le stratège Ptolion a donné une couronne d'or et une robe royale à Horos ».
72 Vandorpe, Waebens 2009 § 47, n° 91 = P. BM EA 10498 (TM 622), éd. Chauveau 2008, p. 34–37 (démotique).
73 Cf. Chauveau 2008, p. 37.
74 Voir Ehling 2008, p. 232–233 et p. 239–240.
75 Voir Olivier, Redon 2020.
76 Chauveau 2008, p. 30 et 32.

tien ? A-t-il envoyé des troupes depuis Damas ? Ou bien a-t-il réussi, depuis Chypre, à susciter des ralliements en Égypte ? L'hypothèse n'est pas si saugrenue lorsqu'on songe que, à l'époque de la guerre civile entre Ptolémée VIII et Cléopâtre II, la reine ne se trouvait probablement dans aucun des lieux de la *chôra* où son autorité a été temporairement reconnue (Héracléopolite, Hermonthis, Edfou, Eléphantine), et que Ptolémée X avait déjà quitté l'Égypte quand son nom continuait d'être employé pour dater les documents dans le sud du pays (voir *infra*). Les périodes de disparition des reçus de taxes, identifiées par K. Vandorpe dans le Pathyrite de 107 à 103, puis de 102 à 94/3[77], sont sans doute au moins en partie liées aux différentes étapes de cette lutte entre les deux frères, dont l'essentiel nous échappe encore, même s'il serait pour autant imprudent de les réduire à une cause unique[78].

Phase 3 – la fuite de Ptolémée X et le rétablissement de Ptolémée IX en Égypte en 88
Le dernier acte de l'affrontement entre Ptolémée IX et Ptolémée X se joua au cours de l'année 88. Comme nous l'avons vu, il est impossible de souscrire à la thèse de Pausanias et Justin, pour qui la mort de Cléopâtre III fut l'élément déclencheur du soulèvement des Alexandrins contre Ptolémée X treize ans plus tard. De son côté, Porphyre livre les informations suivantes[79] :
- Ptolémée X exerça le pouvoir seul après la disparition de Cléopâtre III (en 101), ce qui fait qu'il régna dix-huit années pleines en Égypte à compter de son retour à Alexandrie (en 107), quoique vingt-six années de règne lui aient été officiellement comptées (*i.e.* depuis sa prise du titre royal à Chypre en 114/3).
- la dix-neuvième année (soit 88/87), « en colère contre ses soldats » (τοῖς στρατεύσασιν ὀργισθείς), il partit recruter des troupes à l'étranger pour les retourner contre eux en Égypte (ἐξῆλθε συλλέξων ἐπ'αὐτοὺς δύναμιν εἰς Αἴγυπτον)[80].

---

77 Vandorpe 2000, p. 415 et 433–436.
78 En l'occurrence, il ne nous semble pas que les événements rapportés dans le papyrus Berlin 13608 (TM 308) doivent être rattachés à la guerre civile, et pas non plus qu'ils témoignent véritablement d'une révolte. Ce rapport rédigé par le comogrammate de la toparchie sud du Pathyrite concerne les événements qui se sont déroulés une nuit de septembre 91 (Kaplony-Heckel 1994, p. 82 = Kaplony-Heckel 2009, p. 966) : des individus ont battu à mort Kaies, fils de Pates (le mari d'Apollonia / Senmouthis, l'aînée des filles de Dryton), alors qu'il dormait dans un champ. Quoique les meurtriers soient présentés comme les « hommes du rebelle » (*rmt nty bks*, l. 4), l'affaire nous semble davantage relever de la criminalité ou du brigandage ordinaires ; dans le même sens, voir McGing 1997, p. 298. Le document pourrait être rapproché de ceux qui dénoncent des actes commis « à la manière de rebelles » dans des contextes ne se référant pas à des révoltes : voir Veïsse 2004, p. 143–144.
79 *Apud* Eusèbe, éd. Schoene, p. 164–166. Cf. Van't Dack *et al.* 1989, p. 141–142.
80 C'est probablement dans ce contexte que Ptolémée X rédigea le testament léguant son royaume aux Romains, testament destiné à servir de garantie pour les dettes qu'il avait contrac-

- son départ fut suivi d'une ambassade des Alexandrins auprès de Ptolémée IX pour lui offrir la couronne[81].
- Ptolémée X fut défait une première fois sur mer par le général Tyrrhos (ou Pyrrhos ?[82]), puis il s'enfuit à Myra de Lycie, enfin il disparut dans un nouveau combat naval contre le navarque Chairéas après avoir tenté de débarquer à Chypre[83].

La *Chronique Pascale* présente la même succession événementielle, de manière plus succincte : Ptolémée X fut chassé de son royaume et tué à Myra de Lycie ; Ptolémée IX revint d'exil et recouvra son trône pour huit ans[84].

Ces indications sont globalement conformes au récit livré par le texte historique du temple d'Edfou, lequel évoque successivement la fuite de Ptolémée X, puis le retour de Ptolémée IX (VII 9, 8). Les autres sources directes témoignent cependant d'une situation plus complexe. Premièrement, les monnaies alexandrines datées de l'an 29 de Ptolémée IX permettent de corriger sur un point la chronologie de Porphyre : le roi s'est nécessairement rétabli à Alexandrie dès la « dix-huitième année » de règne de son frère (l'an 26 de Ptolémée X selon le comput officiel : 89/88, Tab. 1[85]),

---

tées auprès d'eux afin de financer la guerre : voir Badian 1967 ; Van't Dack *et al.* 1989, p. 149–150 et p. 156–160.

81 Voir Van't Dack *et al.* 1989, p. 141. Un peu plus loin, Porphyre (*apud* Eusèbe, éd. Schoene, p. 166, version grecque) évoque aussi des violences précédemment commises contre les Alexandrins par Ptolémée X « par l'entremise des troupes auxiliaires juives » (διά τινας Ἰουδαϊκὰς ἐπικουρίας), vraisemblablement les membres loyalistes des garnisons juives d'Égypte.

82 Les versions grecque et arménienne disent toutes deux « Tyr(r)os », mais le nom est rare et il pourrait s'agir d'une erreur de copiste : voir Van't Dack *et al.* 1989, p. 131–132.

83 Les points 3 et 4 sont inversés dans le récit de Porphyre, probablement pour des raisons qui tiennent à la narration, l'auteur ayant présenté les événements se rapportant à Ptolémée X avant d'en venir à Ptolémée IX : voir Van't Dack *et al.* 1989, p. 132.

84 Ed. Migne, p. 449. Porphyre/Eusèbe, éd. Schoene, p. 165–166, est plus précis pour le second règne de Ptolémée IX : 7 ans et six mois.

85 Seuls les documents portant une date bien établie ont été inclus dans ce tableau, et non pas ceux qui peuvent néanmoins aussi être rattachés à l'année 88, comme le *P. Bad.* II 16 (quatrième lettre de Platon). Une stèle démotique de Saqqara (Ray 2011, G1, p. 229–241, « Stèle d'Imhotep » = TM 51405 ; voir Van't Dack *et al.*, p. 144) offre à la fois l'équivalence « l'an 26, qui est aussi l'an 29 » et une allusion au roi hors d'Égypte (« L'an 26 qui est l'an 29, mois d'Hathyr(?), jour 10? du Pharaon qui est hors d'Égypte » : trad. Devauchelle 2014, p. 420). Les deux problèmes concernent la lecture de la saison et l'identification de ce pharaon « hors d'Égypte ». J. D. Ray (Ray 2011, p. 239) donne, pour des raisons paléographiques, sa préférence à la lecture « *3bd-3 3ḥt* » (= mois d'Hathyr), tout en notant que *3bd-3 šmw* (= mois d'Epeiph), « is not to be excluded completely, given the faintness of the original » ; dans le premier cas, la stèle daterait du 22 novembre-1er décembre 89, dans

pas la « dix-neuvième » (l'an 27, débutant le 14 septembre 88)[86]. D'autre part, alors que son autorité était reconnue dans le Fayoum dès le mois de mai au plus tard (*P. Cairo* II 30614, daté du 10 Pachon de l'an 29 = 21 mai 88), les documents en Haute-Égypte ont continué à être datés selon Ptolémée X jusqu'en juin au moins pour Thèbes (*O. Bodl.* I 199 : 5 juin), septembre pour Pathyris (*P. Amh.* II 51 : 6 septembre) et Hermonthis (*Short Texts* II 432 : 22 septembre). Manifestement, Ptolémée IX n'a pas simplement succédé à Ptolémée X après la fuite de ce dernier, comme Ptolémée VIII avait succédé à son frère défunt Ptolémée VI à l'été 145[87] ; bien au contraire, le pays a dû connaître pendant plusieurs mois une situation de guerre civile entre partisans des deux rois, comme au temps du conflit des années 130 entre Ptolémée VIII et Cléopâtre II. La seconde titulature pharaonique de Ptolémée IX, adoptée lors de son retour en Égypte, souligne au demeurant le fait que le roi a repris le contrôle du pays par la force des armes[88].

## 2.2 Le « dossier pathyrite » reconsidéré à la lumière du conflit dynastique

Compte tenu de ce contexte général, on peut estimer que la menace redoutée par Platon en mars 88, quand il écrivit ses premières lettres à Nechthyris et aux Pathyrites, était celle des partisans de Ptolémée IX déjà actifs dans la région, à la fois à

---

le second du 20–30 juillet 88. De même, s'il estime plus vraisemblable que la mention du roi hors d'Égypte se rapporte au détenteur des 29 années de règne (donc, Ptolémée IX), il n'exclut pas formellement qu'il puisse s'agir du détenteur des 26 années (Ptolémée X), compte tenu de l'ambiguïté de la formulation (p. 240 ; voir également Zauzich 1977, p. 193). De fait, la première solution (stèle datée des 22 novembre-1er décembre 89 et faisant référence au règne de Ptolémée IX hors d'Égypte) présente bien des difficultés interprétatives, comme l'auteur le souligne lui-même. La solution inverse (stèle datée des 20–30 juillet 88 et identification de Ptolémée X au « roi hors d'Égypte ») cadrerait en revanche parfaitement avec le contexte général et avec le reste de la documentation. Dans cette hypothèse, la stèle fournirait aussi un *terminus ante quem* pour la fuite de Ptolémée X.
86 Voir Mørkholm 1975 ; Van't Dack *et al.* 1989, p. 143–144.
87 Le retour de Ptolémée VIII sur le trône d'Égypte semble avoir causé des tensions à Alexandrie, notamment parmi les *philoi* de l'ancien roi, comme en témoigne l'affaire Galaistès : voir Veïsse 2004, p. 47–48. Dans la *chôra* en revanche, la succession semble s'être opérée rapidement et sans difficulté majeure : voir Chauveau 1990 ; Lanciers 1995.
88 Voir Traunecker 2013, p. 180–183 : nom des Deux déesses (« Le grand de puissance, *gouverneur de la Grande Verte*, qui s'empare de l'héritage du Double-Pays en toute justification, le généreux auprès des dieux et des hommes, *celui dont la Majesté est invoquée avec joie par ses troupes* ») et nom d'Horus d'or (« Seigneur des très nombreuses fêtes-*sed* comme Ptah-Tatenen, père des dieux, *il a reçu la royauté de Rê en force et victoire*, le prince, qui juge selon Maât, et affermit les lois comme Thot, le deux fois grand »). Voir également Cuénod, Olivier 2020, p. 211, n. 53 et p. 217.

**Tab. 1:** Documents datés selon les règnes de Ptolémée IX ou Ptolémée X au cours de l'année 88.

| Date | Provenance | Doc. | Roi |
| --- | --- | --- | --- |
| 2 janvier 88 | Pathyris | *P. Lond.* III, p. 21–22, n° 883 = TM 88 | Ptolémée X |
| 14 février 88 | Pathyris | Wångsted, *Orientalia Suecana* 12 (1963), p. 48–49, n° 6 = TM 44906 | Ptolémée X |
| 22 février 88 | Thèbes | *O. Tempeleide* 213 = TM 50625 | Ptolémée X |
| 22 mars 88 | Pathyris | Kaplony-Heckel, *Enchoria* 19–20 (1992–1993), p. 61–62, n°12[89]= TM 51156 | Ptolémée X |
| 28 mars 88 | Latonpolis (expédition) / Pathyris (réception) | *SB* 6300 = TM 5653 | Ptolémée X |
| 28 mars 88 | Latonpolis (expédition) / Pathyris (réception) | *P. Bour.* 10 = TM 304 | Ptolémée X |
| 30 mars 88 | ? Pathyris (réception) | *P. Bour.* 11 = TM 306 | Ptolémée X |
| 12 avril-11 mai 88 | Thèbes | Kaplony-Heckel, *Studies Lichtheim* II, p. 588–589, n°18[90] = TM 54079 | Ptolémée X |
| 21 mai 88 | Arsinoïte | *P. Cairo* II 30614 = TM 43282 | Ptolémée IX + double date dans le corps du document : « an 26 = an 29 »[91] |
| 5 juin 88 | Thèbes | *O. Bodl.* I 199 = TM 70952 | Ptolémée X |

---

**89** = Kaplony-Heckel 2009, n° 33, p. 594–665.
**90** = Kaplony-Heckel 2009, n°24, p. 404–519.
**91** Ce contrat est daté selon les années régnales de Ptolémée IX (10 Pachon de l'an 29), mais l'équivalence an 26 = an 29 est donnée dans le corps du document, pour l'intelligibilité de la transaction : voir Van't Dack *et al.*, p. 144 et p.146, n. 147.

**Tab. 1** (suite)

| Date | Provenance | Doc. | Roi |
|---|---|---|---|
| 1 août 88 | Pathyris | Kaplony-Heckel, *Forschungen und Berichte* 10 (1968), p. 145, n° 9[92] = TM 389 | Ptolémée X |
| 10 août 88 | Memphis | *I. Mother of Apis* 123 = TM 130986[93] | Ptolémée IX |
| 6 septembre 88 | Pathyris | *P. Amh.* II 51 = TM 125 | Ptolémée X |
| 22 septembre 88 | Hermonthite (expédition Heka / réception Hermonthis)[94] | Vleeming, *Short Texts* II, n° 432 = TM 48826 | Ptolémée X |
| 4 octobre 88 | Pathyris | *P. Strasb. Dem.*, p. 32–33, n° 8 = TM 119 | Ptolémée IX + double date : « an 27 = an 30 »[95] |
| 5 octobre 88 | Pathyris | *O. Tempeleide* 36 = TM 120 | Ptolémée IX |
| 1er novembre 88 | Pathyris (lieu de réception) | *P. Bour.* 12 = TM 305 | Ptolémée IX |
| 27 novembre 88 | Pathyris (lieu de réception) | *P. Ross. Georg.* II 10 = TM 5281 | Ptolémée IX |
| 13 novembre -12 décembre 88 | Éléphantine | *O. Eleph. DAIK* 287 = TM 74478 | Ptolémée IX |

---

92 = Kaplony-Heckel 2009, n°6, p. 148–201.
93 Voir également *I. Mother of Apis* 105 et 106, datant probablement de la même époque.
94 Voir Vleeming, *Short Texts* II, p. 95–96.
95 La formule de datation de ce document associe de manière curieuse une double date (an 27 = an 30) et le nom du seul Ptolémée IX (« Ptolémée, fils de Ptolémée, le Sôter »). À propos des doubles dates de ce type, voir Chauveau 1990, p. 149, n. 38 : « Des double dates sont occasionnellement utilisées durant de telles périodes troubles (durant la guerre civile entre Ptolémée VIII et Cléopâtre II en 132–130, et celle entre Ptolémée IX et Ptolémée X en 88 [...]), mais elles ne correspondent jamais bien sûr à des directives officielles. Tous ces cas ne font en fait que traduire l'embarras de scribes qui ne savent plus où se trouve la légitimité ». Également Chauveau 1997b, p. 163.

l'intérieur et à l'extérieur de la ville[96]. Les mesures prescrites dans le *P. Bour.* 11 (30 mars 88) laissent penser que le stratège redoutait des difficultés d'approvisionnement, et peut-être un siège. Dans le même temps, le fait qu'il mette aussi en garde Nechthyris contre ceux qui pourraient lui désobéir montre qu'il envisageait des défections internes (*P. Bour.* 10, 28 mars 88). Cependant, ces défections ne se sont pas produites, en tout cas pas à grande échelle, car les documents pathyrites étaient encore datés selon le seul Ptolémée X le 1$^{er}$ août (*Forschungen und Berichte* 10 (1968), p. 145, n° 9) et le 6 septembre 88 (*P. Amh.* II 51), alors que l'autorité de Ptolémée IX était déjà reconnue dans le Fayoum depuis mai et à Memphis le 10 août (au plus tard). Le fait semble plutôt logique, compte tenu de l'histoire récente de Pathyris. Comme sa voisine Crocodilopolis, cette dernière était une ville-garnison depuis les années 160. Après l'éviction de Ptolémée IX en 107, les soldats qui composaient cette garnison ont vécu sous l'autorité de Ptolémée X, pour le compte duquel ils firent campagne en Judée à l'époque de la Guerre des Sceptres, puis, comme nous venons de le voir, dans les environs de Diospolis Mikra en 96–95. Il existait même une association de *philobasilistai* à Pathyris dès 103 (*P. Conflict* 1) et, selon une nouvelle lecture de M. Chauveau, le *P. Conflict* 3, composé également à l'époque du conflit syro-judéo-égyptien, contient des moqueries à l'encontre de Ptolémée IX[97]. Il ne serait donc pas étonnant que la garnison, au moins pour la majeure partie de ses membres, ait longtemps maintenu sa loyauté envers Ptolémée X. On peut également penser que la disparition de la documentation pathyrite et le démantèlement du temple de Crocodilopolis, qui témoignent du dépeuplement des deux localités, furent une conséquence de cette loyauté : soit les forces armées pathyrites et crocodilopolites finirent par s'opposer activement à Ptolémée IX (ceci ayant entraîné une division entre deux partis à Pathyris compte tenu du *P. Bour.* 12) et furent défaites par Hiérax durant la campagne évoquée par Platon, soit elles furent déplacées et réorganisées car le nouveau roi ne leur faisait pas suffisamment confiance[98]. Chacune de ces hypothèses, la seconde paraissant néanmoins plus probable, concorde bien, également, avec l'intégration ultérieure du territoire correspondant à l'ancien nome pathyrite au sein du nome hermonthite. Si l'on se place à l'échelle de l'histoire locale, le retour de Ptolémée IX en Égypte solda donc, au profit des Hermonthites, le long conflit qui les opposait depuis le II$^e$ siècle aux habitants de Pathyris

---

[96] Rappelons que le danger ne pouvait pas venir de Thèbes, qui n'était pas encore en état de rébellion à cette époque.
[97] Cette lecture a été faite lors du séminaire tenu à l'EPHE en 2019.
[98] En ce sens, Pestman 1965, p. 51 ; Devauchelle, Grenier 1982, p. 161–162 et p. 168. Pour ces derniers, les garnisons de Crocodilopolis et Pathyris furent transférées à Ermant et à Tôd ; dans le même sens, Vandorpe, Waebens 2009, p. 50.

et Crocodilopolis[99]. Au cours de la guerre civile entre Ptolémée VIII et Cléopâtre II, les Hermonthites avaient fait un mauvais choix en prenant le parti de la reine : la création du nome hermonthite et la réutilisation de blocs du temple de Crocodilopolis pour le lac sacré de Tôd laissent penser qu'ils furent mieux inspirés à l'automne 88.

## 2.3 Le cas de Thèbes

Le cas de Thèbes fut-il vraiment différent ? Une première manière de lire le passage de Pausanias est de considérer que les Thébains, au sens strict du terme, après avoir attendu durant un siècle l'opportunité de se révolter contre le règne des Ptolémées, profitèrent de la situation politique confuse pour passer à l'action à l'automne 88. Étant donné la pauvreté des sources, cette hypothèse ne peut certes pas être balayée *a priori*. Il existe néanmoins un risque certain à vouloir interpréter, sans autre forme de procès, tout indice d'insurrection comme une révolte dirigée contre le pouvoir ptolémaïque en général, et ce risque peut être illustré par l'expédition menée par le général Paos contre les Hermonthites pour le compte de Ptolémée VIII quarante ans plus tôt. Dans une lettre bien connue, datée du 15 janvier 130, Esthladas, le fils de Dryton, informe ainsi ses parents de l'offensive imminente : « Nous avons appris que Paos remontera le Nil au mois de Tybi, avec des forces suffisantes pour réprimer la populace à Hermonthis (τοὺς ἐν Ἑρμώνθει ὄχλους) et les traiter en insurgés (χρήσασθαι δ' αὐτοῖς {αὐτοῖς} ὡς ἀποστάταις) (*P. Dryton* 36, l. 8–10). Si nous ne possédions que ce témoignage, nous pourrions penser que les Hermonthites s'étaient rebellés contre le pouvoir ptolémaïque, mettant à profit la situation de guerre civile entre Ptolémée VIII et Cléopâtre II. En réalité, ils reconnaissaient à cette époque l'autorité de Cléopâtre II, et l'offensive dirigée par Paos s'inscrivait directement dans ce contexte[100].

De même, l'idée d'une résurgence d'un « nationalisme » ou d'un « séparatisme » thébain n'est guère satisfaisante si l'on considère l'histoire de la ville de Thèbes après la Grande Révolte. Trois éléments en particulier nous semblent devoir être pris en considération :
– Premièrement, nous n'avons connaissance d'aucun soulèvement à Thèbes au cours du deuxième siècle, alors même que les épisodes de conflits dynastiques généraient un contexte *a priori* favorable pour une reprise de trou-

---

[99] Sur les étapes de ce conflit, voir Van't Dack *et al.* 1989, p. 42–43 ; Honigman, Veïsse 2021, p. 325–326 ; Chauveau 2019, p. 8–10.
[100] Voir Honigman, Veïsse 2021, p. 324–325. Le 29 octobre 130, le contrat *P. Bad.* II 2, conclu entre des membres de la garnison d'Hermonthis, était encore daté selon le règne de Cléopâtre II.

bles[101]. Au cours de la guerre civile entre Ptolémée VIII et Cléopâtre II, le contrôle de la ville fut âprement disputé entre partisans du roi et de la reine, mais le supposé « pharaon Harsièsis » qui se serait imposé à cette occasion s'est révélé être un mythe historiographique[102].

- D'autre part, la ville de Thèbes n'a pas été tenue à l'écart du phénomène général de renforcement de l'autorité ptolémaïque en Haute-Égypte dans les décennies qui suivirent la fin de la Grande Révolte : une administration, une banque, un grenier royal, une garnison y furent rétablis, un office notarial grec ouvert vers 174, une deuxième garnison implantée aux Memnoneia dans les années 160, des cavaliers-clérouques installés vers la même époque[103].

- Enfin, il est aussi nécessaire de prendre en compte l'évolution du profil sociologique de la population thébaine au cours du temps : les Thébains de 88 (quel que soit le sens qu'accorde au terme Pausanias) n'etaient certainement pas les mêmes que ceux de 206. La présence d'une élite grecque et/ou hellénisée au sein de la ville a ainsi été spectaculairement mise en lumière par la découverte, en 2007, de deux bains grecs à *tholos* sur le parvis même du temple d'Amon, tous deux pourvus de décors dignes de ceux d'Alexandrie et des palais de Macédoine[104]. La cité de Thèbes n'est pas non plus restée à l'écart du phénomène de cumul de fonctions administratives et religieuses, qui s'accentue dans toute l'Égypte à partir de la fin du IIe siècle. Comme L. Coulon l'a montré, le fils de Platon lui-même, « Platon le jeune », cumulait au début des années 90 des fonctions d'administrateur royal (peut-être celles de stratège de plusieurs nomes) avec celles de « quatrième, troisième et deuxième prophète d'Amon » ; il était aussi chargé de recevoir et d'interpréter les oracles du dieu, ce qui lui donnait probablement la latitude d'orienter la politique locale[105]. Nous ignorons si Amon dit à Platon ce qu'il fallait penser de la rivalité entre Ptolémée IX et Ptolémée X en 88, mais le fait que Platon ait poursuivi sa carrière sous l'aîné des deux frères[106] montre à tout le moins qu'il fit le bon choix à titre personnel.

---

[101] Voir Honigman, Veïsse 2021, p. 323.
[102] Veïsse 2011.
[103] Clarysse 1995, p. 2–3 Winnicki 2001 ; Vandorpe 2011 et 2014, p. 110–113 ; Fischer-Bovet 2014, p. 97.
[104] Voir Redon, Faucher 2015 ; Guimier-Sorbets 2015 ; Marangou, Naguib Reda 2016. Les données céramiques étudiées par A. Marangou et M. Naguib Reda permettent de remonter la construction des bains à la fin du IIIe s.
[105] Coulon 2001, p. 108–110. Également Birk 2023, p. 120–128.
[106] Voir *supra*, n. 15.

## 3 Conclusion

Le 17 avril 29 av. nè, le nouveau préfet romain d'Égypte, C. Cornelius Gallus, éleva à Philae une stèle trilingue (grec, latin, hiéroglyphes) afin de commémorer sa victoire sur des révoltes survenues en Haute-Égypte, ainsi que ses succès contemporains en Éthiopie[107]. La version latine qualifie la Thébaïde de « commun effroi de tous les rois (*communi omnium regum formidine*) » (l. 7) ; quant au texte grec, il va jusqu'à affirmer que le préfet soumit en 29 « la Thébaïde entière, qui n'avait pas été soumise aux rois (σύμπασαν τὴ[ν] Θηβαΐδα μὴ ὑποταγεῖσαν τοῖς βασιλεῦσιν) » (l. 15–16). Quoique ces affirmations aient été très exagérées, il est clair que les révoltes survenues en Haute-Égypte sous les Ptolémées avaient suffisamment marqué les esprits pour être exploitées par la propagande romaine. Pour autant, ceci ne signifie pas qu'il faille les interpréter comme un tout procédant des mêmes causes. Tout bien considéré, il nous semble que les événements de 88 ne s'inscrivent pas dans la continuité de la Grande Révolte des années 206–186, mais que l'expédition mentionnée à la fois par Pausanias et par le stratège Platon fut au premier chef – étant bien entendu que différents types de causes sont imbriqués dans toute révolte – un acte de guerre contre les derniers partisans de Ptolémée X en Haute-Égypte. Sur le fond, cette expédition pourrait être mise en parallèle avec celle menée par le général Paos contre les partisans de Cléopâtre II à Hermonthis en 130 ; dans la forme, il est probable que l'affaire fut réglée par une campagne-éclair plutôt qu'au terme d'une guerre longue de plus de deux ans. Si ces hypothèses sont justes, le soulèvement thébain de 88, loin d'être un nouvel avatar de ce que C. Préaux, il y a quatre-vingts ans, appela « l'inlassable révolte égyptienne »[108], serait plutôt la preuve du succès de la politique menée par les Ptolémées dans la région depuis le II$^e$ siècle, politique consistant en un renforcement et une normalisation de leur contrôle. Cette « ptolémaïsation » de la Haute-Égypte, selon l'expression de J. Manning[109], avait commencé avant la Grande Révolte : elle reprit après elle, et aboutit à la pleine intégration des habitants de la cité de Thèbes dans les jeux politiques de l'État ptolémaïque au début du I$^{er}$ siècle.

---

[107] L'*IG Philae* II 128 donne les textes grec et latin du décret ; on trouvera une traduction française de la version hiéroglyphique par J. Yoyotte dans Yoyotte, Charvet 1997, p. 262–264, et une réédition commentée des trois versions chez Hoffmann *et al.* 2009. Voir également sur ce document Hauben 1976 ; Koenen et Thompson 1984 ; Veïsse 2004, p. 74–76 et p. 241. Strabon mentionne en outre une révolte survenue dans le Delta (Héroônpolis / Pithom) et relie la révolte de Thébaïde au paiement du tribut : « Cornelius Gallus, le premier préfet établi en Égypte par César, attaqua Héroônpolis, la prit avec seulement une poignée (de soldats) et, en peu de temps, brisa une sédition survenue en Thébaïde pour le paiement du tribut » (XVII, 1, 53 ; trad. P. Charvet).
[108] Préaux 1936, p. 552.
[109] Manning 2003, p. 69 et p. 73.

## Annexe : chronologie des luttes dynastiques sous Ptolémée IX et Ptolémée X

*Les faits assurés sont indiqués en caractères droits, les faits hypothétiques en italique.*

| | | |
|---|---|---|
| 109–107 | Ptolémée IX tente d'écarter Cléopâtre III du pouvoir | Porphyre / Eusèbe, éd. Schoene, p. 163–164 ; *IGCyr* 011100 ; Flavius Josèphe, *Antiquités juives*, XIII, 10, 2 |
| septembre 107 | Ptolémée IX est expulsé d'Alexandrie à l'instigation de Cléopâtre III | Porphyre / Eusèbe, éd. Schoene, p. 163–164 ; Pausanias, I, 9, 1–2 ; Justin, XXXIX, 4, 1–2 ; *P. Dion.* 18 = *Pap. Lugd. Bat.* XXII 18 ; Mørkholm 1975 |
| 103 | Début du conflit syro-judéo-égyptien (Guerre des Sceptres) | Van't Dack *et al.* 1989 |
| 102–101 | Invasion du territoire égyptien par Ptolémée IX ; Ptolémée IX reconnu en certains lieux de Moyenne-Égypte *avancée de Ptolémée IX jusqu'à Alexandrie et pillage du tombeau d'Alexandre ?* | Flavius Josèphe, *Antiquités juives* XIII, 351–352 ; Zaghloul 1991 (P. Mallawi inv. 602/7 = TM 47353) ; *P. Hawara* 19 a-b (TM 41474) ? *Strabon* XVII, 1, 8 ? |
| septembre 101 | Mort de Cléopâtre III | *P. Adler Gr.* 12 ; Mørkholm 1975 |
| 96–95 | Opérations militaires dans la région de Diospolis Mikra = *nouvelle tentative de restauration de Ptolémée IX ?* | Chauveau 2008, p. 28–33 (P. Phil. E 16743 = TM 102127) ; *P. Grenf.* II 36 ; *P. Lips.* I 104 ; Chauveau 2002 (P. Claude 2 = TM 44928) ; Chauveau 2008, p. 34–37 (P. BM EA 10498 = TM 622) |
| *printemps 88 ?* | Fuite de Ptolémée X ; ambassade des Alexandrins auprès de Ptolémée IX | Mørkholm 1975 ; *Edfou* VII, 9, 8 ; Porphyre / Eusèbe, éd. Schoene, p. 164–166 ; *Chronique Pascale*, éd. Migne, p. 449 ; Ray 2011 G1 ? |
| 21 mai 88 (au plus tard) | Autorité de Ptolémée IX reconnue dans le Fayoum | *P. Cairo* II 30614 (TM 43282) |
| 4 octobre 88 (au plus tard) | Autorité de Ptolémée IX reconnue à Pathyris | *P. Strasb. Dem.*, p. 32–33, n°8 (TM 119) |

| (suite) | | |
|---|---|---|
| avant le 1ᵉʳ novembre 88 | Mise sur pied d'une expédition dirigée contre « la Thébaïde » (Platon) / « les Thébains » (Pausanias) | *P. Bour.* 12 ; Pausanias I, 9, 3 |
| 88 / 87 | Mort de Ptolémée X dans un combat naval | Porphyre / Eusèbe, éd. Schoene, p. 165–166 ; *Chronique Pascale*, éd. Migne, p. 449 |
| été 87 ? (au plus tard ; plus probablement fin 88) | Fin de la révolte de Thébaïde | *SB* XVIII 13675 et 13677 ? ; *O. Theb. Gr.* 30 ? |

# Bibliographie

Agut, Moreno-García 2016
　Agut, D., Moreno-García, J.-C., *L'Egypte des Pharaons. De Narmer à Dioclétien, 3150 av. J.-C. – 284 apr. J.-C.*, Paris, 2016.
Arlt 2011
　Arlt, C., « Scribal Offices and Scribal Families in Ptolemaic Thebes » in P. F. Dorman, B. M. Bryan (éd.), *Perspectives on Ptolemaic Thebes : Occasional Proceedings of the Theban Workshop*, Chicago, 2011, p. 17–34.
Armoni 2001
　Armoni, C., « Kornlieferung an Soldaten: Bemerkungen zu BGU XVIII.1 2747 », *ZPE* 136, 2001, p. 174–176.
Bagnall 1972
　Bagnall, R. S., « Stolos the Admiral », *Phoenix* 26, 1972, p. 358–368.
Bennett 2013
　Bennett, C., *The Ptolemaic Dynasty*, base de données en ligne, https://www.instonebrewer.com/TyndaleSites/Egypt/ptolemies/ptolemies.htm, consulté le 30 août 2024.
Bergman 1968
　Bergman, J., *Ich bin Isis : Studien zum memphitischen Hintergrund der griechischen Isisaretalogien*, Historia Religionum 3, Uppsala, 1968.
Bielman Sánchez, Lenzo 2015
　Bielman Sánchez, A., Lenzo, G., *Inventer le pouvoir féminin. Cléopâtre I et Cléopâtre II, reines d'Egypte au IIe s. av. J.-C.*, ECHO 12, Berne, 2015.
Bingen 1986
　Bingen, J., « Epigraphie grecque. Les proscynèmes de Louxor », *CdE* 61, 1986, p. 330–334.
Birk 2020
　Birk, R., *Türöffner des Himmels : Prosopographische Studien zur thebanischen Hohepriesterschaft der Ptolemäerzeit*, ÄA 76, Wiesbaden, 2020.

Birk 2023
> Birk, R., « D'un monde à l'autre. Prophètes thébains et fonctionnaires lagides dans la statuaire privée à la fin de l'époque ptolémaïque » in R. Roure (éd.), *Le multilinguisme dans la Méditerranée antique*, collection Diglossi@ 1, Pessac, 2023 [en ligne], p. 115-140, https://una-editions.fr/prophetes-thebains-et-fonctionnaires-lagides, consulté le 30 août 2024.

Brugsch 1886
> Brugsch, H., « Der Apis-Kreis aus den Zeiten der Ptolemäer nach den hieroglyphischen und demotischen Weihinschriften des Serapeums von Memphis », *ZÄS* 24, 1886, p. 32-33.

Calderini 1973-1977
> Calderini, A., *Dizionario dei nomi geografici e topografici dell'Egitto greco-romano*, édité par S. Daris, Volume II, Milan, 1973-1977.

Calderini 1983-1986
> Calderini, A., *Dizionario dei nomi geografici e topografici dell'Egitto greco-romano*, édité par S. Daris, Volume IV, Milan, 1983-1986.

Cassor-Pfeiffer 2008
> Cassor-Pfeiffer, S., « Zur Reflexion ptolemäischer Geschichte in den ägyptischen Tempeln aus der Zeit Ptolemaios' IX. Philometor II./Soter II. und Ptolemaios' X. Alexander I. (116-80 v. Chr.) - Teil 1 : Die Bau- und Dekorationstätigkeit », « Teil 2 : Kleopatra III und Berenike III im Spiegel der Tempelreliefs », *JEH* 1, 2008, p. 21-77 et p. 235-265.

Cauville, Devauchelle 1984
> Cauville, S., Devauchelle, D., « Le temple d'Edfou. Étapes de la construction, nouvelles données historiques », *RdE* 35, 1984, p. 31-55.

Chaufray, Wegner 2016
> Chaufray, M.-P., Wegner, W., « Two Early Ptolemaic Documents from Pathyris » in S. L. Lippert, M. Schentuleit, M. A. Stadler (éd.), *Sapientia Felicitas : Festschrift für Günter Vittmann zum 29. Februar 2016*, CENiM 14, Montpellier, 2016, p. 23-49.

Chauveau 1990
> Chauveau, M., « Un été 145 », *BIFAO* 90, 1990, p. 135-168.

Chauveau 1997a
> Chauveau, M., *L'Égypte au temps de Cléopâtre. 180-30 av. J.-C.*, Paris, 1997.

Chauveau 1997b
> Chauveau, M., « Eres nouvelles et corégences en Égypte ptolémaïque » in B. Kramer, W. Luppe, H. Maehler, G. Poethke (éd.), *Akten des 21. internationalen Papyrologenkongresses*, AfP Beihefte 3, Stuttgart, Leipzig, 1997, vol. 1, p. 163-171.

Chauveau 1998
> Chauveau, M., « Une nouvelle déesse Philadelphe » in W. Clarysse, A. Schoors, H. Willems (éd.), *Egyptian Religion - The Last Thousand Years: Studies Dedicated to the Memory of Jan Quaegebeur*, OLA 84-85, Louvain, 1998, p. 1263-1275.

Chauveau 2002
> Chauveau, M., « Nouveaux documents des archives de Pétéharsemtheus fils de Panebchounis » in K. Ryholt (éd.), *Acts of the Seventh International Conference of Demotic Studies*, CNI Publications 27, Copenhague, 2002, p. 45-57.

Chauveau 2008
> Chauveau, M., « La correspondance bilingue d'un illettré. Petesouchos fils de Panobchouni » in L. Pantalacci (éd.), *La lettre d'archive. Communication administrative et personnelle dans l'antiquité proche-orientale et égyptienne*, suppl. à *Topoi* 9, Le Caire, 2008, p. 27-42.

Chauveau 2019

Chauveau, M., « Démotique », *Annuaire de l'École pratique des hautes études (EPHE), Section des sciences historiques et philologiques* 150, 2019, p. 6–10, https://doi.org/10.4000/ashp.2851, consulté le 30 août 2024.

Clarysse 1984

Clarysse, W., « Theban Personal Names and the Cult of Bouchis » in H.-J. Thissen, K.-Th. Zauzich (éd.), *Grammata Demotika : Festschrift für Erich Lüddeckens zum 15. Juni 1983*, Würzburg, 1984, p. 25–39.

Clarysse 1995

Clarysse, W., « Greeks in Ptolemaic Thebes » in S. P. Vleeming (éd.), *Hundred-Gated Thebes : Acts of a Colloquium on Thebes and the Theban area in the Graeco-roman Period*, P.L.Bat. 27, Leyde, 1995, p. 1–19.

Collart 1922

Collart, P., « La révolte de la Thébaïde en 88 avant J.-C. » in *Recueil d'Etudes égyptologiques dédiées à la mémoire de Jean-François Champollion*, Paris, 1922, p. 273–282.

Coulon 2001

Coulon, L., « Quand Amon parle à Platon (La statue Caire JE 38033) », *RdE* 52, 2001, p. 85–112.

Cowey 2000

Cowey, J. M. S., « Remarks on Various Papyri III », *ZPE* 132, 2000, p. 241–247.

Cuénod 2021

Cuénod, A., *Être reine d'Égypte au IIe siècle avant J.-C. Cléopâtre III à travers les sources égyptiennes et grecques*, thèse de doctorat, EPHE – Paris, 2021.

Cuénod, Olivier 2020

Cuénod, A., Olivier, J., « D'un Ptolémée à l'autre. Ceindre le diadème à Alexandrie (163-80 av. J.-C.) » in T. Faucher (éd.), *Money Rules ! The Monetary Economy of Egypt, from Persians until the Beginning of Islam*, BdE 176, Le Caire, 2020, p. 203–229.

Devauchelle 2014

Devauchelle, D., « Compte rendu de J.D. Ray, Texts from the Baboon and Falcon Galleries: Demotic, Hieroglyphic and Greek Inscriptions from the Sacred Animal Necropolis, North Saqqara (EES-TE 15, Londres, 2011) », *BiOr* 71, 2014, col. 416–422.

Devauchelle, Grenier 1982

Devauchelle, D., Grenier, J.-C., « Remarques sur le nome Hermonthite à la lumière de quelques inscriptions de Tôd », *BIFAO* 82, 1982, p. 157–169.

Ehling 2008

Ehling, K., *Untersuchungen zur Geschichte der späten Seleukiden (164-63 v. Chr.) : Vom Tode des Antiochos IV. bis zur Einrichtung der Provinz Syria unter Pompeius*, HistEinz 196, Stuttgart, 2008.

Eller 2022

Eller, A., *Nomes et toparchies en Egypte gréco-romaine. Réalités administratives et géographie religieuse d'Eléphantine à Memphis*, BdE 179, Le Caire, 2022.

Farid 2005

Farid, A., « Zwei demotische Privatbriefe », *ZÄS* 132, 2005, p. 1–11.

Fischer-Bovet 2014

Fischer-Bovet, C., *Army and Society in Ptolemaic Egypt*, Armies of the Ancient World 1, Cambridge, 2014.

Graslin-Thomé, Veïsse, 2021

Graslin-Thomé, L., Veïsse, A.-E., « Les relations entre Séleucides et Lagides après la Sixième guerre de Syrie : une histoire sans intérêt ? » in C. Feyel, L. Graslin-Thomé (éd.), *Les derniers*

*Séleucides et leur territoire*, Études nancéennes d'histoire grecque 4, Nancy, Paris, 2021, p. 397–438.

Green 1990
    Green, P., *Alexander to Actium : The Hellenistic Age*, Londres, 1990.

Guimier-Sorbets 2015
    Guimier-Sorbets, A.-M., « Les décor architectural grec en Thébaïde. Pavements et peintures murales dans les bains de l'époque lagide » in G. Gorre, A. Marangou (éd.), *La présence grecque dans la vallée de Thèbes*, Rennes, 2015, p. 135–138.

Habachy 2023
    Habachy, M., "L'épithète de culte comme indice de datation. À quel moment les inscriptions hiéroglyphiques ont-elles qualifié Ptolémée IX de « dieu Sôter » ?", JEH 16, 2023, p. 219–249.

Hauben 1976
    Hauben, H., « On the Gallus Inscription at Philae », *ZPE* 22, 1976, p. 189–190.

Heinen 2006
    Heinen, H., « Hunger, Not und Macht : Bemerkungen zur herrschenden Gesellshaft im ptolemäischen Ägypten », *AncSoc* 36, 2006, p. 13–44.

Hoffmann et al. 2009
    Hoffmann, F., Minas-Nerpel, M., Pfeiffer, S., *Die dreisprachige Stele des C. Cornelius Gallus. Übersetzung und Kommentar*, AfP Beihefte 9, Berlin, 2009.

Hölbl 2001
    Hölbl, G., *A History of the Ptolemaic Empire*, Londres, New-York, 2001.

Honigman, Veïsse 2021
    Honigman, S., Veïsse, A.-E., « Regional Revolts in the Ptolemaic and Seleucid Empires » in C. Fischer-Bovet, S. von Reden (éd.), *Comparing the Ptolemaic and Seleucid Empires : Integration, Communication, and Resistance*, Cambridge, 2021, p. 301–328.

Huss 2001
    Huss, W., *Ägypten in hellenistischer Zeit : 332–30 v. Chr.*, Munich, 2001.

Huss 2006
    Huss, W., « Zur Invasion Ptolemaios' VIII. Soters II. in Ägypten (103 v.Chr.) », *ZPE* 157, 2006, p. 168.

Hutmacher 1965
    Hutmacher, R., *Das Ehrendekret für den Strategen Kallimachos*, Beitr. zur klass. Phil. 17, Meisenheim am Glan, 1965.

Kaplony-Heckel 1964
    Kaplony-Heckel, U., *Die demotischen Gebelen-Urkunden der Heidelberger Papyrus-Sammlung*, VHPS 4, Heidelberg, 1964.

Kaplony-Heckel 1994
    Kaplony-Heckel, U., « Demotische Verwaltungsakten aus Gebelein : der große Berliner Papyrus 13608 », *ZÄS* 121, 1994, p. 75–91.

Kaplony-Heckel 2009
    Kaplony-Heckel, U., *Land und Leute am Nil nach demotischen Handschriften, Papyri und Ostraka: Gesammelte Schriften*, ÄA 71, 2009, n° 35, p. 959–975.

Koenen, Thompson 1984
: Koenen, L., Thompson, D. B., « Gallus as Triptolemos on the Tazza Farnese », *BASP* 21, 1984, p. 111–153.

Lanciers 1995
: Lanciers, E., « Some Observations on the Events in Egypt in 145 B.C. », *Simblos* 1, 1995, p. 33–39.

Lanciers 2020
: Lanciers, E., « The Civil War between Ptolemy VIII and Cleopatra II (132–124) : Possible Causes and Key Events » in G. Gorre, S. Wackenier (éds.), *Quand la fortune du royaume ne dépend pas de la vertu du prince. Un renforcement de la monarchie lagide de Ptolémée VI à Ptolémée X (169–88 av. J.-C.) ?*, StudHell 59, Louvain, 2020, p. 21–54.

Laudenbach 2023
: Laudenbach, B., « Guerre de succession et félonie en Haute Egypte », *Les Humanités dans le texte* [en ligne], https://odysseum.eduscol.education.fr/guerre-de-succession-et-flonie-en-haute-gypte, consulté le 30 août 2024.

Laudenbach 2024
: Laudenbach, B., « La fonction de Nechthyris et l'identité de Platon. Le *P.Bour.* 10 en question », *ZPE* 229, 2024, p. 145–154.

Laudenbach à paraître
: Laudenbach, B., « Encore sur les lettres de Platon. Le *P.Bour.* 11 revisité et deux addenda aux *P. Bour.* 10 et *SB* III 63003 ».

Lüddeckens *et al.* 1998
: Lüddeckens, E., Wassermann, R., Erichsen, W., Nims, C. F., *Demotische Urkunden aus Hawara*, VOHD Supplementband 28, Stuttgart, 1998.

Manning 2003
: Manning, J. G., « Edfu as a Central Place in Ptolemaic History » in K. Vandorpe, W. Clarysse (éd.), *Edfu : An Egyptian Provincial Capital in the Ptolemaic Period*, Bruxelles, 2003, p. 61–73.

Marangou, Naguib Reda 2016
: Marangou, A., Naguib Reda, M., « Recherches sur les importations grecques dans la vallée thébaine à l'époque ptolémaïque » in R. David (éd.), *Céramiques ptolémaïques de la région thébaine*, CCE 10, 2016, p. 285–307.

McGing 1997
: McGing, B. C., « Revolt Egyptian Style : Internal Opposition to Ptolemaic Rule », *AfP* 43/2, 1997, p. 273–314.

Mooren 1975
: Mooren, L., *The Aulic Titulature in Ptolemaic Egypt: Introduction and Prosopography*, Bruxelles, 1975.

Mooren, Van't Dack 1981
: Mooren, L., Van't Dack, E., « Le stratège Platon et sa famille », *AntClass* 50, 1981, p. 535–544.

Mørkholm 1975
: Mørkholm, O., « Ptolemaic Coins and Chronology : the Dated Silver Coinage of Alexandria », *ANSMN* 20, 1975, p. 7–24.

Olivier, Redon 2020
: Olivier, J., Redon, B., « Reconsidérer la politique monétaire des Lagides à la lumière des sources numismatiques. Frappes et trésors monétaires aux IIIe et IIe s. av. J.-C. (env. 294–116) » in T. Faucher (éd.), *Money Rules ! The Monetary Economy of Egypt, from Persians until the Beginning of Islam*, BdE 176, Le Caire, 2020, p. 105–139.

Pestman 1965

Pestman, P. W., « Les archives privées de Pathyris à l'époque ptolémaïque. La famille de Pétéharsemtheus, fils de Panebkhounis » in E. Boswinkel, P. W. Pestman, P. J. Sijpesteijn (éd.), *Studia Papyrologica Varia*, P.L.Bat. 14, Leyde, 1965, p. 47–105.

Pestman 1967

Pestman, P. W., *Chronologie égyptienne d'après les textes démotiques (332 av. J.-C. – 453 ap. J.-C.)*, P.L.Bat. 15, Leyde, 1967.

Préaux 1936

Préaux, C., « Esquisse d'une histoire des révolutions égyptiennes sous les Lagides », *CdE* 11, 1936, p. 522–552.

Quack 2022

Quack, J. F., « Eine Abrechnung aus dem Tempelarchiv von Gebeleien : pHeidelberg D 665 » in A. Almásy-Martin, M. Chauveau, K. Donker van Heel, K. Ryholt (éd.), *Ripple in Still Water when There Is no Pebble Tossed. Festschrift in Honour of Cary J. Martin*, GHP Egyptology 34, Londres, 2022, p. 203–217.

Ray 2011

Ray, J. D., *Texts from the Baboon and Falcon Galleries. Demotic, Hieroglyphic and Greek Inscriptions from the Sacred Animal Necropolis, North Saqqara*, EES-TE 15, Londres, 2011.

Redon, Faucher 2015

Redon, B., Faucher, T., « Les Grecs aux portes d'Amon. Les bains de Karnak et l'occupation ptolémaïque du parvis ouest du temple de Karnak » in G. Gorre, A. Marangou (éd.), *La présence grecque dans la vallée de Thèbes*, Rennes, 2015, p. 121–134.

Ritner 2011

Ritner, R. K., « Ptolemy IX Soter II at Thebes » in P. F. Dorman, B. M. Bryan (éd.), *Perspectives on Ptolemaic Thebes : Occasional Proceedings of the Theban Workshop*, SAOC 65, Chicago, 2011, p. 97–114.

Samuel 1965

Samuel, A. E., « Year 27 = 30 and 88 B.C. », *CdE* 40, 1965, p. 376–385.

Strack 1897

Strack, M. L., *Die Dynastie der Ptolemäer*, Berlin, 1897.

Thiers 2015

Thiers, C., « Membra disiecta ptolemaica (III) », *CahKarn* 15, 2015, p. 347–356.

Thomas 1975

Thomas, J. D., *The Epistrategos in Ptolemaic and Roman Egypt – Part 1 : the Ptolemaic Epistrategos*, Opladen, 1975.

Thompson 2012

Thompson, D. J., *Memphis under the Ptolemies*, Princeton-Oxford, 2012 (2e éd.).

Traunecker 1979

Traunecker, C., « Essai sur l'histoire de la XXIXe dynastie », *BIFAO* 79, 1979, p. 395–436.

Traunecker 2013

Traunecker, C., « Thèbes, été 115 avant J.-C. Les travaux de Ptolémée IX Sôter II et son prétendu "Château de l'Or" à Karnak » in C. Thiers (éd.), *Documents de théologies thébaines tardives (D3T 2)*, CENiM 8, Montpellier, 2013, p. 177–226.

Uytterhoeven 2009

Uytterhoeven, I., *Hawara in the Graeco-Roman Period : Life and Death in a Fayum Village*, OLA 174, Louvain, 2009.

Vandorpe 1995

Vandorpe, K., « City of Many a Gate, Harbour for Many a Rebel » in S. P. Vleeming (éd.), *Hundred-Gated Thebes* : *Acts of a Colloquium on Thebes and the Theban area in the Graeco-roman Period*, P.L.Bat. 27, Leyde, 1995, p. 203-239.

Vandorpe 2000

Vandorpe, K., « Paying Taxes to the Thesauroi of the Pathyrites in a Century of Rebellion » in L. Mooren (éd.), *Politics, Administration and Society in the Hellenistic and Roman World* : *Proceedings of the International Colloquium (Bertinoro, 19-24 July 1997)*, StudHell 36, Louvain, 2000, p. 405-436.

Vandorpe 2008

Vandorpe, K., « Persian Soldiers and Persians of the Epigone : Social Mobility of Soldiers-Herdsmen in Upper Egypt », *AfP* 54, 2008, p. 87-108.

Vandorpe 2011

Vandorpe, K., « A Successful, but Fragile Biculturalism: The Hellenization Process in the Upper-Egyptian Town of Pathyris under Ptolemy VI and VIII » in A. Jördens, J. F. Quack (éd.), *Ägypten zwischen innerem Zwist und äußerem Druck: die Zeit Ptolemaios' VI. bis VIII. - Internationales Symposion Heidelberg 16.-19.9.2007*, Philippika 45, Heidelberg, 2011, p. 292-308.

Vandorpe 2014

Vandorpe, K., « The Ptolemaic Army in Upper Egypt ($2^{nd}$-1st centuries B.C.) » in A.-E. Veïsse, S. Wackenier (éd.), *L'armée en Égypte aux époques perse, ptolémaïque et romaine*, Genève, 2014, p. 105-135.

Vandorpe, Waebens 2009

Vandorpe, K., Waebens, S., *Reconstructing Pathyris' Archives : a Multicultural Community in Hellenistic Egypt*, CollHell 3, Bruxelles, 2009.

Van't Dack 1988

Van't Dack, E., *Ptolemaica Selecta. Etudes sur l'armée et l'administration lagides*, StudHell 29, Louvain, 1988, p. 329-385 (= « Recherches sur l'administration du nome dans la Thébaïde au temps des Lagides », *Aegyptus* 29, 1949, p. 3-44).

Van't Dack *et al.* 1989

Van't Dack, E., Clarysse, W., Cohen, G., Quaegebeur, J., Winnicki, J. K., *The Judean-Syrian-Egyptian Conflict of 103-101 B.C.* : *a Multilingual Dossier Concerning a "War of Sceptres"*, CollHell 1, Bruxelles, 1989.

Veïsse 2004

Veïsse, A.-E., *Les « révoltes égyptiennes »*. *Recherches sur les troubles intérieurs en Égypte du règne de Ptolémée III à la conquête romaine*, StudHell 41, Louvain, 2004.

Veïsse 2011

Veïsse, A.-E., « L'"ennemi des dieux" Harsièsis » in A. Jördens, J. F. Quack (éd.), *Ägypten zwischen innerem Zwist und äußerem Druck: die Zeit Ptolemaios' VI. bis VIII. - Internationales Symposion Heidelberg 16.-19.9.2007*, Philippika 45, Heidelberg, 2011, p. 92-102.

Veïsse 2022a

Veïsse, A.-E., « The "Great Theban Revolt", 206-186 BCE » in I.S. Moyer et P.J. Kosmin (éd.), *Cultures of Resistance in the Hellenistic East*, Oxford, 2022, p. 57-73.

Veïsse 2022b
: Veïsse, A.-E., « Ptolémée Apion, roi de Cyrénaïque (v. 101–96 av. JC) » in F. Delrieux, L. Guichard (éd.), *Itinéraire du Nil au Rhône. En mémoire de François Kayser : Docere, Delectare, Movere*, Chambéry, 2022, p. 135–147.

Whitehorne 1995
: Whitehorne, J. E. G., « Ptolemy X Alexander I as "Kokke's Child" », *Aegyptus* 75, 1995, p. 55–60.

Wilcken 1924
: Wilcken, U., « Papyrus-Urkunden », *AfP* 7, 1924, p. 288–314.

Winnicki 2001
: Winnicki, J. K., « Zur Deutung des demotischen Papyrus Erbach » in K. Geus, K. Zimmermann (éd.), *Punica, Libyca, Ptolemaica : Festschrift für Werner Huß zum 65. Geburtstag, dargebracht von Schülern, Freunden und Kollegen*, OLA 104, Studia Phoenicia 16, Louvain, 2001, p. 311–321.

Yoyotte, Charvet 1997
: Yoyotte, J., Charvet, P., *Strabon. Le voyage en Egypte*, Paris, 1997.

Zaghloul 1991
: Zaghloul, E.-H., « An Agreement for Sale from the Reign of Ptolemy IX Sôter II in the Museum of Mallawi », *BIFAO* 91, 1991, p. 255–263.

Zauzich 1977
: Zauzich, K.-Th., « Zwei übersehene Erwähnungen historischer Ereignisse der Ptolemäerzeit in demotischen Urkunden », *Enchoria* 7, 1977, p. 193.

Daniel von Recklinghausen

# Der große Aufstand in der Thebais nach den Aussagen in dem Synodaldekret Philensis II

## 1 Synodaldekrete im ptolemäischen Ägypten

Die Texte der ägyptischen Synodal- oder Priesterdekrete stehen im Interesse der Forschung, seit 1799 der Stein von Rosette zum Vorschein kam, der den Text eines Priesterdekretes aus dem 9. Regierungsjahr Ptolemaios' V. Epiphanes (196 v. Chr., sog. Memphis-Dekret bzw. Rosettana)[1] in einer hieroglyphischen, demotischen und griechischen Version enthält – ein Umstand mithin, der maßgeblich zur Entzifferung der hieroglyphischen und demotischen Schriftsysteme beigetragen hat.[2] Synodaldekrete zählen somit sicherlich zu den bekanntesten und beststudierten Texten in der Ägyptologie wie in den Nachbardisziplinen und sie werden seit jeher als Schlüsseldokumente für ein Verständnis der Beziehungen des (fremden, ptolemäischen) Königshauses mit den (einheimischen) Priestern angesehen. Demgegenüber erfuhren der ihnen intrinsische theologische Aussagegehalt und ihr *Sitz im Leben* in der Forschung früher eher weniger Aufmerksamkeit. Das ist insofern bemerkenswert, als diese Dekrete seit der Regierungszeit Ptolemaios' III. Euergetes für mehrere aufeinanderfolgende Herrschergenerationen nichts weniger regeln als die göttliche Verehrung des jeweils regierenden ptolemäischen Königspaares in den ägyptischen Göttertempeln.

Seit einiger Zeit stehen die Synodaldekrete wieder vermehrt im Fokus des Interesses, was nicht zuletzt den Funden zahlreicher weiterer Stelen(fragmente) sowohl bekannter als auch bis dato unbekannter Synodaldekrete in ganz Ägypten innerhalb der letzten Jahre zu verdanken ist.

---

[1] Die aktuellsten Bearbeitungen bei Pfeiffer 2020, S. 130–145, Nr. 22; Panov 2020, S. 318–373; Bowman et al. 2021, S. 281–298, Nr. 126; Hoffmann, Pfeiffer 2021; Panov 2022, S. 192–268, siehe zudem Birk 2021; Amin et al. 2023.

[2] Siehe dazu jüngst Buchwald, Josefowicz 2020.

---

**Anmerkung:** Den folgenden Ausführungen liegt der Vortragstext in Berlin zugrunde, sie basieren auf den in meiner Dissertation publizierten Ergebnissen, Recklinghausen 2018 (insbesondere Kapitel II, IV.1 und IV.4). An gegebener Stelle wird darüber hinaus vor allem auf seitdem erschienene Literatur verwiesen (letzte Aktualisierung: August 2023).

∂ Open Access. © 2025 bei den Autorinnen und Autoren, publiziert von De Gruyter. [CC BY-NC-ND] Dieses Werk ist lizenziert unter der Creative Commons Namensnennung - Nicht-kommerziell - Keine Bearbeitungen 4.0 International Lizenz.
https://doi.org/10.1515/9783111608051-014

Die ägyptischen Synodaldekrete sind Beschlüsse der ägyptischen Priester, die sich (vermutlich auf Geheiß des Königshauses) einmal im Jahr in Alexandria, seinen Vororten oder in Memphis versammelten, um (mit dem König?) Angelegenheiten der Tempel auf Landesebene zu besprechen.[3] Dazu dürften anlässlich besonderer Ereignisse ebenjene gemeinsamen Beschlüsse zugunsten des Königshauses und ihre Publikation gehört haben. Oftmals steht der Anlass hierzu formal im Kontext eines militärischen Erfolges der Ptolemäer.[4]

Sowohl der Intention als auch der Struktur nach basieren die Texte dieser Priesterdekrete auf griechischen Ehrendekreten, die in der hellenistischen Zeit im östlichen Mittelmeerraum weit verbreitet waren. Vereinfacht gesagt beschloss eine Gemeinschaft, etwa die Bürger einer *Polis*, einer Person bestimmte in ihrem Bereich gültige Ehrungen zu gewähren, weil sich jene Person vorab um die Gemeinschaft verdient gemacht hatte. Hatte z. B. ein Monarch eine *Polis* während einer (militärischen) Krise vor einer drohenden Gefahr bewahrt, konnte diese ihm hierfür eine Ehrung zuteilwerden lassen. Diese bestand oftmals in der Errichtung einer Statue auf einem öffentlichen Platz, konnte aber – je nach Bedeutung bzw. Beurteilung der Tat – auch mit der göttlichen Verehrung der begünstigten Person einhergehen.

Im Fall der Synodaldekrete setzt sich diese Gemeinschaft aus den ägyptischen Priestern zusammen. Aufgrund vorausgegangener Taten des amtierenden Königs (bzw. des Königspaares) fassten die Priester den Beschluss, ihn bzw. in der Regel König *und* Königin[5] in ihrem „Rahmen", vulgo den ägyptischen Göttertempeln, zu tempelteilenden Göttern (*synnaoi theoi*) zu erklären. Sie wurden demnach Teil der Gottheiten, die neben bzw. gemeinsam mit dem Tempelherrn und/oder der Tempelherrin an den Ritualen und den Götterfesten partizipierten und die in hieroglyphischen Tempelinschriften oftmals als „Neunheit" (*psḏt*), also als die Gesamtheit des lokalen Pantheons, angesprochen werden.

Aufbau und Struktur ägyptischer Synodaldekrete sind zwar eindeutig von den griechischen Ehrendekreten übernommen, wurden aber bewusst modifiziert, um sie den Erfordernissen des ägyptischen Tempelkultes anzupassen.[6] Durch diese „Symbiose" eines griechischen Textschemas mit den Vorstellungen und Praktiken der ägyptischen Religion versinnbildlichen die Synodaldekrete die verschiedenen kulturellen Strömungen im ptolemäischen Ägypten. Doch nicht nur die Textstruktur verweist auf die hellenistische Basis, in ähnlichem Maß gilt dies

---

3 Pfeiffer 2020, S. 78 spricht von einer „Plattform der Kommunikation mit dem König".
4 Siehe rezent Pfeiffer 2021b, S. 241.
5 Vgl. zur Königin im ptolemäischen Ägypten Cassor-Pfeiffer, Pfeiffer 2019 und Minas-Nerpel 2022 (mit jeweils weiterer Literatur) sowie den Beitrag von M. Minas-Nerpel in diesem Band.
6 Siehe jüngst Pfeiffer 2020, S. 86; Pfeiffer 2021b, S. 242.

auch für das Konzept einer göttlichen Verehrung des amtierenden Herrscherpaares. Es stellt ein zentrales Element des hellenistischen Herrscherkultes dar und war von fundamentaler Bedeutung für die königliche Legitimation.[7] Allerdings musste sich die Göttlichkeit der Herrscher durch ihre Taten offenbaren (dazu konnten militärische Siege oder Wohltätigkeit gegenüber den Untertanen zählen) und sie musste durch die Untertanen bzw. diejenigen, die ein Ehrendekret verabschiedeten, (an)erkannt werden. Es spricht vieles dafür, dass dem König und der Königin ein göttlicher Status innerhalb eines griechischen bzw. ägyptischen Herrscherkultes jeweils kurz nach einem Regierungsantritt separat zuerkannt wurde.

Für den Bereich der ägyptischen Tempel dienen die Synodaldekrete als das Medium für die Bekanntmachung der königlichen Taten, die daraufhin erfolgte priesterliche Anerkennung der göttlichen Natur der amtierenden Herrscher und, im Ergebnis, deren Integration in den ägyptischen Götterkult. Um eine möglichst hohe Verbreitung der Inhalte zu garantieren, wurde verfügt, die Beschlussinhalte auf einer Stele, die in einem öffentlich zugänglichen Bereich der Tempel aufzustellen war,[8] in drei Versionen zu publizieren (Hieroglyphen, Demotisch, Griechisch).[9] Wie schon angedeutet, war es bei der Komposition eines Dekrettextes von eminenter Bedeutung, nicht nur den Erfordernissen eines hellenistischen Herrscherkultes nachzukommen, sondern vornehmlich auch die Kultpraktiken in den ägyptischen Tempeln zu berücksichtigen und umzusetzen.[10] Kurzum, die Priester sahen sich vor die Aufgabe gestellt, die ägyptische Vorstellung eines göttlichen Königtums (durch den königlichen *Ka* versinnbildlicht) mit dem griechischen Konzept eines gottgleichen Herrschers in Einklang zu bringen. Wie erfolgreich ihnen diese Verschmelzung von eigenen und fremden Ideen gelang, zeigt die Tatsache, dass die Synodaldekrete über ein Jahrhundert lang eine göttliche Verehrung der regierenden ptolemäischen Herrscherpaare in *allen* ägyptischen Tempeln ermöglichte.[11]

---

[7] Für die Umsetzung dieses Herrscherkultes bzw. seine praktischen und materiellen Aspekte siehe die Beiträge in Caneva 2020.
[8] Dazu konnten der Dromos oder der (Fest-)Hof zählen. Vgl. Krapf 2020, S. 164–165 für archäologische Hinweise, aus denen sich womöglich die Zugangsberechtigung in den Hof für ein breiteres Publikums erschließen lässt, vgl. auch Krapf 2019. Vgl. auch den Beitrag von S. Caneva und S. Pfeiffer in diesem Band.
[9] Vgl. rezent Love 2021, S. 60–64; Pries 2023, S. 3.
[10] Vgl. dazu sowie im Hinblick auf die Tempeldekoration jüngst Preys 2022.
[11] Zu den Aspekten, seit wann bzw. wie lange Synoden (jährlich) stattfanden bzw. die Synodaldekrete der Verehrung der ptolemäischen Herrscher in den Tempeln und allgemein ihrer Legitimierung dienten, siehe Gorre, Veïsse 2020.

## 2 Die Synodaldekrete Philensis II und Philensis I

Auch die Synodaldekrete Philensis II, das am Ende des 19. Regierungsjahres Ptolemaios' V. (= 186 v. Chr.) verabschiedet wurde, und Philensis I, kurz danach zu Beginn seines 21. Regierungsjahres promulgiert (= 185 v. Chr.), sind genau in diesem Aktionsrahmen zu lesen und verstehen. Neben dem Stein von Rosette gehörten sie seit ihrer „Entdeckung" auf der Insel Philae (daher ihr Name) in den 1840er Jahren durch Richard Lepsius[12] und andere zu den ersten für die Forschung verfügbaren Textversionen dieser Art von Inschriften. Im Gegensatz zu der üblichen Publikationsform auf einer Stele entschied man sich dort, die Dekrete an der östlichen Außenwand des Mammisis einzugravieren,[13] die zu diesem Zeitpunkt noch nicht mit dem vorgesehenen Reliefdekor ausgestaltet worden war. Das sollte sich aber bald ändern, mit dem Ergebnis, dass alle Textversionen der beiden Dekrete durch diese Arbeiten stark in Mitleidenschaft gezogen wurden und in einem äußerst fragmentarischen Zustand auf uns gekommen sind: Erhalten sind die hieroglyphischen und demotischen Versionen von Philensis II und Philensis I, von denen allerdings ganze Passagen durch die späteren Übergravierungen vollkommen zerstört wurden. Es gibt gleichwohl berechtigte Gründe für die Annahme, dass beide Dekrete ursprünglich vollständig an der Wand zu sehen waren, sie also auch über eine griechische Version unterhalb der beiden ägyptischen Versionen wie eine Darstellung verfügten, die normalerweise den Giebel der Stele schmückte.

Bei näherer Betrachtung fällt die einheitliche Gestaltung ins Auge. Die beiden hieroglyphischen und die beiden demotischen Versionen sind in Textblöcken zu jeweils 16 Zeilen (dreimal) bzw. 14 Zeilen (einmal) angeordnet. Diese Vorgehensweise spricht für eine zeitgleiche Anbringung, die erst nach dem Beschluss von Philensis I, also 185 v. Chr., erfolgt sein kann. Anders lässt es sich auch kaum erklären, wieso der ältere Text (Philensis II) links und der jüngere (Philensis I) rechts positioniert wurde, wenn die Schriftrichtung in allen Fällen von rechts nach links verläuft. Nebenbei bemerkt hat dieser Umstand dazu geführt, dass Lepsius sich bei der Nummerierung der Dekrete für die – chronologisch betrachtet – falsche Reihenfolge entschied; sie wird aber auch hier beibehalten, um jegliche Verwirrung zu vermeiden.

---

[12] Vgl. Gerhardt et al. 2022, für Abschriften aus dem Nachlass von J.G. Wilkinson vgl. Panov 2023.
[13] Vgl. Kockelmann 2020, S. 149.

## 3 Der Aufstand in der Thebais 206–186 v. Chr

Die sehr wahrscheinlich simultan erfolgte Anbringung von Philensis II und Philensis I in Philae dürfte dafürsprechen, in den beiden Dekreten nicht nur eine Einheit bezüglich ihrer Publikationsform und des Layouts zu sehen, sondern vornehmlich auch bezüglich ihres Inhalts. Und dieser inhaltliche Nexus liegt in den Ereignissen, die die Basis für den Beschluss der beiden Dekrete darstellen, nämlich der Niederringung dessen, was – aus der Perspektive der Sieger aufseiten der ptolemäischen Monarchie – als der „Große Aufstand in der Thebais" der Jahre 206–186 v. Chr. bekannt ist,[14] der damit verbundenen vollständigen Rückeroberung Oberägyptens für die ptolemäische Krone (Philensis II) und der im Anschluss getroffenen Maßnahmen für eine Konsolidierung der politischen und sozialen Situation in der ehemaligen Konfliktzone (Philensis I).

Die historische Bedeutung der in den Dekreten enthaltenen Aussagen wurde gleich nach ihrem Bekanntwerden erkannt. Das verwundert kaum, denn Philensis II ist genau auf den Tag datiert, an dem die Nachricht eines Sieges der ptolemäischen Armee über die aufständischen Truppen unter der Führung eines Chaonnophris in der Hauptstadt Alexandria eintrifft. Dieser Sieg beendet einen Zustand, durch den weite Teile Oberägyptens seit der Regierungszeit Ptolemaios' IV. Philopator der ptolemäischen Kontrolle entzogen waren, wiewohl die ptolemäische Armee anscheinend über die meiste Zeit hinweg einige strategische Punkte besetzt halten konnte.

Zunächst wurde die Aufstandsbewegung von einem gewissen Haronnophris (Ḥr-wn-nfr) angeführt, der, von der thebanischen Priesterschaft unterstützt bzw. anerkannt, den Titel eines Königs annahm, wie wir u. a. durch demotische Urkunden wissen.[15] Auf diesen folgte Anchonnophris, oder Chaonnophris, wie der Name oftmals wiedergegeben wird (ʿnḫ-wn-nfr/Ḥr-wn-nfr). In welcher Beziehung die beiden standen, ist nach wie vor eine offene Frage. Letzterer könnte der Sohn des Ersteren, gar nicht mit ihm verwandt oder ein und derselbe Mann gewesen sein, der aus uns unbekannten Gründen mitten in seiner Herrschaft seinen Namen änderte – jedenfalls fällt auf, dass Chaonnophris die Regierungsjahre des Haronnophris fortführt.[16] Auch ist nicht sicher, ob es sich (wahrscheinlich) um einen Ägypter oder (weit weniger wahrscheinlich) um einen Nubier gehandelt

---

14 Aktuelle Übersichten über und Hinweise auf das Geschehen bei Johstono 2016; Armoni, Jördens 2018, S. 85–86; Birk 2020, S. 432–439; Pfeiffer 2021a; Veïsse 2022; Fischer-Bovet 2023, S. 189–190, siehe des Weiteren die Beiträge in diesem Band.
15 Vgl. zuletzt Birk 2020, S. 433; Veïsse 2022.
16 Vgl. rezent Birk 2020, S. 433; Veïsse 2022, S. 58–59; 65–66; Fischer-Bovet 2023, S. 189–190.

hat.¹⁷ Von ptolemäischer Warte aus war Chaonnophris, von dem in Philensis II ausschließlich die Rede ist, vor allem eins: ein Aufrührer.

Nachdem die Herrschaft 204 v. Chr. von Ptolemaios IV. auf seinen noch minderjährigen Sohn Ptolemaios V. übergegangen war, stand das Königreich vor gewaltigen Herausforderungen. Das ptolemäische Heer war vor allem durch den andauernden militärischen Konflikt mit dem Seleukidenreich gebunden. Erst nach einem Friedenschluss mit Antiochos III., der in der Vermählung seiner Tochter Kleopatra (I.) mit Ptolemaios V. 194/193 v. Chr. eine wichtige Bestätigung fand, war es anscheinend möglich geworden, das militärische Engagement in Oberägypten zu intensivieren. Wie genau dabei vorgegangen wurde, ist bis auf wenige Details nicht überliefert. Schlussendlich obsiegte die ptolemäische Krone: Am 23. Epiphi des Jahres 19 Ptolemaios' V. (27. August 186 v. Chr.) gelang einem ptolemäischen Heer unter dem Kommando des Komanos, einem Hofling am Hof in Alexandria, der lang erhoffte Sieg über die Rebellen an einem nicht näher genannten Ort in der Thebais – „im Südland (= Oberägypten) in dem Gebiet von Theben".¹⁸ Deren Anführer Chaonnophris konnte gefangen genommen werden, sein Sohn fand dagegen auf dem Schlachtfeld den Tod. Dieses Ereignis markiert die Rückgewinnung weiter Teile der ägyptischen *Chora* für die ptolemäische Monarchie.

## 4 Der Aufstand in der Thebais und die hierzu relevanten Aussagen in Philensis II

Der Sieg hatte fraglos eine enorme Bedeutung für das politische und soziale Gefüge nicht nur in den eroberten Gebieten, sondern im gesamten Land. Für die ägyptischen Priester, die just zu diesem Zeitpunkt in Alexandria zusammengekommen waren, war es daher ein geeigneter Anlass, mit Philensis II ein weiteres Synodaldekret zu Ehren Ptolemaios' V. zu beschließen. Nach dem Memphis-Dekret des Jahres 9 (196 v. Chr.) bestätigen sie ein weiteres Mal seinen göttlichen Status. Und es sollte nicht das letzte Mal sein, da in kurzer Folge weitere Dekrete verabschiedet wurden, so im Jahr 21 (Philensis I, 185 v. Chr.) und im Jahr 23 nach

---

17 Vgl. Veïsse 2022, S. 64. Pfeiffer 2021a, S. 112 erwägt die Möglichkeit, dass Haronnophris wie Chaonnophris „aus soldatischen Kreisen stammten, es sich also um Männer handelte, die im Ptolemäerheer in Führungspositionen aufgestiegen waren".

18 Philae, Zl. 3–4 (siehe den vollständigen Wortlaut unten auf S. 342). Oftmals wird erwogen (tlw. mit direktem Bezug auf diese Stelle), die Entscheidung sei in der Region von Syene, also ganz im Süden von Oberägypten, gefallen, so zuletzt etwa Johstono 2016, S. 207; Armoni, Jördens 2018, S. 86; 98; Birk 2020, S. 434.

einem weiteren militärischen Erfolg im Delta (182 v. Chr.).[19] Ob die Priester tatsächlich bereits in der Hauptstadt versammelt waren, als die Siegesnachricht zehn Tage nach dem Sieg am 3. Mesore (6. September 186 v. Chr.) durch Aristonikos, einen weiteren Höfling und General der Kavallerie, überbracht wurde, und *ad hoc* ein neues Dekret verabschiedeten, wie uns der Text glauben machen will, ist nicht sicher zu entscheiden. Es ist aber keineswegs auszuschließen; ein Grund für das Versammlungsdatum, wie etwa ein wichtiges religiöses Ereignis (z. B. die Inthronisation des Apis-Stieres), der in den anderen Synodaldekreten regelmäßig genannt wird, fehlt hier jedenfalls. Andererseits wäre eine nachträgliche Rückdatierung auf dieses symbolische Datum ebenso wenig unerwartet.

Da, worauf im Folgenden noch weiter einzugehen ist, der Fokus in Philensis II in jeder Hinsicht auf der Niederringung des Aufstands liegt, erscheint es nur folgerichtig, eine Schilderung der Ereignisse in den Dekrettext zu integrieren. Auch in Philensis I gibt es starke Reminiszenzen an die aktuelle Entwicklung in der *Chora*. Dort liegt das Interesse aber eindeutig in dem Wunsch einer Konsolidierung der Lage nach der Niederschlagung des Aufstands, etwa mittels Verzichtserklärungen auf noch ausstehende Steuern vonseiten des Königshauses[20] sowie der Hervorhebung der Königin, die als Förderin des Tempelkultes gezeichnet wird. Die Betonung dieses Aspektes ist umso dringlicher, als Philensis I im Bereich der Ehrungen eine aktualisierte Fassung der im Memphis-Dekret beschlossenen Ehrungen darstellt. In letzterem Dekret sind diese auf den König allein bezogen (da er bei Beschlussfassung noch nicht verheiratet war), so dass Philensis I nicht zuletzt dazu dient, die dort enthaltenen Ehrungen auf die Königin, Kleopatra I., auszudehnen und das Königspaar gemeinsam zu deren Empfängern zu machen. Dieses Anpassen an aktuelle Entwicklungen könnte, am Rande bemerkt, ein Grund für die dichte Abfolge von Dekreten in der späteren Regierungszeit Ptolemaios' V. sein: Immer dann, nachdem eine Stadt, eine Region oder ein Landesteil Ägyptens für die ptolemäische Krone zurückgewonnen worden war, griff man bewusst auf das Medium des Synodaldekretes zurück, um bereits beschlossenen Kultpraktiken auch in den Tempel der wieder in den Herrschaftsbereich integrierten Gebiete Gültigkeit zu verleihen.[21]

Die Schilderung der Ereignisse wurde an nicht weniger als an drei Stellen in das Textformular von Philensis II eingebunden. Wie weiter unten noch dargelegt wird, sind die Nennung der Daten und der auf der ptolemäischen Seite tatsächlich

---

[19] Siehe zum Dekret des Jahres 23 (182 v. Chr.) zuletzt A. Nespoulous-Phalippou in diesem Band.
[20] Zu weiteren Maßnahmen, die in Philensis I nicht oder wenigstens nicht konkret genannt werden, worunter königliche Amnestieerlasse u. a. für ägyptische, ehemals mit den Rebellen kämpfende Soldaten (*Machimoi*) zählen, vgl. Armoni, Jördens 2018; Pfeiffer 2021a, S. 111–112; 120–122.
[21] Vgl. auch Pfeiffer 2021a, S. 118–119.

in die Kampfhandlungen involvierten Akteure von besonderem historischen Interesse, und auf diesen Details liegt die Betonung in zwei kürzeren Passagen des Dekretes. Daneben gibt es einen äußerst ausführlich gehaltenen Bericht (im Folgenden „Langfassung" genannt), der das Wesen der Rebellion (und der daran beteiligten Personen) sowie das Vorgehen des Königs zu deren Niederschlagung behandelt. Diese Version stellt ein zeitgenössisches Schlüsseldokument unseres Wissens über den Aufstand in Oberägypten von 206–186 v. Chr. aus den Augen der Sieger dar. Gleichwohl sind einem eindeutigen und kohärenten Verständnis dessen, was hier erzählt wird, enge Grenzen gesetzt. Das liegt hauptsächlich an dem äußerst fragmentarischen Charakter aller erhaltenen Textvertreter, ganze Passagen sind gar nicht oder nur bruchstückhaft erhalten. Das gilt aus den bereits erwähnten Gründen insbesondere für die beiden Versionen in Philae (hieroglyphisch und demotisch), aber auch für die einzige bislang bekannte Parallele des hieroglyphischen Textes auf einer fragmentarisch erhaltenen Stele.[22] So ist es nach wie vor an vielen Stellen schwierig bis unmöglich, den Sinn eindeutig zu erfassen. Hinzu kommen der Intention des Berichtes folgend eine mythologisierte Färbung (siehe im Folgenden) sowie die Verwendung zahlreicher inhaltlicher Topoi. Der Gebrauch von allgemein gehaltenem oder selten belegtem Vokabular eröffnet zudem zahlreiche Interpretationsmöglichkeiten. Das gilt vor allem für die hieroglyphische Textversion, die aber insgesamt einen besseren Erhaltungszustand aufweist als die demotische. Bis zum Auffinden einer weiteren, besser oder gar vollständig erhaltenen Textversion dürfte sich an dieser Situation wenig ändern.

Die Langfassung in Philensis II lässt sich in zwei Abschnitte einteilen. Zunächst dient eine Vorgeschichte der Darlegung, warum der König überhaupt gezwungen ist, militärisch in Oberägypten einzugreifen. Der Hauptteil beschäftigt sich in der Folge mit den Maßnahmen des Königs, die zu dem erwarteten Sieg führen werden. Insgesamt ist dieser Bericht ein kunstvoller Einschub in einen besonderen, aber elementaren Abschnitt aller bekannten Synodaldekrete, der eine Neuerung gegenüber den griechischen Ehrendekreten darstellt. Es handelt sich um eine Art von Gegengabe oder Vergeltung (*isw* im hieroglyphischen, *šbt* im demotischen Text), mithilfe derer sich die Götter dem König (bzw. dem Königspaar) für seine (bzw. ihre) Taten erkenntlich zeigen. Dieser Abschnitt dient als Scharnier zwischen den königlichen Taten und den von den Priestern beschlossenen Ehrungen. Vor dieser priesterlichen Handlung erkennen zunächst die Götter und

---

22 Diese Stele befindet sich heute im Ägyptischen Museum Kairo (TR 27/11/58/4) und stammt ursprünglich aus einem Kultort des Amun. Vielleicht Naukratis? Zumindest entdeckte man dort Versionen weiterer Synodaldekrete aus der Zeit Ptolemaios' V., vgl. dazu Recklinghausen 2019, S. 316 (mit weiterer Literatur).

Göttinnen die königlichen Taten an und zeigen sich wohlwollend. In vielen Dekreten ist der Abschnitt relativ kurz gehalten, die Götter gewähren hier Glück, Gesundheit und ein langes Königtum etc. Bei näherer Betrachtung der Abfolge der königlichen Taten und der göttlichen Gegengabe ist man geneigt, hierin eine Umsetzung des *do ut des*-Prinzips zu erblicken, das in den Ritualszenen der zeitgenössischen Tempeldekoration allgegenwärtig ist.[23]

In Philensis II weist dieser Abschnitt eine beträchtliche Länge auf, denn bei näherer Betrachtung entpuppen sich der erfolgreiche Kampf gegen die Rebellen als die göttliche Gegengabe und der Bericht darüber demnach als Narrativ göttlich sanktionierter bzw. gewährter königlicher Sieghaftigkeit. Eine ähnliche Interaktion seitens der Götter findet sich im Rahmen der Synodaldekrete bereits im Raphia-Dekret (217 v. Chr.), sie ist aber auch Teil zahlreicher königlicher Inschriften aus pharaonischer Zeit.

Bereits durch den ersten Satz dieses Abschnittes kommt diese Interaktion zum Ausdruck: Letztendlich ist die Gesamtheit des ägyptischen Pantheons die maßgebliche Instanz, die den König befähigt, siegreich zu sein. Der Bericht beginnt mit der folgenden Aussage:

> Die gesamten Götter Ägyptens und alle Göttinnen haben das veranlasst, was alles der König von Ober- und Unterägypten, der Sohn des Re (Ptolemaios, er lebe ewig, geliebt von Ptah¿, der erscheinende Gott, getan hat gegen den Feind der Götter, Chaonnophris (...). (Philae, Zl. 7–8; Stele Kairo, Zl. 22–23)[24]

Des Weiteren werden wir – gemäß der dem Dekret intrinsischen theologischen Wahrnehmung – über die Hauptakteure in Kenntnis gesetzt: Neben dem ägyptischen Pantheon sind dies der legitime König Ptolemaios V. und der gottlose Rebell Chaonnophris. Der Satz wird mit einer Auflistung der frevlerischen Taten des Letzteren und seiner Kumpane fortgesetzt. Das Bild, das sich hieraus ergibt, spiegelt also den Zustand vor Ptolemaios' Eingreifen wider und dient somit als Vorgeschichte. Der gerade zitierte Satz wird daher wie folgt fortgesetzt:

> (... Chaonnophris), der den Aufruhr in Ägypten begonnen,[25] Betrüger (um sich) versammelt und alle Gebiete Ägyptens in Unruhe versetzt hatte, indem er Böses entstehen ließ mittels

---

23 Siehe rezent Pfeiffer 2020, S. 86; Pfeiffer 2021b, S. 242–243.
24 Alle zitierten Passagen geben die hieroglyphische Version wieder (siehe Recklinghausen 2018, Teil 2, Anhang A: Textsynopse); auf die Kenntlichmachung ergänzter Stellen etc. wurde in diesem Rahmen bewusst verzichtet. Für die textkritische Ausgabe wie für einen philologischen Kommentar siehe Teil 1, Kapitel II; vgl. jetzt auch Panov 2022, S. 269–293.
25 Nimmt man diese Aussage wörtlich, ließe sich hier ein Hinweis darauf erkennen, dass Haronnophris und Chaonnophris ein und dieselbe Person waren, vgl. Veïsse 2022, S. 59.

ihrer Macht (im (?)) Gau von Theben,[26] indem man die Heiligtümer zerstörte (und) ihre Priester sowie die Stundenpriester ihrer Tempel tötete. Geplündert wurden ihre Altäre (und) ihre Ausstattung. Ihr (= der Rebellen) Arm erreichte ihre Schreine und sogar (ihre) Kultbilder. Sie wiesen zurück (= sie kümmerten sich nicht?) die Städte und ihre Leute, bestehend aus Männern, Frauen und Kindern, ebenso wie sie (alles) andere in Unordnung brachten, sie erhöhten die Steuern der Fruchtländer, sie gruben das Wasser ab und legten Feuer (?). (Philae, Zl. 8–9; Stele Kairo, Zl. 23–26)

Einige dieser beschriebenen Unbilden werden in dieser oder ähnlicher Form tatsächlich im Rahmen des Aufstands stattgefunden haben – so scheint beispielsweise die Bau- und Dekorationstätigkeit in den Tempelbezirken Oberägyptens während dieser Zeit weitgehend ausgesetzt bzw. stark eingeschränkt gewesen zu sein, wovon u. a. eine oft herangezogene, zweifach im Tempel von Edfu belegte Textpassage berichtet.[27] Dennoch fällt der stereotype bzw. topische Charakter der Beschreibung ins Auge, denn sie ist ganz typisch für die Schilderung chaotischer, von der Norm der göttlichen Ordnung (Maat) abweichender Zustände, wenn das Land keinen legitimen Herrscher hat. Duktus und Wortwahl in Philensis II sind dem Tenor solcher Beschreibungen durchgehend verhaftet. Dennoch ist das Vokabular im Detail recht treffend gewählt, wenn es etwa darum geht, die Taten der Rebellen auf einer theologischen Ebene mit Seth, dem Götterfeind und Inbegriff des Chaos *per se*, zu verknüpfen. Nicht von ungefähr beginnt Chaonnophris den „Kampf" bzw. den „Aufruhr" (*bꜥr* < der Gott Baal = Seth) im hieroglyphischen Text gegen *Bꜣk.t* – eine Bezeichnung für Ägypten mit einem kultisch-religiösen Konnex.[28] Auch das Wort *npḏ*,[29] mit dem das Gemetzel an den Priestern beschrieben wird, fällt genau in dieses Umfeld. Der Vorbericht schildert also äußerst geschickt und umfänglich Chaonnophris' sündiges und gottloses Verhalten. Aufgrund der Einbindung bekannter Motive, die bereits über Jahrtausende die Wiedergabe ägyptischer Chaosbeschreibungen ausgemacht haben, kann bei niemanden ein Zweifel daran aufkommen, dass die Rebellion und sein Anführer in keiner Weise gerechtfertigt sind und es dem legitimen Herrscher obliegt, diese

---

**26** Zwar liegt jeweils eine unterschiedliche Wortwahl vor, aber diese Ortsangabe dürfte in etwa mit dem Gebiet übereinstimmen, in dem die ptolemäische Armee den Sieg über die Rebellen erringt (siehe oben S. 336).
**27** Hierzu zuletzt Birk 2020, S. 432; Veïsse 2022, S. 58, Anm. 5; zu möglichen Auswirkungen im thebanischen Bereich Johstono 2016, S. 196; Birk 2020, S. 434; Pfeiffer 2021a, S. 110; Ryholt 2022, S. 19–21 sowie der Beitrag von F. Relats Montserrat in diesem Band. Vgl. Silverstein, Littman 2023 zu Auswirkungen im Kontext des in der Rosettana beschriebenen Aufstands in Unterägypten.
**28** Philae, Zl. 8; Stele Kairo, Zl. 23. Dagegen ist im demotischen Text, Philae (dem.), Zl. 7 mit *bks* bzw. *Kmy* eine solche mythologische Gleichsetzung nicht derart vordergründig zu greifen.
**29** Philae, Zl. 8; Stele Kairo, Zl. 24.

Ausdrucksformen „sethischen" Seins zu bekämpfen und zu eliminieren. Es ist also an der Zeit, dass der rechtmäßige König Ptolemaios auf den Plan tritt.

Somit folgt die eigentlich zu erzählende Geschichte, wie es dem Monarchen gelingt, Oberägypten von den Götterfeinden zu befreien und wieder in das ptolemäische Herrschaftsgebiet zu integrieren. Wie zu erwarten, ist dieser Teil umfangreicher gehalten als die Vorgeschichte. Leider ist er aber auch dadurch weit fragmentarischer erhalten, und zahlreiche Details bleiben – nicht zuletzt, weil hier mit der Beschreibung eines spezifischen Ereignisses weit weniger auf ein vorhandenes Formular bzw. Textmuster zurückgegriffen werden konnte – zumindest mir unklar. Einen kohärenten Ablauf der beschriebenen Ereignisse wiederzugeben ist daher für viele Passagen nicht möglich. Dennoch sei an dieser Stelle eine grobe inhaltliche Zusammenfassung der unterschiedlichen Phasen geboten.

Die Schilderung beginnt mit der Versicherung des Königs, sich um das Wohlergehen der ägyptischen Tempel zu kümmern. Dann heißt es u. a.:

> (...) Er setzte griechische Truppen in sie (= Tempel), (...) die Menschen, die in Ägypten umherstreiften (...) Vereinigt waren (?) die beiden Teile seines Volkes, indem sie wie Kinder bei ihnen waren, um sie nicht Rebellion und Unruhe gegen ihn und seinen Vater planen (?) zu lassen und sie wiederkehren zu lassen, um selbiges (erneut) zu tun. Seine Majestät ließ Silber und Gold in unendlich hoher Zahl fortnehmen aus (?) *T3-bh3*, und man ließ Truppen nach Ägypten bringen als Ausgleich dafür, was den Ufern (= den Tempeln?) auferlegt (?) worden war, um wohlbehalten sein zu lassen (...). (Philae, Zl. 9–10; Stele Kairo, Zl. 27–31)

Allem Anschein nach werden vornehmlich griechische Soldaten als Garnison in die durch Umfassungsmauern gesicherten Tempelareale gelegt, vielleicht mit dem Ziel, die umliegenden Gebiete vor marodierenden Banden zu schützen. Es ist nicht auszuschließen, hierin einen Hinweis auf die Situation der 190er Jahre zu sehen, als die ptolemäische Armee nur einige Brückenköpfe halten konnte, aber das ist bloße Spekulation. Darüber hinaus findet sich in der Schilderung kein Hinweis, durch den sich auf eine genaue chronologische Abfolge der Ereignisse schließen ließe. Auf diese ersten Maßnahmen folgen mutmaßlich Handlungen, die zu den entscheidenden Kampfhandlungen überleiten oder bereits zu diesen gehören, aber ein Verständnis des Textes bleibt auch hier aus den bereits genannten Gründen nebulös. Die Erwähnung der Region *T3-bh(3)*, die sich weit im Süden außerhalb Ägyptens befindet, ist aufschlussreich. Aus dieser Region kamen vielleicht Menschen, die Chaonnophris unterstützten, wie eine besser erhaltene Stelle nahelegen könnte. So lautet die Mitteilung an den König, die ihn am 3. Mesore erreicht:

> Sie (= die ptolemäische Armee) haben den Feind der Götter, den Rebellen Chaonnophris in einem Kampf, der mit ihm geführt wurde, gefangen genommen im Regierungsjahr 19, am

> 23. Epiphi, lebend (o. ä.),[30] während sie seinen Sohn getötet haben, (sowie) weitere Feinde und die nubischen Barbaren, weil (?) sie mit ihm gegangen sind (?). (Philae, Zl. 10–11; Stele Kairo, Zl. 32–34)

Dieser Wortlaut, der sich fast identisch auch in der Einleitung findet (siehe im Folgenden), wirkt wie ein Resümee der vorangegangenen Passagen, so dass jene tatsächlich den Ablauf der Kampfhandlungen wiedergeben dürften. Jedenfalls ist das Ergebnis klar: Der gefangen genommene Chaonnophris wird in Ketten vor den König gebracht und danach sehr wahrscheinlich getötet. Die Schilderung schließt mit der Aussage, dass Ptolemaios und Kleopatra den ägyptischen Göttern ihre Reverenz erweisen, weil diese ihnen den Sieg zuteilwerden ließen. Der Hinweis auf die göttliche Gunst, vulgo den Sieg, steht somit am Anfang und am Ende dieser ausführlichen Schilderung und dient stilistisch als rahmendes Element.

Innerhalb der Langfassung wird ein wichtiges Detail bezeichnenderweise ausgelassen, das dafür an zwei anderen Stellen in Philensis II – nämlich innerhalb der Einleitung und den priesterlichen Ehrungen – eine prominente Hervorhebung erfährt: die Namen der beiden Feldherren und Hofleute Aristonikos und Komanos. So lautet der Wortlaut der Botschaft an den König in der Einleitung:

> (Die Priester waren in Alexandria versammelt,) als seiner Majestät berichtet wurde aus dem Mund des Vertrauten seiner Majestät, dem Liebling des Königs, des Obersten der Reiterkommandeure, Aristonikos, Sohn des Aristonikos bezüglich Komanos, der zu den besten Freunden seiner Majestät zählt, mit den Worten: ‚Er (= Komanos) hat gekämpft im Südland in dem Gebiet von Theben mit dem Rebellen, dem Feind der Götter, dem Aufrührer Chaonnophris, und den Soldaten der Nubier, indem sie mit ihm vereint waren. Er (= Komanos) hat sie getötet, dieser Aufrührer (aber) wurde lebend gefangen genommen'. (Philae, Zl. 3–4; Stele Kairo, Zl. 8–12)

Im Kontext der priesterlichen Ehrungen liest sich das Ganze wie folgt:

> Man soll den 3. Mesore – den Tag der Meldung an seine Majestät aus dem Mund des Vertrauten seiner Majestät, des Lieblings des Königs, des Obersten der Kavallerie, Aristonikos, Sohn des Aristonikos, mit dem Wortlaut: ‚Gefangennahme des Aufrührers!' – und den 23. Epiphi – den Tag, als Komanos, der zu den besten Freunden seiner Majestät gehört, ihn (= Chaonnophris) hatte ergreifen lassen – in Ägypten alljährlich (und) zu jeder Zeit als großes Fest begehen. (Philae, Zl. 14–15)

Die Schilderungen des großen Aufstands in Philensis II vermitteln uns demnach wichtige Details eines Schlüsselmomentes der ptolemäischen Geschichte, wie etwa exakte Datumsangaben des Kampfes und der Ankunft der Siegesnachricht

---

**30** Der genaue Wortlaut lässt sich nicht rekonstruieren, siehe aber die Formulierung in der Einleitung (folgendes Textzitat).

in der Hauptstadt, die Namen der beteiligten Personen, oder bestimmte Aktionen, wie die Rekrutierung griechischer Soldaten etc. Dennoch bleibt der Ablauf des Geschehens in vielerlei Hinsicht diffus. Angaben zu Dauer, Intensität und Art der Kampfhandlungen werden uns – wenigstens in den erhaltenen Passagen – nicht mitgeteilt. Welche Manöver waren beispielsweise für den Sieg ausschlaggebend und wie oft trafen die gegnerischen Parteien aufeinander? Ebenso wenig wird auf die Fragen eingegangen, wie Chaonnophris und sein Vorgänger an die Macht kamen, welche Gründe zum Ausbruch der Rebellion geführt haben[31] und warum die ägyptischen Götter all dies haben geschehen lassen. Das ist von theologischer Warte aus nicht ganz unerheblich, ist doch die Niederschlagung der Rebellion letztlich ein durch göttlichen Willen herbeigeführtes Ereignis.

Die Frage stellt sich somit, welchen Zweck die Verfasser, vermutlich doch die Priester oder eine bestimmte Gruppe von ihnen,[32] mit dieser Art von Schilderung in Philensis II intendierten. Ein näherer Blick auf die Komposition des Berichts ist bei der Beantwortung dieser Frage hilfreich und dürfte nicht zuletzt für dessen Einordnung als historische Quelle von Nutzen sein.[33] Wie bereits angedeutet, darf die Hauptintention für den Beschluss von Philensis II nicht übersehen werden. Ebenso wie alle anderen Synodaldekrete dient es vordergründig religiösen bzw. kultischen Zwecken in den ägyptischen Göttertempeln, nämlich der göttlichen Verehrung des amtierenden ptolemäischen Königs(paares). Nicht von ungefähr werden genau diese Tempel in jeder Passage unserer Geschichte wie auch in dem gesamten Dekret immer wieder erwähnt – diese, die dort verehrten Gottheiten und deren Priester sind der Kristallisationspunkt eines jeden Synodaldekretes.

Innerhalb der Struktur von Philensis II dient die Langfassung über den endgültigen Sieg aber zunächst als ein Instrument, den Sieg auf eine göttliche Entscheidung zurückzuführen und den König als den alleinigen Handelnden darzustellen. An dieser Stelle sind daher nur die Details enthalten, die ihn als siegreichen Monarchen wiedergeben. Aus einer innerägyptischen Perspektive lautet der Tenor vereinfacht gesagt: Eine durch einen Rebellenherrscher verursachte Chaossituation wird durch

---

31 Siehe zu möglichen Ursachen Pfeiffer 2021a und Veïsse 2022, die auch die Perspektive der „Aufständischen" in den Blick nehmen. Dezidiert auf Naturphänomene (konkret: weltweite Vulkanaktivitäten), die zu niedrigen Nilüberschwemmungen und damit geringen Ernteerträgen führten, als Auslöser von Erhebungen verweisen Ludlow, Manning 2016; siehe auch den Beitrag von J. Manning in diesem Band.
32 Pfeiffer 2021b, S. 245–246 zufolge spielte die memphitische Priesterschaft bei der Redaktion der Dekrete eine maßgebliche Rolle.
33 Vgl. dazu auch die prägnante Einschätzung bei Pfeiffer 2021a, S. 113.

den legitimen Pharao mit Zuspruch aller Mitglieder des ägyptischen Pantheons abgewendet. Innerhalb dieses Plots geht es also nicht um den Kampf eines Herrschers, der einer fremden Dynastie entsprungen ist, gegen einen (wahrscheinlich) ägyptischen Rebellen bzw. Gegenkönig. Vielmehr ist es ein Kampf zwischen einem frommen und den ägyptischen Göttern ergebenen Mann, der ihrem Willen und Wohlergehen verpflichtet ist und auf diese Weise die göttliche Ordnung (Maat) garantiert, gegen jemanden, der als Feind der Götter das Chaos (Isfet) und somit genau das Gegenteil repräsentiert.[34] Indem in diesem Schema die für die altägyptische Mythologie so typische Dichotomie zwischen Ordnung (Horus [bzw. der amtierende König] als legitimer Herrscher; Ägypten; Tempel) und Chaos (Seth; Ausland; profane Welt) zur Anwendung kommt, das von alters her in vielen Kriegsberichten, Erzählungen, Mythen und Kosmogonien zu greifen und in der zeitgleichen Tempeldekoration in Text und Bild omnipräsent ist,[35] liegt der narrative Impetus der Erzählung eindeutig auf einer mythologisierten (oder theologischen) Ausdeutung und nicht auf dem, was wir nach heutigem Verständnis unter historischer Genauigkeit verstünden. Die Art der Textgestaltung bestätigt diese Sichtweise, denn der Bericht wirkt wie die aktualisierte bzw. mit Bezug auf das spezifische Ereignis kompilierte Variante einer Geschichte, die in der Vergangenheit schon oft erzählt worden ist. Fraglos liegt dem Bericht ein reales historisches Ereignis zugrunde (vgl. die genannten Daten und die namentliche Erwähnung des Gegners bzw. der siegreichen Feldherren), aber der gesamte Aufbau und viele Erzählstränge erinnern auf bemerkenswerte Weise an ältere Aussagen über kriegerische Auseinandersetzungen und Rebellionen. Sie lassen sich mindestens bis in die Ramessiden- und die Spätzeit zurückverfolgen und sind in Königsinschriften, aber auch in autobiographischen Texten einflussreicher Personen aus dem Priestermilieu enthalten, wie beispielsweise Monthemhet[36] in Theben, Udja-

---

**34** Siehe auch die Bemerkungen von Pfeiffer 2021a, bes. S. 110–117 zur (vermeintlichen) Dichotomie „Fremder" und „Einheimischer", die zudem aufseiten der „Rebellen" womöglich ganz anders (nämlich als dezidiert „antigriechisch") erlebt wurde als aufseiten der Ägypter, Griechen etc., die sich nicht auf ihre Seite schlugen. Vgl. allgemein Assmann 2000, S. 91–92 und 227–228.
**35** Mit Pfeiffer 2021a, S. 116–117; Pfeiffer 2021b, S. 243 ist es gut möglich, dass die „Gegenkönige" eine ganz vergleichbare Strategie für ihre eigene Legitimation heranzogen, freilich mit einer invertierten Rollenverteilung, wonach sie die Seite der Maat und die ptolemäischen Könige die Inkarnation des Seth einnehmen. Für Ritualszenen in den Tempeln, welche die Feindvernichtung zum Thema haben, vgl. jüngst Coppens 2021; Preys 2021; Preys 2022, S. 185–186 (auch im Kontext mit den Synodaldekreten).
**36** Krypte des Mut-Tempels von Karnak, Inschrift B, bes. 11–14, Jansen-Winkeln 2009, S. 197, 48.142 (assyrische Invasion?).

horresnet[37] in Sais und Petosiris[38] in Hermupolis, um nur drei der bekanntesten zu nennen.[39]

Zurück zu Philensis II: In diesem Dekret sind alle Abschnitte thematisch auf geschickte Weise miteinander verwoben. In den Wohltaten des Königs, die dem Aufbau der Ehrendekrete zufolge als Basis bzw. Begründung der zu beschließenden Ehrungen dienen, steht die Sorge Ptolemaios' V. gegenüber den Tempeln eindeutig im Vordergrund: Er gibt Geld, um den Kult zu gewährleisten, und bestätigt alte Rechte der Tempel im Steuerwesen, er befiehlt Maßnahmen, die der Wiederherstellung zerstörter oder verfallener Heiligtümer dienen und lässt neue Kultbilder anfertigen. Diese Aufzählung wirkt zunächst wie ein Topos der königlichen Aufgaben, und das ist es zum Teil sicherlich auch. Denn genau diese aufgezählten Handlungen stehen denen entgegen, derer Chaonnophris geziehen wird (denen natürlich ebenfalls ein topischer Charakter nicht abzusprechen ist) und durch welche er sich als Feind der Götter entlarvt. Erneut gehört Ptolemaios in die Sphäre der göttlichen Ordnung (Maat), und Chaonnophris ist die Inkarnation des Seth schlechthin. Obwohl die inhaltliche Abfolge in Philensis II von einer chronologischen Warte aus eine Inversion der Ereignisse darstellt, ist die Intention klar erkennbar, die positiv konnotierten Taten des Königs an den in der Schilderung des Aufstands beschriebenen Gräueltaten des Rebellenanführers zu spiegeln (und umgekehrt).

Da sich Ptolemaios V. bereits durch seine eigenen Handlungen als rechtmäßiger Herrscher erwiesen hat, gewähren ihm die Götter ihrerseits einen Gunsterweis. Besonders hervorzuheben ist in diesem Kontext die Tatsache, dass, ähnlich wie es sich bereits in früheren Texten greifen lässt (eines der bekanntesten Beispiele ist sicherlich der Text der Restaurationsstele aus der Zeit des Tutanchamun), das kö-

---

37 Naophor Vatikan Inv. 22690, 17–23; 31–42, Posener 1936, S. 14–15; 18–20; siehe jetzt auch Jansen-Winkeln 2023, S. 30–31, 63.44 (persische Invasion unter Kambyses?).
38 Grab des Petosiris, Inschrift 81, 26–46, Lefebvre 1923, S. 54–55 (2. Perserherrschaft bzw. den Übergang zur Argeadenzeit?).
39 Auch wenn die Aussagen durchweg vage gehalten sind, fällt doch auch auf, dass sich diese einflussreichen Lokalgrößen rühmen, sich nach einer Zeit der Unruhe und des Chaos für die (erneute) Funktionsfähigkeit der Tempel engagiert zu haben. Zwar mag es sich um einen Topos handeln, es kann aber (contra Colburn 2020, S. 185) wie in Philensis II sehr wohl ein Bezug auf ein konkretes Ereignis vorliegen, wie etwa die Invasion und Besatzung des Landes durch fremde Armeen, in deren Folge es auch zu Plünderungen in Tempeln etc. gekommen sein wird, vgl. hierzu etwa Jansen-Winkeln 2002 (Udjahorresnet); Spencer 2010, S. 479 (Monthemhet); Blöbaum 2020, S. 263 (Monthemhet); McCoskey 2020 (Udjahorresnet, Petosiris); Fazzini, McKercher 2021, S. 48–49 (Monthemhet). Allgemein für private Initiativen im Tempelbau Spencer 2010 (Spätzeit); Thiers 2006 (ptolemäische Zeit). Zur Bedeutung und Funktion der Topik in der antiken Geschichtsschreibung vgl. Free 2020.

nigliche Handeln zugunsten der Tempel und des Götterkultes den Herrscher nicht nur als einen legitimen Herrscher ausweist, sondern darüber hinaus als eine *conditio sine qua non* für die ihm von den Göttern zu vergebende bzw. garantierende militärische Schlagkraft und Sieghaftigkeit verstanden wird.[40]

Die von den Priestern beschlossenen Ehrungen weisen ebenfalls einen klaren Nexus zu dem Sieg in der Thebais auf. Neben einer Statuengruppe, die im Tempelhof zu errichten ist, werden der 23. Epiphi (der Tag des Sieges) und der 3. Mesore (der Tag, an dem die Nachricht hierüber in Alexandria eintraf) zu Feiertagen deklariert, wodurch die Göttlichkeit Ptolemaios' V. und in naher Zukunft auch Kleopatras I. gefeiert wird. Es ist beachtenswert, dass nur in der Dekreteinleitung und innerhalb der Ehrungen die Namen von Komanos und Aristonikos Erwähnung finden, aber in der Langfassung fehlen. Dabei dürfte es sich weniger um eine versehentliche Auslassung gehandelt haben, sondern um eine theologische Notwendigkeit. Denn die Langfassung ist, wie bereits angeklungen, die persönliche göttliche Gegengabe an den König. Nach dieser Lesart sind die Taten der anderen nur eine Verlängerung der Handlungen des Königs selbst. Dennoch soll über die bemerkenswerte zweimalige namentliche Erwähnung der Höflinge keineswegs hinweggetäuscht werden, die ihren herausragenden Status bzw. ihre Machtposition bei Hofe eindrucksvoll unter Beweis stellen – so eindrucksvoll, dass anscheinend auch die Priester ihre Erwähnung für opportun hielten. Nicht zuletzt wird Aristonikos auch in dem aus dem Jahr 23 stammenden Dekret eine bedeutende Rolle zugeschrieben.[41]

Der endgültige Sieg, mit dem der große Aufstand in der Thebais 186 v. Chr. sein Ende fand, ist das konstitutive Element, das zur Verabschiedung von Philensis II zugunsten Ptolemaios' V. führte. Dieser Sieg stellt ein entscheidendes Datum für die ptolemäische Monarchie dar. Die Schilderung der Ereignisse in Philensis II bietet darüber hinaus, so schablonenhaft sie an zahlreichen Stellen erscheinen mag, einen kaum zu unterschätzenden Anknüpfungspunkt für die Legitimation des Königs und die ihm zuerkannte göttliche Immanenz. Dies ist umso mehr der Fall, als hier die Priester, die das gesamte Land vertreten (unabhängig davon, aus welchen Teilen Ägyptens Vertreter tatsächlich zu der Synode angereist waren), ihm diesen Status zuerkennen. Die Darstellung beruht eindeutig auf Motiven, die in der ägyptischen Theologie von alters her tief verankert waren, und es war in

---

[40] Eine prägnante Einschätzung (in Bezug auf die Restaurationsstele) findet sich an eher unerwarteter Stelle: „The point of such historical propaganda was to demonstrate how, through careful attention to the proper maintenance of temples and their cult, the good king regains divine favor. His armies become once more victorious, the land returns to health, and catastrophe becomes prosperity" (Nirenberg 2018, S. 26). Vgl. auch Pfeiffer 2021a, S. 116–117; Pfeiffer 2021c, S. 386–390.

[41] Siehe den Beitrag von A. Nespoulous-Phalippou in diesem Band.

diesem Fall ein Leichtes, (vermeintlich) reale Ereignisse in einem mythologisierten Rahmen zu präsentieren und mit religiösen Vorstellungen zu korrelieren. Der Textaufbau der Langfassung lässt klar erkennen, dass die Redaktoren mit den traditionellen Darstellungsformen von Aufständen und ihren Niederschlagungen in ägyptischen Texten gut vertraut waren und auf diese zurückgriffen. Nichtsdestotrotz stellt die Schilderung eine genuin eigene Textkomposition dar, mittels derer ein spezifisches Ereignis in seinen wichtigsten Entwicklungssträngen vermittelt werden soll. Zieht man die in Philensis II enthaltenen Beschreibungen als Quelle für eine historische Rekonstruktion der Geschehnisse des großen Aufstands in der Thebais heran, so ist dem theologischen Impetus dieser Aussagen immer Rechnung zu tragen.

# Bibliographie

Amin et al. 2023
    Amin, M., Barmpoutis, A., Berti, M., Bozia, E., Hensel, J., Naether, F., „The Digital Rosetta Stone Project" in R. Lucarelli, J.A. Roberson, S. Vinson (Hgg.), *Ancient Egypt, New Technology: The Present and Future of Computer Visualization, Virtual Reality and Other Digital Humanities in Egyptology*, HES 17, Leiden, Boston, 2023, S. 58–84.

Armoni, Jördens 2018
    Armoni, C., Jördens, A., „Der König und die Rebellen: Vom Umgang der Ptolemäer mit strittigen Eigentumsfragen im Gefolge von Bürgerkriegen", *Chiron* 48, 2018, S. 77–106.

Assmann 2000
    Assmann, J., *Herrschaft und Heil: Politische Theologie in Altägypten, Israel und Europa*, München, Wien, 2000.

Birk 2020
    Birk, R., *Türöffner des Himmels: Prosopographische Studien zur thebanischen Hohepriesterschaft der Ptolemäerzeit*, ÄA 76, Wiesbaden, 2020.

Birk 2021
    Birk, R., „Der Rand des Rosettasteins: Eine Neulesung von Z. 1 des hieroglyphischen Texts", *CdE* 96, 2021, S. 10–22.

Blöbaum 2020
    Blöbaum, A.I., „Monthemhet – Priester des Amun und Gouverneur von Theben: Die Selbstpräsentation eines Lokalherrschers im sakralen Raum" in M. Becker, A.I. Blöbaum, A. Lohwasser, *Inszenierung von Herrschaft und Macht im ägyptischen Tempel: Religion und Politik im Theben des frühen 1. Jahrtausends v. Chr.*, ÄAT 95, Münster, 2020, S. 197–312.

Bowman et al. 2021
    Bowman, A.K., Crowther, C.V., Hornblower, S., Mairs, R., Savvopoulos, K., *Corpus of Ptolemaic Inscriptions – Part I: Greek, Bilingual, and Trilingual Inscriptions from Egypt, Volume 1. Alexandria and the Delta (Nos. 1–206)*, Oxford Studies in Ancient Documents, Oxford, 2021.

Buchwald, Josefowicz 2020
    Buchwald, J.Z., Greco Josefowicz, D., *The Riddle of the Rosetta: How an English Polymath and a French Polyglot Discovered the Meaning of Egyptian Hieroglyphs*, Princeton, 2020.

Caneva 2020
Caneva (Hg.), S.G., *The Materiality of Hellenistic Ruler Cults*, Kernos Supplément 36, Lüttich, 2020.

Cassor-Pfeiffer, Pfeiffer 2019
Cassor-Pfeiffer, S., Pfeiffer, S., „Pharaonin Berenike II.: Bemerkungen zur ägyptischen Titulatur einer frühptolemäischen Königin" in M. Brose. P. Dils, F. Naether, L. Popko, D. Raue (Hgg.), *En détail – Philologie und Archäologie im Diskurs: Festschrift für Hans-Werner Fischer-Elfert*, ZÄS Beiheft 7, Berlin, Boston, 2019, S. 199–238.

Colburn 2020
Colburn, H.P., *Archaeology of Empire in Achaemenid Egypt*, Edinburgh Studies in Ancient Persia, Edinburgh, 2020.

Coppens 2021
Coppens, F., „The Ptolemaic Basileus and the Roman Emperor Slaying the Enemies of Egypt: The *sm3 sbi/ḫftyw/ḫ3swt/Stt* Ritual Scene in Context" in F. Coppens (Hg.), *Continuity, Discontinuity and Change: Perspectives from the New Kingdom to the Roman Era*, Prag, 2021, S. 405–489.

Fazzini, McKercher 2021
Fazzini, R., McKercher, M., „The Montuemhat Crypt in the Mut Temple: A New Look" in Y. Barbash, K.M. Cooney (Hgg.), *The Afterlives of Egyptian History: Reuse and Reformulation of Objects, Places, and Texts – A Volume in Honor of Edward L. Bleiberg*, Kairo, New York, 2021, S. 37–53.

Fischer-Bovet 2023
Fischer-Bovet, C., „Hellenistic Warfare and Egyptian Society" in D. Candelora, N. Ben-Marzouk, K.M. Cooney (Hgg.), *Ancient Egyptian Society: Challenging Assumptions, Exploring Approaches*, Abingdon, New York, 2023, S. 182–194.

Free 2020
Free, A., „Bemerkungen zur Topik als unvermeidbarem Element antiker Geschichtsschreibung" in M. Zerjadtke (Hg.), *Der ethnographische Topos in der Alten Geschichte: Annäherungen an ein omnipräsentes Phänomen*, Hamburger Studien zu Gesellschaften und Kulturen der Vormoderne 10, Stuttgart, 2020, S. 27–37.

Gerhardt *et al.* 2022
Gerhardt, M., Helmbold-Doyé, J., Moje, J., „Die Insel Philae: das Tor zum Süden" in S. Grallert, J. Helmbold-Doyé (Hgg.), *Abenteuer am Nil: Preußen und die Ägyptologie 1842–1845*, Berlin, 2022, S. 389–397.

Gorre, Veïsse 2020
Gorre, G., Veïsse, A.-E., „Birth and Disappearance of the Priestly Synods in the Time of the Ptolemies" in G. Gorre, S. Wackenier (Hgg.), *Quand la fortune du royaume ne dépend pas de la vertu du prince. Un renforcement de la monarchie lagide de Ptolémée VI à Ptolémée X (169–88 av. J.-C.)?*, StudHell 59, Löwen, Paris, Bristol, CT, 2020, S. 113–139.

Hoffmann, Pfeiffer 2021
Hoffmann, F., Pfeiffer, S., *Der Stein von Rosetta*, Stuttgart, 2021.

Jansen-Winkeln 2002
Jansen-Winkeln, K., „Die Quellen zur Eroberung Ägyptens durch Kambyses" in T.A. Bács (Hg.), *A Tribute to Excellence: Studies Offered in Honor of Ernő Gaál, Ulrich Luft, László Török*, StudAeg 17, Budapest, 2002, S. 309–319.

Jansen-Winkeln 2009
Jansen-Winkeln, K., *Inschriften der Spätzeit – Teil III: die 25. Dynastie*, Wiesbaden, 2009.

Jansen-Winkeln 2023
> Jansen-Winkeln, K., *Inschriften der Spätzeit – Teil V: die 27.-30. Dynastie und die Argeadenzeit*, Wiesbaden, 2023.

Johstono 2016
> Johstono, P., „Insurgency in Ptolemaic Egypt" in T. Howe, L.L. Brice (Hgg.), *Brill's Companion to Insurgency and Terrorism in the Ancient Mediterranean*, Brill's Companions in Classical Studies. Warfare in the Ancient Mediterranean World 1, Leiden, Boston, 2016, S. 183–215.

Kockelmann 2020
> Kockelmann, H., „The Epigraphy of Philae" in S.C. Dirksen, L.S. Krastel (Hgg.), *Epigraphy through five Millennia: Texts and Images in Context*, SDAIK 43, Wiesbaden, 2020, S. 145–156.

Krapf 2019
> Krapf, T., „Reconstructing the Statuary of the Courtyard of the Temple of Khnum on Elephantine" in A. Masson-Berghoff (Hg.), *Statues in Context: Production, Meaning and (Re)uses*, BMPES 10, Löwen, Paris, Bristol, CT, 2019, S. 147–158.

Krapf 2020
> Krapf, T., „Vom Hofpflaster zur dritten Dimension: Der Kontext der Graffiti des Chnumtempelvorhofs von Elephantine" in S.C. Dirksen, L.S. Krastel (Hgg.), *Epigraphy through five Millennia: Texts and Images in Context*, SDAIK 43, Wiesbaden, 2020, S. 157–167.

Lefebvre 1923
> Lefebvre, G., *Le tombeau de Petosiris. Deuxième partie : Les textes*, BiGen 29, Kairo, 1923.

Love 2021
> Love, E.O.D., *Script Switching in Roman Egypt: Case Studies in Script Conventions, Domains, Shift, and Obsolescence from Hieroglyphic, Hieratic, Demotic, and Old Coptic Manuscripts*, AfP Beihefte 46, Berlin, Boston, 2021.

Ludlow, Manning 2016
> Ludlow, F., Manning, J.G., „Revolts under the Ptolemies: A Paleoclimatological Perspective" in J.J. Collins, J.G. Manning (Hgg.), *Revolt and Resistance in the Ancient Classical World and the Near East. In the Crucible of Empire*, CHANE 85, Leiden, Boston, 2016, S. 154–171.

McCoskey 2020
> McCoskey, A., „Fight the Power: Udjahorresnet and Petosiris as Agents of Resistance", *JAEI* 26, 2020, S. 131–147.

Minas-Nerpel 2022
> Minas-Nerpel, M., „Beyond Boundaries: The Roles of the Queens in the Ptolemaic Ruler Cult" in G. Lenzo, C. Nihan, M. Pellet (Hgg.), *Les cultes aux rois et aux héros à l'époque hellénistique. Continuités et changements*, ORA 44, Tübingen, 2022, S. 117–146.

Nirenberg 2018
> Nirenberg, D., *Anti-Judaism: The History of a Way of Thinking*, London, 2018.

Panov 2020
> Панов, М.В., Исторические надписи из Куша и Кемета (I тыс. до н.э.), Египетские тексты XIV, Новосибирск, 2020.

Panov 2022
> Панов, М.В., Документы по истории государства Птолемеев, Египетские тексты XVIII, Новосибирск, 2022.

Panov 2023
> Panov, M. B. „The Earliest Copy of the Philensis Decrees", *ENiM* 16, 2023, S. 61–68.

Pfeiffer 2020
    Pfeiffer, S., *Griechische und lateinische Inschriften zum Ptolemäerreich und zur römischen Provinz Aegyptus*, EQÄ 9, Berlin, 2020.

Pfeiffer 2021a
    Pfeiffer, S., „Innere Konflikte und herrschaftliche Versöhnungsstrategien im ptolemäischen Ägypten (3.-2. Jh. v. Chr.)" in S. Pfeiffer, G. Weber (Hgg.), *Gesellschaftliche Spaltungen im Zeitalter des Hellenismus (4.-1. Jh. v. Chr.)*, Stuttgart, 2021, S. 107–127.

Pfeiffer 2021b
    Pfeiffer, S., in S. Pfeiffer, H. Klinkott, „Legitimizing the Foreign King in the Ptolemaic and Seleucid Empires: The Role of Local Elites and Priests" in C. Fischer-Bovet, S. von Reden (Hgg.), *Comparing the Ptolemaic and Seleucid Empires: Integration, Communication and Resistance*, Cambridge, 2021, S. 233–261.

Pfeiffer 2021c
    Pfeiffer, S., „'Finding the Gods of Egypt': The Motif of ‚Bringing Home the Statues of the Gods from Asia' as a New Pharaonic Ideal of Ptolemaic Times" in F. Coppens (Hg.), *Continuity, Discontinuity and Change: Perspectives from the New Kingdom to the Roman Era*, Prag, 2021, S. 375–403.

Posener 1936
    Posener, G., *La première domination perse en Égypte. Recueil d'inscriptions hiéroglyphiques*, BdE 11, Kairo, 1936.

Preys 2021
    Preys, R., „Une image de l'hippopotame ... 3000 ans plus tard" in W. Claes, M. De Meyer, M. Eyckerman, D. Huyge (Hgg.), *Remove that Pyramid! Studies on the Archaeology and History of Predynastic and Pharaonic Egypt in Honour of Stan Hendrickx*, OLA 305, Löwen, Paris, Bristol, CT, 2021, S. 899–910.

Preys 2022
    Preys, R., „Le culte des Ptolémées dans les temples égyptiens: Les décrets royaux et la décoration des temples" in G. Lenzo, C. Nihan, M. Pellet (Hgg.), *Les cultes aux rois et aux héros à l'époque hellénistique. Continuités et changements*, ORA 44, Tübingen, 2022, S. 171–194.

Pries 2023
    Pries, A., „Egyptian Writing: Extended Practices" in A. Stauder, W. Wendrich (Hgg.), *UCLA Encyclopedia of Egyptology*, Los Angeles, 2023, online abrufbar unter https://escholarship.org/uc/item/74b3x6s9, abgerufen am 30. August 2024.

Recklinghausen 2018
    Recklinghausen, D. von, *Die Philensis-Dekrete: Untersuchungen über zwei Synodaldekrete aus der Zeit Ptolemaios' V. und ihre geschichtliche und religiöse Bedeutung*, ÄA 73, Wiesbaden, 2018.

Recklinghausen 2019
    Recklinghausen, D. von, „Die Soubassements des Amun-Tempels in Naukratis: ein Zeugnis für die Tempeldekoration in der frühen Ptolemäerzeit" in A. Ashmawy, D. Raue, D. von Recklinghausen (Hgg.), *Von Elephantine bis zu den Küsten des Meeres: die Kulttopographie Ägyptens nach den Gauprozessionen der Spätzeit und der frühptolemäischen Epoche (Soubassementstudien VII)*, SSR 24, Wiesbaden 2019, S. 267–378.

Ryholt 2022
    Ryholt, K., „On the Theban Archive of Amenothes son of Harsiesis and Chibois, and the Acquisition of Ruined Houses after the Great Rebellion" in A. Almásy-Martin, M. Chauveau, K. Donker van Heel, K. Ryholt (Hgg.), *Ripple in Still Water When There is No Pebble Tossed: Festschrift in Honour of Cary J. Martin*, GHP Egyptology 34, London, 2022, S. 3–25.

Silverstein, Littman 2023
: Silverstein, J.E., Littman, R.J., „Archaeological Correlates of the Rosetta Stone's Great Revolt in the Nile Delta: Destruction at Tell Timai", *JFA* 48, 2023, S. 245–263.

Spencer 2010
: Spencer, N., „Sustaining Egyptian Culture? Non-Royal Initiatives in Late Period Temple Building" in L. Bareš, F. Coppens, K. Smoláriková (Hgg.), *Egypt in Transition: Social and Religious Development of Egypt in the First Millennium BCE – Proceedings of an International Conference Prague, September 1–4, 2009*, Prag, 2010, S. 441–490.

Thiers 2006
: Thiers, C., „Égyptiens et Grecs au service des cultes indigènes. Un aspect de l'évergétisme en Égypte lagide" in M. Molin (Hg.), *Les régulations sociales dans l'Antiquité. Actes du colloque d'Angers 23 et 24 mai 2003*, Rennes, 2006, S. 275–301.

Veïsse 2022
: Veïsse, A.-E., „The ‚Great Theban Revolt', 206–186 BCE" in P.J. Kosmin, I.S. Moyer (Hgg.), *Culture of Resistance in the Hellenistic East*, Oxford, 2022, S. 57–74.

# List of Contributors

**Ralph Birk** Freie Universität Berlin

**Stefano G. Caneva** Università di Padova

**Marie-Pierre Chaufray** École pratique des hautes études, Paris

**Laurent Coulon** Collège de France, EPHE, PSL, AOROC, UMR 8546, Paris

**Thomas Faucher** Centre d'Études Alexandrines (CNRS/Ifao)

**Joseph G. Manning** Yale University

**Martina Minas-Nerpel** Universität Trier

**Jan Moje** Ägyptisches Museum und Papyrussammlung Berlin, Freie Universität Berlin

**Alexandra Nespoulous-Phalippou** Université Paul-Valéry – Montpellier 3

**Stefan Pfeiffer** Martin-Luther-Universität Halle-Wittenberg

**René Preys** Université de Namur

**Felix Relats Montserrat** Sorbonne Université

**Anne-Emmanuelle Veïsse** Université Gustave Eiffel

**Daniel von Recklinghausen** Eberhard Karls Universität Tübungen

Open Access. © 2025 the author(s), published by De Gruyter. (CC) BY-NC-ND This work is licensed under the Creative Commons Attribution-NonCommercial-NoDerivatives 4.0 International License.
https://doi.org/10.1515/9783111608051-015

# Names and Places Index

## Divine Names

Amun  33, 41, 59–60, 77, 92–94, 102, 165, 236, 261–262, 283, 286, 306–307, 320, 338
Amun-Kematef  67
Amun-Nakht  59
Amunrasonther  63
Amun-Re  55, 61, 63, 106, 113, 171, 173
Aphrodite  159, 161
Aphrodite Euploia  161
Apis  207, 245, 337
Apollo  74, 230
Asklepios  66

Baal  340
Bukhis  117

Caesar Augustus  70
Chnoubis  72

Dionysos  105

Goddess Rome  70

Hapy  67
Harendotes  238, 241
Haroeris  172, 245, 276
Harpocrates  230
Harsiesis  220, 235
Harsiesis-Harpocrates  116
Harsomtus  178
Hathor  99–100, 102, 161, 178
Hathor-Tefnut  68
Hera  158, 168
Heracles  278
Horus  97, 156, 173, 175, 178, 216, 230, 234–236, 344

Ipet-weret  234
Isis  59, 68, 106, 135, 158, 161, 166, 168, 171, 179, 190, 236, 241, 278

Khnum  161, 191, 276
Khnum-Haroeris  197
Khonsu  164–165, 172
Khonsu-Thoth  241

Mnevis  208, 219
Montu  61, 95, 164, 245, 255, 257–259, 263, 269, 276, 278, 286
Montu-Re  275
Mut  165

Nehemetaway  65
Nut  234

Osiris  4, 38, 65, 68, 105–118, 158, 168, 194, 220, 234–236, 238, 241, 247

Pakaouraashespses  270

Re  216

Serapis  105, 155, 179, 235, 261
Seshat  231, 233, 241
Seth  150, 340, 344–345
Shai  67
Shentayt  114
Sobek  172, 302
Sobekneferu  166
Sokar  106, 111
Sokar-Osiris  107–108, 116, 163
Soknebtynis  99
Sothis  68

Theoi Adelphoi  162–163, 165
Theoi Epiphaneis  241–242
Theoi Euergetai  33, 242–243
Theoi Philadelphoi  243
Theoi Philometores  241

*Theoi Philopatores* 169, 234, 266
*Theoi Soteres* 174, 178
Thoth 231, 233, 242, 244

Zeus 66, *74*, 158, 168, *262*
Zeus Megistos 70
Zeus-Ammon 135, 261

## Royal Names

Alexander IV Aegos 62, 112, 229
Alexander the Great 156, 158, 170, 177, 229, 310
Amenhotep II 258, 264
Amenhotep III 109–110
Amenmesse 109
Antiochos III 336
Antiochos IV 139, 151, *283*
Antiochos IX *308*
Antoninus Pius 258
Arsinoe II 157–158, 162–164, 166–171, 175, 178, 221
Arsinoe III 114, 169–170, 174, 176, *243*, *266*
Arsinoe IV 266
Arsinoe Philadelphos *76*
Augustus 161, 193, *236*, *280*, 286
Ay 109

Berenice I 169, 178
Berenice II *67*, 162–171, 174, *178–179*, *269*, *273*
Berenice III 246–247

Caesar, Gaius Julius *67*
Cambyses 259, *345*
Chaonnophris 4, 27, 40, 100, 117, 145, 189, 195, 198, 209, 236–240, 282, 297, 335–336, 339–343, 345
Cleopatra Berenice III *303*
Cleopatra I 114, 168, 175–177, 206–207, 232, 240, 336–337, 342, 346
Cleopatra II *76*, 112, 117, 164, 168, 172, 176–177, 232, 240–247, *284*, 307–*308*, *311*, 313, *317*, 319–321
Cleopatra III 168, 170, 172, 176–177, 241–247, 303–*304*, 307–310, 313, 322
Cleopatra III and Ptolemy IX Soter II 112
Cleopatra Selene 308
Cleopatra VII 58–59, 61, 64, 75, 131–132, 136, 162, 168, 176, 286

Demetrios III 312
Domitian *258*, 283

Haronnophris 4, 27, 35–38, 43, 47, 100–101, 117, 145, 189, 199, 236–240, 282, 297–298, 335, *339*
Hatshepsut 156, 166, *282*
Horemheb 109

Lysimachos *73*

Magas *74*
Marcus Aurelius 191
Merenptah 109, *267*
Montuhotep II *257*

Necho II 113
Nectanebis 109–110, 274
Nero *258*, 285

Paos 319
Philip I 312
Philip III Arrhidaios 65
Ptolemy (Memphites) 245
Ptolemy Eupator *242*, *265*, 284, 286
Ptolemy I Soter 62, 66, 109, 112, 129, 136, 155, 157–158, 169, 178, 190, 229, 237, 261, *272*
Ptolemy II Philadelphos 28, *32*, 37, 94, 109–110, 112, 130, 136, 155–158, 163–164, 168, 178, 242, 244, 255, 257–258, *261*, 263, *265*–266, 268–*276*, 279–280, 286–287
Ptolemy III Euergetes I 29, 32, 35, 37, 44, *74*, 92, 99, 105, 109–110, 115, 118, 147, 162, 164–165, 167, 169, *171–172*, 178–179, 190, 233–236, 242, 244, 247, 258, 260, 263, 265–266, 268–271, 273–275, 279, 286, 331
Ptolemy IV Philopator 27, 100, 109, 111, 113–118, 134, 158, 161–163, 166, 169–175, 178–179,

189–192, 194, 203, 207, 234–238, 241–245, 255, 257, 259, 261–262, *265*, 269–270, 273–275, 279–280, 283, 286–287, 335–336
Ptolemy V Epiphanes  27, 36, 41, *99*–100, 114, 117, 157, 170, 173–176, 189, 193–194, 196–197, 203, 209, 220–221, 232, 238–239, 241–242, 244, 255, 258–260, 262, 264–265, 267–269, 273, 283, 286, *306*, 331, 334, 336–339, 341–342, 345–346
Ptolemy VI Philometor  36, *73*, *76*, 109, 112, 115, 136, 173, 175–177, 193, 195, 207, 232, 237, 240–243, 258, 260, 265, 269, *272–274*, 276, 279–280, 284, 286, 288, 297–298
Ptolemy VIII Euergetes II  *73*, 109–110, 112, 136, 164, 172–173, 175, 177, 192, 236–237, 240–245, 247–248, *258*, 260, *262*, 265, 276, 280, 284, 288, 297, *307–308*, *311*, 313, *315*, 317, 319–320
Ptolemy VIII Euergetes II, Cleopatra II and Cleopatra III  *99*
Ptolemy IX Philometor Soter II  58, 66, *73*, 177, *193*, 245–248, 260, 265, 286, 297, 301–308, 320, 322
Ptolemy X Alexander I  *73*, *173*, 177, *241*, *258*, 261, 284, 297, 299–*304*, 306–309, 310–323
Ptolemy XI Alexander II  *303*

Ptolemy XII Neos Dionysos  64, 112, 114–115, 163, 190, *193*, *258*, 260, *265*, *266*, 269, 274, 276, 279–280, 284–285, *302*, 306
Ptolemy XIII  58
Ptolemy XV Kaisarion  61, 75

Ramesses I  109
Ramesses II  68, 109, 173, *267*
Ramesses III  109, *267*
Ramesses IV  109, *267*
Ramesses VI  109
Ramesses VII  109–110

Sesostris I  68, *282*
Sesostris III  *257*–258, *262*, *267*, 286
Sethnakht  109
Seti I  109, *267*
Seti II  109, *267*
Siptah  109

Tausret  109, 166
Thutmosis III  257–258, 264
Thutmosis IV  264
Tiberius  114
Trajan  255, *258*, 283
Tutankhamun  *282*, 345

Vespasian  *258*, 285

## Private Names

Achaios  74
Aetos  *73*
Amasis  *65*, 92–93
Anemher II  29
Apollodoros  *59*, 277
Apollonia  *313*
Aristokrates  *72*
Aristomenes  220
Aristonikos  27, *70*, 209, 211–214, 216, 218–221, 337, 342, 346

Bakchios  175
Barkaios  72

Berenepthis  97–99
Boethos  72–73, 75

Chaireas  314
Chapochonsis  30, 92–93
Chapochrates  *65*, 118

Daimachos  40
Dikaiarchos  174
Diodoros Pasparos  *70*
Dionysios Petosarapis  *73*
Drakon  *72*
Dryton  *313*, 319

Esbendetis 96
Eschnoumpmetis 198
Eschonsis 94
Eshyris 96
Esminis 92–93, 100
Espmetis II 43
Esthladas 319
Estphenis 97–98

Gallus, C. Cornelius 1, 285, 321

Hakoris *237*
Harendotes 29, *41*
Harmachis 29
Harnuphis 33
Harpaesis 100–101
Harsiesis 92–93, 97, 100
Harwa 65, *67*
Heliodoros *41*
Heniochos 175
Herodes *70*, *75*
Hersenef 45
Hierax 301, 304, *306*, 318
Hippalos 175
Hones 97
Horos 64–65, 92–93, 95, 197, 312
Horos III 29
Horpakhepesh *237–238*

Inaros 194
Iry-iry 95
Iufaa 95, 110

Kaies *313*
Kallikrates 159, 161
Kallimachos 168
Kallimachos I 59
Kallimachos II 10, 55, *307*
Kapefhakhonsou 45
Kapefhamonthu *65*
Kleitomachos 174
Kolluthos 197
Komanos 27, 195, 211, 215–216, 218, 221, 336, 342, 346
Kronios 59, 76

Labeo, L. Vaccius *71*
Lusanias 175

Marres 92–93
Milon 98–99
Montemes 30, 259, 344
Montemes III 29

Nachtefmut 95
Nechthyris 299–*301*, 315, 318
Nechtminis 100–101
Nechtmonthes *43*, 96
Nechtmonthes I 29, 45
Neferpres 196
Nikanor 175
Nikias *70*

Olympichos 74
Onnophris 92–93, 96
Osoroeris 29, *31*, *46*
Osoroeris I 42
Osoroeris III 29
Osoroeris IV 42

Pacharchonsu 96
Paches 99
Pachnum 34, 36–42, 48
Pakebkis 100
Pamonasis 196
Pamonthes *65*
Panebchunis 311
Panechates 101
Panemerit 64
Paninuthis 92–93
Paos 319, 321
Parates 194, 196
Paris 72
Pasherenptah 36
Pasomtus 92–93
Pates *313*
Patus 38–42, 48
Pemsais 40
Petamunis 96–97
Peteharoeris 99–100
Peteharpochrates 97

Peteharpres 92–94
Peteharsemtheus 97, 99–100, 102, 311
Petemestus 92–94, 96
Petesuchos 311–*312*
Petimuthes *65, 304*
Petosiris *65, 172*, 345
Phagonis 93
Phibis 38–42, 101
Philotas 149
Philoxenos 302
Pinyris 97–98
Platon 298–302, 304, 307, 315, 318, 320–321
Platon (the Younger) 302, 320
Polycrates 220
Psemminis 93, 100–101
Psenchonsis 33
Psenmonthes *301*
Psenpachered 96
Psentesoys 31
Ptolion 312
Ptomphis 97–98

Senmuthis *313*
Serapion *124*
Sesoosis 100–101

Shepenupet II *280*
Sosibios 169
Sosos 175
Spotus 29, 30
Spotus I 30, 42
Spotus II 31
Spotus III 31, 42, 43, 47
Spotus IV *42*
Spotus V 43

Tachybiat 118
Teos *31*, 65, 67
Themnestos *41*
Theon *41*
Thotmosis 97
Thotortaios 100–101
Totoes 64, 159, 167
Tsenonpmus 40

Udjahorresnet 345
Ursenuphis *124*

Xenon, C. Julius *70*

# Toponyms

Abbad 125
Abusir 106, 110–111, 116
Abydos 125, 194
 – *W-pkr* 195
Ain Birbiyeh 59
Alexandria 55, 131–132, 135, 139, 144, 157–159, 164, 169–170, 174, 178–179, 192, 209, 220–221, *303*, 308, 310–311, 313–*315*, 320, 322, 332, 335–336, 343
Apameia 212
Arados 212
Armant 117, 125, 313, 317–319, 321
Arsinoe (Cilicia) *73*
Aswan 125, 161, 166, 190
Athens 303

Baba Kome *74*
Behbeit el-Hagar 167
Berenike 125
Bi'r Samut 125, 221
Buto *62*

Cape Zephyrium 159, 168
Cleopatra 72
Coptos 116, 125
Cos *70*
Crocodilopolis 298, 302–*303*, 311, 318–319
Cyprus 308, 313–314
Cyrenaica *74*
Cyrene 72, 313–314

Dakka 265
Damascus 312–313
Deir el-Medina 255
Dendera *31*, 111–112, 125, 161, 207, *285*
Diospolis Mikra *see* Sema-Behdet
Dodekaschoinos 195, 241

Edfu *31*, 34, *56*, *67*, 91, 94, 97–99, 102, 125, 138, 173, 175, 189, 230, 235–236, 238, 243, 249, 255, *265*, 283, *285*, 305, 313–314, 340
– Enclosure Wall 248
– Hypostyle Hall 235
– Naos 236, 242–243, 245
– Pronaos 247
Elephantine 72, 91, 125, 189–200, 206, 276, *282*, 313, 317
Elkab *46*, *302*
el-Sheikh Fadl 106
Esna 8, *265*, 299, 304, 322
Euhemeria *124*

Fayum *40*, *309*, 315, 318, 322

Gaza 309
Giza 106, 108, 110–111, 115–116
Gurnet Murai 116

Hawara *310*
Heka 317
Herakleopolis 65
Hermonthis *See* Armant
Hermopolis 64–*65*, 345
Hut-Nesu 309

Ioppe 137

Judaea 309, 318

Kalabsha 161
Karnak 31, 33, 35–36, 44, 55, 59–60, 63, *65*, 75, 77, 92, *105*–106, 117, 124, 128, 130–132, 139, 173, 306
– Akh-Menu 114
– Bubastite Portal 125, 134, 138–139, *237*
– Chapel of Achoris 125, 135
– Chapel of Osiris of Coptos 114, 118
– Chapel of Osiris Wennefer Neb-Djefau 135, 139

– *Chapelle rouge 282*
– Enclosure Wall 125, 138
– First Pylon 131, 135, 137–138
– Granary of the Temple of Amun 34
– Karnak North 125, 139
– Kiosk of Taharqa 171–175, 179
– Osirian Catacombs 113–114
– Osirian Chapels 125
– Propylon of Khonsu (Gate of Euergetes) 165, *171*–172, 178–179, 234–*235*, *243*
– Propylon of Montu 167
– Ptolemaic and Roman Baths 125
– Ptolemaic Baths 139
– Residential quarter east of the sacred lake 28, 43
– Residential quarter of the "House of the Cow" 44
– Second Pylon 134, 167, 173, 232, *236*, 241–242, 265
– Sphinx Alley *138*
– Temple of Akhenaten 128
– Temple of Khonsu 165
– Temple of Mut 135, *344*
– Temple of Opet 133, 138
– Temple of Ptah 125, 134
– Treasury of Shabaka 125
Keramike 278
Keramos 72
Kiddiou Kome *74*
Kom Ombo 72, 172, 239, 241
– Hypostyle Hall 245
Kyme *71*

Lake Borollos 213
Lake Tana 147
Lepidoton Polis 91
Luxor 68, 124–125, 128, 130, *133*
– First Pylon 125
– Sphinx Alley 125
Lykopolis 36

Medamud 95, *238*, 255–288
– Bark Sanctuary 258, 265
– *Chambre d'Arsinoé 272*, 274
– *Chapelle d'Arsinoé* 269
– Enclosure Wall 269, 275
– *Péribole 272*, 274, 280

- *Petit Pylône* 270
- *Porches* 274
- *Porte de Tibère* 267, 269, 272, 276, 280, 286
- *Pylône* 269, 274
- *Salle* XVI 265
- *Salle* XVII 265
- *Salles* XVI–XVIII 268–269, 271, 273–274
- *Temple latéral* 257, 259–263, 267
- Temple of Montu 264–266

Meidum 106
Memphis 40, 48, 110, 301, *306*, 317–318, 332
- Serapeum 305
Moeris *283*
Mylasa 74
Myra 314

Nag Hammadi 125
Naukratis *338*
Nome
- Arsinoites *34*, 316
- Eileithyiaspolites 302
- Heracleopolites 313
- Hermonthites 302, 317–318
- Memphis 39
- Pathyrites 302, 313
- Peritheban 40, 55, 59
- Thebes 39, *59*
Nubia 198

Oxyrhynchos 110–113, 116–117
- Per-khefa 106, 112

Pathyris 35, 91–92, 99–102, 298, *301*–304, 311, 315–318, 322
Pella 163
Pelousion 308–309
Pergamon *70*, 74
Philae 59, 91, 125, 190, 194, 197, 207, 241, 321, 334–335
- Naos *236*
Philometoris 72
Pithom *321*
Pr-w-qr 194
Psenamosis 72
Ptolemais Hermiou 55, 58–59, 72, 76–77, 144, 157, 169, 174–175, 178, 221

Qena 125, 136
Qus *241*, 247, 276

Raphia 138
Ro-Setau 106–*107*, 110
Rosetta 334

Sais 64, 345
Sema-Behdet 212–213, 220–222, 311, 318, 322
Speos Artemidos *282*
Syene 91, 196, 199, *336*
Syria 309, 311

Tanis *31*, 45, 64–65, 67
Taposiris Magna 207
Tebtynis 99
Tehne 106, 111
Telmessos *73*
Thebaid 1, 3, 10, 13–15, 19, 27, 35, 40–41, 44–45, 47, 55–60, 62–*63*, 69, 72–73, 75, 78, 91–92, 94, 97, 102, 105, 114, 117, 119, 123, 125–126, 128–129, 131–133, 136, 138–140, 145, 155, 157, 162, 167, 171–*173*, 175, 178, 189, 195, 209, 216, 221–222, 236–238, 255, 277, 283, 286, 288, 297–299, 301, 303–304, 307, *321*, 323, 336, 346
Thebes 28, 33–35, 48, 55, 60, 62–63, *65*–68, 71, 75, 91–97, 102, 123–124, 129, 131, 178, 189–190, 195, 212, 220, 222, 278, 297, *301*, 304–307, 315–316, *318*–319, 344
- Djeme 93, *274*, 275, 283
- Medinet Habu 306
- Memnoneia 320
- Qasr el-Aguz 265
- Qurna *267*
- Ramesseum 125
Thyateira *70*
Tod 164, *270*, 278, *282*, 302, 318–319
Triakontaschoinos 72
Tuna el-Gebel 106, *172*, 189

Wadi Qubannet el-Qirud 106

Xois 31

# Sources Index

## Ancient Authors

Aristotle 2
Athenaeus
– XII, 73 *303*

*Chronicon paschale* 314, 323
– P 449 310, 322

Diodorus Siculus
– Book XX, §§ 99–100 158

Flavius Iosephus 309, *311*
– *Antiquitates Iudaicae*, XIII, 10, 2 *308*, 322
– *Antiquitates Iudaicae*, XIII, 348 *311*
– *Antiquitates Iudaicae*, XIII, 348–355 *304*
– *Antiquitates Iudaicae*, XIII, 351–352 309
– *Antiquitates Iudaicae*, XIII, 351–352 322
– *Antiquitates Iudaicae*, XIII, 369–371 312
– *Ap.* 2.60 *58*

Galen 1

Herodotus
– *History*, II, 63 *218*
Hesychius *310*

Justin 308
– XXVII, 1 10
– XXVII, 1, 9 149

– XXXIX, 3 *307*
– XXXIX, 4 *303*
– XXXIX, 4, 1–2 *308*, 322

Pausanias 8, 17, 298, 303–308, 319–321
– I, 8, 6 *158*
– I, 9, 1 *307*
– I, 9, 1–2 *308*, 322
– I, 9, 3 *58*, 323
Pliny
– *Naturalis historia* 34, 148 159
Polybius
– *History*, V, 107 8
– *History*, XV, 25,3 *207*
– *History*, XVIII, 55,3 *207*
– *History*, XXII, 17 213, 216, 219
Porphyrius 304, 306, *308*, 310, 313–314, 322–323
– *FGrHist*, 260 F43 149
Posidippus 163
– *AB* 63.9 *163*
– *Epigrams* 116; 119 159

Seneca
– *Q.Nat.* 4.2.16 *58*
Strabo *310*
– *Geographica*, XVII, 1, 16 *159*
– *Geographica*, XVII, 1, 8 310, 322

## Papyri, Ostraca and Editions

Inscriptions
– CGRN 143 *74*
– I. Keramos 5b *72*
– I. Keramos 9 *72*
– I. Kyme 19 *71*
– I. Louvre 14 *73*
– I. Mother of Apis 105 *317*
– I. Mother of Apis 106 *317*
– I. Mother of Apis 123 *317*

– I. Philae I 52 *59*
– I. Philae I 52, 53, 56 *59*
– I. Philae I 57 *59*
– I. Philae I 58 *59*
– I. Philae I 61 *59*
– I. Prose 21 *72*
– I. Prose 40 *72*
– I. Th. Sy. 302 (= OGIS 111) *72*
– IG XII 4.2, 682 *70*

- IGCyr 011100 308, 322
- IGR IV 292 *70*
- OGIS I 90 *99, 146*
- PHRC 010 *73*
- SB V 8202 *278*
- SB V 8878 *73*
- SEG IX 4 *72*
- SEG LII 1462 *73*
- SEG LIV 1020 *70*
- TAM V 2, 1098 *70*

Mummy Labels
- Vleeming, Short Texts II, no. 432 315

Ostraca
- Kaplony-Heckel, Enchoria 19-20 (1992-1993), pp. 61-62, No. 12 316
- Kaplony-Heckel, Forschungen und Berichte 10 (1968), p. 145, No. 9 317-318
- Kaplony-Heckel, Studies Lichtheim II, pp. 588-589, No. 18 316
- O. Berlin P 9389 *193*
- O. BM EA 29719 100-*101*
- O. BM EA 5730 93
- O. BM EA 5734 93
- O. Bodl. 371 93
- O. Bodl. I 199 304, 315-316
- O. Cairo JE 38258 35, 37, *189*
- O. Cairo JE 51449 102
- O. Cairo without no. (= TM 51237) 102
- O. Cambr. Fitzw. GR.P.47 *193*
- O. Eleph. DAIK 287 317
- O. G. Michaelides 204 *91*
- O. G. Michaelides 206 *91*
- O. Karnak L.S. 462.4 28
- O. Mattha 272 *93*
- O. Taxes II 117 93
- O. Taxes II 123 93
- O. Tempeleide 213 316
- O. Tempeleide 36 317
- O. Theb. dem. p. 39 no. D 51 96
- O. Theb. gr. 30 *305*, 323
- O. TT 32 93
- O. V DO Uppsala 1027 37
- O. Vleem. 53 93, 95
- O. Wilck. 1535 *299*

- ODL 133 *91*
- Wångsted, Orientalia Suecana 12 (1963), pp. 48-49, No. 6 316

Papyri
- BGU III 993 *311*
- BGU VIII 1730 *58*
- BGU VIII 1843 *58*
- BGU XIV 2378 *302*
- BGU XVIII.1 2747 *305*
- P. Adler gr. 12 *303*
- P. Amh. II 51 *301*, 315, 317-318
- P. Ashm. 22 *177*
- P. Bad. II 16 300-301, 304, *314*
- P. Bad. II 2 319
- P. Baraize (= SB V 8033) 40
- P. Berlin P 13564 194-195
- P. Berlin P 13567 196
- P. Berlin P 13593 192
- P. Berlin P 13596-7 193
- P. Berlin P 13608 *313*
- P. Berlin P 15515 *195*
- P. Berlin P 15527 *195*, 197
- P. Berlin P 15609 195
- P. Berlin P 15802 195
- P. Berlin P 21690 *193*
- P. Berlin P 23571 196
- P. Berlin P 23625 196
- P. Berlin P 23641 198-199
- P. Berlin P 9068 100
- P. BM Andrews 1 93
- P. BM Andrews 11 36
- P. BM Andrews 13 93, *95*
- P. BM Andrews 5 36
- P. BM EA 10226 157
- P. BM EA 10486 *100*
- P. BM EA 10498 *312*, 322
- P. BM EA 10529 93
- P. BM EA 10555.5 A *100*
- P. Bour. 10 299, 304, 316, 318
- P. Bour. 11 300, 304, 316, 318
- P. Bour. 12 301, 304, *306*, 317-318, 323
- P. Brooklyn dem. 153 96
- P. Bürgsch. 13 97, *98*
- P. Bürgsch. 14 97, *98*
- P. Cairo II 30614 315-316, 322

- P. Cairo II 30670 *302*
- P. Cairo II 30704 *101*
- P. Cairo II 30768 + P. Cairo II 30771 *302*
- P. Claude 2 *312*, 322
- P. Conflict 1 318
- P. Conflict 3 318
- P. Conflict 5 *301*
- P. Dion. 18 308, 322
- P. Edfu 8 149
- P. Eheverträge 22 *33*
- P. Eheverträge 37 *311*
- P. Eleph. dem. 8 97
- P. Eleph. gr. 25 *97–98*
- P. Eleph. gr. 27a + P. Eleph. dem. 10 *98*
- P. Fam. Theb. 24 93, *95*
- P. Freib. III 12–33 *176*
- P. Grenf. II 36 *311*, 322
- P. Hawara 19a–b *309*, 322
- P. Hawara 20 *310*
- P. Hawara 21a–b 177
- P. Heidelberg D 655 *299*
- P. Heidelberg dem. 750a *301*
- P. Joseph Smith *31*
- P. Lips. I 104 *312*, 322
- P. Lond. III 316
- P. Louvre gr. 2390 (= P. Salt 5) *193*
- P. Mallawi inv. 602/7 309, 322
- P. Oxy. XX 2258C *168*
- P. Oxy. XXVII 2465, fr. 2 *76*
- P. Petr. III 53p *99*
- P. Phil. E 16743 *311*, 322

- P. Ross. Georg. II 10 302, 317
- P. Ryl. dem. 2 100
- P. Ryl. dem. 32 *100*
- P. Ryl. dem. III 12–13 94
- P. Ryl. gr. 2 125 *124*
- P. Ryl. gr. 4 572 *34*
- P. Strasb. dem., pp. 32–33, No. 8 317, 322
- P. Tebt. III 781 *282*
- P. Tor. Amen. 11 93
- P. Tor. Botti 1 157
- P. Tor. Choach. 7 42
- P. Tebt. I 5 *99*
- PSI IV 389 *162*
- PSI IX 1092 *168*
- SB I 2264 *59*
- SB I 3926 *59*
- SB III 6300 299, 304, 316
- SB V 8031 *72*
- SB V 8036 *59*
- SB VI 8993 *76*
- SB XVIII 13675 305, 323
- SB XVIII 13677 323
- SB XVIII 13678 305
- SB XX 14659 *145*
- SB XXIV 16161 *309*

Wooden Tablets
- T. Cairo JE 51437 100
- T. Hess dem. 1 100–*101*
- Vleeming, Short Texts II, no. 432 317

# Hieroglyphic Texts

Dendera
- XII, 2, 6 *162*
- XII, 28,13–32,7 *67*
- XIV, 146, 8 *162*

Edfu
- I, 26, 17–28, 4 *235*
- I, 517 *175*
- I, 526–527 178
- II, 158–159 *175*
- II, 40, 2–12 *235*

- III, 130, 13–131, 11 *242*
- III, 140, 9–141, 8 *242*
- III, 181, 12–182, 10 *242*
- III, 191, 9–192, 5 *242*
- IV, 248, 15–17 *244*
- IV, 249, 3 *244*
- IV, 249, 5–6 *244*
- IV, 249, 8 *244*
- IV, 340, 11–12 *246*
- IV, 8, 4–5 173
- IV, 92, 8 *244*

- IV, 93, 1-2  *244*
- IV, 93, 4  *244*
- VI, 277, 2-11  *248*
- VII, 6, 6-8  173
- VII, 9, 8  *305*, 322
- VIII, 22  *265*

Esna
- II, 13, l. 7  *265*

Karnak
- *Ka2Pyl* 20  232
- *Ka2Pyl* 24  232

- Propylon of Khonsu (= Urk. VIII, 69 a)  *67*
- Propylon of Khonsu (= Urk. VIII, 78-79)  164
- *TahKiosk* E04  171
- *TahKiosk* E10  172

Kom Ombo
- I, 14  *241*
- I, 462  *172*

Tod
- II, 318  *242*, *265*

Tombs
- Siut I, 264  *68*

## Monuments

Architectural elements
- Block Karnak, 7373.22  *43*
- Medamud, inv. 1146  *266*, *273*
- Medamud, inv. 1431  *258*, *267*
- Medamud, inv. 1446  *267*
- Medamud, inv. 1496  *258*, *267*
- Medamud, inv. 1619  *266*
- Medamud, inv. 2259  *266*
- Medamud, inv. 2469  *259*
- Medamud, inv. 2629  *268*
- Medamud, inv. 3072  *268*
- Medamud, inv. 4359  *272*, *276*, *279*, *284*
- Medamud, inv. 4476  *259*
- Medamud, inv. 4477  *259*
- Medamud, inv. 4507  *269*, *273*
- Medamud, inv. 4508  *273*
- Medamud, inv. 4552  *279*-*280*, *285*
- Medamud, inv. 4827  *277*
- Medamud, inv. 4885  *271*, *273*, *279*
- Medamud, inv. 5252  *271*
- Medamud, inv. 5548  *272*, *276*
- Medamud, inv. 5549  *272*, *276*
- Medamud, inv. 5901  *270*
- Medamud, inv. 5959  *270*
- Medamud, inv. 5960  *270*
- Medamud, inv. 5961  *270*
- Medamud, inv. 6025  *270*
- Medamud, inv. 6027  *270*
- Medamud, inv. 6239-6240  *270*
- Medamud, inv. 8729  *270*

- Medamud, inv. 8730  *270*
- Medamud, inv. 8731  *270*
- Medamud, MAG/O/ 72  *269*
- Medamud, MAG/O/116  *268*, *272*

Mosaics
- Alexandria, Graeco-Roman Museum, inv. no. 21739 (Sophilos-Mosaic)  168

Objects from excavations
- Medamud, inv. 5310  *277*
- Medamud, inv. 5859  *260*
- Medamud, inv. 5860  *260*-*261*
- Medamud, inv. 5861  *260*
- Medamud, inv. 5862  *260*
- Medamud, inv. 6105  *277*
- Medamud, inv. 6389  *262*
- Medamud, inv. 6390  *262*
- Medamud, inv. 6391  *262*
- Medamud, inv. 6392  *262*
- Medamud, inv. 6393  *262*
- Medamud, inv. 6394  *262*
- Medamud, inv. 6395  *261*
- Medamud, inv. 6396-6397  *262*

Osiris coffins
- Barcelona, Museu Egipci, Inv. Nr. E 476  109
- El-Ahram storerooms no. 502  109
- El-Ahram storerooms no. 503  109
- Freiburg, Galerie Puhze  109

- London, Charles Ede Limited  109
- Vienna, KHM ÄS 10090  109

Sculptor's models
- Vleeming, Short Texts III, no. 2087  97

Statues
- Abu-Gud-Storeroom, Register of Mut & Khonsu Chapel in Luxor temple, Nr. 121  *31*
- Baltimore, Walters Art Museum 22.213  *31*
- Berlin, ÄMP 2271  *64*
- Berlin, ÄMP 8163  *66*
- Cairo, CG 689  *31*
- Cairo, CG 48606  *65*
- Cairo, CG 48621  *95*
- Cairo, JE 36576  *32*
- Cairo, JE 37436  *38–42*
- Cairo, JE 37448  *95*
- Cairo, JE 37452  118
- Cairo, JE 37456  *36*
- Cairo, JE 38004  *38–42*
- Cairo, JE 38013  *95*
- Cairo, JE 67094  *64*
- Cairo, SR 218  *30*
- Cairo, TR 20/2/25/4  *30*
- Cairo, TR 25/12/26/2  *39*
- Ex-Cairo, JE 37982  *96*
- Lausanne, Musée des Beaux-arts, EG 7  *33*
- London, BM EA 48038  *96*
- London, BM EA 55306  *65*
- Medamud, inv. 6399 (fragment)  *262*
- New York, MMA 1980.422  *33*
- New York, Private Collection  *30*
- Paris, Louvre A 84  *65*
- Vatican, Museo Gregoriano Egizio 22690  *345*

Stelae
- Alexandria 21352 (Stela of Noub Taha)  206
- Cairo, CG 22181 (Mendes Stela)  159
- Cairo, CG 22186 (Canopus Decree, Kom el-Hisn)  233
- Cairo, CG 31088 (Stela of Nobareh)  206, 215, 239
- Cairo, JE 44901 (Memphis Decree of 182 BCE)  208, 212–213, *239*
- Cairo, TR 2/3/25/7 (Memphis Decree of 182 BCE)  208, 212, 218, 239
- Cairo, TR 2/4/80/1  275
- Cairo, TR 27/11/58/4 (Philensis II)  207, *210*, *338*
- Famine Stela  9
- Florence, Museo Egizio 2540/2  *68*
- Konosso Stela (= Urk. IV, 1546, 13)  *68*
- London, BM EA 24 (Rosetta Stone)  206
- London, BM EA 886  36
- Medamud, inv. 3172  *269*
- Moscow, Pushkin Museum of Fine Arts, I.1.a. 3015 (= C.Ord.Ptol. 67)  *59*
- Paris, Louvre AF 10077–10078  206
- Paris, Louvre E 12677 + AF 10006-7  206
- Paris, Louvre E 12929 (= Medamud, inv. 1720)  278
- Philae 143 (Stela of Gallus)  285, 321
- Satrap Stela (= Urk. II, 13, 2)  62
- Stela of Imhotep, Saqqara (ed. Ray = TM 51405)  *314*
- Stela of Totoes (Private Collection)  159, 160, 167
- Turin, Museo Egizio 1764 (= I. Prose 46)  55, *59*, 307

# Res Notabiles Index

Army (ptol.)
- Machimoi  8, *337*
- Misthophoroi  8, 298

Book of the Dead
- BD 125  64
Byssos-linen  98–99

Coins
- Circulation of  124
- Hoards  124, 129, 133
- Series  129–133, 262
- Single finds  125
Continuities and breaks
- Breaks induced by fire  285
- Coinage  129–140
- Cultic activity  105, 113, 117
- Dynastic cults  155–156, 178
- Genealogies  42, 102
- Recycling of monuments  279
- Temple building  256, 282, 287
- Temple decoration  172
Crisis
- Concepts of  1–6
- demographic  146
- dynastic  113, 240–245, 248, 307–319
- environmental  3, 9, 58, 60, 146–150
- Famine  62, 65, 75, 196, 214
- Impact on cults  105, 117
- Impact on temple building  255, 282, 340
- Impact on temple decoration  236
- Literary reflections  149–151
- Revelatory nature  5
Cultural hybridity  204

Decorum
- Ptol. Queens in ritual scenes  164, 176
Demotic literature
- Demotic Chronicle  4
- Oracle of the Potter  144, 149–151
Dynastic cult  110, 115–116, 119, 155–180, 204, 206, 216, 218–219, 231–248, 286–287, 333, 343
- *Synnaoi theoi*  157, 159, 163, 204, 220, 232, 286, 332

Egyptianising  75
Epithets (divine)
- Lord of Ro-Setau  107
Epithets (royal)
- Agathos Daimon  67
- Bright star  67
- Euergetes  70
- Euploia  161
- Female Horus  12, 165–168
- Female vizier  166
- *nb nfr.w*  206
- Pelagia  161
- Philometor  240
- Soter  66, 70
- *wḏꜣ(.t) bꜣ*  161
Eponymous days  72
Eponymous priests  40, 157, 169, 171, 174, 176–179, 204
Ethnicity  8
Euergetism
- private  55, 62–66, 75
- royal  204, 207, 215, 219–220, 332, 345

Festivals
- Arsinoeia  178
- Introduction of national  218, 221
Fifth phyle  29
Figurine of Sokar  110–111

*Grammaire du temple*  230, 234, 242
Greek communities
- Medamud  278
- Soldiers  341
Greek vs. Egyptian  7, 77, 151, 193, 220, 229, 320, 331
Gymnasion  71–72

Honorific and cultic statues  71, 332, 346

Ideology
- Description of chaos  340, 343
- royal (Ptolemies)  105, 144, 150, 179, 215, 229, 231, 344
- royal (rebel kings)  35, 105, 117
- royal (role of queens)  157

Khoiak figurines 111

Land survey 28

Medamud
- Chronology of temple construction 276
- Recycling of monuments 279

Messianism 4, 145
Monetisation 123, 125, 237
Multilingualism 149, 193, 205, 331
Mutilation
- of royal images 247
- of statues 45
Myths
- Myth of the Divine Birth 136
- vs. history 344

Narratives
- historical (in Synodal Decrees) 214, 337–347
- teleological 6–10
Nationalism 7, 143, 151, 238, *282*, 287, 319

Osirian cemeteries 105–118
Osiris coffins 110

Priesthood 27–48, 60, 63, 65, 75, 91–92, 98, 100–102, 106, 134, 137–138, 144, 149, 156, 162, 165, 179, 198, 204–205, 210, 214, 216, 218–221, 229–230, 233–235, 237, 240, 249, 282, 300–*301*, 306–*307*, 332, 335–336, 340, *343*, 346

*Prostagmata*
- Cleopatra VII and Ptolemy XIII 58, 76
- Ptolemy V 41
- Ptolemy IX and Cleopatra Selene 308

Raphia, Battle of 6, 8, 138, 169, 235
Reforms
- fiscal 34
- of Ptolemy III 45
- Temple administration 3–4, 28–34, 45–46
Refugees 190, 198
Regionalism vs. central control 76
Revenue Laws 136
Revolts 173
- *seditio domestica* (Ptol. III) 92, *99*, 102, 147

- Alexandria (203 BCE) 144
- Causes of 143
- Collateral effects 284
- Gallus' campaign (29 BCE) 285
- Great Theban Revolt (206-186 BCE) 6, 27, 42–43, 46–47, 92, 99, 114, 119, 129, 134, 137–138, 140, 144–145, 173, 178, 189, 195–197, 221, 230, 236, 255, 264, 267, 279, 282–283, 287, 297–298, 319, 321, 335
- Lykopolis 36, 207, 214
- of 88 BCE 58, 60, 297
- of Dionysios Petosarapis *73*
- Scale and nomenclature 144–146
Ritual
- Coronation 35, 207, 282, 305
- *do ut des* 339, 346
- of dynastic cult 232, 339
- of Khoiak 105–106, 111–112, 114, 118
- of lighting the lamps (λυχναψία) *218*
- of the four balls 110–111, 115
- Transmission of the *jmj.t-pr* 164, 172, 231, 239, 241–243, 245
Royal and Synodal Decrees
- Ptolemy I
  - Satrap Stela 62, 229
- Ptolemy II
  - Stela of Sais (266/265 BCE) *32*
- Ptolemy III
  - Alexandria (243 BCE) 35, 162, 167
  - Canopus (238 BCE) 3, 10, 29, 32–33, 35, 44, 118, 147, 164, 167, 216, 233–235
- Ptolemy IV
  - Raphia (217 BCE) 234–235, 239, 339
- Ptolemy V
  - Decree of 199–194(?) BCE 206
  - Memphis (182 BCE) 208, 212–214, 218, 220, 239, *281*, 337
  - Philanthropa (Ptol. V) 221
  - Philensis I (185 BCE) *36*, 176, 207, 221, *238*, 334, 336–337
  - Philensis II (186 BCE) 42, 44, 173, 176, 195, *198*, 207, 209–210, 214, 216, 218, 221, *238–239*, *281–282*, 334–347
  - Rosettana (196 BCE) 34–*36*, 42, 176, 193, 206, 214–216, 239, *281*, 331, 336, *340*

- Ptolemy VI
  - Decree of 161 BCE  *32*, *36*, 240
  - Synodal Decrees (general)  32, 35, 47, 147, 149, 233
  - Synodal Decrees (Ptol. V)  238, 281, 331–347
Royal vs. private roles  64, 75, 216, 219

Seleucid Empire  73–74
Social models of Ptol. Egypt  145
Statues
- private  32–33, 36, 38, 45, 71–72, 94–95, 118, 231, 233–234
- royal  159, 176, 216, 238
- Striding Draped Male Figure  231
Syrian Wars  8, 148
- Third Syrian War  92

Taxes and payments  151, 237, 337
- Apomoira tax  136
- Epigraphe  102
- Salt tax  136
- Syntaxis  34
- Tax farming  91
- Tax receipts
  - Elephantine  190, 192–193
- Yoke tax  136
Temporality  2
- Annual rhythms  111
- of crisis  1–6
- Synchronising divine and royal regnal years  116
Titles
- 1st and 3rd Prophet of Banebdjed (ḥm-nṯr dpi ḥm-nṯr 3.nw n B3-nb-Ḏd)  32
- 1st Prophet of Amun (ḥm-nṯr dpi n Ỉmn)  29–31, 36, 42–45, 47, 93
- 2nd Prophet of Amun (ḥm-nṯr 2.nw n Ỉmn)  45, 320
- 3rd Prophet of Amun (ḥm-nṯr 3.nw n Ỉmn)  30–46, 320
- 4th Prophet of Amun (ḥm-nṯr 4.nw n Ỉmn)  29–30, 45–46, 320
- 4th Prophet of Hathor (ḥm-nṯr 4.nw n Ḥw.t-Ḥr)  99–101
- 5th Prophet of Amun (ḥm-nṯr 5.nw n Ỉmn)  29, *45*
- Acquaintance of the king (rḫ-nsw)  32
- Administrator of domains (ḥḳ3-ḥw.t)  32
- Agent (rd)  28
- Archiereus  32, *70*, 98
- Archiprytanis  59
- Archisomatophylax  72
- Athlophoros  169, 174
- Chief of the Prophets in Thebes (ỉmỉ-r' ḥm.w-nṯr m W3s.t)  30–32
- Chief of the Temple Domains (ỉmỉ-r' gs.w-pr.w)  32
- Epi ton prosodon  59
- Epistates  *34*, 101–102, 221, *302*
- Epistrategos  59, 81, *307*
- God's father (ỉt-nṯr)  95
- Great Governor in Thebes (ḥ3tỉ-' wr m W3s.t)  29–32, 34, 45
- Gymnasiarch  *59*, 72
- hereditary vs. non-hereditary  34
- Hipparch  *59*
- Kanephoros  158, 169, 175, 221
- Lesonis (mr-šn)  32, 91–102
- Monopolisation of  34
- Nautes  159
- Navarch  314
- Notary  34
- One who is alone with the king of the gods (w' w'.w ḥn' nsw nṯr.w)  46
- Overseer of Prophets in Ḥw.t-nswy.t (sḥḏ ḥm.w-nṯr m Ḥw.t-nswy.t)  32
- Pastophoros  159
- Praktor  98
- Priest of Augustus  72
- Prophet (ḥm-nṯr/προφήτης)  32
- Prophet of Amunrasonther (ḥm-nṯr Ỉmn-R' nsw-nṯr.w)  95
- Prophet of Khonsu who governs in Thebes (ḥm-nṯr n Ḫnsw p3 ỉrỉ sḫr.w m W3s.t)  46
- Prophet of Min who massacres his enemies (ḥm-nṯr n Mnw sm3 ḫrw.w=f)  46
- Prophet of the Theoi Euergetai (ḥm-nṯr n nṯr.w mnḫ.w)  33, 118
- Prophet of the White One (ḥm-nṯr ḥḏ(.t))  96
- Reporting prophet of Amun (ḥm-nṯr wḥm n Ỉmn)  31
- Royal accounting scribe of the king of the gods (sḫ3w nsw ḥsb n nsw nṯr.w)  36, 39
- Royal scribe (sḫ3w nsw)  34, 37, 48

- Royal scribe of the nome of Thebes (and) of Memphis (sḫ3w nsw n t3š Nỉw.t Ỉnb.w-ḥḏ) 39
- Royal scribe of the nome of Thebes (sḫ3w nsw n t3š Nỉw.t) 41
- Royal Scribe of Upper Egypt (sḫ3w nsw m Šmʿw) 33
- Scribe (sḫ) 28
- Scribe of the directive (sḫ n p3 wḫ3) 35, 37
- Scribe of the divine seal (sḫ3w ḫtm.t-nṯr) 96
- Scribe of the god's book (sḫ3w mḏ3.t-nṯr) 46, 95
- Scribe of the phylae (sḫ3w s3.w) 93
- Scribe of the trench of the water of Thebes (sḫ n t3 ʿ.t p3 mw Nw.t) 37
- Second Governor in Thebes (ḥ3tỉ-ʿ m-ḫt m W3s.t) 29–32, 34, 45

- Strategos 20, 40, 55, 59, 72–73, 308, 312, 318, 320, 321
- Syngenes 46, 59, 72, 77
- Ton proton philon 46
- Wab-priest (wʿb) 28, 197
- Who-is-in-his-month (ỉmỉ-3bd=f) 29

Topos
- of destroying cult statues 281
- of temple destruction 281, 345

Trade networks 277

Violence against temples and priests 44–45

War of Sceptres 309, 318, 322

www.ingramcontent.com/pod-product-compliance
Lightning Source LLC
Chambersburg PA
CBHW070806300426
44111CB00014B/2438